Global Value Chains and Uneven Development

International Labour Studies – Internationale Arbeitsstudien

Edited by Klaus Dörre and Stephan Lessenich

Volume 36

Christin Bernhold is a post-doctoral researcher at the Institute of Geography at the University of Hamburg.

Christin Bernhold

Global Value Chains and Uneven Development

Corporate Strategies and Class Dynamics in Argentinian Agribusiness

Campus Verlag
Frankfurt/New York

This book is based on a PhD thesis submitted to the Faculty of Science, University of Zurich (UZH) in mid-2019. The research was partly funded by the UZH Candoc Grant, through which the University of Zurich supports its junior scholars at the doctoral level.

ISBN 978-3-593-51637-0 Print
ISBN 978-3-593-45177-0 E-Book (PDF)
ISBN 978-3-593-45178-7 E-Book (EPUB)

Cover design: Campus Verlag GmbH, Frankfurt am Main
Typesetting: le-tex xerif
Typesettig-Fonts: Alegreya
Printed in the United States of America

www.campus.de
www.press.uchicago.edu

A Christian y los compañeros del pasado y presente

Contents

1. Introduction: Who's Upgrading?

Together we add value. This is a catchphrase used by El Agro[1], a leading agribusiness group in Argentina. The company is widely regarded as a role model in this South American country for its success in firm-level upgrading. What began as a locally born family-run firm at the beginning of the twentieth century has grown into a billion-dollar agribusiness group. Today, it owns multiple subsidiaries active in various links of agro-industrial value chains.[2] El Agro's former chairman Santiago in particular has made a name for himself by pioneering the restructuring of agriculture in the Pampean region, the main hub of grain and soybean production in Argentina, into a highly technologized, network-like industry. The company was among the first to employ no-till farming methods and other forms of process upgrading in Argentina, including new forms of organizing primary production, all of which I will explore throughout this book.

The catchphrase *Together we add value* conveys the sense that these achievements entail a win-win situation for all kinds of actors. In this scenario, partners add value together, and no one is appropriating the fruits of someone else's labor. In this vein, El Agro refers to itself as the managing nucleus of an innovative, knowledge-based network that promotes modernization and progress in a way that serves broader socioeconomic development. The company is just one case in point. Its description of itself mirrors the notion propagated by pro-agribusiness state, corporate, and media representatives that agribusiness-led growth can benefit all actors in the respective value chains, provided the right measures are taken by state and private actors (see Tort 2010, 108).

---

1 Due to anonymization, this is a fictitious company name (see Chapter 5 for data handling).

2 This book mainly refers to the production, processing, and trade of grains and oilseeds, such as soybeans, maize, and wheat.

In fact, studies on agrarian change have shown that grain and oilseed production in this country has generally undergone significant changes over the past three decades. Among other transformations, scholars have pointed to the technologizing of primary production using genetically modified organisms (GMO) and to the advent of modern large-scale agribusiness. Extensive soybean cultivation has received particular scholarly attention (Acosta Reveles 2008; Delvenne et al. 2013; Giarracca and Teubal 2008; Gras and Hernández 2013a; Leguizamón 2014).

Grain production has long played a crucial role in Argentina's economic, political, and social history. However, it began to skyrocket around the turn of the millennium. The harvested area for important grains and oilseeds (soybeans, wheat, maize, and sunflower seeds) more than doubled from approximately 14.5 million hectares (ha) to nearly 32 million ha between 1990 and 2019. In this same period, the production of these commodities more than quadrupled from approximately 30 million tons to 135 million tons, and the average yield has grown from 2.16 tons/ha to 3.33 tons/ha in the case of soybeans and from 3.5 tons/ha to 7.9 tons/ha in the case of maize (FAOSTAT). Accordingly, productivity has increased significantly. The cultivation, processing, and trade of soybeans in particular have grown in importance to Argentina's political economy (Lence 2010). In 2020, soy and its derivatives alone accounted for approximately 27.1 percent of all the country's exports, compared to 18 percent in 1993, while all grains and oilseeds and their derivatives totaled nearly 48 percent of all exports in 2020 (INDEC). In this context, Argentina has also become an important player on the world scale. Today, it ranks third in producing raw soybeans after Brazil and the US (USDA 2022, 17). Furthermore, the country has developed a considerable processing industry for these oilseeds. In 2020, 38.8 out of 48.8 million produced tons of soybeans (more than 75 percent) where crushed in Argentina and thus underwent at least a first step of industrial processing in situ (ibid., 33). That same year, Argentina was the fourth biggest crusher of these oilseeds after China, the US, and Brazil and the world's top exporter of soybean oil and soybean meal (ibid., 18 f.).

It is in this context that some agriculture companies of Argentinian origin have managed to grow to such an extent that they are able to integrate their investment activities within larger parts of agro-industrial value chains, including technology development, the production and sale of agrochemicals, the provision of financial and other agro-related services, the commercialization of crops, and the operation of processing plants. At the same time, these actors have changed the dominant model of capitalist farming in the Pampean region. For much of the 20th century, the region saw both big farmers and so-called *Chacareros*. The latter have been described as traditional capitalized farmers who own the agriculture machinery needed for production, with a strong participation of family labour in direct production for both subsistence and the market. Until the mid-20th century, many of them leased-in land. Later, they gradually acquired land property (Muzlera 2021). Today, agricultural enterprises mostly outsource rural labor associated with primary production, such as sowing and harvesting. They lease in land and machinery, contract labor, and manage primary production on large scales.

Here, companies like El Agro come into the picture as local actors who are driving the historically changing patterns of agro-industrial value chain development in Argentina. For a time, this company alone cultivated agricultural goods on several hundred thousand hectares. Today, it concentrates on making investments all along agro-industrial value chains, as Chapter 9 analyzes in depth.

One could stop at this point and interpret these developments as an example of modernization and success. But is the performance of agro-industries in Argentina really a success story? And if so, for whom? This book takes a closer look at these developments to understand whose interests are ultimately vindicated in the wake of agro-industrial upgrading in Argentina, what kinds of strategies are being enforced on the ground, and by whom. In this context, I also examine whether, where, and how the respective actors face limitations, and what implications particular strategies entail for other actors.

In Argentina and beyond, opinions on the matter have to date differed sharply. As mentioned above, some accounts are optimistic: Policy makers, academic scholars, and corporate actors have maintained that agribusiness involves much more than the mere production and export of primary goods. This debate has been influenced by the global value chain (GVC) approach (Gereffi and Kaplinsky 2001), which introduced upgrading as a key development strategy. Upgrading, which I will discuss in greater detail in Chapter 3, is commonly understood as a process whereby firms or regions "shift to more secure or more profitable niches within or between industries through organizational learning facilitated by networks" (Werner 2012, 403). At the same time, it has been implicitly or explicitly linked to the prospect of broader socioeconomic development. The World Bank recently claimed that GVCs can "boost incomes, create better jobs, and reduce poverty" (World Bank 2020). In this spirit, key actors in Argentina have come to regard agro-industrial upgrading as a potential driver of socioeconomic development in situ.

However, there is also a vast body of literature that is far more critical. Scholars have, for example, diagnosed a (re)primarization of the Argentinian economy, and pointed to increasing social and spatial inequalities, environmental and health problems caused by the use of agrochemicals, as well as poor labor conditions in the agriculture sector. In what follows, I provide a brief description of both perspectives.

1.1 Argentinian agribusiness and value chain upgrading

GVC research originated with a critical analysis of the global political economy from a world-systems perspective. Hopkins and Wallerstein (1977) introduced the commodity chain approach as a means for analyzing how socioeconomic inequality is necessarily reproduced across chain links in a capitalist world-system, though in ever changing historical and geographical constellations. However, much of the current value chain literature sidelines issues of exploitation and uneven development. Instead, scholars as well as policy makers frequently use the GVC approach to focus on upgrading. As a "new paradigm for development," the "'GVC paradigm' of upgrading" (Gereffi and Fernandez-Stark 2016, 24) is based on the premise that moving to higher value activities in GVCs does not necessarily require a transformation from traditional agriculture to manufacturing or service industries. It is rather aimed at a development from a low-skilled, labor-intensive towards a higher value added, technology, skill, and knowledge-intensive production within any industry, including agriculture (ibid.). In this vein, Gereffi (2012, 34) points to economic upgrading, for example by moving "beyond extraction of raw materials to additional processing and commercialization." As regards the actors believed to be potentially driving this development forward, GVC literatures have at first mainly focused on firms and state actors (see Humphrey 2006b; Kaplinsky and Morris 2001; Trienkens 2011).

Building on this debate, some Argentinian GVC scholars have been optimistic about agro-industrial development in Argentina, pointing to upgrading opportunities provided by the respective value chains. Among other things, these voices highlight the state-of-the-art technology driving soy production. They also point to the role of industrial processing and domestic value added both as a possible source of upgrading and an engine of development, and they hint at the job creation capacity of agro-industrial chain development (Anlló et al. 2013a; Bisang et al. 2013; Llach et al. 2004; Lódola et al. 2010). According to this view, social impacts that have so far accompanied agrarian change, such as land conflicts or crises among small producers, can potentially be overcome by GVC upgrading. For Bisang et al. (2008, 33), existing economic and technological asymmetries may even represent a potential basis for dynamic mechanisms and permanent renegotiations, a dynamism that is seen as conducive to the adoption and adaptation of innovation. In any case, these literatures see a development potential in Argentina's capturing of higher rents within global value chains" by moving "towards chain links with higher technical complexity" (Anlló et al. 2010, 10, own translation).

A second group of actors emphasizing the potentials of agro-industrial GVC upgrading are policy makers from different government administrations[3] who have pointed to perceived value added possibilities along the whole value chain and across different geographical regions. A case in point is the *Federal and Participative Agri-Food and Agribusiness Strategic Plan 2010—2020* (PEA) (Ministry of Agriculture 2011). This government document conveys that the vitality of the sector "is not exclusive to the Pampa's agriculture; it stretches along the value chain" (ibid., 59). It lauds agribusiness for having the potential to boost "the national and regional development of our country" (ibid., 62). Similar to El Agro's production model, particular emphasis is given to the modern rural entrepreneur who employs both state-of-the-art technology and managerial knowledge, and who acts "in a complex network of agents connected to each other by a variety of contracts" (ibid., 43; see Chapter 7 for an in-depth analysis of the PEA).

Third, there are companies and agribusiness associations in Argentina that reference the value chain metaphor in fairly positive terms. For example, representatives of the Argentinian soy and wheat chain associations (ACSOJA, ArgenTrigo) problematize the current limits of agro-industrial value chain development. At the same time, however, they point to value chains both as a plane of common business organization and as a way to sound out economic potential. In a joint press release, these associations have argued that agro-industrial value chain development has the potential to generate

3 See Berndt and Bernhold (2018) for a discussion of continuities in agricultural policies between neoliberal and so-called post-neoliberal agendas in Argentina.

economic growth for Argentina in a way that "has a favorable impact on the whole society," and that "the value chains have to be the pivot for this transformation."[4]

In fact, as I will show throughout this book, agro-industries in Argentina and various firms in particular have undergone major transformations that can well be described in the terms of the GVC upgrading agenda. And yet, being on the ground and talking to representatives of companies and business associations, state actors, unionists, and small farmers, I encountered much that contradicts the presentation of GVC upgrading as a path to general development.

Based on my research into upgrading strategies in Argentinian agro-industries and their ramifications, this particular, updated form of modernist belief in capitalist progress forms the object of discussion and critique in this study.

1.2 Argentinian agribusiness and its adverse effects

In contradiction to these optimistic accounts, Argentinian agribusiness has often been subject to scholarly critique. A vast body of scholarship has analyzed how global dynamics of agrarian change, such as the development of a "corporate food regime" (McMichael 2005, 269; 2016, 650; see Delvenne et al. 2013), the financialization of agriculture and increased accumulation by dispossession (Cáceres 2015; Constantino 2016; Svampa and Viale 2014), as well as class dynamics (Bernstein 2010; see Villulla 2015) have played out in practice in Argentina. From a variety of empirical and theoretical perspectives, scholars have asked, for whom is the current mode of agricultural production in this country a success story, and at whose expense?

Studies have raised reasonable doubts about crafting success stories, especially around soy mono-cropping based on GMOs, and a related shift away from the production of foodstuffs towards the extensive cultivation of fodder and biomass for export (Teubal 2006). This shift has often been referred to as the *sojización* or soy-ization of Argentina's political economy (Acosta Reveles 2008; Ainsuain and Echaguibel 2012; Basualdo 2013; Bravo et

4 http://www.argentrigo.org.ar/2014/pdf/4CadenasEnExpoagro_consolidado.pdf, last accessed March 29, 2022, own translation.

al. 2010; Fernández 2013a; Martínez Dougnac 2013). Scholarly contributions have analyzed negative socioeconomic, cultural, and environmental trends (Barri 2009; Domínguez and Sabatino 2006), as well as adverse health effects (Ávila-Vázquez and Difilippo 2016; Domínguez and Sabatino 2010), and they have argued that the country has turned into an "open-air laboratory" (Gras and Hernández 2013c, 27, own translation; see López et al. 2008; Romero 2016) for biotechnology and agrochemical interests controlled by only a handful of profiteers. In what follows I briefly highlight six key issues dealt with by scholarly critics of the currently dominant model of agro-industrial production in Argentina.

First, studies have pointed to a changing social fabric in Pampean agriculture. This includes the observation of an ongoing economic concentration in primary production, which is fueled by increasingly capital-intensive production, economies of scale, and state policies (Fernández 2013b), and the resulting dominance of large-scale agribusiness led by entrepreneurial figures able to mobilize advanced organizational and technical knowledge (Gras and Hernández 2016a). This has been associated with an increasing displacement of family agriculture (Giarracca and Teubal 2008; Gras 2012; Gras and Sosa Varrotti 2013; Palmisano 2014) and a resulting "agricultura sin agricultores" (Teubal 2006, 81; see Poth 2010), which means an agriculture without farmers and peasants. Scholars have also pointed out that local farmers who have been driven out of the market are frequently reabsorbed into agribusiness networks in new ways. They are transformed, for instance, into salaried service providers or small rentiers (Acosta Reveles 2008; Craviotti and Gras 2006; Gras and Hernández 2013b). However, these actors often cannot "control the terms and conditions of their incorporation" (Craviotti 2016, 344).

A second body of literature has analyzed how the expulsion of actors can take on existential and in some cases life-threatening importance, especially as agribusiness has advanced the soy frontier into the north and the northwest of the country, where peasant and indigenous communities have long predominated (Leguizamón 2014). In this context, research has focused on violent dispossession and displacements (Cáceres 2015; Féliz 2014), often resisted by peasant and indigenous communities and local movements (Berger and Ortega 2009; Carrizo and Berger 2012; GEPCyD 2011; GER 2004). Both market and violent displacements have been accompanied by the mobilization of modernization discourses, which—together with the depiction of small-scale production as an ineffective mirror of modern agroindustries and the characterization of community land on the edge of the agribusiness frontier as unused or unproductive—have served as an ideological justification for concentration and dispossession (Flammini 2001; Gras and Hernández 2016b).

Third, research has focused on how these transformations have been strongly influenced by finance capital invested in the soy industry. There are obvious global dimensions to this, not least the dominance of the Chicago Board of Trade and stock market speculation in soybean price formation, which leaves large corporations less vulnerable to volatile prices than smaller producers. Furthermore, national and international capital has flowed towards Argentinian agribusiness following the opening of the economy and the liberalization of export regimes, especially in the 1990s. These investments have fueled the explosive growth of soy production (Fernández 2014; Grosso et al. 2010; Pertierra Cánepa 2014).

In connection to the changing social fabric in Pampean agriculture, a fourth sizeable body of critical scholarly research has dealt with rural labor relations and working conditions. Contributions include investigations of job losses in an increasingly capital-intensive agriculture (Acosta Reveles 2012; Lattuada and Neiman 2005; Neiman 2010b; Otero 2012), labor flexibilization (Neiman and Quaranta 2004), precarious working conditions, the increase in subcontracted, seasonal labor, overexploitation, and low levels of union organizing (Bardomás et al. 2010; Neiman 2010a; Neiman et al. 2006; Villulla 2015).

Fifth, Argentina's dependence on primary production and on a limited number of foreign firms that control the commercialization of seeds and other inputs, as well as the processing and export of soybeans, has prompted critiques of a "reprimarization" (Teubal 2006, 79, own translation) and "foreignization" (Giarracca and Teubal 2006, 79, own translation; see Romero 2016) of the Argentinian political economy. Heterodox economists have argued that the country has suffered a loss of domestically oriented manufacturing industries, as it has simultaneously reoriented itself on industries that hardly offer incentives for productive investments in situ, including agro-industries (Azpiazu et al. 2011; Azpiazu and Schorr 2010; Ebenau and Gatica 2013; Gaggero et al. 2014; Schorr 2013; Schorr et al. 2012).

Finally, many studies have analyzed in depth the ways that people and environments are affected by the increasing destruction of the environment and loss of biodiversity, among many other things through the increasing use of agro-toxics and vast deforestation (Alonso et al. 2014; Ávila-Vázquez and Difilippo 2016; Paganelli et al. 2010; Pengue 2004; 2005; Rodríguez and Jacobo 2010; Ronco et al. 2016; Sarandón and Flores 2014).

Ultimately, there is an incredibly rich body of academic literature in Argentina and beyond, impressive in its empirical depth, that has adopted a critical stance towards agribusiness in this South American country and its socioeconomic and nature destroying effects. My study broadly shares these views that challenge optimistic assessments of agribusiness as an engine of sustainable development in Argentina.

Connecting critical research on Argentinian agribusiness to the GVC upgrading paradigm

However, there has been a tendency in critical scholarly contributions to focus either on socioeconomic changes in certain steps in the production process, and here mainly on primary production, or on the role of individual actors, such as foreign seed or export companies. Despite a strong influence of the GVC upgrading paradigm in academic, political, and corporate circles in Argentina, the GVC approach has so far only drawn limited scholarly attention from critics of this country's export-oriented agribusiness. This lack of accounting for the concept and practice of value chain development in situ leaves critiques of the mode of primary production vulnerable in the face of ideological confrontations where the positive effects of GVC development elsewhere in the chain are posited optimistically. For example, ACSOJA and ArgenTrigo have tried to overwrite analyses of poor labor conditions and job losses at the point of primary production with an alternative view according to which positive effects arise along the whole value chain.

So how can we understand the successes, limitations, and ramifications of corporate-led upgrading in Argentinian grain and oilseed value chains from a critical perspective? Who are the drivers and beneficiaries of the dominant upgrading strategies within and beyond primary production? And at whose expense are they proceeding? There is a need for a critical research agenda that traces upgrading strategies in agro-industrial value chains in Argentina, as well as their ramifications and potential contradictions. Therefore, my study pays particular attention to the respective approaches taken by state actors, firms and agribusiness associations, which the GVC approach designates as key developmental actors.

1.3 An empirical critique of upgrading as a development strategy

One of the main aims of my research is to cast a critical light on the assumption that upgrading in general, and in agro-industrial value chains in Argentina in particular, can yield general socioeconomic development. To this end, I draw on and seek to complement the referenced literature on the adverse effects of agribusiness in this country. At the same time, I also suggest approaching agro-industries from a different angle. My perspective considers examples of successful upgrading (as in the case of El Agro, which I introduced above) and, beyond that, more ambitious approaches to value chain development on the ground, while taking the limits and contradictions of these strategies into account. In this context, I also reflect on ideological recourses to the value chain metaphor that serve to justify corporate action.

Value chain research, exploitation, and uneven development

Given the above-mentioned fact that value chain research was originally designed to trace uneven development in the capitalist world-system (Hopkins and Wallerstein 1977), I was at first surprised by the ways in which companies and agribusiness associations in Argentina positively reference this approach when I began my research. This represented the impetus for a closer exploration of the theoretical development of the chain analytic since its introduction. In view of today's mainstream version of GVC research, I became interested in investigating the extent to which its theoretical principles allow state and corporate actors to use it as a tool for designing capitalist development strategies.

I situate my work within a body of literature that has raised similar questions. From different theoretical and empirical perspectives, scholars have criticized the modernist assumption implicit in the GVC approach, according to which firm upgrading can be conceived of as a strategy for achieving general socioeconomic development (Bair 2009; Campling and Selwyn 2018; Werner et al. 2014). A detailed analysis and critique of the GVC approach is contained in Chapters 3 and 4. Suffice it at this point to give a brief glimpse into inquiries broadly inspired by critical political economy perspectives, which have elaborated on what can be conceived as critical chain studies. In considering the issue from different perspectives, they share the goal (a) of contradicting the contention by mainstream GVC studies that anyone can climb up value chains to development, and (b) of revitalizing the analysis and critique of uneven patterns of capitalist development in its place.

In this vein, Bair and Werner (2011a, 989) have adopted a feminist approach to highlight the "inclusionary bias" of GVC research. From a dis/articulation perspective, they argue together with Berndt and Boeckler (Bair et al. 2013) that social inequalities, exclusion, and uneven spatial development in many cases are rather enhanced through value chain development, often unfolding along the lines of social difference, including race and gender. Here, attention is directed to how struggles over production, redistribution, and control are led by agents included in commodity networks in asymmetric power relations, as well as to the everyday practices of exclusion (see Berndt 2013).

Bair (2014) was also among those who have called to restore the big picture of the global political economy back in response to narrow, firm-centered network analyses that focus on detecting upgrading possibilities. She has reminded us of the roots of commodity chain research that underlie an analysis of how activities in different chain links are systematically attributed with unequal gains. In contrast to an understanding of GVCs as ladders that can be climbed by actors at the bottom rungs, this research again suggests that socioeconomic stratification is an immanent feature of global capitalism, its historical and geographical alterations notwithstanding (see Brewer 2011; Parnreiter 2019).

In this context, Ouma (2017, 502 f.) has also argued that given its "origins in world-systems theory and the dependency tradition, one would expect to learn more about the classical concerns of critical political economy in the chain literature: the labour process, patterns of uneven development and social stratification, or questions of extraversion, income distribution, and exploited nature" (see Fischer et al. 2021). Furthermore, scholars have highlighted the need for GVC analysis to theorize the capitalist state and peripheral positions in geopolitics in particular, instead of merely presupposing the state as a neutral developmental actor (Fernández and Trevignani 2015; Glassman 2011; Neilson 2014). Understood as a "neoliberal device," Fernández (2015, 209) has argued that the GVC approach refuses to analyze power in terms of domination. Consequently, it does not allow for an in-depth analysis of the Argentinian state's involvement in agro-industrial chain development, for instance. As elsewhere, this has happened in the context of a need to mitigate the negative impacts of neoliberalism after the 1990s, when the value chain turned into a policy template that came to pervade state structures, promising socioeconomic improvements and the possibility of remedying institutional voids, as well as orienting policy interventions towards market integration (see Berndt 2015).

Alongside a critical engagement with these reformulations of GVC analysis, especially Marxist, class-analytical studies have helped me focus the analytical gaze of my research. Here, scholars have underpinned research into uneven power relations and unequal economic gains, using a social-relational theory of capitalism. Campling et al. (2016, 1745) have considered class dynamics to be "at the heart of developmental processes," and thus sought to view the uneven development between actors in different chain links and the capitalist exploitation of labor together, in the same light. In this line, scholars have emphasized that the role of labor (not only as a mere input factor) and capitalism's antagonistic class relations need to be re-considered to understand why workers' situations do not necessarily improve when firms upgrade. Firm strategies are instead accompanied by shifting patterns of exploitation (Selwyn 2016b, 5; see Bair and Werner 2015; Smith et al. 2002). Furthermore, Selwyn (2016a) has pointed to the class-relational basis of competitive capital accumulation and the resulting relations between firms, which are not arbitrary, and which are instead forged by capital strategies. According to this research, analyzing interclass struggles over the production and distribution of surplus value can help elucidate broader dynamics of uneven capitalist reproduction as it embraces the "dynamic, integrated, but nonetheless structured global economy" (Werner 2018, 2). In this context, studies have analyzed how capital power constrains workers but can also be influenced by labor agency (Selwyn 2013; 2017; Taylor et al. 2015; Werner 2012; 2016a).

This literature helps me to conceptualize actual social relations in agro-industrial chains in Argentina, and how they are organized in a way that facilitates differentiated growth. However, while empirical studies have mainly concentrated on capital-labor relations and the developmental power of labor struggles (Selwyn 2012), less is known about how successful firm-level upgrading in GVCs can work within and through a process of class differentiation. This includes changes in capital-labor relations, and how a myriad of social actors in between the positions of capital and labor are included in the process of production.

Research gaps in critical chain studies

Based on a Marxian social-relational perspective, my study aims at a closer examination of how exploitative relations between capital, labor, and intermediate classes are created and reproduced in the wake of value chain development, and how these relations influence the struggle over the benefits to be gained from upgrading. Considered from the standpoint of their political *economic* character, these social relations are class-based, that is, they can be defined by the actors' relations to the means of production and by the question of who produces and who receives which part of the social product. To do so, I refer to works on both class analysis and agrarian change, which I find helpful for understanding the ever-changing social dynamics of capitalist development in general and of Argentinian agro-industrial networks in particular (see for example Bernstein 2010; Bernstein and Byres 2001; Carchedi 1998; PKA 1974). Considered from a *political* economic standpoint, the actual manifestation of these social relations is a question of historical struggles on different terrains. In this instance, especially by seizing upon Gramsci's thinking, I am also interested in the way that the specifics of social development depend on the strength of actors in class struggles on economic as well as on political and ideological terrains. Without claiming that class relations are the only important factors in value chain development, I do think that they are essential, and I hope to provide ways of employing them in empirical investigations.

With respect to the quoted critical chain studies, my study supports the aim of these scholarly contributions to use commodity or value chain analysis not as a means for designing upgrading strategies but, instead, to reclaim the tools it provides to analyze exploitation and uneven development. At the same time, I identify two further research gaps. First, while the GVC approach has explicitly considered upgrading towards a technology, skill, and knowledge-intensive agriculture as an element of the "new paradigm for development" (Gereffi and Fernandez-Stark 2016, 24), highly technologized and capital-intensive grain and oilseed value chains have so far received little attention from critical chain scholars (for an exception, see Soendergaard 2018).

Second, while I share the critique of the narrow, firm-centric focus of mainstream GVC research, I identify a need for an immanent, ideology-critical and at the same time empirical analysis of the premises on which this approach is based. This is because (a) the ways in which firms and other business actors use the GVC analytic for their purposes, practically and ideologically (as in the case of Argentinian agribusiness), have, to my knowledge not yet been the subject of close scrutiny. Such an analysis would entail understanding whether or how the GVC approach itself entails omissions that enable political and economic actors to use it to uphold their particular interests, masked as universal interests. An empirical and ideology-critical account of the GVC approach is also necessary, (b) because of the way it addresses states and firms as developmental actors.

Therefore, given that corporate actors employ GVC analysis for their own vested interests, I deduce the need to design a research strategy that examines two assumptions of GVC research into the empirical world: (a) that upgrading can engender general socioeconomic development within capitalism, provided the right institutional or business environment, and (b) that state and corporate actors are key developmental figures in this process. I ask, what kinds of strategies do firms and, in my case, agribusiness associations actually formulate with regard to GVC development? How do they use the GVC approach to design their upgrading strategies? What are these actors' actual practices in GVCs? What limits do they identify? And in this light, what contradictions arise from these strategies and their ramifications with respect to the assumption in the GVC approach that firm upgrading can engender general development?

Hence, while I agree that an analysis and critique of the global political economy (instead of a mere firm-centered analysis) is needed to understand uneven development, I argue that, by bearing these general capitalist dynamics in mind, the analysis of individual, micro-scale, capital-led upgrading strategies has the potential to reveal the contradictions of GVC upgrading. Such an analysis makes it possible to challenge mainstream GVC analyses "by singing their own tune to them" (Marx 1975 [1844], 178). Understood as an empirical ideology critique, it requires elucidating both immanent contradictions of the GVC approach and where it comes into conflict with social reality.

This endeavor does not preclude the possibility of an economic and social development in value chains that entails improvements for other actors than just firms.[5] Instead, first, I scrutinize to what extent the mainstream GVC

5 In this context, it is not my concern to define what exactly constitutes development. First, there is no universal and commonly accepted definition of the forms of economic growth and of the increase of social, political, and cultural freedom and justice necessary to justify the use of the

approach considers the factors on which such improvements depend. Second, based on theoretical as well as empirical grounds, my study challenges the assumption that GVC upgrading as a "new paradigm for development" (Gereffi and Fernandez-Stark 2016, 24) can engender general socioeconomic development within capitalism.

In summary, this study aims at contributing to a critical analysis of agro-industrial value chains in Argentina, as well as to an in-depth theoretical and empirical analysis and critique of the GVC upgrading paradigm. While this forms the conceptual context of the book, the analysis of my empirical work requires both further theoretical considerations and an embedding in further, specific debates, which I will introduce where I use them to make sense of my findings.

Research questions

I derive the following research questions from the debates that I have so far introduced. By employing a methodology that I choose to call an empirical ideology critique (the contours of which I define in Chapter 2), I first pose questions for the GVC upgrading paradigm on a theoretical level.

To what extent is the GVC approach designed to grasp the social conditions under which uneven development—which it intends to remedy by upgrading—is reproduced in global capitalism?

term. Moreover, this has long been a topic of fierce debate. Nohlen and Nuscheler (1993, 64 ff., own translation), for instance, have included five interrelated elements: economic growth, improvements in labor conditions, social equity/justice, participation, and sovereignty/independence. I agree that development is more than economic growth. At the same time, what people define as development is historically and geographically specific. Selwyn (2016a, 1768 f.) critically quotes Amartya Sen's "advocacy of development as a process that expands human freedoms by increasing individuals' abilities and choices." With him, I agree that the expansion of freedoms for members of different social classes "depends on myriad factors, including [...] the balance of class power between labour and capital" (ibid., 1769). However, viewed from my perspective on what development needs to be, this would include the making of a society free from exploitation and domination, in which no socially produced suffering persists. In any case, my study does not require a precise definition of what constitutes development in empirical terms. Given that the GVC framework includes not only economic growth but also social improvements for workers and broader populations, this represents the yardstick for my analysis.

My study seeks to examine this question by (a) tracing contradictions inherent to the GVC approach as well as omissions and obstructions in its relation to the empirical world; (b) scrutinizing to what extent its conceptual development allows corporate actors to build on this approach in a way that justifies their own vested interests; and (c) tracing the advantages of using this approach to analyze uneven development.

Rather than only arguing at a theoretical level, I shall ground my discussion in in-depth, empirical research into upgrading strategies and practices in agro-industrial value chains in Argentina and their ramifications. This Argentinian case strikes me in particular because, as I outlined above, while it can be read as a textbook example of possible and in some ways successful upgrading, it also leaves many questions unanswered. In this vein, my study is inspired by the following broader conceptual question: What can successful upgrading strategies of particular local players within agro-industrial value chains teach us about the reproduction of socioeconomic antagonisms in global capitalism, and how does that contradict the GVC upgrading paradigm?

To operationalize this overarching question, my empirical research was guided by the following two sets of more concrete research questions. With the first set of questions, I follow a crucial premise of the GVC upgrading paradigm, i.e., the presumption of states and firms as development actors, into the empirical world and ask:

What are the upgrading strategies and strategic approaches to GVC development adopted by state representatives, business associations, and companies in agro-industrial value chains in Argentina? To what extent are these strategies successful, and where do they face limitations or entail contradictions with respect to upgrading as a development strategy?

Second, in light of the assumptions that upgrading strategies cannot automatically be associated with broader positive social effects, and that uneven development is an immanent moment of global capitalism, I ask:

In what ways are upgrading strategies shot through with class and power relations and the ensuing unequal socioeconomic outcomes? Who benefits from upgrading in these relations, who does not, and on what does the ability to gain from upgrading depend?

In the remainder of this introduction, I provide an outline of how I will address these research questions in the following chapters.

1.4 How this book unfolds

Chapter 2 can best be understood as a theoretical-methodological note on the design of this book as an empirical ideology critique of the GVC upgrading paradigm. Inspired by historical materialist approaches, including Critical Theory in the Frankfurt School tradition and the work of the Italian Marxist Antonio Gramsci, it methodologically underpins my objective of tracing the contradictions within the (implicit) assumption that upgrading can engender general socioeconomic development within capitalism. This methodological chapter precedes the theoretical ones for the reason that I conceive my conceptual discussion of the GVC upgrading paradigm already as a part of this ideology-critique, such that it requires reflections on this methodology in advance. Thus, in Sections 2.1 and 2.2, I discuss various aspects that add to grasping ideology from a historical materialist perspective. Based on these considerations, Section 2.3 explains how ideology critique, understood as an immanent critique, aims at unveiling justifications of particular interests that are portrayed as general interests. In doing so, it does not aim simply to reject a theory. Instead, it takes its claims seriously, reacts to the contradictions that arise within it and in its relation to the empirical world, and at the same time it seeks to maintain its strengths.

Chapter 3 then provides an overview of the conceptual development from commodity chain analysis in the world-systems tradition (3.1) to the global commodity chain (GCC) approach that dominated chain research throughout the 1990s, leading up to the current mainstream GVC approach. I show how these changes in name went along with conceptual amendments, and a shift away from analyzing and criticizing global capitalism's immanent tendency to reproduce uneven development. In this line, in Section 3.2.1, I discuss GCC research in terms of (a) its legacies from the world-systems perspective, (b) a shift of focus to chain governance, and (c) the role it ascribes to upgrading. I then trace the GVC framework's movement towards transaction cost economics and micro-level network governance (3.2.2.). Section 3.2.3 portrays how GVC analysis today mainly focuses on upgrading, driven by a consideration to craft policy tools and strategies for firm-led development. Section 3.2.4 shows in more detail how this approach has also influenced scholarship on agro-industrial chains in Argentina. These chain analytics are part of the theoretical framework of this study and object of analysis at the same time. I highlight their key strengths, which inform my own research. At the same time, from an ideology-critical perspective, I analyze theoretical shortcomings and omissions as well as the contradictions arising in the GVC upgrading paradigm where they become apparent already at the theoretical level.

Chapter 4 revisits critiques of mainstream GVC analysis and alternative conceptions as they have been formulated in academic discussions in the past years. I situate my own work within these debates, which provided me with analytical tools that I consider useful for looking at upgrading strategies in the context of Argentinian agribusiness. Section 4.1 briefly looks at the global production networks (GPN) approach, since it has introduced the academically most visible reformulation of chain-like approaches to studying development issues above the plane of national units. Section 4.2 introduces the "disarticulations perspective" (Bair and Werner 2011a, 989) that seeks to remedy the "inclusionary bias" of GVC analysis. Section 4.3 discusses recent approaches that again refer back to world-systems analytical approaches to investigating uneven development in global chains, followed by a discussion of different Marxist perspectives on the matter. Here, I also substantiate my understanding of class relations and why class matters as a category for analyzing the perpetuation of inequality in GVCs. In the final Section 4.4, I present literatures that point to the importance of theorizing the capitalist state and geopolitics for chain analysis.

Before commencing with the analysis of the data that I gathered in Argentina, in Chapter 5, I provide a detailed account of the design of my multifaceted empirical research, and of the methods I used for my data collection and analysis.

Chapter 6 is designed as a contextual chapter that gives a rough overview of the political economy of agro-industrial value chains in Argentina. First, Section 6.1 hints at the (dis)continuities in agribusiness-related economic policies implemented in Argentina under different governments (until the transfer of office to then President Mauricio Macri in 2015), and how these have formed the political environment in which local agro-industries and the corporate strategies that I analyze have evolved. Section 6.2 considers crucial economic developments as well as the dominant corporate actors in different links of grain and oilseed value chains, including the production and trade of seeds, biotechnology, and agrochemicals (6.2.1), the agricultural machinery industry (6.2.2), agricultural production in the Pampean region (6.2.3), as well as processing industries and trading (6.2.4). This chapter provides background information, which the subsequent empirical chapters now and then invoke.

As pointed out above, the core of my study and the basic concept of my empirical research design is to follow key presumptions associated with the GVC upgrading paradigm into the empirical world. The results of this research are presented in Chapters 7–10. Here, I analyze actually existing upgrading strategies set out by different sets of actors in agro-industrial value chains in Argentina, the successes they have spawned as well as their limitations, the standpoints from which these strategies are formulated, how they are accompanied by unequal ramifications, and how the notion of the value chain is used both for the political organization of firms and on the ideological terrain.

In this vein, I start with an analysis of the government's approach to agro-industrial chain development issued under then President Cristina Fernández de Kirchner (2007–2015) (Chapter 7). I delineate the general objectives set out by government employees and in the most important governmental strategy paper covering the 'Kirchnerist' approach to grain and oilseed value chain development (7.1) and the role assigned to the state in this process (7.2). This official approach strongly asserted the potential of social inclusion and the environmental, economic and social sustainability arising from an expansion of agribusiness and further processing in situ. In this context, Section 7.3 scrutinizes this image and discusses how it uses a GVC concept to design strategies tailored to economic interests, while excluding exploited and marginalized actors and omitting aspects that are relevant to the perpetuation of inequality and exploitation through agro-industrial upgrading.

Chapter 8 shifts the focus to analyzing agribusiness federations' strategies for GVC development. On the basis of interviews with representatives of ACSOJA, ArgenTrigo, and various member organizations, the first part of the chapter examines upgrading strategies as they are discussed by the above informants (8.1). I depict how they have agreed on a common, practical approach to agro-industrial development, pushed by chain-wide organizations that unite business groups operating along grain and oilseed value chains. For them, the value chain is not only an analytical tool but also a level of common organizing, which is, however, characterized by intra-firm coordination and intra-capitalist competition at the same time. The second part examines limits and barriers to upgrading as they are explicitly or implicitly addressed by my interlocutors (8.2). Section 8.3 looks at how business federations have aspired with some success to strengthen particular discourses on agribusiness in the public arena and to broaden their voice in Argentinian politics. All three sections scrutinize capital-led upgrading as a development strategy in that they (a) identify economic, political, and ideological strategies proposed by corporate actors (who consider themselves as drivers of value chain development); (b) draw attention to implicit assumptions and omissions, such as obstructions or contradictions that are blanked out in the identified strategies; and (c) indicate how business agents use the value chain concept from the ideological standpoint of capital's vested interests, which differ from a socioeconomically and ecologically sustainable development.

Chapter 9 builds directly on this analysis, but it shifts the focus to examine the competitive strategies of three case companies, which I have named Agrigood, El Agro, and LAgricola in this book. All three grew with the commodity boom, and have upgraded processes and functions at the firm level. This chapter hence underlines that successful upgrading, as understood by the GVC approach, is indeed possible, as I depict in Section 9.1. However, I do not view this as a success story about corporate development, rather as a way to challenge the assumption that firm-level upgrading generally entails broader socioeconomic gains. Therefore, this chapter argues that, if firm-level upgrading is equated with development, the result may instead contradict the goal of achieving broader social development and entail the assertion of vested interests accompanied by ideological justifications (9.2) and persistent processes of concentration and centralization of capital fueled by upgrading strategies (9.3). Furthermore, firm level strategies can entail geographical profit transfers away from Argentina (9.4), such that they are not necessarily oriented at development in situ, as well as a dismissive stance towards organized labor and social movements that struggle against the adverse effects they experience as a result of particular corporate action.

After having looked at upgrading strategies at the level of business associations and various case companies, Chapter 10 zooms in closer to interpret a case study, namely a production network controlled by the above introduced company El Agro, through the analytical gaze of what I call 'upgrading in and through class differentiation.' The chapter shows how El Agro's capacity to upgrade its processes and to invest in different links of agro-industrial value chains has been built upon a clear transformation from an agriculture dominated by independent farmers to modern agribusiness, which has entailed the reorganization of the local social relations of production and changing relations of exploitation and domination. I therewith aim to contribute to a better understanding of how, why, and for whom upgrading may entail advancement and for whom it instead entails either simple reproduction under the wings of big capital and/or different forms of exploitation. To this end, Section 10.1 first recalls some theoretical key points of the class dynamics of upgrading (10.1). I then focus on how El Agro's strategies work in and through a process of class differentiation, which entails cooperative and at the same exploitative relations with intermediate classes, which are often masked as a co-equal network-partnership (10.2). Section 10.3 examines the ways in which El Agro does not neutrally coordinate but instead dominates and shapes these relations to its own benefit in the wake of upgrading, and how this is accompanied by strong consensus-building and the widespread rationalization of the analyzed social edifice as characterized by reciprocity. Finally, Section 10.4 looks at relatively poorly paid rural labor and working conditions in the fields. It shows, how and why the outsourcing of seeding, fumigation, and harvesting is key in this context, given its adverse effects on the conditions for labor struggles that could achieve social improvements. This section also includes an excursus to the vegetable oil industry, where a combative union has more successfully struggled for better wages. In sum, Chapter 10 examines how upgrading does not automatically lead to a process of social equalization, and how, on the basis of class relations, it is also likely to perpetuate inequality, though in changing forms, unless class struggles from below demand and achieve social improvements.

Finally, I discuss in my concluding chapter how all the small examples examined contribute to a general ideology-critical view of the GVC upgrading paradigm. Furthermore, I outline what this may mean for the use of the GVC agenda from a social-relational, political economic perspective, and where I see the need for further connections with theoretical discussions on questions of uneven development, debates that I could not address in this book.

Altogether, I hope to provide readers with arguments and ideas for how GVC analysis can and should be fruitfully employed to analyze and critique patterns of exploitation and uneven development in capitalism, globally and locally, instead of as a tool for designing capitalist development strategies.

2. Empirical Ideology Critique—A Theoretical-Methodological Note

This study has been conceived as what I choose to call an empirical ideology critique of the GVC upgrading paradigm. I have developed and pursued a research agenda that traces the contradictions within the (implicit) assumption that upgrading can engender general socioeconomic development within capitalism, provided the right institutional or business environment. My research design comprises both a theoretical critique of mainstream GVC analysis in reference to previous scholarly discussions (Chapters 3 and 4) and, specifically, in-depth, empirical research into the contradictions of upgrading (strategies and practices) in agro-industrial value chains in Argentina (Chapters 7–10).

To substantiate my endeavor, this chapter offers introductory reflections on my understanding of ideology and its immanent critique. Taking inspiration from historical materialist approaches, including from critical theory in the Frankfurt School tradition (hereafter referred to as Critical Theory) as well as from the work of the Italian Marxist Antonio Gramsci, it is intended as a first part of the theoretical-methodological basis of this book. I build on this to ask: To what extent does the GVC approach adopt a critical position on the social conditions under which uneven development—which it intends to remedy by upgrading—is reproduced in global capitalism? The presentation of the empirical methods I have used and the fieldwork I have conducted in the course of this study follows in Chapter 5, which directly precedes the empirical sections.

In general, the remarks made in this chapter are of twofold relevance to this book. Alongside their epistemological and methodological significance for my critique of the GVC approach itself, this concerns the role of ideology more broadly, inasmuch the latter works to justify or conceal social relations of exploitation and domination and contributes to perpetuating them

(Hawel 2008). I will address this in different sections of my empirical chapters where I examine (a) how corporate actors act on the ideological terrain to promote approval of particular upgrading strategies in agro-industrial global value chains and (b) patterns of ideological rationalizations and consensus building in a sample case of upgrading (Chapters 8–10).

Because of this double relevance, I elaborate on some characteristics of ideology in greater detail than a depiction of the ideology-critical method alone would require. In addition, defining ideology entails further mid-range thinking tools which form a part of my understanding of a Marxist social theory and which inform this study more broadly. That being said, this chapter does not in itself provide a sufficient theoretical framework, since the methodological reference to ideology critique does not mean that ideology is the main subject of my study. Further theoretical considerations will be elaborated in the respective sections where I need them to make sense of my findings.

As an initial remark, ideology is a contested concept among various Marxist, post-structuralist, and other scholars and it may be interpreted in distinct ways. It is not my aim here to retrace this debate in detail; I will instead outline my own reading of the issue to the extent of its relevance to my work.

When you look up the term ideology in a lexicon, you find a range of synonyms, including doctrine, *Weltanschauung*, or credo. In everyday parlance, it is mainly used in a broad and abstract manner, describing any form of viewing the world and reflecting upon it. In this instance, I am employing the concept of ideology in a more complex, and at the same time more concrete way. From a historical materialist perspective, defining ideology as an intellectual framework that includes language, notions, imageries, theories, and representation systems "in order to make sense of, define, figure out and render intelligible the way society works" is a starting point (Hall 1983, 59). This definition, however, is not in itself sufficiently concrete; hence, the following discussion of elements that I consider crucial for making sense of ideology, its role, and the consequential necessity of its immanent critique.

2.1 Ideology and the (lacking) aspiration of social liberation

As an important point of departure, my understanding of ideology is tightly connected to the aspiration to put an end to exploitation and domination in their manifold expressions within the capitalist social formation. In this vein, reasoning on ideology in the traditions of both Critical Theory and Gramsci's work stems from the question of why exploited classes and oppressed or marginalized groups do not inevitably seek to change a status quo that entails their own exploitation, oppression, and uneven development.

To address this problem, the Frankfurt School takes the critique of ideology as one of its starting points. Even though Marx and Engels were aware of the importance of ideology, Adorno (1973) argues that their critique of political economy and notion of social change does not in itself suffice to explain the lack of emancipatory practice. He makes this consideration against the background that building a social formation based on the dictum "from each according to [their] abilities, to each according to [their] needs" (Marx 1989 [1875], 87) is in fact both possible and overdue in terms of historical and economic conditions, and yet, such a liberated society has still not been created.[1] At the same time, theory production that contradicts this goal continues. However, this is not an unconditional call for philosophy. Adorno has agreed with Marx especially about the need to criticize theory building which is detached from historically given social conditions and contradictions.

While Critical Theory rather looks at the problem of ideology from a Freudian-Marxist psychoanalytical perspective, Gramsci's approach is somewhat different. He asks how and why exploitation and oppression can often build upon a passive or even active consensus, including of the exploited and oppressed, to the hegemonic "historical bloc," (Gramsci 2012 [1975]-e, 1249) even if this is not built on direct coercion.[2] As I will detail below, Gramsci explores how ideology contributes to the stability of hegemony, i.e., predominance by consent. Vice versa, his concept of hegemony contributes to an understanding of how particular ideologies, entangled with material interests and concessions, come to dominate. His work on

1 For Adorno, the necessity of ideology-critical thinking had been catastrophically shown by the temporary negative culmination point within the history of capitalism, namely German fascism and the singular crime against humanity committed against European Jews. In fact, he not only sees a need to consider the absence of a broad-based liberating practice, but also the relapse into barbarism (Stache 2017, 40).

2 Gramsci understands a historical bloc as a strong coalition of the ruling political and economic forces in a particular historical and geographical constellation, which—all potential differences among themselves notwithstanding—come to agree upon a specific project of capitalist development. (All passages quoted or paraphrased from Gramsci's prison notebooks are taken from the German version and translated by the author.)

this issue concerns the ways in which consensus is organized politically-economically in class struggles, and how the respective ruling classes contend for dominance not only by controlling the means of production, but also by achieving a socioeconomic, political, and ideological-cultural hegemony that transcends antagonistic social relations.

Gramscian thinking shares Critical Theory's concern of how ideology serves the particular interests of those who benefit from sustaining the status quo of global capitalism. However, in both approaches, ideology is not the only or main reason for lacking aspirations of liberation; it cannot be understood independently of its social basis. But inversely, capitalism necessarily relies on ideological justification. The exploitation and/or domination of people in historically and geographically specific forms, and the social acceptance thereof, indispensably rely on racist, gendered, and other ideological justifications (see Werner 2016a). This also includes affirmative ideological patterns, such as Margaret Thatcher's *There Is No Alternative* or the belief that no social formation could possibly inhere greater potentials of human development than capitalism. Žižek once quipped that most people today suffer from an inability to imagine a world without capitalism, as if it were our inescapable fate.

So far, this raises two issues with respect to challenging the GVC upgrading paradigm. First, throughout this book, I will examine to what extent the GVC approach contributes to or rather obstructs an understanding of (a) the social conditions for, and contradictions of, value chain development and (b) possible ways to social liberation from exploitation and inequality. In this context, I will discuss points at which this paradigm works on the basis of ideological assumptions insofar as it abstracts from actual social contradictions that impede the goal of general socioeconomic upward mobility within global capitalism.

Second, I will scrutinize the extent to which the political and conceptual development of the mainstream GVC debate allows economic actors to build on this approach in a way that justifies vested interests rather than identifying the opportunities of bottom-up struggles and developments for social change.[3] This will now be explained in more detail.

3 Chapter 8 analyzes how GVC development strategies are actually defined in the corporate realm in Argentinian agribusiness.

2.2 Ideology in dialectical relation to the social relations of production

What makes a notion, imagery, or theory an ideology? Various aspects are relevant to define this from a historical materialist perspective. A first issue is how particular phenomena are understood in relation to the historically specific actual social praxis.

Marxism has often been accused of deploying a "too simple correspondence between the economic and the political ideological" (Hall 1983, 70). Stuart Hall, for instance, criticizes "classical" Marxism for assuming that the economic structure generated a guaranteed set of dependent ideological effects (ibid., 66). However, my interpretation of historical materialism is somewhat different. Indeed, Marx and Engels (1976 [1846])—and after them Gramsci and the Frankfurt School—have argued that the political and the ideological originate on the basis of a historically specific social reality (Gramsci 2012 [1975]-b, 456). Yet, this does not imply a rigid determinism, according to which the economic structure exists as a sphere detached from human agency, which then descends in what people do, and predefines their politics, cultures, thoughts, and theories.

Instead, as Engels puts it, people make their own history and social reality, but only under definite historically produced conditions. Among these conditions, the economic ones—understood very broadly as the dominant social praxis in which humans produce and reproduce 'actual life' and relate to one another and to nature in production, exchange, and consumption—are regarded the ultimately decisive driving forces in the making of history. Yet political, ideological, and cultural conditions develop in relative autonomy and have their own impact on the course of historical struggles (Engels 2001 [1890], 34 f.). In this vein, in *The German Ideology*, Marx and Engels (1976 [1846]) assert that consciousness can never be anything other than conscious being, and the being of people is their actual life-process.[4]

Gramsci has therefore argued that it is essential for theory formation to detect the adequate relation between the organic whole of the capitalist social formation on the one hand and particular political conditions on the other to avoid "depicting root causes as immediately operative which in fact

4 Ideologies in this sense are "objective and effective reality, but they are not the driving force of historical development, that is all" (Gramsci 2012 [1975]-b, 475).

only work indirectly" or asserting that "immediate causes are the only operating causes." The first case leaded to an "excess of economism," the second, to "ideologism" (Gramsci 2012 [1975]-f, 1557) or to an overestimation of the individual element of human action based on free choice (Gramsci 2012 [1975]-b, 494). In essence, reasoning and conscious political agency are dialectically linked to actual, specific conditions of organizing social life (Hawel 2008, no page).

The dialectics of structure and (conscious) agency

To illustrate that in more detail, Dieter Wolf (2013) emphasizes that, on the one hand, the economic structure or the capitalist mode of production with its imperative of ever more surplus value production (Marx 1990 [1867]) asserts itself independently of individual human will. Yet on the other hand, the socioeconomic reality does not exist as a self-contained sphere: As pointed out above, it is nothing other than the aggregate of social relations, produced and reproduced by acting humans endowed with reason who can thus also change these relations, again, under specific conditions (see Lütten 2015; Sommer and Wolf 2008). However, Wolf argues that consciousness, which determines people's agency, has itself a conscious and an unconscious side and that the relationship of social being and consciousness is, hence, a particular form of the relationship between structure and agency (Wolf 2013, 5 f.): People act consciously, but in doing so, they are not necessarily entirely aware of the socioeconomic forms they reproduce, because a part of what constitutes the capitalist social formation is not directly apparent on its surface; it remains hidden from social actors, as long as they do not become actively involved with the topic (Hall 1983, 68; Wolf 2013, 2).[5] One

5 Wolf therefore argues that what people know about the world motivates what they do, and with what they do, they impose the social forms, including the economic processes of which they may be (partly) unaware. For example, everyone knows that money is needed to buy commodities. On the basis of this knowledge, people reproduce the structural conditions of capitalism. What does not appear on the surface of the social relations, however, is that money is a manifestation of value, that value is produced by workers, and that capital accumulation is based on the appropriation of a part of this value and, hence, on exploitation (Wolf 2013, 8). In this context, Marx has described three different forms of the fetish character: commodities, money, and capital. He depicts as 'commodity fetishism' the mediation and perception of the social relations among people as phantasmagoric social relations among things (commodities) in a market exchange (Marx 1990 [1867]). This is ascribed to the fact that in capitalism, social labor is done individually, meaning that producers produce commodities independently of one another and only relate to one an-

task of critical theory is therefore to uncover these socioeconomic forms that constitute actual global capitalism.

For example, Marx has argued that while commodities appear to have an intrinsic value, the latter in fact needs to be understood in terms of a social relation. In order to grasp value, he says, we have to enquire about the common third that makes commodities generally interchangeable. This common third is the "property […] of being products of labor" (Marx 1990 [1867], 127). By exchanging commodities on the market, people implicitly compare the labor time that is socially necessary to produce them. Only the social relation (of exchange) thus assigns meaning to value. At the same time, Marx reveals that the essence of the valorization of value consists of a process that is intrinsically based on the exploitation of labor by capital. Exploitation, here, is understood as the appropriation of surplus value by those who essentially control the means of production, whereas surplus value is defined by the value produced by workers in the time that exceeds the labor time necessary for their reproduction under given historical conditions (Marx 1990 [1867], 274, this is further elaborated in Chapter 10). As Hall nicely illustrates, "the market brings together, under conditions of equal exchange, consumers and producers who do not—and need not […] know each other. Similarly, the labour market brings together those who have something to sell (labour power) and those who have something to buy with […]: a 'fair price' is struck" (Hall 1983, 68). 'Fairness' or 'equality' hence offer idealized or one-sided expressions of exchange relations in capitalism. They conceal exploitation or the fact that individuals take part in actual political equality from particular class and power positions (see Chapter 10).

In the same vein, the production of surplus value appears to be a naturally inherent property of capital itself, fruitfully harnessed by people endowed with business talent or a good nose for innovations. Money apparently becomes more money, but the process that mediates both extremes (the production of surplus value by workers and its appropriation by capital) remains hidden on the surface. This needs to be unhidden by critical theory and practice.

---

other through the exchange of their labor products. Hence, the social character of their private labors only appears in the moment of exchange (Wolf 2013, 29 f.). The 'mysticism' lies exactly in the concealment of the social relations of production behind commodity exchange, and hence, of the question what 'value' is and where it comes from.

This has the following implications for my discussion of the GVC approach: first, to what extent are its theoretical tools designed to grasp the social relations that constitute global capitalism and their immanent social conflicts? I will argue that the GVC framework rather tends to neglect and therefore contributes to veiling capitalist relations of production and exploitation, the analysis of which, however, is crucial when examining upgrading in global value chains and its contradictions and ramifications. Second, I will argue that mainstream GVC scholarship tends to have a narrow understanding of governance power in global value chains, from which it derives upgrading possibilities. Power, here, is detached from its socioeconomic conditions, including the uneven control over capital in competition, and the dialectics of social structure and agency.

This is not to say that a study on GVCs is ideological when it does not address every aspect that could possibly influence the matter being analyzed. No scholarly research is capable of doing that. However, the question is whether it is designed to be able to address crucial social relations, or whether it instead obstructs their understanding. I argue that an approach that is designed to neglect social relations of exploitation and domination can be described as ideological.

Ideology as false consciousness

Based on the above, I follow Hawel (2008, no page) and Stache (2017, 41) in their interpretation of Critical Theory, and further define ideology as a historically and geographically specific, but necessary and, at the same time, false consciousness. This is certainly a much-disputed understanding of the issue, and there are Marxist scholars who reject the objective of depicting ideology as a mystified and hence false conception of the social relations of production. A case in point is Althusser's school (see Reitz 2004, 707 f.).[6] Stuart Hall (1983), on the other hand, criticizes the denotation of ideology as false

6 Althusser conceptualizes ideology in the sense of ideological power, practices, and rituals within "ideological state apparatuses." People, here, are subjected to (or subject themselves to) particular ideologies, a process that is referred to as "interpellation." This is helpful for understanding how subjects impose a particular consciousness on themselves. However, Althusser understands the creation of ideology as a trans-historical process. Its dialectical relation to a historically specific reality is therewith, by trend, dissolved (Reitz 2004, 708).

consciousness without entirely rejecting the underlying conceptualization.[7] For him, the term implies a patronizing pattern and smacks of elitism: Why should "we," the privileged, "with our superior wisdom, or armed with properly formed concepts" (Hall 1983, 66) see through distortion without illusion? Reitz (2004, 710 f.) counters, however, that ideology critique in the Marxian tradition in fact criticizes the self-delusion of intellectual elites above all. Either way, Hall proposes not to understand ideology as false, but instead as a "one-sided" or "only *partially* adequate" account of social relations: "One-sided explanations are always a distortion. Not in the sense that they are a lie about the system, but in the sense that a 'half-truth' cannot be the whole truth about anything" (Hall 1983, 73, emphasis in the original).

"Is the worker who lives his or her relation to the circuits of capitalist production exclusively through the categories of a 'fair price' and a 'fair wage' in 'false consciousness'? Yes, if by that we mean there is something about her situation, which she cannot grasp with the categories she is using. [...] No, if by that we mean that she is utterly deluded" (ibid.).

However, even if ideology cannot be satisfactorily portrayed as a trick that only an intellectual elite can see through, calling an idea partially adequate is not necessarily more or less elitist than calling it false. Furthermore, Hall's change of terms indicates a turning away from the concept of reality. I instead seek to preserve an understanding of a historically and geographically specific, socially produced reality. As mentioned above, I pose that every scholarly work can always only be half-true (no one can encompass every possible aspect), and yet this sense of incompleteness is different from when particular social relations are structurally omitted or veiled.[8]

7 Hall agrees in that bourgeois ideology can be understood as false because it does not adequately explain the social relations of production. On the other hand, he says, it "can't be false in the simple sense either, since these practical bourgeois men seem capable enough of making profit [...] without benefit of a more sophisticated or 'truer' understanding of what they are involved in" (Hall 1983, 61). However, false consciousness in my understanding of Marxist Critical Theory does not mean a total delusion or deception that prevents capitalists from acting successfully.

8 There is a third point that distinguishes Hall's understanding from mine: While Gramsci's work is characterized by a concurrent understanding of ideology as an instrument of domination on the one hand, and as a terrain of struggle on the other (see Section 2.3), Hall tends to dissolve this problem in favor of the war of position conception (for a critique see Reitz 2004, 710 f.). What tends to get lost here is both the dialectics of social structure and conscious agency described above, and the necessity of ideological justification in class societies: As I have argued before, the contradictions of capitalism, including exploitation and social inequality, could not be maintained without its ideological justification, provided that it is not merely based on coercion or material concessions.

On these grounds, I adhere to the above-cited understanding of ideology as false consciousness. I will briefly specify what I mean by that. First, I have already pointed out that my conceptualization of ideology is not without preconditions. Rather, it operates on the premise of actual social conditions. It presupposes definite individuals who are active in a definite way and enter into definite social and political relations in an active life-process: "Not in any fantastic isolation and fixity, but in their actual, empirically perceptible process of development under definite conditions" (Marx and Engels 1976 [1846], 37). However, a historical materialist conception of ideology sharply criticizes positivist positions that accept the existing social conditions as a naturally given norm; it understands reality as socially produced over time and space and, hence, changeable (Gramsci 2012 [1975]-e, 1412; see Stache 2017, 42).

Second, I agree with Adorno on the need to question a seamless identity of reality and its depiction. A subject cannot depict the object in an unmediated, position-less manner. However, the precondition for getting closest to truth is the "need to lend a voice to suffering" (Adorno 1973, 17 f.). In this vein, Critical Theory stands in sharp contrast to a mainstream theory that conditionally or unconditionally accepts the social whole as pre-given and thereby duplicates the real existing social conditions of suffering within the sphere of reasoning (Hawel 2008, no page; Stache 2017, 41; see Chapter 5).[9] Based on such a conception of reality, Adorno sees in ideology an amalgam or entanglement of truth and untruth. On the one hand, it is objectively necessary in the sense that a society that systematically creates suffering cannot continue existing without ideological explanations; "ideology is justification" (Adorno 1997 [1972], 465, own translation). It is hence true in the sense that, even if it does not adequately express reality, it still reveals something about the state of society (Stache 2017, 47). And yet, it is false, not as a matter of false thinking from an opposed moral or normative point of view, but instead because it mystifies historic social reality and thus objectively serves those who have an interest in maintaining this reality. In other words, ideology is not false in the sense of being a total delusion, but rather in that it pretends to coincide with reality. There is a chasm between ideological principles and real socioe-

9 In his seminal essay *Traditional and Critical Theory*, Max Horkheimer (1988) criticizes mainstream theory for presenting reality as positive, reasonable, and, as such, seamlessly depictable, although it is in fact historically and socially produced. Consequently, it affirms the existing social relations as the ideal or at least normal state of social being.

conomic practice (Reitz 2004, 698; Stache 2017, 42). In brief, "the untruth of ideologies must [...] be traced to social conditions" (Hawel 2008, no page).[10]

For example, the idea of liberty is not false, but the idea that we have achieved it is. It is not false to say that most workers in capitalist societies are free in the sense that they are not anyone's personal property. But is wrong to ignore that they have to sell their working force since they do not own any means of production. The idea of social equalization is not false, but the idea that it can be thoroughly achieved by GVC upgrading may well be.

However, ideologies provide reasons for the general rightness of maintaining the capitalist relations of production, and thus de facto serve the particular interests of those in power. In this sense, Gramsci figuratively calls ideologues roosters that announce a day that will never come (Gramsci 2012 [1975]-g, 1918) insofar as they veil what needs to be done for this day to dawn.

This section has added to my ideology-critical approach to GVC upgrading in the following ways. First, when I argue that the latter can be criticized from an ideology-critical perspective, this does not mean that this particular form of conceptualizing development is a guaranteed and pre-determined efflux of capitalism, immutably made-to-order. Generally speaking, particular ideologies that are potent in a specific historic moment are not the only possible forms of digesting these conditions. Rather, they are particular forms of intellectually dealing with actual social conditions. Historically, the GVC upgrading paradigm has asserted itself as a mainstream approach against other approaches, such as chain scholarship in the tradition of world-systems analysis.

Second, and consequently, I analyze the GVC approach as false, not in the sense that it is entirely wrong. I will rather demonstrate that upgrading as a general path out of uneven development entails various contradictions and structurally omits particular social root causes of inequality. Therewith, the approach comes into conflict with its own aspiration, namely to generally enhance the socioeconomic situation of so-called developing countries.

10 In their *Dialectic of Enlightenment*, Horkheimer and Adorno (2004 [1944]), for instance, have argued that the progressive ideas of the French Revolution—liberty, equality, fraternity—historically developed according to the already changing social conditions that were headed towards overcoming feudalism. Since the revolution, however, did not create the social conditions for the fulfillment of these ideas, they turned into idealism in the sense that they pretended to coincide with reality, even if social relations ever since have not done justice to the ideas of liberty, equality, and fraternity.

Ideology, hegemony, class, and struggle

I have not yet addressed the question of how ideological elements actually come to be dominant. In this regard, Marx and Engels have formulated a controversial dictum, saying that the "ideas of the ruling class are in every epoch the ruling ideas" (Marx and Engels 1976 [1846], 59). The controversy surrounding this concerns the class character of ideological elements in general, and the question of whether ideas can be ascribed to particular classes. Hall (1983, 62, 77) criticizes *The German Ideology* for assuming a fixed correspondence between class and associated ideas. However, as I interpret it, it is not about claiming a fixity. Its essence is rather that historically specific social conditions provide the ruling classes "which [have] the means of material production at [their] disposal" with an unequal control over the "means of mental production" (Marx and Engels 1976 [1846], 59). In a similar line, Wallerstein, for example, has analyzed liberalism as the temporarily dominant geoculture, pushed by the hegemonic forces of the capitalist world-system (Wallerstein 2012b).

However, it is necessary to differentiate between a tendency of spontaneous attraction to specific ideas depending on particular material interests on the one hand, and the dominance of ideologies as an outcome of historic struggles on the other. As regards the first issue, it can be argued that the objective position of a class or class fraction may be related to "the limits and horizons of thought to which they would be 'spontaneously' attracted" (Hall 1983, 80) due to material interests. Class analysts have argued that capitalists, for instance, are unlikely to be attracted to ideas of social revolution (PKA 1974).[11] On the other hand, exploited classes may have an objective interest in overthrowing the capitalist mode of production. And yet, the question of how objective interests translate into subjective ideas and perceptions, which does not happen in a fixed or inevitable way (Hall 1983, 81), is very different. Apart from the aforementioned systematic mystification of exploitation, there are material conditions that can prevent working class members from sharing a class-specific consciousness. Wage earners are far from being in the same economic situations. Some enjoy considerably more material concessions than others and there is a hierarchical order, for instance, along lines of (a) varying qualifications, (b) (geographically) differentiated wages

11 See Chapter 10 for a more detailed discussion of class analysis.

or working conditions, (c) gender inequality, or (d) racist justifications (PKA 1974, 257 ff.).

Consciousness can neither be analyzed independently of its material conditions, nor can particular ideas be ascribed to class positions in a formulaic manner. Whether a major part of the working classes consciously seeks to overcome exploitation, or thinks that only individual effort leads to success, or is dominated by racist ideas, cannot merely be explained by the class position itself. It is a question of social struggles.

Gramsci's theory of hegemony helps closing this chasm. Hegemony is a fundamental concept of political and state theory. However, while Arrighi (2010) and Wallerstein (2012a) have used it to analyze cycles of hegemonic leadership on the plane of the capitalist world-system, it especially speaks to questions of cross-class consensus building (in my case, around agro-industrial upgrading; see Chapter 10).

Gramsci encourages analyzing the historical agency of social classes in relation to the development of their political culture, and to conceive class struggle beyond its economic aspect by considering political, ideological-cultural, and military struggles. For Gramsci, hegemonic class power cannot be sufficiently explained by economic and direct political supremacy. Rather, it requires moral-intellectual leadership and consent. For a class to be hegemonic, non-economic relations are crucial. In other words, gaining hegemony is not only a question of controlling the means of production, but also of adequately representing the moral and cultural standpoint of a society at a given historic moment to convince the subaltern classes.

From this viewpoint, the ruling classes dominate the ruling ideas, because they have historically gained the capacity to organize the dominant ideologies, which form "the innermost cement" of the society (Gramsci 2012 [1975]-e, 1313). Hegemony and class alliance do not just merely exist; they have instead been historically forged. This implies that ideological elements can be articulated into discourses across different classes and social groups (Gramsci 2012 [1975]-b, 492). Consequently, Gramsci understands ideology as one part of a contested but class-structured terrain on which people attain (a possibly false) consciousness of the basic structural conflicts that are manifested in the economic world (Gramsci 2012 [1975]-f, 1568 ff.). Therefore, the ideological terrain is part of the broader terrain of class struggles. But according to Gramsci, very importantly, the respective correlation of forces in these struggles cannot be understood in an abstract-tautological manner.

"In historical narratives, one often reads the common expression: favorable or unfavorable 'correlations of forces.' Formulated this abstractly, the expression, however, hardly explains anything. In this manner, one just tautologically repeats a fact that should actually be explained" (Gramsci 2012 [1975]-b, 495).

Power relations are closely connected to the social forces, and the terrain of struggle is structured historically and geographically. This means that in political and cultural-ideological struggles, members of different social classes do not have the same material conditions for enforcing ideas and putting them into practice. Without analyzing the social positions that different actors and social groups occupy within production, it is, for instance, hardly possible to estimate the degree to which particular ideas can be implemented under definite conditions (ibid.).

Ideology, therefore, has become a "practical instrument of governance and domination" (ibid., 1246), inasmuch the economically and politically ruling classes are ahead in the struggle for consciousness. Gramsci therewith implicitly reconnects to *The German Ideology* in that he understands the capacities of the ruling classes to rule in the world of ideas as a temporary result of historic struggles that leave economically dominating groups and their intellectuals with greater means of mental production. To what extent and to whom ideological/political arguments may seem convincing, and whom they serve on a broader political level is, in short, a question of the struggle for hegemony. Hence,

"ideologies are anything but arbitrary; they are real historical facts that need to be fought and revealed in their essence as instruments of domination, not for reasons of morality etc., but rather for reasons of political struggle: in order to make the governed intellectually independent of the governing" (Gramsci 2012 [1975]-e, 1325).

Importantly, the manufacturing of "active or passive consensus" (Gramsci 2012 [1975]-a, 411)[12] is not merely an issue of ideas. Active consensus means that the subaltern voluntarily become allies and cooperate in the reproduction of existing structures of exploitation and domination not simply because they are coerced, but rather because they are convinced that this is the right thing to do. It requires (a) taking the interests at least of parts of the subaltern classes seriously including (b) material concessions that enhance the legitimacy of the "historical bloc" (Gramsci 2012 [1975]-e, 1228) and

12 In other instances, Gramsci speaks of "direct" and "indirect" consensus, the latter understood as "political passivity" (Gramsci 2012 [1975]-b, 481).

strengthen the belief in the advantages of capital accumulation not only for capitalists. Coercion, however, always plays a role as background music.[13] In summary, the manufacturing of consent cannot be understood as mere ideological persuasion, rather it entails the offering of possibilities for personal advancement (or economic and social upgrading) to a wider range of social actors.

This approach also helps answering the question of how one can account for subversive ideas if ideology is considered a necessary mystified understanding of the capitalist mode of production (Hall 1983, 64). The social structure does inherently entail mystifications of the character of these social relations. However, while people tend to be spontaneously attracted by variegated false or half-true concepts, this is, as much as the structure itself, a result of historical contestation. Hegemony is never sealed; it must be constantly earned and the ways in which people intellectually digest the capitalist mode of production is contested in an ongoing struggle for hearts and minds.[14]

These considerations are useful in my context of study in different ways. First, I come back to the role of ideology and consensus building in Chapter 10, where I analyze a case of network upgrading based on exploitation and domination that is nevertheless broadly conceived as a win-win situation that benefits all actors involved. Gramsci's work allows me to assess the importance of cultural, ideological, and moral elements in the analyzed social configuration without abstracting from or eluding existing capitalist so-

13 Gramsci notes in this context that "this means that incurable contradictions have come to light within the structure, and that the political forces who positively work to maintain the structure endeavor to heal these contradictions within certain limits" (Gramsci 2012 [1975]-b, 493). For him, Fordism serves as an example, in that the adaption to new production and work methods cannot be realized merely by means of social coercion. Coercion rather has to be combined with persuasion and consensus. Given the forms inherent to the current society, this can for instance be achieved by higher pay that allows for a certain living standard. Such concessions, however, tend to be temporary and tied to particular groups rather than to all workers (Gramsci 2012 [1975]-g, 2093).

14 By way of an illustration of the historical character of these struggles, Gramsci describes how the 19th century was characterized by a considerable many-sided critical awareness of the class structuring that characterizes capitalist societies. More than is the case today, people tried to make their own histories in the hope that these can be made as histories of freedom (Gramsci 2012 [1975]-c, 1005). Historically, working class organizations have lost influence, however, also on the terrain of ideas.

cial relations as class relations—an issue that I argue needs to be brought to the fore in the discussion of (global) capitalism.

Second, the above considerations lead to the question of whose interests the GVC upgrading paradigm serves. Chapter 3 will show how the emergence of the GVC approach itself has included theoretical-conceptual changes to the commodity chain concept in the world-systems tradition. These changes have made the approach mainstream-compatible not just in scholarly debates. On Gramsci's ideological terrain, the GVC approach has also become suitable for use by institutions like the World Bank, as well as by corporate actors. In this vein, Chapter 8 analyzes how business associations in agro-industrial value chains in Argentina refer to the GVC metaphor to justify their vested interests.

The remainder of this chapter summarizes the aims of immanent ideology critique.

2.3 An ideology-critical method of immanent critique

In the past years, a number of contributions on the ideology-critical method of immanent critique have been published (Hawel 2008; Jaeggi 2009; Korf 2018; Reitz 2004; Stache 2017; Stahl 2013). In some cases, this has primarily been oriented at a critique of social practice (see, for instance, Stahl 2013). However, the method is also relevant to the critique of scholarly approaches and theories, as to the GVC approach in this case. Here, I draw on a particular version of immanent critique based on the above considerations on ideology and on the methodological assumption that critical social theory should not develop its principles independently of a historically and geographically specific social reality. Instead, it seeks to inquire into this social reality. This is a very basis of the method of immanent critique in a Marxian perspective.

Whether it deals with social practice or with a particular theory, it seeks to unveil "veiled justifications, that is, essentially particular interests masked as universal interests" (Hawel 2008, no page). As Reitz (2004, 690) puts it, ideology critique is the disclosure of how particular patterns of understanding serve domination. It examines how ideologues blank out disturbing counterfacts (ibid., 700) and thus announce a day that will never come (under definite conditions). It asks: Whom does it serve? In this vein, for Gramsci, critique opposes ideology (Gramsci 2012 [1975]-e, 1478) by showing how it is a one-sided practical political tendency (Gramsci 2012 [1975]-d, 962). It claims the invalidity of ideas inasmuch they conceal the reality of "the struggle and the contradiction" and therewith de facto serve as instruments of domination (Gramsci 2012 [1975]-e, 1326). Consequently, critique seeks "to understand and to evaluate the arguments of the opponent in a realistic manner" while taking "a 'critical' position" (Gramsci 2012 [1975]-e, 1276).

Immanent critique

What does immanence mean in this context? Immanent critique seeks more than simply claiming that its own criteria are right from the outside (Stache 2017, 39 ff.). It does not only establish external criteria; it instead criticizes—in my case the GVC upgrading paradigm—by using particular immanent standards (see Jaeggi 2009, 283 f.)—in my case, the assumption that upgrading can lead to general socioeconomic development.

This also implies that, in methodological terms, it is not the objective of ideology critique to reject every written word of the criticized approach. Instead, it seeks to preserve fruitful contributions while at the same time unfolding the extent to which it relates to the existing social order in an affirmative manner (Stache 2017, 42). In this way, critique aims to prove its point by portraying the analyzed theoretical positions, pointing out inconsistencies, internal contradictions, omissions and shortcomings, and "reflecting on their truth, particularly with regard to their social significance" (Hawel 2008, no page).

For the present study, this would mean questioning the premises and aims of the upgrading paradigm and how they relate to a historically and geographically specific reality. Hence, an immanent critique of the GVC approach confronts it against its own claims, such as the assumption that upgrading can generally remedy uneven development when "economic actors—firms and workers—move from low-value to relatively high value activities in GVCs" (Gereffi 2014, 18; see Chapter 3). In the course of this book, I will encounter points at which this assumption neglects or implicitly accepts socioeconomic structures that oppose this very purpose or through which upgrading itself reproduces uneven development.

In brief, immanent critique takes the claims set by a theory seriously, reacts to the contradictions that arise in it and in its relation to the empirical world, and seeks to gain from this the potential to reach beyond the approach while maintaining its strengths (see Jaeggi 2009, 258).

On that note, immanent critique does not mean that only the internal concepts, claims and categories of an approach can be applied as a criterion; it is not internal critique. Both have in common that they work on the basis of standards that are, in some way, already embodied in the criticized approach (ibid., 277). However, a central difference to internal critique lies in the fact that immanent critique points beyond the existing theoretical framework; it is thus transformative. Accordingly, "as analysis, it is critique (and not a mere description of the existing) and as critique, it is analysis" (ibid., 280, own translation). This entails its examining particular claims as they encounter actual social contradictions and "aims at critical overcoming" (ibid., 283). The aim of immanent critique is therefore to explain why the criticized approach must systematically and not only accidentally come into conflict with actual social praxis. It "does not naively claim that the norm could also easily be met, but reveals why the violation of the norm is not accidental, but necessary" (Stahl 2013, 49, own translation).

Consequently, the immanence of ideology critique has its limits, not least because it does not seek to spin around and remain wedged within the criticized paradigm (Stache 2017, 49). Instead of navigating only within the criticized approach, it needs a "good theory" (Jaeggi 2009, 300, own translation). It is never entirely capable of pursuing its purpose without "knowledge from outside" (Adorno, cited in Stache 2017, 50, own translation). Indeed, even the very aim of diving into an approach and criticizing it is preconditioned and has its origin in specific standpoints. Critical thinking finds its impulsion in the perception of socially produced suffering, in the urge to remedy it, and in prior knowledge and reflections. As follows from the above, ideology critique can only determine contradictions within an approach to the extent that its subject matter comes into conflict with social reality (Stache 2017, 55). Critique, hence, depends on an exploration of the contradictory character of the social reality (Adorno 1973, 205).

For my study, this means taking the concern of the upgrading agenda—the provision of socioeconomic improvement—seriously, but also analyzing the contradictions of upgrading. It does not confine itself to the theoretical instruments that are explicitly recognized by mainstream GVC scholars, but instead looks at the obstacles that stand in the way of a general upward mobility within global capitalism and uses the theoretical instruments that are needed to make sense of it. In Selwyn's words, it does not take historically and geographically specific socioeconomic structures for granted but "calls them into question by concerning itself with their origins" (Selwyn 2016b, 3).

As a case in point, neither Marx's nor Wallerstein's critique of the contradiction between formal equality or liberalism on the one hand and social inequality or uneven development on the other hand would work without their respective theories of exploitation. At the same time, Marx's critique of classical political economy insists that the latter was a powerful, substantial scientific body of work, which nevertheless contains an essential limit in that it assumes that economic development had achieved its final conclusion, apogee, and natural form. It "*assumed* the categories of bourgeois political economy as the foundations of all economic calculation, refusing to see the historical determinacy of their starting points and premise" (Hall 1983, 67, emphases in the original). Here, the distortions within bourgeois theoretical ideology are not false in the sense of breaking the rules of scientific work. "On the other hand, the distortions limit its scientific validity, its capacity to advance beyond certain points, its ability to resolve its own internal contradictions, the power to think outside the social relations reflected in it" (ibid.).

Empirical critique

In this book, my ideology critical approach to GVC upgrading as a development strategy provisionally follows the presuppositions of this paradigm and, on this basis, seeks to carve out the ensuing contradictions and shortcomings. However, my study is not designed primarily as a theoretical critique; I do not criticize the upgrading-paradigm merely on a conceptual level. Instead, I follow its assumptions with my empirical work, analyzing actual upgrading strategies in agro-industrial value chains in Argentina. Based on this analysis, I identify contradictions of upgrading strategies as they arise and are formulated on the ground.

This method meets the assumption that theory formation does not take place independently of historical geographical social reality and must therefore be evaluated according to the empirical. With Gramsci, it can be said that the quality of criticism lies in its search for "the real identity under the apparent differentiation" and the "substantial diversity underneath the apparent identities." This requires working "on the basis of real and of actual experience" (Gramsci 2012 [1975]-h, 2177 f.). For Wallerstein, ideology critique and an empirical look at the world therefore go hand in hand. He positively refers to Marxism in that it calls attention to the contradictions of the system and also "to those of its ideologists by appealing to the empirical evidence of historical reality which unmasked the irrelevancy of the models proposed for the explanation of the social world" (Wallerstein 2000a, 71). In this sense, "to be historically specific is not to fail to be analytically universal. On the contrary, the only road to nomothetic propositions is through the historically concrete" (Wallerstein 1974c, 391).

While engaging with my empirical findings and their relation to theoretical concepts, my critique seeks to maintain those elements of GVC analysis that are useful to a critical theory of uneven development. At the same time, it (a) requires conceptual tools that go beyond the theory building of mainstream GVC analysis and (b) rejects particular concepts of the GVC approach that facilitate its use in a way that portrays particular interests as universal development interests.

In brief, I therefore call my research design an empirical ideology critique of the GVC upgrading paradigm.

The positionality of ideology critique

Finally, the foregoing implies that ideology critique is not neutral; it pushes towards progressive social practice "without degenerating theory to a mere instruction manual" (Stache 2017, 43, own translation). Even though ideology critique may be in a powerless position historically, it nevertheless aspires for social emancipation. Based on the assumption that the social order provides a fertile ground for ideologies, the decisive factor in redeeming the aims of the "struggle against the lie" (Adorno, cited in Stache 2017, 43, own translation) is, in the end, social agency. On the other hand, revolutionary practice is not possible without a critical reflection on society. One can argue, as Gramsci did, that ideology critique may be a means of liberation inasmuch it is part of class struggles over hegemonic consciousness (see Reitz 2004, 691).

In a recent contribution, Korf (2018, 151 f.) has warned us a "moralization of critique" that knows what to do more than the agents of a particular social practice themselves. Following Jaeggi, he argues that immanent critique wants to show the inherent contradictions of a social practice, without a "know-it-all attitude" (ibid., 162, own translation). However, radical critique is not to be equated with being complacent or a 'know-it all.' It does not aim to predetermine social praxis from the ivory tower, but it is necessary for exposing the actual conditions for an aspired social change, including potential obstacles that can be removed by a specific social praxis.

With regard to GVC analysis, my critique is not directed against the general aim of socioeconomic development. It instead focuses on this framework's voluntaristic approach to development, meaning that its proposals for social praxis, i.e., economic and social upgrading, neglect its actual, existing socioeconomic conditions. Here, my study takes a Marxist position and argues that class dynamics, exploitation, and resulting material interest need to be brought to the fore when analyzing upgrading and its actual ramifications. I make conflicts and contradictions visible, which I argue must be consciously dealt with when thinking about an alternative social praxis. In this line, for instance, I will critically examine the GVC approach's presupposition of states and capitalist firms as bearers of socioeconomic development, and I will argue in favor of an emancipating social praxis that bears in mind the dialectics of the socioeconomic conditions of historically and geographically specific capitalism on the one hand and the possible courses of agency on the other.

Conclusion

In summary, this chapter has provided a methodological-theoretical note on the design of my study as an empirical ideology critique of the GVC upgrading paradigm. In Sections 2.1 and 2.2, I discussed various aspects that add to grasping ideology from a historical materialist perspective. As a starting point, this concerns the role of ideology in contradicting or omitting possible ways to emancipatory social practices. Second, I have problematized the detachment of theories on socioeconomic development from the historically and geographically specific capitalist social relations of production and their inherent contradictions. It is essential (a) to uncover socioeconomic forms under which uneven development reproduces itself in actual global capitalism and (b) to detect the adequate relationship between the organic whole of the capitalist social formation on the one hand and particular political conditions on the other hand.

Third, I have followed an understanding of ideology as a historically and geographically specific, necessary and at the same time false consciousness, in other words, as an entanglement of truth and untruth. It is necessary and true in the sense that (a) a society which systematically builds on exploitation and domination necessarily relies on justification and (b) it reveals the societies' dominant forms of thinking. And yet, it is false, not merely from an opposed moral or normative point of view, but because it contributes to mystifying historic social reality and de facto serves those who have an interest in maintaining the status quo. With Gramsci, I have argued that there is a chasm between ideological principles, as in the analyzed case of socioeconomic development through upgrading, and actual socioeconomic practice. This makes ideologues roosters that crow a day that will never come—under particular conditions— (Gramsci 2012 [1975]-g, 1918) as they veil what needs to be done for this day to dawn. Sharply criticizing positivist positions that accept the existing social conditions as a naturally given norm, a historical materialist conception of ideology understands reality as socially produced over time and space and, hence, changeable.

Fourth, I have explored the question of ideology in the context of class struggles and hegemony formation, and argued that the GVC approach can itself be understood as a theoretical tool on a class-structured terrain of ideological struggles.

Based on these considerations, I have argued in Section 2.3 that ideology critique aims at unveiling veiled justifications and particular interests that are portrayed as general interests. It examines how ideologues blank out disturbing counter-facts and announce a day that will never come, and it asks: cui bono? (To whose benefit?) It claims the invalidity of ideas that conceal the reality of "the struggle and the contradiction" and can therewith serve as instruments of domination (Gramsci 2012 [1975]-e, 1326). This critique is immanent critique in the sense that it does not merely establish external criteria; it criticizes—in my case the GVC upgrading paradigm—using particular immanent standards (see Jaeggi 2009, 283 f.). It seeks to preserve theoretical elements that are needed for a critical social theory while at the same time unfolding the extent to which a particular approach relates to the existing social order in an affirmative manner and systematically comes into conflict with both its own objectives and actual social praxis.

On this basis, I have posed questions that scrutinize the correspondence between the assumption that anyone can climb GVCs within capitalism provided the right institutional context, and actual social practice or corporate strategies in agro-industrial value chains in Argentina. In more general terms, my study challenges the GVC understanding of development both theoretically and by "appealing to the empirical evidence of historical reality" (Wallerstein 1974c, 487). Based on my empirical work I ask, to what extend does the GVC approach adopt a critical position on (a) the social conditions (and their immanent conflicts) under which uneven development is reproduced in global capitalism and on (b) the related possible ways to counteract exploitation and inequality?

Following upgrading strategies on the ground, my study examines how the premises and aims of the GVC approach relate to these actual strategies. It points to contradictions of upgrading and discusses how this approach blanks out counter-facts that obstruct equalization via firm-level upgrading. Furthermore, it scrutinizes the extent to which the conceptual development of the mainstream GVC approach enables a justification of vested corporate interests rather than identify the chances of bottom-up struggles for social change.

At the same time, I have pointed out that the critique of the GVC framework as ideological is not merely due to missing aspects that could also have an influence on the analyzed matter. Rather, the question is whether it is designed to be able to address crucial social relations of exploitation and domination, or whether it obstructs their understanding. Furthermore, I analyze the GVC approach as false not in the sense that it is entirely wrong. I will, in sum, instead demonstrate that positing upgrading as a general path out of uneven development entails contradictions, structurally omits particular social root causes of inequality, and thus comes into conflict with its own aspiration.

In conclusion, and as a bridge to the next chapter, I agree with Gramsci that emancipatory ideas, which are "in the air" (Gramsci 2012 [1975]-b, 460) at a certain point in time, like the idea of commodity chain analysis, may be appropriated by ideological positions, neutralized, and used for affirmative political strategies. In this line, I argue that while critical thinking in the tradition of world-systems analysis (WSA) has been, more than just today, in the air since the late 1960s, some of its ideas have been assimilated and modified by mainstream GVC analysis over the past decades and converted into a paradigm that applies to affirmative practice. This theory development will be depicted and criticized on the following pages.

3. From Commodity Chains to GVC Upgrading as a New Paradigm for Development

Global commodity or value chain analysis can look back on a history spanning decades during which different approaches using different underlying epistemological assumptions and research foci have been designed and applied in case studies. This is not solely a matter of conceptual and methodological further development; it is accompanied by an academic controversy in which a particular form of chain analysis has become mainstream. In concrete terms, while chain analysis has its roots in the critique of global political economy in the tradition of world-systems analysis (WSA), one can observe that global value chain (GVC) research with a focus on upgrading as a "new paradigm for development" (Gereffi and Fernandez-Stark 2016, 24) has become dominant. Upgrading, here, is defined as "the process by which economic actors—firms and workers—move from low-value to relatively high-value activities in GVCs" (Gereffi 2014, 18). This GVC approach has gained importance not only in academic but also in policy circles such as state-run development agencies or the World Bank (Werner et al. 2014). The latter has recently even posed that GVCs "boost incomes, create better jobs, and reduce poverty" (World Bank 2020, 3; see Selwyn and Leyden 2021a for a critique). And as Chapters 8 and 9 exemplify, corporate actors have used the approach for their own purposes, too. Now, one of the two building blocks of the GVC literature along with chain governance (Lee and Gereffi 2015, 320), upgrading is considered a device for enhancing so called developing countries' competitiveness. According to scholars at Duke University, host of some key protagonists in the GVC research community, "the challenge of economic upgrading in GVCs is to identify the conditions under which developing and developed countries and firms can 'climb the value chain'" (Gereffi et al. 2015, 3).

This chapter proceeds by giving an overview of the conceptual development from commodity chains in the WSA tradition to the global commodity chain (GCC) approach to today's dominant focus on upgrading in GVCs. It then defines more precisely what is meant by upgrading and how the GVC approach designates upgrading as a development strategy. Following this description and in line with my ideology-critical approach, I will address the key strengths of chain research as well as inconsistencies, contradictions, and omissions, especially with regard to the implicit assumption of general upward mobility within GVCs. Following on from this, Chapter 4 then revisits critiques of mainstream GVC analysis and alternative conceptions as they have recently been formulated in scholarly discussions—including the global production networks (GPN) approach—and situates my own work within these debates.

A limitation of my presentation and critique is to be considered at the outset: the plethora and theoretical eclecticism of GCC and GVC scholarship makes it difficult to do justice to the variety of thematic and theoretical backgrounds gathered under these conceptual roofs. However, it is not the aim of this book to provide a complete account of all chain and similar constructs used to analyze the functioning and the geographies of global capitalism. A variety of approaches have been sketched more comprehensively by Jennifer Bair (2005; 2008,;2009), to which readers can refer. The present study focuses on the most influential contributions to GVC analysis and to its direct predecessors, because, as stated above, it has evolved into the dominant chain approach both in development studies and as a political-practical development tool (Bair 2014, 2; Newman 2012, 155). This also corresponds to experiences I had during my fieldwork in Argentina, where interlocutors from both agribusiness and state bodies frequently referred to the value chain metaphor.

In the following section, I start with a description of the origins of commodity chain research as an approach to analyzing, understanding, and criticizing the functioning of global capitalism—or rather its functionality for some at the expense of others—from the perspective of WSA.[1]

1 WSA is not understood as a homogenous theory. Contributions by scholars like Immanuel Wallerstein or Giovanni Arrighi vary in several points including the conceptualization of capitalism itself. However, these differentiations do not impact the arguments made in the present book. For varieties of WSA, see Schmalz (2009).

3.1 Commodity Chains as the *warp and woof* of the capitalist world-system

At the beginning of his four-part opus *The Modern World-System*, Wallerstein writes that "to the extent that we want a more egalitarian world and a more libertarian one, we must comprehend the conditions under which these states of being are realizable" (Wallerstein 1974b, 10). This assertion unites two objectives: first, it is a declared goal of WSA not to pursue critical science only as an end in itself. Instead, it is tightly connected with the aspiration to change the social conditions of life for the better. Second, to achieve this goal, scholars and political actors are nevertheless encouraged to overcome illusive, modernist, and technocratic development proposals and to focus instead on holistically-minded analyses of the world economy's dynamics and inherent contradictions to understand (a) the very conditions of capitalist development and (b), based thereon, how to overcome it. To this aim, WSA has interpreted the historical course of the capitalist social order. Unlike other Marxist interpretations of the rise of capitalism, it understands the world economy as a system that came into existence at latest in the sixteenth century. Ever since, it has been dominated by "owners who sell for profit" (Wallerstein 1974a, 3) and who seek to acquire extra profits. In this view, it began as a European world economy (Wallerstein 1974b) and came to span the entire world in the nineteenth century (Wallerstein 1974a, 1). Until today, it has evolved in hegemonic cycles and long waves of economic expansion (A-phases) and contraction (B-phases). Note that these boom-bust cycles are regarded a hallmark of the world-system—capitalism without cyclical crises is inconceivable from this perspective.[2]

One of the central tenets of WSA is that the dynamics of global capitalism lead to a steady reproduction of uneven development, to a geographical stratification into centers, peripheries, and semi-peripheries in a cohesive world economy marked by a global division of labor and a geopolitical division into separate states. Pursuing this argument, centers are where highly profitable, i.e., relatively monopolized activities converge, while the oppo-

2 "Capitalism is not a stasis; it is a historical system. It has developed by its inner logic and its inner contradictions. In another language, it has secular trends as well as cyclical rhythms" (Wallerstein 1988, 103). For a brief explanation of the so-called Kondratieff-cycles, which measure expansions and contractions in the average rate of profit in global capitalism, see Wallerstein (1994, 8 f.; 2004, 30 ff.).

site is true for peripheries (Arrighi and Drangel 1986). In other words, WSA refers to centers as those zones that concentrate the most productive activities and higher value appropriating capabilities, and which thereby emerge as winners of the distribution of surplus value (Parnreiter 2011, 192).[3]

It is against this background that the idea of analyzing commodity chains was first introduced by Hopkins and Wallerstein (1977, 128). It was intended as a theoretical and analytical means to investigate how processes of production and exchange are linked in a way that systematically reproduces geographic inequality. By commodity chain the authors mean "a network of labor and production processes whose end result is a finished commodity" (Hopkins and Wallerstein 1994, 17; see Wallerstein 200b, 2; Hopkins and Wallerstein 1986, 159). More precisely, this means to take "an ultimate consumable item and trace back the set of inputs that culminated in this item—the prior transformations, the raw materials, the transportation mechanisms, the labor input into each of the material processes, the food inputs into the labor" (Hopkins and Wallerstein 1977, 128). To differentiate this approach from the subsequent modifications of chain analysis, with which some decisive strengths of the world-systems perspective were relinquished, the following recalls seven key premises of commodity chain research in the WSA tradition.

First, in contrast to the GCC debate that evolved in the 1990s, Hopkins and Wallerstein (1977; 1986) maintain that the global scope of the organization of commodity chains is not qualitatively new (see Komlosy 2021). They understand the tendency towards globalization (a) as a hallmark of capitalism since its emergence, which has (b) always been an imperialist globalization of chains of exploitation, though its *forms* and characteristics have changed historically and geographically (see Wallerstein 2000b).

Second, the world-system is explicitly not considered to be the sum of self-contained national economies (Arrighi and Drangel 1986, 12). While dependency theory, against modernist conceptions, had rejected the nation-state as the appropriate level of economic analysis and focused instead on the relations between states and their social classes (Gereffi 1983, 9; see Frank 1969), WSA sees the world-system as marked by a world-scale division of

3 In the words of Arrighi and Drangel (1986, 17): "[T]he nodes or economic activities of each and every commodity chain tend to become polarized into positions from which the pressure of competition has been transferred elsewhere (core-like activities) and positions to which such pressure has been transferred (peripheral activities)."

labor, "integrating labor processes dispersed across territorial boundaries" (Hopkins and Wallerstein 1986, 168; see Wallerstein 2000b, 2). Accordingly, commodity chains are usually geographically extensive and tightly interwoven; they are the "warp and woof" (Hopkins and Wallerstein 1994, 17) of the structure of the world-economy, and in their totality, they are the world-economy. From this perspective, research must not be limited to national units, decontextualize chains from one another, or look at particular firm activities without understanding them in relation to other actors.[4] Accordingly, analyses of single chain 'boxes' or 'nodes'[5] are best conducted by considering their relations with other nodes (Hopkins and Wallerstein 1994, 18 f.; 1986, 162).[6]

Third, and in concomitance with this understanding of the world-economy as marked by a global division of labor, the center of attention is not on the commodity as a thing. The term commodity chain was rather assigned "for want of a better conventional term" (Hopkins and Wallerstein 1977, 128). Instead, the focus lies on (a) the tasks in component production in relation to other activities in a chain (functional division) and (b) these activities' uneven geographic distribution (geographical division).[7] Whether activities are core-like or periphery-like is explicitly defined by their profitability compared to other activities, not by the produced commodity as such. In other

4 Wallerstein (2000b, 3 f.) gives an example for the difficulty to mark starting points and ends of commodity chains: "Let us take [...] the oft-described 'world car' [...]. The cars that are sold are assembled in places called automotive plants. Each plant has essentially three elements: machines, inputs, and workers. Each element may be traced back beyond the plant. The machine was in turn assembled in a locus where there were other machines, inputs and workers [...] And so it goes. [...] Let us think of [the] food production as the essential input to workers [...]. This is, of course, an endless chain." It is equally difficult to exactly define the contours of single chain links (ibid., 5). Korzeniewicz and Martin (1994, 69) have therefore argued that any "claims derived from commodity chain analysis regarding the structure of the global division of labor would require the accumulation of a very large set of commodity chains."

5 Such analyses can ask, for example, to what extent the boxes are core-like and how they spread geographically, what are the property-like arrangements and the dominant relations of production, what are the modes of labor control, and so forth. Here, the terms "links," "boxes," and "nodes" will be used synonymously.

6 However, Bair and Werner (2011a) have noted that commodity chain research has not yet thoroughly considered how different chain links are actually forged or how exactly core-like nodes appropriate a part of the surplus produced in the periphery. Daviron and Gibbon (2002, 140) even ask, what a singular box or chain node is. "How specific does a process have to be before it is considered distinct, and how can this specificity be confirmed?"

7 As core-like activities are predominantly located in certain geographic areas, the functional division of labor reiterates in the geographical division of labor.

words, what remains decisive is the differentiated distribution of surplus value between chain links and across loci (Bair 2009, 8; see Wallerstein 2000, 7). As Arrighi and Drangel (1986, 11 f.) put it, "core activities are those that command a large share of the total surplus produced within a commodity chain and peripheral activities are those that command little or no such surplus" (see Wallerstein 1994, 7; Korzeniewicz and Martin 1994).[8] Hopkins and Wallerstein (1982, 125) therefore speak of "cores-in-relation-to-peripheries and peripheries-in-relation-to-cores."

Fourth and consequentially, the focus on the underlying processes and relations between core and periphery is necessarily a focus on inequality. Core-like actors monopolize[9] and produce with high profitability, because peripheral actors are being outplayed and cannot do the same.

Fifth, the assumption that the complex world-division of labor leads to a constant perpetuation of uneven development does not imply that centers will always be centers and peripheries are necessarily trapped in their position for all and forever. The configuration of commodity chains and their nodes is rather subject to historical and geographical change. It is a matter of "constant social redefinition" (Wallerstein 2000, 5). The reason is seen in an above-mentioned tendency: highly profitable chain links are commonly characterized by relative monopolization and account for above-average profits secured through entry barriers. But this can only be a temporal

8 Consequently, Hopkins and Wallerstein (1982) interpret the initial dependency theory's assumption that peripheral zones produce raw materials whereas core-like zones produce manufactured goods as too simple. In a similar vein, Appelbaum et al. (1994) argue that it is not the degree of industrial processing that accounts for the wealth of a country but the relative value produced and captured in it. A country can possibly be industrialized—but still captured in a peripheral position due to "geographical transfer of value" (Hadjimichalis 1984). This is an important point, also for analyzing agro-industrial chain nodes that are located in Argentina. Romero (2016) has argued in this context that a significant part of the value produced in the Argentinian soy processing industry is realized elsewhere and that the majority of high value and capital-intensive means of production are import goods (see Chapters 8 and 9). However, it has not been systematically discussed from within the commodity chain approach that whole chains can be more profitable than other chains.

9 The underlying definition of monopolization is: "a situation in which, because of the absence of competition, the transactor can obtain a high profit, or one could say a high proportion of the surplus-value generated in the entire commodity chain of which the monopolized segment is a part. [...] [Capitalism] has never known widespread free enterprise precisely because capitalists seek profits, maximal profits, in order to accumulate capital, as much capital as possible. [...] Capitalists do not want competition, but monopoly. They seek to accumulate capital not via profit but via rent" (Wallerstein 1988, 103).

situation and in the long run, any highly profitable chain link is potentially "subject to competitive pressures that tend toward its demonopolization over time" (Bair 2009, 8; see Wallersetein 2000b, 8). New producers can enter into the world market "however well politically defended is a given monopoly" (Wallerstein 2009a, no page). From the viewpoint of WSA, this tendency of relative monopolies to break down sooner or later steadily causes shifts in the division of labor, in the distribution of social wealth, and thus in the functional and geographical restructuring of chain nodes, all of which are linked to the "cyclical rhythms of the world-economy" (Hopkins and Wallerstein 1994, 18).

But, and this is a sixth point, while upgrading and geographical shifts of periphery-like activities are regarded as possible, this does not imply the feasibility of harmonization, equalization and even development within the capitalist world-system. The latter is *necessarily* based on the unequal distribution of rewards and on the corresponding perpetuation of uneven development (Gereffi and Korzeniewicz 1990, 47).[10] Core-ness can move around geographically but the prospect of general upward mobility is a "developmentalist illusion" (Arrighi 1990, 11) and "the some that rise are at the expense of others that decline" (Wallerstein 1974a, 7). Put differently, within capitalism this is a "zero sum game" (Wallerstein 1994, 15).

"As the rise of an activity to core status implies the decline of one or more other activities to peripheral status (i.e., it implies that competitive pressures have been shifted from one activity to other activities), the success of an enterprise in upgrading its mix of core-peripheral activities always implies a more or less generalized downgrading of the mixes of other enterprises" (Arrighi and Drangel 1986, 20).

Finally, a seventh—and important—characteristic of thinking in the world-systems tradition is the analysis of the world-scale integration of production on the one hand and the geopolitical organization in national units on the other. States, in this conception, cannot be understood as neutral ac-

10 It is a merit of dependency theory and especially Frank (1969a; 1969b) to have analyzed the historical making of metropolis-satellite relationships as a development of underdevelopment. However, while *dependistas* have argued that development was most feasible when the respective region was most delinked from global capitalism (in B-phases), Arrighi and Drangel (1986, 58) instead argue that even if peripheralization was historically not widened in B-phases, it was deepened. Furthermore, Frank tended to theoretically immobilize center-periphery relations or to reify them at a particular point of historical development. Arrighi and Drangel (1986, 58) have attached importance to changes within the world economy over time.

tors: WSA points to the strength of core states to support 'their' capitals and to influence both local prospects of accumulation and the allocation of specific chain nodes, for instance, through tax policies or protectionism (Arrighi and Drangel 1986; Wallerstein 2009a). Inspired by Gramsci, the WSA conception of capitalism as reproducing in cyclical rhythms includes struggles over, and cycles of, geopolitical and geocultural hegemony. Accordingly, strong imperialist states compete against each other (in phases of a descending hegemony) and use their power against weak states (Hopkins and Wallerstein 1977, 120; see Arrighi 2010; Wallerstein 2012a).[11] Vice versa, firms can exert pressure on states, for instance, by threatening the relocation of particular chain nodes. Without this international character of the world-system, Wallerstein argues, "the likelihood of serious accumulation of capital would be radically reduced. In consequence, one cannot make sense of decisions by particular producers in a commodity chain without first taking into account the geopolitical situation" (Wallerstein 2009b, 87).

In summary, commodity chain analysis in this tradition is designed to analyze a deeply contradictory capitalist world-system especially with respect to the inherent uneven distribution of surplus value between peripheries and centers through mechanisms of unequal exchange within a global division of labor. One of the mayor strengths of WSA lies in the analysis of how necessarily uneven development plays out on the ground in variegated and ever-changing ways, without losing sight of systematic characteristics of global capitalism (Wallerstein 1974; see Hopkins and Wallerstein 1977). However, the assumption that center-periphery relations cannot be generally dissolved within the capitalist world-system has been largely abandoned by mainstream GVC scholars.

With respect to my case study, successful upgrading strategies deployed by firms in Argentinian agro-industries (see Chapter 9) can indeed only satisfactorily be interpreted when understanding 'periphery' as something historically and geographically alterable. Economic actors can move towards higher profit activities. At the same time, my empirical chapters support WSA's assumption that upgrading cannot trigger an overall catch-up development. However, commodity chain analysis in the world-systems tradition also has shortcomings (for a friendly critique, see ten Brink 2008). I briefly

11 See Quark's (2014) study on how the intensification of inter-state and inter-firm competition in the cotton commodity chain has destabilized but not undermined the hegemonic position of the US both economically and politically as China's position has grown and consolidated.

address three aspects that are relevant for the discussion of my empirical work and which I will discuss in greater depth in the respective chapters.

Three considerations

A first point is of relevance for my analysis of upgrading in and through class differentiation in Chapter 10: While WSA is characterized by a great historiographical narrative power that in fact includes the role of capital strategies and social struggles in the development of global capitalism, class relations remain underexposed in theory. Labor does play a role here, especially with respect to differentiated systems of labor control, working conditions, and wages, which are assumed to be worse in peripheral chain nodes than in capitalist centers (Hopkins and Wallerstein 1982, 126; see Soendergaard 2018, 71). However, Wallerstein ultimately sees these differences as distributional matters and as dependent on center-periphery relations. As outlined above, WSA understands commodity chain analysis primarily as a means to explain "how the system of 'unequal exchange' worked in practice" (Wallerstein 2000a, 221; see Wallerstein 1979; 2009a).[12] It therewith theoretically suspends the question of where the unevenly distributed value actually comes from or how it is produced. More precisely, WSA theoretically prioritizes the structure of uneven exchange between center and periphery over the social relations of production. The underlying understanding of capitalism as a system in which capitalists "seek to accumulate capital not via profit but via rent [that is, above-average profit enjoyed due to monopolization, CB]" (Wallerstein 1988, 103) reduces the explanatory power of the concept of exploitation to profiteering among chain nodes, and neglects class dynamics[13] as drivers of historical development (Hadjimichalis 1984, 331; Selwyn 2012). This results in a limitation of WSA's conceptual tools for an analysis of how

12 In a similar vein, Arrighi and Drangel (1986, 16 f.) grasp accumulation differentials that underlie the center-periphery relation in terms of an uneven distribution of rewards among chain nodes, due to monopoly power. They use the term 'surplus' as a "short-hand designation of the differential between the total product of a commodity chain and the total rewards that would accrue to factors of production if they were remunerated at the rates obtaining in peripheral activities."

13 Wallerstein (1975) tends to understand class formation mainly in terms of political class formation and power relations, thus letting aside political economic class relations.

value is produced and distributed also *within* particular chain links (in the wake of upgrading).[14]

A second, though related aspect concerns the concept of monopolization (through entry barriers). The way in which WSA understands the latter as an immanent though historically and geographically altering feature of the world economy is useful, in particular, in that it does not reify the formation of (relative) monopolies in time or space. Yet it does not theoretically explain monopolization as a process. Wallerstein (2009a, no page, emphasis in the original) defines that

> "[c]apitalism is a system in which the endless accumulation of capital is the *raison d'être*. [...] In a situation of perfect competition, it is absolutely impossible to make significant profit. [...] Any time the world-economy is expanding significantly, one will find that there are some 'leading' products, which are relatively monopolized. It is from these products that great profits are made and large amounts of capital can be accumulated."

This conception is inspired by Schumpeter's (2003 [1943]) understanding of value in terms of rent (as mentioned above) and of capitalism as existing in a constant process of reshaping through innovation that temporarily and unequally raises minorities into economically powerful positions (see Selwyn 2014b, 104; Werner 2018, 5). However, this approach expounds monopolization one-sidedly as the capacity to outplay other producers by controlling scarce products and innovations. Competitive innovation appears as the driver of historical change. Therefore, it does not theoretically account for how capitalists seek to produce and sell above the competitive level by increasing the rate of exploitation, i.e., the surplus value compared to labor costs. As Selwyn (2014b, 113) points out from a value-theoretical perspective, Marxist and WSA conceptions of monopolization are compatible in the assumption that leading capitalists seek to gain super profits from leading in innovation or from enjoying resource-monopolies. However, in contrast to an understanding of profits as primarily returns on entry barriers, Marxist theory (a) emphasizes the roots of both average and super profits in the exploitation of labor and (b) finds in this process of valorization a

14 For example, why is it that core-like activities entail greater 'trickle down' effects at some times and places than at others? Beverly Silver has acknowledged that while the WSA perspective emphasizes the "very real constraints that the totality imposes on the range of possible action open to local actors [...] its weakness is that it excludes a priori a situation in which local action [for instance, decisions forced through by either capital or workers, CB] significantly impacts local outcomes" (Silver 2003, 39).

reason for the tendency of capitals to innovate and concentrate. Marx (1990 [1867], 429 ff.) argues that capital—without innovation—faces constraints with respect to the need to increase the appropriation of surplus value, i.e., to increase the time wage earners work beyond the reproduction of their wages. For instance, the working day cannot be extended indefinitely, wage dumping has its limits, and workers may defend their interests. However, these constraints can temporarily and geographically be bypassed; through the development of the productive forces, be it via technological innovation or more effective forms of organizing production, the valorization of value can be increased by endowing "a given quantity of labour with the power of producing a greater quantity of use-value" (Marx 1990 [1867], 431). The rate of exploitation can thus increase without extending the absolute working day or cutting wages, but by reducing the labor time necessary for commodity production (Altvater 1975, 133 f.).[15] As long as an innovation in production has not been socially established, leading firms can thus produce commodities below the average cost price, sell them at the market price, and hence make extra profits (Altvater 1975, 149; Selwyn 2012, 23 f.). With respect to such upgrading processes, the consideration of class relations and the underlying understanding of exploitation are necessary for the theorization of uneven development.

A third point that requires further consideration is the way WSA conceptualizes the state. It tends to reduce the theory of the state to describing its functionality in the capitalist world-system. I agree with Bair (2005, 156) that examining the antinomy between the world economy and its organization in core-like and peripheral (nation-)states is a fundamental concern. For instance, this concerns analyses of how core states shape the economy by different means that include free trade agreements[16], standards, and protectionism (Bair 2014; Quark 2014; Wallerstein 2009b). Furthermore, it is important to consider the relationship between the economic position within global capitalism and the political capacities of a state. However, the theorization of the (peripheral) capitalist state itself remains weak, especially

15 This is because the surplus labor grows in relation to the time that is socially necessary for a worker to work for her reproduction. Marx has called this an increase of the relative surplus value, which leaves a greater share of the produced value in the hands of capital. I will come back to this point when analyzing strategies of process upgrading and related capital concentration in Chapters 8 and 9.

16 As I will take up in Chapter 8, Wallerstein has therefore analyzed free trade as "free trade imperialism" (Wallerstein 2012b, 145, own translation).

with respect to the questions of (a) how and why the dominance of particular social classes within states develops, and (b) how and why the ways in which state policies benefit the interests of capital, workers, or other social groups have differed historically, also within core-like or peripheral states respectively. Recourse to state-theoretical considerations is needed to explain actual state agency, also in view of GVC scholars' understanding of the state as a promoter of upgrading (see Chapters 4 and 8; the debate on the (non)existence of national economies has to be excluded from this study).

Bridging to the next section, I maintain that the portrayed conceptual roots of chain research in WSA bear strengths that have been sidelined by contemporary commodity or value chain research. As regards the analyzed shortcomings, I would differentiate between approaches that, like WSA, put the critique of exploitation and domination on a scholarly footing and in doing so neglect crucial aspects (differences between WSA and other strands of Marxism bear room for fruitful debates) and other approaches, which can de facto serve as a conceptual basis for affirmative projects of capitalist development. The following sections discuss a theory development through which mainstream chain research has taken the second path over the past decades.

3.2 From GCC research to GVC upgrading as a new paradigm for development

Scholars have comprehensively reviewed the growth of commodity chain research's importance in the academic world throughout the 1990s. However, the conceptual access was modified under the GCC framework and further-reaching alterations were made under the GVC perspective in the 2000s (Bair 2005; 2009; 2014; Newman 2012; Selwyn 2012; Sturgeon 2009).[17] As mentioned above, both approaches—though especially the GVC version—have extended their influence to academically informed policy circles that aim at engendering "investment policies for growth and sustainability" (Fessehaie and Morris 2018, 27; see Frederick and Gereffi 2009; Gereffi and Bair

17 There is no overall agreement among scholars working with chain-like concepts about the exact distinctions between these approaches. Studies are often comparable in key assumptions and methods (Bair 2009, 12). Furthermore, CC, GCC, or GVC research have not replaced one another over time; "literature overlaps, and work in all three traditions of chain research continues" (ibid., 13). I cite the concepts according to the quoted authors.

2010; Gereffi and Luo 2014; Gonzalez 2016; Psilos and Gereffi 2011; Taglioni and Winkler 2016; World Bank 2020).

In what follows, I trace the most influential conceptual changes made by GCC and GVC scholars, which have partly enriched the tools of critical chain research. At the same time, however, the theory development has successively contributed to an ideologization of chain analysis and to its use for a scholarly-based affirmative paradigm of capitalist development (see Parnreiter and Bernhold 2020).

First, I delineate GCC research, with (a) its legacies from the world-systems perspective, (b) a shift of focus to chain governance, and (c) the role it ascribes to upgrading (Section 3.2.1). In Section 3.2.2, I trace the GVC framework's movement towards transaction cost economics and micro-level network governance. Section 3.2.3 then offers a detailed portrayal of upgrading as a development strategy. At the end of each section, I submit aspects of an immanent critique.

3.2.1 Global Commodity Chain Analysis

In the mid-1990s, Gereffi and Korzeniewicz (1994) published a path-breaking anthology named *Commodity Chains and Global Capitalism* to which Hopkins and Wallerstein (1994) contributed a paper on commodity chain research.[18] What was genuinely new was the introduction of the GCC framework. Gereffi and his colleagues have defined GCCs as the infrastructure of international trade consisting of "sets of interorganizational networks clustered around one commodity or product, linking households, enterprises, and states to one another within a world-economy" (Gereffi et al. 1994, 2).[19] Under this umbrella, they claimed to reformulate the basic conceptual categories needed for analyzing new patterns of global economic organization (ibid.).

18 In the same book, this paper was used by Özveren (1994) and Pelizzon (1994) as a lens for analyzing cyclical fluctuations of monopolization and de-monopolization in shipbuilding and grain flour commodity chains respectively.

19 GCC scholars understand as a network the linkage of firms to one another across space in a dynamic division of labor, connecting producers to national, regional, and global markets (Gereffi 1996, 428). This is not understood in contrast to chains; the latter rather comprise inter-firm networks.

Legacies from the world-systems perspective

The GCC approach has maintained the WSA's focus on "world-economic spatial inequalities" (ibid.) and "unequalization" (Kaplinsky 2000). As its direct predecessor, it regards uneven development as causally related with the global integration of production, which can only be grasped by moving across different levels of analysis both above and below the plane of national economies. Furthermore, GCC analysis shares the assumption that a country's export structure or level of industrialization does not in itself reveal much about its integration into the world economy; "'industry' is not always a motor of development" (Gereffi et al. 1994, 4). In this line, scholars have proposed to analyze the *mode* of the integration of firms and countries into global production and "the specific linkages that connect industries to global markets and transnational corporations" (Appelbaum et al. 1994, 187; see Kaplinsky 2000, 119). GCC scholars therewith aimed at responding to the reorientation of many so-called developing countries towards export-oriented industrialization (EOI) throughout the 1970s, buttressed by neoliberal governments and supranational institutions. Concurrently, the framework was conceived as a means to critically interpret "industrial upgrading by established exporters among the newly industrialized countries (NICs)" (Gereffi 1994a, 211). Some East Asian countries were depicted as beneficiaries from their integration into GCCs. In most cases, however, research indicated that a peripheral incorporation into the global division of labor was consolidated despite or rather precisely because of EOI strategies, since high-value products for export continued to be based on low-waged assembly tasks in situ, such as the automotive industry in Mexico (see Appelbaum et al. 1994; Bair and Dussel Peters 2006; Gereffi and Korzeniewicz 1990; Lee and Cason 1994; Parnreiter 2007; 2013).

In brief, GCC research seeks to address "who controls global trade and industry, how they do so, and with what consequences for producers in developing countries" (Daviron and Gibbon 2002, 141). Yet apart from analytical legacies of the WSA, Bair (2005, 154; 2009, 9 ff.) has worked out important splits that have existed between the two frameworks from the beginning, which I will depict and complement in the following.

Shifting the focus to governance in global commodity chains

First, GCC (and GVC) scholars regard the global integration of production in commodity chains as something qualitatively new.[20] This assumption is based on the premise that the organizational and geographical fragmentation of production as well as the importance of trading components in lieu of finished products have reached a new quality—a process that simultaneously inhered a de-verticalization of production and a yet increasing control over commodity chains exercised by lead firms (Dicken 2003; Gereffi 1994a, 211 ff.; 1994b, 95 f.; 1996, 434; Humphrey 2004; Kaplinsky 2000; Sturgeon 2009, 111).[21] GCC scholars hence assume that socioeconomic polarization, today, can be attributed to qualitatively new patterns of globalization. The assertion of WSA, according to which cyclical dynamics of global reorganization and a concomitant reproduction of uneven development belong to capitalism like the rain to a cloud is no longer part of the GCC-research basis. The strong emphasis on the world-economy as a holistic social order and on *system-immanent* features that make equalizing development an illusion was discontinued, such that the focus on organizational features of commodity chains (Gereffi 1996, 428; see Daviron and Gibbon 2002; Gibbon et al. 2008, 316) is a substantial departure from the WSA tradition (see Bair 2009).

Throughout the 1990s, GCC scholars started placing greater emphasis on the argument that "regions, countries, and individual localities *can* improve their relative position in the global economy" (Sturgeon 2009, 110, emphasis in the original) and on the question of how this can be achieved (see Kaplinsky 2000, 126). However, the main research focus was on the problem that finding levers for a more sustainable development requires an understanding of how uneven development is actually organized in GCCs, and how these organizational characteristics often prevent peripheral countries, regions, and firms from upgrading.

20 More precisely, Gereffi et al. (2001a, 1) differentiate between internationalization, defined as the spread of economic activities between states, and recent processes of globalization, the functional integration of economic activities. Newly, for them, capitalism "is not only international in scope, it is also global in organization" (ibid.).

21 The work of both Dicken (2003) and GCC scholars on intra-firm trade and outsourcing strategies can also be read as a critique of assumptions in the style of Nigel Harris (1987), according to whom a new division of labor that includes industrialization in the Global South paved the way for "The End of The Third World," leaving aside how firms outsource, move production loci, and resort to low wage labor to "escape the core economy profitability crisis of the 1970s" (Selwyn 2016b, 10).

Similar to WSA, one decisive aspect of defining the (im)possibility of upgrading consists of the (in)capacity to set entry barriers. In this view, the ability to control strategic assets or scarce attributes (and thus to evade the pressure of competition) is decisive to profitability. As indicated in Section 3.1, this emphasis is strongly based on a Schumpeterian understanding of how firms gain high returns when they are ahead in the context of "creative destruction" (Schumpeter 2003 [1943], 81 f.; see Gereffi and Korzeniewicz 1994, 4; Kaplinsky 2000, 122; for a critique see Selwyn 2014a) and have a decisive lead in innovation. GCC (as well as GVC) scholars then understand value added as rent accruing from returns on innovation[22] or from "barriers to entry (that is, scarcity)" (Kaplinsky 2000, 122; see Dedrick et al. 2009; Gereffi 1992; 1999; Kaplinsky 2006).[23] For Kaplinsky (2000, 127), high value activities increasingly stem from "governorship itself."[24] In this respect, I refer to my critique of the conceptualization of value added through entry barriers as briefly formulated in Section 3.1.

In accordance with this importance ascribed to governorship, the GCC framework has made a shift towards analyzing especially the role of lead firms in present-day inter-firm networks (Gereffi 1996; 1999). Scholars have specified analytical tools that help make sense of how the uneven distribution of profits is organized in commodity chains. Gereffi outlined three dimensions along which GCCs can be analyzed, the first two being directly based on WSA: the geographic scope of commodity chains and their input-output structure, that is, "a set of products and services linked together in a sequence of value-adding economic activities" (Gereffi 1994b, 96 f.).[25] The newly introduced and most employed dimension, however, is chain governance. A basic assumption is that GCCs are shaped by structures of com-

22 See for instance the empirically very rich study by Dedrick et al. (2009, 82) on how Apple has captured a great deal of "value from innovation embodied in the iPod" in comparison to other notebook makers.

23 Raikes and Gibbons (2000, 66) consequently assume that the preparation of commodities for international transport (drying, hulling etc.) is not a value-adding process, since it does not belong to the activities with relatively high margins. In a similar vein (and in contrast to a Marxian understanding of value), Fernandez-Stark (2011, 32) argue that value added in the production of fruits and vegetables only takes place when industrial processing is incorporated.

24 Kaplinsky and Morris (2001, 28) differentiate between Schumpeterian rents (based on better technology, human resources, organization, and marketing), relational rents (arising from beneficial relationships), and rents external to the chain (policy rents, infrastructural rents, financial rents).

25 GVC scholars later added another dimension, namely institutional structures (Sturgeon 2009, 114; see Gereffi and Fernandez-Stark 2016).

mand and control, even in dominantly market-like relations, and it describes the asymmetric power of lead firms to shape chain nodes' configurations, set barriers to entry, specify what is to be produced, by whom, where, and how, and hence, to appropriate relatively higher profits. Accordingly, lead firms therewith establish the parameters for upgrading capacities of other actors in GCCs (Gereffi 1994b; Gereffi et al. 2001a).

Gereffi (1994b) has famously defined governance in terms of driving, distinguishing between producer-driven and buyer-driven chains (PDCCs and BDCCs respectively). This difference is defined by the sites of key entry barriers within the commodity chains[26] and the ways in which lead firms outsource low-profit activities. In PDCCs, which are largely associated with capital-intensive industries, "large integrated industrial enterprises play the central role in controlling the production system" (Gereffi 1994b, 97; 1996, 430 ff.; see Raikes et al. 2000). BDCCs, on the other hand, concern labor-intensive industries in which large retailers and brand firms set up "decentralized production networks in a variety of exporting countries, typically located in the Third World" (Gereffi 1994b, 97; 1996, 430 ff.).[27]

GCC scholars have used this governance-framework, for instance, to map the growing power of oligopolistic commercial capitals in "a web of independent but interconnected enterprises" (Gereffi 2001a, 32). There are plenty of studies analyzing how chain drivers have used their market power to lower prices for goods or components, dictate standards, reduce labor costs via subcontracting and outsourcing, and shape overseas production networks by determining the terms and conditions of participation, even without having equity relations of any kind with contractors. On the other side of the chain, the implications for downstream exporters have often been "not so

26 The outlined Schumpeterian understanding of surplus is also relevant to the distinction between BDCCs and PDCCs: PDCCs rely on "technology rents" (arising from scarce control over key technologies) and "organizational rents" (arising from entry barriers set via specific patterns of organization). BDCCs, in contrast, rely on "relational rents" (arising from supply chain management), "trade-policy rents" (arising from scarcity created by state policies), and "brand-name rents" (arising from higher returns based on prominence) (Gereffi 1999, 43 f.).

27 One of Gereffi's basic assumptions is that a reorientation of so-called developing countries towards EOI went along with a growing importance of BDCCs, which came along with transitions in monopolized profit making from tangible activities to intangible (knowledge and skill-based) activities such as design and branding that are tacit in nature and thus provide strong entry barriers.

promising" (Gereffi 1994b, 116).[28] As for agriculture, Raynolds (1994) examined how 'traditional' agriculture activities in the Dominican Republic have been upgraded throughout the 1980s to technology-intensive, non-traditional exports, such as horticultural crops. Yet she concludes that the local returns remained limited because of the low tax rates to be paid by lead firms and rock-bottom wages (ibid., 158; see Section 3.2.4 for a review of further agriculture-related GCC/GVC studies).

GCC research and upgrading

It can be recapitulated that GCC analysis was initially performed mainly to examine how the organization of global production often impedes upgrading and equalization in commodity chains—especially for those who act under the wings of lead firms that set entry barriers. At the same time, however, it was no longer emphasized that general upgrading is a developmentalist "illusion" (Arrighi 1990, 11; see Wallerstein 1994). The shift of focus to organizational features of GCCs implied the implicit assumption that a different organization of capitalism could possibly remedy socioeconomic polarization. In fact, Gereffi highlights that "one of the major hypotheses of the global commodity chain approach is that development requires linking up with the most significant lead firms in the industry" (Gereffi 2001b, 1622). Accordingly, upgrading can occur "to products that are organizationally related through the lead firms in global commodity chains. The microfoundations of this upgrading pattern involve both forward (marketing) and backward (sourcing) linkages from production, and the kind of learning that occurs across these segments" (Gereffi 1999, 39). In this vein, the framework was used early on, albeit not primarily, to investigate organizational conditions that can possibly facilitate upward mobility for suppliers, and to explore the prospective development of peripheral regions through "informational flows and learning potential" (Gereffi 1999, 52; see Dolan and Tewari 2001; Gibbon 2000; 2001b). This includes studies on how lead firms transfer internet technology by forcing "their rivals and suppliers alike to bear the costs of adapting to new technologies in the information age" (Gereffi 2001b, 1634).[29]

28 A vast body of literature has expanded the BDCC/PDCC distinction between two different forms of chain governance. For a review see Bair (2009, 20 ff.) and Section 3.2.2 of this book.

29 In a similar manner, Gereffi has studied how apparel manufacturers in East Asian newly industrialized countries (NIC) used networks to enhance their competitive advantages. In "triangle man-

In summary, GCC research was designed to focus on specific modes of integration into global commodity chains and especially on chain governance and related power differentials. The research interest was shifted to determine (a) (organizational hindrances of) upgrading possibilities in global commodity chains and (b) mechanisms by which organizational learning can occur.

What drives the drivers? An ideology-critical note

Many scholars have pointed out how the GCC framework and in particular the analysis of chain governance has advanced the study of commodity chains. It offers tools to map and describe (a) the articulation of firms that are globally dispersed across chain links as well as (b) related geo-economic power differentials and their ramifications for development prospects in peripheral chain links. Methodologically, it enables a strong empirical depiction of the coordination and control strategies of lead firms in chain nodes with high entry barriers. Therewith, GCC analysis can illuminate "how corporate decisions and practices in one part of the world impact upon developmental processes in another part of the world" (Selwyn 2016b, 4), putting the spotlight on the making of a "growing disjuncture between the global spread of activities and incomes" (Kaplinsky and Morris 2001, 41; see Bair 2005; Daviron and Gibbon 2002; Kaplinsky 2000a; Taylor 2007). As an approach that has thus been used in numerous case studies, the GCC research agenda has sprouted substantial empirical insights into the organization of global production and trade, intra-capitalist relations, the geographies of the distribution of pieces of the cake, and the resulting constraints faced by peripheral actors. All this material reveals with a global view and "with empirical clarity the fallacy of the idea of the 'free market'" (Selwyn 2016b, 4) and of perfect competition (see Selwyn 2016a, 1769). The global economy is not just the sum of arms-length relations between firms; it is coordinated among firms with different levels of power. Furthermore, it is a merit of GCC research to have exemplified that development and industrialization are not synonymous and that uneven development is a question of how firms or regions are integrated into global production in relation to one another.

---

ufacturing," first-tier suppliers (positioned between lead firms and offshore-factories in low wage countries) could upgrade from the assembly of imported goods to a more domestically integrated and "higher value-added form of exporting" (Gereffi 1999, 38).

The narrow focus on organizational features and governance structures in single chains has contributed to the feasibility of research "because it takes a significant but still manageable slice of the world economy as its object of study" (Sturgeon 2001, 9). Thus, the power of GCC analysis lies in its potential to analyze capitalism—not how it systematically works as a social order, but how its organization plays out in situ. However, "if we lose sight of the entities from which the 'slice' is extracted" (Bernstein 1996, cited in Bernstein and Campling 2006a, 262), we also lose sight of the dialectical relation of the practices in such slices to the structural characteristics of global capitalism. In this respect, the focus on chain governance is often accompanied by a systematic neglect of central findings of both the Marxian critique of political economy and WSA, which brings with it omissions and theory-immanent contradictions. Here, I address the question of chain governance, while the next section will focus more closely on upgrading.

Chain research in the GCC tradition contradicts its own agenda to a certain degree. I have traced in this section how the approach aims to offer theoretical-methodological tools to explain uneven patterns of economic development and to study socioeconomic polarization. However, while this undertaking requires an understanding of the underlying socioeconomic relations, the GCC approach tends towards politicistic arguments in that it confines the explanation of political economic phenomena to a question of political power relations among economic actors. It is thus reductionist specifically because it prioritizes the articulation of economic actors endowed with differentiated access to power over economic processes and constraints that influence these actors' power, rather than integrating both.

This finds an expression in a tautological explanation of power or chain governance, and therewith of a phenomenon that lies at the heart of the GCC framework's analysis of commodity chains. The tautology lies in that power is, on the one hand, associated with chain drivers: those who have power control scarce resources and coordinate the chain to their own benefit. In other words, governance power determines "how financial, material, and human resources are allocated and flow within a chain" (Gereffi 1994b, 97). On the other hand, power is supposed to accrue from the monopolization of scarce resources which again arise from "governorship itself" (Kaplinsky 2000, 127). Put differently, power arises from the control over scarce resources, and the control over scarce resources arises from power. What needs to be explained is, thus, instead repeated. A parallel can be drawn to Gramsci's note that the correlation of forces in social struggles cannot be understood in an abstract-tautological manner but need to be related back to socioeconomic forces (see Chapter 2). The GCC framework herewith loses explanatory power to not only describe how lead firms develop certain strategies to gain competitive advantages but also to explain why and on what political economic basis they do so. I will argue throughout this book for an understanding of competitive advantages and therewith economic power as a historically specific outcome of class dynamics and competition in capital accumulation (see Campling and Selwyn 2018, 427 f.).[30] Without a theory of the capitalist social relations of production and exploitation, GCC research is only partly equipped to explain how capitals can or cannot gain the power to lead.[31]

To sum up, GCC research looks at power differentials, depicts unequal patterns of control over the organization of global industry and trade, and captures the consequences for actors in peripheral chain links. At the same time, however, it systematically excludes the social relations of production and neglects class dynamics as well as the power of core-like capitals as a historical result of gaining control over the means to increase the rate of exploitation (see Hadjimichalis 1984). It therefore lacks a part of the basis to explain the power to govern a chain.

The next section analyzes how these omissions have been accentuated by mainstream GVC scholars' focus on upgrading. The GCC framework, however, with its deviations from WSA and a narrow explanation of political economic relations, has already contributed to blanking out counter-facts that contradict upgrading as a viable path for capitalist development to the benefit of all, even though it has delivered helpful tools to analyze global chains as well as comprehensive information that contradicts such an affirmative turn. Some shifts already made under the GCC conceptual roof helped push chain research into the mainstream (Taylor 2010, 611) and for its use to map

30 In contrast to WSA, GCC scholarship furthermore abstracts from structural patterns of economic crisis that influence strategic decision-making. However, the validity of crisis theory in the WSA tradition compared to other theories of capitalist crisis cannot be discussed within the scope of this book.

31 I have discussed above how the GCC theory of entry barriers and extra profits would gain from the conceptualization of labor exploitation. This is a similarity to WSA. Yet in contrast to the latter, which empirically highlights the role of labor or different forms of labor control, GCC studies have long been characterized by an absence of issues of labor in general. I will discuss this in Section 3.2.3 in terms of social upgrading.

out upgrading as a "key strategy" (Appelbaum et al. 1994, 188) for so-called developing economies (see Bair 2009, 11; Bernstein and Campling 2006a).[32]

3.2.2 The Global Value Chain framework

Further substantial modifications of the chain construct were undertaken throughout the 2000s under the label of GVC analysis (see Bair 2005; 2009). According to involved scholars, the new denomination was introduced, first, due to a widespread connotation of the term commodity with raw materials and, second, to highlight the importance of value added within chains. Third, the term GVC was considered as a basis for gathering different currents of chain analysis under one conceptual umbrella (Sturgeon 2009, 117; see Gereffi et al. 2001a, 2).

The term value chain is more precise than former denominations in the sense that, with respect to uneven development, it is not the commodity as a product that is critical, rather the production and distribution of value—or value as a reified social relation. Yet despite the change in name, critical scholars have noted that the GVC perspective does not actually work with a coherent theory of value, let alone one that deals with exploitative social relations (Quentin and Campling 2018; Selwyn 2013; Werner 2012). When exploitation is considered in mainstream GVC research, it is portrayed as a situation where workers are very poorly treated and paid, rather than as a systemic feature of capitalism. GVC analysis rather centers on how value added as returns on investments through the "application of human effort" (Sturgeon 2009, 117) grows by way of innovations. Earlier in this chapter, I have outlined why I do not consider this a sufficient explanation for the production and uneven appropriation of surplus value. Following up on this, this section traces how the GVC approach has further moved in the direction of an understanding of value added as something that can generally be increased by upgrading in/of value chains. GVC analysis is typically conducted from the vantage points of two key concepts: governance and upgrading (Lee and Gereffi 2015, 321). Both are mutually related and will be discussed in the two following sections.

---

32 Bair (2009, 11) points out that institutions such as the UN Economic Commission for Latin America and the Caribbean (ECLAC) have already taken up the GCC framework for assessing development prospects.

GVC-Governance, transaction cost economics, and micro-level network analyses

The GVC framework was developed as a modified theory of chain governance in the course of a series of workshops held by policy makers and academics from different disciplines (Sturgeon 2009, 112). Their stated goal was to solve "real-world policy problems" related to the widespread recognition that the gains from global capitalism are unevenly distributed within and between economies and to "develop a theory that could help policymakers explain and predict governance patterns in cross-border production networks. With such tools in hand, our thinking went, interventions aimed at upgrading the position of local workers, firms, and industries within global-scale production systems could be more finely crafted and effective" (Sturgeon 2009, 112; see Gereffi and Fernandez-Stark 2016). Fittingly, the first publication launched from this initiative was titled *The Value of Value Chains: Spreading the Gains from Globalisation* (Gereffi and Kaplinsky 2001).

The theoretical roots of chain research in the WSA tradition were now widely superseded by a conjunction with literatures on international business, management, and industrial organization. Especially transaction-cost economics are central for the GVC-understanding of governance (Lee and Gereffi 2015; Sturgeon 2009; for a critical review see Bair 2008; Taylor 2010). In very simple terms, transaction cost theory (Williamson 1989) looks at how economic operations imply varying transaction costs according to different conditions. A key concept is "asset specificity," in which assets are regarded as specific depending on the degree to which they can only be reasonably deployed in particular contexts, tying business partners into a mutually dependent relationship. This creates "opportunities for either party to take advantage of the other" (Sturgeon 2009, 120). Accordingly, asset specificity accrues in networks and transaction costs are high where, for instance, opportunistic behavior and cheating are likely or where complex and delicate information is crucial. On this basis, it is assumed that firms then tend to work towards forms of direct control over production to prevent high transaction costs (Gereffi and Luo 2014, 3; see Sturgeon 2009, 120; for a critical assessment see Taylor 2010). GVC scholars argue, however, that even complex production does not necessarily require a vertical integration of operations under a single company roof; instead, coordination costs can also be managed via inter-firm divisions of labor.[33] Accordingly, network actors can dampen opportunism through mutual dependence and trust, or "through the effects of repeat transactions, reputation, and social norms that are embedded in particular geographic locations or social groups" (Gereffi et al. 2005, 81; see Humphrey and Schmitz 2001, 20).[34] In this line, GVC research focuses on inter-firm coordination and resulting forms of network governance in consideration of institutional environments in which economic activities are embedded[35] "to understand how industries function within particular localities" (Sturgeon 2001, 10). Kaplinsky (2000, 125) for instance argues that the parameters of production and distribution can be strongly influenced by state institutions. Yet the framework's main objective is to analyze chain governance "by isolating those industry-level characteristics that affect inter-firm linkages" (Bair 2008, 357). Instead of theorizing state or other institutions in relation to the economy, the focus lies on depicting the context that they provide "for firm-specific action" (Neilson et al. 2014, 3).

In conjunction with these considerations, scholars have scrutinized the twofold model of producer-driven and buyer-driven chain governance as dichotomous and too static, and they have argued that coordination in value chains can take various forms beyond market-led or hierarchical models (Gereffi et al. 2001a, 4; Sturgeon 2009, 16). Five forms of inter-firm governance were identified, applicable to any industry and ranging from low to high levels of power asymmetry:

"Simple *market* linkages, governed by price; (2) *modular* linkages, in which complex information regarding the transaction is codified and often digitized before being passed to highly competent suppliers; (3) *relational* linkages, in which tacit information is exchanged between buyers and highly competent suppliers; (4) *captive* linkages, in which less competent suppliers are provided with detailed instructions; and (5) linkages within the same

33 Dolan and Humphrey (2004, 439) pose that firms may prefer outsourcing over intra-firm vertical integration also due to the complementary competencies provided by independent suppliers.

34 In Chapter 8, I exemplify how this view influences firm-level upgrading strategies in the agro-industrial chain in Argentina. Especially my case company El Agro directly builds upon network analysis and transaction cost economics.

35 Embeddedness is understood here as an "effect of the institutional environment on transaction specific governance" (Bair 2008, 346; see Dolan and Tewari 2001; Sturgeon 2009). The concept is taken from Granovetter's economic sociology. However, Gereffi and Hamilton (2009) criticize the latter for underestimating the relevance of entry barriers and governance structures. Moreover, they reject an understanding the global economy as a sum of national economies.

firm, governed by management *hierarchy*" (Sturgeon 2009, 118 f., emphasis in the original).[36]

Accordingly, the type of chain governance is determined by (a) the complexity of and the ability to codify transactions, (b) the capabilities of suppliers in relation to the requirements of a given transaction, and (c) social/institutional embeddedness. A central interest of GVC research then lies in analyzing how power dynamics related to these types of linkages play out in different situations. Power asymmetries are assumed to be higher in GVCs with a predominance of captive linkages than when market or modular relations prevail (ibid., 130); on the other hand, they are supposedly lower when suppliers wield competency and thus power due to a specific supply that is indispensable for a lead firm.

In brief, GVC analysis seeks to depict "the complexity of inter-firm relationships and the extent to which they involve investments specific to a particular transaction—asset specificity" (Gereffi et al. 2005, 80; see Humphrey and Schmitz 2001). The aim is to map how global production is linked contingent on issues of coordination and related power asymmetries. Bair (2005, 153) points out that the GVC approach has thereby shifted the analytical interest of chain research away from a holistic understanding of the global political economy to "the meso level of sectoral logics and the micro level objective of industrial upgrading." In contrast to the GCC conception of governance as drivenness, command, and control, that includes an understanding of (market) power as domination and inter-chain-link inequality (see Section 3.2.1), the GVC conception looks at power in terms of coordination in network junctures (Gereffi et al. 2005, 85; Sturgeon 2009, 119; see Bair 2008).

---

36 Ponte and Gibbon (2005, 3) note that there has yet to exist a "single and relatively coherent model of overall governance." Accordingly, GVC governance consists of three levels: first, the micro level of governance as understood in GVC research. Second, they refer to convention theory and analyze how conventions, normative frameworks, and standards regulate GVC participation at the meso-level. Here, they analyze governance as "normalizing" (i.e. how norms and standards are passed on between different chain links, making firm agency compatible). Third, the macro level is about governance at the level of the whole chain (ibid.; see Ponte 2009; Ponte and Sturgeon 2014; Ouma 2010). Gibbon (2008), for example, examines African clothing production for US and EU markets and how conventions of culturally specific forms of organization influence chain governance. He argues that taking conventions and trade regulations into consideration solves the problem of the GVC framework's narrow understanding of governance. However, these authors do not problematize how certain conventions actually evolve in historical social and political (class) struggles.

So far, the World Bank's *World Development Report 2020* marks the culmination of chain research's mainstreaming, in the wake of which the significance of exploitation and power in terms of domination has been increasingly neglected. As Selwyn and Leyden (2021a, 3) criticize, "the report is as full of praise for the developmental potential offered by GVC inclusion as it is empty on [...] power relations." It takes the concept of *relational* chains from GVC analysis whilst ignoring the latter's discussion of captive chains (see World Bank 2020, 3, 14, 32), and it "uses the language of comparative advantage trade theory to assert that GVC-led development generates mutual gains for both lead firms (concentrated in developed countries) and supplier firms (concentrated in developing countries), thus benefiting workers in both rich and poor countries alike" (Selwyn and Leyden 2021a, 6).

Critical reflections on the GVC approach to chain governance

One of the stated aims of GVC scholars is to further contrive elements of a "generic, industry-neutral" (Sturgeon 2009, 135) theory. This is a needed undertaking within development studies, especially for research that understands the dynamics of contemporary global capitalism as more than a mere sum of cases from different industries and that attempts to be both historically and geographically specific and "analytically universal" (Wallerstein 1974c, 391).

However, the portrayed analytical tools proposed by the mainstream GVC current of chain research are somewhat at odds with its stated objectives: On the one hand, the perspective seeks to explain patterns of uneven "gains from globalization" (Gereffi and Kaplinsky 2001) as well as power asymmetries in global value chains and, on this basis, to find levers to remedy inequality. In this context, chain governance is regarded as causal, meaning that it can explain "organizational and spatial features of GVCs" (Sturgeon 2009, 128) and resulting development prospects. On the other hand, the portrayed conceptual modifications have limited the analytical view of chain research to the level of inter-firm coordination in networks. As Bair (2008, 339) remarks, the proposed empirical analysis on a micro-socioeconomic level "is a problematic concept for analyzing economic organization at a global level," particularly when case studies are not discussed in the context of political economic dynamics.

Building on my critique of the GCC approach to governance (Section 3.2.1), I thus argue that the GVC analysis has further narrowed the understanding of chain governance. The added dimensions of chain governance notwithstanding, the perspective one-sidedly assumes governance structures to be the cause of uneven upgrading opportunities, leaving aside how they are themselves an effect of political economic practices that require explanation. It has moved global economic dynamics, systemic exploitation, and power (as power-over) further off the scholarly radar.[37] Therefore, it has systematically excluded analytical tools that have informed generic theories of uneven development and helped explain why the gains of globalization are unequal.

In detail, one implication of the theoretical turn towards transaction cost economics is that GVC analysis tends to neutralize power as a social category. While it problematizes power asymmetries, governance power as such is no longer analyzed in terms of domination structurally exercised by core-like actors to enlarge their share of the cake. Rather, it is considered an organizational feature that accompanies any economic action, while asymmetries then accrue through adverse forms of network organization. Humphrey and Schmitz (2000; 2001), for example, portray governance as a technical necessity that closes the rift between market requirements and (lacking) capacities of suppliers or that avoids the risk of supplier failure to comply with labor or other standards. In this respect, they do recognize that profit squeeze is likely to lead to wage pressure. However, they argue that this in turn increases the need for chain governance. Here, the cat bites its own tail, as the authors neglect that chain governance as an enforcement of profit interests may itself lead to wage pressure. As I discuss in the next section and in my empirical Chapters 8 and 9, one consequence of understanding governance one-sidedly as coordination, detached from structural socio-economic conditions, is the implicit assumption that firms are development partners interested in general upgrading—unless conditions are adverse.

A second shortcoming that results from the omission of capitalist socioeconomic relations concerns the explanation of power asymmetries and the assumption that the latter are high in captive chains and low in market or modular linkages. The GVC perspective does not offer valid grounds for hypothesizing a linear causal relation between the five types of governance and power asymmetries. It posits that the form of chain governance is contingent upon different factors, namely institutional context, complexity and codi-

37 Kaplinsky and Morris (2001, 50), for instance, mention exploitation not as a general feature of GVCs, but rather with respect to "women, children and other marginalized and exploited groups."

fiability of transactions, and "suppliers' capability to meet buyers' requirements" (Lee and Gereffi 2015, 322). However, economic relations can be "governed by price" (Sturgeon 2009, 118) and at the same time characterized by exploitation and differentiated capital power. Take, for instance, the purchase of labor force at the market price and its exploitative use in production; or relations in which firms buy, say, machinery from large corporations at market prices while uneven gains and decision-making power still exist due to differentiated capital concentration, i.e. not merely due to a lack of competency or of a transaction's complexity. Here, the GVC framework's attribution of weaker power to scarce skills and competencies reduces its capacity to explain who is able to develop competencies and govern a chain and why. In Chapter 10, I use an example to discuss this issue.

A third issue concerns the GVC framework's conceptualization of embedded chain governance. It identifies, with good reason, state and other institutions as entities that influence value chain development (Gereffi 2014, 13). However, the employed concept of embeddedness presumes states as given factors. In this respect, the GVC perspective loses analytical strength, as it does not conceptualize states with their historically and geographically specific relations to socioeconomic dynamics and class and other social struggles. Consequently, it does not ask how and why state actors at specific times and places do or do not have the power or interest to shape GVCs in a particular way. I return to this in my discussion of the upgrading paradigm.

In summary, the GVC approach explicitly aims to formulate a generic theory that contributes to addressing questions of global development; however, the analytical tools it has introduced rather describe firm and network-level coordination (see Bair 2009, 25). Scholars have shifted chain research away from examining governance as the power to organize exploitation to a technocratic understanding of governance as the "non-market coordination of economic activity" (Gereffi et al. 2001a, 4; see Ponte and Sturgeon 2014, 206). The GVC framework's neglect of exploitation and domination incapacitates it from explaining anti-developmental outcomes of GVCs (Selwyn and Leyden 2021a, 14). In these ways, GVC approaches hide key social relations and processes from view. This conceptual turn is tightly intertwined with an understanding of upgrading as a development strategy.

3.2.3 Upgrading as a new paradigm for development

As mentioned before, mainstream GVC scholarship is explicitly driven by the consideration to craft "effective policy tools related to industrial upgrading, economic development, employment creation, and poverty alleviation" (Gereffi et al. 2005, 79). In this light, upgrading has been described as a "stepping stone" and vital condition of both economic and social development (Gereffi and Fernandez-Stark 2016, 6).[38] According to Lee and Gereffi (2015, 321), the concept focuses on "bottom-up strategies" that can be used under definite governance arrangements "by countries, regions, and local firms to maintain or improve their positions and outcomes in the global economy" (see Cattaneo et al. 2010; Gereffi 2014; Gereffi and Fernandez-Stark 2016; Gereffi et al. 2011; Psilos and Gereffi 2011).

GVC literatures generally refer to upgrading as a process by which firms or regions and workers advance from low-value into "relatively high-value, sustainable niches" (Gereffi et al. 2001a, 5). This can occur through innovations that allow for higher returns (Gereffi 1999, 52; see Anlló et al. 2010; Gereffi and Fernandez-Stark 2016). Kaplinsky and Morris (2001, 38, emphasis in the original) identify four possible trajectories commonly adopted by GVC researchers:

"*Process upgrading*: increasing the efficiency of internal processes such that these are significantly better than those of rivals, both within individual links in the chain (for example, increased inventory turns, lower scrap), and between the links in the chain (for example, more frequent, smaller and on-time deliveries)[.]

Product upgrading: introducing new products or improving old products faster than rivals. This involves changing new product development processes both within individual links in the value chain and in the relationship between different chain links[.]

Functional upgrading: increasing value added by changing the mix of activities conducted within the firm (for example, taking responsibility for, or outsourcing accounting, logistics and quality functions) or moving the locus of activities to different links in the value chain (for example from manufacturing to design) [...]

---

38 In the awareness that there are also critical studies that work with the GVC vocabulary, the arguments portrayed in this section are aimed at mainstream analyses.

Chain upgrading: moving to a new value chain (for example, Taiwanese firms moved from the manufacture of transistor radios to calculators, to TVs, to computer monitors, to laptops and now to WAP phones)."[39]

These types of upgrading correspond to four Schumpeterian forms of innovation: (1) new methods of production and organization, (2) new commodities, (3) new sources of supply, and (4) new markets (Selwyn 2012, 17). Duke fellows have furthermore defined the mere entry in value chains and movements into larger end-markets as upgrading (Gereffi and Fernandez-Stark 2016, 12).

As a "*new* paradigm for development," the "'GVC paradigm' of upgrading" (Gereffi and Fernandez-Stark 2016, 24, emphasis added) argues that moving to higher value niches does not necessarily require a transformation from traditional agriculture to manufacturing and service industries. It rather means a development from low-skilled, labor-intensive towards higher value added, technology, skill, and knowledge-intensive production within any industry, including agriculture (ibid.; see Salido and Bellhouse 2016; Taglioni and Winkler 2016).[40]

However, most scholars acknowledge that upgrading is not a straightforward process. For example, studies have suggested that in captive chains, process or product upgrading are likely facilitated by learning from lead firms, whereas this is not the case with functional upgrading (see, for example, Schmitz 2006). Other surveys have indicated that upgrading capacities tend to be geographically concentrated in old as well as new centers of political and economic power, while this does not necessarily entail technical

39 From within GVC scholarship, Ponte and Ewert (2009, 1638 f.) have criticized this four-type classification. They argue (a) that product and process upgrading cannot easily be distinguished in agribusiness GVCs, (b) that profits can be enhanced without upgrading (by economies of scale), and (c) that higher profits "can actually entail product 'downgrading'" (ibid., 1639; see Section 3.2.4). They also point out that product upgrading does not necessarily entail better prices per unit; it may simply be necessary in the face of competition or not to fall out of the system at all (ibid., 1640).

40 Corresponding studies have been published, for example, on Latin America and the Caribbean, where GVC authors aim at guiding future competitiveness and economic development by capturing greater value from export activities, enhancing the respective industries via organizational learning or workforce development. Examples include coffee in Central America, automobiles in Mexico and Brazil, and horticulture in different countries, among others (Fernandez-Stark et al. 2014; Gereffi 2012; Gereffi et al. 2013; Gereffi et al. 2015).

spillover to low-value chain links (Gereffi 2014; Gereffi and Fernandez-Stark 2016; Humphrey 2004; Lee and Gereffi 2015).[41]

Yet although such problems are raised, the GVC perspective presupposes that analyses of the conditions under which firms and countries are integrated in GVCs generally allow for the creation of suitable strategies for value chain development. As I have portrayed in the previous section, factors that are assumed to determine the odds of upgrading include socio-politico-spatial dynamics and forms of chain governance (Gereffi 2014; Gereffi and Fernandez-Stark 2016; for agriculture and agro-food GVCs see Fernandez-Stark et al. 2011; Humphrey 2004).[42] The analysis of these conditions then serves to explain (with a view to practical development) "whose behavior needs to change if different outcomes are to emerge" (Kaplinsky and Morris 2001, 44; see Schmitz 2004).

The (at least implicit) premise is that economic advancement can be achieved anywhere (at least to some degree) when the right instruments are defined according to the local conditions for improving knowledge, productive capacities, products, and functions in GVCs, or by accessing new

41 Lee and Gereffi (2015, 325) have argued that emerging countries, such as China, India or Brazil, managed to develop new competencies. They pose that "rising power firms" and south-south value chains with lower entry barriers, reshape the geographies of GVCs, and provide new, though not secure, upgrading advantages. "The business press is full of entrepreneurial initiatives being launched by innovative companies all around the world [...] which are empowered by the use of the Internet, pervasive digital technologies and crowd-sourced venture capital to solve basic development problems" (ibid.; see Cattaneo et al. 2010; Kaplinsky and Farooki 2010). However, the authors also assume that rising power firms such as Foxconn hardly transfer knowledge and technology to smaller firms (or improve labor conditions) (Lee and Gereffi 2015, 331). Similarly, Kaplinsky et al. (2011) find that upgrading in China goes along with downgrading in other regions, including Thailand and Gabon, from where China prefers to import unprocessed products. Therewith, it negatively affects upgrading possibilities in "less-developed countries," since "the buyer has the power to either create a path to upgrading or kick away the development ladder" (Cattaneo et al. 2010, 14).

42 To name two examples, Humphrey and Schmitz argue that although knowledge transfers "are by no means automatic" (Humphrey 2006b, 582), firms that gain access to chain leaders in highly governed chains "tend to find themselves on a steep learning curve" (Humphrey and Schmitz 2001, 20). Stamm (2008) indicates in a study on agribusiness in Sri Lanka that there are cases of organic agribusiness where the business objective is to "supply high value products to challenging markets" (ibid., 29) and where relational linkages prevail that are characterized by "low levels of power inequalities" and "rather positive socioeconomic outcomes" (ibid., 25). He concludes that "in the best case relational chains can have an important outreach to smallholders and especially where the chain integrators are willing to share their knowledge and enable joint learning and upgrading" (ibid., 33).

markets. This already contains an inherent contradiction: On the one hand, upgrading has a "comparative component," meaning that it refers to the *relative* improvement of a firm's competitive position compared to others: "Sustainable income growth requires the capacity to protect oneself from competition" (Kaplinsky and Morris 2001, 76; see Anlló et al. 2010; Gereffi et al. 2001a). Here, the search for possibilities to escape the "tyranny of the normal rate of profit" (Kaplinsky and Morris 2001, 27) is the fuel that drives capitalist innovation processes, and therewith upgrading. On the other hand, especially policy-oriented analyses neglect that this comparative element in fact implies the *im*possibility of upgrading for all, since in competition, one can only win at the expense of others; regardless, studies focus on upgrading opportunities for individual firms or countries. In other words, while gaining a competitive advantage necessarily means outpacing other actors, mainstream GVC scholars purport a general possibility to make "global value chains work for development" (Taglioni and Winkler 2016) through "private sector development strategies" (Pietrobelli and Staritz 2013, 2). In contrast to the WSA's concern with how uneven development changes in form and place and yet necessarily reproduces in global capitalism, the GVC paradigm for development thus de facto assesses capitalist competition as a possible motor of general development. Instead of a structural feature of the dominant economic system, inequality here is understood in terms of an "uneven distribution of upgrading opportunities" (Lee and Gereffi 2015, 319; see Cattaneo et al. 2010, 19) that can potentially be tackled by meeting "national competitive goals" (Psilos and Gereffi 2011, 3) and by helping "developing-country firms" (Gereffi et al. 2001a, 2) understand how GVCs operate in order to explore the potentials to better participate in the capitalist profits to be reaped (see Anlló et al. 2010; Gereffi and Fernandez-Stark 2016; Pietrobelli and Rabellotti 2006). Participation in GVCs is regarded as a potential funnel for corresponding development strategies (Gereffi 2012, 6 f.; Humphrey et al. 2004, 63).

Here, the GVC upgrading paradigm shows similarities to modernist assumptions about the 'way up' in economic development[43] and related positive social outcomes. Yet in response to both modernization theories and also to the "one size fits all" solutions of the Washington Consensus, GVC analysis gears towards more tailored solutions "directed at firms in a particular sector or along a specific supply chain" (Werner et al. 2014, 1239). However, the perspective on development remains within localized technocratic policy approaches to global socioeconomic problems. It proposes that questions of development can be tackled by adjusting screws, managing the insertion of firms and regions into GVCs, and paying "explicit policy attention" (Dolan and Tewari 2001, 102; see Gereffi et al. 2001a; 2001b; Humphrey 2004; Pietrobelli and Rabellotti 2006) to spreading upgrading capabilities.

Realpolitik and its protagonists

Since sustainable development is not regarded as a straightforward process and value chains span national boundaries, scholars argue that developmental actors may need to "learn how to upgrade producers in low income countries" (Kaplinsky 2000, 126). As Humphrey and Schmitz (2001, 21) put it, "some buyers may require 'mentoring' in order to fulfill this funnel and transmission function." Correspondingly, realpolitik-oriented GVC research aims at assisting "in formulating appropriate policies and making necessary choices" (Kaplinsky and Morris 2001, 22) that promote desirable development outcomes.

When it comes to actors considered as the subjects of development who potentially make the local best of globalization, literatures have at first mainly focused on firms and state actors as well as development institutions (see Humphrey 2006b; Kaplinsky and Morris 2001; Trienkens 2011). These parties are considered responsible for setting the rules of the game in GVCs or, in the case of donor organizations, who ought to understand these rules and draw the respective practical conclusions. According to Humphrey

43 For instance, Fernandez-Stark et al. (2011, 23 ff.) depict stages of functional upgrading in horticulture value chains. Once countries enter a GVC via primary production, they "can begin to offer services in the packing and storage segment." Since climbing on to processing industries is regarded more difficult "previous success in the production stage" is a precondition, according to the authors. Then, distribution and marketing, "the final stage of the value chain" can be taken over from global buyers by actors from "larger and more capable developing countries."

(2006b, 584), for instance, donors intervening in agribusiness GVCs need to base their agendas on an understanding of the local private sectors' interests to ensure that firms support (or at least do not undermine) development strategies.

State institutions are supposed to create fruitful surroundings for upgrading and (a) "proactively assist the private sector workers' organisations and other stakeholders to recognise the opportunities and threats posed by participating in global value chains" (Kaplinsky 2000, 141 f.); (b) assist economic actors in accessing GVCs; and (c) use its available policy instruments to support corporate actors in moving to high-value niches and meeting the required standards. Concrete measures extend from providing support for skill enhancement, to the provision of infrastructures and the development of workforce or human resources, and to facilitating helpful trade policies (ibid.; see Gereffi and Fernandez-Stark 2016; Humphery 2004; Psilos and Gereffi 2011).[44] In the words of Gereffi et al. (2015, 22), it is central how states "can move up the value chain by engaging local firms, assimilating new knowledge and improving employment conditions, with appropriate policies and institutions to facilitate economic, social and environmental upgrading."

In this vein, the improvement of countries' upgrading capacities is supposed to take place in cooperation between value chain links and in dynamic public-private partnerships to ensure "systemic efficiency" (Kaplinsky 2000, 126) or "systemic competitiveness" (Kaplinsky and Morris 2001, 9).[45] Here, additional "stakeholders" come into play, for which GVC research analyzes the potential to act "in concert" (ibid., 131), including education, finance and scientific institutions, workers organizations, and others. However, the ex-

---

44 Kaplinsky and Morris (2001, 78) identify blockers that need to be tackled to promote upgrading, such as "poor IT infrastructure," "lack of skills in the economy," "intellectual property rights," "buyers who block suppliers from using own designs," among other things.

45 These ideas show strong similarities with the concept of "systemic competitiveness" as envisioned by Latin American neo-structuralism, a development approach designed by the ECLAC as a response to criticism of neoliberalism (Figueroa 1993; Sunkel 1993; Sunkel and Ramos 1993). Fernandez-Stark et al. (2011, 32) analyze Chilean horticulture industries and positively reference this country's government's "economic openness, political stability, and concerted efforts by both the private and public sectors to improve competitiveness." Chile is one of the countries that referred closely to neo-structuralist recommendations (for a critique see Leiva 2008; Webber 2010). The latter have also been as a source of agro-industrial value chain strategies followed by Argentinian governments throughout the 2000s.

act relation between all these actors remains rather undefined, as I will further discuss in the next section on social upgrading.

The realpolitik-focus on public-private "synergistic partnerships" that supposedly correct for "market failures such as information asymmetry and under-investment in innovation and technology" (Werner et al. 2014, 1240) has made the chain construct and especially the upgrading paradigm deployable as a development strategy for institutions such as the World Bank (Cattaneo et al. 2010; Farole and Winkler 2014; Taglioni and Winkler 2016; World Bank 2020), which had hitherto been eyed with suspicion by critical chain scholars. Further policy-oriented studies have been commissioned, to name but a few examples, by the International Labor Organization (ILO) (Humphrey 2004), the United States Agency for International Development (USAID) (Gereffi and Bair 2010)[46], the World Trade Organization (WTO) (Elms and Low 2013), the Organization for Economic Co-operation and Development (OECD 2014), the ECLAC and the German Society for International Cooperation (GIZ) (Hernández et al. 2014; Pérez 2017), the United Nations Industrial Development Organization (UNIDO) (Gereffi 2015), and the Inter-American Development Bank (IDB) (Pietrobelli and Rabellotti 2006; Pietrobelli and Staritz 2013).[47] Scholars have also worked with RTI International, an institute that offers policy consultation to the U.S. government, among others (Psilos and Gereffi 2011, 2). As Gereffi and Lee (2012, 24) cheerfully state, the GVC framework has been "adopted by many of the major international donors and peak organizations concerned with economic development."

Conversely, critical scholars note that the corresponding political agendas of these institutions have gained entry into the GVC framework that is now widely used as a tool for correcting market failures such as under-investment in innovation and information asymmetry and to "promise both to consolidate, and to advance beyond, the market fundamentalism of the Washington Consensus" (Werner et al. 2014, 1219). While Gereffi (2014, 24) interprets the adoption of GVC concepts by neoliberal institutions as an in-

46 For a USAID report that explicitly uses the value chain framework for detecting opportunities of small enterprises in agribusiness chains, see Steen et al. (2005).

47 Note that these institutions use the GVC approach differently, according to their particular policy goals. Werner et al. (2014, 1240) therefore point out that especially World Bank studies have deployed the GVC framework while painting the state as an obstacle to market functioning. Other institutions more closely related to scholarly GVC research have outlined state institutions as co-facilitators of business environments (see Pietrobelli and Staritz 2013).

dicator of positive change and a growing openness to heterodox models of development thinking, Werner et al. (2014) instead view them as a co-optation and neutralization of critical theory, endowed with cosmetic changes made to neoliberal policies (the WDR 2020 even overtly imagines a comparative advantage world). Their critique follows Neilson's (2014) argument that the actual mainstream use of chain research ends up stabilizing a developmental paradigm, which at its core is not designed to challenge but to reinforce the belief in capital-led development. Fernández (2015, 2) argues that the GVC framework has de facto contributed to a legitimization of exploitative patterns of GVC integration controlled by international capital fractions, and thus become a "neoliberal device." In a similar vein, Selwyn situates the GVC framework in the domain of "problem-solving" as opposed to critical theory, where the latter does not take "institutions and social and power relations for granted but calls them into question" (Robert Cox, cited in Selwyn 2016b, 3).

The social upgrading agenda

Scholars from different currents have soon criticized the GVC approach for both its focus on firm-level development and its "labour blindness" (Taylor 2007, 529; see Bair and Werner 2015; Newman 2012; Selwyn 2012a; 2012b; 2013; Werner 2012). Tellingly, labor disappeared (also graphically) from depictions of the input-output structure of value chains (see Fernandez-Stark et al. 2011, 22; Gereffi and Fernandez-Stark 2016, 8; Kaplinsky and Morris 2001, 4 ff.).[48] Yet at the same time, the GVC perspective has implicitly (or even explicitly, as in the WDR 2020) assumed that upgrading translates into social enhancement and more and better jobs (see Werner et al. 2014). Workers have often appeared as beneficiaries of capital-led development, in abstraction from de facto "the anti-developmental outcomes" of GVC participation for them (Selwyn and Leyden 2021a, 3).

Later in this book (Chapters 4 and 10), I discuss questions of labor and class relations in more detail. With regard to the upgrading paradigm, however, it is necessary at this point to briefly outline how GVC scholars have themselves responded to such critiques of firm centrism and trickle-down

48 Sturgeon (2011, 14) lists as productive actors "different kinds of firms that participate in value chains and production networks," whereas labor appears as an endogenous or a priori factor of production, and in terms of labor costs.

assumptions. Corresponding studies have taken issue with the real-existing disjuncture between economic upgrading and social gains and with the de facto negative effects of GVC-dynamics on wages or working conditions.[49] Knorringa and Pegler (2006, 470) have argued, for instance, that processes of immiserizing growth have made improvements in labor conditions especially in low-skilled production "very unlikely," and that strategies like ethical sourcing often only benefit core workers in key firms. In a similar vein, Barrientos et al. (2011a) have found that employment by suppliers in GVCs can have adverse effects on working conditions and salaries (see Bernhardt and Milberg 2011).

Related research has led to the supplementing of the concept of upgrading with the social upgrading agenda, which encompasses improvements in labor conditions and wages, gender equality, economic security, and other benefits of workers in GVCs, including their right to organizing and collective bargaining. Maintaining upgrading as a general development strategy, scholars have used this heading to examine the conditions under which capturing the gains of upgrading can be made possible in situ for more than just firms (Barrientos et al. 2012; 2011a; 2011b; Barrientos and Smith 2007; Gereffi 2014; Lee et al. 2011; Milberg and Winkler 2011). According to Barrientos (2019), social upgrading as a concept helps analyzing up- and downgrading trajectories and their consequences for workers, to whom the pressure that lead firms exert on suppliers is often passed on (see Flecker 2021, 149 f). This perspective understands upgrading as a segmented process that creates new development opportunities and at the same time possibly exposes local firms and workers to new risks resulting from lead firm requirements, international (sustainability) standards, or competitive pressures that may entail a social race to the bottom. Informal workers, women, and migrant workers are considered most likely to be employed under highly precarious conditions, often without the possibility or the right to contest their situations (Gereffi and Luo 2014).

To counter this situation and to secure social upgrading, GVC scholars have proposed to adhere to the ILO Decent Work Agenda (Barrientos 2007). With reference to Polanyi's double movement, Barrientos and colleagues

49 Studies have indicated that especially work in apparel and agriculture in so-called developing countries is poorly paid and precarious (Bamber and Fernandez-Stark 2013; Gereffi and Fernandez-Stark 2016). See Anner (2015a) on the relation between the international dispersion of apparel production and labor control regimes.

have advanced the objective to "improve the position of both firms and workers within GPNs" (Barrientos et al. 2011a, 320; see Barrientos et al. 2011b). Gereffi and Luo (2014, 19) have posed that socioeconomic win-win scenarios can by created through "public-private-civil society partnerships, as well as regional partnerships involving countries and firms that lead international production networks". Firm-level upgrading, in this view, is one of the conditions for social upgrading, the others being corporate social responsibility (CSR) and deliberate actions that seek to introduce better standards and regulations, possibly enforced in collaboration with the ILO, governments, firms, business associations, consumer groups, and also by workers and their trade unions (Barrientos et al. 2011a; Gereffi and Luo 2014, see Dünhaupt and Herr 2021).[50] From the perspective of the regulation school, Palpacuer (2008, 410) has called for the search of "sustainable improvements" through "an institutional view of GCC governance" that includes the participation of corporate accountability movements, transnational trade unions, community groups, and others as governance-makers.

Critical assessments of the social upgrading agenda

However, Gereffi and Luo, among other GVC scholars, stick to firm upgrading as a development strategy, assuming that "the likelihood of enforceable standards" rises "as one moves up value chains" (Gereffi and Luo 2014, 13). As Selwyn has criticized, one underlying assumption here is that poor salaries and working conditions are primarily an effect of employment in low-productivity economic sectors (Selwyn 2016b, 14), neglecting capitals' systemic interest in appropriating as much surplus value produced by workers as possible. In fact, much of the labor controlled by core-like firms in peripheral regions is poorly paid, also when employed in highly productive factories (Selwyn 2016b; Suwandi 2019). Even though the social upgrading perspective has taken up the issue of deleterious effects upon workers, it does not "identify the roots of such processes" (ibid., 5) in class relations, and therefore risks obscuring as much as it explains. As a consequence, the idea of achieving social upgrading through public-private-civil society partnerships is somewhat naïve: first, due to a belief in the state as a neutral actor and in

50 In this vein, Stamm (2008, 24) concludes that upgrading in agribusiness GVCs can lead to pro-poor development, if the right institutional setting is given and societies count with "institutional control of power asymmetries."

the time and space spanning will of public institutions to transform labor control regimes to the benefit of workers; second, due to the non-recognition of capitals' often hostile responses to the demands of workers and their organizations—not only in peripheral chain links or regions (Selwyn 2012, 7). Even though unions are regarded as actors who have a role in social betterment, this is often being attached to the co-operation with corporate actors in social partnerships—in contrast to an understanding of antagonistic capital-labor relations, where gains must be struggled for against capital interests.

On this note, the contradictions that are inherent to the GVC-upgrading paradigm cannot be resolved by merely adding on a social-upgrading agenda. Marxist scholars have instead proposed to renew value chain analysis on the basis of a social-relational understanding of global capitalism (Campling et al. 2016). This implies abandoning an all too optimistic belief in companies as social partners. Negative social outcomes are not just by-products but can rather be conditions of successful upgrading.

Scholars have also advocated the notion that analyzing the conditions of workers' collective action (and how both developments in capitalism and corporate strategies may constrain them) is key when it comes to achieving better salaries and working conditions (Marslev et al. 2021; Selwyn 2013; 2017; Taylor et al. 2015). An often-discussed constraining factor is lead-firm pressure passed on to workers in peripheral chain links by suppliers, who often use violent means to enforce low wages and a high labor intensity (Anner 2019; 2021). However, the notion that lead firms impose poor working conditions on supplier firms in peripheral chain links (Flecker 2021, 149) sometimes seems to suggest that suppliers would otherwise act in favor of workers' interests (see Bernhold 2022). In general, critical social upgrading literatures tend to have capital power and other constraining factors in mind when analyzing possibilities of workers to struggle for better salaries or working conditions. However, research that generally analyzes the political economy of GVCs from a class relational (not merely a power relational) perspective is rare.

I will come back to these arguments in Chapters 4 and 10, where I discuss how class matters as a category for critical GVC-research. In Argentina, for example, agro-industrial development has entailed the reorganization of the local social relations of production: upgrading has taken place in and through class differentiation, meaning that it is by shaping the exploitative social relations of production it is achieved, not just by innovation.

3.2.4 Agro-industrial GVC upgrading

In view of the empirical focus of this study, it is of particular interest to trace how the GVC upgrading paradigm is reflected in debates around agro-industrial chain development.[51] As in other empirical fields, there are studies that predominantly concentrate on uneven development and, especially in the past 20 years or so, ones that mainly focus on upgrading and policy-advice. As noted earlier, the development industry, and in particular the focus on upgrading as a new paradigm for development, has increasingly emphasized agriculture as a target of GVC initiatives and "market-driven policy interventions" (Berndt 2018, 1; see Berndt 2015; Werner et al. 2014).

Concurrent to these different foci, agriculture-related chain studies vary in their theoretical sources. For instance, Fernandez-Stark et al. (2012) look at agro-food value chains through the above portrayed policy oriented GVC-approach (see Bamber et al. 2014; Daly et al. 2018); Gibbon and Ponte (2005) supplement GCC/GVC concepts with Convention Theory; Challies and Murray (2011) refer to the livelihood approach; Barrientos et al. (2003, 1511) employ feminist theories for a "gendered value chain approach"; Fold and Pritchard (2005) use the regulation approach of food regime analysis (see McMichael 2005); and Bernstein and Campling (2006b) have called for a class-conscious take on the political economy of agrarian value chains (see Selwyn 2016a).

Thus, there is no general agreement on the extent, causes, and consequences of uneven development in global agriculture industries or the best way to deal with it. With the awareness that research in this field is diverse, this section provides a brief account of dynamics of inequality commonly recognized among different scholars before focusing on the mainstream debate's orientation on upgrading. This includes optimistic assessments of agribusiness in Argentina.

Talbot (2009) has argued that the point of primary production should receive more scholarly attention with respect to issues like the uneven distribution of profits along agricultural chains, economies of scale and their socioeconomic effects, as well as multiple governance structures that include the impact of global lead firms, states and social movements. Like him, various scholars have analyzed blatant inequalities among direct producers, mainly in the Global South, and processors or retailers of agricultural

51 Corresponding scholarly discussions partly overlap with debates on agrarian change (see Bernstein and Campling 2006a; 2006b; Fold 2002).

export commodities. Studies have spawned rich material by examining the journeys of these commodities along "chains driven by massive corporate capitals" (Bernstein and Campling 2006a, 245). Be it processors in the case of cocoa and coffee chains or retailers in the case of horticulture, lead firms' control over production and distribution and their capacity to pocket the lion's share of profits have been comprehensively researched in the 2000s (ibid.; see Daviron and Gibbon 2002; Dolan and Humphrey 2000; 2004; Fold 2002; Gibbon and Ponte 2005; Losch 2002). Here, scholars have mainly concentrated on tropical crops and fresh fruits and vegetables. Grain and oilseed value chains have long received less attention, especially with regard to critical GCC/GVC studies.[52]

Examples include Kaplinsky's (2000) analysis of canned deciduous fruit-chains. Though the latter is often regarded an ideal industry for low-income countries to diversify and increase their share of return, the author has found that the profits acquired by core-countries' retailers were more than double those of local producers. He concludes that the question cannot just be whether but "how and on what terms" (Kaplinsky 2000, 124) agricultural actors participate in global chains.

Dolan and Humphrey (2000) have illustrated how arm's-length trade of fresh fruits and vegetables in Kenya and Zimbabwe in the 1990s has been widely replaced by sales to UK retailers that determine the conditions under which local producers are included (companies able to deal with stringent standards) or rather excluded from participation in GVCs (especially small growers). Examining how lead-firm-drivenness in tropical agro-commodity trade took shape throughout the 1980s, Daviron and Gibbon (2002) have similarly found a growing oligopolistic power of TNCs on the buyer side and a complementary rise of specialized contract farming on the local primary production side (see Dannenberg and Kulke 2014). Analyses have also focused on how lead firms control information flows, standard demands and quality certification schemes, and in general the terms and conditions of production that contract farmers must meet (Dolan and Humphrey 2004; Ponte and Gib-

52 One exception is a paper by Gómez Lende and Velázquez (2018) that explicitly refers to the agricultural value chain metaphor to analyze socioeconomic, ecological, and health effects of the soy industry in Argentina, and the increasing subordination of local farmers under lead firms. Pro-agribusiness research on value chain development in this country will be summarized below in this section.

bon 2005). In this context, Ouma (2010) has analyzed how contested private standards impact Kenyan horticulture industries.[53]

In these and similar ways, there are numerous case analytical contributions that can prompt and inform a critical look at agriculture-related GVC development.[54] However, as Bernstein and Campling (2006a; 2006b) note, this empirical material is hardly related to critical political economy analyses of how the social relations of production forge global chains and are forged in them. I will come back to this in the next chapter. At the same time, and parallel to the course of the GVC debate described above, the focus on upgrading has taken hold as the mainstream approach to agro-industrial value chain development during the 2000s. Here, again, chain analysis serves as a device for elaborating case-specific accounts "of conditions for economic upgrading in DCs [developing countries]" (Gibbon 2001b, 345). As Dolan and Tewari (2001, 94) put it, "the issue of upgrading has become central to debates on how traditional, labour-intensive sectors restructure themselves to maintain competitiveness in a more trade-liberalised environment."

53 Scholars have argued, however, that while retailers do play a major role controlling agro-industrial chains, this is not necessarily the only determining factor (Daviron and Gibbon 2002; Humphrey 2006b; Raikes et al. 2000). For instance, Fold (2002) points to the power of processors in cocoa and chocolate chains, concluding that there are "more complicated patterns of power relations between lead firms in global chains—or, at least those for agroindustries" (ibid., 230). Raikes and Gibbon (2000) have analyzed how primary commodities like cocoa tend to be exported in unprocessed form from Africa (see Prowse and Moyer-Lee 2014 on Malawi's burley tobacco exports) while the processing industry is controlled from outside the continent, the respective value chains remaining "largely polarized in classic nineteenth-century forms" (Raikes and Gibbon 2000, 86; see Fold 2002; Losch 2002). Furthermore, research has directed the view to the influence of political blocks like the EU (Gibbon and Ponte 2005) and to the co-mediation of chain governance by state policies and regulation more generally (Daviron and Gibbon 2002; Ponte 2002; Raikes et al. 2000). Daviron and Gibbon (2002, 138) emphasize the elimination of state-led agriculture organizations, marketing boards, and price stabilization in the course of neoliberalism, and the concomitant suspension of policies that to a certain degree had reflected the interests of smallholder-producers (see Gibbon 2001a). Similar changes in state policy have played a role in Argentina, as Chapter 6 will briefly outline. Prowse and Moyer-Lee (2014, 324) argue for the case of burley tobacco in Malawi that state interventions such as minimum prices can help smallholders to gain higher profits. However, "the US has not reformed its trade regime to allow Malawian burley producers to compete unhindered against its own tobacco farmers" (ibid., 344). In this line, Challies and Murray (2011) explore how raspberry production can entail positive effects on rural livelihood improvement in Chile. They conclude that "the survival of small-scale growers" is not just a technical but also a political question (ibid., 56).

54 Contributions to the debate under the label of "dis/articulations" (Bair and Werner 2011a) will be introduced in Chapter 4.

Ponte and Ewert (2009, 1637) distinguish between two different perspectives on upgrading in agricultural value chains: first, research that is interested in detailed case studies to understand rural livelihoods and the sources, constraints, and "real-world patterns of upgrading" (Gibbon and Ponte 2005, 92) instead of drafting normative guidelines for climbing up a chain. Upgrading, here, is rather understood as an improvement of the possibilities to reach "'a better deal' for developing country firms," as Ponte and Ewert (2009, 1637 ff.) argue for the case of South African wine. This may also include dynamics "that would otherwise be termed 'downgrading'," for instance, in the sense that for some firms and regions "lower value products sold in larger amounts may be the most profitable strategy" (ibid.). Second, there are studies based on a more explicitly modernist and normative understanding of upgrading as moving up value chains to higher value activities through technology and knowledge transmission (see Da Silva et al. 2009; Fernandez-Stark et al. 2012).

As to the first perspective, Daviron and Gibbon (2002) and Gibbon and Ponte (2005) look at how upgrading opportunities have changed with restructurings in African export agriculture and in international trade regulations during the 1990s. Accordingly, increasing control over much of Africa's agriculture by oligopolistic buyers (and decreasing space for autonomous and domestically regulated smallholder production for local consumption) have attenuated the odds of functional upgrading for local actors in different agro-food chains. At the same time, "old upgrading opportunities have become more restricted and new ones have opened up" (Gibbon 2001a, 64), especially as regards process upgrading towards modern production systems. However, small farmers often tend to be at a disadvantage due to a lack of finance, modern techniques, and access to global companies (Daviron and Gibbon 2002). In this context, the authors deliberate on how local suppliers can best tailor their strategies to these changes. The opportunities for economic development that exist, they argue, are often due to "trading down" (Gibbon and Ponte 2005, 203; see Bernstein and Campling 2006a, 259; Gibbon 2001b; Ponte and Ewert 2009) to labor intensive production technologies and economies of scale.

Dolan and Tewari (2001, 94), on the other hand, argue for Kenyan export horticulture that local firms have succeeded in upgrading into more efficient processes, new products and functions with higher value added. In general, the authors agree that upgrading is "key to generating increased employment and sustained incomes." Yet at the same time, only firms that have "the knowledge and competences" to meet global buyers' demands are able to stay in the market and "the governance and nature of global markets may circumscribe the opportunities for more broad-based development, unless explicit policy attention is focused on the mechanisms of diffusing these capabilities more widely across the sectors" (ibid., 102).[55]

This is the point of departure for policy-oriented studies that take a definitely affirmative stance towards upgrading in agricultural chains as a development strategy, many of which are commissioned by state and supranational institutions including the World Bank (Farole and Winkler 2014), the FAO (Da Silva et al. 2009; Kaplinsky 2006) or the ECLAC (Bamber and Fernandez-Stark 2014). The focus in most of these studies lies in determining possibilities for agricultural firms and/or local processors in so-called developing countries to improve their positions in global markets.

In line with the GVC approach, the corresponding scholars agree that the "poverty reducing effects of the formation of agribusiness value chains" (Stamm 2008, 25) is often constrained, especially for small producers, by entry barriers and specific governance structures. Broad-based benefits from upgrading are therefore not regarded as an automatic process.[56] However, these constraints are not analyzed as geographically differentiated features immanently rooted in the political economy of global capitalism, rather as remediable market failures that result from an uneven distribution of information or a lack of local competitiveness (see Bamber et al. 2014, 143; Da Silva and Baker 2009, 2; Kuijpers and Swinnen 2016, 1407). Thus, instead of drawing conclusions towards a critique of political economy, these scholars advance proposals for local value chain policies that are supposed to remedy development constraints. Accordingly, the odds and outcomes of upgrading in

55 Mather (2008, 10) comes to a similar conclusion with respect to upgrading in the South African squid value chain after the mid-1980s, when the industry developed into a "sophisticated sector producing a high value product for export" in response to demands from European buyers. In the late 2000s, however, this sophistication had become a very condition for chain participation without necessarily entailing social improvements in situ (ibid.). Humphrey et al. (2004, 79) pose, on the other hand, that horticulture exports to the UK market have had a "poverty reducing effect," particularly due to further processing in situ. This has increased "employment to a far greater extent than any possible shift to smallholder production, even when optimistic assumptions are made about the labour intensity of the latter."

56 Studies have also included geographic differences. While for Fernandez-Stark et al. (2011, 60) upgrading trajectories generally indicate "that the export of fruits and vegetables represents an opportunity for low-income countries to drive economic development," they differentiate between newcomers such as Honduras, who face more constraints, and veterans like Chile or Kenya.

agricultural chains depend on the extent to which systemic efficiency can be achieved and "all stakeholders" can be involved "in processes of rapid and sustained continuous improvement" (Kaplinsky 2006, 377). In this vein, changing local perspectives for the better can also include "strategies for offsetting the effects of market power" (Humphrey 2006a, 41). However, this should be achieved not by imposing restrictions on large capitals but, for instance, through (a) local public-private partnerships to promote industry associations through which support for the export sectors can be channeled or (b) quality improvements, product differentiation, and "branding from below" (ibid., 41 ff.). This implies that growers have to "take action to imbed place-specific characteristics in the product's positional features" (Kaplinsky 2006, 377) to find market niches. In a word, strategies to restrict capital power and its consequences are deferred in favor of initiatives to improve local business (environments) within the status quo. Humphrey (2006b, 584 ff.) explicitly argues that donors intervening in agribusiness GVCs should base their agendas on an understanding of lead firms' interests in formulating policies that do not undermine them. The latter can include "allowing small farms to decline and focusing instead on improving conditions for waged employees in agricultural production and postharvest processing" (ibid., 588).

Proposed concrete policies for upgrading—primarily technocratic solutions to rural uneven development and poverty—then range from infrastructure development, technical assistance, knowledge transmission, and support for local producers to gain market access and competitiveness, e.g. through product innovation into fair trade agriculture (ibid., 43 ff., see Humphrey 2006b), and to value adding through new packing services and further processing in situ (Farole and Winkler 2014; Fernandez-Stark et al. 2011; Humphrey et al. 2004; Stamm 2008).

To name a few studies with a modernist leaning, Fernandez-Stark et al. (2011, 61) argue that through "institutional capacity building," producers of fruits and vegetables can gain "a degree of expertise during the production stage to increase output to a level that will enable the country [Chile] to upgrade to the fruit and vegetable processing stage."[57] Da Silva and Baker

57 Bamber and Fernandez-Stark (2014) argue in a study on the inclusion of small producers in high-value agriculture chains that GVC analysis can help donor institutions reveal what can be produced that is commercially viable and thus mitigate (market) failures. Interventions should then be designed to facilitate finance, technical assistance training and market access. In different examples for "value-chain interventions," including Central American coffee, Paraguayan Stevia and Peruvian organic cacao, fruits and vegetables, these authors stress the effectiveness of tech-

(2009, 2) argue that fighting poverty requires that "economic growth and development are brought to rural areas." Accordingly, agro-industrial value chains are "known to be efficient engines of growth and development" (ibid.) when they successfully upgrade from raw-material-production to processing, packing, and other tasks: "With their forward and backward linkages, agro-industries have high multiplier effects in terms of job creation and value addition" (ibid.). And Farole and Winkler (2014, 163) generally assume that investments in agribusiness GVCs offer "a significant opportunity to raise productivity levels by adopting new knowledge, technology, and techniques, from farming, through processing and manufacturing." The fact that prospects differ across countries, these authors argue, underscores the importance of "complementary and cross-cutting policies to improve skills and address supply-side constraints to competitiveness in the sector" (ibid.). For Trienkens (2011), (mainly endogenous) constraints on agricultural value chain upgrading lie in market access restrictions, weak infrastructures, a lack of resources, and institutional voids that can be changed through local interventions. He argues that if trade rents result from production scarcities, trade policies, and market intelligence, if technological rents result from command over technologies, and organizational rents from management skills, and so on, government policies and private-private or public-private partnerships can make actors in agricultural GVCs better in all these areas to become "more efficient and value adding" (ibid., 53; see Da Silva and Baker 2009).

Stamm (2008, 25) concludes that there is no "clear-cut division" between winners (the Global North) and losers (the Global South) in agribusiness chains. Instead, governments and donors can set incentives for the formation of competitive agro-industries that are a "promising sector for pro-poor growth [...] as it allows developing countries to capitalize on their natural production advantages, while reaching out to the rural poor through backward linkages" (ibid., 23). "In the best case relational chains can have an important outreach to smallholders and especially where the chain inte-

nical assistance and the creation of links with foreign buyers (Bamber and Fernandez-Stark 2014; Fernandez-Stark et al. 2012). These studies give the impression that such strategies can benefit local actors in general. However, see Berndt (2018, 7) on longstanding discussions on commodity chains and the agrarian question, including on poor labor relations in "an increasingly fragmented agricultural production system," including for high-value foods.

grators are willing to share their knowledge and enable joint learning and upgrading" (ibid., 33).

What all these studies have in common is their focus on national upgrading policies as a development strategy. Although problems faced especially by smallholder producers in different contexts are widely acknowledged, the political economic reasons for these problems are just as widely factored out, especially when it comes to proposed solutions. Even authors like Gibbon and Ponte (2005), who sharply criticize lead firm governance and oppose normative guidelines for upgrading in GVCs, focus on national strategies to find the best possible deal for firms in situ, sidelining the social relations of capitalist production and (international) exploitation when it comes to proposals for political action. To quote Ouma (2017, 502 f.), given its

> "origins in world-systems theory and the dependency tradition, one would expect to learn more about the classical concerns of critical political economy in this literature: the labor process, patterns of uneven development and social stratification, or questions of extraversion, income distribution, and exploited nature. Sadly, because of a number of intellectual shifts over the past 20 years, this body of work has largely failed to engage with some of the key social processes that make up capitalist landscapes as well as with the disarticulations that come along with the integration into commodity chains often dominated by lead firms from the Global North."

Most importantly, though, studies with a rather modernist understanding of stages of upgrading emphasize technocratic solutions to development problems and hold out the prospect of a catching-up-development towards agro-industries that are "competitive, equitable and inclusive" (Da Silva and Baker 2009, 2). It is noteworthy that the policies proposed in these studies often resemble one another, although their authors stress the importance of (chain and place) specific analyses to understand upgrading opportunities. Furthermore, companies are assumed to be actors of national or regional GVC development. In case of doubt, they can be steered into the right direction by appropriate state action. But what if firms are not interested in upgrading strategies to the benefit of local firms and workers, or when actual capital interests instead undermine positive socioeconomic development? Or if local upgrading strategies reproduce tendencies towards a concentration and centralization of capital and thus uneven development in situ? I discuss these types of questions on the basis of my empirical work in Chapters 8–10.

Optimistic assessments of agro-industrial chain development in Argentina

The belief in the opportunities of upgrading to spread the gains of capitalist progress can also be observed in scholarly contributions to debates on agro-industrial development in Argentina that draw on the GVC framework and optimistically point to agricultural paradigm shifts and related upgrading opportunities. Studies have argued that this South American country, which is an important supplier of grains, oilseeds, and processed derivatives to international production networks (Anlló et al. 2013c, 23), has the potential to "capture greater benefits" (ibid.) by exporting more processed products, such as foodstuffs or biofuels. But even for the current situation, these voices positively highlight the already implemented state-of-the-art technology driving soy, maize, and wheat production, point to the role of industrial processing and domestic value added as an engine of development, and hint at the job creation capacity of agro-industrial chain development (Anlló et al. 2013a; 2013c; Bisang 2003; 2007; Campi 2013; Llach et al. 2004; Lódola and Brigo 2013).

In fact, the respective authors assume that the positives of agribusiness in Argentina, as in every process of creative destruction "at least in its early stages" (Anlló et al. 2013c, 28, own translation) still stand in opposition to ongoing adverse events, such as land conflicts, enduring crises, and victimization among small producers who cannot keep up, as well as rural poverty in general. Furthermore, studies have pointed to the concentration of tacit knowledge in the hands of large corporations that control the development of biotechnology and "tend to capture a larger share of the generated rents than in the past" (Campi 2013, 143, own translation). But here too, this is considered in terms of resolvable market imperfections, the need for further local technology development, and fillable institutional voids.

To analyze and overcome such issues, scholars have compiled "*Keys to Rethinking Argentinian Agriculture*" (Anlló et al. 2013a, own translation) from a GVC perspective. They emphasize that Argentinian agribusiness has undergone profound changes in the past decades, a path that they say must be further developed. This includes the ongoing refinement of biotechnology and high-tech machinery as well as patterns of organizing production that have changed from the vertical integration of small farming entities to a network model that strongly relies on (labor) subcontracting (see Chapters 6 and 10)—developments that blur the boundaries between primary production, services, and industrial production (Anlló et al. 2013b; Cohan and Costa 2011).

Here, in contrast to old fashioned conceptions of farming, "economic agents as diverse as input suppliers, contractor networks, and agencies (public or private) for the development and diffusion of technology ensure a well-oiled mechanism of adoption and adaptation of new technologies for the sector" (Cohan and Costa 2011, 7, own translation). Accordingly, to be of the countryside today is to be involved in a modern business "with its very diverse and complex sub-activities" (ibid., 8, own translation). As a consequence of these upgrading processes, Cohan and Costa say, sales and value added "in *all the companies involved* in the business showed a remarkable evolution" (ibid., emphasis added, own translation).

In this context, scholars have asked the rhetorical question whether Schumpeter is visiting the Pampean region in Argentina, the main hub of the country's grain and oilseed production. Following the idea of creative destruction, they argue that old production schemes and old, tacit bodies of knowledge were being replaced by new or renewed entrepreneurs who (a) readily pioneer the risk of implementing new technologies, (b) form the new, network-like organizational patterns of production, and hence (c) "push the economic cycle towards a positive phase" (Anlló et al. 2013c, 28, own translation; see Anlló et al. 2013b; Bisang and Campi 2013; Campi 2013). In this view, such inter-firm networks, characterized by a separation of machinery/land ownership and control over production, allow for a rapid economic and territorial expansion of agricultural production companies, since they do not have to fix capital in land or equipment. Instead, service providers (so-called *contratistas*) own the necessary machinery and hire workers (Anlló et al. 2013b, 193). For Lódola and Brigo (2013, 249), the existence of these *contratistas* has helped relieve market restrictions and inefficiencies, improve the quality of rural labor, and increase the productivity of agriculture production in general (see Chapter 10 for an empirically informed critique of these assumptions). As a result of all these changes, Argentinian agribusiness "operates at the vanguard of the so-called biological revolution" (Bisang and Campi 2013, 92).

In such an environment, participants are required to cooperate and compete at the same time (Bisang et al. 2008, 195 ff.). As mentioned before, existing inequalities are not denied in this context. However, the idea is that cooperation holds the potential of win-win situations, since "on the one hand, each party (even with its structural asymmetries) wants to maximize income/benefit, but on the other hand, their income/benefit levels depend on the collective performance" (ibid., 195, own translation). More precisely, participation in networks or GVCs provides "challenges and opportunities" (Bisang et al. 2013, 286, own translation); the structuring of the global economy via competing GVCs provides incentives for participants to cooperate to make their chain competitive in the global market, but at the same time, it fosters intra-chain competition over the distribution of profits (Anlló et al. 2010, 41). However, Bisang et al. (2008, 33) understand existing asymmetries as a basis for dynamic mechanisms and permanent renegotiations that are conducive to innovation:

"The existence of economic and technological asymmetries, both between nodes (and/or critical activities in the network) and between economic agents, lays the foundation for a very dynamic mechanism with a permanent rebalancing (which is attentive to regulatory frameworks and local and international market conditions). These different nodes from which the network is mobilized are complemented and counterbalanced by the demands of exporters and the early stages of industrial processing, where economic and technological asymmetries can also be found. This functional structure has its productive counterpart in the form of adopting and adapting innovations" (ibid., 198 f., own translation).

Beyond modern soybean production, Bisang et al. (2013, 328) argue that changes within global markets (including demand not only for raw soybeans but also for processed derivatives) hold development opportunities for countries with good natural conditions. "Argentina is one of the countries with the potential to benefit from this scenario" (ibid., 309). However, to harness this potential even more, industrial processing in situ must be expanded (ibid.).[58] Accordingly, upgrading possibilities can be identified and strengthened in order to "capture higher rents within global value chains and move towards chains links with higher technical complexity" (Anlló et al. 2010, 12, own translation; see also Lódola et al. 2010 with a view to linkage effects).

In line with the policy-oriented upgrading debate cited above, the proposed measures to secure further positive outcomes of agro-industrial chain development in Argentina include continuing education and advanced training (Campi 2013, 144), technology development, infrastructure

58 The authors analyze the composition of Argentinian agro-industrial exports, and Argentina's participation in global trade involving both primary and processed products. They conclude that, in 2013, 54 percent of agro-industrial exports from Argentina underwent an initial step of processing (mainly soybean oil and meal, that is 5.7 percent participation in the world market), 30 percent correspond to unprocessed primary products (5.1 percent of the world market), and 15.4 percent underwent more than one step of processing (1.1 percent of the world market) (Bisang et al. 2013, 313 ff.).

programs, and facilitating political environments, among other elements. Bisang et al. (2013, 328 f.) furthermore point to constraints that need to be removed, including (a) private and public standards that affect, for example, Argentinian biodiesel production, (b) subsidies for local further processing, for instance, in the EU, and (c) other political entry barriers, like restricted market access staggered by the degree of processing (China demands imports of primary more than of processed products).

Finally, in emphasizing social spillovers, Llach et al. (2004) map out downstream employment effects of functional upgrading in agriculture value chains in Argentina that are supposed to compensate for job losses at the point of primary production.[59]

In sum, GVC scholars in Argentina assume that especially the soy value chain has performed successfully and opened a "window of opportunities" (Anlló et al. 2013c, 13, own translation) for development and for "the local society" (Anlló et al. 2013a, 352, own translation). However, they point to the need of further upgrading in order to maximize these positives. "A double challenge appears, the meeting of which preponderantly depends on *the Argentinians*: take advantage of this window of opportunity to take the model of the country into the future and work intensely on a new generation of innovations" (ibid., own translation, emphasis added). Chapters 8–10 offer an in depth-analysis and empirically informed critique of these assumptions.

3.3 Interim conclusions

This chapter traced and reviewed from an ideology-critical perspective the conceptual development of chain analysis from its origins in the world-systems tradition to the GCC framework, and to the focus on GVC upgrading as a new paradigm for development. I portrayed chain analysis as an important

59 The argument goes that functional upgrading does not only create employment in links that are directly part of agro-industrial chains. Instead, it also has an indirect impact on employment created through the net demand of inputs in each chain link, and a secondary indirect impact, for instance, through public employment created with taxes paid by agro-industrial companies as jobs that are generated due to consumption financed with incomes generated within agro-industries (Llach et al. 2004, 8). Other scholars have criticized this study for using both the GVC framework and questionable methods to lobby against taxes (Rodríguez 2006). Since the study is frequently cited not only by Argentinian GVC scholars but also by agribusiness associations, I take a closer look at it in Chapter 8.

tool for mapping power relations and uneven gains in global production and trade and to portray how corporate strategies in one part of the world impact socioeconomic developments in other places (Section 3.2). However, as Bair (2009, 29) has noted, chain analysis through the lens of upgrading shifts the view away from the reproduction of inequality to "trade and production networks as opportunity structures for organizational learning." The former secretary general of the Organization for Economic Co-operation and Development Ángel Gurría argues that "everyone can benefit from global value chains," and "encouraging the development of and participation in global value chains is the road to more jobs and sustainable growth for our economies" (cited in Werner et al. 2014, 1220). As Selwyn and Leyden (2021b) put it, the World Bank "takes this hyperbole to a new level." It "represents the culmination of almost two decades of pro-global value chain ideological projection." Although evidence shows otherwise, the WDR 2020 states, for example, that "global value chains boost incomes, create better jobs and reduce poverty" (World Bank 2020, 3).

I have argued in this chapter that the conceptual foundations of mainstream chain research and especially the focus on GVC-development and upgrading have put it at odds with the goal of explaining uneven development and power asymmetries and, based thereon, finding levers to remedy inequality. The following summarizes crucial points that can be made already at this point.

The conceptual evolution of the chain framework towards a tool for designing development strategies has been accompanied by a renunciation of key theoretical considerations that marked early commodity chain analysis' critical stance towards the capitalist world economy (Bair 2009). WSA points out that capitalism is not a static system and that upward mobility is possible, but only within historical and geographical limits and at the expense of other actors or regions (Section 3.1). The underlying premise is that a general upgrading within global capitalism is not possible, since uneven development is inscribed in its DNA. By contrast, mainstream GVC scholars have shifted the view to identifying upgrading opportunities that can provide so-called developing countries with development prospects and social spill-over effects. The underlying conceptual change can be seen even in the wording: policy-oriented studies speak of developing countries instead of periphery. This further mirrors a shift away from the analysis of peripheralization as an outcome of genuinely exploitative relations, towards a proposition of the possibility of a catching-up development. Brewer (2011,

309, emphasis in the original) remarks that "ironically, commodity chain analysis [...] was first constructed as a means of illustrating precisely why *general* developmental progress is, at best, highly unlikely within the institutional structures of the capitalist world-system." Thus, the GVC approach has gone from a methodology for analyzing and critiquing global capitalism to an ideologized, pro-capitalist development tool.

This is not to say that WSA-commodity chain research is without theoretical shortcomings (see Section 3.2). However, mainstream GVC research has reinforced these shortcomings and discarded the critical strengths of WSA by taking the systematic reproduction of inequality and power as power-over off its agenda, thereby converting chain analysis into a normative paradigm; its policy suggestions no longer deviate from the status quo of capitalist development.

In detail, a first critique (made in Section 3.2.1) is that the GCC framework tends to reduce chain governance—a root of inequality—to a question of political power relations and to explain the power to govern in tautological terms. This was reinforced by GVC scholars' myopic understanding of governance as inter-firm coordination in embedded networks (Bair 2008), which went along with a systematic exclusion of critical theory tools that can help unravel why some actors have more power than others (see Section 3.2.2). In particular, it is striking that GVC scholarship is conceived to deal with value chains as relational phenomena of global capitalism while at the same time abstracting from issues of the global political economy.

Second, the GVC approach is contradictory in that, on the one hand, it assumes that upgrading has a competitive component. It requires setting entry barriers against other actors. This implies that upgrading through innovation and skill enhancement cannot logically be possible for all (see Section 3.2.3). On the other hand, upgrading is its general development strategy. This inner contradiction is largely ignored by policy-oriented case studies which assume that policies can be implemented "to enable individual producers and countries to increase their share of the gains" (Gereffi and Fernandez-Stark 2016, 6), without asking (a) what happens to those who held that share before, or whether they would peacefully give it away, or (b) who carries out the low-profit tasks when some firms upgrade within the overall structure of the capitalist world-system?[60]

60 Schrank (2004, 124) identifies a further contradiction: a generalized transfer of technology and skills to suppliers in peripheral regions creates overcapacity, the author argues, such that replica-

Third, scholars have noted the GVC perspective, despite its naming, does not work with a coherent theory of value, let alone one that theorizes the capitalist social relations of production (Quentin and Campling 2018; Selwyn 2013; Taylor 2007; Werner 2012).[61] Throughout this book, I will discuss in more detail how I consider a Marxian, social-relational perspective on the issue to be an important basis for chain research. Suffice it at this point to recall that rather than tracing the origin of value along chains, GVC scholars proceed from an understanding of value added as rent accruing from scarcity, which increases with upgrading. However, this leaves them unable to explain, for example, why firms may decide not to invest in innovation but instead to relocate production to sites where exploitation and thus value appropriation can be increased by paying lower salaries or by extending working days (Suwandi 2019). In this context I refer back to Hadjimichalis' (1984, 338, emphasis in the original) argument that participation in the fruits of capitalist production is a question of "*class struggle between capital and labor* over the production of surplus value, and of *competition between capitalists* over the distribution of surplus value." Moving to a relatively higher value niche may thus well imply that firms increase the exploitation of workers and/or win over a greater piece of the pie at the expense of other firms elsewhere.

This brings me, fourth, to the question of capitalist firms as key drivers of development, as presupposed by GVC scholars. The upgrading agenda addresses firms as actors interested in development for the benefit of all, unless conditions are adverse, abstracting from both capitalist competition and capital interests in profit making. Thus, it ignores counter-facts that contradict the upgrading agenda. At any rate, it presupposes that individual capitalists can be led to subsume their interests to intended policy formulation or prioritize them over immediate accumulation interests (and that state actors have both the will and the power to promote the required systemic competitiveness). In Chapters 8 and 9, I analyze on empirical grounds how strategies

ble development strategies tend to undermine entry barriers set by actors in so-called developing countries, which makes a general theory of industrial upgrading a "contradiction in terms."

61 Bernstein and Campling (2006a) have remarked that the GVC scholars' choice to speak of value chains instead of commodity chains is an expression of the assumption that a variety of products "lack commodity features," as they quote Gibbon and Ponte (ibid., 241). From a Marxian, value-theoretical perspective, however, capitalist commodity production is not limited to particular use values. What lies at its center is rather the valorization of capital, the social relation of the production and appropriation of value that is realized when a commodity is sold on the market—be it a ton of wheat, a loaf of bread, or a car.

for GVC development are actually defined in the corporate realm and what kinds of contradictions arise from that.[62]

Bair (2005, 166) notes a fifth contradiction in this context, namely between firm-centered micro-level of analysis and the aspiration of socioeconomic development that refers to larger spaces. Certainly, micro and meso-level institutional differences do matter, for example, when it comes to investment decisions. However, this does not imply that those who keep their house in order can develop. Brewer (2011, 308) has called this an "upgrading paradox," that is, a faith in development, underpinned mainly with firm-level research, combined with a neglect of systemic socioeconomic inequality and their effects on development issues that go beyond firm-, network-, or even chain-level analysis. This concerns both the question of how upgrading is supposed to lead to broader social progress, be it local, regional, or national, and how labor relations play out within upgrading firms.[63]

62 As I have outlined in Section 3.2.4, imposing restrictions on large capitals' strategies is explicitly not a part of this approach. As Selwyn (2016b, 4) writes, "it takes as given the existence of transnational corporations and does not seek to disempower them vis-à-vis poorer countries, and/or the labour forces employed by/for them. Rather, [...] it ideologically and practically enhances TNC power by advocating that potential supplier firms 'link up' with them." The abstraction from exploitation and capital power, and competition, can be observed in the following quote taken from the 2002/03 UNIDO report. It creates the impression that industriousness and the right strategy for organizational learning is what makes the difference: "Global value chains spanning functions, processes and countries provide a means for accelerating the development of enterprises and countries, providing openings that developing country enterprises can exploit to upgrade their capabilities. For such enterprises, or local clusters of enterprises, the task is to insert themselves into the wider networks. This takes discipline, to attain the higher world standards. It also takes an initial base of technological capability, built through purposive innovation and learning. But the effort should be worth it, for it offers access to markets and the knowledge of players in the world economy" (UNIDO 2002, 105).

63 Fernández (2016) argues in this context that GVC scholars tend to ignore the contradictory and immanently conflict-ridden logics of capital accumulation, which have reproduced differentiated spaces of capitalist (re)production. In a similar vein, Dussel-Peters (2008, 13) states, that "while GCC analysis tends to focus on firm-level upgrading within a chain, the challenges for 'upgrading' from a territorial perspective are different." Accordingly, the importance that GVC scholars ascribe to processes within individual chains ignore the fact that countries like Mexico rather struggle with the challenge not to fall in the "commodification trap associated with particular links (e.g. assembly) in many different chains" (ibid., 14). He concludes his analysis of the yarn-textile-garment GCC in Mexico to say that even though GCC integration may have permitted Mexico to increase exports and technology absorption, this has not translated into benefits for broader segments of firms and workers, since specialization was only possible in chain segments that rely on cheap labor and imported inputs (see also Parnreiter 2013).

In point of fact, several GVC scholars have admitted that development is not straightforward and that, for example, economic upgrading does not unconditionally translate into social improvements. In this context, the upgrading paradigm has been supplemented by the social upgrading agenda (see Section 3.2.3). It assumes that upgrading can engender broader national development, including the generation of "more and better jobs to reduce unemployment and poverty" (Gereffi and Fernandez-Stark 2016, 6)—although this does not happen automatically. The social upgrading agenda juxtaposes risks and opportunities of upgrading and finds what is best for firm-development is not necessarily the best for workers. However, it does not explain why that is. Scholars assume that the risks can be overcome when proper action is taken by public-private-civil society partnerships. In this context, different institutions (including state and supranational institutions, labor unions, NGOs, and others), firms, and consumers are considered as stakeholders. However, questions of indecent labor are not analyzed as existing in-relation-to-capital, and the framework lacks the theoretical means to explain when, where and why particular actors at particular places may or may not have the power to influence chain coordination to their own interest. As Selwyn (2013) argues, GVC scholars neglect capitalist valorization and lack a conception of class relations. They tend to deny "the reality of labour's exploitation by capital" and are therefore "only partially equipped to explain the existence of indecent work" (ibid., 75).

In this light, studies have questioned the absence of state and class theory in mainstream GVC research and, concomitantly, an often all too optimistic belief in companies or states as providers of social upgrading. This tends to neglect geopolitics (Glassman 2011), capitalist imperatives of profit-maximization (Taylor et al. 2015), and the problem that workers cannot "simply impose their demands on capital without the latter responding in kind" (Selwyn 2012, 7). In the words of Bernstein and Campling (2006b, 440), some versions of GVC analysis take relations of power between firms into account, but "this is systematically, if tacitly, detached from structures and dynamics of class inequality and social inequality more broadly." My next chapter discusses approaches to remedy these shortcomings.

Eventually, Webber's (2010, 218) description of Latin American neo-structuralism holds true for the mainstream GVC debate, too. It distances itself from orthodox neoliberalism while "continuing to promise a high road to capitalist globalisation in which a rising tide will lift all boats, and conflict, crisis, and instability will be avoided," factoring out the actual broader socioeconomic conditions that may obstruct such a development. In this way, the idea of upgrading as a general development strategy becomes ideological in the sense of the Gramscian rooster that crows a day that will never come (Gramsci 2012 [1975]-g, 1918). It mobilizes the idea of "a seemingly 'gentler capitalism'" (Berndt 2018, 8), but in spite of its (partial) deviation from the one-size-fits-all solutions of the Washington Consensus and the focus on local social embeddedness, it "adopts a linear conception of development—where 'correct' policies are transformed into successful developmental outcomes [...] [and] simplifies the social world to such an extent that it generates a distorted understanding of it" (Selwyn 2016a, 1769–71).

In closing, it should be recalled that GCC/GVC studies have been compiled from different perspectives and cannot easily be lumped together. There are also differences within studies that focus on upgrading. For instance, some justify interventions by neoliberal development institutions, and others simply pursue the honest target of finding a better deal for local economies. Ultimately, though, both is accompanied by a shift away from the analysis and critique of the structural reproduction of exploitation and inequality.

However, commodity or value chain analysis has the potential to be both historically and geographically specific and "analytically universal" (Wallerstein 1974c, 391), and thus to foster an understanding of uneven development that considers both structural capitalist developments and agency, local detail, and case specificity. The next chapter discusses alternative conceptions of chain research that have blossomed from a critical engagement with the GVC approach in an attempt to uncover the hidden issues of exploitation and uneven development.

4. Revisiting Alternative Approaches to Analyzing Chains and Networks

Scholarly work thrives on controversy, and the variant of global value chain (GVC) research that I portrayed and critiqued in the previous chapter certainly does not represent the last word in the debate on global commodity or value chains. Its prevalence as the mainstream approach has not made it uncontroversial, and there have been extensive academic discussions in recent years in which critical scholars have spawned different proposals to remedy the limitations of GVC analysis. A considerable body of chain and production network literature has taken issue with the narrow focus of firm-centered GVC research as well as its use as a "neoliberal device" (Fernández 2015, 2) and suggested reformulations "of the hitherto dominant assumption of felicitous inclusion" (Werner 2018, 2).

However, the studies gathered under this umbrella of alternative approaches are not built on common theoretical and methodological grounds either, "and any review will necessarily be partial and selective," as Bernstein and Campling (2006a, 240) point out for commodity chain studies in general. This chapter discusses such a selection of GVC-critical, alternative contributions. The selection criterion is quite simple: critically exploring and discussing these contributions has helped me find analytical tools that I consider useful to look at upgrading strategies in the context of Argentinian agribusiness.

Section 4.1. briefly discusses the Manchester-Singapore school of global production networks (GPN), which has introduced the academically most visible reformulation of chain-like approaches to studying development issues above the plane of national units. Section 4.2 introduces the "disarticulations perspective" (Bair and Werner 2011a, 989) that seeks to remedy the "inclusionary bias" of GVC analysis, which considers who the potential winners of value chain development are, but it leaves aside questions of who loses or who is excluded. Section 4.3 then gives an account of recent approaches that again refer back to world-systems analytical approaches to analyzing uneven development in global chains, followed by a discussion of different Marxist perspectives on the matter. In the final Section 4.4, I will present literatures that point to the importance of theorizing the capitalist state and geopolitics for chain analysis.

Further theoretical considerations that are not well situated in this chapter, but which contribute to my analytical perspective, will be introduced later in this study where I use them to make sense of my empirical work.

4.1 Global Production Networks

In parallel and in response to the GVC approach, a body of scholars has developed the GPN school[1] to overcome shortcomings identified in GVC research. First and foremost, GPN scholars have criticized the vertical/linear focus on inter-firm relations and governance. In this connection, they have also questioned a crude, deterministic relation between governance structures and upgrading. In general, they argue that firm-centric analyses do not adequately consider (a) socio-territorial differences, (b) complex relations between different groups of actors, and (c) the interplay between local and global dynamics (Coe 2011; Coe et al. 2008; Coe and Hess 2013; Henderson et al. 2002; Murphy 2012; Neilson et al. 2014; Yeung 2015).

Instead, by encompassing all stakeholders that shape production networks, GPN research seeks to go beyond the linearity of inter-firm relations (Coe et al. 2008, 272). From this perspective, there is a need for a multi-dimensional approach able to analyze both vertical and horizontal networks "that interconnect producing firms and nonfirm actors (e.g., consumers, labor, civil society, and the state)" (Murphy 2012, 209). The aim is, first, to assess how relationships between all these actors shape the organization of industries and the global distribution of value-added activities (ibid.). Second, though, it holds that the relations between these actors are marked by power differentials. Third, studies attach importance to how economic action is embedded in contingent spatio-temporal contexts, which scholars

1 GPNs are defined as organizational arrangements "comprising interconnected economic and noneconomic actors coordinated by a global lead firm and producing goods or services across multiple geographic locations for worldwide markets" (Yeung and Coe 2015, 32).

often understand in line with the concept of "variegated capitalism" (Peck and Theodore 2007).[2]

In this vein, GPN research is concerned with the organizational and geographical formation of global networks as "complex circuitr[ies] with a multiplicity of linkages and feedback loops" (Hudson, cited in Coe et al. 2008, 272). Accordingly, comprehending place-specific development dynamics requires analyzing not only how capital flows, labor, and power relations transform places, but also how these "places (or more specifically their institutional and social fabrics) are transforming those flows as they locate in place-specific domains" (Henderson et al. 2002, 438). Firms, then, cannot be understood as black boxes (Coe et al. 2008, 284); they are "networks embedded within networks, with varying degrees of imbrication and interconnection" (ibid., 277).

A GPN is thus considered as an economic, political, and cultural phenomenon and a field of contestation in which actors struggle over the tying of economic relations, social and political norms and rules, as well as discourses (Coe et al. 2008, 274). Methodologically, this means directing attention to the practice through which value is created and distributed in these broader contexts of asymmetrical power relations and socio-institutional situations (Henderson et al. 2002, 447). Therefore, it is especially the agency of business people, local and international state actors, workers, consumers, NGOs, and others that receives scholarly attention.

In research practice, however, GVC and GPN studies are often hardly differentiable. Some scholars have also used these labels interchangeably (Bair 2008, 358). Furthermore, as in the case of GCC and GVC studies, there are variants of GPN research that take a critical political economy view (Glassman 2011; Mahutga 2014; Selwyn 2013) alongside mainstream research that ultimately differs little from the GVC upgrading paradigm.

As for the latter, GPN studies have promoted the concept of "strategic coupling" (Coe et al. 2008, 280) instead of upgrading (for a review see Werner 2018). Strategic coupling is understood as a process where domestic firms' strategic action (innovation, capacity building, etc.) helps them couple with global lead firms in GPNs (Morgan 2018, 458). In this sense, local development is understood as a "globalized relational process dependent on the ability of local actors [...] to enhance the value of ties to international markets" (Murphy 2012, 210). In other words, the approach seeks to show how local so-

2 This concept points to connections and divergences between different forms of capitalism (ibid.).

cioeconomic benefits can result from complementarities between "regional assets" (technological and institutional resource bases, labor, etc.) and the global "logics" of GPNs (Yeung 2015, 1). At stake is the "intentional convergence and articulation of actors in both regional economies and GPNs for mutual gains and benefits" (ibid., 5).[3]

Strategic coupling, in this view, does not necessarily shield against negative effects, such as uneven value capture or the breakup of local socioeconomic systems. As a contested process, it "may also include the options of de- and re-coupling in various ways" (Coe and Hess 2013, 7). As a consequence, there can be a "dark side" (ibid.) of strategic coupling, and it "is unrealistic for regional policy-makers and practitioners to expect such global-regional coupling process to be always inclusive" (Yeung 2015, 13). The odds of a broad-based success of strategic coupling then depend on the agency of all state and non-state actors in a social and political system. Accordingly, regional institutions and civil society groups of actors need to commonly engage in promoting policies that are designed to (a) transform "regional assets" (ibid., 6) so that that they can foster development and (b) mitigate possible dark sides.

This study follows some of the critical points leveled against early GVC research by GPN scholars, for instance, regarding the neglect of issues such as the role of the state and labor. Scholars have helped bringing (back) actors other than firms into chain or network debates (which is also reflected in the social upgrading agenda portrayed in Chapter 3). They have thereby also contributed to highlighting the possibility of workers struggling for better pay and working conditions. In general, it is a merit of GPN scholars to have once again drawn attention to the fact that particular social, economic, and political geographies matter. Finally, they have drawn attention to how inequality does not only accrue along chains but is as well reproduced within particular nodes or networks.

---

3 Coe and Yeung (2015, 29) have added what they call a more dynamic theory of GPNs or "GPN 2.0" that is supposed to better grasp the exact relations between value added, embeddedness, and power. The authors argue that they can explain the odds and outcomes of strategic coupling from an explicitly actor-centered perspective. Accordingly, firms that stem from different places, corporate cultures, and ownership structures (ibid., 53) adopt diverse strategic choices ("intrafirm coordination, interfirm control, interfirm partnership, and extrafirm bargaining" (ibid., 32)) in response to different competitive pressures ("optimizing cost-capability ratios, sustaining market development, and working with financial discipline" (ibid., 32)). Thus, they say, varying results of strategic coupling and "the differentiated organization of global production networks in diverse industries and territories" (ibid., 33) emerge.

However, especially the mainstream variant of GPN research on strategic coupling does not considerably differ from the upgrading paradigm. It, too, has moved the analysis of systemic inequality and uneven development into the background (Werner 2018, 4). In this context, Werner (2012, 405) criticizes the fact that GPN scholars have dropped earlier calls by Henderson et al. (2002, 448) to include analyses of the capitalist labor process and systemic exploitation.

More abstractly, GPN scholarship emphasized different actors involved in the making of production networks, but in doing so, it tends to dissolve the dialectical relation between social structure and agency one-sidedly in favor of agency. Networks here appear as nodal points of social, political, and economic agents endowed with differentiated power. But this leaves the relation between 'the economic,' 'the social,' and 'the state' relatively undefined. Furthermore, it remains unclear how the differentiated power(lessness) of actors to co-shape GPN development can be explained.[4] Coe et al. (2008, 276) answer that the relative power of actors within networks depends on the extent to which each possesses assets (or has access to them) sought by others. Social asymmetries here are understood as an outcome of mal-development that could be smoothened out by bargaining over the distribution of these assets (Selwyn 2016a, 1772). But why do some have more assets than others? Answering because of their power, one would enter in a tautological loop of explanations. I therefore agree with Selwyn that "GPN notions of power, value creation and local-level embeddedness, while intuitively necessary for a deeper comprehension of development, lose analytical purchase in application because they are not founded in an internally integrated conception of capitalist reproduction" (ibid., 1770). While including workers as actors, for example, the approach does not take account of structural capital power and its systemic maintenance through exploitation. Furthermore, it tends to dismiss geopolitics and "macro-geographies of uneven development" (Werner 2018, 4). In fact, it rather plays off local specificity against broader dynamics of the capitalist world-system. While it seeks to avoid a reduction of actors and localities to their functional position in the world-system (ibid.), it reduces the global economy to a sum

4 Coe et al (2008, 289) call for a "conceptualization that operates at the interface of structure and agency." In a similar manner, Coe and Hess (2013, 7) argue that the agency of labor is shaped by both GPN structures and the local labor control regimes in which it is embedded; however, the authors do not specify what they mean by structure.

of individual networks. Places—though historically, geographically, and socially mediated—then tend to be conceptualized as place-monades in relation to other place-monades. Bair and Werner (2015, 120) sum up that, "because capitalism is not reducible to discrete networks of particular firms, GPNs and labour's mobilization within these circuits cannot stand in for political economic analysis in toto."

The formulation of a critical theory of global political economy lies beyond the scope of this book. But throughout the next chapters, I resort to theoretical tools that have not only helped me analyzing my empirical data but which I argue must form part of the foundation of such a theory.

4.2 Dis/articulations and the role of social difference

As I have previously sketched out, part of what has gone lost in the GVC approach is the question of winning and losing in capitalist development. Taking that to heart, another group of scholars points to the "inclusionary bias" (Bair and Werner 2011a, 989) of GVC analysis with its focus on how the incorporation of actors and places into value chains can possibly enable upgrading. From what they call a "dis/articulations" (Bair et al. 2013, 2545) perspective, Bair and Werner, together with their colleagues Berndt and Boeckler, argue that, first, GVC scholarship does not examine processes of exclusion from developmental paths. Second, they note that social inequalities and uneven spatial development in many cases are enhanced rather than eliminated through the dynamics of value chain development. Accordingly, integration in capitalist commodity chains never occurs universally or to the benefit of all actors involved. Uneven creation, appropriation, and distribution of value across and within spatial borders instead constitute the norm.

These authors' attention is thus directed to the everyday practices of production, distribution, and exclusion that reproduce the uneven geographies of global capitalism (Bair and Werner 2011a; Bair et al. 2013; Werner 2016b). As Bair and Werner (2011a, 990) put it, "the power of a disarticulations perspective lies in connecting an analysis of global commodities to the politics of disinvestment, devaluation, place-making, and subject-making which make their production possible." Elsewhere in their writing, this is supplemented by the role of dispossession (Bair and Werner 2011b, 1000).

The theoretical sources of this perspective include, first, Harvey's (2003, 137 ff.) concept of "accumulation by dispossession," a reinterpretation of

Rosa Luxemburg's (1913) work on both primitive accumulation and capitalism's need for its own exteriority in order to maintain the capability to accumulate. Second, to make sense of the exclusion of workers from GVCs, the authors use Marx's understanding of an industrial reserve army only seized upon by capital when needed for further valorization (Marx 1990 [1867]), 787).

However, it was the work of Stuart Hall that was acknowledged in the name of the dis/articulations concept. The term hints to the fact that commodity circuits always involve a double movement of articulation—the conjunctural linking of actors and places—and disarticulations—processes of separation and exclusion (Bair et al. 2013, 2545).[5] In this context, the authors deploy Hall's understanding of "articulation"[6] as a process of linking social, political, ideological, economic, and, they add, spatial practices (Bair and Werner 2011a, 993).

This proposal to chain research attaches particular importance to how dis/articulations often work along lines of social difference including race and gender (Bair et al. 2013; Berndt 2013). By further reference to Massey (1995) and Wright (2006), the scholars ask, what difference does social difference make to capital and to the spatial division of labor? A core concern here is how the making of disposable labor, often on differential pay and conditions, justified through discursive constructions, both emanates from and influences the relations of capitalist production within particular historical and spatial contexts (Bair and Werner 2011a, 991; see Bair (2010) and Werner's (2016b) book on the making of uneven development in the Caribbean). In sum, what is needed from this point of view is the analysis of commodity chains "as expressions of an ongoing and continuous interaction between the production of goods, places, and subjects and their iterative incorporation and expulsion from primary circuits of capital accumulation" (Bair and Werner 2011a, 989).

Taking on this task, Brown (2013), for example, has used the prism of the dis/articulations perspective to look at how the Fairtrade banana complex in Colombia could easily be read as a win-win story, while it concurrently en-

5 In 2011 called "disarticulations" (Bair and Werner 2011a), the perspective was renamed (a slash was inserted) in the 2013 paper co-authored with Berndt and Boeckler to emphasize this double movement.

6 It is beyond the scope of this book to discuss the origins of this debate in discussions of the articulation of modes of production. For a summary, readers can refer to Herrigel (2018, 30–44).

tails devaluation, marginalization, and elite control, expressed even through armed conflict. It thus reproduces local uneven geographies in new forms. Wilson (2013) uses the perspective to propose a potential, alternative view of the 2000–2005 coffee crisis in Nicaragua, which, he says, is often explained by overproduction and resulting price cuts, namely one of the disarticulation of actors from production through corporate land dispossessions. And Debbané (2013) analyzes how agrarian capital in the South African deciduous fruit industry has disarticulated or in part adversely included racialized and marginalized small farmers and workers.

For my own work, the criticism of the inclusionary bias of the GVC debate and the reminder of the fact that upgrading never occurs to the benefit of all actors involved are especially valuable. In Chapter 10, I will discuss how upgrading in Argentinian agribusiness has entailed the expulsion of small-scale production over the past decades. Some outcompeted farmers have been re-articulated to agribusiness networks, not as independent producers but, for example, as salaried service providers under the control of big agrarian capital.

However, the dis/articulations perspective and its conceptualization of the commodity chain as "a constantly shifting boundary that demarcates an outside within and reproduces uneven relations at a variety of scales" (Bair et al. 2013, 2544) remains vague in some ways. The authors introduce this understanding in demarcation from the conception of commodity chains in WSA.[7] At the same time, Bair and Werner maintain the assumption of a global capitalist political economy.[8] Against this background, the dis/articulations approach does not really explain how exactly the contingencies and everyday practices of dis/articulating actors and places that reproduce the geographies of uneven development relate to one another and to structural properties of (global) capitalism. How are everyday agency, the "region as 'conjuncture'" (Werner 2018, 7), and contingent political, ideological, economic, and, spatial practices related to capitalism as a mode of production and as a social formation? Are they ex ante categories that exist indepen-

7 They differentiate themselves from what they describe as a WSA conceptualization of commodity chains in terms of advancing frontiers that proceed "by incorporating territorial and social relations inside a hierarchical core-periphery structure of global capitalism" (ibid.).

8 Bair (2005) has also criticized that mainstream adaptions of the chains framework increasingly refrain from "focusing on the broader political-economic environment in which chains operate" (ibid., 154) and encouraged a closer look at the "structural properties of contemporary capitalism" (ibid., 170). Yet, she does not elaborate here on what is meant by these structural properties.

dently of one another, and are subsequently articulated? And how exactly are capitalist exploitation and oppression (along lines of social difference) related?

In Chapter 2, I very briefly set forth my understanding of the dialectics of structure and agency. In this vein, I think that the relation between (a) the capitalist social relations of production and its structural properties and (b) both contingency in agency and social difference needs to be elaborated further from a Marxist perspective. However, a corresponding literature work would go beyond the scope of this book.

4.3 A return to WSA and Marxist approaches to analyze uneven development

Over the past years, scholars from different theoretical currents have once again problematized that analyzing chain-slices in isolation can obscure much when attempting to contribute to an understanding of contemporary capitalism (see Chapter 3). Referencing both the large looming legacy of world-systems contributions and Marxist theory more generally, scholars have argued that the upgrading of some actors and regions goes hand in hand with a (world-scale) reinforcement of inequality. Bair (2014) was among those who have called to bring the big picture back in. In 2014, she edited a special issue of the *Journal of World-Systems Research* titled *The political economy of commodity chains*. The contributing authors explicitly draw on WSA.

In her introduction, Bair reminds the research community of the original intention of commodity chain analysis: to trace the worldwide division of labor and to ascertain where the respective activities are carried out, "and how the unequal returns to these activities created a stratified world-system" (ibid., 2). Together with other contributors (Clelland 2014; Mahutga 2014; Quark 2014; Sowers et al. 2014), she calls for renewed attempts to use commodity chain analysis in this vein for illuminating "the complex and concrete determination of a capitalist world-economy" and its "contours, composition, and character" (Bair 2014, 2; see Smith and Mahutga 2009 on agriculture industries and world-system inequalities).

In contrast to the GVC understanding of chains with sequential steps of value added that can possibly be climbed by actors at the bottom end, Bair

(2014) refers back to Arrighi and Drangel's (1986) work on the stratification of the world-system. She recalls that economies in certain regions are dominantly periphery-like *because* others are core-like, even though the geographies of center-periphery relations are not set in stone. Climbing commodity chains is possible within the capitalist world-system, as the example of China shows (Arrighi 2010). David Harvey (2010b, 3) once stated that economic crisis cannot be solved within capitalism, instead only moved around geographically. Likewise, the geographies of exploitation may be altered (geographically) within this system, but not dissolved (see Section 3.1 for a more detailed review).

Along similar lines, Brewer (2011, 309, emphasis in the original) has evaluated recent world income inequality literatures and argued that the structure of income distribution across the capitalist world-system has remained quite stable "even if the positions of individual nations within that hierarchy (can) shift over time as a result of *either* upgrading or downgrading." The author supports the WSA-hypothesis that a durable, three-tiered "distribution of world income will be a persistent structural reality within the modern world-system, *even if there is mobility on the part of individual countries or groups of people within them*" (ibid., 314, emphasis in the original).

Soendergaard (2018) has also used the lens of WSA, in this case for analyzing periphery formation in one particular commodity chain, namely the Brazilian soy complex. He concludes that WSA offers useful tools for highlighting the structural character of problems attached to the political economy of this chain. This includes the strong presence of global players such as Bayer, Cargill, and ADM in different chain nodes, which "also means that a range of significant value-added activities bypass Brazilian actors within the soy sector" (ibid., 86). Furthermore, he finds a low degree of soybean processing in situ. He argues, though, that further theoretical tools are needed, for example, to consider the work of local social agency in potentially mitigating the negative social and environmental effects of this agribusiness (ibid., 78).

Another example for contemporary research informed by the world-systems perspective is Parnreiter's (2019) work on the role of global cities as nodes in GCCs. Crucially, he argues, global cities as core places are not just hot spots where financial flows converge. Instead, as loci where producer service firms are clustered which help to protect their clients from competition, global cities are "strategic governance places" from where "the transfer of wealth towards the centres of the world economy is organized" (ibid., 91).

This book supports the aim of these scholarly contributions to use commodity or value chain analysis not as a means for designing upgrading strategies but, instead, to reclaim the tools it offers to make the structural reproduction of inequality inherent in the capitalist world-system visible. Although my own research is not designed to address issues surrounding the reproduction of a stratified world-system at a global scale, the reproduction of uneven development at different scales is a key aspect of my analysis of the contradictions in GVC-development in Argentinian agro-industries. Here, WSA has shaped my thinking about how uneven development necessarily reproduces itself in the wake of upgrading. Even though upgrading refers to local strategies, it does not take place in a political economic and geographical vacuum. In this vein, using world-systems analysis has helped me identify and discuss the limits and contradictions of upgrading in Argentinian agribusiness industries.

However, there is a need for a renewed discussion of the nexus of capitalism's stratification into centers and peripheries and the social relations of production—or the dialectics of local/national class relations and global uneven development. Among other things, this includes socioeconomic and political class formation (see Bair and Werner 2017, 608) as well as interclass and intraclass struggles over the production and distribution of surplus value (Hadjimichalis 1984, 333). Bearing in mind the shortcomings of WSA that I discussed in Section 3.1, I draw on Marxist theoretical considerations for my own research. This concerns studies that have theorized the role of the state(s) in global chains as well as, most importantly for my study, responses to WSA's theoretical focus on exchange-based conceptualizations of capitalism with a relative inattention to the social relations of production and the capitalist production process.

4.3.1 Value theoretical approaches

Certainly, I am not the first to try to evaluate the GVC framework from the point of view of Marx's critique of political economy. Studies include Taylor's (2007) work on how GVC analysis can make sense of the global relations of production and Starosta's (2010) structuralist theory of *Global Commodity Chains and the Marxian Law of Value*. Purcell et al. (2018) have furthermore elaborated on agrarian GCCs and ground rent, and Selwyn (2016) has made an effort to develop a class relational framework of global value chains and human development (see Campling et al. 2016). Yet, there are different forms of Marxism and a brief discussion of these approaches is necessary to situate my own work, especially because working on global chains from a Marxist perspective is often perceived as a homogeneous affair.

Taylor's (2007, 531) proposal to rethink "the global production of uneven development" is based on the argument that capitalist reproduction is not solely embedded in local institutions and social relations, as if these were separated from capitalist reproduction. Instead, he seeks to consider "the dialectical relationship between social embedding and social abstraction" and "the ways in which socially embedded economic activities undergo a repeated process of abstraction and re-embedding within the context of global capitalism" (ibid., 535). In his view, social labor and everyday practices of production are, on the one hand, concrete and private and as such embedded in unique social contexts. On the other hand, they are social and abstract "because every private and concrete process of production forms one moment of a social division of labour that is mediated through the exchange of commodities on a global level" (ibid., 536). The market, Taylor says, acts as an abstract disciplinary mechanism through which concrete productive activities are compared.

> "When the socially embedded relations of production for a specific firm no longer meet the social ascription of value, production must be dis-embedded from its existing social context, and those social relations must be restructured before production can be profitably re-embedded. A focus on social abstraction, therefore, helps us put social embedding in motion" (ibid., 537).

I agree with Taylor that the capitalist mode of production inheres structural characteristics, from which locally specific processes in commodity chains cannot be understood separately. For instance, capitalist competition compels local social organization and production in a struggle to maintain profitability, while local processes, in turn, constantly change the global social average and co-produce the social relations of production in toto.

At the same time, I beg to differ with Taylor's understanding of this dialectical process as an "embedding-abstraction relationship" (ibid.). I will come back to the problem I see in analyzing capitalism as an abstract mechanism after looking at another contribution made by Starosta (2010), which accentuates this shortcoming.

Referring to the Marxian law of value, Starosta argues that there is a need to uncover the inner connection between (a) the valorization of value on an ever-increasing scale and (b) the historic and geographic concrete relations between particular capitals within GCCs (ibid., 441). Echoing my critique elaborated in Chapter 3, he remarks that GVC studies use typological descriptions of lead firms' power in their relation to other capitals to determine the characteristics of chains, without explaining how such power is produced and reproduced within the social relations of production.

To solve this theoretical problem, Starosta argues that the power relations in GVCs are "concrete mediations of the inner laws regulating the indirect social relations among individual capitals: the process of global competition through which the formation of the general rate of profit asserts itself" (ibid., 433).[9] Differentiated power in GVCs, he says, is not the result of "differential valorization capacities" (ibid., 448) manufactured by particular capital strategies. Instead, he maintains that capitalist power has an impersonal and abstract character and "is actually strictly and objectively determined in accordance to the laws of movement of capital as whole" (ibid.). In sum, "the 'concrete' power that each actor in a commodity chain exercises [...] is actually an expression of the 'abstract' power that capital exercises over all of them" (ibid., 449).

In contrast, for instance, to GPN scholars, Starosta thereby dissolves the dialectical relation between social structure and agency one-sidedly in favor of an allegedly 'abstract' structure. He seems to assume that there is an abstract power exercised by the law of value (as though it arose independently of human agency) over all actors, and that the 'concrete' power exercised by actors in commodity chains is nothing but an expression of an abstract system.

In my understanding of Marxism, however, capitalism cannot be analyzed as an abstract system (see Lütten 2015). This would imply that social forms exist, as a "creatio ex nihilo" (Wolf 2013, 12), detached from concrete action which then nearly divinely determine people's actions (see Chapter 2 on the relation between economic structure and social praxis). In fact, Marx methodologically abstracts from human agency at some points.[10] But the

9 The valorization of small capitals in GVCs, Starosta argues, deviates from the average rate of profit. Instead, it is regulated by their self-paid wages after deducting expenses on input-expenses and interest payments (ibid., 445).

10 For example, at the beginning of *Capital*, he abstracts from concrete qualities of human labor to explain how value is a social relation. What makes two commodities interchangeable, he says, is that they are both product of a certain quantity of socially necessary labor, no matter the particular form of the labor.

use of abstraction as a method does not make social processes themselves abstract. It is instead always the people who produce and reproduce the social structure, that is, the (reified) aggregate of the social relations "which the bearers of production have towards nature and towards one another" (Marx 1991 [1894], 957). The thus created structural conditions for specific action are "on the one hand the presuppositions of the capitalist production process, on the other its results and creations" (ibid.). Strictly speaking, the social relations of production *as class relations*—and capital interest in profit making though exploitation—cannot play a role in Starosta's theory, where all agents in capitalism are governed by an abstract system.

I do ultimately agree that uneven development is "an integral rather than incidental feature of capitalist growth," to borrow Peck's (2012, 120) words. I also agree that the social relations of production and capital power need further theorization for GVC analysis from a Marxist, value-theoretical perspective. What I draw especially from Taylor's (2007) work is the importance of considering the dialectics of the capitalist socioeconomic structure and historic and geographic specific agency, the "unity of the diverse" (Marx 1986 [1857–61], 38), through which capitalism is socially produced and reproduced in ever changing forms.

Class matters

I have recurrently remarked on a relative inattention to class dynamics. My concern to promote a social-relational, class analytical approach to analyzing GVCs in global capitalism sits well with the insistence of Campling et al. (2016, 1745) that "class dynamics are at the heart of developmental processes." These authors highlight that the laws of motion of capital (they especially highlight to the imperative of profit-making through exploitation and capitalist competition) do not play out the same way in every historical and geographical situation. Nevertheless, profit-making based on the exploitation of workers by the owners of means of production is a general feature of capitalism and thus needs to be at the heart of value chain analysis. In this vein, I endorse the notion that a class analytical approach—and therewith also the question of social property relations—is essential to any research on capitalist development that seeks to uncover the social relations behind uneven profit-making, and that considers that social structures do not act by themselves while social agency does not take place in a vacuum.

The debate on capital-labor relations in GVCs has partly evolved through discussions on the social upgrading agenda, which I briefly portrayed in Chapter 3. Here, scholars have pointed out the need to understand how surplus value is actually produced (Selwyn 2016a, 1769; see Smith 2016; Taylor 2007). Echoing this debate, this book employs a Marxian conception of value. In what follows I therefore briefly insert a few lines on what that means.

Marx has argued that value it is a characteristic attributed to commodities when they are exchanged and thus implicitly related to each other on the market as equals. But what makes them equivalent? The value of commodities—the equivalent that remains when abstracting from their use values—is the embodiment of human labor measured by the time that is socially necessary for their production. Importantly, thus, to see how value is produced and thus "how capital itself is produced," one has to look into the "hidden abode of production" (Marx 1990 [1867], 279 f.).

In capitalist production, the dominant social relations are exploitative class relations. They are exploitative in the sense that those who essentially control the means of production appropriate the surplus value produced by workers. Surplus value, here, is defined by the value workers produce during the period that exceeds the labor time necessary for the reproduction of their labor power's value under given historical conditions (Marx 1990 [1867], 274). This means that wage earners work longer hours than socially necessary (under given productive forces) to secure the reproduction of their labor power and their wellbeing. This produced surplus is the basis of capitalist profits, which are consequently always a result of the appropriation of alien labor.

With this in mind, scholars have questioned the social upgrading agenda's lack of capitalism's systematically antagonistic class relations and instead encouraged researchers, first, to identify the roots of indecent labor in strategies to maximize profits through intensified exploitation (Selwyn 2016b, 5). This requires paying greater attention to the shaping of capital-labor relations (Bair and Werner 2015, 42; Smith et al. 2002) and elucidating shifting patterns of exploitation that accompany firm's strategies, as well as the imperatives of capitalist competition. It also entails showing how the conditions of uneven capitalist development as well as class struggle from above constrain workers but are possibly also influenced by labor agency (Selwyn 2013; 2017; Taylor et al. 2015; Werner 2012; 2016a). Second, this implies abandoning an all too optimistic belief in companies or states as providers of social upgrading (see Section 3.3). Instead, there is a need to understand how class struggles shape development.

Tying into these discussions, and in line with my critique of the GVC upgrading paradigm, I find, however, that the issue of how upgrading itself can be gainfully analyzed as a process in and through class differentiation has not been explicitly studied so far. To substantiate this conceptual contribution, Chapter 10 analyzes how firm upgrading in Argentinian agribusiness is accompanied by changes within the manifestation of the social relations of production in situ. This requires analyzing class relations beyond the capital-labor antagonism. Although production here is based on capitalist exploitation, the myriad of social actors involved do not necessarily directly fit into the categories of capital or labor respectively. The sometimes complex ways in which means of production and labor power are combined—not necessarily under the roof of single capitals—can play an important role in capital's strategies for gaining power. In Chapter 10, I will therefore explore class analysis and conceptualize class differentiation in greater depth. Suffice it to say at this point that the corresponding look at who owns and controls capital encompasses the role of intermediate classes that "occupy a continuum of positions that straddle the capital-labour divide" (Campling et al. 2016, 1753).

This analytical prism helps me to grasp (a) how property or class relations as relations of exploitation and domination work as catalysts of uneven development, which can change in form but at the same time be reproduced in the wake of upgrading, (b) to whose benefit and at whose expense that happens, and (c) how, if at all, it is contested by labor. My study thus takes class-based strategies both from the capital and the labor side into account.

Trained with a class-relational gaze on the structural dynamics of capital accumulation, scholars have furthermore revisited the issue of capitalist competition, which has not played a role in the GVC conceptualization of governance (see Chapter 3). Accordingly, competitive and profit maximizing strategies of lead firms based on increased labor exploitation, on a growing control over means of production, and on the appropriation of value produced elsewhere under other capitals' control needs to (re)acquire a central role in chain analysis (Quentin and Campling 2018; Selwyn 2016b). This diagnosis is not arbitrary; it is instead based on the notion that, within the capitalist social formation, firms need to be profitable on the penalty of being outcompeted. The power to govern a chain, thus, needs to be considered as the class power of leading capitalists (core-like capitals) to outcompete periphery-like capitals[11] in controlling the development of the productive forces and enhancing strategies to appropriate profits.

The implications of this for my research will be more thoroughly analyzed in Chapters 8 and 9, where I look at how corporate actors develop upgrading strategies to enhance their competitive positions—from the standpoint of vested capital interests.

4.3.2 Geopolitics and the (peripheral) state

As I have previously mentioned, scholars have remarked that the role of state(s) and geopolitics remains underexposed in GCC/GVC literatures (Neilson et al. 2014, 3 f.).[12] Chapter 3 has shown how especially the GVC approach has abandoned WSA's preoccupation with the world-scale integration of production and the related geopolitical organization in state units (Bair 2005, 156).[13] GVC scholars have answered their critique of state-centric economic analyses with a non-theorization of both the capitalist state and many states' peripheral integration into the prevalent world order (Dicken et al. 2001; Fernández and Trevignani 2015; Neilson 2014).

In fact, the GVC approach has presupposed states as actors that set entry barriers, for example via trade policies (Kaplinsky and Morris 2001, 43), often to the detriment of so-called developing states.[14] However, first, it does not

11 This can be conceived both geographically and in the sense of capitals within a local network.

12 The state has often received relatively little theoretical attention in critical theories of uneven development, also beyond commodity chain analysis. In Harvey's (2006) theory of geographically differentiated growth, for example, the author deals with how capital's tendency to act across space meets spatio-temporal differences in (a) a tiered control of spatially fixed means of production and (b) other conditions of the valorization of value. This includes a spatial concentration of key infrastructures and the ratio of capital and labor power, among other aspects. The geographical concentration of capital and an opposed tendency towards fragmentation and disintegration lead to meandering motions and geographies of capitalist development, where capital preferably invests in particular spaces that it may also abandon. Historically, these conditions of valorization have grown in a system of multiple states. Harvey (2007, 67) admits, however, that he did not do a "very good job" in theorizing the role of state agency in development issues.

13 As a reminder, Wallerstein stresses the differentiated functions of core-like and peripheral states and their respective strengths in co-shaping the world-economy (Wallerstein 2012a). Here, core states shape commodity chains by different means reaching from free trade agreements to protectionism (Bair 2012, 2; Quark 2014; Wallerstein 2009).

14 See Stevens (2011), who argues that EU trade policies can prevent non-preferred states from emulating upgrading strategies—or contribute to the dominant positions of particular horticulture-

provide for analyses that extend past a mere description of what state institutions do or do not do to promote economic development. Second, in abstraction from the reasons of how, why, when, and where states (do not) endeavor or (do not) have the capacity to bring 'their' economies forward, states are addressed as key actors when it comes to promoting upgrading initiatives. Accordingly, as a consequence of the silence on the character of capitalist states in general and geopolitical positions in the global political economy in particular, GVC scholars all too easily reduce the political environment of economic action to "access restrictions, weak infrastructures, lacking resources and institutional voids" (Trienkens 2011, 51) that can be enhanced.

A number of studies have tried to counter such an understanding of the state as a neutral developmental actor and put it (back) on the chain research agenda (Fernández and Trevignani 2015). For example, opposed to illusive requests to state actors nurtured by a non-theorization of capitalist states and an abstraction from actual imperialism, Glassman (2011) calls for an analysis of geopolitical power that shapes regional processes of both upgrading and downgrading. He analyzes how Korean firms were historically able to expand their geographical reach by collaborating with the US war in Vietnam, helping to build a Cold War regional economy while simultaneously derailing Vietnam's economy. Glassman directs attention to the importance of inter-state competition and even imperialist war for the question of whether or how economic performance is successful in specific regions. Geopolitics, he argues, cannot be understood as something exterior to the development of global production networks. Rather, there is a need to explain the "power that capital has in relation to such state agencies and the interpenetration of capital and states" (ibid., 157).

However, the questions of why state actors do what they do and how peripheral positions translate into specific political capacities or weaknesses still require further elaboration within chain research. By that token, it is helpful to recall Wallerstein's diagnosis that the extent to which state action can have a critical influence on upgrading possibilities and not just for the benefit of particular companies depends on a state's strength, which in turn cannot be understood independently of center-periphery relations (see

exporting countries. However, he does not discuss the character of capitalist or imperialist states and simply concludes that these policies have to be changed, without considering what kind of struggle might be necessary to achieve such goals. Does it suffice simply to remind the EU that it conducts erroneous policies?

Chapter 3). Yet as I have briefly discussed in Section 3.1, this does not allow one to infer state action merely based on the state's position in the global division of labor (see Selwyn 2012, 26). Wallerstein sidelines questions of class struggle and hegemony formation within states. He does not analyze how and why the ways in which state policies benefit the interests of capital have differed historically, also within core like or peripheral states respectively (see Chase-Dunn 1998, 132 f. for early versions of this debate).

This book has not been conceived as a contribution to state theory. However, my critique of the GVC upgrading paradigm's illusive understanding of developmental state action raises the questions of (a) to what extent and why states with particular social structures and positions in the imperialist world-system have the capabilities and willingness to promote specific developmental paths and influence the position of 'their' capitals, and (b) to what extent and why state actors are (not) oriented at a national development that includes broad concessions to the working classes. These questions are of particular relevance for Chapter 8, where I analyze corporate strategies on GVC development and their limits and contradictions. This makes it necessary to set out my understanding of capitalist sates, at least cursorily.

States are understood in this book as *relatively* independent and autonomous political forms of the capitalist social relations and an institutionalization of their inherent struggles between classes (and marginalized groups), as well as between fractions of capital. The economically ruling class is not fully identical with the politically ruling one and they each operate in different spheres. In other words, the economy and the state formally fall apart. There is, as Marx says, a "particularization of the state" (Marx 1975 [1844], 78). However, this particularization does not imply that the state is neutral or independent from the capitalist economy. Instead, it is based on the capital relation. "It is always the direct relationship of the owners of the conditions of production to the direct producers [...] which reveals the innermost secret, the hidden basis of the entire social structure, and with it the political form of the relation of sovereignty and dependence, in short, the corresponding specific form of the state" (Marx 1991 [1894], 778).

Capitalist states monopolize the use of force, and they guarantee the acts of selling and buying commodities, as well and the private property of the means of production. Thus, while the capitalist state does not provide the economically ruling class with formal political privileges, it is nevertheless a class state. Its rule of law applies across classes, yet the bourgeois form of rule de facto upholds the capital relation.

It is, in this sense, a structural expression of class relations and capitalist competition, the condensation of which shapes its development dynamics. As "material condensation[s] of a relationship of forces" (Poulantzas 2000 [1978], 129) between these social actors, states and their apparatuses are always contested. Yet in historically and geographically specific political economic constellations, the ruling classes have gained hegemonic control over states, which perpetuate the overall conditions for capitalist reproduction.[15] Here, I agree with the WSA understanding of core-like states as "organizations which are often utilized by the classes that control them to help appropriate shares of the world surplus value" (Chase-Dunn 1998, 137), if necessary by pursuing political-military goals (ibid., 134).

The extent to which particular capitals' interests directly translate into state action (as might have been the case when, for instance, a former Monsanto manager led the Ministry of Agriculture in Argentina's province of Buenos Aires) or hegemony in a state is based on broader social compromise can vary over space and time.

To grasp hegemony, Gramsci emphasized the importance of analyzing how it is manufactured politically, culturally, and ideologically in the civil society, and how this is rooted in actual social structures, the social relations of production. Here, coalitions among the capitalist fractions are formed, material and other concessions are struggled over with exploited classes and marginalized groups, and cultural life, ideas, and beliefs are (re)produced. Given its contested character, hegemony can be more or less stable, but it is never sealed. It can be challenged by dissensions among the dominant economic actors or by struggles from below by those who do not accept the respective status quo as a given. When stable intra-capitalist coalitions can be built to formulate a common strategic project or development path—and when at the same time economic, political, and ideological consent is manufactured among the forces in the civil society—Gramsci calls such relative hegemonic alliances a "historical bloc" (Gramsci 2012 [1975]-e, 1228, 1249).

15 Bourgeois states thus enforce hegemonic projects (which can inhere setting limits for individual capitalists or designing policies fought for by marginalized groups), the historically and geographically specific manufacturing of which depends on both general political economic conditions and social struggles. Yet for as long as the social relations based on exploitation are not effectively called into question by class struggles from below, the political societies necessarily have a bourgeois character. Conversely, the state also uses political, ideological, and coercive means (police, military, etc.) to intervene in struggles in the civil society.

Importantly, hegemony is (re)produced in historically and geographically specific political economic constellations with different conditions for the formation of a historical bloc and for the definition of longer-term development strategies. As for the question of the relative weakness of peripheral states to build stable historical blocs and corresponding feasible strategic projects for development, Fernández and Ormaechea (2018) point out that this requires a grasp of different interrelated aspects, namely, how do nationally specific political economies with the productive forces of 'their' capitals, class dynamics and social struggles intertwine with (a) the historical dynamics of global capitalism, (b) globally differentiated control over capitalist production and distribution, (c) barriers set by core-like capitals as well as other territorial strategies to gain or perpetuate economic superiority over (peripheral) regions and the ensuing (im)possibilities for peripheries, and (d) geopolitical rivalry? This speaks to the problem of how the relationship of forces may condensate differently in peripheral states due to the influence of core-like capitals and imperialist states. All of this has a decisive impact on the extent to which state actors have the will and capacity to "manage the demands of maintaining both cohesion and competitiveness in both the international and their specific national political economies" (Rolf 2015, 140).

I will discuss the problems and contradictions of optimistically addressing states as potent partners in promoting both economic and social upgrading in Chapters 7 and 8.

But before commencing with the analysis of my empirical data, the following Chapter 5 serves to delineate the methods I employed and to provide insight into the empirical work that I carried out in Argentina to answer my research questions.

5. Methods and the Field

I situate my research within the confines of what I call an empirical ideology critique, the contours of which I presented in Chapter 2. Gazing through this "conceptual kaleidoscope" (Bhaskar and Callinicos 2003, 101), my study engages with the GVC upgrading paradigm. I hitherto discussed this approach on a theoretical level, grounded in a notion of critique as a method that is mindful of the claims and (implicit) assumptions of its object and, at the same time, points to the contradictions that may arise immanently in theory as well as in relation to social practice.

Following on from this, the present chapter introduces the design for my empirical research. The basic concept has been to follow key presumptions associated with the upgrading paradigm into the field and to analyze actually existing upgrading strategies in agro-industrial value chains in Argentina. In this vein, in my empirical chapters I first argue on the basis of strategies and practices set out by different sets of actors in these chains. Secondly, I trace the concomitant limitations, contradictions, and implications of value chain development. To substantiate my research strategy in this endeavor, in the remainder of this chapter, I will first briefly address some epistemological aspects of my study design (with reference to Chapter 2). Then, I provide an account of the fieldwork that I conducted in Argentina between 2014 and 2016 and of how I worked with the gathered data. Finally, I offer reflections on my empirical research in the last section of this chapter.

5.1 Epistemological considerations

I argued in Chapter 2 that scholarly thinking never takes place in isolation from a historically and geographically specific social reality. Furthermore, I proposed that critical research works "on the basis of real and of actual experience" (Gramsci 2012 [1975]-h, 2177 f.) and, at the same time, it takes the dialectic between the social whole and particular phenomena into account. In this sense, ideology critique goes hand in hand with "appealing to the empirical evidence of historical reality" (Wallerstein 2000a, 71). That being recalled, the following provides an account of the epistemological premises that underlie my empirical analysis.

Inherent to my research design is the epistemic, counter-positivist assumption that critical science, which is "engaged in understanding the social world" (Bhaskar and Callinicos 2003, 95), cannot "view reality from some neutral standpoint" (Isaksen 2018, 98). At the same time, the framing of my study implies that critique is not only a "method of argumentation" but that it also provides "grounds for knowledge" (ibid.). On the basis of both theoretical discussion and empirical research, I argue that key theoretical principles of mainstream GVC analysis render this approach inadequate to do justice to particular phenomena within social reality. Said another way, I analyze social relations and practices that contest the basic assumptions of the GVC upgrading paradigm.

So how do I make sense of the relation between scholarly positions and social reality of which my research seeks to understand an extract? A point of reference that I find helpful is Bhaskar's (2008) critical realism that can be read from a historical materialist perspective. In brief, Bhaskar's epistemology is conceived as a critique of and an alternative to positivism, "to which contradictions are anathema" (Adorno 1977 [1969], 5). Bhaskar understands as science a "systematic attempt to express in thought the structures and ways of acting of things that exist and act independently" of what scholars think (Bhaskar 2008, 250). This implies that the "truth-conditions" for our knowledge of an object of study are not the same as the "truth-conditions" for this object (ibid.).[1] This is based on two interrelated premises.

As regards the first premise, historical materialists start from the assumption that there is a "complex, structured, and multi-levelled" (Bhaskar and Callinicos 2003, 90) social reality that exists independently of how science digests it, that is, of scholarly thought. But this is not a naturally given social reality with a supra-historical, unchangeable set of problems.

1 In other words, "knowledge may change without objects and objects change without knowledge. [...] Things exist and act independently of our descriptions, but we can only know them under particular descriptions" (ibid.).

Instead, it is socially produced and thus historically and geographically specific (Gramsci 2012 [1975]-e, 1412; see Stache 2017, 42). This includes, for example, the social reality of capitalist production as being based on endless accumulation through exploitation, though in forms that have varied over time and space.

The second premise is that "there could not be knowledge without antecedents" (Bhaskar 2008, 250) and scholars are no unmediated recorders of given conjunctures (ibid., 242). As perceiving subjects, they are themselves part of—and related to—a social world. Knowledge production hence cannot happen in an unmediated manner, utterly detached from the social practice. In that sense, Horkheimer (1972 [1937], 200) has emphasized that even the way we see and hear "is inseparable from the social life-process." Accordingly, the world is real but not seamlessly knowable. It is necessarily understood from a particular position, because both the object of interest and the subject are ultimately historical. "The facts which our senses present to us are socially preformed in two ways: through the historical character of the object perceived and through the historical character of the perceiving organ. Both are not simply natural; they are shaped by human activity" (ibid.).

The premise that ideas do not develop in a vacuum is commonly accepted within different perspectives on historical materialism. Gramsci, for instance, emphasizes the relationship between the subject and reality and concludes that searching for the latter outside of the historical human being is a paradox. "For historical materialism, thought cannot be detached from being, man from nature, (historical) activity from matter, the subject from the object" (Gramsci 2012 [1975]-b, 505). There is, thus, no such thing as objectivity that transcends history. In a similar vein, Adorno (1973) emphasized the historicity of truth. It "is suspended and frail, due to its temporal substance" (ibid., 34). Beyond that, he questioned a seamless identity of reality and its perception. A subject cannot depict reality in an unmediated, position-less manner.

This is not only due to the social conditions of knowledge; when one describes social realities, one necessarily makes abstractions and leaves things out. One must furthermore speak of them "and know them under particular descriptions, descriptions which will always be to a greater or lesser extent theoretically determined" (Bhaskar 2008, 249). As a consequence, it is not only necessary for scholars to remember that research not neutral. Theory must also allow for a reflection on the dialectic between the social whole and particular phenomena, and on how theory is necessarily an incomplete construction in terms of its ability to capture reality.

That being said, I have previously argued that theories can be more or less adequate to explain (a part of) social reality. Concepts can "only be justified by their capacity to render intelligible a certain domain or phenomena" (ibid.). Otherwise, Bhaskar argues, they can also be incapable of explaining "a range of phenomena that takes on a special significance for the agents that participate in the forms of social life they define" (ibid., 246). He takes as an example how mass unemployment in the 1930s showed the inadequacy of neo-classical theories. An example from my own study is my analysis of corporate upgrading strategies and practices, which suggests the inadequacy of upgrading as a new paradigm for development.

In brief, the epistemic premise that social reality and the concepts for analyzing it are not identical requires a researcher to critically reflect on his or her work and thought. Nevertheless, "the self-reflection of enlightenment is not its revocation" (Adorno 1973, 158).

Points of view and empirical research

With this meta-theoretical approach in mind, what can my empirical research offer? In my study, I do not aim to and I cannot comprehensively describe the social reality of agro-industrial chain development in Argentina as a whole. Instead, I can take a close look at specific aspects of upgrading in these chains, consider some of their ramifications, and refer to actual contradictions arising within the GVC upgrading paradigm. This allows me to reflect on how particular social practices and resulting problems that I have studied cannot be adequately captured by the mainstream GVC approach, or resolved by its upgrading paradigm.

Conceptual frameworks and points of view inherent to my ideology-critical scheme do not stand in conflict with a careful reflection on my findings. It is not about outright categorically opposing everything, for instance, that business actors tell me. For example, many of my interlocutors themselves pointed to certain limits to upgrading rather than telling a mere success story. I picked up on such matters and, at the same time, I considered from which standpoints and with which interests such problems were raised (see Chapter 8). A second example refers to cases in which I analyzed a reproduction of uneven development that appeared to go hand in hand with upgrading strategies. Here, my analysis took into consideration how many of my interlocutors who are not staying ahead of the competition, but who are instead in a dependent relationship with one of my case companies, in fact appreciate their status quo (see Chapter 10).

Thus, I took care to do justice to my empirical data and to reflect what my interlocutors told me in interviews. But, obviously, I read these interviews through my eyes, not theirs. I have disclosed the theoretical, partisan standpoint from which I did so from the beginning of this study.

5.2 Setting up my research field in Argentina

When I first came to Argentina for exploratory fieldwork in 2014, my research design was not yet planned in detail. From the beginning, my project proposed to investigate competitive strategies of companies in agro-industrial commodity chains in this South American country. In the back of my mind, I thought I would deal with issues of monopolization, and I was keen to investigate what these competitive strategies could teach me about the (re)production of uneven development. These initial questions still remain at the heart of my interest, yet they are somewhat vague, and so was my initial fieldwork. In retrospect, however, this 2014 research stay yielded a part of the empirical data on which my analysis builds. It also coined the further formation of my research field and contributed to sharpening the analytical lens through which I have interpreted my findings.

One observation in particular was formative in this respect. I noticed that while the GCC/GVC perspective hardly played a role in the rich and comprehensive critical scholarship on agribusiness in Argentina, the corporate actors I interviewed frequently referenced the value chain metaphor fairly positively. Most of my interlocutors mentioned current difficulties and limits of agro-industrial value chain development, as I will analyze in Chapter 8. At the same time, however, they pointed to value chains both as a plane of common business organization and as a possibility space for sounding out economic potential. This observation, first, led me to more comprehensively engage with the GVC approach on a theoretical level, as the previous chapters illustrated. Second, it resulted in my decision to make a critical analysis of how this approach is reflected in corporate strategies and practices a key guide for my empirical research (see Chapters 8 and 9).

During two further research periods in 2015 and 2016, I then pursued in a more structured manner what I had started in 2014. To put my research design into practice, my empirical study followed the upgrading strategies of different actors, in modification of the approach of following a commodity to unveil patterns of exploitation and uneven value appropriation. I tracked trajectories, discourses, and practices, as well as stated purposes and doubts regarding agro-industrial value chain development in Argentina. My research thus revealed multi-faceted contradictions that come along with an unreserved invocation of state and corporate actors as bearers of economic and social upgrading. As my empirical chapters will analyze in detail, this includes (a) the ideological use of the GVC approach for vested interests and related omissions; (b) obstructions and structural limits to upgrading; and (c) discrepancies between business interests and social upgrading. Beyond that, I traced concomitant ramifications of upgrading strategies, including capital concentration and the reproduction of exploitative relations in situ in changing forms.

With respect to the methods I employed, my study represents a multi-faceted endeavour that relies mainly on four sets of data: (1) semi-structured in-depth interviews with different actors in the field; (2) text corpora (policy analysis, homepages and other company materials, media articles, etc.); (3) participant observation; and (4) quantitative data provided by case companies and public databases. In addition, several conversations held with scholars in situ have helped sharpen my view. Table 1 below provides an overview of the methods I used. The following sequentially gives a glimpse into these different parts of my fieldwork and illustrates how they nourished my analysis.

Interviews as sources of information and forums for perceptions

Semi-structured, problem-centered interviews (Helfferich 2009, 36) are the main source of my analysis. Problem-centered in this context refers to research that focuses on a socially relevant question and aims to understand both the interview partners' actual practices and their ways of reflecting social reality (Flick 2006, 135). It leaves room for respondents to comprehensively express their views, interests, concerns, aspirations, and objectives. A semi-structured interview at the same time allows one to address theory-guided interests.

Interviews	Representatives of the Argentinian soy and wheat chain associations (ACSOJA, ArgenTrigo) and of member organizations	15 respondents
	Representatives of the Argentine Federation of Freight Transport (FADEEAC)	2 respondents
	Representatives of three case companies	14 respondents
	Representatives of small firms related to case company El Agro (labor contractors; service providers; small producers; land owners)	11 respondents
	Representatives of state institutions: Ministry of Agriculture (MAGyP); National Institute for Agriculture Technology (INTA)	6 respondents
	Representatives of labor unions	4 respondents
	Representative of an association of regional peasants in the province of Buenos Aires	1 respondent
	Members of the Latin American Coordination of Rural Organizations (CLOC)–La Vía Campesina	2 respondents
	Total respondents: 55	
Discussions with Argentinian scholars who work on related topics		
Text corpora	– Governmental strategy papers – Homepages – Press releases – Company documents (annual reports of my case companies) – Union documents (collective agreements)	
Participatory observations	– 2014: 22nd congress of the Argentinian No-Till Farmers Association (Aapresid) – 2015: Congress of the CLOC–La Vía Campesina – 2015/2016: Expoagro (agricultural fair) – 2016: ArgenTrigo congress – Farm visits	
Quantitative data	– Company information – Public databases	

Table 1: Overview of data sets for multi-faceted research

Source: own elaboration

During three phases of fieldwork (July–August 2014; April–May 2015; March–August 2016), I conducted a total of 51 interviews with 55 respondents. In some cases, interviews were held with more than one interlocutor at a time. Usually, interviews lasted between one and two hours. The selection of my interlocutors followed the logic of my research design. State and corporate actors are referred to as the main drivers of upgrading in mainstream GVC literatures; thus, following that assumption into the field meant first analyzing state and corporate strategies.

State institutions

Four interviews conducted with six respondents from state institutions served to supplement my study of policy documents (see below). Together, these sources formed the basis for my analysis of the strategic governmental[2] approach to agro-industrial value chain development in Argentina, which I present in Chapter 7. At the time of my fieldwork, the then Ministry of Agriculture had established secretariats that were responsible for higher value-added activities and for small-scale family agriculture. Interviewing representatives of both, I sought to account for possible controversies among these different areas of responsibility within the ministry. The other two interviews were held with representatives of the National Institute for Agriculture Technology (known as INTA, in Spanish), one of the most important state institutions that drives the ministry's goals forward. Together, this material offers detailed elaborations on how state actors defined prospects for GVC development in Argentina and on which strategies they aimed to enact. They also provide a basis for analyzing omitted aspects regarding the perpetuation of socioeconomic inequality and exploitation in the wake of agribusiness development (see Chapter 7).

Agribusiness associations and case companies

For various reasons, I decided to put my main empirical focus on analyzing the strategies of corporate actors, as it is reflected in Chapters 8 and 9. I already mentioned the relevance attached to firms as developmental actors by the GVC approach. But there were also reasons that concerned my particular field of research. First and foremost was the extremely transparent access to some companies and to most of the business associations organized within the Argentinian soy and wheat chain associations (ACSOJA,

2 This refers to the former government under president Cristina Fernández de Kirchner.

ArgenTrigo, in Spanish). Second was the importance attached to the value chain agenda by these business associations, which have come to organize and present themselves as parts of larger chains rather than as mere individual actors. I was therefore interested in exploring their discourses on this subject more closely. Third, some of the strategies pursued by my case companies Agrigood, LAgricola, and especially El Agro can be read as textbook cases of upgrading as defined by GVC scholars (see Chapters 3 and 9). My critical political economy-guided interest in these strategies entails the aim to increase awareness to the contradictions surrounding firm-level upgrading, especially regarding the broader positive effects that are anticipated in GVC literatures.

The interviews I held with representatives of both business associations and case companies were inspired by Schoenberger's (1991, 180 ff.) reintroduction of the "qualitative corporate interview," the goal of which is to understand the behavior of firms in light of their histories and economic conditions as well as other considerations such as competitive strategies and class relations, among others. These interviews serve both as sources of information and to reconstruct how corporate actors discursively frame their actions and relations (intra-capital, to workers, and to other actors).

I was interested in what my respondents said, and also in what they didn't say. What kinds of issues were left out or only addressed selectively? For example, I explored the ways in which my respondents talked about social upgrading and also how they neglected certain aspects of it at the same time.

I conducted 16 interviews with 17 representatives of ACSOJA and ArgenTrigo, as well as of member organizations that organize firms in different chain nodes, and FADEEAC. This footage builds the foundation for Chapter 8. It offers detailed interpretations of agro-industrial value chain development in Argentina and of perceived problems that may obstruct upgrading strategies. At the same time, it provides an in-depth analysis of class-biased strategy formulation and related omissions or one-sidedly defined problems.

In a similar vein, I conducted 14 interviews with representatives of my case companies Agrigood, LAgriciola, and El Agro (three of the biggest agribusiness companies in Argentina at the time, which have taken different upgrading trajectories). They offered insight into the competitive strategies of these firms and some of their socioeconomic ramifications, which I discuss in Chapter 9. Especially El Agro granted me a fairly open access to the company and allowed me to conduct interviews with its then president (in

2014 and 2015 respectively) and vice president (in 2016), as well as with staff of different sections within the company.

A case study on the class dynamics of upgrading

This relative openness allowed me to zoom in further and to conduct a case study on the relationships that El Agro has established to other actors in the course of its upgrading strategies. In Chapter 10, I discuss the related findings through a class-analytical lens.

El Agro granted me contact to various of its clients and contractors, including small capitalist labor contractors and agricultural producers, land owners who lease out to the company, and self-employed management service providers. Respondents were asked to discuss different facets of their relationship to El Agro. These interviews helped me to explore some of the implications of capital-led value chain development with respect to class dynamics. Furthermore, I used interviews with unions, which allowed me to obtain insights into how organized labor has struggled for the benefits to be gained from upgrading. At the same time, my case study data shows how social upgrading is not an automatic result of value chain development, and that it does not work so readily in any historical and geographical (class) constellation either. In this context, I also benefitted from lively scientific exchange with Juan Manuel Villulla (University of Buenos Aires), who conducted in-depth ethnographic research on labor relations and working conditions in Argentinian agribusiness.

Data handling and analysis

I conducted my interviews and their analysis in Spanish, and I only translated into English the quotes that I used in this study. For all my interview footage, the names of both persons and case companies were anonymized. I had already assured that in email enquiries to my desired interlocutors. Although many of the business people I interviewed in fact encouraged me to use their full names, I decided to stick to anonymization for all my respondents. I hoped that some of them would speak more openly in the knowledge that they did not have to fear reading their names in studies. Furthermore, especially regarding the interviews I conducted with actors related to my case company El Agro, I did not want the company to be able to read about 'who said what' in my study. In the case of business associations, I anonymized the persons but not the institutions. What these institutions do in particular is important for my analysis and a change of designation, in these cases, would not have changed their recognizability.

All my interlocutors were given first names as pseudonyms. This may seem somewhat strange to readers, since I do not have a personal relationship with my respondents. In Argentina, however, people hardly address each other formally. Even company representatives sometimes asked me to address them on a first-name basis when I kept calling them by their last names out of habit.

As for the analysis of my interviews, I organized them with the aid of a qualitative data analysis software and analyzed them by multiple rounds of close reading and coding. Here, I used the method of structuring qualitative content analysis (Kuckartz 2012, 77 ff.). This method combines analysis informed by theory-driven research questions with inductive coding and creating categories along topics addressed by interview partners. What Charmaz (2006, 43–45) has pointed out for Grounded Theory holds true for inductive coding in general: it is "the first step in moving beyond concrete statements in the data to making analytic interpretations [...] As we code, we ask: which theoretical categories might these statements indicate?" Guided by theory, I analyzed my data at the same time by asking categorizing questions related to my research objective. For example, how is GVC development discussed? What are the stated competitive strategies? Where do my interlocutors see limits to upgrading and what do they propose to overcome them? What do my interviews (not) say about exploitation and power relations? What are the (possible) contradictions that arise within the key assumptions of the GVC upgrading paradigm?

Supplementing data with document analysis

The same method of analysis was used for documents. As noted before, Chapter 7 works through the cornerstones of the roadmap that the former government under then President Cristina Fernández de Kirchner had promoted for agro-industrial value chain development in Argentina. Here, the analysis is mainly derived (a) from the governmental strategy document *Argentina Agribusiness Leader. Federal and Participative Agri-Food and Agribusiness Strategic Plan 2010–2020* (PEA) (Ministry of Agriculture 2011) and (b) from a policy paper which presents the strategic objectives of the INTA (2004).

It should be noted that these documents do not reveal the actual political practice. However, they do disclose strategic governmental plans and discourses on GVC development. On that basis, I contrast the claims made here both with statements made by my interlocutors from state agencies and with scholarly literature on the effects of agribusiness development in Argentina. As mentioned above, my main interest here was in analyzing the defined strategies and prospects for GVC development in Argentina, as well as omitted aspects regarding the perpetuation of socioeconomic inequality and exploitation (see Chapter 7).

Throughout my research, I also included further text corpora into my analysis. Homepages of companies and business associations, including press releases and media coverage placed there, provided information about the featured histories and public appearances of these actors, which became pivotal as context knowledge and for the preparation of my interviews.

Later, annual reports of the case companies became an important part of my analysis, for two main reasons. First, they served to analyze the quantitative data of the financial statements and thus to depict whether or how these companies upgraded into more profitable activities. Second, company reports are insightful because they are at least partly written for a particular purpose, namely to convince potential investors. Accordingly, discourses in these reports often differ from those in interview footage or media texts with which companies aim to address a wider public. Examining these documents revealed, for instance, discrepancies between public or interview statements on a firm's social upgrading goals and how this issue was addressed in the financial reporting.

Observing-as-participant

ACSOJA and ArgenTrigo were created as chain-like entities that coordinate various business associations operating along the respective value chains. On this plane of organization, common strategies and political positions are dealt out, controversies among the members are put on the agenda, technical, political, and economic problems and challenges are discussed, and external criticism is addressed. These issues are discussed at meetings and conferences, among other spaces. ACSOJA and ArgenTrigo helped me schedule interviews with member associations and granted me access to key conferences in the field, to fairs, and in one instance, even to an internal meeting of ArgenTrigo.

This allowed me to couple my interview data with observations. Mattisek et al. (2013, 149) have called researchers in such settings "observers-as-participants." Compared to other forms of participatory observation, scholars here focus on attendance and observation without being intensively integrated into the research context.

At these events, I was able to capture how the actors I analyzed present themselves in their business environments and what kinds of topics they address there (without being asked in interviews). My attendance at conferences in particular offered a better vantage point for evaluating (1) how different actors represent their interests in shaping value chain development; (2) how they promote particular positions on different sets of problems; and (3) how they discuss common approaches to dealing with protests and criticisms, for instance, from environmentalist groups. In particular, these observations fed into my analysis of how corporate actors organize themselves along chains and how they promote their interests (see Chapter 8). Furthermore, they allowed me to interpret the analyzed strategies against the background of their ideological embedding into corporate promotions of GVC upgrading as a national development strategy. A further, incidental advantage was that the conferences also served as sites for interviews and as places where I could obtain additional contacts to potential interlocutors.

At an event on farming technologies organized by my case company El Agro, I interviewed two clients of El Agro, who then invited me to spend a day with them on their farms. These visits gave me a glimpse into the everyday practices and struggles of farmers, who still work and live in the countryside despite today's dominantly large-scale agribusiness in Argentina. These encounters have enriched my analysis of socioeconomic relationships in the production network controlled by El Agro (see Chapter 10). Through a day of informal conversations, I was also able to get a better insight into how my hosts perceived their relationship to El Agro in this connection.

Finally, I contrasted my observations made in the agribusiness world with insights gained at a conference held by the Latin American Coordination of Rural Organizations (CLOC)–La Vía Campesina, an internationally operating organization that brings together peasants, rural workers, landless people, among others, and which opposes corporate-driven agriculture.

Quantitative data

In addition to my qualitative research, some parts of my study required the use of quantitative data. For instance, data provided by the Argentinian National Statistics Institute (INDEC) allowed me to trace issues such as economic concentration in Pampean agriculture, as well as changes in the share of wage workers in the economically active population in that region.

Other sets of data, such as on registered jobs and average wages, are published by the Argentinian Ministry of Labor, Employment and Social Security (MTEySS). I was additionally granted unpublished data by the Employment and Business Dynamics Monitoring Centre at MTEySS that allowed me to roughly quantify formal employment in different industries, and to compare this data with optimistic statements made by agribusiness actors on the job-creating capacity of agro-industrial chain development. Collected agreements published by labor unions provided an overview of wage trends in different nodes of soybean value chains.

Finally, I consulted databases of intergovernmental organizations such as the Food and Agriculture Organization (FAO) on the evolution of harvested areas and crop yields. A detailed list of databases can be found in the Annex.

5.3 Reflections on my empirical research

This section engages in general considerations about my fieldwork. I begin by discussing some caveats and difficulties that have emerged as my research took shape. This is followed by a reflection on my work in Argentina.

Research does not always proceed as planned or desired

A first aspect concerns the access to quantitative data. Many of my interlocutors—from scholars to business actors—drew attention to an overall poor data situation in Argentina. Different governments have accused each other of openly using the INDEC for political purposes, and data series are often discontinued. A similar situation arises with respect to company data. Wallerstein once pointed out that

"The opacity of the distribution of the surplus-value in a long commodity chain is the most effective way to minimize political opposition, because it obscures the reality and the causes of the acute polarization of distribution that is the consequence of the endless accumulation of capital, a polarization that is more acute than in any previous historical system" (cited in Bair 2014, 7).

Yet tracing value in commodity chains is not only challenging with respect to the distribution of value. Its production is already opaque.

A first reason is that companies publish data only selectively. Asked whether they had information on the average cost structure in their industry, my respondents at CIARA (a business association that groups large oilseed processors) answered that companies do not share that kind of information. "They argue that almost all their information is very sensitive [...] even we don't have the real values of each company, say, how much they invested in what."[3] I also unsuccessfully asked for data such as averages of gross value-added in particular chain nodes. INDEC publishes the respective numbers according to categories like 'agriculture' and 'industry.' Asking business associations whether they managed this kind of data within their organization, the answer was "no" in every case, except for data on exports or tons of processed raw material.

Second, data published by companies and related institutions (if published at all) is not necessarily designed to be approached using the categories of critical political economy to accurately trace exploitation. For instance, (1) capital invested in labor power and means of production respectively is most often not reported by these categories in annual reports, (2) data is sorted by business year and not by the turnover time of invested capital, and (3) value transfers within or among companies are not necessarily trackable. This is specifically relevant to Chapter 9. Here, I discuss how the data I use can provide an approximation.

In general, however, missing or insufficient data has only marginally affected my work, because the focus of my research is on qualitative methods. As I have elaborated above, my study is not designed to trace precisely the value produced and appropriated along agro-industrial value chains in Argentina. However, in an awareness of the described problems, I did use available data wherever it is important for my argument. At the same time, the research I conducted has increased my interest in future studies to deepen my analysis in terms of the production and distribution of value along chains.

A further difficulty surfaced with respect to interview footage. I noted above that my case companies were extremely open to giving interviews.

3 Interview with two representatives of CIARA-CEC, June 2, 2016, Buenos Aires.

However, I did not receive access to all companies that I had initially planned to include in my research. In one case, a company representative answered that his firms' business policy is not to give interviews at all. In a second case, I encountered delaying tactics until I left Argentina. That said, I still believe that the analyses I am able to make stand on solid ground. The material I gathered allows me to capture how strategies on GVC development are defined by different corporate actors in agro-industrial chains. Thus, I can support the critical arguments I produce regarding the GVC upgrading paradigm. However, actors and upgrading strategies are manifold, such that my analysis only refers to a fragment of reality.

After the companies, getting access to representatives of labor unions proved to be more difficult than anticipated. For example, the Argentinian Union of Rural Workers and Stevedores (UATRE, in Spanish) never answered my requests. As described above, my research plan entailed starting with corporate actors and then zooming further in to identify the contradictions surrounding firm-level upgrading. Therefore, conducting interviews with firms and agribusiness associations was my first priority. In retrospect, I would have liked to take more time from the beginning to contact more workers and trade unionists. As noted above, however, other scholars conducted in-depth ethnographic research on labor relations and working conditions on which I was able to draw especially for my case study analysis of the class dynamics of upgrading in Chapter 10.

Me as a researcher in and on Argentinian agribusiness

When I arrived in Argentina in 2014, I was struck by the variety and quantity of critical research that has been conducted on agribusiness-related topics in this country. As a result, I initially struggled to find out what my role could be in such a research environment. Why should I be conducting fieldwork in Argentina, where plenty of researchers with longstanding local expertise work on similar issues? However, with the above described experiences from my first period of fieldwork, it became clearer to me that my contribution could best lie in an analysis and critique of how the GVC upgrading paradigm plays out in local grain and oilseed value chains. I was glad to hear that many of the scholars I spoke to thought this was a helpful undertaking, especially because the GVC metaphor is increasingly used by business actors (and pro-agribusiness scholars), while this has not been thoroughly reflected yet in critical research.

For this study, my background provided several advantages. First, there is the general privilege of conducting fully financed fieldwork on the other side of the earth, which is unequally granted to researchers situated in the capitalist centers. But there were also advantages directly related to my fieldwork. As regards the interviews with business actors, my position as a female researcher (then from the University of Zurich) helped me in various respects. First, agribusiness is a fairly controversial topic in Argentina. In this context, I believe that my respondents were not suspicious of me, due to my provenance. This intertwined with the above-mentioned fact that the GVC term was coined positively for them. As a result—at least this was my impression—they saw me as an ally, rather than a critical researcher, without their asking many questions. Second, I had the impression that some interlocutors took much more time to explain their contexts to me as a foreigner than they may have done if I were Argentinian.

Challenging interview situations

There were nevertheless some difficult interview situations. In her article on corporate interviews, Schoenberger (1991, 182 ff.) points to different challenges posed by this method. This includes the potential problem that in these interviews, investigators often talk to people who are experts in public representation and in keeping a conversation under their control. Especially from the second period of fieldwork on, I therefore tried to be as prepared as possible before entering an interview situation, especially through intensive internet-based background research on the companies' histories and strategies.

In some cases, it was even an advantage that I did not appear as a business or agronomy expert to my respondents. Thus, they explained 'their world' to me in greater detail. In other cases, however, I found it extremely difficult to encourage my counterpart to talk about issues that he or she had not already promulgated in press releases or on homepages. In this context, it was helpful talking to several employees within the same company. For example, while El Agro's former president had told me—without lying—that his company does not own any land, it was another employee who reported that the owner family, however, does own land that is leased out to the firm.

In yet other cases, respondents made pretty clear to me that they would answer 'this far and no further.' In one instance, at the very end of an interview, I asked a respondent about his opinion on an issue. He had appeared negatively in some headlines, and I wanted to know what was behind these media articles. But my interlocutor just smiled amicably and said: "That's all lies." In this vein, I often experienced a stunning cordiality with which interview partners welcomed me, combined with a subtle but crystal-clear demarcation of what was askable and what was not.

These contacts to very nice people who obviously would not want to talk about some of their not-so-nice actions, and whose roles as business representatives I would criticize, was at times also challenging for me. I never lied to anyone about the framework of my study (though admittedly, people hardly asked me). However, I sometimes felt out of place and it would have been easier for me to interview actors who are closer to me in my partisanship.

In one case, difficulties included the need to clearly distance myself from an interview partner while still being as friendly as an interview situation requires. Soon after commencing with my questions, he explained that he was running out of time. With a wink he said that he would invite me to have a drink with him later that night. Surely, he would have taken me more seriously as a researcher—not a company for a night out—if I was not a woman.

Co-selection of interview partners

A last issue that I would like to address regards the co-construction of data by way of selecting interview partners. During fieldwork for my case study on the socioeconomic relations in the production network controlled by El Agro, I was confronted with this methodological problem. I had difficulties in independently finding interview partners that are directly connected to this company, because it monopolizes this sort of information. The respective actors often live and work in a geographically atomized capacity, such that it was not possible to approach them by just spending time in a particular village. After a process of negotiation, El Agro agreed to connect me with regional staff that in turn made appointments with different respondents. This whole process took quite a lot of time. In some cases, company staff participated in interviews or waited outside, passing by the door from time to time. Thus, whether intentionally or not, some of my interviews were accompanied by a certain surveillance of what was being said and by whom.

In closing, I can say that despite or in part also because of these challenges, three successive periods of fieldwork in Argentina allowed me to improve my qualitative research in situations that were new to me. Even if I would do some things differently in retrospect, the resulting findings allowed me to elaborate the empirical chapters of my study. They follow after the subsequent brief contextual chapter on the political economy of grain and oilseed value chains in Argentina.

6. The Context of the Study: Grain and Oilseed Value Chains in Argentina

After then Argentinian President Mauricio Macri took office in December 2015, scholarly and political critics of this former government widely shared the diagnosis that the then new administration had quickly begun to alter the country's political economy in a way that benefited highly concentrated capitals and disadvantaged workers and marginalized groups (Schorr 2016).[1] However, there is some disagreement when it comes to assessing the extent of the political sea change from the previous governments of Néstor Kirchner (2003–2007) and his successor Cristina Fernández de Kirchner (2007–2015), especially with respect to agribusiness related policies. The Kirchner governments had positioned themselves as an antithesis to the neoliberalism promoted by right-wing Peronist Carlos Menem, whose presidency (1989–1999) ended with a deep economic crisis and the country's insolvency in the early 2000s. They made the case for a neo-developmentalist[2] program. Many elements of the latter can be found in the so-called neo-structuralist development paradigm by the UN Economic Commission for Latin America and the Caribbean (ECLAC), which promotes a "renewed development strategy from within" (Sunkel 1993, 1; for a critique see Leiva 2008; Webber 2010), as I will explain in more detail below. In this context, the Kirchner governments at-

1 This book is based on a PhD thesis submitted in mid–2019. Debates concerning the presidency of Alberto Ángel Fernández (since 2019) are not included, and most of the data used in Section 6.2 does not extent beyond that year. However, I included results of the National Agricultural Census published in late 2019.

2 The term was first coined by Brazilian economist Bresser-Perreira, who aimed to promote a path to development that could avoid the negative effects of the Washington Consensus. Very briefly, its core is a national capitalist development program, which aims to achieve macroeconomic stability and full employment through a combination of economic liberalism with state intervention oriented at systemic competitiveness and pro-poor policies to increase domestic demand (Ban 2013, 300 ff.).

tached importance to both primary production and agro-industrial processing as a lever for local progress (see Gras and Hernández 2016b, 15).

Critical scholars have pointed out that the Kirchner administrations made a de facto difference for broader populations through redistributive social policies and poverty reduction, among other measures (Basualdo 2006, 173). Yet at the same time, their policies helped to deepen (a) the dominance of industries related to the expanded production and export of agricultural commodities and their derivatives, as well as (b) the power of large corporations operating in different nodes of their respective value chains (Lapegna 2017, 314; see Azpiazu et al. 2011; Féliz 2013; Fernández 2013b; Romero 2016; Schorr 2013).

As I have said before, my study follows upgrading strategies within grain and oilseed value chains and discusses some of their ramifications. On that note, this chapter is not designed as an in-depth analysis of the political economy of agro-industrial GVCs in Argentina; rather it seeks to provide a rough panoramic view on the latter to contextualize my empirical work.

To this end, the next section (6.1) briefly summarizes the (dis)continuities in agribusiness-related economic policies implemented in Argentina by the military junta (1976–1983), under President Menem (1989–1999), and by the neo-developmentalist Kirchner governments (2003–2015). These policies form the political environment in which the corporate strategies that I analyze have evolved.

Section 6.2 then provides a panoramic view of grain and oilseed value chains in Argentina. It considers economic developments as well as dominant corporate actors in different chain nodes, including the production and trade of seeds, biotechnology, and agrochemicals (Section 6.2.1), the agricultural machinery industry (Section 6.2.2) the production of soybeans, wheat, and maize in the Pampean region (Section 6.2.3), and processing industries as well as trading (Section 6.2.4).

In this chapter, I include the most important crops produced and processed in Argentina: soybeans, maize, and wheat. However, the main focus remains on the production and trade of soy and its derivatives, which have become key to Argentina's industrialized and export-oriented agriculture, especially since the 2000s. It was necessary to make this selection to remain within the scope of this study, even though the business associations and case companies I analyze in Chapters 8–10 are involved in producing other commodities, too. Issues related to social upgrading and capital-labor relations have largely been left out of this contextual chapter. They are analyzed in the subsequent chapters.

6.1 (Dis)continuities in agricultural economic policies

Agro-export commodities have long played a crucial role in Argentina's political economy, especially in the fertile Pampean region, which became the main hub of an export-oriented agrarian economy in the late 19th and early 20th century (Lapegna 2017, 315). In contrast to the country's north, where descendants of indigenous populations had not been displaced and people produced agricultural goods for both subsistence and regional markets, the Pampean region was dominated by a class of landowners with a commercial focus on wheat and cattle exports to the capitalist centers (ibid.; see Sábato 1988, 49 ff.).

Towards the 1930s, the agro export-oriented development model entered a crisis, partly due to a general decline in international trade in the face of two world wars, falling prices for agriculture commodities, and protectionist policies implemented by capitalist centers. Roughly put, this led to an amplification of local industrial production, which was later institutionalized as import substitution industrialization (ISI). It was in this historical context that Army General Juan Domingo Perón embarked on his first presidency (1946–1955). Economic policy was now designed to support the establishment of urban industries pillared by national capitals, and to increase domestic consumption by a relatively well-situated working class. During this time, agriculture policies, oriented at low-cost domestic supply, were not straightforward. ISI continued to support extensive agriculture and cattle breeding, which benefited large landowners (Lattuada 2002, 5; see Kay 2016, 5 ff.). But concurrently, Perón's initial rural policies were oriented at winning over small producers and rural workers. His administration improved leasing contracts and prices for tenants, salaries, and the rural labor law for workers. It also strengthened the bargaining power of rural unions. Furthermore, the government created the Argentine Trade Promotion Institute (IAPI, in Spanish), which centrally controlled all grain exports and used the generated surplus for state subsidies (later, this institution was renamed into National Grain Board, JNG). Through state-guaranteed prices, it offered a certain security to small and medium-sized producers (Lapegna 2017, 315 f.; Lattuada 2002, 6 ff.). At the same time, Perón's campaign promises had included a land reform that was never realized and big landowners and large international grain traders continued to benefit the most from state subsidies (Lattuada 2002, 9 f.; see Lapegna 2017, 316).

From the military dictatorship to Menem

Between 1976–1983, a civil-military[3] dictatorship rolled up Argentina's socioeconomic landscape to what Harvey (2005, 14) called the "restoration of upper class power" in the wake of both economic crisis and a relatively strong, organized workforce in the 1970s. The military junta contributed heavily to consolidating the rule of big capital in Argentina. It quickly started to dismantle protectionist, pro-labor, and social policies, and it launched political measures that favored an intensification of capital concentration and a growing influence of large corporations in Argentinian agro-industrial value chains (see Berndt and Bernhold 2018).

The privatization of the ports at the end of the 1970s was a first step towards the deregulation of agricultural trade. At the same time, the military junta initiated financial liberalization (Teubal 2008, 172), deregulated production (for instance, through the elimination of minimum prices guaranteed to producers), lifted taxes on agricultural exports called *retenciones*, and privatized state-owned processing companies, which "had supported the production of small farmers" (Lapegna 2017, 316). In 1976, it also passed Law 21,382, which ended the protection of Argentinian companies from foreign capital. It kept regulating foreign investments in the new millennium, and has therewith set the political background for the dominance of transnational corporations in the commercialization of grains and oilseeds (Villulla 2015, 35), which I describe below. One of the architects of these policies was then Minister of Economy José Martínez de Hoz, an important figure in the Argentine Rural Society (SRA, in Spanish). The SRA is an influential association of large landowners founded in 1866 (Lapegna 2017, 316).

Also in 1976, agricultural workers were excluded from the labor law. In 1980, a new law (Law 22,248) was enacted for agriculture only, which explicitly no longer contained a legal limitation of daily working hours. Until 2011,

3 The term civil-military dictatorship is widely used in Argentina to highlight that the coup was not only supported by army members but also more broadly by economic and political actors who had an interest in the political-economic changes to come.

this was the legal framework that "regulated labor relations in agriculture to the benefit of companies" (Villulla 2010b, 21, own translation). As further discussed in Chapter 10, this is still mirrored in the non-fixing of hourly wages in the collective agreement for rural labor and in wages and labor conditions more generally. Although a new Agricultural Labor Law (26,727) was enacted in 2011, which currently regulates the eight-hour day, actual practice has not changed much in many instances. Importantly, in this context, organized agricultural labor has never regained the position it held before the military dictatorship began persecuting and assassinating unionists (see Section 10.4). All in all, Lapegna (2017, 316) concludes that the military dictatorship allowed the dominant class in agribusiness to expand its power in Argentina.

After 1989, then President Carlos Menem (1989–1999) deepened economic liberalization. His administration rigorously implemented the structural adjustment requirements made by the International Monetary Fund (IMF) (Boris 2002; Lapegna 2017). This included implementing an agenda of privatization and general labor flexibilization, as well as cutting social spending. The Convertibility Plan of 1991 pegged the Argentinian peso to the US-Dollar (Grugel and Riggirozzi 2007, 91). This policy benefitted big agrarian capital over family farms, as it cheapened imported means of production (such as agricultural inputs) compared with living expenses (Azcuy Ameghino 2000; Peretti 1999). Furthermore, the government facilitated the commercialization of land, dismantled trade barriers, and lifted import tariffs on agricultural inputs, such as seeds, agrochemicals, and machinery. In this context, it also eliminated price controls and completely dissolved public regulatory bodies (such as the National Grain Board) that had offered state-guaranteed prices and subsidies to small producers (Giarracca and Teubal 2008) but were already quite deteriorated when Menem took power. With these measures, state control over grain exports and secured prices was "replaced by oligopolistic companies, which henceforth dominated exports [...]. From that moment on, Argentina's agricultural sector became one of the least regulated in the world" (Ainsuain and Echaguibel 2012, 84, own translation).

Financial deregulation also reduced small producers' access to cheap credit (at subsidized interest rates), and promoted a growing presence of *fideicomisos*, which are comparable to trusts (Gras 2013b, 77). In the 2000s, the most prominent forms were so-called *pools de siembra*, which then came to dominate Pampean agriculture, as I discuss in Section 6.2.3. Small farmers as well as indigenous and other peasants who previously "were a subordinated but integral part of regional development became increasingly marginalized" (Lapegna 2017, 318) during the 1990s.[4]

The Menem administration governed by maintaining close ties to powerful agribusiness associations. The SRA, for example, pushed biotechnology-based agriculture development and publicly formulated the goal of preventing state regulation of any kind in this context (Palmisano 2014, 126). Menem consequently supported the endeavor of GMO-based process upgrading. In 1996, his government authorized the use of the genetically modified seed RoundupReady (RR).[5]

In this context, the production of agro-export commodities, especially soybean cultivation, expanded geographically (Lapegna 2017, 316; see Section 6.2.3).[6] This process was further supported by a state co-financed infrastructure development, which opened provinces north of the Pampean region to the ports in Rosario and Buenos Aires (Schnepf et al. 2001, 22).[7]

A vast literature has looked at how these political changes went along with an increase in the importance of primary products and processed derivatives with low value added in situ to Argentina's political economy. It also entailed an ongoing concentration and centralization of capital, and a consolidation of the control of large international corporations over crucial links of agro-industrial chains, as well as in other industries (Lapegna 2017, 314; see Azpi-

---

4 Lapegna (2017, 318) notes in this context that "the state regulated its own deregulation." This means that the government, in parallel to the described policies, initiated various measures designed to remedy its impacts. This roll out in rural areas included programs to enhance the market integration of smallholders via credits and technical assistance, financed through loans by the World Bank and the Inter-American Development Bank, as well as by the United Nations Food and Agriculture Organization's International Fund for Agrarian Development.

5 RR is a genetically modified (GM) soybean seed developed by the former US company Monsanto, now Bayer. It is resistant to the glyphosate-based herbicide Roundup, originally also produced by Monsanto/Bayer.

6 An analysis of the global political economic factors that stimulated the growing importance of agribusiness and especially the production and trade of soybeans and derivatives for the Argentinian economy is beyond the scope of this book. For different accounts see Turzi (2017) and Gras and Hernández (2016b, 85 ff.). Both include (a) changes in global demand especially for soybeans used for animal feed and the production of biofuels, (b) rocketing soy prices, and (c) over-accumulated international capitals in search of profitable investment options, which they have found in agribusiness development.

7 The radical move away from ISI has thus not entailed a complete withdrawal of the state. In some areas, the state has even played a more active role, but the question remains, to whose benefit? The named measures to improve transport infrastructure, for example, benefited mainly export-oriented agribusiness (Berndt and Bernhold 2018, 32).

azu et al. 2011; Féliz 2013; Fernández 2013b; Romero 2016; Schorr 2013). Examples will be provided below. Readers can refer to Boris and Tittor (2006) for an in-depth analysis of the socioeconomic effects of the policies propelled in the last two decades of the 20th century, including a deep economic crisis erupting by the end of the 1990s, high national debt, and a massive impoverishment of large parts of the population, followed by massive protest movements. After a succession of five presidents after 1999, Néstor Kirchner took office in 2003, followed by Cristina Fernández de Kirchner in 2007.[8]

Kirchnerismo and agro-industrial development policies

The neo-developmentalist policies implemented by the Kirchner governments entailed substantial changes in social and economic policies, which are explored elsewhere.[9] The following refers to the agro-industrial development orientation, which entailed some modifications, although in many respects, it has perpetuated the previous political economy of agribusiness, especially regarding the domination of agro-industrial chains by highly concentrated capitals (Romero 2016).

8 Before, President Duhalde (2002–2003) had repealed the Convertibility Law. The associated devaluation of the Argentinian Peso favored export-oriented parts of the economy, including agribusiness. At the same time, inflation reduced real wages. Combined with rocketing international soy prices, post-convertibility resulted in high profits for agribusiness and associated export capitals (Romero 2016, 115 ff.). These actors also benefited from the conversion of private debt into Pesos; debts were 'pesified' at a rate of one Peso per US-Dollar, while deposits in US-Dollars were exchanged at a rate of 1.40 Pesos/ 1.00 US-Dollars. This de facto private debt relief facilitated the upgrading strategies of my case company El Agro (see Chapter 9).

9 Kirchner's neo-developmentalism partially re-focused on strengthening domestic industries and public services, the funding of which was aided by high global prices for the country's principal exports, including soy (Grugel and Riggirozzi 2007, 97 ff.). The government discontinued the debt service and replaced its close relationship with the US with one with Venezuela, Brazil, and Bolivia through the Mercosur (ibid., 99). Accompanied by anti-neoliberal counter-discourses, redistributive social programs were launched, small producers received financial and technical assistance, and some industries were nationalized. Between 2002 and 2009, the Gini coefficient dropped by 10 points, and according to official data, unemployment declined from 21.5 percent to 7.9 percent in the same period. "As a consequence, the percentage of people living below the poverty line in Argentina declined from 54.3 percent of the population in 2002, to 9.9 percent in 2010" (Rivera Quiñones 2014, 67). With respect to the culture of memory, human rights organizations like the *Madres de Plaza de Mayo* were supported in the reappraisal of the military dictatorship (Basualdo 2006).

Policies were inspired by a development model delineated by ECLAC-scholars that seeks a third way between ISI's inward-directed development and neoliberalism à la Washington Consensus. Governments should engender a "development from within" (Sunkel 1993, 8) that combines market-led growth with equity and democracy (see Leiva 2008; Webber 2010). The state is supposed to create systemic competitiveness (much like in the GVC upgrading paradigm, see Section 3.2). Ideally, it creates a good business climate not only through macroeconomic policies, but also by providing education and infrastructure, among other things. It creates a broad social consensus by articulating contradictory interests of various social groups and classes. In brief, it supplements the invisible hand of the market with social, political, and economic coordination and thus supports technological and social development (Sunkel and Ramos 1993, 16 ff.).

Agro-industries are at the center of this model. Industrialization and technical progress are regarded as crucial by neo-structuralists, but the goal is not necessarily to substitute imports with locally manufactured consumer goods. Instead, the aim is to add as much value as possible to natural resources before export. To counter the dependency on capitalist centers and their technology development, the neo-structuralist recommendation is to align agricultural economic policies on modernization and productivity increase from within. "If agriculture itself is the way to bridge the external gap [...] then agricultural productivity has to increase" (Figueroa 1993, 301). Resonating with the above quoted GVC literature on Argentinian agribusiness, the development recipe includes state-led infrastructure development, technological and organizational innovations, the development of modern financial and insurance markets, a transformation of traditional farmers into modern entrepreneurs who readily take risks and are eager to invest (ibid., 304).[10] Many of these suggestions can be found in the governmental *Argentina Agribusiness Leader. Federal and Participative Agri-Food and Agribusiness Strategic Plan 2010–2020* (PEA, in Spanish) (Ministry of Agriculture 2011; see Chapter 7).

Under Néstor Kirchner, the government launched different programs in favor of small-scale agriculture. For example, the Secretariat of Family Agriculture, Coordination, and Territorial Development was instituted within the Ministry of Economy, and the National Institute for Agriculture Technol-

10 For a critique of neo-structuralism, its modernist promises to lift all boats with a rising tide, and related state policies in Latin America, see Leiva (2008) and Webber (2010).

ogy (INTA, in Spanish) opened regional centers to support family agriculture (Lapegna 2017, 321). It also started a dialogue with the National Peasant-Indigenous Movement, which was allowed to participate in the state-led Social Agriculture Program (PSA, in Spanish). This program provided credits to smallholders, until the members of its management were changed in 2007 (ibid.). However, it quickly became apparent that the governmental priorities lay with large scale grain and especially soybean production and adherent processing industries.

The most important change in macroeconomic policies after Menem was the reintroduction of *retenciones*, through which a part of agricultural profits was redirected towards the public budget. Export taxes on processed soybeans were lower than on raw material.[11] This tax policy was the main reason for the negative stance taken by large parts of agribusiness actors towards the Kirchner administrations (see Chapter 8 for a further discussion of the issue).[12] In 2008, disaffections were openly articulated by the dominant bloc, and agribusiness associations and farmers demonstrated their capacity to raise political pressure. When Cristina Kirchner aimed to introduce flexible *retenciones* that fluctuate from day to day depending on world market prices, this undertaking was stopped due to fierce protest (Giarracca and Teubal 2011; Teubal and Palmisano 2010). The change would have meant a further increase in export taxes on soybeans of nine percentage points at the time. While Kirchner rhetorically went against the agrarian oligarchy during this conflict, *retenciones* were in fact never levied according to farms' sizes. Since their implementation in 2002, they had affected small producers relatively more than large agribusiness companies (Fernández 2013b, 86). This was one of the reasons why entities grouping small and medium-sized agricultural producers, such as the Argentine Agrarian Federation (FAA), had long criticized the government for "an alliance […] with the concentrated [agribusiness] groups," as FAA president Eduardo Buzzi put it (Clarín 2008, own translation). Furthermore, big trading companies were allowed to "pass the tax burden on to growers […]. The government, in short, benefited the

11 *Retenciones* were reintroduced by President Duhalde in 2002, initially at the rate of 23.5 percent. In January 2007, Néstor Kirchner raised them to 35 percent. Lower export duties were levied on processed soy products; from 22 percent in 2002, they were raised to 24 percent in January 2007, and to 32 percent in November 2007 (Palmisano 2014, 149 ff.).

12 To counter agribusiness-led discourses, according to which agriculture financed the state, Lapegna (2017, 325) and Teubal and Palmisano (2010, 231 f.) emphasize that agro-exports only made up for 7.8 percent of the state revenues in 2008.

largest or more powerful players, to the detriment of the lower echelons of the soybean chain" (Lapegna 2017, 323). In fact, the 2008 protests united 'the countryside' against Kirchner. At the same time, however, they were mainly driven by medium-sized farmers who feared the existential consequences of higher *retenciones*. Large landowners and agribusiness corporations, which wanted to prevent the government from appropriating larger parts of the agrarian profits but which also have an interest in maintaining an uneven agrarian structure, combined their participation with efforts to marginalize voices that demanded a differentiation in *retenciones* according to farm sizes (Villulla 2009, 19 ff.).

Another continuity to its predecessors is that the Kirchner governments completely focused on productivity increases through GMO-based agriculture. Between 2004 and the transfer of office to President Mauricio Macri, the National Advisory Commission on Agricultural Biotechnology (CONABIA, in Spanish) approved the use of 37 new transgenic organisms (ISAAA GM Approval Database). As my interlocutor Alfredo from the soy chain association ACSOJA puts it: "Never has an expanding producer lacked a GM variety in Argentina."[13] GMOs are also an integral part of the development as it is envisioned in the PEA (Ministry of Agriculture 2011). Argentina thus continued to be an "open-air laboratory" (Gras and Hernández 2013c, 27, own translation) for biotech companies. Under the Kirchner administrations, Monsanto (now Bayer) and other biotech companies were able to standardize the production of crops, soy, and maize in particular, and to control the terms and conditions of their production (see Section 6.2.2). At the same time, however, the Argentinian seed law, which was enacted in 1973, sets limits on these corporations. It grants seed developers like Monsanto/Bayer the exclusive right to commercialize new seed varieties for a certain period of time. In contrast to other Latin American countries, however, it also allows farmers to reuse parts of their harvest as seeds in later plantings without having to pay royalties anew (Pengue 2005). As I discuss in Chapter 8, biotech corporations and agribusiness associations have been lobbying for a new seed law that prohibits this practice.

Cristina Kirchner already took up the issue in 2012 and started negotiating a new law. Shortly after, Monsanto put the GM soy RR2 Intacta on the Argentinian market. But attempts to change legislation have provoked large protests (Vicente 2014, 188 f.) and until now, it has not been possible to push

13 Interview with a representative of ACSOJA, August 7, 2014, Rosario.

any amendments through Congress. In 2012, then President Kirchner stated that

> "Monsanto's investment is incredibly important and is going to help in the realization of our Agro-Food 2020 industrial plan [...] And today, the head [of Monsanto] told me that they were very impressed by the support that our government is giving to science and technology. You should all be certain that we are going to continue in the same line" (cited in Lapegna 2017, 324).

There are further examples of the support that large corporations received from the Kirchner administrations, including subsidies. According to Palmisano (2014, 134), more than 55 percent of the subsidies granted to companies in the agri-food complex in 2007 were given to only ten corporations, including Cargill. Besides, Lapegna (2017, 324) reports that "in 2013, the national government dropped a long-running investigation into tax evasion by Cargill."

According to Cáceres (2015), land conflicts and dispossession have also accelerated with the expansion of agribusiness, especially of the soy frontier into non-Pampean areas under the Kirchner administrations. In several cases, land was taken from peasants and indigenous communities by violent, even life-threatening means (Teubal 2006). Critics say that the Kirchner administrations did little about these land seizures (Poth 2010, 271). According to Lapegna (2017, 315), they rather supported local governments that participated in the suppression of peasant movements. The rural land law implemented in 2011 (Ley 26.737) has not changed that trend either.[14] Among other problems, Gras (2013a, 67 ff.) argues that it has only partially addressed the land issue, as it is not accompanied by a legal instrument to address the role that land leasing plays for a processes of capital concentration in primary production.

In summary, it can be noted that the agribusiness-related economic policies implemented by the Kirchner administrations, despite all changes, were designed to support a corporate-driven agro-industrial development, and to redirect a part of the profits made in these industries into the state budget for retroactive redistribution. Therefore,

14 This law determines that no more than 15 percent of the rural land in Argentina can be owned by foreigners. Furthermore, foreigners cannot buy more than a thousand hectares in Argentina's farming heartland, or an equivalent to be determined by the provinces in other areas (ibid., Article 9).

"the dominant sectors of agrarian Argentina clashed politically with the Kirchner administrations, yet the Kirchner governments did not address the material basis of rural inequalities and the uneven distribution of power at the subnational scale. Rather, their administrations supported the expansion of agribusiness by favouring global agribusiness corporations and promoting the adoption of agricultural biotechnology" (Lapegna 2017, 315).

In a word, the poverty alleviating policies coincided with a political environment that facilitated an expansion of capital concentration and of the power of mainly multinational corporations in agro-industrial chains (Romero 2016, 116; see Bernhold and Palmisano 2022).[15]

6.2 An overview of grain and oilseed value chains in Argentina

The next sections seek to contextualize my research by providing a rough overview of important dynamics and corporate actors in soy, maize, and wheat value chains in Argentina. Figure 1 shows key chain nodes addressed in this chapter, taking the soybean value chain as an example. More than any other agriculture product in Argentina, soy stands for the transformation from a traditional family-based farming model to capital-intensive agro-industries.

In 2016, 8.9 out of 58.8 million produced tons were exported as raw soybeans, mainly to China. That same year, 44.5 million tons (more than 75 percent) underwent at least a first step of industrial processing in situ. Out of 29.1 million produced tons of soybean meal, 8.4 million tons were exported to the European Union (EU).

Grain and especially soybean value chains dominate the Argentinian export structure, such that this country's foreign exchange earnings are highly dependent on volatile grain and oilseed prices. Table 2 shows that the soybean complex, which includes raw soybeans, soybean oil and meal, biofuels, and other soy-based products, alone accounted for up to 32.8 percent of total

15 Scholars have come to similar conclusions on the development of Argentinian industries during post-convertibility in general. According to Azpiazu et al. (2011, 21), the participation of the first 100 top-selling companies in manufacturing industries in the gross production value increased from an average of 33.1 percent between 1993 and 2001 to an average of 40.9 percent between 2003 and 2009.

	2012	%	2015	%	2016	%	2018*	%	2020*	%
Oilseed complex	**18,645**	**23.2**	**20,174**	**35.5**	**20,731**	**35.8**	**16,639**	**26.9**	**16,730**	**30.5**
Soy complex	17,377	21.7	18,615	32.8	18,911	32.7	15,054	24.4	14,865	27.1
Cereal complex	**10,541**	**13.1**	**5,399**	**9.5**	**7,528**	**13.0**	**8,151**	**13.2**	**9,539**	**17.4**
Maize complex	4,952	6.2	3,211	5.7	4,242	7.3	4,301	7.0	6,151	11.2
Wheat complex	3,499	4.4	1,332	2.4	2,184	3.8	2,839	4.6	2,471	4.5
Soy, maize, and wheat complex	**25,828**	**32.2**	**23,158**	**40.8**	**25,337**	**43.8**	**22,194**	**35.9**	**23,487**	**42,8**
Exports (total)	**80,246**	**100.0**	**56,784**	**100.0**	**57,909**	**100.0**	**61,782**	**100.0**	**54,884**	**100.0**

Table 2: Export shares of selected products (in millions of US-Dollars and percent)
* Provisional data
Source: own elaboration based on INDEC data

Argentinian exports in the last decade. Together with maize and wheat and their derivatives, export shares amounted to up to 43.8 percent.

Overall, Argentina's trade balance has been on average positive in the past 20 years (with some exceptions, such as in 2018); however, for finished goods, such as machinery and chemical products, it was negative. In 2019, for instance, the trade deficit for machinery and chemical products amounted to 8.7 billion US-Dollars (UN Comtrade). These imports are highly relevant the chain nodes described below.

6.2.1 Seeds, biotechnology, agrochemicals

The development of the means of agricultural production in Argentina has been widely associated with the introduction of a "technological package" (Leguizamón 2014, 151) for capital—not labor—intensive production. It is based on a biotechnology-agrochemical complex, and on no-till sowing to which I will come back below. Today, especially the production of soy and maize is based almost exclusively on GM varieties. As mentioned before, scholars have criticized that Argentina has become an "open-air laboratory" (Gras and Hernández 2013c, 27, own translation) for biotech companies after Menem authorized the first RR soy.

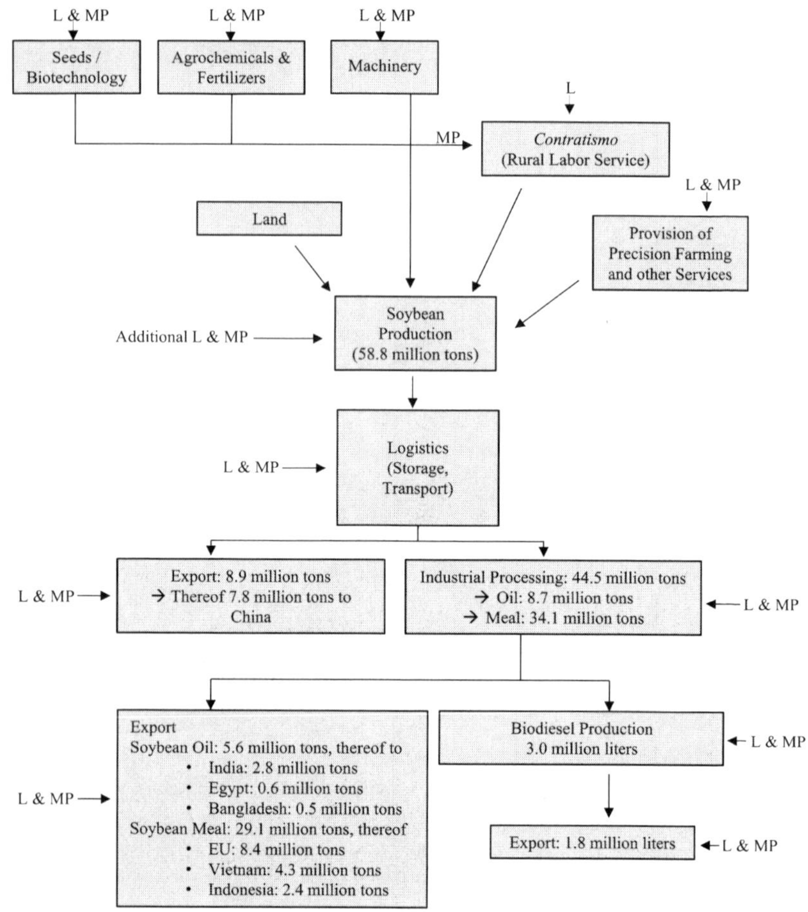

Figure 1: Soybean value chain in Argentina
L & MP = Labor power and means of production; production and export data for the 2015–2016 season
Source: own elaboration based on data provided by CIARA and the Ministry of Production and Labor

For 2019, the International Service for the Acquisition of Agri-biotech Applications (ISAAA 2019, 6) listed Argentina third after the US and Brazil in a ranking of "biotech mega countries," with 24 million hectares under GM-crop cultivation. For Turzi (2017, 25), GMO based process upgrading was

"the result of a corporate strategy before anything else. In the 1980s, agrochemical corporations were experiencing declining profit margins and dwindling expansion opportunities as a result of increased regulations and fewer markets in which to expand. In response, they built on their existing relationships with farmers to enter into another, more promising agricultural input industry: the seed industry."

The development of GM agriculture, he further argues, happens in a perfect logic of the Schumpeterian "creative destruction." Agrochemistry giants like Monsanto/Bayer or Syngenta seek to increase their market shares through the "permanent innovation" (ibid.) of new seed varieties and associated agrochemicals.

In Argentina, the biotechnology, seed, and agrochemical industries are firmly in the hands of oligopolistic gatekeepers, mainly multinational corporations, over which the INTA was never able to gain an advantage. "In consequence, Argentina held no incentives to create synergies or spillovers with local agents, or to partner with the private sector to extend the range of products or to support small and medium seed producers organized around local foundations" (Turzi 2017, 32).[16]

The biotechnology for GM seed in Argentina is largely controlled by Monsanto/Bayer and Syngenta (see Table 3). According to the ISAAA GM Approval Database, out of 79 events approved in Argentina between 1998 and 2019, 51 were developed by Monsanto/Bayer and Syngenta. For the case of maize, Monsanto/Bayer and Syngenta developed 36 of the 52 varieties approved in Argentina; for the case of soy, Monsanto/Bayer and BASF developed 9 of the 18 approved varieties. Turzi (2017, 34) highlights, however, that almost all legal GM soybean seed that is actually sold in this country is based on biotechnology by Monsanto. As I show below, these companies also hold significant shares in the agrochemical market in Argentina.

As mentioned above, to strengthen their positions and their capacities to raise entry barriers, companies like Monsanto/Bayer have strongly lobbied not only for the implementation of a new seed law, but also for tighter controls, in response to an apparent loss of royalties collected by the biotech giants. In addition to the legal right of farmers to reuse their own harvests as seed, there is also a black market for GM seeds, referred to by farmers as *bolsa blanca*, "organized by farmers who store retained seeds for subsequent

16 Note that when I give an insight into this concentrated corporate landscape in the following, the data I use at least partly refers to the time of my field work and, thus, to corporations that do not necessarily exist anymore as such due to the acceleration of centralization. As I have mentioned before, Monsanto was acquired by Bayer in 2018, and Syngenta was bought by ChemChina in 2017. However, I refer to company-names according to the data I use.

	Soy	Maize	All GM Crop Events approved in Argentina
Monsanto	5	14	23
Bayer	2	1	7
Syngenta	0	21	21
BASF	4	0	4
Dow	3	8	11
DuPont	1	8	9
INDEAR	2	0	2
Verdeca	1	0	1
Technoplant Argentina	0	0	1
Total	18	52	79

Table 3: Approvals of GM crop events in Argentina, 1998–2019
Source: own elaboration based on ISAAA GM Approval Database

sale, often using crop that has been taken out of circulation by underreporting harvests" (Berndt et al. 2019, 10). Estimates indicate that the legal Argentinian seed market represents only between 20 and 35 percent of the total market (Leguizamón 2014, 151; Turzi 2017, 34).

Monsanto has also tried to circumvent the seed law. After failing to collect royalties for its RR technology to the extent desired, this company has been trying to urge farmers into 'voluntary' waivers or into elicit statements attesting reused seed, such that Monsanto could issue a debit note for royalties. It "established a private system to collect royalties" on saved seeds grown from its second-generation biotechnology for soy, the "Intacta RR2" (Turzi 2017, 35; see Berndt and Bernhold 2018). The private control system includes testing of soybeans before being loaded at ports. Farmers are then charged an extra fee when crops test positive for Monsanto's GMOs. "Exporters such as Cargill, Bunge, Dreyfus, Vicentín, and ADM-Toepfer have agreed to act as inspectors in order to avoid having problems when handing over the grains" (Turzi 2017, 35). Monsanto even took measures such as stopping shiploads of soy in European ports, arguing that they illegally contained genes that were its property (Vicente 2014, 188). I will return to such controversies in Chapter 9, showing how agribusiness associations support a new seed law as a necessary measure for process upgrading, while entities that group small producers, such as the FAA, have sharply criticized Monsanto's methods.

As for the production of the seeds, the legal market is again divided among few companies. Turzi reported in 2017 that it is led by Nidera (with a 48 percent market share), a company whose seed division was bought up by Syngenta/ChemChina in 2018. Don Mario, an Argentinian breeding company, holds 29 percent of the market, followed by minor players: La Tijereta (5 percent; the company is owned by Monsanto), Santa Rosa (4.6 percent) and SPS (2.5 percent). The latter was also acquired by Syngenta in 2008 (Turzi 2017, 34).[17]

With the spread of corporate-driven industrial agriculture, the 'technological package' and the expansion in cultivated land and especially in GM soy production (see Section 6.2.3), sales of agrochemicals in Argentina have increased significantly over the past 20 years (see Cáceres 2018). As Figure 2 shows, agrochemicals worth around 600 million US-Dollars per year were officially sold in this country at the beginning of the new millennium, a number that went up to nearly 2.5 billion US-Dollars in 2016.

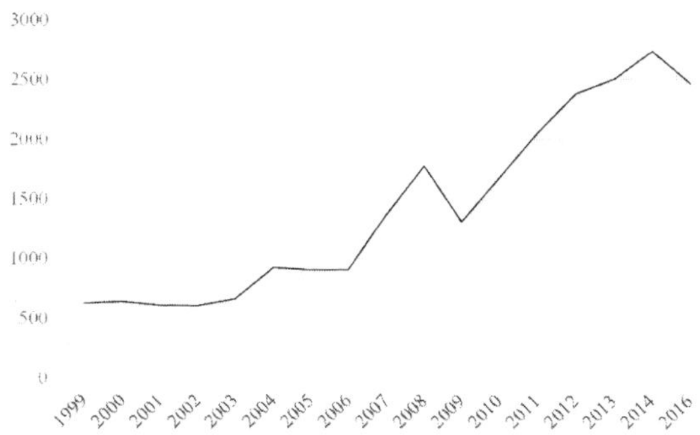

Figure 2: Increase in sales of agrochemicals in Argentina (in millions of US-Dollars)
Source: own elaboration based on data published by the Chamber of Agricultural Health and Fertilizers (CASAFE)

According to the Argentinian Chamber of Agricultural Health and Fertilizers (CASAFE 2016), prices have dropped in recent years, such that the graph line for the usage of agrochemicals would be even steeper. Fernández (2017, 106) indicates that the productive consumption of agrochemicals in Pampean agriculture has multiplied by 7.2 between 1992 and 2010. A study

17 Note that these data refer to soybean seeds. The seed markets for grains are similarly concentrated. According to a development manager of Don Mario, the company held 40 percent of the wheat seed market in 2018. (See https://efarmnewsar.com/2018-11-23/don-mario-already-accounts-40-of-wheat-seed-market-share-its-strategy.html, last accessed May 24, 2022.)

commissioned by the World Bank even estimates that it has increased nearly tenfold, from 26,000 tons in 1992 to 256,000 tons in 2011. "Among the agrochemicals, the herbicide Glyphosate accounts for 75 % of the use in 2006 compared with only 50.1 % in 1991" (World Bank 2016, 27).

With respect to the biggest players in this market, the corporate landscape shows a strong overlap with the above-mentioned multinational biotech giants. As Table 4 shows, after Monsanto, which held a 15.3 percent market share in agrochemicals in Argentina in 2015, second place went to Syngenta that year (12.4 percent), and the third to Dow (11.3 percent) (see Poth 2010, 265). Bayer, which held a market share of 8.4 percent in 2015, is now by far the biggest player, following its acquisition of Monsanto.[18]

	Market Share, 2015 (%)
Monsanto	15.3
Syngenta	12.4
Dow	11.3
Bayer	8.5
Atanor	6.7
BASF	5.8
Dupont	5
ChemiAgro*	4.8
Others	30.2

Table 4: Shares in the Argentinian agrochemical market (2015)
* Name changed; ChemiAgro is a subsidiary of El Agro
Source: own elaboration based on data provided by El Agro

As Turzi (2017, 30) puts it, "agrochemical and seed companies are reinforcing market power from the top through deals and alliances that render futile the notion of competition" and increases their power to appropriate a sizeable portion of the value generated in agribusiness. One example is a 1.2 billion-dollar "R&D and commercialization collaboration agreement in plant biotech [between BASF and Monsanto], characterized by ETC Group as a 'nonmerger merger'" (ibid.).

According to Pengue (2005, 318), 16.6 percent of the pesticides used in Argentina are produced in situ, 43.6 percent are imported, and the remain-

18 When only considering glyphosate, the most important herbicide, Monsanto/Bayer held a 65 percent market share in 2008, according to Romero (2016, 251).

ing 39.8 percent are chemicals produced abroad and mixed in Argentina (see Romero 2016, 249 for a similar estimation).

In Chapter 8, I revisit this GMO-based form of process upgrading when I discuss strategies of value chain development as they are portrayed by agribusiness associations.

6.2.2 Machinery

Advanced agriculture machinery has played another important role in upgrading primary production. This includes the use of state-of-the-art harvesters, fumigators, and equipment for no-till sowing. According to the Argentinian No-Till Farmers Association (AAPRESID), 91 percent of this country's cultivated land was farmed by direct sowing in the 2016–17 season, compared to 0.4 percent in 1990 and 44.3 percent in 2000 (Nocelli Pac 2017, 11). With no-till technology, farmers sow seed directly onto the field, without ploughing, thus saving labor time. This also allowed for the introduction of wheat-soybean double-cropping, which means that a double-crop soybean variety is planted after wheat has been harvested in that same season, instead of leaving fields fallow (Cohan and Costa 2011, 16; Turzi 2017, 24). The direct sowing model is closely coupled to the above-mentioned technological package; without ploughing, the use of agrochemicals becomes essential for weed control.

Apart from this particular technology, the capital-intensive agricultural machinery industry in general is often referred to as a key sector of the Argentinian economy (Romero 2016, 126). The corresponding means of production are partly produced in situ and some local firms have managed to take advantage of the increasing demand of sophisticated equipment (Lavarello 2012, 52). According to the Ministry of Treasury (2016, 5), this branch accounted for 25.2 percent of the gross value added in Argentina's machinery and equipment industry that year, and for 1.1 percent of the gross value added in all manufacturing industries in this country.

However, Romero (2016) poses the rhetorical question of whether its development has been primarily characterized by a "promotion of national innovations or [by] subsidies for foreign capital" (ibid., 190, own translation). By the same token, Lavarello (2012, 52, own translation) highlights that important parts of the industry are "dominated by subsidiaries of multinational companies," which entails "a low national integration that limits learning processes and explains the persistent deficit of the sector's trade balance."

According to Romero (2016), the local production of agricultural equipment played an important role during the ISI period, reaching a record high in 1977. But since the mid-1950s, this was accompanied by a process of capital concentration[19] and the growing impact of global players like John Deere. After the military coup in 1976, the on-site production of tractors and harvesters was affected by both economic liberalization and a decrease in state support for the industry. Romero shows that until 1978, "the production [of tractors and harvesters] fell by 77 percent and domestic sales by 70 percent, while imports increased in importance" (ibid., 191, own translation). The author sees in this a period of "reprimarization" of the Argentinian agro-export structure (ibid.).

This trend strengthened during the 1990s, concurrent with an increase in demand for machinery towards the end of that decade (Lavarello 2012, 52). At the same time, "the tendency to import parts of disassembled machinery increased, such that the local manufacture of new units was, in fact, often merely their assembly by use of a labor force that was cheaper than in the US or in Brazil" (Romero 2016, 192, own translation).

After 2002, sales of agricultural equipment rose as grain and oilseed production increased (for detailed information see Ministry of Treasury 2016, 16 ff.).[20] This was accompanied by a "partial reactivation of the local production of machinery" (Romero 2016, 177, own translation) and of tractors, in particular. The participation of locally manufactured tractors, including those that are merely assembled in Argentina, in the domestic market went up from around 15 percent in 2004 to an average of 21 percent in 2007 (ibid., 186). This was partly due to state subsidies for on-site technology development and for wages. Furthermore, the Kirchner governments issued favorable credit lines to support the acquisition of locally produced capital goods at preferential rates, backed by Law 25,924, which regulates the "promotion of investments in capital goods" (ibid., 179, own translation). On the other hand, around 80 percent of the tractors and harvesters sold in Argentina during that period were imported. This negative balance was

19 In 1960, 28 Argentinian companies produced harvesters in this country, a number that fell to 13 in the 1970s (ibid., 152).

20 In 2008, production temporarily collapsed due to an economic crisis, the above-mentioned disputes with the government, and drought.

reinforced by the partial relocation of assembly plants run by large US corporations from Argentina to Brazil in the new millennium (Lavarello 2012, 52), from where 60 percent of the machinery imported to Argentina originates.[21] By 2017, however, the participation of locally manufactured tractors in the domestic market had risen to around 67 percent. In the case of harvesters, 59.6 percent of the machines sold in Argentina were manufactured locally that year, and in the case of sowing machines, 85.7 percent. As mentioned above, the government of Cristina Kirchner had promoted machines made in Argentina with subsidized credit lines.

However, a representative of CAFMA bemoans in an interview that machinery also counts as national production when produced by US companies like John Deere, whose on-site activity mainly consists in the assembly of imported semi-finished parts. CAFMA estimates that only 20 percent of the US company's machinery labeled "Argentinian production" is actually produced within the country; it is "nearly finished already when it arrives in Argentina."[22] The association demands that 60 percent of the final product has to be local production in order to be labeled Argentinian production. I will come back to this issue in Chapter 8.

The agriculture machinery market in Argentina is highly concentrated and dominated by large corporations, though the degree of concentration is different according to the type of machinery (Table 5).

	Tractors	Harvesters	Sowing machines	Fumigation machines
Concentration of sales, first two companies (%)	66.4	53.5	39.6	86.2
Share of multinational corporations in total sales (%)	80.3	74.3	–	–

Table 5: Concentration in the Argentinian agricultural machinery market, selected machines
Source: modified from Lavarello (2012, 54)

Approximately 80 percent of all tractors and harvesters sold in Argentina originate from the US companies John Deere and AGCO, and from the Dutch CNH (Ministry of Treasury 2016, 25). The manufacturing activities

21 Information extracted from a PowerPoint presentation forwarded to me by a CAFMA-representative.

22 Interview with a representative of CAFMA, May 13, 2016, Buenos Aires.

controlled by these players in Argentina are mainly limited to assembly tasks and are characterized by a "low interaction of national suppliers" (Lavarello 2012, 54 f., own translation).[23] The production of sowing and fumigation machines is dominated by Argentinian companies. In the case of fumigators, two local players (Metalfor and Grupo Pla) control more than 80 percent of the market. The fabrication of sowing machines is a bit more atomized and divided among various Argentinian companies. However, here, too, a somewhat more moderate oligopoly has prevailed in competition over no-till technology, led by the Argentinian Agrometal (see Ministry of Treasury 2016, 26).

A trade deficit in agriculture machinery persists according to INDEC data (Table 6). The balances in agricultural machinery have been negative over the past decades, with the exception of sowing machines, the trade balance of which became positive in the mid-2000s.[24] Later, however, it turned negative again.

	1998			2008			2017		
	Import	Export	Trade Balance	Import	Export	Trade Balance	Import	Export	Trade Balance
Harvesters	97.26	0.14	-97.12	277.83	19.38	-258.45	101.04	3.34	-97.7
Sowing Machines	11.84	2.38	-9.46	3.84	35.41	31.57	16.9	8.28	-8.62
Tractors	108.62	2.01	-106.6	285.42	19.9	-265.52	237.23	0.82	-236.41
Total	217.72	4.53	-213.2	567.09	74.69	-492.39	355.17	12.44	-342.73

Table 6: Argentina's trade balance in selected agricultural machinery (in millions of US-Dollars)
Source: own elaboration based on INDEC data

23 John Deere runs a plant in the province of Santa Fe, where it produces motors and provides financing for buyers. AGCO has two fabrics in Rosario, where it produces motors and tractors. CNH owns a plant in Córdoba, where it produces tractors and harvesters (Ministry of Treasury 2016, 27).

24 Between 2002 and 2008, Argentina increased its exports in agricultural machinery, mainly to Venezuela (Lavarello 2012, 188 f.; Romero 2016).

6.2.3 Developments in grain and oilseed production

In Argentina, the production of grains and in particular of soybeans and maize has increased significantly over the last twenty years. As Figure 3 indicates, the production of soybeans, wheat, maize, and sunflower seeds has risen from approximately 30 million tons in 1990 to 135.4 million tons in 2019. Soybeans alone accounted for 55.3 million produced tons in 2019, compared to 10.7 million tons in 1990. Maize also experienced a significant increase, from 5.4 to 56.9 million tons in the same period. Wheat production has fluctuated between ten and 19 million tons. Today, Argentina is the world's third largest producer of soybeans after the USA and Brazil (USDA 2022).

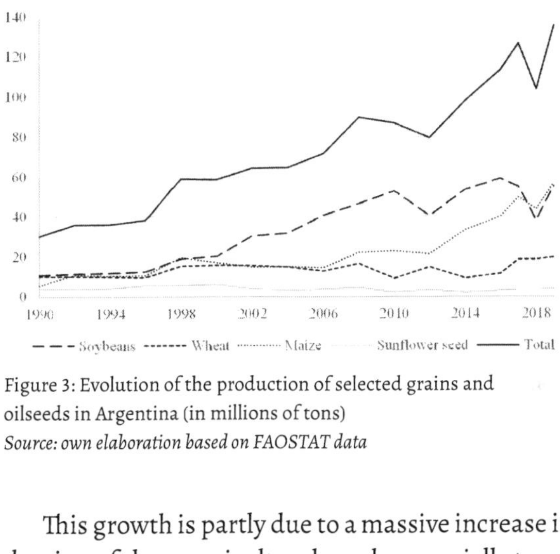

Figure 3: Evolution of the production of selected grains and oilseeds in Argentina (in millions of tons)
Source: own elaboration based on FAOSTAT data

This growth is partly due to a massive increase in land devoted to the production of these agricultural goods, especially to soybean cultivation. Figure 4 shows that in 2019, approximately 32 million ha, an area nearly 8 times the size of Switzerland, were dedicated to the production of soybeans, wheat, maize, and sunflower seeds, of which 16.6 million ha for the cultivation of soybeans alone, 7.2 million ha for the cultivation of maize, and 6.1 million ha for the cultivation of wheat. In 1990, these numbers totaled 14.5 million ha (all listed grains and oilseeds) and 4.9 million ha (soybeans) respectively. The area used for the industrial cultivation of soybeans has grown especially since the authorization of RR seeds.

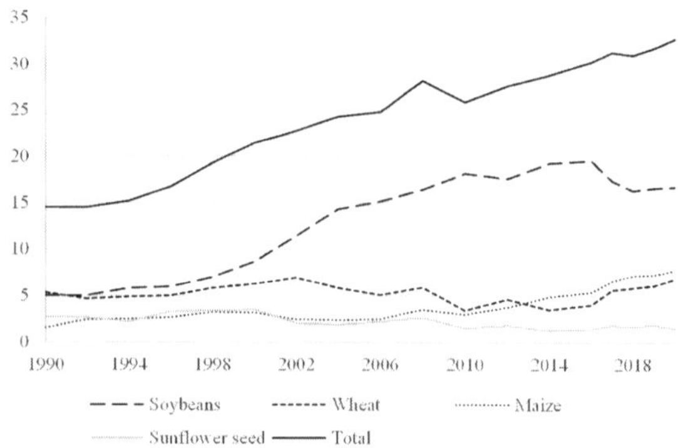

Figure 4: Evolution of the harvested area in Argentina, selected grains and oilseeds (in millions of ha)
Source: own elaboration based on FAOSTAT data

Cultivation was first intensified in the Pampean region, Argentina's agricultural heartland, where fields previously used for cattle breeding were transformed into soy plantations.[25] In 2017, 75 percent of all soybeans were produced in the Pampean provinces Buenos Aires, Santa Fe, and Córdoba (Ministry of Treasury 2017, 10). But the agribusiness frontier was also extended towards provinces in the north and northwest (Santiago del Estero, Chaco, and Salta), which had until then hardly been integrated into capital-intensive agriculture (Leguizamón 2014). As I have mentioned above, this has been associated with the often violent appropriation of land that was previously inhabited and/or cultivated by others, as well as with ecological destruction and deforestation (Pengue 2005; Sarandón and Flores 2014; Teubal 2006).

In addition to geographical expansion, the growth in production is a result of process upgrading and a resulting increase in productivity. Figure 5 shows that the production volume of the most important grains and oilseeds has grown by 350 percent, while the harvested area has 'only' grown by 118 percent. In the case of soybeans, average yields rose from 2.2 tons/ha to 3.3 tons/ha between 1990 and 2019. The average productivity in wheat cultiva-

25 Interview with a representative of ACSOJA, August 7, 2014, Rosario. According to Cohen and Costa (2011, 14), 86.1 percent of Argentina's grains and oilseeds are produced in the Pampean region.

tion has increased similarly from 1.9 tons/ha to 3.2 tons/ha, and maize yields increased from 3.5 tons/ha to 7.9 tons/ha.[26]

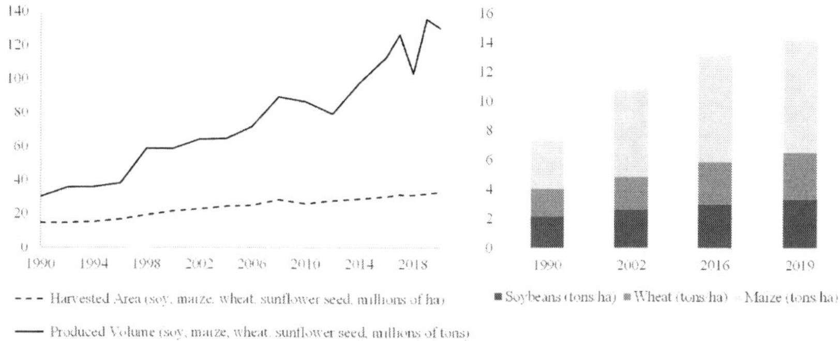

Figure 5: Relation between harvested area and output & average crop yields, 1990–2019
Source: own elaboration based on FAOSTAT data

Process upgrading: technological and organizational changes

The improvements in productivity can be explained by various aspects. First is the technological package introduced above.[27] Second, in addition to the described innovations, especially large-scale farmers have increased the use of precision farming technology, including drones and remote sensing analytics. Aerial crop sensors monitor the exact conditions on the planted fields and processed data provide information on the demand for fertilizers and chemicals with spatial accuracy (Berndt and Bernhold 2018, 37).

With the development of the productive forces, the social structuring of agriculture production changed, too, and new forms of organizing production were introduced. In Chapter 10, I will discuss this from a class-analytical perspective. At this point, a brief overview shall suffice in the meantime.

26 Yields in soybean cultivation are above the world average and compare to those in the USA and Brazil. In wheat, they fluctuate around the world average and compare, again, to those in the US, but they are by far lower than those, for example, in the EU (5.8 tons/ha in 2017) or China (5.5 tons/ha in 2017). As for maize, yields in Argentina are above the world average, but, again, lower than those in the USA (11.08 tons/ha in 2017).

27 Yields also vary according to natural conditions such as soil properties and rainfall. The influence of developing productive forces refers to the average increase in yields in Argentina.

Before the growth of capital-intensive agribusiness, next to big farmers, so-called *chacareros* or *colonos* played an important role in 20th century Pampean agriculture. *Chacareros* have been described as traditional capitalized farmers who own the machinery needed for grain cultivation and cattle breeding, with a strong participation of family labor in direct production for both subsistence and the market. Until the mid-20th century, many of them leased-in land. Later, they gradually acquired land property through market purchases or colonization policies (Muzlera 2020; see Archetti and Stölen 1975; Balsa 2007; Barsky and Gelman 2001).

Especially from the 2000s on, production became increasingly controlled by large agribusiness firms. The 1990s had already seen the emergence of an Argentinian particularity that should later turn out to play a crucial role in the new millennium. *Pools de siembra* (sowing pools, in English)[28] mushroomed, which led the expansion especially of soybean production. Comparable to trusts, the organizational cores of these pools, mainly agricultural companies, but also finance capital, gather capital to invest it mainly in soy production (Fernández 2012a, 103).[29] In this connection, a *relative* independence of land ownership and control over production developed, which is now characteristic for Pampean agriculture. Property keeps being the most important form of land control. However, its participation has decreased by 20.1 percent between 1988 and 2018. Especially large companies have expanded by leasing-in land in addition to the land they own. This way, they do not have to fix capital in land and gain the flexibility to quickly change investment decisions (Bernhold and Palmisano 2022).

Agribusiness companies mainly lease-in land for the duration of only one or two agricultural seasons, often from former *chacareros*, some of whom became small rentiers, as independent production ceased to be profitable or even possible. First, they had faced debt crises in the late 1990s and second, the growingly capital-intensive cultivation models restricted the competitiveness of farming on a smaller scale. As Hernando, a representative of the

28 Amongst other things, *pools de siembra* have been criticized for hit and run monocropping, and as a form of spatio-temporal fix of over-accumulated capital (Berterretche2015) that causes soil degradation, depopulation of rural areas and the expulsion of small producers either by direct violence or by market displacement (Féliz 2014; Gorenstein and Ortiz 2017; Gras 2012).

29 This was not only readily embraced by Argentinian and also international capitals as a tool for investing in large-scale production. It also played a crucial role in the above-mentioned movement of the soy frontier into the north and the northwest of the country (Fernández 2012a; Leguizamón 2014; Pertierra Cánepa 2014).

grain stock exchange in Rosario, puts it in an interview: "Soy is more competitive when produced on a large scale [...] There is a gradual withdrawal of the traditional producer, to make room for a more capable producer, who is much more aggressive and much more innovative; this is a producer who leases-in fields."[30]

Another transformation that has begun in this context and by now become established is that many agribusiness companies do not own all the machinery needed for agricultural production. Instead, they outsource rural labor to *contratistas*, mainly small firms that own tractors, harvesters, or sowing machines, and who hire wage workers, as I discuss in depth in Chapter 10. This way, the "incursion of financial capital, in the way of 'Pools de Siembra' [...] and land letting, has allowed corporations to enter into agribusiness without having to sink in any capital in machinery and land" (Féliz 2014, 4; see Gras 2012).

Thus, the *pools de siembra* "changed the logic of Pampean agriculture [...] and created very efficient networks by leasing in land and machinery," as ACSOJA representative Alfredo puts it. "In contrast to the small producer, the basis of the pool is efficiency, cost reduction, and economies of scale."[31] The resulting production model resembles the ideas of the Argentinian GVC scholars discussed in Section 3.2.4 above, who take a positive view of these changes away from the vertical integration of small farming entities to a network model characterized by labor subcontracting and a separation of machinery/land ownership and control over production.

Today, many companies have modified their strategies further, such that land, machinery, etc. is no longer simply leased at fixed rates. Instead, small producers, landowners, *contratistas*, and other actors are often formally integrated as network partners, who receive a share of the harvest instead of a previously fixed price for rents or services (see Chapter 10 for an in-depth analysis of such arrangements). As Alfredo puts it, "when I can withdraw the rents, then I have a much better result. [...] Today there are still *Pools*, but the types of contracts that are made in the countryside have diversified" (ibid.). According to Gras and Hernández (2016b, 17), approximately 80 percent of agricultural production in Argentina works through such "networks".

The described developments have entailed a profound transformation of the social structure in rural areas. This includes a process of class differentia-

30 Interview with a representative of the grain stock exchange in Rosario, August 12, 2014, Rosario.
31 Interview with a representative of ACSOJA, August 7, 2014, Rosario.

tion as well as cultural changes and upgrading through a professionalization or "managerialization" (Gras and Hernández 2013a, 42, own translation) of agriculture. Grain and oilseed producers often do not live in the countryside anymore, and agriculture is increasingly managed by professionals who live in cities (ibid., see Chapter 8). Labor relations have also seen major transformations in this setting, as Chapter 10 analyzes in depth.

Capital concentration in grain and oilseed production

One final aspect that needs to be considered more closely at this point is the concentration and centralization of capital[32] in agricultural production, which accompanies the development of the productive forces. Some of the mega-companies that have pushed the described organizational changes have leased-in several hundred thousand hectares of land for soybean production (Gras and Sosa Varrotti 2013) and outcompeted smaller producers by exploiting economies of scale (see Chapter 9).[33]

In late 2019, the INDEC published a first set of results of the National Agricultural Census (NAC) held the year before. This first fully usable census data since 2002 registered 250,881 farming units (FU) nationwide, approximately a quarter less than at the beginning of the millennium. Preliminary estimates for the Pampean region—Argentina's heartland of agricultural production—indicate that 28 percent of the local farms have disappeared between 2002 and 2018. At the same time, the number of production units

32 Both notions highlight the property-based capacity to extendedly appropriate surplus-value, either directly from workers or from other capitals. In Capital, Marx describes that with "the increasing mass of wealth which functions as capital, accumulation increases the concentration of that wealth in the hands of individual capitalists" (Marx 1990 [1867], 776). In this sense, the term concentration refers to the reproduction of capital on an extended scale and to the related growing control and command over means of production and labour by individual capitalists. The mutual competitive repulsion of these individual capitals, Marx goes on, tends to be "counteracted by their attraction" (ibid., 777). This refers to a trend towards the centralization of capital as an immediate form of overcoming the limitations of corporate growth. "It is concentration of capitals already formed, destruction of their individual independence, expropriation of capitalists by capitalists, transformation of many small into few large capitals. [...] Capital grows [...] in a single hand in one place, because it has been lost by many in another place. This is centralization proper, as distinct from accumulation and concentration" (Marx 1990 [1867], 777). Although 'concentration' can thus be read as an umbrella term, the notion of centralization explicitly highlights the transformation of many small into few large capitals.

33 The following paragraphs are based on Bernhold and Palmisano (2022).

bigger than 2,500 ha has grown (Azcuy Ameghino and Fernández 2019, 1). Although primary production is the most atomized node in grain and oilseed value chains in Argentina these data indicate an ongoing trend towards the concentration and centralization of agrarian capital.

In fact, the number of FU has already been in sharp decline since the last decades of the 20th century. As Table 7 shows, it has almost halved between 1988 and 2018. Strikingly, the decline in FU was of similar extent in the periods 1988–2002 and 2002–2018, such that the centralization of production can be interpreted as a general trend in Pampean capitalist agribusiness, irrespective of different political-economic contexts over time. Small farmers in particular have gone out of business in the Pampean region.[34]

Farming Units (ha)	1988	2002	2018	Variation 1988–2018	Variation 1988–2018 (%)	Variation 2002–2018	Variation 2002–2018 (%)
Up to 100	83,591	49,469	31,179	-52,412	-62.7	-18,29	-37.0
100–500	70,11	50,763	36,604	-33,506	-47.8	-14,159	-27.9
500–1000	14,226	13,658	11,478	-2,748	-19.3	-2180	-16.0
1000–5000	10,725	11,417	10,474	-251	-2.3	-943	-8.3
More than 5000	882	1,031	1,172	290	32.9	141	13.7
Total	179,534	126,338	90,907	-88,627	-49.4	-35,431	-28.0

Table 7: Variation in number of farming units in the Pampean region according to size
Source: own elaboration based on INDEC data

Another eye-catching aspect is that this has affected farms of different sizes in an unequal manner. Whereas FU smaller than 100 ha have vanished considerably (-62.7 percent) between 1988 and 2018, farms bigger than 5000 ha have even grown in number (+32.9 percent), and the relative importance of production units sized 1000–5000 ha has increased (Table 7).

Census data furthermore reveal a process of land use concentration in big farms. Table 8 illustrates the extension of the land controlled by FU of different sizes. Between 1988 and 2018, the total land used for agriculture produc-

34 This analysis includes the provinces Buenos Aires, Santa Fe, Córdoba and Entre Ríos. Note that the Pampean region furthermore covers some departments located in La Pampa and San Luis. However, data on the department level are not available, and including these provinces, the socio-economic structure of which is very different from that of the Pampean region, would distort the data (see Azcuy Ameghino and Fernández 2019).

tion has shrunk in the context of increasing urban growth in the Pampean region, where around 65 percent of all Argentinians live today. The share of the area cultivated by the smallest FU has decreased the most. Although in 1988 farms smaller than 500 ha controlled more than one third of the area under cultivation, in 2018, it was only a fifth. In contrast, FU bigger than 5000 ha have expanded their share in land use from 13.53 percent to 22.08 percent.

Farming Units (ha)	1988		2002		2018	
	ha	%	**ha**	%	**ha**	%
Up to 100	3,532,850.3	6.06	2,203,828.3	3.96	1,361,049.3	2.71
100–500	16,367,778.6	28.08	12,338,180.3	22.18	9,092,840.8	18.10
500–1000	9,946,554.7	17.07	9,633,523.1	17.32	8,131,454.3	16.18
1000–5000	20,550,490.2	35.26	22,086,086.9	39.70	20,565,817.3	40.93
More than 5000	7,882,375.3	13.52	9,374,474.5	16.85	11,092,401.7	22.08
Total	58,280,049.1	100	55,636,093.1	100	50,2435,63.4	100

Table 8: Share in land use among farming units in the Pampean region according to size
Source: own elaboration based on INDEC data

The slight decrease in land use by 500–1000 ha farm units is also a display of a process of concentration, "which is expressed not only in the highest social ranks" (Barsky and Gelman 2009, 495, own translation). Estimations of how large a farming operation in the region must be, as a minimum, to be viable are rare. At any rate, Fernández (2013, 95) calculated in 2009 for the case of soy plantations that only around 11 percent were then smaller than 600 ha (down from over 40 percent in 2002). The frontiers of what constitutes a medium-sized producer are thus shifting within the present mode of agricultural production. However, as I will explore in more depth in Chapter 10, these producers do not cease to exist entirely. Yet their reproduction is increasingly contingent on dependent relations to large agribusiness companies, whose value capture strategies in fact work best if there are smaller actors who lease-out land, and buy inputs and services. Beyond that, these 'partners' often become ideological-cultural transmitters that help maintaining the agribusiness *status quo* (Bernhold and Palmisano 2017, 129).

Ultimately, process upgrading has brought with it a growing importance of constant capital in relation to human labor force and a thus decreasing profitability of small-scale production. This was reinforced by economic policy, for instance the imposition of *retenciones* without differentiating between the sizes of producers (Fernández 2013b, 86; Gras and Hernández 2016b, 116).

6.2.4 Processing and commercialization

As I have shown above, Argentina has become an important player on global markets especially for soybeans and their derivatives. However, as in other chain nodes, the profits from processing industries and trading are appropriated by a concentrated group of large corporations. Many of them do not only run processing plants but also own and operate ports lined up along the Paraná, a river that flows into the large estuary Río de la Plata. However, the exact picture varies according to the export commodity in question.

Wheat

Of the agricultural goods analyzed in this chapter, the production of wheat is the least export-oriented. According to the Ministry of Treasury (2018, 3), of the 18 million tons produced in 2017[35], six million were consumed domestically. With a 7 percent share in global wheat exports, Argentina ranked 7th after Russia, USA, EU, Canada, Australia, and Ukraine that year (Figure 6). Its wheat exports were primarily shipped to Brazil.

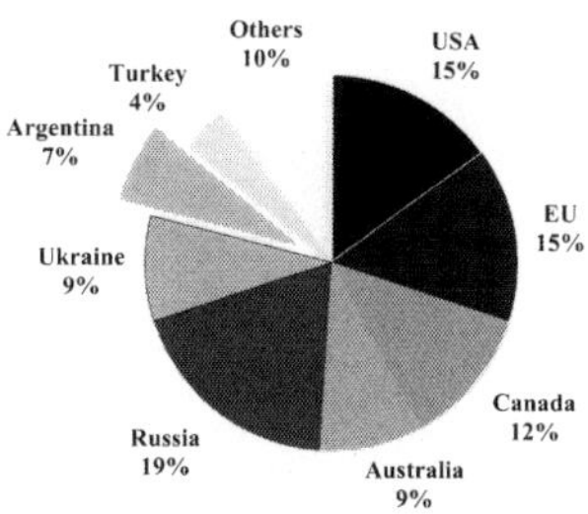

Figure 6: Participation in global wheat trade according to exported tons (2017/2018)
Source: Ministry of Treasury (2018, 6)

35 With a 3 percent participation in global wheat production, Argentina ranked 7th in 2018—after the EU (20 percent), China (17 percent), India (13 percent), the USA (6 percent), Russia (11 percent), and Canada (4 percent) (Ministry of Treasury 2018, 6).

66 percent of these exports were controlled by five companies: Bunge, Cargill, COFCO (ex-Nidera), Louis Dreyfus, and the Glencore subsidiary Oleaginosas Moreno, followed by the Argentine Cooperatives Association (Aca, in Spanish).

With respect to the processing industry, the Ministry of Treasury (2018, 9) suggests that 3 percent of the companies in this chain link mill approximately 35 percent of the wheat and 81 percent of the firms mill 39 percent of this cereal. Industrial bread production is monopolized by the Bimbo group; beyond that, however, bread baking is atomized and divided among more than 15,000 small firms. The production of dry pastas is largely controlled by the Argentinian Molinos Río de la Plata, which produces more than 80 percent of this good (ibid.).

Maize

In the case of maize, of the 43 million tons that were produced in 2018, 53 percent were exported, 39 percent were used as animal feed in Argentina, and 8 percent went into the production of bioethanol and seeds, among other things (Ministry of Treasury 2019, 8). Globally, Argentina was the fifth largest producer[36] and the third biggest exporter of maize that year (Figure 7). The three main destinations were Vietnam (18 percent), Algeria (14 percent), and Egypt (11 percent). As in the case of wheat, five companies controlled 66 percent of these exports, according to the Ministry of Treasury (ibid., 13): Cargill, Bunge, COFCO, Louis Dreyfus, and ADM. These are followed by the Argentinian Aceitera General Deheza (AGD), Molino Cañuelas, and ACA.

The processing industry is divided into the technologically more sophisticated wet-milling (fabrication of syrups and other food stuff) and dry-milling (fabrication of maize meal). 54 percent of the former is dominated by the US based company Ingredion, which runs two plants in Argentina. It is followed by the Argentinian Arcor (31 percent) and Glucovil/Cargill (13 percent). In dry-milling, Arcor holds a 37 percent market share, followed by FyA Basile (12 percent) and Rivara (12 percent) (Ministry of Treasury 2019, 10).

36 The shares are as follows: USA (55 percent), China (22 percent), Brazil (8 percent), EU (6 percent), Argentina (3 percent), India (3 percent) (Ministry of Treasury 2019, 11).

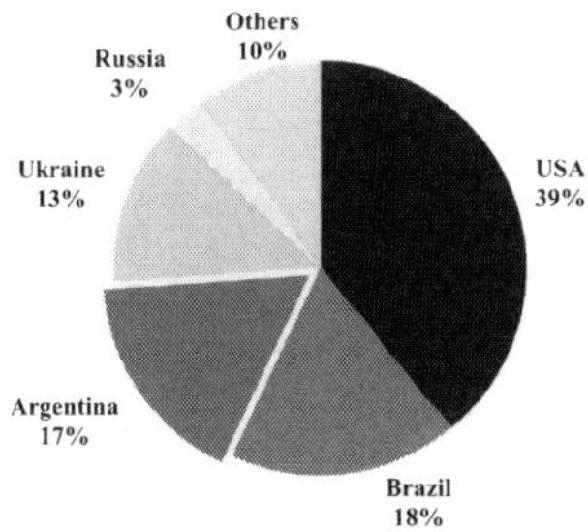

Figure 7: Participation in global maize trade according to exported tons (2017/2018)
Source: Ministry of Treasury (2019, 11)

Soy

As mentioned before, soybeans and their derivatives are almost completely produced for export. Of the roughly 9 million tons sold abroad in 2016, China bought nearly 8 million tons (see Figure 1 above). This made Argentina the third largest exporter of unprocessed soybeans after Brazil (54.4 million tons) and the USA (52.9 million tons) (USDA 2019, 26). At the same time, with 44.5 out of 58 million produced tons, more than three quarters of the soy cultivated in this South American country underwent at least a first step of industrial processing in situ. In 2016, Argentina was the third biggest crusher of these oilseeds after China and the USA, where 81.5 and 51 million tons respectively were crushed in 2016 (USDA 2019, 26). In 2020, Argentina was the fourth biggest crusher of soybeans after China, the US, and Brazil and the world's top exporter of soybean oil and soybean meal (USDA 2022, 18 f.).[37]

Here, again, the dominance of corporate conglomerates is very pronounced with respect to both processing and trade. As Table 9 demonstrates, nine companies produced and exported nearly 90 percent of the soybean oil and meal in 2016. Three of them (Vicentín, Aceitera General Deheza, and Molinos Río de la Plata) are of Argentinian origin.

37 Exports of soybean oil amounted to 5.6 million tons in 2016, 2.8 million tons of which went to India. That same year, exports of soybean meal, which has found its strongest application as fodder in animal industries (Turzi 2017, 5), amounted to 29 million tons, thereof 8.4 million tons to the EU, 4.3 million tons to Vietnam, and 2.4 million tons to Indonesia (see Figure 1).

Top exporters of soybean oil			Top exporters of soybean meal		
	Tons	Share (%)		Tons	Share (%)
Vicentín	887,901	14.5	Vicentín	4,879,552	15.4
Aceitera General Deheza	850,392	13.9	Aceitera General Deheza	4,817,932	15.2
Cargill	772,076	12.6	Bunge	3,980,421	12.6
Bunge	635,913	10.4	Cargill	3,512,461	11.1
Oleaginosa Moreno (Glencore)	627,242	10.2	Oleaginosa Moreno (Glencore)	3,137,167	9.8
Nidera (COFCO)	451,516	7.4	Louis Dreyfus	2,715,941	8.5
Molinos Río de la Plata	400,863	6.6	Molinos Río de la Plata	1,796,208	5.6
Noble	377,142	6.2	Nidera (COFCO)	1,713,332	5.4
Louis Dreyfus	333,104	5.4	Noble	1,583,097	5
First 9 companies	5,336,149	87.2	First 9 companies	28,136,111	88.6

Table 9: Main producing and exporting companies of soybean oil and meal, 2016
Source: own elaboration based on CIARA data

Summary

The data compiled in this chapter supports what Bernstein and Campling (2006b, 443) have suggested for agricultural commodities in general: "concentration of capital and scale of operation are much greater in sourcing, processing and sales (via increasingly internationalized retail corporations) than in their production." In agro-industrial value chains in Argentina, capital concentration is by far more pronounced in upstream and downstream chain links. However, it has increased in grain and oilseed production throughout the past decades. On that note, asked in which parts of the soy value chain in Argentina most profits are made, ACSOJA representative Alfredo answers that,

> "other than the state who pockets the *retenciones*, without any doubt the crushing and export companies [...]. They deal with very large volumes, shared among few players and although their returns per unit are small, this is multiplied by volume. [...] And although the soy market is very transparent, there is obviously a difference between the price paid to the producer and the sales price. I would say the biggest share of the money stays here. [...] And from there we can say that it's the input companies, seeds, and agrochemicals."[38]

38 Interview with a representative of ACSOJA, August 7, 2014, Rosario.

As a result of the oligopolistic power held by companies like Monsanto/Bayer and Syngenta upstream, and processors and traders like AGD, Cargill, and Bunge downstream, small producers "have less and less control over what they produce, how they produce it [...] and what price they can get for it" (Otero 2012, 286). This situation has consolidated over the past decades. It is both the result of and the background for the state and corporate-led GVC upgrading strategies analyzed in the next chapters.

7. “Argentina Agribusiness Leader”—A Governmental Strategic Plan

The third phase of my fieldwork in Argentina started after the 2015 presidential elections, won by Mauricio Macri. As I sketched in the previous chapter, the then new president was determined to liberalize agribusiness exports. He quickly confirmed the elimination of *retenciones* on most crops, including wheat and maize, and a gradual reduction of withholding taxes levied on soy exports—a fact that led Miguel, co-director of my case company Agrigood (see Chapter 9), to compare the new political situation to “Christmas, birthday and honeymoon, all at once.”[1] Shortly after the then new administration took power, it renamed the former Ministry of Agriculture, Livestock, and Fisheries (MAGyP, in Spanish) into the Ministry of Agroindustry. This was aimed to inspire confidence in the development of an agro-industrial value chain that goes beyond agriculture and serves as an engine for broader national development. Underlining the then government’s commitment to this objective, a TV spot published shortly after by the Presidency presents a whole set of production steps taken in Argentina that result in an *empanada*, the stuffed pastry that is one of the mainstays of Argentinian cuisine. It suggests that “everything is possible”[2] when all economic actors stand together to reinforce the country’s economic performance. The advertisement and the ministry renaming suggest a radical sea-change in politics, institutions, and the discourse on agro-industry-led progression.

However, Macri’s predecessor Cristina Fernández de Kirchner had already identified grain and oilseed value chain development as an engine of Argentinian development, and this is the focus of the present chapter. Corresponding strategy papers launched during the Kirchner administra-

---

1 The comment was part of an informal chat preceding an interview with Miguel, Agrigood manager, July 20, 2016, Buenos Aires.

2 https://www.youtube.com/watch?v=HtvDBXle-68, last accessed 25 May, 2022.

tion resemble the idea of global value chain (GVC) upgrading, which I have traced in Chapter 3. First and foremost, this applies to the argument that upgrading creates possibilities for sustainable development in Latin America by moving "beyond extraction of raw materials to additional processing and commercialization" (Gereffi 2012, 34). Or as Taglioni and Winkler (2016, 22) put it in a World Bank study: "Upgrading does not necessarily mean transitioning from an agricultural to a service economy […] It can instead mean increasingly embracing higher value-added production with the contribution of better skills and know-how, capital and technology, and processes."

Yet how governmental strategies on Argentinian agribusiness can be understood as theoretical-policy expressions of the GVC upgrading paradigm has rarely been featured. On these grounds, closer empirical attention needs to be paid to the question of how strategies on agro-industrial value chain development are actually defined by state institutions and which priorities are set. From an ideology-critical perspective, this entails considering omissions and implicit silences, as well as asking whose interests are or are not reflected in these strategies, and how they do or do not deal with obstructions and contradictions that may arise in the wake of upgrading. On that note, while the previous chapter gave an overview of the political economy of grain and oilseed value chains in Argentina, this chapter shifts the focus to critically discussing the most important governmental strategy paper covering the 'Kirchnerist' approach to agro-industrial value chain development: *Argentina Agribusiness Leader. Federal and Participative Agri-Food and Agribusiness Strategic Plan 2010–2020* (PEA) (Ministry of Agriculture 2011). In this connection, it also takes the corresponding stance of the National Institute for Agriculture Technology (INTA) into account, which is one of the most important state institutions driving forwards the goals of the Ministry of Agriculture.

The next section (7.1) describes the general objectives set out in the PEA and by the INTA. Following on from that, I then discuss contradictions and depict omitted aspects relevant to the perpetuation of inequality and exploitation in the wake of agro-industrial upgrading.

7.1 General objectives of the PEA

With the mainstreaming of GVC analysis, its concepts have been increasingly incorporated into strategy papers and statements by the Kirchner administration, especially where this approach fits well with neo-developmentalist policies. As José, an employee at the MAGyP commented, "before 2000, no one talked about chains and value added; the topic has only come up since 2002, 2003. Before, nobody took notice."[3]

In 2010, the government launched a discussion process with the participation of state, academic, and business actors, which resulted in the publication of the 160-page PEA (Ministry of Agriculture 2011), the first governmental strategy plan for agriculture since 1984 (Carballo González et al. 2012, 2). Basically, it defines cornerstones for the development of agro-industrial value chains as an engine for national development. The INTA has also published documents that refer to GVC development (Giancola et al. 2009; INTA 2004) and regard "Global Value Chains as a strategy" (Iglesias 2002, 1, own translation).

The PEA in particular focuses on the articulation of an increase in both the area under cultivation and labor productivity in export-oriented grain and oilseed production on the one hand, with a process of further industrialization and value added in situ on the other (Ministry of Agriculture 2011, 24). It maintains that agribusiness involves much more than the export of primary goods, and points to development opportunities upstream and downstream along the value chain to be achieved by economic actors of all sizes. The vitality of agribusiness "is not exclusive to the Pampas' agriculture; it stretches along the value chain" (Ministry of Agriculture 2011, 59) and can boost "the national and regional development of our country" (ibid., 62). The general vision is that

> "Argentina will be a world leader in the production of quality agri-food and agribusiness goods and services with added value [...] within a framework of territorial equity, social inclusion and environmental, economic and social sustainability. [This is to the benefit of] the producers, businessmen and workers involved in the production process and of all the Argentinean people, who are the ultimate beneficiaries of greater growth and a sustained and sustainable process of development" (ibid., 83 f.).

Thus, the forecasts made about agro-industrial upgrading for the benefit of all people in Argentina are quite comprehensive. However, the approach to achieve these goals does not envision major deviations from corporate-driven agribusiness development since the 2000s, which has often been crit-

---

3 Interview with a representative of the MAGyP, Sub-secretariat for value added, April 21, 2015, Buenos Aires.

icized for it has led to environmental, economic, and social *un*sustainability (see Chapter 6).

According to the PEA, a part of the targets defined has already been achieved through the successful modernization of processes and technologies. Basically, this refers to the growth in grain and particularly soy production both in "quality and quantity (more productivity per unit of surface and incorporation of new cultivable lands), based on a greater generation and adoption of technology" (Ministry of Agriculture 2011, 64). The PEA concludes from this that Argentina does have what it takes to profit from an ever-growing global demand of agro-food and biofuels. Yet, to stay competitive, it depicts a need to improve further by generating more growth. In particular, the area under grain and oilseed cultivation should grow from 32 to 42 million ha between 2010 and 2020 (ibid., 90). In the same period, production should increase from approximately 100 to 157.5 million tons (ibid., 96; these goals were not fully achieved). The PEA also aspires to a further growth in productivity (ibid., 103 f.) and to an increase in exports (ibid., 110). Here, the country should sell more processed products of agrarian origin. This means an increase of "added value in the industrial manufacturing of rural products" (ibid., 89). Further objectives for functional and chain upgrading include the production of sundry foodstuffs, industrial meat production, and an expansion of the biofuels industry.

To be a world leader in the sustainable production of agro-food products and services, characterized by an articulation of social humanism with innovation, business, entrepreneurship, competitiveness, and increasing capital accumulation (INTA 2004, 26 ff.; Ministry of Agriculture 2011, 86), the former government depicted some improvements still to be made.

Fostering process upgrading

The respective concepts for such improvements comply with mainstream GVC approaches to process upgrading (as defined in Chapter 3) in various ways. First, the technological and organizational changes at the point of primary production are positive reference points for the PEA, above all, for their capacity to massively increase both absolute primary production and productivity, as well as export capacities. The PEA aims to build upon and to deepen these forms of process upgrading, which put rural producers "at the center of a transformation that not only implies a change in the technological paradigm […] but also an organizational restructuring" (Ministry of Agriculture 2011, 43). The strategy reiterates the picture in which the 21st century agrarian subject is not just a farmer. Particular emphasis is put on the modern rural entrepreneur as an idealized figure, who readily takes risks against all odds, employs the latest managerial knowledge, and acts within "a complex network of actors connected to each other by a variety of contracts," thereby erasing the boundaries among "the primary, the industrial and the service sectors" (ibid.), and broadening the scope of agrarian actors to service suppliers and well-educated managers at the point of primary production. The PEA seeks to further strengthen "an associativity that promotes a strong integration of the diverse links and actors" (ibid.) and that creates possibilities for small producers to stay in agriculture, the required economies of scale notwithstanding. The idea is that former family agriculture units can organize in networks and grow into "pocket multinational companies" (ibid., 45). In this view, a deepening of the ongoing modernization process redistributes the risk among different actors and "brings power back to balance in the processes to generate and capture rent" (ibid., 43).

The quite technocratic idea here is that the use of "innovative ways and the appropriate technology" (ibid., 44) will guarantee opportunities for anyone. In addition to a positive attitude towards the use of technology, farmers need "a clear spirit for productivity" and the will to be part of a modern global value chain rather than to seek "shelter under the state protection" (ibid.).

In sum, rural entrepreneurs should be innovative, well educated in agricultural engineering or organization studies, and well associated with other economic actors to meet the needs of modern agribusiness management (ibid.).

These ideas recorded in the PEA are very similar to the conceptions of Argentinian GVC scholars, which I depicted in Section 3.2.4. The perceptions of technological and organizational process upgrading also meet the ideas and expectations formulated by both agribusiness associations (see Chapter 8) and the case companies in this study (see Chapter 9). In Chapter 10, I use a case study to challenge this idea that upgrading via network association benefits all actors involved; I show how upgrading works in and through a process of class differentiation.

Besides the consolidation of these forms of organizing production, the PEA attaches importance to furthering science and technical innovation, especially bioengineering, and developing ever new information technologies for precision farming (Ministry of Agriculture 2011, 28). In the case of soy, the bean as such should be upgraded genetically into a product that contains an improved amount of proteins and oil (Giancola et al. 2009, 100). The dissemination and adoption of technology and knowledge transfer through institutional learning in networks, as well as "training of human resources" (INTA 2004, 24) is supposed to guarantee closing the technological divides among producers. As INTA-employee and coordinator of the national program Agroindustry and Value Added Vanessa puts it, "the issue is that many of the producers don't know how things work; perhaps they learn with the time."[4] At the same time, better "commercial technologies" (INTA 2004, 48) should enhance small producer's access to the markets.

For those who are entirely excluded from the value chains or live below the poverty line, the INTA seeks to enhance the food security situation by means of support for subsistence production, and to train and inform people so that they can build up a small-scale microenterprise or improve their qualification for the labor market (ibid., 45).

First and foremost, however, GMO-based technological innovation, the dissemination of knowledge, and the consolidation of organizational changes form the basis for state strategies to foster process upgrading in agriculture. This is to "gain higher international rent" (Ministry of Agriculture 2011, 45), supposedly to the benefit of actors of all economic positions, which should then be invested to create the possibilities for greater value added in situ.

These (bio)technology-based upgrading strategies are very similar to those formulated by agribusiness associations (see Chapter 8). They remain committed to the concerns of large-scale farmers and companies whose profits are tied to doing business with GM-seeds and accompanying chemicals. While the PEA thus widely mirrors the positions of these economic actors, alternative forms of production that could be considered, or the fact that organized small farmers on the ground have opted for agroecology go tacitly ignored (see section 8.1).

Expanding functional and chain upgrading

Functional and chain upgrading are also part of the PEA. With regard to already achieved upgrades, it mainly refers to the worldwide competitive performance of the soy processing industry, and to the respective exportable

4 Interview with a representative of the INTA, April 22, 2015, Buenos Aires.

products (soybean oil and meal, and biofuels): "Argentina's soybean processing is characterized by the constant adoption of innovation and technological improvement; [...] the industrial plants for processing are the most modern and largest in the world" (Giancola et al. 2009, 18, own translation).

Furthermore, the PEA highlights exports of agricultural machinery made in Argentina (Ministry of Agriculture 2011, 53; for a critique see Section 6.2.2). My interviewees have also positively referred to agribusiness companies which have managed to invest in activities upstream and/or downstream of primary production. Josè, for instance, mentions my case company El Agro (see Chapter 9), which "offers services and financing, counseling, these kinds of things more than production."[5]

However, being more competitive internationally with higher value added products is still regarded as a pending issue, one "which requires further investments in the agri-food and agro-industrial industries" (INTA 2004, 26). As José puts it,

"I believe that value added at the point of origin is very important if we want to differentiate ourselves from the world [...] and generate more jobs, and export higher value products. [...] We have soy. Let's no longer sell soybeans, let's sell the industrialized soy: transform it into meal, into oil. These are the first steps, and then, if you want, you can amplify but this is the first step of value added [...] Then with the meal you can produce animal feed, you can produce different animals, and afterwards you can make cold cuts. [...] With every step you add value. This is how we understand value added."[6]

In the view of INTA, the key factors for the success of these kinds of upgrading are the development of innovative ventures, the provision of highly qualified services, and a form of technology development that benefits companies of all sizes. As Benicio explains, this does not have to be only tailored to globally competitive companies. According to him, the first step is regional development.

"We are not only working in the global value chain; we also work in value added in short chains, local chains in the territories [...] so that the producers start to have an entrepreneurial vision of how to develop and get connected to the market, and after that, in the future, yes, commercialize at the level of the global chain, but then already with a high value product."[7]

5 Interview with a representative of the MAGyP, Sub-secretariat for value added, April 21, 2015, Buenos Aires.

6 Ibid.

7 Interview with three representatives of the INTA, May 05, 2015, Buenos Aires.

The entrepreneurial vision and the competitiveness of many local producers is regarded as something that is still up in the air. For example, INTA representatives explain that the production of biofuels in cooperatively organized plants run by small producers focuses merely on local small-scale production for subsistence to replace more expensive diesel. Yet, this is supposed to change step by step, as Bruno indicates:

> "We are starting to see what we need locally so that it [the economy] can start to grow from the bottom up [...]. We start to work with this focus on territorial demand. And from there, people demand that they want to start having a more industrialized country, and get out of the commodities."[8]

In a similar vein, Vanessa states that

> "The concept of value added in situ aims to encourage the producer, show him some kind of development, some kind of processing, at least a first step [...]. One typical example is when soy is sold as a bean, as a commodity. Now four or five producers get together, buy equipment, produce oil, and sell it as a first step. After that, if you want, you can make a lot more things with the soy. I don't know, protein yarns, for instance, soy concentrate. This is difficult at the point of origin, but hey, at least start with one step."

She goes on to explain that everyone can possibly improve their situation in value chains provided they have the necessary knowledge and equipment.

> "When you are capable of differentiating yourself, even if you're small, be it in terms of quality, be it for a different kind of food, you will have opportunities [...] a niche in the market that the other doesn't have [...]. What you need is economic knowledge and the equipment to start, isn't that true? [...] The small producers here in Argentina have to reinvent themselves."[9]

In brief, the government has aimed to foster functional upgrading for both big business and local small producers. It has acknowledged that it is not easy for small producers to catch up with the development of big agribusiness players and compete in global value chains. However, the ideas for upgrading local production remain within a modernist framework of technocratic solutions to social problems. For instance, the PEA does not address competitive capital accumulation in which large corporations have asserted themselves—there has been an ongoing process of concentration and centralization of capital. Consequently, it does not contain parts, for instance, on restrictions of capital power as a possibility to protect small producers.

---

8 Ibid.

9 Interview with a representative of the INTA, April 22, 2015, Buenos Aires.

Instead, upgrading is thought to be achieved through science, innovation, technology development, and the dissemination of knowledge. I will come back to these issues in Section 7.3.

Social Upgrading

The depicted strategy is tightly connected to the objective of social sustainability. First and foremost, this is about job creation. The PEA seeks to increase the "number of producers, rural employees working directly for the Agrifood Sector and workers linked to the agribusiness production by 35 % by the year 2020" (Ministry of Agriculture 2011, 127). According to José, this can also be made possible through upgrading in networks:

"When you're constantly producing and expanding, you are generating more work and jobs [...] So, when I lease-in land, I will need contratistas and machinery, or I'll need more employees for the management. It depends on the type of production you're doing, but you will be linked to other sectors, and after you have harvested, you need a buyer for your grains. This will be someone who does livestock or an agro-exporter [...] and so on, and so on."

José admits that sometimes

"More profitability can also mean to kick out people, yes. But for me, to generate more profitability as a state institution means to help with the purchase of machinery, help with a better tax rate, with a credit. In that sense, this will generate greater profitability for the company, such that it does not need to reduce jobs. Rather, for instance, it is about generating a new product line, and thereby more direct and indirect employment."[10]

The jobs to be generated by agro-industrial development are supposed to be "steady, law-abiding, qualified and well paid" (Ministry of Agriculture 2011, 24). In this context, the PEA supposes that the incorporation of regional production into global value chains can cause companies to adapt to both national and international regulations "in detriment of unethical labor practices" (ibid.). Thus, not only the quantity, but also the quality of jobs is assumed to enhance and to make rural life more promising. This includes

"Securing access to food for every Argentinean, [...] encouraging the rural population to settle, [...] increasing safeness and health care within rural employment, [...] contributing to the observance of the local goals (The Millennium Goals) [...]. Finally, this vision pro-

10 Interview with a representative of the MAGyP, Sub-secretariat for value added, April 21, 2015, Buenos Aires.

poses, as an objective, the need to create the proper conditions to generate wealth together with social, organizational, environmental and human development across and along our nation, prioritizing equity, inclusion, settlement and respect for cultural diversity" (ibid., 45).

In sum, economic upgrading in grain and oilseed value chains is supposed to be accompanied by new and better sources of employment in rural areas. As a result, "people can have interesting prospects to facilitate them access to a decent life that, in turn, will boost concrete, comprehensive and sustainable development processes" (ibid., 123). In Chapter 3, I analyzed the assumption that economic upgrading automatically leads to social upgrading as an ideological claim. In Argentina, state and corporate actors alike have disseminated this assumption and I will return to it throughout the next chapters.

7.2 The role of the state in agro-industrial development

The role of the state in all this, as far as it has been addressed in the analyzed documents and interviews, first, regards commercial policies. By its own account, the then Kirchner government implemented macroeconomic policies to privilege the domestic market while simultaneously opening "more dynamic markets by integrating the driving family farms into a driving, associative and cooperative model" (Ministry of Agriculture 2011, 28). On the one hand, this refers to the differentiated *retenciones* to support industrial processing in situ. Functional upgrading should be incentivized by levying higher export taxes on raw soybeans than on processed derivatives. On the other hand, the Kirchner administration had implemented export restrictions on products that are needed on the domestic market at cheap prices, such as wheat. The official idea was to benefit from a high global soy demand and assure cheap wheat for domestic markets at the same time. In Chapter 8, I analyze how farmers and agribusiness associations have responded to these policies.

A second governmental task emphasized by the PEA involves investments in infrastructure development (Ministry of Agriculture 2011, 117). My interlocutors repeatedly emphasized that the state of Argentina's infrastructure was a major reason for a lack of local competitiveness. In this vein, the INTA (2004, 67) points out that 84 percent of all agrarian goods are being transported in trucks on poor roads, though this means of transport is much more expensive than cargo trains. José seconds that "we believe that we can add value by paving a road which used to be mud [...]. Why? Because we prevent the commodity from breaking and we help it arrive in a better condition, right? This is also value adding for us."[11]

Third, INTA representatives highlight the role of the state in the above-mentioned facilitation of state-of-the-art technology and innovation. According to my interlocutors, this is not only thought to be usable by large companies. Instead, it is supposed to benefit of all kinds of actors. For instance,

"we have the national program of agro-industries and value added, and our center has two institutes: food-stuff technology and rural engineering. Rural engineering is machinery, there is an area of agro-electronics, very important, agro-sensors for precision farming. Another area is for mechanical seeding, we have an area for fumigation, and another one for agrochemicals [...]. We have an area that works on bioenergy and biofuels made of crop waste. [...] We are working a lot with family agriculture, in order to make small machinery for family agriculture, to alleviate their work [...] because there are some machines that are too big for them."[12]

Among other things, the INTA is investigating nanotechnology. However, Emma argues that in Argentina's north, where people lack water, "they are not interested in nanotechnology, because it does not solve any problems for them. But by bringing them water, you do solve their problems." But this statement is also embedded in an argument about the possibility of gradual regional modernization and value chain upgrading through the diffusion of technology and innovation. Emma goes on to say that

"when they have access to water, there will be another problem to be solved and hopefully step by step they reach the issue of nanotechnology at some point [...]. And like this we add small innovations that may not have an impact at the commercial or entrepreneurial level immediately, but they do have an impact at the level of development and people's quality of life. And as they advance and improve, they will reach a moment when there will be a development and a more important movement in the region. And when the regions are more developed, this will have an impact on the national development [...]. Therefore, we are thinking about those who need more assistance, but without forgetting the big producer [...] but we also see those who need help the most."[13]

11 Interview with a representative of the MAGyP, Sub-secretariat for value added, April 21, 2015, Buenos Aires.

12 Interview with three representatives of the INTA, May 05, 2015, Buenos Aires.

13 Ibid.

In this context, the state also seeks to find private actors for public-private partnerships, because the defined goals can be achieved "together with the business sector, which we should help to become more profitable, and which should help us to create greater employment and in better conditions" (Ministry of Agriculture 2011, 24). One example here is biotechnology development, where the INTA (2004, 29) maintains that state and private actors together can put "the country in line with the world trends of recent years."[14] Another example is the state-owned high-tech company INVAP, which founded a joint venture with my case company El Agro to articulate aerospace technology, software, and rural engineering to intensify precision farming (however, the joint venture has already been dissolved again). A consequential pillar of INTA policies is the dissemination of these newly developed technologies and management systems (INTA 2004, 37), and the provision of assistance to actors according to their problems (ibid). As Vanessa explains, the INTA organizes "trainings, demonstrations, and conferences when there are new things to learn [...]. There are courses in software and precision agriculture. They show farmers how to use the tractors with the precision equipment, and thus there are courses and specific demonstrations of experiments made for the producers."[15]

7.3 Contradictions, implicit assumptions, and omissions

Both the analyzed governmental strategy papers and my interview partners also address problems with respect to enhancing the socioeconomic situation of the (rural) Argentinian population through the development of agro-industrial value chains. A case in point is José's above-quoted remark that the lack of infrastructure in Argentina can obstruct upgrading. High-tech agribusiness does not necessarily make this country's farmers more competitive when the issue of paving roads is neglected. Other problems are rather implicitly addressed. For example, an implicit premise of the asserted need to produce and appropriate more value in situ is that Argentina occupies a peripheral position in the global political economy that needs to be changed.

14 Despite extensive academic and political criticism of bioengineering and the related massive use of agro-toxics, the PEA positively mentions the role of the state and the National Institute of Seeds (INASE) as a driver of GMO-driven value chain development (Ministry of Agriculture 2011, 49).

15 Interview with a representative of the INTA, April 22, 2015, Buenos Aires.

The strategy to develop grain and oilseed value chains as an engine for national development, which is supposed to allow all kinds of actors to move out of adverse positions, and to participate in the capitalist reaps, inheres several contradictions and omissions. In some respects, this concerns the same issues discussed with regard to the GVC upgrading paradigm (Chapter 3). One example is the belief in capitalist firms as key drivers of development, interested in progress for the benefit of all. Like the mainstream GVC approach, the PEA abstracts from profit interests and therewith from possible counter-facts that may contradict a socially and ecologically sustainable development.

Furthermore, the PEA tends to equate firm-development in agro-industrial GVCs with national development. In this context, it avoids any notion of systemic social and power differences both at global and local levels. As noted before, Brewer (2011, 308) has called this an "upgrading paradox," that is, a faith in development combined with a neglect of systemic socioeconomic inequality and its effects on development issues that go beyond firm-, network-, or even chain-level analysis.

In this vein, exploitative social relations of production as well as conflicting interests among different actors in GVC's and capital fractions in Argentina go tacitly ignored in the strategic plan. As a consequence, it also does not consider that inequality and exploitation may be perpetuated at local levels or even increased, possibly also as a result of upgrading, regardless how innovative the used technology is.

The PEA does not take into account those who remain outside agro-industrial GVC development, for instance, because they have been displaced from the market due to capital concentration (Fernández 2013a; 2013b) or even violently displaced; for a critique of the PEA in this regard see Carballo González et al. (2012). Thus, it reiterates what Bair and Werner (2011) have criticized as an inclusionary bias (see Bair et al. 2013; Werner 2016b). The remainder of this section highlights four aspects in detail.

Tackling socioeconomic power differences with technocratic solutions

Redistributive policies that include the allocation of funds for assistance to small producers surely have the potential to enhance individual socioeconomic situations. At the same time, however, the PEA refers to such policies only within a political economic framework that has caused the adverse situation of small producers vis-à-vis powerful economic actors in the first place. The plan does not imply to impose restrictions on the strategies of large agribusiness companies, traders, and biotech corporations to counteract the unequal production, distribution, and appropriation of value. What Selwyn (2016b, 4) writes with respect to the GVC approach holds also true for this strategy document: "it takes as given the existence of trans-national corporations and does not seek to disempower them."[16]

The PEA proposes an increase in the local processing of agricultural products by small producers. Yet it does not ask the question of how this aim may be impacted by oligopolistic processing industries run by large corporations, which have not aligned their activities with local integration benefitting small-scale manufacturing industries (see Chapter 6). Asked about state policies to restrict the power of large corporations, José answered, "I don't think we want to restrict companies. We have discussions and points of view, but the government won't oblige companies not to do something, unless it is very harmful to the country, but it is all a question of conversation, and luckily, dialogues are open today."[17]

In this context, Carballo Gonzales et al. (2012, 9) point to the contradiction that the PEA emphasizes its assistance to small producers while it pursues exactly a model of productivity increase in agriculture, which makes production profitable only on ever larger scales, with a growing number of farmers being displaced from the market or becoming highly dependent upon large companies. Here, INTA-representatives, do acknowledge a de facto rift between small producers and big capitals in primary production. Benicio says that

> "symbolically we could say that the big fishes eat the smaller ones [laughter]; thus, in a competition, the more powerful actors dominate the smaller ones […] and there are the famous *pools de siembra* and all these problems you maybe have heard about […] but the INTA cannot… What it can do is offer technologies and help with technologies, with which these small fishes can be calm […] and if these small fishes can develop, and transform themselves in a big fish in order to compete with the other big fishes, this would be a very valid objective. It seems to me that this is what people think, that there is a need to work with the small fish […].[18]

16 Agribusiness-related policies of the Kirchner government have rather fueled the trend towards capital concentration and centralization in different links of the agro-industrial value chains in Argentina (see Chapter 6).

17 Interview with a representative of the MAGyP, Sub-secretariat for value added, April 21, 2015, Buenos Aires.

18 Interview with three representatives of the INTA, May 05, 2015, Buenos Aires.

Accordingly, while the INTA regards economic concentration a problem, it does not deal with it in terms of the underlying socioeconomic relations and capital-led productivity development. Instead, the problem is supposed to be solvable by further innovation and catch-up-development efforts.

In this context, interviews also covered another related issue, namely that the INTA often develops new technologies, which many small producers are not able to use due to a lack of capital or because they can only be profitably employed on large scales. Thus, contradictorily, such innovations are considered necessary for improving the competitiveness of small producers, while at the same time they potentially widen the rift between big capital and small producers under the status quo. Benicio says that a private company once even patented an invention made by the INTA, privatizing the results of public Research & Development. In the same interview, Bruno admits that innovations can thus be good for some, and "potentially very bad" for others. "Nothing is perfect," he continues, "money talks, money talks [loud laughter]." And Benicio adds that "the technology is not neutral." However, these admissions do not influence the described technocratic development strategy.

The same applies to the awareness that the INTA cannot compete with the innovative capacities of large international corporations. As Bruno says,

> "Well, we are just not as sophisticated as they are. [...] For example, Monsanto is working on this or that and we want to compete [...] but we can't. Even if we knew what they are working on, we could not replicate it or do something similar. It would cost us a lot of money, and we can't. This is a disadvantage that we may have."

And Benicio seconds that

> "Yes, totally, there are large corporations, the multinationals, [...] they have laboratories with the latest equipment. They're not here; they are in Europe or in the United States. Thus, with their research capacity, not so much the intelligence of their investigations, but with their equipment capacity, they can advance much faster than we can. Well, our equipment is not as sophisticated and there is a disadvantage compared to these big companies."[19]

José gives another example and argues that it is not easy for Argentina to compete with manufactured products internationally, since "globalization made finished foodstuff cheap during the 1990s" and it has been more conve-

19 Ibid.

nient to import finished goods than to produce them locally.[20] However, the implicit assumption in these statements is that nothing can be done about the capital power that outplays local actors except for own, though lower-level technology development.

With respect to geopolitical dynamics, Benicio mentions that there are always disputes over "what I buy, what I don't buy, raw wheat, flour, or processed pastas. Let's say there is always a commercial bid for different countries."[21] China, for example, penalizes the import of higher value soy derivatives, buys raw soybeans instead of oil, and prefers to extend its own processing industry (Giancola et al. 2009, 105). In this context, INTA-representative Vanessa argues that

> "you also have to be careful, because on the one hand you teach the producer to produce this, but you must assure this producer that he will be able to sell the oil he produced. But Argentina is a commodity exporter. It is very difficult to compete with other countries, to put products other than commodities on the international market. I do not say that it is not possible, but you have to work on it. You need to have a particular quality and differentiate yourself [...]."[22]

Here, again, the struggle for change in global political economic relations does not appear on the political radar. Instead, the proposed solution is to find niches that are not yet occupied. While translating a critique of global political economy into state policies is certainly not an easy task, such considerations are completely absent from the economic strategies set forth by the PEA and the INTA.

In summary, in my interviews with state representatives, the problems of global capitalist competition, capital concentration in Argentina, and geopolitics played a role. Yet, there was always a sentiment that such problems cannot possibly be tackled, except with the described technocratic approaches. In practical terms, the solutions discussed in both the analyzed strategy papers and in my interviews mostly focus on innovation, technology, and training.

With respect to the assistance provided to small producers, Lea, then an employee at the Secretariat of Family Agriculture, even argues that although it is mentioned as a part of the PEA, the de facto allocation of funds has not

20 Interview with a representative of the MAGyP, Sub-secretariat for value added, April 21, 2015, Buenos Aires.

21 Interview with three representatives of the INTA, May 05, 2015, Buenos Aires.

22 Interview with a representative of the INTA, April 22, 2015, Buenos Aires.

livd up to the rhetoric of social sustainability. Her team within the Ministry of Agriculture, she says, worked "with a spectrum that goes from indigenous groups to small producers who are a bit more capitalized." She worries about a political prioritization of large-scale agribusiness in Argentina. She generally welcomes goals such as the development of infrastructure and trainings, the promotion of gender equality and of sustainable production for family agriculture. However, she complains that now and again her secretariat has been shunted into a siding.

"We have not had a specific financing for our working area for years now [...] The secretariat is part of the ministry, but it is something that does not have priority within the ministry, so that we always have problems of financing. For example, since the secretariat has existed, there has never been something like a universal plan for all working areas. [...] I would say that there is a dispute over the de facto non-support of family agriculture [...]."

When I asked her what was financed instead, she answered: "cattle raising, big soy, and grains, basically everything that is thought of as for export."[23] These observations coincide with stories told by Tomás, a petty commodity producer in the province of Buenos Aires, and a member of a small cooperative, about several experiences involving the unsuccessful fulfillment of promises made by the state.[24]

Does capital necessarily seek strategic upgrading?

The PEA rests upon the assumption that private actors generally have an interest in upgrading within agro-industrial GVCs. Resembling Argentinian GVC scholars' works on agribusiness (see Chapter 3), the document is characterized by a strong belief in a Schumpeterian creative entrepreneur, who takes pleasure in creating innovations and steadily seeks to diversify his/her production capacities in a way that serves 'the country.'

Yet at the same time, Benicio bemoans that there is "a lack of entrepreneurial vision to reinvest profits" in Argentina.[25] This statement has two dimensions. First, capital is not primarily interested in national development but in the profitability of investments, which may be higher

23 Interview with a representative of the Argentine Ministry of Agroindustry, Secretariat of Family Agriculture, June 17, 2016, Buenos Aires.

24 Interview with a petty commodity producer and representative of APER, an association of regional peasants in the province of Buenos Aires, July 28, 2016, Parque Pereyra Iraola.

25 Interview with three representatives of the INTA, May 05, 2015, Buenos Aires.

somewhere else. But such considerations do not play a role in the PEA. Second, Benicio's statement alludes to ongoing rentier economic structures. In this line, José argues that many former *chacareros* today prefer to live from the rent they get from leasing out their land, rather than try to produce something and look for investment options. Yet, he also recognizes that capital (credits) and profitable investment options for these actors do not abound and that making risky innovations in an unstable Argentinian economy is not necessarily attractive.[26]

In brief, capital does not necessarily invest in industrial upgrading in case this is less profitable than merely appropriating ground rent or putting money in soy cultivation. However, the PEA suggests a coincidence of national and firm-level interests in agro-industrial value chain upgrading. In Chapter 8, where I analyze how strategies for GVC development are actually defined in the corporate realm, I come back to the question of whether companies are necessarily interested in upgrading. In this context, I also challenge the assumption, which the PEA shares with mainstream GVC analysis, that they can generally be assumed as partners in development.

Social upgrading without the exploited and displaced as subjects of development

Depending on the actual historical and geographical situation of class struggles, technology development and productivity increases can affect workers positively or negatively. However, the PEA avoids any notion of exploitative social relations and of the fact that the interests of workers are not served automatically in the wake of upgrading. As I will illustrate throughout the following chapters, this governmental strategy and corporate actors share the notion that an expansion of agribusiness and economic growth in different links of agro-industrial value chains would directly lead to more and better jobs.

In a similar vein, the PEA states that the state's strategy arises "as an expression of the society's general interests and politics" (Ministry of Agriculture 2011, 27). However, the situation and the struggles of peasants and indigenous communities against often violent displacement, among other things, are not mentioned at all. In this context, Carballo González et al. (2012, 9) have criticized that many groups of actors, such as workers and

26 Interview with a representative of the MAGyP, Sub-secretariat for value added, April 21, 2015, Buenos Aires.

trade unions, organizations of landless people, and indigenous communities, were not involved in the development of the strategy paper, even if it carries 'participative' in its name. Lapegna (2017, 324) therefore argues that "the ultimate goal of this plan, […] was to increase agricultural production and expand the area used for agriculture, which could only be achieved at the expense of a further marginalization of peasants in favour of agribusiness."

At the INTA, one of my interlocutors proudly told me that "we have a very significant level of public oversight." He referred to the fact that the institute's highest authority that controls the implementation of INTA-strategies is a board of directors, which is made up of several members:

> "First, there are the president, the legal representative of the INTA, the vice president and the representative of the Ministry of Agriculture. These three are appointed directly by the President of the nation, and then there are several members representing the different agricultural associations of the country […] well, these are the big organizations, […] and then there are two more members from the national universities […]. The advisory board approves everything that we are working on, the projects, the plans."[27]

In addition to state representatives, the INTA is, thus, overseen by university representatives and various business associations, actor groups that have also participated in the conceptualization of the PEA, excluding different exploited and marginalized groups that may have an interest in alternative kinds of policies.

Summary

The outlined governmental strategies rest upon a belief in capitalist growth and upgrading as an engine for sustainable socioeconomic development. They are predominantly oriented at niches and competitiveness, and they remain respectful of prevailing relations of capital power. The questions of who benefits and who loses out remain widely excluded. State actors mention various challenges, but the problem-solving approaches remain conditioned by a technocratic belief in the feasibility of socioeconomic change via top-down innovation and educational advancement. At the same time, social conflicts, power relations, and other obstructions of a socially and environmentally sustainable catch-up-industrialization are omitted.

27 Interview with three representatives of the INTA, May 05, 2015, Buenos Aires.

The PEA widely uses GVC concepts to design strategies that are primarily tailored to particular (corporate) interests.

This contradicts the GVC approach's take on states as actors concerned with the well-being of all, engaging "local firms assimilating new knowledge and improving employment conditions, with appropriate policies and institutions to facilitate economic, social and environmental upgrading" (Gereffi et al. 2015, 22). This assumption of states as neutral actors who generally promote consensus among all social actors to ensure harmonious growth neglects existing class structures and corporate interests strongly represented in the case of the PEA.

The next chapter analyzes corporate strategies on GVC development and revisits the issue of the state with respect to the question of how agribusiness associations in Argentina have lobbied to push through their particular interests vis-à-vis the state—an issue that demands rethinking capital- and state-led upgrading as a development strategy.

8. Corporate Strategies—Business Associations on GVC Development

When applying for interviews with agribusiness associations in Argentina, I expressed my interested in agro-industrial GVC development with a specific focus on learning more about the strategies of different actors within these chains. In general, I found that the representatives I interviewed responded to and referenced the value chain metaphor very positively. Companies are designated in the mainstream value chain literature as key carriers of upgrading and thus believed to engender development, as I have sketched out in previous chapters. However, it has hitherto rarely been featured how economic and political-ideological strategies of business actors in general and of agribusiness advocates in Argentina in particular can be understood as corporate expressions of the GVC upgrading paradigm. Chain research has paradoxically paid little attention to how businesspeople use its concepts. On these grounds, closer empirical attention needs to be paid to the question of how strategies on GVC development are actually defined in the corporate realm.

Within the scope of my work on an empirical ideology critique of the upgrading paradigm (see Chapter 2), this chapter thus shifts the focus to the empirical world of industry federations' competitive strategies. More precisely, it considers the strategic approaches of the Argentinian Soy Chain Association (ACSOJA), its equivalent for wheat, ArgenTrigo, as well as various of their member organizations that represent firms in different chain nodes.[1] It thereby carves out how they interpret agro-industrial value chain development and depict problems regarding their roles within these chains. At the same time, it draws attention to implicit assumptions and omissions, such

1 Since they are operating in related areas, the members of both chain-associations partially overlap. The same is true for other chains, e.g. maize, which are not specifically considered in this context. Suffice it to say that they cooperate and work in very similar ways.

as obstructions or contradictions that are blanked out in the identified narratives. This includes a focus on how these agribusiness actors address value chain development from a class-biased perspective, meaning that they approach the matter from the ideological location of capital's vested interests.

Following on the discussion of the GVC upgrading paradigm in Chapter 3, this analysis is inspired by research which has found that, although the GVC literature includes factors within and outside firms which may enable or block upgrading (Kaplinsky and Morris 2001, 78), advocates of the upgrading paradigm tend to neglect the imperatives of intra-capitalist competition inherent to the capitalist relations of production (see Selwyn 2016a). In this respect, (power) relations among firms are not only shaped by forms of coordination, but more concretely by capital strategies to control production and exploitation in the most lucrative ways and by struggles over surplus value. This may well entail intra-firm cooperation, for instance, to work around adverse effects of anarchic competition or to gain a stronger position vis-à-vis state institutions. Yet it calls into question the *general* possibility of molding relations among capitalist firms such that barriers are removed and upgrading is enabled for everyone. This chapter demonstrates that relations within the capitalist class can be "collaborative and antagonistic" (Campling et al. 2016, 1751) at the same time.

The first part examines upgrading strategies as they are discussed by the above informants (8.1). I depict how they have arranged for a common practical approach to agro-industrial development, pushed by chain-wide organizations that unite business groups operating along grain and oilseed value chains. For them, the value chain is not only an analytical tool but also a level of manufacturing a "gradual perception of common interests" and "organizational structure(s) to advance these interests," to borrow Wallerstein's (1975, 370) words. The second part discusses limits and barriers to upgrading as they are explicitly or implicitly addressed by my interlocutors (8.2). Based on Gramsci's analysis of the historical work ("Wirken") of ruling classes not only in the economic sphere in the strict sense but also in political and ideological arenas (see Chapter 2), Section 8.3 discusses how business federations have aspired with some success to strengthen particular discourses on agribusiness in the public sound space and to broaden their say in Argentinian politics.

This chapter adds to critical debates on GVC upgrading and to a scrutiny of capital-centered development in that it, first, identifies economic and political-ideological strategies proposed by corporate actors, who consider themselves drivers of value chain development in the empirical world. Second, it discusses how their interests may shape or confine upgrading beyond the company level. Third, it indicates how business agents use the value chain concept from the standpoint of vested interests, which may differ from socioeconomic development in the chains' peripheries as envisaged in GVC literatures. Thus, it confronts the theoretical aim of firm-led GVC upgrading with the reality of its interpretation by business actors.

8.1 Organized value chain development for everyone? Interests, obstructions, and omissions

Similar to the first appearance of GVC concepts in governmental strategies in the new millennium, the value chain construct started gaining importance for Argentinian agribusiness associations at around the same time. Since then, Lucas, whose organization UIFRA groups pasta companies, says,

> "people have started to talk of chains. Only recently. [...] Lately, the government has started to call us in as a chain. When it wants to take wheat-related measures, it doesn't call only the millers; instead it summons the entire chain. So, the chain issue is fashionable."[2]

In practical terms, individual industry federations that operate along grain and oilseed value chains have started to group in larger associations, as my examples of ACSOJA (founded in 2004) and ArgenTrigo (founded in 2007) illustrate. According to the latter's representative Diego, organizing as a chain is a crucial condition for the success of agribusiness:

> "You have to start analyzing how to improve competitiveness. [...] When you go out to bargain and compete, then you have to think more chain-like than individually. [...] What is individual is individual, but it is important to understand that there are issues that affect all of us, right? [...] There are issues which we have to take on as a chain."[3]

ACSOJA and ArgenTrigo have materialized this position in chain-wide business associations that aim to reinforce the economic and political influence of agro-industries in Argentina. In other words, their aim is to forge alliances among individual capitals in order to assert common concerns or dominant interests within the chains more effectively (see 8.3). With this conscious

2 Interview with a representative of UIFRA, April 27, 2016, Buenos Aires.
3 Interview with two representatives of ArgenTrigo, May 12, 2016, Buenos Aires.

"alignment of forces" (Wallerstein 1975, 370), they are an empirical expression of political class-formation.

Both institutions declare that they seek to consolidate agribusiness as the "most important sector in the economy, projecting a future characterized by sustainability, competitiveness, and growing value added."[4] The following sections detail how they seek to achieve this aim through, inter alia, proper chain coordination, scientific progress, a further development of (bio)technology, commercialization strategies for international markets, upgrading to new related chains, and by fighting for a facilitating political background.

Chain coordination and institutional learning

ACSOJA and ArgenTrigo attach a similar importance to promoting agro-industrial value chain upgrading as an engine for national economic and social development. It is their stated goal to "add sustainable value,"[5] to the benefit not only of the direct chain constituents but also of the society as a whole, "if we all work together."[6] On closer examination of the addressed 'all,' the subject of this development is confined to an agribusiness-related "coordination between private actors, the scientific-technological sector, finance, and the public sector."[7] While workers and subalterns remain outside of this conception of the subject of progress, they are considered as objects of socioeconomic enhancement: ArgenTrigo's official strategy includes the "generation of development and jobs in all the territories," and thus "the success will be the success of everyone." In this context, value chain development is also associated with the development of peripheral areas: "We know that our sector has the possibility to generate rapid growth and that this growth has a favorable impact on the whole society, because it facilitates development within the territories themselves," ACSOJA and ArgenTrigo stress in a joint press release, and "the value chains have to be the pivot for this transformation."[8]

Different suggestions are put forward on how to achieve this, many of them broadly reflecting the above-discussed idea of institutional learning in GVCs (Chapter 4). ArgenTrigo-representative Diego contends that using the

---

4 http://www.acsoja.org.ar/quienes-somos/ last accessed May 26, 2022, own translation.

5 http://www.argentrigo.org.ar/2014/asociacion.php, last accessed May 26, 2022, own translation.

6 http://www.argentrigo.org.ar/2014/pdf/4CadenasEnExpoagro_consolidado.pdf, last accessed May 26, 2022, own translation.

7 Ibid.

8 Ibid.

chain concept to this effect "means that we have to diminish transaction costs and align all the actors involved so that the chain can be competitive vis-à-vis a demand that is very differentiated, and we need people who interpret this information and disseminate it along the chain." A concrete example he mentions is the multinational food company Bimbo, which is headquartered in Mexico City. It helps coordinating the chain and serves local producers to learn by fleshing out its wheat demand and sharing the knowledge with primary producers: "These are the actors we're trying to use so that they tell us [what/how to produce]." Diego goes on to say that "you need role models for innovation," and he proposes following Bimbo's example, for instance, in "exporting pastry for empanadas." To achieve that, "we need trainings, science, and support for new SMEs [Small and Medium Enterprises]."[9]

Resembling what Werner (2018, 2) has depicted as GVC studies' "predilection for exploring the largely beneficial effects of linking supplier firms and regions to contracting chains coordinated by multinational corporations," Diego's suggestion contains the implicit assumption that large corporations seek to coordinate value chains in a way that allows actors lower down in the hierarchy to learn and upgrade. Accordingly, he says,

> "the most interesting thing about having a chain is that large parts of its links start learning [...] you say, well, which wheat will I seed, who is going to be my buyer [...] what do they want? [...] This should improve the functioning of the chain because all actors win. It's a win-win, isn't it?"[10]

Carlos, a chief economist at the grain stock exchange in Buenos Aires, describes the importance of chain-wide organization in a similar manner:

> "A chain [organization] works on the problems that arise from linking along a chain without coordination, let's say, and it achieves improvements in competitiveness, information, access, and transaction costs. Just like it says in the corresponding literature, right?"[11]

In short, they argue that in a transparent, well-coordinated and innovative chain, the competitive positions of all actors can be improved; in other words, everyone can upgrade.

However, this idea of proper chain coordination, which helps local producers to learn and upgrade, as an engine for regional development is based

9 Interview with two representatives of ArgenTrigo, May 12, 2016, Buenos Aires.
10 Interview with two representatives of ArgenTrigo, May 12, 2016, Buenos Aires.
11 Interview with an economist at the grain stock exchange in Buenos Aires, May 26, 2016, Buenos Aires.

on a myopic understanding of corporate agency. The belief that, for example, the demands of buyers are primarily an opportunity for local producers to improve their performance rests on the tacit premise that lead firms in GVCs generally have an interest in coordinating the relations among firms to the benefit of other chain actors. As discussed above, such a focus on supplier upgrading tends to abstract from both capitals' systematic interest in exploitation and from intra-capital struggles over surplus value (see Selwyn 2014a). Critical commodity chain analyses have provided vast empirical material that shows how large corporations do not neutrally coordinate, rather control production and distribution in commodity chains according to their profit interests, and that rewards are reaped unevenly (see Quentin and Campling 2018 and early GCC studies discussed in Chapter 3). The contradictory unity of coordination and competitive struggles over surplus value includes core-like capital's attempts and relative capacity to "obtain the lion's share of the profits from the transaction between […] firms" (Nolan, cited in Selwyn 2016b, 14), not just to reduce overall transaction costs. However, such phenomena as well as the possibility that attempts to upgrade within value chains may reproduce "asymmetrical relations between […] different units of capital" (Selwyn 2014a, 261) were not mentioned in my interviews. More precisely, some of my interlocutors in fact gave me examples of how lead firms act to the detriment of other actors in the chain. A frequently mentioned example is the strategy of Chinese companies to purchase raw soybeans instead of processed products (see 8.2), at the disadvantage of companies operating in Argentina. But such criticism is voiced only at very specific instances where respondents stand lower down in competitive struggles themselves. Despite observing such particular stumbling blocks, ACSOJA and ArgenTrigo generally depict value chain development as a way up for everyone. Such contradictions, I suggest, are an expression of the fact that their members by and large benefit from agro-industrial value chain development in Argentina, which is why an upgrading rhetoric that abstracts from concrete political economic power relations suits them, while at the same time they face the pressure of global capitalist competition and, thus, problems that deviate from the overall story.

Promoting competitive advantages through process upgrading

When it comes to concretizing what is meant by GVC development, a first action that ACSOJA and ArgenTrigo perceive as necessary is ongoing process upgrading at the point of primary production to counter declining yields. Above all, this refers to the further development of the productive forces, including modern patterns of organizing production based on management techniques.

As Gras and Hernández (2016b, 126 ff.) have highlighted, business associations in Argentina have promoted technology development as a strategy that goes beyond relying on differential rents based on the possession of fertile soils. Here, differential rent refers to "the result of varying productivity of equal capital investments on equal land areas of different fertility" (Marx 1991 [1894], 812). In other words, it is determined by "the difference between the yield of capital invested on the worst, non-rent-bearing land, and that of capital investment on better land" (ibid.). Yet agrarian capital can make a surplus profit from a second type of differential rent, when the natural fertility of the soil is increased above average through higher capital investments in the development of the productive forces—or in the GVC vocabulary, through process upgrading (ibid., 813 ff.; see Fernández 2011). The following discusses three main fields of process upgrading highlighted by my informants: technological progress, management techniques, and financial management.

First, my interlocutors regard ongoing investment in technological progress as an essential premise of agro-industrial development. Particular emphasis is placed on bioengineering, especially the development of new resistant seed varieties, and on crop protection via precision farming based on drone and satellite technology.[12] Drones, for instance, are thought to apply pesticides according to information collected from remote sensing. All in all, the GMO-based production model is endorsed but productivity needs to be constantly improved.

Agribusiness federations have complained that this need for process upgrading is because harvest yields tend to stagnate in Argentina while expenses on agrochemicals and other production costs have skyrocketed. As a representative of the SRA (Argentine Rural Society, an influential association of large landowners founded in 1866) puts it, the "soil fertility is decreasing [...] The levels of phosphorus that we have in the Pampean region are decreasing sharply."[13] One problem mentioned, which makes

12 Information extracted from a PowerPoint presentation forwarded to me by ACSOJA-representatives.

13 Interview with a representative of the SRA, August 7, 2014, Rosario.

the technology improvements necessary, is the soil leaching effect of soy-monocropping.[14]

Interestingly, thus, while environmental and health effects of the currently dominant agribusiness model are, if mentioned at all, attributed to individual misconduct by particular farmers, my interlocutors clearly acknowledge that it is reaching its limits in terms of economic growth. Much research has shown how productive forces under the existing social relations of production easily turn into socially and ecologically "destructive forces" (Marx and Engels 1976 [1846], n. p.; see Foster et al. 2010; Malm 2016; Stache 2017). This is not always an immediate threat to capital itself, provided that the destruction of nature does not instantly threaten accumulation. But in Argentinian agribusiness, soil leaching has become such a threat. And thus, while on-site studies have long analyzed environmental effects of biotechnology-based large-scale agriculture without being acknowledged by corporate actors (Alonso et al. 2014; Ávila-Vázquez and Difilippo 2016; Paganelli et al. 2010; Pengue 2005; Rodríguez and Jacobo 2010; Sarandón and Flores 2014), agribusiness associations now tackle the problem because it is setting a limit to their accumulation interests: the exhausted soils do not produce the desired results.

However, this does not mean that they aim to change anything fundamental. Instead, the targeted solutions, i.e., process upgrading as listed above, are based on the current agribusiness model. Thus, they remain strongly committed to the concerns of large-scale farmers and companies whose profits are tied to doing business with GM-seeds and accompanying chemicals. Such companies, including Monsanto/Bayer, Syngenta, BASF, among others, are themselves organized in federations that are members of ACSOJA and ArgenTrigo. It would thus be rather surprising if these organizations were to advocate sustainable solutions to agriculture development.

14 From the point of view of most of my interviewees, soy-monocropping was caused by commercial policies under the Kirchner administration, which did not make crop rotation profitable (see Section 8.3). Yet stock-exchange economist Hernando adds that capital interests in soy production have not been unimportant in this context. With the growing influence of *pools de siembra* (see Chapter 6), large-scale production has mainly taken place on leased land and thus "the soy producer has not been so preoccupied with sustainability." Due to high rents and profit expectations, producers reduced "investments in everything that has to do with long term crop protection. And well, this has generated a stagnation of yields per ha" (Interview with a representative of the grain stock exchange in Rosario, August 12, 2014, Rosario).

It is important to note, though, that this is not due to a lack of alternative forms of production that could be considered. Studies on agroecology, for instance, have long been gaining momentum not only in eco-socialist movements or NGOs, but also as a scientific discipline. One main argument is that it does provide a potential for the optimization, though not short-term maximization, of yields (Altieri 2018 [1995]; Pretty et al. 2003; Silici 2014). But such considerations do not play a role for the kind of biotechnological innovation for which ACSOJA and ArgenTrigo have advocated. Furthermore, the fact that some organized small farmers on the ground have opted for agroecology also goes tacitly ignored. One example are members of La Vía Campesina (a worldwide organization that groups peasants, small farmers, landless, indigenous people, and rural workers). Their critique of exploitative social relations and environmental effects of capitalist agribusiness does not entail a fundamental opposition to technological change. Feminist and small-farmer activist Celina, for instance, states that "of course, we also want productivity to progress and work to become easier, but these changes must not be aimed at enriching individuals."[15]

Thus, while alternative forms of enhancing processes in agriculture have not won out against the dominant agribusiness forces so far, it is nevertheless erroneous to say that the latter has been without alternatives—unless the focus of production is on quick maximum profits and not on the needs of humans and nature (see Giarracca and Palmisano 2013).

Management techniques represent a second instrument used to upgrade processes and thereby strengthen the global position of Argentinian grain and oilseed producers. One private organization to disseminate these techniques to primary producers is AACREA, the Argentine Association of Regional Consortiums of Agricultural Experimentation. Aside from its political-ideological work (see Section 8.3), this influential organization instructs farmers on how to draw a comparative advantage from cutting edge technology and management techniques rather than merely relying on differential rents based on the possession of fertile soils (Gras and Hernández 2016b, 126 ff.). In an interview, AACREA representative Renerio repeatedly drew my attention to the importance of management techniques:

"In reality, it seems to me that the important thing in Argentina apart from that [biotechnology and no-till farming] was the administration of the business itself. Business man-

15 Interview with a member of the CLOC–La Vía Campesina, April 13, 2015, Buenos Aires.

agement [...] The advantage that we have here is that the multinationals are investing a lot of money in technology in Argentina [...] and management is part of adapting to these changes [...] People lease-in land and machinery. I do too, and you can mismanage [...] but if you are able to do it well, that is the big difference that allowed for big Argentinian companies to emerge, which used to be very small."[16]

This and similar statements in my interviews convey the notion that anyone can succeed in doing agribusiness—even without possessing capital—if he/she is a proficient manager. What goes unquestioned in such assessments is how management techniques usually go hand in hand with an increased grip of large capitals on agriculture, which rely on managers to mediate their interests on the ground (see Gras and Hernández 2016b). Furthermore, the fact that agribusiness companies do not possess parts of the constant capital (machinery and land) does not imply that the latter is unimportant for production. Instead, investments in machinery and related economic risks are often outsourced to small capitalists, while large capital organizes and controls the production process with the help of management skills (see Chapter 9 for an in-depth analysis and Campling et al. 2016 on the role of managers from a class-analytical view).

As a third and related form of process upgrading, ACSOJA and ArgenTrigo attach great importance to financial management. First and foremost, they aim at strengthening futures markets as "a fundamental tool that enables large investments from different sectors."[17] Simply put, these are contracts for the future delivery of commodities at previously agreed prices. As my informants argue, they can be used by primary producers or traders as tools for hedging transactions or to control price risks. Futures are often also supposed to generally increase commodity prices. According to the United Nations Conference on Trade and Development (UNCTAD), soy and wheat are among the commodities for which futures prices indeed play a particular role in affecting local market prices (Berndt and Bernhold 2018, 39; UNCTAD 2011, 7).

Critics, however, have pointed to the problem that, especially in deregulated futures markets, speculation has led to an increasing price volatility

16 Interview with a representative of AACREA, August 27, 2014, Buenos Aires.

17 http://www.argentrigo.org.ar/2014/pdf/CuatrocadenasenExpoagro2015.pdf, last accessed May 26, 2022, own translation.

with which smaller producers in particular have problems in dealing.[18] Studies on similar cases have furthermore shown that large traders and agribusiness companies are generally more successful at reaping the profits of such instruments than small producers (Höffler and Owuor Ochieng 2009). The presentation of futures markets as a risk prevention tool that allows primary producers to upgrade thus factors out how it may also abet processes of unequalization and capital concentration at the point of primary production.

In view of the GVC upgrading debate, the present discussion of proposals for process upgrading has so far identified two generally crucial points to consider. First, one must examine how the specific forms that upgrading may take depend on the prevailing social forces moving them forward, as demonstrated by the example of (bio)technology development, which is in the interest of large-scale farmers as well as seed and agrochemical corporations. Second, strategies for process upgrading considered by business actors may conflict with the consideration of possibilities for a progressive development of the productive forces, which is not primarily thought to serve large capitals' interests.

Factoring out such considerations, ACSOJA and ArgenTrigo portray themselves as pure modernizers that are not just keen to be at the cutting edge of (bio)technology and business management: "Today the producer uses genetics, high added value [...]. Today it is much more complex. You have the whole chain [...]. It is a well-managed network."[19] In this vein, they also seek to move attention from simple agriculture to agro-industrial global value chains that offer development opportunities by "promoting and fostering the generation of value added."[20]

Climbing up the chain for development

The fact that Argentina has already succeeded in becoming an important player not only as an exporter of soybeans but also in the soy processing industry is often positively raised in my interviews. However, ACSOJA and ArgenTrigo consider further functional and chain upgrading important and

18 https://www.oxfam.de/system/files/281112_nahrungsmittelspekulation_fragen_und_antworten_final.pdf, last accessed May 26, 2022.

19 Interview with two representatives of ArgenTrigo, May 12, 2016, Buenos Aires.

20 Information extracted from a PowerPoint presentation forwarded to me by ACSOJA-representatives.

define different goals that are similar to those stated in the above discussed governmental strategy (Chapter 7). First, this concerns a further expansion of on-site processing industries. Second, the primary focus is on expanding exports. The overall goal is thus to foster an export-led industrialization of agribusiness products.

As regards the first point, the analyzed associations most prominently express the need to leverage Argentina's potential to become a leader in bio-economy and foodstuff production. This way, the country could generate "hundreds of products derived from flours and oils, and thus create more value and the consequent sources of labor."[21]

With respect to food production, particular attention is paid to a modern meat industry that does not rely on pasturage for animal feed but which instead uses grain proteins. Although globally "people with increasing purchasing power have the capacity to eat chicken and pork," Alfredo bemoans, "in Argentina, the only thing that has really grown so far has been soy."[22] Luis seconds that "we have to develop pig, poultry, and beef cattle chains."[23]

Concerning bio-economy, the potentials of increasing the production of biofuels and bioplastics are highlighted. In 2019, Argentina was already a top exporter of biodiesel, the production of which is mainly dominated by the same companies that control the soy processing industries.[24] Yet according to stock-exchange economist Carlos, there's more to it:

> "Bioplastics [...] The demand for products from the field, natural resources, will be increasingly important and will have more and more uses. Then, to see Argentina 10, 15 years ahead as a supplier of flours and oils for food, is to see only a small part of the picture, because there will probably be much more industrial demand for these other products."[25]

Cristian, representative of the Argentine Biodiesel Chamber (CARBIO), adds that "every new industry is always a huge engine upstream or downstream,

---

21 http://www.argentrigo.org.ar/2014/pdf/4CadenasEnExpoagro_consolidado.pdf, last accessed May 26, 2022, own translation.

22 Interview with a representative of ACSOJA, August 7, 2014, Rosario.

23 Interview with a representative of the bank association ABA, August 26, 2014, Buenos Aires.

24 Both CARBIO and CIARA-CEC, a business association that groups large oilseed processors and grain traders, group oligopolistic corporations, some of which operate in both the vegetable oil complex and biodiesel industries, including AGD, Bunge, Cargill, Louis Dreyfus, Glencore, Molinos Rio de la Plata, and Vicentin (http://carbio.com.ar/index.php/integrantes/; https://www.ciaracec.com.ar/ciara/Institucional/Asociados, last accessed May 26, 2022).

25 Interview with an economist at the grain stock exchange in Buenos Aires, May 26, 2016, Buenos Aires.

either because new industries are created, in this case the catalyst industry, or also new services [...]. You have to generate new know-how, new skills and... thus new virtuous circles are generated, right?"[26] He mainly refers to the production of both glycerin (a biodiesel by-product) and the catalyst sodium methoxide. In Argentina, the production of both is dominated by German corporations Evonik and BASF.

In addition to these most emphasized examples for the incorporation of new functions and the expansion of agro-industrial chains in Argentina, business associations state the goal of increasing the local production in their respective industries. With regard to this envisaged quantitative expansion of already existing local production, the Chamber of Agricultural Machinery Manufacturers (CAFMA), which groups Argentinian firms, takes a particular position. In contrast to other interviewees, representative Fabio very explicitly connects the need to expand its production to Argentina's present peripheral insertion into global production:

"Let's see which are the suppliers that sustain this activity [agriculture] and then which are the processing sectors of all that and there you have the value chain [...]. This is what allows us machinery manufacturers to be in a position which allows for expectations, right? [...] If we are a country that has to buy the seeds outside, if we have to buy the fertilizer and the machinery, ultimately others will reap the real profit of our business."

In this context, he goes on to criticize that international competitors who "count on a high level of technological development in all of their machines," have too easy of a time in Argentina. For instance, the government has promoted machines made in Argentina, but Fabio bemoans that even John Deere's machinery partly counted as national production. As mentioned before, CAFMA estimates that only 20 percent of the US company's machinery labeled 'Argentinian production' is actually produced within the country. It rather imports semi-finished parts that are then assembled on site. "If I bring in machines from a multinational company, and I put the same financing conditions on it, [...] I give public resources to a multinational company that in fact does not need them."[27]

Fabio's concern about Argentina importing means of production instead of producing them on site arises from the fact that local production of machinery is the very economic basis of companies organized in CAFMA.

---

26 Interview with a representative of CARBIO, June 6, 2016, Buenos Aires.

27 Interview with a representative of CAFMA, May 13, 2016, Buenos Aires.

However, he expresses a minority position within the analyzed agribusiness associations. In contrast to his critique, other interviewees who aim to expand production in their respective industries do not problematize the origin of the means of production they use. In response to my explicit question, Dalina says that the technology used in the milling industry is partly imported from China but mostly from Europe.[28] In the same vein, CARBIO answers that, with some exemptions, the technology used in the biofuels industry is imported from Germany, Belgium, or the USA. The chamber stresses that "local suppliers provide engineering, assembly and ancillary services."[29] The same is true for the vegetable oil industry, where the means of production mainly stem from the Belgian company DeSmet.[30] However, questions such as, first, where the used constant capital is produced, second, how a part of the value contained in oils, meal, or biofuels is thus produced elsewhere, or, third, whether machinery imports incentivize or impede economic development in Argentina beyond assembly tasks and beyond the gates of individual companies have not been raised by these actors in interviews. After all, in these cases, in contrast to CAFMA, such questions do not have an impact on their own accumulation basis.

Second, as mentioned above, all my interviewees are anxious to expand exports of their respective products and either remain a global leader in selling abroad, as in the case of vegetable oils and meals, or become it to climb up the chain for development. The world market is their main envisaged destination, since Argentina's domestic market does not allow for accumulation on an expanded scale. For instance, the Argentine Milling Industry Federation (FAIM, according to its initials in Spanish) argues that, even if a growing local production of cookies or pastas should increase domestic consumption of wheat flour, "for us, the way towards growth goes through exports."[31] CAFMA, too, seeks to sell Argentinian-made agriculture machinery abroad. Interestingly, Fabio mainly mentions peripheral economies on the African continent as a destination. "We will always have a large domestic market. But in turn, if we win markets outside [...], we will gain in competitiveness [...] in Africa in general we have a huge potential through Argentinian technology."[32]

28 Interview with a representative of FAIM, May 26, 2016, Buenos Aires.
29 Email received by a representative of CARBIO, June 13, 2016, own translation.
30 Interview with two representatives of CIARA-CEC, June 2, 2016, Buenos Aires.
31 Interview with a representative of FAIM, May 26, 2016, Buenos Aires.
32 Interview with a representative of CAFMA, May 13, 2016, Buenos Aires.

A critical note may be slipped in here: judging Fabio by his own argument cited above, i.e., Argentina suffers from its dependency on imported means of production, CAFMA-companies would then capture 'the real profit' in Africa. Ultimately, his criticism of Argentina's peripheral relation to seed, fertilizer or machinery companies is expressed from a capital position that faces difficulties vis-à-vis global competitors. It reaches its limits when it comes to profits gained from shifting the periphery of the chain elsewhere.

To sum up, the proposals for functional and chain upgrading, expanding local processing industries and getting access to global markets—in other words, export-oriented agribusiness industrialization—is commonly regarded the right path to development. As a general remark, a developmental problem that is tackled in the presented strategies of functional and chain upgrading, even if only implicitly, pertains to Argentina's peripheral position within the global economy based on the production of primary products or processed derivatives, which are eventually further processed somewhere else or the production of which is heavily based on capital goods produced somewhere else. However, several issues fall from view when socioeconomic development is easily linked to particular capitals' upgrading in agribusiness in the manner described above.

Contrary to the prospect of development via participation in global markets with industrially processed products, GCC studies on other cases have shown that the success of particular exporters cannot be equated to a process of dynamic economic development. Export oriented industrialization is not per se an indicator of a non-peripheral insertion of countries or regions into global capitalist production and distribution, depending on "the specific linkages that connect industries to global markets and transnational corporations" (Appelbaum et al. 1994, 187; see Kaplinsky 2000, 119; Parnreiter 2013). As described above, for instance, biofuels exported from Argentina are produced with imported high value means of production and thus contain value that was produced elsewhere. Furthermore, the imported constant capital hardly creates incentives for local producers who just assemble the machinery. Most of my interviewees do not take this into consideration as a problem, since it does not affect their firm-level accumulation basis—except for CAFMA, whose concerns, however, do not seem to arise from a general critique of center-periphery relations, but instead from its economic basis, which depends on the capacity to produce means of production locally.

Adding to these qualms, while relying on a global expansion of meat industries and bioenergy is in general problematic from an eco-socialist perspective[33], various scholars in Argentina have questioned the country's particular export orientation and its dependence on the dominant agribusiness-related industries as an overall development strategy. Criticism includes that profits tend to be disproportionally reaped by concentrated multinational capitals. In this context, studies have pointed to the mentioned technological recourse of agro-processing industries to imported technology and related it to profit-transfers to capitalist centers (Romero 2016). Accordingly, the success of a few powerful companies in Argentina is not paralleled by a dynamic and socio-spatially deconcentrated economic development within the country (Azpiazu et al. 2011; Azpiazu and Schorr 2010; Schorr 2013; Schorr et al. 2012). In fact, studies have shown that the development of small capitals, who are often named as major job creators, has been curtailed in Argentina since the 1990s and also under the Kirchner administration (Fernández and Seiler 2016). Finally, Fernández and Ormaechea (2018) have more generally pointed to the fact that an adequate assessment of national development capacities in the periphery implies more than spotting the success of individual firms in individual chains. It requires an integrative understanding of the historical dynamics of global capitalism and ruling-class interests, possible geopolitical, geo-economic, and internal constraints faced by peripheral states, as well as the resulting (lack of) their capabilities to limit the power of concentrated capitals and enable a dynamic development (ibid.). Thus, while the possibility of catch-up development via technology transfer depends on several variables—including capitals' interest in investing in local markets combined with the capacity of states to channel them to create a "territorial assemblage able to compete with more advanced productive forces" (Rolf 2015, 139), as has been possible in the Chinese context (see Liu and Dicken 2006), this cannot be generalized to any political economic context (Quentin and Campling 2018).

However, it is not the aim of this chapter to discuss the Argentinian economy holistically or to sound out possible policies that inhibit big businesses'

33 This concerns both industrialized meat production and the above-mentioned ecological problems entailed by agribusiness, such as the serious lack of nutrients in the soils, compensated for with mineral fertilizers which do not recuperate the organic structure. A critique of animal industries would go beyond the scope of this study. Analyses of how the destructive forces of capitalist production tend to condense in meat industries, including the (over)exploitation of workers, alienation, the systematic destruction of natural bases of life, and the millionfold killing of animals which are capable of suffering and possess tormentable bodies, have been provided elsewhere (Bernhold and Stache 2021, Nibert 2017).

vested interests and allow for a more inclusive economy. The point I rather make here is that the proposals made by ACSOJA and ArgenTrigo for functional or chain upgrading by and large do not impact these issues or only from a limited perspective of vested interests. This includes the quandary that Argentina's peripheral insertion into the global economy does not necessarily change with further industrial production and exports. While referring to development true to the motto 'our growth is good for everyone,' the question who benefits from real existing capitalist agency and who does not, is eventually factored out, unless it concerns particular issues that negatively affect the consulted actors themselves. With a view to the GVC upgrading, I argue: it is precisely because the actors analyzed in this chapter argue from a class position that they do not consider these issues that may contradict general upgrading. This again demonstrates the fallacy of all too easily regarding corporate actors as key players in broad-based development projects.

Social upgrading—a by-product of corporate upgrading?

According to ACSOJA and ArgenTrigo, the described forms of upgrading eventually lead the way to social upgrading. In particular, they refer to job creation, which is presented as an essential result of agro-industrial value chain development. In a joint press release, the agribusiness associations write that in Argentina "the only way to create genuine employment is through the generation of wealth based on an increase in the production of raw materials and its derivatives."[34] This essentially draws on a modernist trickle-down logic according to which (agri)business wealth generation ultimately leads to social development.

In fact, many of my interlocutors repeat a criticism that is widespread among critics of agribusiness in Argentina, according to which the increased mechanization at the point of primary production has diminished employment in rural areas (see Neiman 2010b). SRA representative Eugenio, for instance, explains that farmers today usually do not live in the countryside and hardly create jobs. "Why should I pay employees?", he asks.

"My family has 1,500 hectares in two regions [...] and we use machinery for sowing, fumigation, harvesting, we have three trucks for transport [...] a small part of the staff is permanent, [...] and then we hire people temporarily [...] but the direct occupation in the

34 http://www.argentrigo.org.ar/2014/pdf/4CadenasEnExpoagro_consolidado.pdf, last accessed May 26, 2022, own translation.

countryside has diminished with the soy production [...] I also do not see the middle class or the small producer prospering."

However, along with ACSOJA and ArgenTrigo, he argues that people should not only take primary production into account when evaluating agribusiness' job creation capacity. Instead, the latter lies in the agro-industrial value chains as a whole. "All these people that leave agriculture go to transport, to the processing plants, to services that are important for agriculture."[35] Argentinian agribusiness associations state that more than one third of all jobs created in Argentina can be attributed to agro-industrial value chains. One respondent says that "for each direct employment generated in agriculture, four are generated indirectly." Even if human labor tends to be replaced by machines, he goes on, "someone needs to design it, produce it, sell it, sell related services, so that the change is perhaps going to consist in the composition of [...] employment."[36]

However, according to their own information, the business associations do not generate data on job creation in agribusiness. Their source goes back either to rough estimates or to the above-mentioned study by Llach et al. (2004), according to which 35.6 percent of all employment in Argentina was attributed to agro-industrial chains in 2003. More current data does not exist, they say.

Three main problems may be highlighted about my interviewees' use of this study. First, Llach et al. do not only include grain and oilseed value chains, but also other agriculture industries that are much less mechanized and more labor intensive. ACSOJA and ArgenTrigo, however, identify agriculture with grain and oilseed value chains and use the study's data for a positive portrayal of their branches. Second, Llach et al. have been validly criticized, among other things, for their very broad understanding of indirect jobs (Rodríguez 2006). According to their method, even the labor spent on the production of a TV bought by a trucker who transports soy can be assigned to the soy chain as indirect employment. Applying this method to other chains, most of the jobs in Argentina would be counted twice and

35 Interview with a representative of the SRA, August 7, 2014, Rosario.

36 Interview with an economist at the grain stock exchange in Buenos Aires, May 26, 2016, Buenos Aires.

triple.[37] Third, my interlocutors adopt the notion of indirect employment in an idiosyncratic sense. To illustrate the importance of indirect jobs, they often instance qualitative changes in local labor relations—that is, the outsourcing of rural labor to labor contractors, so called *contratistas* (see Chapter 10). Diego, for example, explains that

> "a majority of the producers do [...] not seed but contract a *contratista* for that, who in turn has employees. [...] So, one thing is direct employment and another thing is total work [...] we are not talking about direct employment but also about indirect jobs, right? Because you need more and more services all the time and these services are not direct employment." [Question: "What kinds of services are we talking about?"] "Transport, *contratistas*, consultancy, the person who controls the quality, all this cannot be in-house, so the issue of services is becoming more important than direct employment."[38]

SRA representative Eugenio more concretely points to the outsourcing of rural labor to *contratistas* as "a strategy to lower labor costs".[39] Yet while this labor is directly spent in agriculture, though the relation to capital is intermediated by *contratistas*, he also lists such services as indirect jobs. Thus, specific forms of rural labor are unduly invoked as an example for the extra job-creation capacity of modern agribusiness.

One exception regarding the depiction of job creation capacities downstream along the value chain is UIFRA, whose representative Lucas regrets the fact that both job creation and the sustainment of small firms in the pasta industry has become increasingly difficult with an advancing technology development. "Technology naturally replaces labor, so if there is no increase in total production... We are working on an increasing consumption, but this is going very slowly... the only faster possibility would be export." His colleague, who appeared during the interview, seconds that "we need more exports, which I think would help, if anything, not to not to destroy jobs and not to create jobs."[40] These two in fact see the contradictions between capital-led process upgrading and the interests of wage-dependent workers. Yet, they remain within a logic of individual capitalist competition: only their export-growth can provide relief.

37 It is valid to study spillover effects. However, Llach et al. (2004) instead only randomly consider industries as multiplier effects of agriculture, which may stand in relation to, but do not exist because of, agriculture.

38 Interview with two representatives of ArgenTrigo, May 12, 2016, Buenos Aires.

39 Interview with a representative of the SRA, August 7, 2014, Rosario.

40 Interview with a representative of UIFRA, April 27, 2016, Buenos Aires.

This discussion is not meant to downplay the number of people working in agro-industrial chains in Argentina. In fact, determining the exact number of jobs is not an easy endeavor. Of data on registered jobs in the private sector in 2014, which I received from the Employment and Business Dynamics Monitoring Centre at MTEySS, I selected all categories that stand in relation to grain and oilseed value chains. Summed up, these jobs account for 9 percent of all registered jobs (see Table 10). However, these data are not accurate. First, they do not count informal labor. Second, some of the activities listed here, such as transport, do not exclusively refer to agro-industrial chains. Third, data can vary according to the source. For the production of agricultural machinery, for instance, the MTEySS counted 12,000 registered jobs in 2014 (see Table 10), whereas the Ministry of Treasury (2016, 24) counted 30,000 "direct jobs." The Agricultural Foundation for the Development of Argentina (FADA, in Spanish) estimates that in 2016, 17 percent of all employment in Argentina's private sector was attributed to all agri-food chains[41] together. Out of this, the institution attributes 35 percent to grain and oilseed value chains (FADA 2017, 9 f.)

However, what becomes evident is how chain-wide agribusiness associations present themselves as promoters of social upgrading via economic growth, based on the job-creation capacity of agribusiness networks, while at the same time, the emphasis put on the latter is clearly not based on well-founded analyses. The sparse substantiation of the data disseminated by dominant agribusiness associations suggests that their discourse on social development pushed by agro-industrial chains stems from an ideological strategy to present themselves in a positive light rather than from an endeavor to determine the real number of wage dependent people making a living in agribusiness. In this context, agribusiness associations have used the value chain metaphor to whitewash their business rather than act on a serious concern for social upgrading.

It is also striking that quantitative job creation is the only concrete aspect of social development that is positively mentioned. Here, the unsaid is revealing. In none of my interviews did interlocutors talk about issues such as economic security or about any other aspects of social upgrading, like social infrastructure, elderly care, labor conditions, gender equality, or income distribution. In other words, their discourse is tailored to quantitative em-

41 This includes oilseed and grain value chains, meat and dairy industries, bio-ethanol and biodiesel production, and other agriculture chains.

Economic activity	Number of registered Jobs in 2014
Seed production	8,129
Production of fertilizers	948
Production of agrochemicals	17,446
Production of agricultural machinery	11,692
Rental of machinery and equipment	6,212
Agricultural services	43,957
Cultivation of cereals and oilseeds	69,279
Storage	7,654
Trucking	144,584
Rail transport	33,638
Maritime transport	5,882
Fluvial transport	3,229
Cargo handling services	9,257
Wholesale of agricultural raw materials, live animals, and processed products	47,238
Wholesale of machines and equipment	14,184
Wholesale of non-specified goods	27,092
Processing of vegetable oils and fats	23,950
Milling	11,940
Starch Production	1,305
Bakery	55,376
Pasta production	10,074
Retail of bread and other bakery products	20,966
Financial services, excluding banks	3,809
Subtotal	**577,836 (9 % of all registered jobs)**
Cattle breeding and milk, wool, and hair production	85,066
Farm production and animal breeding, excluding cattle	13,671
Livestock services other than veterinary services	2,960
Production and processing of meat	69,242
Production of dairy products	35,932
Total	**784,707 (12.2 % of all registered jobs)**
Total registered jobs in Argentina	**6,410,595**

Table 10: Registered jobs in Argentina according to economic activity (2014)

Source: own elaboration based on MTEySS data

ployment only. The only further aspects mentioned are salaries and the right to organize. But, as the following shows, both salaries and unionizing when it is connected to demands on capital made by organized workers are discussed as limits to social upgrading that lie outside capital's responsibility.

8.2 Limits to upgrading

An analysis of corporate approaches to GVC-development as capital-biased does not insinuate that the corresponding actors depict agro-industrial value chain development as a seamlessly straightforward process or that they are blind to limiting factors. This section goes on to analyze the depiction of different disruptions and limits to upgrading as they emerged in my interviews.

Limits to social upgrading

Following on from the previous section, I start with the depiction of the limits to social upgrading. Mostly, when my interviewees detect limits to social upgrading, these are traced back to factors that are beyond any corporate control—a question of macroeconomics rather than of capital-labor relations—and hence lie outside their field of influence. A case in point are poor salaries, which Alfredo depicts as inflation driven: "Salaries are constantly being adjusted to inflation, right? In reality, salaries are not good in Argentina. Inflation is higher than wage adjustment."[42] However, inflation is not the only determinant of wage levels in Argentina. They are also the result of class struggles.

Interestingly, most of my informants depict relations between business associations and labor unions as tranquil, as long as the unions do not demand much. Dalina, Lucas, and Fabio, for instance, explained that

> "negotiations [between companies and unions] often take place here. […] Our federation also participates in some events of the UOMA [the responsible union for the milling industry], and I mean there is dialogue that takes place when there are questions to be resolved. It is carried out in a cordial manner. Yes, obviously there is always a disparity regarding the search for one's interests [aughs] but there is always dialogue."[43]

---

42 Interview with a representative of ACSOJA, August 7, 2014, Rosario.
43 Interview with a representative of FAIM, May 26, 2016, Buenos Aires.

"[The relation between the chamber and the union] is good, it's very good, yes. Super cordial. […] Without a doubt, the union wants the best for the sector. It is not just looking how it can squeeze the sector […] it is aware that if the sector does better, that's also better for them. […] There's a friendship besides having a professional relationship."[44]

"They [the companies] have a commitment with the community […] they buy things in the same supermarket, go to the same club, their children go to the same school… so there is a social commitment […]. And also the relationship with the union tends to be very good. What happens is that the union, the metalworker's union, knows that it can't push too hard, because then all this reality would fall down."[45]

Where unions are combative, in contrast, some respondents even regard them as a limit to social upgrading. CIARA-CEC, for instance, has a more negative opinion of unions. The association groups high-profit multinational companies with high organic compositions of capital, which face off against one of the most combative unions in Argentina (the Workers' Federation of the Industrial Oilseed Complex, F.T.C.I.O.D. y A.R.A), as I will expand on in Chapter 10. Marcos identifies a problem with the fact that this union affiliates workers in the Rosario port area, while in another export hub further north, San Lorenzo, workers are organized in a different union: "When either of them achieves an enhancement, the other wants it, too." He explains that "the relation [with the union] used to be very good [laughs loudly] […]. Ten years ago it was a fairly quiet relationship, quite easy. When there was a conflict, we talked on the phone and we quickly found a solution… today there are no such things." Julieta agrees that "the oil workers have strong unions that usually get what they ask for, because they have a lot of power of action […] they can easily blockade the entry to the plants."[46] CIARA's negative opinion of organized oil workers is supported by ACSOJA and ArgenTrigo. Alfredo and Diego portray even the large processing companies as downtrodden by unrealistic demands. According to Alfredo, who has a managing position in a soy processing company in addition to his representative function in ACSOJA,

"oil plants, for example, have union pressure, strikes, production stops. The same happens in ports. […] There is a situation with the unions who want more and more, but the prices

44 Interview with a representative of UIFRA, April 27, 2016, Buenos Aires.
45 Interview with a representative of CAFMA, May 13, 2016, Buenos Aires.
46 Interview with two representatives of CIARA-CEC, June 2, 2016, Buenos Aires.

we gain are not more and more. So, the labor cost today [...] is high because there is a lot of constant conflict with the unions in the oil industry."[47]

For Diego, unions are even the drivers of economic concentration (their demands drive small companies into bankruptcy). This omits the fact that small companies are unable to compete with the state-of-the-art technology and the scale of production in the soy processing industry in any case. Furthermore, he believes that unions force companies into employing workers informally: "The labor unions sit down with the large companies and dictate how much the salary will be, and the small company cannot compete, so what happens? It has to have informal workers."[48]

But, in this view, unions are not the only culprits of informality. As Diego argues, it is also reinforced by the Argentinian labor law, which does not create incentives to employ workers formally. If you want to dismiss someone, he explains, you have to pay the person a monthly salary for every year he had worked for you. Therefore, companies are virtually pushed into hiring workers informally. CIARA, however, admits that while on average 20 percent of labor in Argentina is informal, the companies it groups generally employ workers formally—not on their own initiative but rather because the "unions with a lot of power" fought for this.[49]

In conclusion, my interlocutors have not associated limits to social upgrading with corporate strategies. According to their logic, capital is not responsible for doing anything for social development, except for growing. Where limits to social upgrading are depicted, they are located outside capital's responsibility. With an eye to the GVC literature, this poses a question with respect to the supposed carriers of social upgrading. As discussed in Chapter 4, the mainstream social upgrading agenda excludes class conflict from its theoretical framework and regards "public-private-civil society partnerships, as well as regional partnerships involving countries and firms that lead international production networks" as common facilitators of social development, as Gereffi and Luo (2014, 19) put it in a World Bank working paper. As the above discussion of my interviews shows, capital's stance towards such an endeavor, however, can well be indifferent (denying responsibility) or hostile.

47 Interview with a representative of ACSOJA, August 7, 2014, Rosario.

48 Interview with two representatives of ArgenTrigo, May 12, 2016, Buenos Aires.

49 Interview with two representatives of CIARA-CEC, June 2, 2016, Buenos Aires.

With one exception, the analyzed actors have only shed light on the antagonistic relation between capital and labor when unions actively struggle for better salaries or labor conditions. In that case, the agribusiness associations not merely position themselves on the side of capital. They even portray unions and labor rights as limiters to social upgrading, even though (or because) they have fought for higher salaries. This stands in contrast to the social upgrading agenda, which aspires to improvements in the terms of employment, remuneration, worker rights, and the like (Barrientos et al. 2011a).

So, what if companies are not interested in forging the kind of social partnership with organized workers who raise demands that are supposed to yield social upgrading? I conclude that the assumption according to which corporate actors can generally be seen as social partners for achieving social upgrading tends to ignore capitalist imperatives of profit-maximization (see Bernhold 2022). It also neglects that capital may well react in a hostile manner when workers impose their demands on it (see Selwyn 2012, 7) and that firms may not consider themselves responsible for concrete measures for enhancing the social situation of workers.[50]

(Not) interested in upgrading?

Do firms *necessarily* have an interest in functional or chain upgrading at all? The following argues that business interests may rather be opposed to moving 'up' the chain if individual accumulation can be best secured otherwise.

Studies on agrarian change in Argentina have shown how national and international capital investments have enhanced the country's dependence on soy production (Giarracca and Teubal 2008; Gras and Hernández 2013a; Hernández 2009; Martínez Dougnac 2016). Especially the so-called *pools de siembra*, which I have previously described as capital pools for investment in crop farming, have been criticized in this context for pushing a hit-and-run monocropping focused on quickly reaping extraordinary profits and benefitting from high differential rents (Féliz 2014; Gras 2012), at the expense of an economically and ecologically sustainable development. This has also included processes of "accumulation by dispossession" (Harvey 2003, 137 ff.),

50 A question that needs to be discussed elsewhere is how far agribusiness capital's interest in paying higher salaries, for instance, as a material concession in the wake of hegemony building may be diminished by the fact that export industries do not rely on people's purchasing power on the domestic market.

especially in areas where agribusiness is based on the "private appropriation of traditionally common lands" (Féliz 2014, 7). These authors suggest that agribusiness interests have been largely opposed to an economically sustainable and dynamic development in Argentina that seeks to change the country's peripheral role in the global economy. They thus implicitly challenge the depiction of capital as a cross-locational and cross-historical subject of GVC upgrading.

Adding to this, my interviews indicate that the dominance of agribusiness in Argentina has reinforced the contentment of firms and landowners with a logic of rentier capital accumulation and ground rent appropriation. Alfredo, for instance, notes that "the *pool* [*de siembra*] became a group of managers, production in rented fields was common [...] and they really paid a lot for renting the land [...] Well, give me the Dollars and I won't do anything else."[51]

AACREA-representative Renerio, for his part, rightly points to the fact that the opportunities to climb up agro-industrial chains in Argentina have been very much limited to large corporations. He notes that some "big companies that crush soybeans do add a lot of value, but yes, they do it and not the small producer." He questions that there are a lot of investment opportunities in processing for small and medium producers. But he does not say that to discuss the lack of upgrading opportunities as a problem. What he wants to point out in the interview is rather that people should appreciate Argentina's competitive advantage and value the merits of primary production instead of only craving activities downstream in the chains.

> "In reality, the primary producer is adding value... when he plants, he adds value, doesn't he? Putting in a soybean seed... everyone thinks that this doesn't add value, but it has a lot inside: it has genetics, it has a lot of people working on it, it has a lot of experimentation and so on [...] he is actually already adding value, you know? It's a bit more philosophical... but it's true."[52]

However philosophical this statement—the economic value of GMO-seeds is not produced and appropriated by Argentinian farmers but by companies upstream in the chain. Nonetheless, Renerio has a point when he says that value is generated in capitalist agriculture. Both in policy-oriented GVC literature and in my interviews, value is often understood as something

51 Interview with a representative of ACSOJA, August 7, 2014, Rosario.
52 Interview with a representative of AACREA, August 27, 2014, Buenos Aires.

that is somehow added with every step of production appended to primary products. This ignores that, first, in any capitalist industry, including agriculture, capital appropriates the surplus value produced by workers, and that, second, some capitals are able to appropriate greater shares of the total social wealth produced than others. However, this is not what Renerio wants to point out. He instead uses his statement that agriculture, too, produces value, to level down the importance of functional upgrading in Argentina beyond primary production. Furthermore, by mingling activities from bioengineering to farming into the term primary production, he overlooks the question as to which capital fractions in the chain have the relatively strongest capacity for controlling the hubs of production and appropriation of value.

These considerations on firms' possible disinterest in functional or chain upgrading lead back to Ponte's and Ewert's (2009, 1638 f.) argument that the way up in global value chains may not always be the best option for local companies, since "lower value products sold in larger amounts may be the most profitable strategy for some firms, at least in the short term." These authors seek the most profitable solution for "developing country firms," which can at least temporarily include "dynamics that would otherwise be termed 'downgrading' in the GVC literature" (ibid., 1637). I, in contrast, emphasize here that capital (dis)interests may be a structural, though time- and space-specific, hindrance to functional or chain upgrading as a development strategy that not only serves individual short-term accumulation interests but also alters the insertion of peripheral actors and regions into commodity chains. The argument, here, is not that economic development is a question of attitude in the first place. As posed before, the question of how actors or regions can profit from capitalist development at a particular point in time depends on an interplay of cyclical developments of capitalism, global and local political economic class dynamics, and related state capabilities (see Campling et al. 2016; Fernández and Ormaechea 2018). Inspired by André Gunder Frank, however, I find it essential in view of the GVC upgrading paradigm to consider that capital operating in peripheries may not only be outmatched by global players or lack (state) incentives. Firms may also not be *interested* in altering the functional integration into global capitalism when individual accumulation is "economically fed and politically sustained" (Frank 1973, 129, own translation) by the status quo. With an eye to firm-upgrading as a development strategy, the possibility must be considered that locally dominant capital fractions may see no need to change the local composition of economic activities. This adds to the reasons why the reliance on capital as a subject of equalizing development is problematic. A GVC-theory that abstracts from concrete capital (dis)interests is likely to result in illusive assumptions about capital-led development.

Geo-economic and -political limits to upgrading

Chapter 4 discussed critiques of the GVC framework that point to capitalist centers' geopolitical and geo-economic strategies and their importance for understanding the shaping or the lack of development at the periphery (see Fernández and Ormaechea 2018; Glassman 2011). Below I discuss how geo-economic constraints appear on the radar of the agribusiness actors analyzed in this section.

In reflecting upon growth opportunities for soy and wheat processing industries in Argentina, many business associations address the problem that 'their' companies are globally competitive but at the same time face idle capacities, which cannot be remedied due to a limited domestic market and a lack of export opportunities. As Lucas expounds, "we should be behind Brazil, which is the largest pasta industry in Latin America. [...] And why are we in zero export? It's crazy."[53] Similar issues are raised by local biodiesel and oilseed-crushing industries. The latter belongs to the most competitive industries of this kind worldwide. But, as Julieta explains, it deals with an average of 30 percent in spare capacity. She explains that the companies involved had expected consistently higher soy harvests when they built the plants.[54]

On-site counter-strategies to prevail against oligopolistic competitors in the capture of commodities for further processing have alleviated but not solved this problem in the oilseed processing industry. AGD, for instance, is now vertically integrated in soybean chains in order to forge closer relations with primary producers and enlarge their base for procuring raw materials. It has invested in in-house soybean production and storage, and in a railway for transport.[55] With the same goal, the grain and oilseed dealers and processors Nidera (bought by the Chinese COFCO in 2014, which sold the

53 Interview with a representative of UIFRA, April 27, 2016, Buenos Aires.
54 Interview with two representatives of CIARA-CEC, June 2, 2016, Buenos Aires.
55 Interviews with a representative of ACSOJA, August 7, 2014, Rosario and with a representative of the grain stock exchange in Rosario, August 12, 2014, Rosario.

seed business to Syngenta/ChemChina in 2018) and Luis Dreyfus have become traders of seeds and agrochemicals, since "this was an opportunity to generate a proximity to the supplier of primary products."[56] These individual strategies to secure production are compounded by calls on the government to facilitate inflows of primary products from surrounding countries.[57]

However, my interview partners stress that their overcapacity problem exceeds the scope of local competition or access to inputs. More important constraints are seen, especially in the long run, in geo-economic and -political barriers that are set elsewhere. Here, China and the EU are most prominently mentioned. As regards the first, business actors are concerned by China's policy to buy raw soybeans instead of processed derivatives, despite the fact that

> "the costs of processing are much lower in Argentina than in other countries. [...] The raw beans go to China and they end up processing them with much higher costs. But well, they have the policy that they crush internally [...]. For now, it isn't a problem. But it could be 10 years from now, because a gigantic industry has been built here, and [...] China is a market that puts a lot of pressure on increasing the trading of raw beans."[58]

> "China used to be one of the main recipients of oil exports, and since 2010, exports have been falling [...]. The Chinese industry has a certain protection, a differentiated import tariff, which favors soybean imports compared to processed products. Then it has internal subsidies and a good promotion of local industries. [...] With regard to meal.... we could also sell to China at a more reasonable price. But China does not buy, and there are estimates that China will become an exporter of soybean meal to the region. It will become a competitor of ours in Asian countries."[59]

Accordingly, China, creates opportunities for controlling core-like activities in soy GVCs, which alarms processing industries in Argentina, who fear the possibility of a re-peripheralization of the country's position in this chain.

In the case of the EU, my interlocutors report politically imposed economic restrictions such as commercial policies designed to protect European processing industries. Diego, for instance, stresses that "many countries are putting barriers to more processed products. [...] They put environmental barriers on the emission of greenhouse gases. This is affecting countries which are more competitive in agriculture and derivatives than the in-

56 Interview with a representative of CIARA-CEC, August 29, 2014, Buenos Aires.
57 Interview with two representatives of CIARA-CEC, June 2, 2016, Buenos Aires.
58 Interview with a representative of the grain stock exchange in Rosario, August 12, 2014, Rosario.
59 Interview with two representatives of CIARA-CEC, June 2, 2016, Buenos Aires.

dustrial countries."[60] CARBIO representative Cristian expounds that the EU applies double standards due to geopolitical interests: "If countries that produce raw materials keep producing very cheap raw materials without giving work to the people, that's ok. They [the EU] don't even notice when we are deforesting. With primary production there is no preoccupation at all with sustainability." Cristian's legitimate point is to see some hypocrisy in socio-ecological claims made by the EU to justify economic barriers against the import processed products. He says: "But when *we* add the value, then the preoccupation with all types of regulations begins... then they ask for environmental issues, which in reality are tariff barriers [...], such as the one that Europe unjustifiably imposed on Argentina."[61] He explains that the EU has levied high import duties on biofuels while imposing none on raw materials. The EU has called this policy anti-dumping duties due to the Kirchner administration's policy of raising higher withholding taxes on raw soybeans than on processed products. Biodiesel industries in Argentina could thus unfairly purchase raw materials at cheaper prices than their competitors. Cristian also states

"When Argentina applies a mirror policy and puts differentiated export tariffs [...] to favor value added at the point of origin, then this is dumping. When they do it to favor the entry of unmanufactured products and add the value at the point of destination, that's fine. There is a great hypocrisy, and the struggle is to see where to add the work, the value."[62]

Alejandro endorses that "the European industry looked for a way to protect itself against an efficient producer and convinced its government to start a dumping investigation. This was an artificial story that generated a huge tariff in Europe and cut off the flow of biodiesel exports to Europe."[63]

In sum, these actors validly criticize geopolitical measures that are designed to protect EU-based industries against competitors and are hypocritically justified with anti-dumping and socio-environmental arguments. It may be critically remarked, though, that uncovering double standards held by the EU does not imply that GMO-monocropping in Argentina and socio-environmental effects are not actually worthy of criticism. The disapproval of hypocrisy, for instance, becomes ideological itself when it is raised from

60 Interview with two representatives of ArgenTrigo, May 12, 2016, Buenos Aires.

61 Interview with a representative of CARBIO, June 6, 2016, Buenos Aires.

62 Ibid.

63 Interview with a representative of CIARA-CEC, August 29, 2014, Buenos Aires.

the standpoint of vested interests with limited concerns for sustainable development and social upgrading, as I have discussed in the precious section.

When it comes to political counteractive measures to these geo-economic and -political barriers, my interlocutors demand that the Argentinian government "protects the local industry so that we generate value and labor here," as Alejandro says. "I think that this is one of the arm-wrestling matches that exist [...] because each of the countries wants to add that value locally and it is important that we defend that here." He goes on to argue that Argentina needs to

> "generate the conditions for the industry to exist here [...]. If buyers insist on processing at the point of destination, we would have to put mirror policies, as we call them here, in a way that [...] does not turn us into suppliers, against the re-primarization of our expectations."[64]

His demand of protective state measures complements ACSOJA's and ArgenTrigo's call on the state to participate in free-trade agreements that benefit Argentina's competitive grain and oilseed industry (this is further discussed in Section 8.3). Julieta, however, questions whether such mirror policies could be easily pushed through from Argentina's geopolitical position. While she, too, argues that the government has to negotiate favorable international regulations "that help us to sell," she complains that "it is very difficult to change their minds. For example, in the case of China, it is very difficult to negotiate China waiving the development of its own industrial sector."[65]

With this, she implicitly points to a general dilemma that arises when political demands on international commercial policies are raised to the level of abstraction from real international political economic power relations. The importance of both international disputes over commercial policies and the geographically differentiated power of states to enact these policies has long been discussed. Scholars have argued that economic actors with a definite competitive advantage "are usually the most enthusiastic advocates of free trade" (Chase-Dunn 1998, 136; see Section 8.3). At the same time, research has unmasked how, throughout the history of the capitalist world-system, free trade policies have included protectionist measures most effectively enforced by core-like states to patronize their own industries, which has re-

64 Ibid.

65 Interview with two representatives of CIARA-CEC, June 2, 2016, Buenos Aires.

inforced geographically differentiated capacities to control production and trade (Shaikh 2006; Wallerstein 2012b). Wallerstein has therefore argued that free trade in the capitalist world system has always been "free-trade imperialism" (Wallerstein 2012b, 142 ff.). Following on these arguments, my interviews underscore that GVC research needs to consider how geopolitical measures and geo-economic power serves to restrict higher value activities at the periphery.

However, more discussion is needed about how exactly the development of such measures is determined within capitalist states. While such an endeavor exceeds the scope of this study, I may briefly highlight an example of how protectionist measures by global powers are not just naturally carved in stone. They may also be contested among core-like capitals and change in conjunction with conflicting interests—not only between Argentina and the EU, but also between industries headquartered in capitalist centers. As the following example succinctly shows, business actors headquartered in the EU, for instance, may themselves have an interest in altering political regulations to strengthen processing industries located in Argentina. After a WTO ruling, the EU massively reduced the above-mentioned anti-dumping duties on Argentinian biodiesel in September 2017. European biodiesel producers have heavily complained about this decision. Elmar Baumann, managing director of the German Biofuels Industry Association VDB, argued in 2017 that "it is a very weak situation that the European Commission and its member states do not see any possibility for effectively protecting the domestic biofuel industry."[66] His association has lobbied for a renewal of the duties. Other German companies, however, have an interest in the growth of Argentina's biodiesel industry and its export capacities. This holds true, for instance, for Evonik and BASF, which run plants in Argentina to produce catalysts for biodiesel production, and which supply agrochemicals for farming.

In summary, the positions formulated by the analyzed associations on geo-economic constraints tackle a problem for their global competitiveness, namely their relatively underpowered positions vis-à-vis global competitors and related commercial policies. This results in a critique of corresponding decisions taken for instance in the EU or in China. Such criticism is voiced in the context of a juxtaposition between different capital's ambitions to

66 http://www.biokraftstoffverband.de/index.php/detail/items/europaeischer-markt-wird-von-unfair-gefoerdertem-argentinischen-biodiesel-ueberschwemmt.html, last accessed May 26, 2022, own translation.

control the core-like activities in agro-industrial GVCs. This adds to calls on GVC research to consider how geopolitical measures serve to restrict higher value activities in the periphery. While a detailed discussion of intra-capitalist struggles over such measures exceeds the scope of this study, I argue that further research is needed to fully grasp the making of geopolitical environments, by taking underlying conflicting capital interests into account. There is an ongoing need not only to reflect on the institutional environments of GVC-development, but also to analyze the political economic context in which these environments are manufactured.

Upgrading only for some? Neglected capital concentration

Critical scholarship on agrarian change in Argentina has studied capital concentration and the wide-ranging displacement of independent units of petty commodity production (Bernhold and Palmisano 2022; Fernández 2013a; Giarracca and Teubal 2008; Girbal-Blacha 2013; Gorenstein and Ortiz 2017) or their inclusion into production networks controlled by large companies (see Chapter 10). The concentration and centralization of capital—though being a matter of "constant social redefinition" (Wallerstein 2000b, 5)—is also a crucial aspect for critical commodity chain analysis. The main argument is that highly concentrated capitals tend to reap relatively great shares of the total produced social wealth, to the detriment of other actors in commodity chains (see Bair 2009, 8). Here, the analysis of monopolization is closely connected to the impossibility of economic equalization within the capitalist world-system (see Chapters 3 and 4).

In contrast, most of the business associations analyzed in this chapter do not regard such tendencies as a problem. Instead, they downplay the issue, justify and naturalize it, or insist that the whole chain is characterized by free competition. Carlos, for instance, says that

"large parts of Argentina's agro-industrial sectors are small and medium enterprises and in many cases family companies." [Question: "In which chain links?"] "Importantly, all chain links operate in free competition or at very low levels of oligopoly. But clearly, they work more in free competition. […] One often hears that there are few companies in the export sector. In reality, when you draw up the indices of concentration, the results never say that the sector is concentrated. [...] At the level of primary production, the largest company does not even have one percent. This is totally deconcentrated."[67]

While Carlos rightly states that the level of concentration at the point of primary production is comparably low, he leaves aside the process of capital concentration over the past decades (see Bernhold and Palmisano 2022; Section 6.2.3). Furthermore, the assurance of free competition in every chain link justifies the political economic status quo in the soy processing industry, for instance, where only a few lead firms compete—leaving unsaid that these capital-intensive enterprises make much higher profits than smaller capitals in the chain. For Carlos, concentration and centralization become a problem only when monopolistic power violates official rules. Other actors state more clearly that there are high levels of concentration and monopolization in some chain links:

"Monsanto is the devil [ABA representative Luis states and laughs loudly] [...] but you have the possibility, if you want, at least in Argentina to look for another seed, another herbicide that is not produced by Monsanto [...]. So I say, I think Monsanto has a political burden above all [...] independently, well, of them being obviously an important player, there is a certain concentration in this type of activities, just like in the financial sector. In the financial sector there are not so many banks, 80 percent of the market must be controlled by ten banks in Argentina, but that's just how it is in the world."[68]

"In the soybean chain, I believe that the positions, speaking of the export sector, I think it is oligopolistic. [...] There are six or eight companies that control the market. If we look at the seeds, there are two companies that control 90 percent of the market [...]. The genetics today are 100 percent Monsanto [...]. So, from this point of view, you might think that it is monopolistic."[69]

Similarly, CIARA-CEC admits that the soy processing industry is largely controlled by concentrated export companies. "The plants that crush soybeans are usually large plants [...] they are always competing with each other to improve the efficiency. They produce a product that cannot afford to stay behind in terms of the incorporation of technology."[70] Yet for these informants, relative monopolization is not a problematic issue either. In the first quote, ABA representative Luis trivializes the matter, proclaiming that calling Mon-

67 Interview with an economist at the grain stock exchange in Buenos Aires, May 26, 2016, Buenos Aires.

68 Interview with a bank employee and representative of ABA, August 26, 2014, Buenos Aires.

69 Interview with a representative of ACSOJA, August 7, 2014, Rosario.

70 Interview with two representatives of CIARA-CEC, June 2, 2016, Buenos Aires.

santo a monopoly is above all politically motivated. For him, there is no real political economic problem and he goes on to portray economic concentration as something that just naturally belongs to "the world," abstracting from the historically specific social relations of production. Instead, in the second quote, Alfredo says more clearly that there are oligopolies and monopolies in the chain, but he does not describe that situation as problematic either. CARBIO representative Cristian, for his part, finds that it is a normal economic process when corporations that already control the soy crushing industry also become the main biodiesel players.

"It is very difficult to compete with someone who already produces oil or has plants with an adjacent port, very difficult [...], these are very big competitive advantages [...]. Those who are producing oil are also operating on biodiesel and glycerin [...] and just like in any industry, economies of scale give you an advantage [...]. It is not the same thing to have a very small plant in the middle of the country, which has to bring the oil from many kilometers away with a very high cost in freight and then send the biodiesel back to the ports."

He goes on to argue that small biodiesel producers "in the middle of the country have their function in terms of [...] industrial development that gives work to people in the area, and so on." However, through the lens of CARBIO—an entity that groups large corporations—small-scale production in the country's interior just does not make sense, because it "has comparatively high costs."[71] The concentration and centralization of capital, here, is examined from the perspective of capitalist rationality as being economically viable.

At the same time, in Cristian's view, small producers are not primarily limited by their incapacity to compete, but by the state. He argues that the use of biofuels on the domestic market is limited by law. Otherwise, small producers in the countryside could serve local markets. This line of argument, however, omits that a larger domestic market would not *necessarily* reverse the trend of the concentration of processing industries under the roofs of a few corporations.

Thus, many of my interview partners either deny the impact of capital concentration or naturalize it. They do not consider the tendency of capital to concentrate as something to criticize, rather they evaluate it from the standpoint of cost-effectiveness. This view factors out the relative economic power held by advanced capitals in relation to other actors or their capacity to win in competitive struggles. In other words, the questions of how con-

71 Interview with a representative of CARBIO, June 6, 2016, Buenos Aires.

centrated capitals benefit unevenly, and to whose detriment, are largely ignored. This might be explained by the fact that the associations mentioned so far speak for actors who belong to the winners of concentration. In contradiction with the idea of capital-led GVC development, these actors do not seem to be interested in unveiling, let alone dismantling, the unequal appropriation of value, unless their own interests are affected.

Lucas' story is a bit different. His association UIFRA maintains a tradition of small or medium-sized family-run pasta companies, and he is concerned that these companies tend to be swallowed up as a result of increasing market concentration.

> "Obviously there are fewer and fewer companies. But in the long run, if you look at the early 90s, there were a hundred and some companies, and today there are 55. [...] This is happening very slowly. But for example, in 2014, Molinos Rio de la Plata bought brands from the company Mondeléz, which used to be Kraft. [...] The brands in Argentina were either Mondeléz or Molinos. [...] Knorr has recently appeared, which is the only brand name [...] comparable to Molinos. Everything else is, let's say, 'everyone for himself'. [...] This year [in 2016], three noodle companies have closed down in crisis. [...] Of those three, perhaps one is a more family-related problem [...] the other two are due to the market context. In other words, they are disappearing, yes."

He goes on to explain how large companies in the sector have been trying to expand their market shares. They "have been selling below cost. They're doing some sort of internal dumping." Yet despite this assessment, UIFRA adheres to individual capitals' increasing competitiveness on global markets as the only possible solution. "There's nothing we can do about it. Because these are situations of supply and demand that are uncontrollable. What can we do about it? Promote exports."[72]

In sum, capital concentration and resulting power asymmetries within nodes of agro-industrial value chains in Argentina are broadly neglected by the analyzed business associations. Only less powerful informants for whom these tendencies have negative effects make more critical remarks. But the latter, too, tend to remain within the logic of capitalist competition (on export markets) as a way of possibly holding out against rivals. State policies to restrict the power of large corporations—among other possible measures—are not addressed as a possibility. The tendency of capital to concentrate lies at the heart of capitalist competition, which impedes a cooperation among capitals in GVCs that is free from antagonistic elements (Campling et al.

72 Interview with a representative of UIFRA, April 27, 2016, Buenos Aires.

2016, 1751). As my discussion underscores, it should thus be part of GVC analyses.

8.3 Manufacturing consent and lobbying for influence in the state

As depicted in Chapter 4, scholars have identified the need for chain analysis to engage with state theory. As a lens for interpreting the political-ideological work of agribusiness associations, the following refers to aspects of the struggles over hegemony within the extended state, in Gramsci's (2012 [1975]-c, 783, own translation) terms, encompassing both the "civil society" and the "political society."

Section 4.3.2 outlined this study's understanding of capitalist states. As a brief reminder: States are understood here as relatively independent political forms of the capitalist social relations and an institutionalization of their inherent struggles between classes and marginalized groups, as well as between fractions of capital. As "material condensation[s] of a relationship of forces" (Poulantzas 2000 [1978], 129) between these social actors, states and their apparatuses are always contested. Yet in historically and geographically specific political economic constellations, the ruling classes have gained control over states, which perpetuate the overall conditions for capitalist reproduction.[73]

Gramsci's notion of the capitalist state includes the (potential) use of force, i.e. domination in the narrow sense, and the organization of consent. His concept of the extended state encompasses this double character of bourgeois rule (Stache and Bernhold 2021). He has suggested that the organization of consent or hegemony cannot be reduced to the state apparatuses, and emphasized the importance of analyzing how hegemony is rooted in

73 This does not mean that bourgeois states are the direct instruments of particular capitalists. They enforce hegemonic projects, which can inhere setting limits for individual capitalists or designing policies fought for by marginalized groups, the historically and geographically specific manufacturing of which depends on both general political economic conditions and the above-mentioned relationship of forces. Yet for as long as the social relations based on exploitation are not effectively called into question by class struggles from below, the political societies necessarily have a bourgeois character. Conversely, the state also uses political, ideological, and coercive means (police, military, etc.) to intervene in struggles in the civil society.

the socioeconomic relations, including the capacity to make material concessions to the subaltern classes. However, the class conflict for hegemony is not confined to the economic terrain. It is also fought on political, cultural, and ideological terrains in the civil society. Here, coalitions among the capitalist fractions are formed, material and other concessions are struggled over with exploited classes and marginalized groups, cultural life, ideas, beliefs etc. are produced, and so on. When stable intra-capitalist coalitions can be built—and when at the same time economic, political and ideological consent is manufactured among the forces in the civil society—Gramsci calls such relative hegemonic alliances a "historical bloc" (Gramsci 2012 [1975]-e, 1228, 1249).

Given its contested character, hegemony can be more or less stable, but it is never sealed. It can be challenged by dissension among the dominant economic actors or by struggles from below by those who do not accept the respective status quo as something naturally given. In this context, economic actors like the analyzed agribusiness associations work in the extended state to maintain or improve their influence therein and to achieve a facilitating ideological and economic policy background that serves their interests.

Hegemony embodied in the extended state (re)produces in historically and geographically specific political economic constellations and with varying stable consensuses. As Fernández and Ormaechea (2018) point out, understanding the building of a historical bloc and corresponding viable strategic projects or agreements upon a general path of development especially at the periphery requires a grasp of how nationally specific processes intertwine with the historical dynamics of global capitalism and the ensuing possibilities for the peripheries, its class dynamics, and geopolitical/geo-economic power relations. This also relates back to Wallerstein's argument that center-periphery relations, geopolitics, and the strength of a state are interrelated matters, such that the odds of upgrading do not merely depend on the capable management of government representatives. According to Fernández and Ormaechea, in Argentina, across import substitution, neoliberal-, and neo-developmentalist approaches, no strong state or historical bloc has emerged with the capability or will to develop a strategic project oriented at fundamentally altering the country's peripheral insertion into the capitalist world system (ibid.). In this particular historical bloc, struggles over the political economic orientation of the state are often remarkably overt. In parallel, the Argentinian sociologist Adrian Piva (2015, 24) has described the local situation as a "weak hegemony" or a "negative consensus,"[74] which is repeatedly and massively questioned by labor struggles, organized unemployed or other protest movements, and on the other hand by capital fractions that try to mold the state to suit their own particular interests.

Building on these remarks, the following sections are not designed as a fully-fledged analysis of hegemony formation in my field of research—which would include a broad study of how the dominant class in Argentinian agribusiness works to generate the approval of the subaltern classes on economic and other terrains. Instead, this chapter discusses how agribusiness associations in Argentina have seeked to gain influence both in the civil society and on state policies, in order to change the political environment and to secure the type of policy sought by the dominant actors within ACSOJA and ArgenTrigo. First, it looks at one particular constituent of hegemony building, namely the creation of unity between different fractions within the dominant class. This includes—to a certain degree—overcoming fractional egoisms, as well as building a common political ideology. Such a framework does not exclude disputes or conflicts about its concrete design (Stache and Bernhold 2021). Thus, I analyze internal consent building and the political alignment of different capitals along value chains, which makes common political action 'as a chain' possible despite existing differences of opinion. I then analyze how corporate actors engage on the ideological terrain to build a counterpoint to anti-agribusiness protests and to gain ideological consent in the broader civil society. After discussing this, I exemplify fields in which ACSOJA and ArgenTrigo have striven for influence on the state.

Contradictory unity in value chain associations

At the beginning of this chapter, I set out that ACSOJA and ArgenTrigo were founded with the aim to forge alliances among companies operating in agro-industrial chains in Argentina. The following shows how different actors endorse their participation in these chain-wide associations, even if some are skeptical about internal power differences and question whether they are gaining any direct economic benefits. At the same time, controversies and potential antagonisms continue inwardly.

All individual member organizations I talked to emphasize that participating in chain-wide associations is crucial for them. The mentioned advan-

74 According to Gramsci, forms of consent can range from "endurance" to active consent.

tages include access to information flows and the possibility of broadening their own sound-space, for instance via contributions at ArgenTrigo-conferences in the presence of media and political decision-makers.

Several interviewees highlight the importance of replacing the "selfish" distrust among competitors with political cooperation. Julieta, representative of the influential grain and oilseed wholesalers and processing industries organized in CIARA-CEC, stresses that ArgenTrigo "seeks a balance, that all sectors are represented and that one does not prevail over the other; this is the logic we are looking for in Argentina." Her colleague Marcos adds in the same interview that "within the entities, there is an equilibrium, although outside it may seem that there isn't."

"We have played a driving role in the organization [...] especially in ACSOJA and ArgenTrigo [...]. We believe that it is very important in that different sectors which normally have opposing interests can sit down at one table: buyers, sellers, and other sectors linked to the business. It allows us to be informed about the problems these other actors face [...] and it is good to know what happens in the other related business areas, because they are our clients, they sell to us, they buy from us, because they have the inputs, etc."[75]

Similarly, Diego and Lisa point to the importance of internal consensus building to strengthen the whole chain:

"Diego: The different links distrust one another. Generally, they do not believe that there is a big advantage at first [...]. But when you start having serious problems like a lack of wheat or lack of quality or you can't export, then they understand that you have to work together.

Lisa: In general, when there is a problem in one of the links, people discover that presenting themselves as a chain they can achieve a better consensus in favor of the chain. It is a kind of demonstration that they are not selfish, as if to say, 'we are for the chain, not just for our portion of the chain'."[76]

The wheat milling industry federation FAIM endorses that ArgenTrigo provides advantages in terms of political representation and as a space for coordinating what is produced and how: "Wheat has different uses, for export, for milling etc. Thus, discussions on what kind of wheat is produced in Argentina are good [...] this is why ArgenTrigo is a necessary space."[77]

75 Interview with two representatives of CIARA-CEC, June 2, 2016, Buenos Aires.
76 Interview with two representatives of ArgenTrigo, May 12, 2016, Buenos Aires.
77 Interview with a representative of FAIM, May 26, 2016, Buenos Aires.

On the other hand, UIFRA in particular, as a less influential member organization grouping small and medium pasta companies, doubts that this form of cooperation brings them economic advantages. Lucas stresses that it is vital for UIFRA to be part of ArgenTrigo, mostly for political reasons: "Now we are the wheat chain, and people talk a lot about that. And it looks good. [...] It strengthens us as an institution and it puts us on the radar." At the same time, however, he stresses that he does not expect a genuine economic cooperation among chain constituents that entails benefits for the pasta industry. "Maybe information [...] but beyond talking to each other, benefits for the concrete business? I don't know [...] No, no, no, no, no, no. The only advantages are political [...]."[78]

For representative reasons and the political importance to appear as a chain, ArgenTrigo was eager to gain UIFRA's participation, according to Lucas. He explains that his organization had to be called 25 times to be persuaded to come to a meeting. "They were obsessed with continuing downstream. And we were the key to that. Because in terms of industrial processing, in the second level of transformation, we are the biggest, together with cookies. So, for them our presence was politically very significant." At the same time, he explains that relations between different companies in the chains have often been antagonistic. One issue he raises is the strength of the milling industry in the wheat chain and its capacity to determine prices, for instance by holding back wheat flour to drive up prices.

> "In fact, we used to fight among the members of the chain. A lot of mistrust and a lot of, uh, like us seeing the other links in the chain not as partners but as culprits of what happens to us. For example, this is very typical in the case of the milling industry. In the wheat chain in Argentina the mills are, I would say, the strongest [...]. They're always in the eye of the storm, let's say."[79]

Before ArgenTrigo was founded, "the truth is that, if there was something that we could do or say against the milling industry, we did say it."[80] Lucas

---

78 Interview with a representative of UIFRA, April 27, 2016, Buenos Aires.

79 Ibid.

80 Ibid.; Manilo, representative of the Argentine Federation of Freight Transport (FADEEAC, in Spanish), which according to Manilo was not asked to participate in ArgenTrigo or ACSOJA, said that this kind of confrontation is still commonplace between them and other agribusiness actors. They complain, for instance, that ACSOJA had published a statement in the newspaper La Nación a couple of days before the interview, putting the transport sector in a bad light by portraying transport costs as being much higher than they really are and, thus, blaming them for high wheat prices. "This is crazy, we are not the ones who set prices [...] don't tell me that freight is the cul-

goes on to explain that such open disputes previously held in the media are now often resolved within ArgenTrigo. "When they realized that they were always being attacked from one side and the other, they reconsidered and started to modify their discourse and to generate a much more pro-chain discourse." He stresses that now, "outwardly, we are all friends. For the people outside. I think it's all right. I think something good came out of it." However, he expresses doubts about the stability of this construct. "When things are going well it's easy [...] when there are complications, [...] we'll see."[81]

In the end, the wheat value chain—here understood as a level of organizing—has been initially promoted by the economically most influential actors within it, who stress both economic advantages and the importance of being publicly perceived as a chain. All member associations agree that despite internal contradictions, cooperation in a chain-wide organizational structure serves them for different reasons. These include representation and political lobbying beyond individual business organizations. Through the building of an internal consensus towards the importance of participating in chain-wide associations, ACSOJA and ArgenTrigo manufactured projects of political class-formation despite ongoing internal antagonisms. As mentioned above, the aim is to assert common interests—or those interests that are dominant within these chains.

Further below this section shows how some of the political claims that ACSOJA and ArgenTrigo have tried to enforce are in fact more in the interest of agribusiness and seed corporations or grain dealers and do not necessarily support, for instance, the further industrialization of wheat. In other words, they de facto serve some interests more than others. Nevertheless, and despite persisting competitive conflicts, working on an internal consensus among actors who all benefit from being part of political chain formation in one way or another, has allowed them to act on the political stage as a chain—countering the image of self-serving agribusiness companies.

Agribusiness on the ideological terrain

Carla Gras and Valeria Hernández (2016b, 17, own translation) have comprehensively analyzed the efforts of agribusiness associations in Argentina to

prit," Manilo's colleague Roberto says. And Manilo seconds that: "For me, this is so otherworldly." (Interview with two representatives of FADEEAC, June 6, 2016, Buenos Aires)

81 Interview with a representative of UIFRA, April 27, 2016, Buenos Aires.

posit the possibility of a sustainable and inclusive "development that goes beyond a mere economic growth" and thus to win over large parts of the civil society as allies. Elsewhere, scholars have analyzed how politico-ideological positions of capital-intensive agribusiness are regularly reproduced in the most influential media in Argentina, including the daily newspapers Clarín and La Nación or their weekly rural supplements, which celebrate agriculture's high-tech solutions or modern network-like farming as opposed to the traditional oligarchy (Berndt and Bernhold 2018; Palmisano 2014). The following section contributes examples of how agribusiness associations engage on the ideological terrain. It is mainly based on interviews and field notes taken during my participatory observation at the 22nd congress (2014) of the Argentinian No-Till Farmers Association (Aapresid) titled "The Mission."[82]

ACSOJA had invited me to this conference, saying that it was one of the most important events regarding agro-industrial chains in Argentina. It is a highly recognized forum with the annual participation of the biggest and most powerful agribusiness companies, chemical-, seed-, and agricultural engineering corporations, and pro-agribusiness politicians, among others. Here, they discuss technical and economic innovations and their application, as well as political ideas, discourses, and challenges.

The advertising video shows a young hippie-style woman who plays the *cajón* and connects her hands with the earth. In terms of aesthetics, this video could well be footage in support of social movements that struggle against agribusiness in Argentina. At the same time, a pleasant voice talks about new forms of connecting with the earth though generating technological innovation and knowledge, and producing foodstuffs, fibers, and bioenergy in a sustainable manner. "We integrate an extensive learning network in order to strengthen the mission [...]."[83]

Remarkably, many of the lecturers and panelists talked about political protests from do-gooders and environmentalists, and addressed the general doubts in the civil society about agribusiness' practices and health effects. The above-mentioned video is well suited for what, in my impression, was one of the missions of this conference: to approach mistrust and criticisms that are raised against agribusiness, embrace them, and to work on

82 Agribusiness conferences are important platforms for strengthening such ideas internally and externally, since the messages spread there are not only self-referential but widely spread to the broader public through the media.

83 shorturl.at/nwR18, last accessed May 25, 2022, own translation.

a general consent among economic actors in the field on how to deal with these criticisms—not by ignoring critics, but rather by integrating particular claims made by social and environmentalist protestors, turning their arguments against them, and concluding that "those who are not in favor of transgenic planting are against progress" (Teubal 2006, 71, own translation).

A noteworthy aspect of agribusiness' actors on the ideological terrain is work on the "inside" with economic actors in the field. This includes the encouragement of farmers and other agribusiness actors to push specific legitimizing discourses forward into the broader civil society. The named Aapresid conference is one space where agribusiness elites work on such discourse strategies. As a first part of that, conference lecturers have badmouthed political opponents or denied them the seriousness, accountability, and integrity of their actions. On a panel on the Kirchner governments' agrochemicals-related legislative framework and affected farmers, an Aapresid representative, who is also an area manager of one of my case companies analyzed in Chapter 9, bemoaned that some physicians, journalists, and politicians together try to evoke a feeling of fear, and, therefore, that the members of agricultural value chains, "all of us who are affected," have to stand together to counter such calumny.[84]

In an opening speech, US-agronomist and co-initiator of the 'green revolution' in Latin America Norman Borlaug's granddaughter Julie Borlaug described those who are worried about increasing incidences of cancer in rural areas as "moms with young children who believe everything on Facebook." According to her, environmentalists who demonize biotechnology have never been close to those who suffer hunger—an argument that was put forward by several speakers, which implicitly silences the fact that most of the industrial grain and oilseed production in Argentina is not for human consumption, rather for animal feed and biofuels. "I strongly believe in biotechnology," she said and then assumed that those who do not share this belief have never been "in Africa" to see how hard it is to farm without technology. Therefore, anti-GMO movements (or "Anti-Science-Movements" as Borlaug calls them), their "powerful social media campaigns," and their hysteria are "a backlash against modern production."[85]

While activists and scientists alike are portrayed as irrational deniers of progress, this discussion among agribusiness actors neglects serious social

---

84 Transcript of field notes, 22nd Aapresid-congress, August 7, 2014, own translation.
85 Ibid.

and academic debates, for instance, on the health effects of agrochemicals. While scientific opinions on the damaging effects of glyphosate and other agrochemicals differ, a large body of literature has indicated a real increase in the number of cases of cancer, birth defects and malformations in inhabited environments close to fumigated areas (Arancibia 2013; Delvenne et al. 2013; Lapegna 2016; Paganelli et al. 2010). Indeed, malpractice was mentioned by agribusiness actors both at conferences and in my interviews—but always as a problem of misconduct by individuals who only need to learn the safe use of agrochemicals. Agroecologist Liam Finnegan (2017, 2) has analyzed this narrative of undertrained or underequipped farmers as "a powerful tool for the pesticide industry to keep their product in the market"—thus detracting from the problem that agribusiness is a highly competitive industry that incites this very (mis)use.

As a second argument, by drawing a line of distinction around both critics of agribusiness and individual mistakes made by farmers, the analyzed agribusiness actors present themselves as modernizers and promoters of social and ecological sustainability within value chains. In other words, publicly raised doubts are not simply ignored, but the agro-industry itself is characterized as the better socio-environmentalist. In the opening ceremony, speakers emphasized that it is important to show the world how technological development does not only increase the profitability but also social and ecological sustainability and earth conservation. (To underline this aim, the 2018 Aapresid congress was named "sustentología,"[86] a Spanish word mix of sustainability and technology.) On a panel on the impact of agriculture on the environment and human health, an Aapresid representative highlighted that with modern science, "every time we understand the nature a bit more," and because biotechnological development and precision farming leads to a more accurate use of agrochemicals, "we entrepreneurs are environmentalists by virtue of our own interests."[87] Julie Borlaug herself called her grandfather a "warrior against famine," biotechnology being his weapon. She went on that agribusiness needs to do a better job of explaining its capacity to fight hunger to the public, which needs to hear that "we will not be able to feed a growing population without GMO's."[88] Particular interests are thus presented as universal socio-ecological interests.

86 http://2018.congresoaapresid.org.ar/, last accessed May 26, 2022.

87 Transcript of field notes, 22nd Aapresid-congress, August 7, 2014, own translation.

88 Ibid.

In some instances, this also involves recourse to the chain metaphor. During the three days of panels, it was accentuated many times as a discourse strategy for making people understand that Argentina does not merely produce soybeans but foodstuffs in agro-industrial value chains. This was also the joint message of chain organizations at the world's largest open-air agricultural exhibition, Expoagro, in 2016: "Our most important message to the world must be that we are producers of abundant, healthy and safe food."[89] And in a similar vein, ACSOJA has held a conference in 2018, where representatives of some of the largest corporations along the soy chain together with government members discussed on seven panels how the soy value chain is "an engine for sustainable Argentinian development."[90] Thus, the business associations use such conferences to render both internally and externally plausible the notion that their economic agency is of universal interest to both people and the environment.

This is not only directed at politicians and at the media. It is also accompanied by the call on participants to spread the word. A speaker at "The Mission" who was indicted due to fumigation himself, argued that a better communication strategy is needed to respond to a lack of social acceptance of the agricultural industry. This would include the confession that "we are not as good as we say," combined with the assurance that "we are not as bad as the others say either." His plea to the audience is that the good cooperation in networks and along the value chains should be supplemented by closer relations with society as a whole: "We have to go out to the villages and talk to people, because if we don't do that, others will occupy these spaces." A colleague in the panel also argued that "we have to go and knock on people's doors. Don't go as an individual—go as an institution." Another Aapresid representative endorsed that there is a need to actively approach people. "Why should the society trust us just like that," he asked. "I wouldn't trust the businesspeople." He went on that there is a need to "build an agenda together with the civil society, together with the environmentalists, and together with the government [...] then we can take away fields from the environmentalists." The aim is to pick up on disagreements among these actors while making clear to the public that there is no unbridgeable antagonism.[91]

---

89 http://www.argentrigo.org.ar/2014/pdf/4CadenasEnExpoagro_consolidado.pdf, last accessed May 26, 2022, own translation.

90 http://seminario.acsoja.org.ar/programa/, last accessed May 26, 2022, own translation.

91 Transcript of field notes, 22nd Aapresid-congress, August 7, 2014, own translation.

In sum, this section has shown how agribusiness actors both work on their internal ideological unity and discuss how to assure consent within the broader civil society, and thus to let protest run into a void. In other words, they knead an organic ideology. As they call on their colleagues to present themselves as the real environmentalists or authors of social achievements, they articulate various ideological elements and bridge the gap between discourses emanating from both the agribusiness world and from subaltern groups. Thus, they embrace the fact that the ideological terrain forms a part of social struggles, in which they try to bring forth their strategies. In this context, the value chain metaphor appears as one of several ideological arguments.

So far, no counter-hegemony has been built up from below, as Gras and Hernández (2016b) have argued. Critical debates on agribusiness in Argentina have been restricted "to certain academic areas or to limited political spaces" (ibid., 19, own translation).[92] Indeed, companies repeatedly face drawbacks. One example is Monsanto, who had to give up on the construction of a new GMO seed plant after strong local protests, which included blockades of the access roads (Agosto 2014). However, agribusiness' advocates have reached a degree of consent that "is nothing other than the construction of hegemony" (Gras and Hernández 2016b, 17, own translation).

Lobbying for free trade policies—as a chain

Prior to the presidential election won by Cristina Fernández de Kirchner's political companion and predecessor Néstor Kirchner in 2003, class and social struggles from below had responded to the profound 2001 crisis

92 This is not to downplay existing protests. Most of today's relevant protests do not take place in Argentina's farming heartland and the hub of grain and oilseed production. The latter had seen protests among producers who were facing difficulties in raising the capital necessary to keep up competition and, hence, in integrating themselves into a grain and oilseed production that was increasingly dominated by big capital. In the province of La Pampa, the Movement of Agricultural Women in Struggle (MML for its initials in Spanish), for instance, had fought against land foreclosures (Giarracca 2002; Gras and Hernández 2016b, 19 f.). Yet, such movements were silenced after president Néstor Kirchner decided to put an end to foreclosures. "Thus, towards the mid-2000s, the struggle in the region was abandoned, causing the internal rupture of the MML and its demobilization" (Gras and Hernández 2016b, 20, own translation). From then on, movements against capital concentration as well as protests against environmental effects were rather active along the frontiers of large-scale agribusiness production, such as Santiago del Estero, Chaco, and in the north of Cordoba (ibid.).

(Boris and Tittor 2006). The vigor with which these movements demanded "Que se vayan todos (They all must go)" was cushioned through a new compromise within the historical bloc, reflected in improvements in social and democratic policies and a greater downward redistribution of social wealth (Berndt and Bernhold 2018). At the same time, however, the neo-structuralist-inspired economic path taken by the government of Cristina Kirchner allowed agribusiness and other economic forces characterized by capital concentration and low on-site surplus reinvestment to consolidate their power in the country (see Chapter 6).

In this context, ACSOJA and ArgenTrigo have undertaken targeted lobbying and tried to ensure that the economic importance of agribusiness is followed by adequate influence on the state. "The chain" has been a helpful tool for achieving this aim: "In weak political systems, so to speak [...] each chain link tries to have the telephone number of a decision-maker, but people need to understand the strength of making the chain better as a whole," Diego explains. He argues that the combined strength of the chain association increases the power to push through demands: "Being able to agree upon certain issues with the different actors of the chain turns out to be very positive, very positive."[93] Marcos seconds that "we believe that this type of entity is a good thing when it comes to dealing with the authorities. It represents diverse interests and aligns them to face the authorities with a balanced position [...]. I think that this alignment of interests is the value added of this entity."[94] Carlos adds that "the private agreements that are achieved," are then transmitted to political decision-makers by both the chain associations and by the stock exchange, which is a "direct interlocutor with the government."[95]

Before former President Mauricio Macri took office in December 2015, ACSOJA and ArgenTrigo campaigned for a market-radical sea change in Argentinian policy. Certainly, the Kirchner administration never fully scrapped Argentine neoliberalism (Berndt and Bernhold 2018) and its strategy of agro-industrial value chain development strongly resembles corporate visions (see Chapter 7). Yet especially the external trade policies were a thorn in the side of agribusiness actors.

93 Interview with two representatives of ArgenTrigo, May 12, 2016, Buenos Aires.

94 Interview with two representatives of CIARA-CEC, June 2, 2016, Buenos Aires.

95 Interview with an economist at the grain stock exchange in Buenos Aires, May 26, 2016, Buenos Aires.

Criticizing then president Cristina Kirchner, Lisa enunciates that "you need an institutionally strong government but also the ability to understand how the market works [...] to recognize what a government should do."[96] ABA representative Luis describes the Kirchner government as the only real disturbance to an otherwise perfect market, without mentioning, though, for whom it works perfectly: "In the soy industry, the market is kind of perfect, that is, [...] you have various exporters, many plants, you have a market that's perfect and very transparent." The only corporate actions that are "not holy," as he puts it, resulted from state policies. In particular, restrictions of wheat and corn exports distorted the market, leaving the government "instead of the free market" to decide who gets to export.[97] For Eugenio, whose organization SRA groups large landowners and has long been a strong lobbyist for free market policies, this has accelerated the power of the big grain dealers.

> "I wouldn't bring a penny to our agriculture if I were a foreigner. Except for grain trading, yes, this is tremendously profitable, because with a distorted market like the one we have today, what does the exporting industry do? When the wheat or maize market remains closed because there are no permits, they have the capacity to buy grain from the producer at cheap prices and store it. When the government loosens restrictions on exports, they sell at a much higher price."[98]

Accordingly, free trade policies are needed. Diego seconds that "our chain organization was constructed in a very bad political climate." It is thus a necessary corrective for a government that "does not understand its role well" and impedes innovation and competitiveness.[99] Besides high inflation and a lack of infrastructure development, all these remarks refer to an allegation repeatedly voiced against then President Cristina Kirchner, i.e., that her policies did not provide incentives to produce anything other than soy. In particular, this concerns the above-mentioned *retenciones* and the export permit system (ROE), which included temporary export stops for wheat. While supporters of the ROE have maintained that it impedes increases in food prices by securing a sufficient domestic supply, ArgenTrigo argues that export restrictions in fact prevented farmers from growing any wheat at all. Accordingly, this did not only enlarge soy-monocropping, it also jeopardized the future of industrial plants developed around grains: "With that, you also neg-

96 Interview with two representatives of ArgenTrigo, May 12, 2016, Buenos Aires.
97 Interview with a bank employee and representative of ABA, August 26, 2014, Buenos Aires.
98 Interview with a representative of the SRA, August 7, 2014, Rosario.
99 Interview with two representatives of ArgenTrigo, May 12, 2016, Buenos Aires.

atively affect the agricultural inputs business [...] You diminish all the economic movement related to this part of the chain."[100]

ACSOJA and ArgenTrigo have lobbied for the elimination of both the *retenciones* and the ROEs, and described these intended changes as a reintroduction of clear rules which only allow agribusiness chains to reach the governmental goals formulated in the agribusiness strategic plan (PEA) and to access "external markets, which are the ones that can sustain a stable growth over time."[101] Accordingly, through an elimination of tax withholdings, "the entire value chain and, finally, the whole country benefits."[102] In a joint press release, they also maintained that "we know that an elimination of the ROE [...] will create reasonable conditions to incite the first chain link, i.e. primary production, and to realize investments that allow agro-industries to develop their power."[103]

Interestingly, they present their rejection of the *retenciones* as both a general observation and a chain-wide position, while in fact, this was a highly controversial issue in Argentina, even within ACSOJA and ArgenTrigo. UIFRA representative Lucas, for instance, does not regard differentiated *retenciones* on primary and processed products as the only possible measure to support manufacturing (UIFRA today rather opts for export refunds for processed products). Yet he remarks that

> "the only measure we had were the differentiated retenciones. [...] More industrialized, less withholding tax. Well, it was a measure that after all helped a bit. Even if we could not export much anyways. And it is getting worse and worse. Now with the new [Macri] government with a more liberal stance, it has eliminated the retenciones on wheat [...] That made us lose even more competitiveness. Before, we could access the raw material more economically."[104]

---

100 Ibid.

101 http://www.argentrigo.org.ar/2014/pdf/4CadenasEnExpoagro_consolidado.pdf, last accessed May 26, 2022, own translation.

102 http://www.argentrigo.org.ar/2014/pdf/Comunicado4C31032014.pdf, last accessed April 17, 2018, own translation.

103 http://www.argentrigo.org.ar/2014/pdf/CuatrocadenasenExpoagro2015.pdf, last accessed February 23, 2018, own translation.

104 Interview with a representative of UIFRA, April 27, 2016, Buenos Aires. This possibly represents a single opinion within UIFRA, or the union's public opinion was changed after Macri's election. In later documents, UIFRA has stated that with Macri's presidency, extolled by agribusiness actors for its free trade posture, "for the first time in years, the state has stopped being an obstacle and is encouraging Argentine companies to go out, to open themselves to the world" (http://uifra.org.ar/home/downloads/ANUARIO2017.pdf, last accessed May 26, 2022).

When I mentioned that Macri had advocated for value chain development and I asked, whether the then new government had taken other measures to this end, Lucas answered that

"He always says we shouldn't export wheat, that we have to export noodles. [...] This was part of his election campaign. [...] Now, we haven't really seen any, any kind of willingness to make that happen. What's more, we belong to the wheat chain, and in ArgentTrigo we talk to the producers, and we see that the wheat producers are going through very good times now, with great expectations, while we are in the same situation as last year. Or maybe even worse."[105]

Statements of other actors, too, suggest that the withholding taxes had benefited the processing industry. In 2014, stock exchange economist Hernando told me that

"the industry has an important leverage, which is the tax structure. For seven years now, we have been exporting soybeans with a 35 percent duty, but only 32 percent on soybean flour and oil and 11 percent on biodiesel. [...] This has led to the construction of the largest crushing plants in the world."[106]

In a similar vein, CARBIO sees the danger of a loss of competitiveness for the biofuels industry in the absence of protectionist measures.

"We are going to find ourselves without the differentiated retenciones. As I said, Europe and other countries have tariffs that can obviously affect us. Unless someone says 'ok, let's stop all that,' at least we need to have something similar so that we can compete at equal conditions. Unless the world says 'good, we are now all taking off all tariffs.'"[107]

In a 2014 interview, Alejandro told me that CIARA never had a problem with the *retenciones*, because they could just pass down the pressure. "Well, let's see, we don't have a strong opinion here. It's a tax but the only thing it affects negatively is primary production. [...] When the export price is 100 and the withholding tax is 35, we pay 65 [...] But the bad thing is that producer has less incentives to produce."[108] Julieta even considers it possible that a revocation of the *retenciones* could lead to a reprimarization of the Argentinian economy. "Yes, yes, the elimination of export duties or the reduction in the case of the

105 Interview with a representative of UIFRA, April 27, 2016, Buenos Aires.
106 Interview with a representative of the grain stock exchange in Rosario, August 12, 2014, Rosario.
107 Interview with a representative of CARBIO, June 6, 2016, Buenos Aires.
108 Interview with a representative of CIARA-CEC, August 29, 2014, Buenos Aires.

soy complex [...], in fact, it does not benefit the industry; it benefits the primary producer."[109]

However, the crushing industry is mainly controlled by the same companies that dominate grain and oilseed trading. Thus, at a company level, potential losses in further processing might be compensated by greater profits made with wheat or corn exports. Furthermore, with an eye to the powerful agricultural lobby, Alejandro responded to the question why CIARA supports free-trade claims within ACSOJA and ArgenTrigo: "We have to reach an equilibrium, we don't want to kill the goose that lays the golden eggs."[110] At any rate, CIARA welcomed the political changes accompanying Macri's presidency (2015–2019). Fabio, for his part, had purely positive expectations for the agriculture machinery industry: "Due to cancelled or reduced *retenciones* and new exchange rates, the profitability of agricultural production in general changes notably, and [...] we noticed a surge of people interested in buying machines."[111]

For the sake of completeness, it should be mentioned that the critics of Kirchner's *retenciones* have also included scholars. As mentioned before, one of the main objections was that the withholdings were levied on large corporations and petty commodity producers in equal percentages. This has accelerated the process of capital concentration in agriculture which had started under neoliberal conditions in the 1990s (Fernández 2012b, 2013a; Martínez Dougnac 2013).

The lobbying against ROE's and *retenciones* tie directly into the above-discussed postulation that Argentina needs to give up bad international negotiations and participate in free trade agreements to counter geopolitical barriers. However, the mixed opinions on these measures show the contradictory character of both Kirchner's commercial policies and the (dis)advantages arising for different capitals from them. Nevertheless, ACSOJA and ArgenTrigo use the metaphor of chain unity to present particular positions on commercial policies as common and general interests. Apparently, actors interested in free market policies and corresponding international agreements are able to assert their position within these agribusiness associations. In

109 Interview with two representatives of CIARA-CEC, June 2, 2016, Buenos Aires.

110 Interview with a representative of CIARA-CEC, August 29, 2014, Buenos Aires.

111 Interview with a representative of CAFMA, May 13, 2016, Buenos Aires. There have also been controversies on the ROEs. In 2013, for instance, in contrast to the demands of primary producers and trading companies to free up exports, the Federation of Bakers blamed the latter for holding back wheat in speculation and called on the government to punish such action (Rebossio 2013).

contrast to the cited critical analyses of Kirchner's *retenciones*, their claims of free trade tend to blur differences between big business and smaller capitalist producers and to neglect the mechanisms of "free-trade imperialism" (Wallerstein 2012b, 142 ff.).

Trying to change the rule of the game: a new seed law

The speedy adoption of a new seed law has been another topic on the table of negotiation between agribusiness associations and the government. As mentioned in Chapter 6, the previous seed law in force was enacted in 1973. It grants companies like Monsanto/Bayer the exclusive right to commercialize new seed varieties for a determined period of time. At the same time and in contrast to other Latin American countries, however, it allows farmers to reuse parts of the harvest as seeds in later plantings without having to buy a new permission. Together with the Argentinian Seed Producers' Association (ASA, a member of both ACSOJA and ArgenTrigo), its affiliate Monsanto/Bayer has lobbied for a new seed law that guaranties the legal security of investments or, in other words, which obliges farmers to pay royalties every sowing season. To build pressure, the company had taken measures such as stopping shiploads of soy in European ports, arguing that they illegally contained genes that were its property (Vicente 2014, 188). Then President Kirchner took up the issue in 2012 and started negotiating a new seed law. But the discussion of the changed legislation has provoked large protests (ibid., 189).

ACSOJA and ArgenTrigo have strongly supported the lobbying for the new seed law, not only because Monsanto/Bayer is a member of its affiliate ASA, but also because the company had announced that it would otherwise not launch new soybean varieties in this country. Furthermore, according to their arguments, a new "up-to-date and powerful legal tool benefits the chain as a whole,"[112] as it should better be able to guarantee intellectual property and incite biotech developers to produce ever better variations. As a consequence, Argentina remains at the forefront of the use of state-to-the-art biotechnology and, thus, further increases the productivity in primary production: "The new biotechnological products [...] will better tolerate drought and saline soils, and resist insects and diseases. They will also be more efficient in the use of environmental resources, produce better

112 http://www.argentrigo.org.ar/2014/pdf/4CadenasEnExpoagro_consolidado.pdf, last accessed May 26, 2022, own translation.

yields, and have a better quality […]."[113] Diego also emphasizes that ArgenTrigo is putting pressure on the state to pass the law because it would bring new investments to Argentina. "Our chain [association] believes that seeds should be paid for. You want to save your seeds? But you have to pay a royalty […] this is a rule of the game […] and once it's a business, the investors will appear."[114]

Finally, a new law should also standardize the payment of royalties to Monsanto/Bayer and therewith settle a dispute between Monsanto/Bayer and trading companies on what is known as the "Monsanto clause." Monsanto/Bayer had demanded that grain and oilseed dealers charge royalties on their behalf in the event that primary producers did not do so correctly.

This measure has been rejected by entities that group small and medium sized producers, such as the Argentine Agrarian Federation (FAA). The latter has also opposed the new seed law, arguing that it defends Monsanto/Bayer's interests over those of small and medium primary producers in Argentina.[115] Furthermore, as shown in Chapter 6, there is informal resistance via black market seeds (*bolsa blanca*) (Berndt et al. 2019, 10). Other small farmer organizations and social movements have also been fighting against the legislative change, arguing that it will probably drive even more small farmers out of the market. It "seeks to privatize seeds and criminalize small farmers for their use, conservation, exchange and reproduction" (Vicente 2014, 181, own translation).

Diego Andreucci and others (2017, 28) have argued that such moves (in this case initiated by Monsanto/Bayer) can be understood as "value grabbing," or as expressions of a contradiction over the appropriation of rent. In other words, capital strategies by Monsanto/Bayer and others to acquire a greater share of the surplus value produced in agriculture can be understood as "class struggles over value appropriation" (ibid.). ACSOJA and ArgenTrigo have clearly positioned themselves on the side of big capital in this struggle, and lobbied for a new seed law, even though it would not benefit all actors in the grain and oilseed value chains.

113 http://www.argentrigo.org.ar/2014/pdf/CuatrocadenasenExpoagro2015.pdf, last accessed May 26, 2022, own translation.

114 Interview with two representatives of ArgenTrigo, May 12, 2016, Buenos Aires.

115 http://faa.com.ar/mobile/noticia.asp?idNoticia=8221, last accessed May 26, 2022.

Christmas, birthday, and honeymoon?

In my interviews with agribusiness associations in 2016, nearly all my interlocutors celebrated the end of Kirchner's presidency as a victory, and expressed the belief that they could push through their claims much more easily with then new President Macri. Already in 2014, Eugenio had told me that the SRA "is keeping an eye on what's coming and we are now working with the next candidates [...], to inform them so that when they enter office, they know what the problems of the agricultural sector are."[116]

Shortly after President Macri took office in December 2015, he announced the elimination of export taxes on all agriculture commodities, except for soybeans and its derivatives, for which export taxes were initially only reduced by 5 percent. The ROEs were replaced with a mechanism that merely tracks exports (Affidavits of Foreign Sale). Lisa, therefore, hailed that "now, finally the market governs: supply, demand, and opportunity."[117] In a press release, the chain associations expressed their success and thanked the then new government, as "these are fulfilled promises that will once again give us clear rules." Argentina could

> "now focus on attracting investment flows to an Argentina that lowers transaction costs and develops the competitiveness of its value chains, so that it can place its products on the world markets again and contribute to global food safety, job creation, and guaranteeing opportunities to every inhabitant of the country."

What they demand, then, was a "confirmed plan" for a gradual further reduction that allows for an "adequate profitability."[118]

It cannot be determined how much agribusiness association's lobbying against former President Kirchner really contributed to the change of government in 2015. At any rate, some of the capital representatives from their environments became a part of the government under President Macri. For instance, then minister of agricultural affairs of the largest soybean-producing province Buenos Aires, Leonardo Sarquis, used to be an executive at Monsanto/Bayer. Befor Macri's election, he had participated in various conferences organized by the chain associations and its members. At the 2014 Aapresid conference, he lectured on agro-industry related state poli-

116 Interview with a representative of the SRA, August 7, 2014, Rosario.

117 Interview with two representatives of ArgenTrigo, May 12, 2016, Buenos Aires.

118 http://www.argentrigo.org.ar/2014/pdf/4CadenasEnExpoagro_consolidado.pdf, last accessed May 26, 2022, own translation.

cies, and he argued for the new seed law and that "we have to eliminate the *retenciones*, not just reduce them."[119] Another example is Luis Miguel Etchevehere, who was the president of the SRA until he became National Minister of Agroindustry in 2017.

8.4 Interim conclusions

Chapter 8 has examined the strategies for, and the limits to, value chain development as they are formulated by business associations organized along agro-industrial chains in Argentina (ACSOJA and ArgenTrigo) as well as by various of their member organizations. It has also analyzed how leading agribusiness actors in these associations work to increase their political and ideological influence in the extended state. This analytical focus was derived from the purpose to consult the empirical world of corporate strategies to reflect upon a key premise of the mainstream GVC-literature from an ideology-critical perspective. This concerns the assumption that business actors are key carriers of value chain upgrading and thus of national socioeconomic development. I have therefore scrutinized, first, how business actors themselves portray both value chain upgrading and their roles therein and, second, which contradictions, inconsistencies, or omissions are inhered in these approaches, particularly regarding their significance for socioeconomic enhancements and equalization.

In detail, in the first part (8.1), I analyzed ACSOJA and ArgenTrigo as corporate-practical expressions of the GVC framework and looked at their conceptions of development via chain-coordination, process upgrading, functional or chain upgrading, and social upgrading.

A first noteworthy point is how positively my informants generally refer to and make use of the value chain metaphor—especially considering that chain research, depending on the respective academic traditions, ranges from assessments of upgrading possibilities to analyses of exploitation and uneven development in the capitalist world system. Yet, its affirmative use has been adopted by capitals' advocacy groups as a tool for defining business strategies and as an ideological instrument for embedding their agency in a development discourse. My discussion has shown that there

119 Transcript of field notes, 22nd Aapresid-conference, August 6, 2014, own translation.

is a class dimension in the assessment of GVC upgrading. The concept of value chain development is used from the ideological standpoint of capitals' vested interests. At the same time, critical analyses are largely factored out, and concrete explanations of how exactly these individual strategies serve broader socioeconomic interests are lacking.

In general, my interlocutors regard export-oriented agro-industrial value chain development as the most solid ground for national socioeconomic enhancements in Argentina. However, their understanding of the latter is myopic in that the way up-the-value chains is presented as being generally possible for anyone, as long as it is well organized. Impeding factors such as inter-firm struggles over production and surplus value appropriation, which implies that global lead firms are not necessarily interested in helping actors lower down on the chains to upgrade, or the fact that capitalist (agribusiness) growth is based on exploitation go largely unmentioned. For instance, the problem that local industrialization does not necessarily alter Argentina's peripheral insertion into the global division of labor is factored out, except by actors whose immediate accumulation interests are negatively affected by the import of high value means of production.

As regards the assessments of process upgrading, the envisioned technological and organizational improvements are tailored above all to the interests of multinational biotech and seed companies and of large-scale farmers. Alternative proposals for an improvement of the productive forces—oriented at socio-ecological sustainability—are omitted. And when it comes to social upgrading, the discourse is, first, narrowed down to quantitative job creation. Second, my analysis suggests that the emphasis placed on the capacity of agro-industrial value chains to create employment stems from an ideological strategy to whitewash agribusiness rather than from a serious concern to improve the social situation of wage-dependent people in Argentina. My argument here is that the GVC approach falls short when it counts on the developmental role of business actors, neglecting their acting in value chains from a class position.

In the second part (8.2), I analyzed how agribusiness associations depict different disruptions and limits to upgrading. Again, the ways in which such limits are addressed are strongly shaped by particular business interests. This includes various aspects.

First, with respect to factors that constrain social upgrading, it is noteworthy that capital agency does not play a role for my interview partners.

They see themselves in charge with respect to social improvements only as far as their own economic growth is concerned, which then allegedly trickles down to reach other parts of the society. In this logic, anything that stands against their individual accumulation interests also hinders social upgrading. At the same time, capital as an antagonistic social relation appears in these presentations when unions act as combative antagonists. In fact, organized workers and also national labor law—two factors that have indeed guaranteed greater social security for some workers—are designated as the real constraints to social upgrading.

Second, with respect to functional or chain upgrading, it needs to be considered that business actors may refer to the concepts of value chain development but at the same time be satisfied with the political economic status quo, as long as it serves their individual accumulation interests. In the case of Argentina, for instance, it is important to note that there is a strong agriculture lobby that is in fact oriented towards free trade policies that contradict a value chain development that could benefit broader parts of the population.

Third, when it comes to geo-economic and geopolitical limits to upgrading, my interviewees tackle such problems in the context of a juxtaposition between different capital's ambitions to control the center-like activities in agro-industrial GVCs. However, this shows once more that they address global political economic drawbacks not as a systemic problem, but rather as an anomaly to an otherwise well-functioning free market. Geopolitical constraints on upgrading opportunities are furthermore only addressed to the extent that the respondents are themselves affected, that they, at some point, stand below in struggles vis-à-vis global competitors.

Fourth, the discussion about capital concentration and resulting inner-chain power differences has brought me to a similar conclusion. In short, both are broadly neglected, with the exception of actors for whom economic concentration has negative effects. If, as I assume, the tendency of capital to concentrate lies at the heart of capitalist reproduction and competition, this impedes an equal cooperation among capitals free from antagonistic elements (Campling et al. 2016, 1751). Accordingly, concentrated capitals do not have an interest in exposing their privileged position.

Throughout the third part (8.3), I have discussed how agribusiness associations act in the extended state. This entails the creation of internal consent among actors that have particular interests in common, while these joint concerns at the same time do not set aside inter-capitalist competition. In practical terms, ACSOJA and ArgenTrigo have promoted a process of political (chain-like) class-formation, forging alliances among individual capitals in order to assert common concerns or in instances those interests of the dominant actors within these chains more effectively. With respect to lobbying for a political sea change after the last Kirchner-administration, ACSOJA and ArgenTrigo have first and foremost represented the opinions of particular powerful actors in the agro-industrial chains. At the same time, they have mixed the GVC metaphor with typically neoliberal demands, e.g. for free trade.

The policies lobbied for by these associations are not uncontroversial in Argentina. Yet until now, large agro-industrial capital has not had to fear a fundamental questioning of its dominant position. Nonetheless, the analyzed federations do not consider a broad social consent towards its interests as a sure-fire success. Rather, they regard ideological work as a crucial field of activity. I have shown how the corresponding strategies for creating positive discourses on their actions are discussed, for instance, at large conferences. However, an in-depth analysis of these actors' influence in the extended state requires further study. In this chapter, this aspect was included in a portrayal of business strategies in the width. To thoroughly analyze how hegemony is produced, a comprehensive study of their representation in the media, their work in schools and universities, the exact nature of their influence on politicians, and the like would be necessary.

In sum, my analysis shows how, on the one hand, exploitation, intra-capitalist struggles over surplus value and related social and spatial patterns of winning and losing tend to be omitted by my informants. GVC upgrading is generally portrayed as a driver not only of firm-level but of national and territorial socioeconomic development. On the other hand, this does not imply that my interviewees operate and speak with a single voice. Their portraits of value chain development are not straightforward; rather, they are characterized by a concomitance of common and conflicting interests. Yet power asymmetries, environmental problems or other challenges are part of the analyzed narratives only inasmuch they work against my interviewees' own interests.

In the end, capitals first and foremost aim at developing themselves. This can but does not necessarily entail cooperation or national economic development, and even less so, social development. In closing, I propose some general implications for the debate on GVC development.

First, when analyzing process upgrading, that is, the development of the productive forces, it needs to be considered which specific forms technological or organizational productive developments may take, depending on the prevailing social forces moving them forward, as demonstrated by the example of (bio)technology development. Accordingly, particular forms of process upgrading may help particular actors increase their profits but at the same time conflict with opportunities for a progressive development of the productive forces.

Second, it is questionable to assume capital as a subject of social upgrading. In line with Ben Selwyn's (2017) critique of capital-led development, my research shows that business actors may locate any aspect of social upgrading that does not come along with mere growth outside of their responsibility. Capital may thus not consider itself responsible, or it may even react in a hostile manner to struggles for better social or working conditions. The GVC approach abstracts from capitalism as an antagonistic relation when suggesting that social partnerships among firms, organized workers, and the state should be forged to promote social upgrading.

Third, there is a need for a broader discussion of how corporate actors use the narrative of value chain upgrading. In this vein, policies lobbied for under the label of chain-wide interests may even obstruct functional or social upgrading.

Fourth, the same problems recur on another level if one believes that the state is a neutral mediator to create an environment which alleviates all these problems or channels capital agency into a project of national development. The perspective taken here on the extended state and corporate agency therein contradicts the presumption that states are quasi-neutral public partners and that they "move up the value chain by engaging local firms assimilating new knowledge and improving employment conditions, with appropriate policies and institutions to facilitate economic, social and environmental upgrading" (Gereffi et al. 2015, 22).

Fifth, with respect to studies on geopolitical constraints, I have argued that there is a need to further analyze the making of geopolitical environments, taking underlying conflicting capital interests into account, and thus, to not only reflect on the geopolitical institutional environments of GVC-development, but also to analyze the political economic context in which these environments are manufactured.

Finally, to summarize all these aspects, GVC analyses fall short when they ignore real capital interests, which may turn out not to be at the service of broader socioeconomic development strategies. The analysis of real capital (dis)interests and strategies is an important means of scrutiny of firm-level upgrading as a driver of socioeconomic development to the benefit of more than just specific capital fractions. According to my analysis that business representatives approach the concept of value chain development from the standpoint of vested interests, general conclusions must be drawn about capital-led development. Building on capital representatives as subjects of development is loaded with contradictions. This does not exclude the possibility of local upgrading but it highlights the necessity, first, to move the research focus away from firm-level upgrading or, as Brewer (2011, 319) puts it, "'sub-systemic' units of activity," and, second, to acknowledge the contradictions that even emerge at this very level, as this chapter has shown. Otherwise, the GVC approach may today be at the service of capital, rather than at the service of development.

At any rate, the development of agribusiness in Argentina has allowed firms to upgrade. This does not only concern the soy processing industry. Some primary producers, for instance, have been able to accumulate enough capital to invest in different parts of grain and oilseed value chains, as the next section will discuss based on three case companies.

9. On Contradictions of Firm-level Upgrading

As portrayed in previous chapters, the deepening of economic deregulation and trade liberalization in Argentina during the 1990s, along with other locally-specific neoliberal reforms and global economic developments, has created the conditions for the restructuring of agriculture and a growing importance of agribusiness corporations (see Gras and Hernández 2013a; Sosa Varrotti 2015). The legal framework for land leases, the promotion of biotechnology, the removal of state-regulated grain prices, and a business-friendly rural labor law have coupled with a boom in the global demand for commodities, especially for soy, and a growing interest of international capitals to invest in farming industries in the global south. In result, the rules of the game have changed for agriculture in Argentina (Sosa Varrotti 2015, 46). This has also paved the way for some locally born companies to upgrade and grow into multinational corporations.

Looking at the development of such corporations, this chapter directly builds on the preceding one. It continues to address upgrading as it is pursued by agribusiness actors. But it changes focus to analyze the competitive strategies of three case companies: Agrigood, El Agro, and LAgricola.[1] All three were founded in Argentina, grew with the agricultural commodity boom, and have upgraded processes and functions at the firm level over the past decades. Throughout the 2000s, they have been among the largest grain and oilseed growers on the South American continent.

In 2015, the representatives of these companies that I interviewed expected even greater growth potentials in a post-Kirchner scenario. Although the Kirchner administration had never fully scratched agribusiness-friendly policies (Berndt and Bernhold 2018), my informants welcomed the political

1 This study tracked the strategies of the above companies until about 2018.

sea change following Macri's election, like the associations analyzed in Chapter 8. Forbes magazine said in 2018 that "it might be time to get out of Argentina" (Rapoza 2018), and critical voices expected disinvestment and capital flight already in 2016. Manager Rogelio, however, considers that economic liberalism endorses development. As long as companies are not disturbed by the state and are free to develop their businesses, he argues, they will invest in upgrading. "We did everything we could to make it [Macri's election] happen. Now we are living a paradise […], we cannot wipe the smile from our faces [laughs]. […] Now there is a unique opportunity for value chain development, after 12 years of attacks and closed policies."[2] In this view, when agriculture is doing well, everything else follows suit.

In contrast to this estimation, the following analysis into my case companies suggests that this and similar statements reflect interests in re-increasing private agribusiness profits vis-à-vis the state rather than concerns about development in general terms. In contrast to the Argentinian economy in general (Fernández and Seiler 2016; Schorr 2013), the companies analyzed in this chapter have developed considerably over the past decades, and they all have carried out functional upgrading in firm-specific ways. On that note, the following is not conceived as a success story about corporate development, rather as a contribution to an empirical ideology critique of the GVC upgrading paradigm. I follow mainstream chain studies by analyzing firm-level upgrading. At the same time, however, I challenge their underlying assumption, according to which firm-level upgrading generally entails gains for so called developing countries, "by singing their own tune to them" (Marx 1975 [1844], 178). The firm-level stories told in this chapter can well be read as success stories, based on how the GVC approach understands upgrading (see Chapter 3). However, I show that the analyzed strategies are first and foremost capital strategies, which may as well contradict the aim to achieve broader social development. From a critical political economy perspective, this may not be too surprising. The point I seek to make, however, is that this fundamentally challenges the GVC upgrading paradigm to the extent that it regards firms as key subjects of development.

Paths of upgrading are processes within the capitalist world system that both restructure and reproduce uneven development (see Chapters 3 and 4). The following further substantiates the doubts raised about both the assumed generalizability of upgrading and the positive link to favor-

2 Interview with the executive director of LAgricola, July 18, 2016, Buenos Aires.

able socioeconomic outcomes. My research confronts these assumptions with contradictions that arise from the upgrading strategies of Agrigood, LAgricola, and El Agro.

The chapter is structured as follows. The first section depicts the upgrading strategies of my case companies (9.1). El Agro is described in most detail because Chapter 10 of this book contains an in-depth analysis of the social relations of production within its network. I then briefly discuss how these firms assess potential limits to upgrading and at the same time ideologically justify their strategies (9.2). Subsequently, I analyze how firm-level upgrading contributes to persistent processes of concentration and centralization of capital and thus to a local reproduction of uneven development (9.3). In Section 9.4, I show how economic upgrading on a firm level can be linked to a "geographical transfer of value" (Hadjimichalis 1984) away from Argentina. Finally, I discuss how capital interests, functional upgrading in situ, and social upgrading are not necessarily compatible endeavors (9.5).

9.1 Cases of firm-level upgrading

In the wake of the agricultural commodity boom, my case companies have played a key role in adopting new technologies and they have at least partly altered their roles within agro-industrial value chains. To this end, they have also attracted external investors, resembling a general trend described by Ouma (2016, 86), wherein investments in agribusiness are made increasingly through private equity or corporate structures, combined with local management control. As the following depicts, their strategies show similarities, but their areas of capital diversification also differ from each other.

9.1.1 Agrigood

Agrigood was initially founded during the 2001–2002 crisis in Argentina by local agricultural engineers who had previously held positions in agribusiness, consulting, investment, trading, and farmland management firms. As manager Miguel comments, "no investor, not even Argentinians, wanted to put money in this country at that time." Yet Agrigood found backers who expected agriculture to be a profitable business. "We knew that it could have even better results and more productivity simply by applying good technologies."[3] Since its incorporation, the company has grown considerably. By the mid-2010s, it was involved in a range of businesses in Argentina and its neighboring countries.

Growing with international capital investments

While Agrigood is often referred to as an Argentinian giant, today, the bulk of the company's capital is of international origin. As manager Miguel explains,

> "after we started in 2002, [...] the company wanted to grow, and we looked for investors. The existing ones could have put more money, but we were also looking outside. Not only did the capital of the company grew, but so did the number of investors, and we began to welcome investors from the United States, Brazil, and Europe."[4]

In 2011, Agrigood was transformed into a joint stock corporation based in Luxembourg, where the income tax rate (26 percent) was nine percentage points lower than in Argentina (Agrigood 2018, F-34). According to Miguel, it had to go public to gain greater capital flexibility and liquidity. As a first step, an international holding was founded in Delaware (USA) in 2010 to facilitate the initial public offering at the New York Stock Exchange (NYSE). This holding acquired all shares of Agrigood, which was converted into a limited partnership (Agrigood LP). That same year, a *Société Anonyme* (S.A.) was set up in Luxembourg (Agrigood S.A.), to which the Delaware holding transferred 98 percent of its shares. In 2015, Agrigood LP was officially transferred to Luxembourg, too (Agrigood 2018, 42). In 2018, the CEO and directors owned approximately 5 percent of the shares, while the principal holders were hedge funds and investment companies based in Qatar, Europe, USA, and Singapore (ibid., 123).

Miguel argues that during the conversion into a stock company, Agrigood was able to draw positive effects from the 2008 economic crisis, "because there we said 'let's not grow too fast, let's analyze the best opportunities [...] and let's take advantage of this moment.' [...] So, we slowed down and we started to dedicate ourselves to internal restructuring in 2008–2009."[5] In fact, capitalist crises do not necessarily cause long-term damage to everyone. They can also "lead to reconfigurations, new models of development,

---

3 Interview with an Agrigood manager, April 22, 2015, Buenos Aires.
4 Ibid.
5 Interview with an Agrigood manager, April 22, 2015, Buenos Aires.

new spheres of investment and new forms of class power" (Harvey 2010a, 11). Agrigood is an example of how such reconfigurations can work at the firm level, provided that the firm is strong enough to withstand such crises. Table 11 shows the development of Agrigood's sales, which according to company information rose from 183 million US-Dollars in 2009 to almost one billion in 2017.

Year	**2009**	**2011**	**2013**	**2015**	**2016**	**2017**
Sales	183.386	365.857	644.624	674.314	869.235	933.178

Table 11: Agrigood's sales in agricultural and processed goods (in millions of US-Dollars)
Source: Agrigood's 2013, 2015, and 2018 annual reports; numbers vary in the reports, this table uses the latest available data until the 2018 report.

The following details the underlying strategies to increase sales and profits through different forms of upgrading, including changes in "the mix of activities conducted within the firm" (Kaplinsky and Morris 2001, 38). This has involved geographic diversification of investments, the acquisition, transformation, and resale of land for profit, and a "vertical integration in key segments of the agro-industrial chain" (Agrigood 2018, 44).

According to Miguel, the GVC concept has been helpful in this context.

"It seems to me that it is super important to understand value chains, how they are built, where the efficiencies or inefficiencies lie, which type of long-term policy is required. Analyzing the value chain as a whole is essential. For a company like ours that seeks efficiency, it is important to know to what point it can or should be integrated, and where integration does not make sense."[6]

He understands GVCs as a tool to identify the best investment decisions and to understand up to what point it actually makes sense for a company to climb up the value chain.

Expanding agriculture—controlling the production costs

In 2002, Agrigood started off with the acquisition of a farming company. The deal included over 74,000 hectares of land. In the first years following this acquisition, it focused on increasing the productivity of grain and oilseed farming. Miguel explains that "you can still optimize the technology, inputs,

6 Interview with an Agrigood manager, July 20, 2016, Buenos Aires.

fertilizers, seeds, and the process of sowing, harvesting, irrigation in the case of rice. [...] It is the same as in processing industries."[7]

"As primary producers we are price takers. But we can control the production costs. So, we said 'Let's produce commodities at low cost, so that we can always capture the maximum profit.' [...] What we know is that our investors are looking for returns, they are looking for scale, they are looking for efficiency and we are going after that objective: long-term high returns."[8]

Process upgrading has thus laid the foundations for the company's expansion. One example for an in-house innovation for precision farming is an "Irrigation Surveillance Methodology" for rice production, which is based on the use of drones instead of human labor. It is supposed to "improve water management efficiencies and [...] rice yield performance" (Agrigood 2018, 112).

The efficiency strategy has furthermore included a reorganization of the production process. Miguel highlights that an increasingly well-trained staff is working for the company, running computer analyses to specify, for example, where soils need fertilization. As for the remaining work in the fields, Agrigood relies on *contratistas*, as is now common for agribusinesses in Argentina. Since the *contratistas* are the direct owners of the agriculture machinery, this also allows for a reduction of fixed capital. For farming operations in Argentina, "we don't own a single sowing machine, harvester, anything."[9] Agrigood has therewith shortened the turnover time of its capital, since it is not fixed in capital-intensive means of production, and it has enhanced its "efficient allocation [...] in our core productive activities" (Agrigood 2018, 74).

Through increased productivity and by attracting investors, the company was able to expand its business. First, this concerns a growth in farming and its geographical diversification. In contrast to other companies, Agrigood has maintained a focus on landownership in Argentina, where 80 percent of its farming business takes place on company-owned land. Furthermore, it has expanded regionally into Uruguay and Brazil to reduce the volatility of returns and natural risks, and to minimize political uncertainties and tax exposure.

7 Ibid.
8 Interview with an Agrigood manager, April 22, 2015, Buenos Aires.
9 Ibid. As detailed below, this, however, does not apply to rice production in Argentina and to the operations in Uruguay and Brazil.

By 2005, it had purchased a total of 120,000 ha. By the end of 2010, this number had grown to over 320,000 ha (almost 8 percent of the size of Switzerland). 19 of the acquired farms are located in Argentina, eleven in Brazil, and one in Uruguay. During the 2016–2017 season, the company controlled primary production on 367,000 ha, of which nearly 100,000 for soy and 138,000 for sugarcane cultivation, the latter on leased land in Brazil. 60,000 ha of the company-owned land were leased out to cattle farmers (Agrigood 2018, 45).

Intra-firm integration

According to Ouma (2016, 88), agriculture related investors increasingly do "not only invest in landowning, production-oriented companies, but also place their capital along the whole agricultural value chain from input, over production to logistics and retailing." In a similar vein, Agrigood has invested in several links of agribusiness value chains.

First, to reduce logistics costs and to enhance commercial strategies, it has storage and conditioning facilities that provide an advantage over smaller producers. It can thus temporarily hold back harvests from the market and "capitalize on fluctuations in the prices of commodities." It also sells storage services to third parties (Agrigood 2018, 83).

Another upgrading strategy is the land transformation business. Agrigood buys and gentrifies land that lies outside of Argentina's farming heartland by "implementing cutting-edge production technology and agricultural best practices" (ibid., 47). According to company information,

> "land transformation is an important element of our business model and a driver of value creation. [...] We optimize land use and increase the productive potential and value of our farmland. Our [...] model consists of changing the use of underutilized or undermanaged agricultural land to more profitable cash generating agricultural activities" (ibid., 66).

Here, the capital is valorized by purchasing land at prices below its fair value and increasing its value and the differential ground rent by enhancing the soil-productivity. The transformed land is partly used for in-house production or, when high profits beckon, resold (ibid., 67). By the end of 2017, Agrigood had generated 210 million US-Dollars in profit with the sale of 77,000 ha (ibid., 44).

In addition to the expansion of its agribusiness and land transformation activities, Agrigood has been investing in industrial processing in Argentina and Brazil since 2015. As maintained by Miguel, "sometimes, a way to achieve more efficiency is by chain integration, capturing value further ahead in the agriculture chain."[10]

A first area of investment in processing industries is a sugarcane-ethanol-energy complex in southern Brazil. In 2005, Agrigood bought a functioning mill that processes sugarcane both from in-house production and purchased from other farmers. As of 2017, it runs "one of the most mechanized [sugarcane] harvesting operations in Brazil" on 138,000 ha, approximately 94 percent of which was leased in[11] (Agrigood 2018, 61). In 2007 and 2015, the fixed capital invested in sugarcane processing was enlarged with the inauguration of two new plants with a total crushing capacity of 11 million tons. The three factories in Brazil produce sugar, ethanol, and electric power from bagasse. Miguel says that these investments happened almost automatically because sugarcane has to be

> "processed immediately if you don't want it to lose quality. There has to be coordination with the industry anyways. It is not a commodity that can be easily stored and traded. Either way, it goes from the field to the industry. [...] You have to process it, transform it into a commodity, into ethanol, sugar or electrical energy."

However, he says, an expansion was planned from the beginning. The first small plant "allowed us to gain the know-how" and following on that, "we travelled all over Brazil, looking for greater potential, lower costs, and greater scales." Asked why Agrigood decided to invest in this business in Brazil instead of looking for further investment opportunities in Argentina, Miguel answers that "the sugar cane business is really very, very efficient in Brazil."[12]

Another example for Agrigood's chain integration is rice processing and branding. From 2007 on, Agrigood invested in a fully integrated rice operation from seed production to processing plants in Argentina. The starting point was the acquisition of an existing company. "What we did was: we redesigned it, we invested in processing machinery, we changed the people that had to be changed, we re-engineered the company to be more efficient."[13] In 2017, it produced rice on over 40,000 ha, accounting for 21 percent of the total Argentinian production (Agrigood 2018, 44 f.). As in the

10 Interview with an Agrigood manager, July 20, 2016, Buenos Aires.
11 In contrast to Argentina, here, land can be leased in on a long-term basis.
12 Interview with an Agrigood manager, April 22, 2015, Buenos Aires.
13 Ibid.

case of sugarcane, Miguel explains that the company had to invest in the processing industry because

> "there is no market for paddy rice that comes directly from the field. The commodity that can be sold is milled white rice, so either way we needed to be integrated [...]. Obviously with a previous analysis of the returns on our investments, right? [...] The strategy is to pursue a commodity only if it's profitable. The analysis was done; it was profitable, and that's why we got involved."[14]

According to the company's 2018 business report, by then, it owned three rice mills that process both in-house production and rice purchased from third parties. It controlled 19 percent of the total white rice production in Argentina and 25 percent of the exports (Agrigood 2018, 44). "Our vision is to open us up to the world [...] and to new markets."[15]

Another business line Agrigood absorbed with the 2007 acquisition is the production of rice seeds. Ever since, it has invested in bioengineering rice varieties adapted to local conditions. It does not have competitors in the Argentinian rice-seeds market; therefore, "it's a very important business unit, and we realized that if we did not invest in genetic development [...] we'd be left without a source of genetics. So, we invested." Since 2007, they have put three new varieties on the market "and we are constantly analyzing how to further improve the genetics."[16] Agrigood has cooperated with the German BASF in producing a new herbicide-resistant variety. The seeds are also sold in Paraguay, Uruguay, and Brazil (Agrigood 2018, 56). Additionally, the company incorporated its own brand, which sells sorts of rice, pastas, and rice snacks. In sum, it gew to be the principal rice producer in Argentina, integrated in this chain from the production of its own seeds and genetics, to processing and branding.

Finally, Agrigood has invested in animal industries. Initially, it constructed a facility with the capacity to milk 3,000 cows in 2007. This was more than doubled with the construction of a new 'free stall' in 2012. According to company information, it plans to invest 50 million U-Dollars in another two facilities to exploit a total of 14,000 cows that do not "eat outside" as a "form to add value to the grains."[17] Agrigood claims to be Argentina's leading dairy producer in terms of using cutting-edge technology

14 Interview with an Agrigood manager, April 22, 2015, Buenos Aires
15 Interview with an Agrigood manager, July 20, 2016, Buenos Aires.
16 Interview with an Agrigood manager, April 22, 2015, Buenos Aires.
17 Interview with an Agrigood manager, April 22, 2015, Buenos Aires.

Property / Operation	Purpose and Capacity (rounded numbers)
Land ownership	246,000 ha – 85 percent in Argentina (grains, oilseeds and cattle) – 14 percent in Brazil (sugarcane, grains, oilseeds, and cotton) – 1 percent in Uruguay (oilseeds)
Real estate	– 77,000 ha sold until the end of 2017
Farming operations	– Crops on 190,000 ha (Argentina, Brazil, and Uruguay); – 652,000 tons in 2016/17 – Rice on 40,000 ha (Argentina): 235,000 tons in 2016/17 – Sugarcane on 138,000 ha (Brazil)
Seedbed and stockpiling plants (Arg.)	29,000 tons storage capacity; 2,400 tons per day drying capacity
Seedbed plant (Arg.)	Rice genetic engineering
Three rice processing and drying plants (Arg.)	– 15,500 tons of white rice per month – 5,100 tons of husk rice drying per day
Two Free Stalls (Arg.)	Exploitation of 7,000 cows for milk production (93 thousand liters in 2017)
Bio-digester (Arg.)	Energy production
Sugar and ethanol plants (Brazil)	Production per year: – 11.1 million tons of sugarcane milling – 661,000 tons of VHP sugar – 592,000 cubic meters of ethanol – 720,000 MWh
Foodstuff brand	A variety of rice, pastas, and snacks sold on the domestic market (Argentina)

Table 12: Agrigood's property: ownership of land and plants in 2017
Source: own compilation based on interviews and Agrigood's 2018 annual report

and of productivity per cow (nearly 37 liters per day). In 2017, it also built a plant for the combustion of biogas that generates electricity for both own use and a local power grid (Agrigood 2018, 45). Table 12 summarizes Agrigood's current operations.

According to a common understanding, upgrading involves the shift of firms to higher profit activities "within or between industries" (Werner 2012, 403; see Chapter 3). As maintained by Miguel, the chain integration strategy portrayed in this section has clearly increased both Agrigood's profits and profitability. Asked which is its core business, he answers that "it is the sugar business, integrated from the field to the industry, and the final commodities are ethanol, sugar, and renewable energy. All three products have interesting returns."[18] The rice processing and bioengineering business need more time, but he expects them to grow in the long term.

This is supported by company data, which indicates that the earnings before interest, tax, depreciation, and amortization (EBIDTA) are higher in the sugarcane processing industry than in farming (Table 13).

	2015		2016		2017	
	Millions of US-Dollars	%	**Millions of US-Dollars**	%	**Millions of US-Dollars**	%
Total sales and other incomes	783.749	100	1,002.648	100	1,056.455	100
...thereof crops	197.415	25.2	190.914	19.1	230.951	21.9
...thereof rice	88.09	11.3	107.462	10.7	97.438	9.2
...thereof dairy	40.523	5.2	39.059	3.9	49.954	4.8
...thereof farming (total)	326.678	41.7	338.092	33.7	379.923	35.9
...thereof sugar, ethanol, and energy	439.745	56.1	657.397	65.6	664.828	62.9
Costs (goods*, services, administration)	-679.164	100	-824.142	100	-919.425	100
...thereof crops	-166.631	24.5	-164.821	20.0	-206.784	22.5
...thereof rice	-84.803	12.5	-98.53	12.0	-89.11	9.7
...thereof dairy	-35.623	5.3	-34.306	4.2	-38.748	4.2
...thereof farming (total)	-287.304	42.3	-289.421	35.2	-335.825	36.6
...thereof sugar, ethanol, and energy	-369.821	54.5	-514.562	62.4	-561.976	61.2
EBIDTA	215.902	100	298.049	100	276.293	100
...thereof crops	33.211	15.4	26.093	8.8	24.167	8.8
...thereof rice	6.274	2.9	8.932	3.0	8.328	3.0
...thereof dairy	6.356	2.9	4.753	1.6	11.206	4.1
...thereof farming (total)	46.518	21.4	48.671	16.4	44.098	16.0
...thereof ethanol, sugar and energy	167.18	77.4	142.835	47.9	102.852	37.23
Profit before interest payments and taxes	104.585	–	178.506	–	137.03	–

18 Interview with an Agrigood manager, April 22, 2015, Buenos Aires.

	2015		2016		2017	
Finance costs (interests)	-116.89	–	-165.38	–	-131.349	–
Profit (after investments and interests) before tax	-12.305	–	13.126	–	5.681	–
Income tax benefit/expense	7.954	–	-9.387	–	6.068	–
Profit after investments, interests, and taxes	-4.351	–	3.739	–	11.749	–

Table 13: Agrigood's earnings, costs, and profits (in millions of US-Dollars and percent)
*This refers to the share of the means of production immediately consumed in the production process, thus not to fixed capital.
Source: own calculations based on Agrigood's 2018 annual report

Furthermore, both the sugarcane and dairy industries have achieved higher returns than crop farming. According to the numbers provided, the ratio of EBIDTA to expenditures on production has been more lucrative in the sugar-ethanol-energy complex, for instance, than in farming (Table 14). Hence, the expansion into higher profit niches has so far been successful for the company.

	2016	2017
Sugar, ethanol, energy	27.7	18.3
Rice	9.1	9.3
Dairy	13.9	28.9
Crops	15.8	11.7
Farming (total)	16.8	13.1

Table 14: Agrigood: ratio of EBIDTA to direct expenditures on production (in percent)
Source: own calculations based on Agrigood's 2018 annual report

It is important to note, though, that these data can only provide an approximation. As a comment on this and on company data used in this book in general, the exact amount and rate of profits earned are hardly knowable for an outsider. Company data is sorted by business year and not by the turnover time of invested capital. Furthermore, constant capital, fixed capital, and variable capital are not differentiated in these data sets. They do not reveal exactly how much of the annual profit is reinvested in fixed capital. Such investments do not appear as company profits, but they are, in fact, not just current costs but reinvested profits that enlarge the company's capital basis. When looking at the information on net profits distributed to the shareholders, the problem is reinforced and real profits are probably higher than the data suggests, since managerial bonuses as well as the interest paid to creditors also form part of the industrial profits. Finally, there is the problem that in holdings with subsidiaries, money can be shifted back and forth internally and labeled as service payments when it is useful for the balance sheets, although such in-house "services" are not necessarily real production costs (see 9.4). Money flows to the holding are thus impossible to detect.

9.1.2 LAgricola

LAgricola is another big player in Argentinian agribusiness, mainly in the large-scale production of soy and grains. With regard to process upgrading at the point of primary production, it bears many similarities with Agrigood. The following outlines some particularities of its strategies.

LAgricola was founded in 1996. Since 2013, it has been listed on the Buenos Aires stock exchange. Like El Agro (see 9.1.3), its foundations were laid by a family who started farming in Argentina at the beginning of the 20th century. Executive director Rogelio recounts that the family business grew significantly throughout the 1990s and 2000s, mainly on leased land. "Anyone could lease in land and *contratistas* cheaply at that time. [...] And that's what the [owner] family did. They owned land but since they couldn't expand buying fields, which requires a lot of capital, they started leasing-in."[19]

LAgricola was created to professionalize the management of these growing farming operations. The family kept their owned 13,400 ha in a separate business. LAgricola bought another 13,000 ha in Chaco and in Salta, but it has always kept the focus on leasing-in.

While other farming giants have invested in buying land (Agrigood), LAgricola's strategy has been to take advantage of a shrinking interest in the leasing market and to produce "on the good fields left by those other companies."[20] Rogelio says that it is worth it to wait out bad times and that LAgricola used decreasing competition on the leasing market to improve their position vis-à-vis small landowners.

"We have been working hard on adjusting what we pay to lease land. [...] Before [...], the one who took most of it [the profit] was the owner of the field. We were the ones who ran

19 Interview with the executive director of LAgricola, March 31, 2015, Buenos Aires.
20 Ibid.

the risk, [LAgricola]. That doesn't make a lot of sense, does it? When the commodity prices fell, we managed to adjust the lease prices. In the past two years, they must have shrunk by 30 percent."

He goes on to explain that LAgricola's size is an advantage in the struggle over rent "between the two extremes," landowners and agrarian capital. The company can exert more pressure than smaller players, and in high-risk agriculture, landowners also prefer to deal with bigger companies that have a more reliable solvency. Put differently, they prefer to receive less rent over running the risk not to receive any at all. "And if we don't come to a common ground, if he doesn't reduce the rent, we leave. [...] But normally [the cultivated area] does not change in size." In addition to working on lowering lease prices, the company bet on the change of government from Kirchner to Macri in 2015 and the associated tax reliefs for agribusiness. In 2015, Rogelio told me that "we are going to sow with one government but we expect to be harvesting with another."[21]

Farming season	**2007–08**	**2009–10**	**2011–12**	**2013–14**	**2016–17**	**2017–18**	**2018–19**
Total ha	84,194	108,040	130,444	154,466	125,760	147,222	167,549
Total tons	**366,258**	**396,417**	**432,709**	**669,510**	**728,994**	**710,661**	–
...thereof soy	148,521	197,611	147,237	255,170	227,791	227,105	–
...thereof maize	148,113	145,970	182,309	288,976	387,220	390,955	–
Soybean yields (tons/ha; national average in brackets)	3.0 (2.8)	3.0 (2.9)	2.3 (2.3)	3.1 (2.8)	3.5 (3.2)	3.1 (2.3)	–
Maize yields (tons/ha; national average in brackets)	7.5 (6.4)	7.4 (7.8)	6 (5.7)	7.8 (6.8)	8.6 (7.6)	8.1 (6.1)	–

Table 15: LAgricola: agricultural production in Argentina (in hectares and tons)
Source: own elaboration based on LAgricola's 2010–2018 annual reports and FAOSTAT data

Agriculture has thus remained at the heart of LAgricola's accumulation strategies. In the 2018–19 season, it produced mainly soy, maize, and wheat on nearly 170,000 ha in Argentina (LAgricola 2018, 18). Table 15 shows that the company nearly doubled its agricultural production between 2007–08

21 Ibid.

and 2018–19 (some fluctuations over time notwithstanding). Furthermore, its yields per hectare have significantly exceeded the national average, according to the company's information. This indicates a productive advantage for large corporations with "agronomic technologies that guarantee high productivity" and "large-scale agriculture production as a means of efficiency" (ibid., 15) over smaller farming companies.

Geographic and investment diversification

As in other examples, LAgricola has diversified its investments geographically. In total, it produced on approximately 300,000 ha in Argentina, Brazil, Paraguay, and Uruguay in 2018. The operations in neighboring countries are not directly controlled by LAgricola S.A., but by a holding located in Spain, which was founded in 2009. When asked for the reason for this, Rogelio explains that "in 2009, a European pension fund entered [LAgricola] with a minority share" and "the European investor demanded Spanish jurisdiction."[22]

Beyond primary production, LAgricola has set up a management services business, which according to Rogelio is now its most profitable project. It sells services to the company Juaquimana, which was founded in 2007. The latter is a land fund owned by European investors and headquartered in the US. It does not have any own staff and LAgricola is its exclusive provider of management services. "We do not participate in the company; unfortunately, we do not have any equity. But we provide them with management services, 100 percent."[23]

As off 2018, Juaquimana owned approximately 70,000 ha of land in Argentina, 9,200 ha in Paraguay, 5,000 ha in Brazil, and 10,300 ha in Uruguay. The fund buys relatively cheap land at the edges of industrial agricultural activities in Argentina and other Latin American countries. LAgricola's staff is responsible for seeking out suitable land and transforming it for grain and oilseed cultivation or cattle breeding. It also manages the whole process of agriculture production for Juaquimana, "100 percent of the operation in the field, 100 percent of the administration, marketing, everything. The company does not have any employees; all employees are from [LAgricola] [...]

22 Interview with the executive director of LAgricola, March 31, 2015, Buenos Aires.
23 Ibid.

and we charge [Juaquimana] a fee."[24] In fact, LAgricola thus runs another company.

According to company information, some of these fields have already been resold with profits as high as 80 percent (LAgricola 2015, 16). Rogelio says that

"the model of this business line is: I buy a field that is abandoned or under-produced [...] and I apply technology to turn it into a profitable field that produces grains. So, you buy a field at one price to sell it to another. In the meantime, with agricultural production, you will gain in some years, and you will lose in others. The cash flow is not so attractive for grain production. Today, the view points more towards the real estate business."

He further states that in a scenario where leasing-in land has become comparatively risky and political changes are unpredictable, "we keep producing but our energy is more focused on developing the management of agricultural assets for investors." Rogelio calls these assets undeveloped or under-managed land:

"Our expertise [...] is in those places that are not so developed and where investors need a reliable player. [...] This is a very difficult business to understand. Although it's not rocket science, [...] you might have projected a 10 million US-Dollars profit, but there was maybe a drought, too much rain, or the commodity prices dropped and you end up with two million or maybe 15 million. That's how it works. [...] And you might have an investor with a German mentality who is used to know how much he will earn 10 years out. [...] And well, we have the expertise and we are mostly developing projects in places where there are new agricultural frontiers, in developing countries. [...] This is where you have opportunities today to get cheap land with good productive potential."[25]

Like other, larger, agribusiness corporations, LAgricola has thus morphed into an intermediary "providing asset management services" (Ouma 2016, 88) to real estate investors. It is a "vehicle that earns investors an annual operating income [...]. At the same time, [LAgricola] is able to capture the increasing value of the managed land without immobilizing capital, which represents a higher return for investors" (LAgricola 2015, 8).

To facilitate this business in Argentina, LAgricola expected the then Macri administration to change the rural land law implemented in 2011 (Ley 26,737). The latter determines that no more than 15 percent of the rural land in Argentina can be owned by foreigners. Furthermore, foreigners cannot

24 Ibid.
25 Interview with the executive director of LAgricola, March 31, 2015, Buenos Aires.

buy more than a thousand hectares in Argentina's farming heartland, or an equivalent to be determined by each province in other areas (ibid., Article 9). Consequently, the land management business could only grow in neighboring countries. "Argentina is not open for that market. This is going to change, but today, it is still not an option."[26]

Rogelio says that LAgricola did not participate in writing a draft for a new law but "we had meetings with officials to look over ideas. [...] If the law becomes more flexible, we believe that this is the area where we're going to grow," because in this real estate and land management business, one does not depend so much "on taxes, on Chicago, and on the rain."[27]

He summarizes that "this is an upgrading process." Although the profits the company makes with these management services are still "low in proportion, the margins are very high. The profitability is very high. With [LAgricola] I think our sales from primary production reach 170 million US-Dollars. With the sales of services, we make only 8 million. But the profitability is so much higher."[28]

Table 16 above shows LAgricola's increases in both sales and gross profits until 2018. On average, the ratio of gross profits on expenditures shows that the managements services are indeed more profitable than agriculture production (Table 17). These data, however, only include LAgricola's operations in Argentina, as I do not have access to data for the holding's other subsidiaries.

In 2016, the family which founded LAgricola started running another business: LAgricola Energy, controlled by a holding based in the UK. By 2017, it operated three thermal power plants run with turbines built by General Electric. The plants then generated electricity with a total capacity of 450 MW (LAgricola Energy 2017). In 2017, its sales amounted to 22.4 million US-Dollars, and its operating profit (before interest payments), to 7.2 million US-Dollars (ibid., 3).

In a nutshell, LAgricola has managed to grow and to upgrade to higher profit activities. Yet the company's accumulation strategies have stayed closely attached to the expansion of grain and oilseed production on leased land. As Rogelio puts it, "we have started to offer management services, but [primary] production is still our core business." However, "we believe that having been large-scale producers will give us advantages at the moment

26 Interview with the executive director of LAgricola, March 31, 2015, Buenos Aires.
27 Interview with the executive director of LAgricola, July 18, 2016, Buenos Aires.
28 Interview with the executive director of LAgricola, March 31, 2015, Buenos Aires.

	2013		2014		2017		2018	
	Millions of ARS	%	Millions of ARS	%	Millions of ARS	%	Millions of ARS	%
Earnings	578.78	100	907.11	100	2,164.75	100	2,976.05	100
...thereof agriculture production	545.06	94.2	876.94	96.7	2,089.61	96.5	2,920.99	98.2
...thereof management services	33.72	5.8	30.17	3.3	75.14	3.5	55.06	1.9
Direct costs during production season	-544.97	100	-802.05	100	-1,922.38	100	-2,519.91	100
...thereof agriculture production	-524.61	96.3	-772.38	96.3	-1,857.6	96.6	-2,478.62	98.4
...thereof management services	-20.36	3.6	-29.67	3.7	-64.78	3.4	-41.29	1.6
Total gross result	33.81	100	105.06	100	242.37	100	456.14	100
...Gross result agriculture production	20.45	60.5	104.56	99.5	232.01	95.7	442.37	97.0
...Gross result thereof management services	13.36	39.5	0.5	0.5	10.36	4.3	13.77	3.0
Finance costs	-24.43	_	18	_	-65.36	_	-45.16	_
Profits (Losses) before tax	9.36	_	123.06	_	177.01	_	410.98	_
Income tax	-5.19	_	-39.83	_	-66.67	_	-81.43	_
Net result	4.17	_	83.23	_	110.33	_	329.55	_

Table 16: LAgricola Argentina: earnings, costs, and profits (in millions of Argentine Pesos, ARS)
Source: own calculations based on LAgricola's 2013–2018 annual reports

	2013	2014	2017	2018
Agriculture production	3.9	13.53	12.49	17.85
Management services	65.65	1.69	16.01	33.35

Table 17: LAgricola: ratio of gross profits to expenditures on production in percent
Source: own calculations based on LAgricola's 2013–2018 annual reports

of further upgrading." In the future, LAgricola plans to "upgrade, implement new business lines to add value to our produce [...] and open more management businesses for investors in different countries."[29]

9.1.3 El Agro

El Agro is one of the most well-known agribusiness corporations in contemporary Argentina. This is not only because it has grown from a locally born, family-owned farming and storage firm to a business group with several subsidiaries. Company representatives have also engaged in business associations and participated prominently in public debates on a wide range of issues, including questions of social and economic development.

Santiago, El Agro's former president, has managed in particular to become a figurehead in this South American country, because he has been a pioneer in restructuring the agriculture sector, no-till farming and other forms of process upgrading. He might be understood as an "intellectual" of Argentinian agribusiness in terms of Gramsci, for whom intellectuals are not mere scribes. Rather, they play an organizing role in the generalization of particular interests (Gramsci 2012 [1975]-f, 1500), articulating the interests and experiences of a particular social group and strengthening consent not only in the economic sphere but also through politics and social culture.

Also known as the 'king of soy' or as the 'Steve Jobs of agribusiness,' Santiago has promoted the image of modern agro-industries which are at least partly detached from old rentier-like rural oligarchies. His family is well connected, and the husband of Carolina (El Agro's vice-president and Santiago's sister) used to be mayor of the town where El Agro is headquartered (in 2021, he became a provincial senator). Beyond such political ties, Santiago is often asked to share his thoughts in the media, at conferences, in ministries, and at universities. In these and other public spaces, he has often talked about what to do to develop Argentina. He ponders on capitalism's inequality problem and the necessity of a free society without shackles and hunger. In his view, these problems can best be solved by modern entrepreneurship and the keys to common progress are free competition and, above all, innovative companies that create technological and organizational solutions to social problems. What entrepreneurs need, in his opinion, are clear rules of the game

29 Interview with the executive director of LAgricola, March 31, 2015, Buenos Aires.

(see discussion on state policies in Chapter 8) and a facilitating state that stimulates economic growth through the provision of education and infrastructure instead of through export tax-based social redistribution. From his perspective, social difference lies between those who actively stay tuned in an ever-changing knowledge society and those who do not. In other words, those who keep up with the times can develop. And El Agro presents its own history as an example.

Global value chains and production networks are crucial for the company's idea of development, and according to Santiago, Argentinian companies need to play a more important role in these chains. In accordance with the idea of capital-led chain coordination, he argues that multinational corporations "are the ones that pull small companies into global value chains," and he explains that "we have to fight globalization with more globalization to generate resources, work, and employment."[30] In this view, large corporations become a quasi-natural condition of existence for all other actors: "The jungle needs ants but it must also have elephants and giraffes. Multinationals are the ones who open the paths, who engender research and development. They work on forward and backward integration so that later on, smaller companies can be multinationals, too, or work in the networks."[31] However, Santiago says that Argentina needs to develop these multinational corporations itself.

By that token, El Agro describes itself as a multinational of Argentinian origin that leads in innovation. "There is great growth potential in our business and there is constant technological transformation. [...] We want to be leaders in both of these processes. We want to grow and we want to grow with a new agriculture."[32] Its declared aim is a socially and naturally sustainable development "and we are committed to continue deepening it in each of the value chains in which we participate" (El Agro 2018, Message from the president).

Similar to LAgricola (see 9.1.2), El Agro's roots lie in a family business that started operating at the beginning of the twentieth century. Santiago's grandfather started cultivating 15 ha of land in the Argentinian Pampas in 1915. In the 1950s, he was able to buy 150 ha, and another 10 years later, he

30 Quote from an interview given by Santiago to students of the University of Buenos Aires (UBA) for the local journal of social sciences in 2016, own translation.

31 Santagio, anonymized speech, March 14, 2009, own translation.

32 Interview with El Agro's former president, April 27, 2015, Buenos Aires.

left his children with 550 ha. By the end of the 1970s, the family owned 4,500 ha of arable land in the Pampean region. In 1984, the family business was split and Santiago's father founded El Agro, keeping 3,500 ha of the family-owned land. Ever since, agriculture-related activities have stayed at the core of its business strategies. However, the operations as agrarian capital does not build the core of its activities anymore. It has simultaneously outsourced agricultural production to *contratistas* and integrated itself into agribusiness value chains with a variety of investments as industrial, finance, and commercial capital.

Season	**93/94**	**94/95**	**96/97**	**97/98**	**01/02**	**03/04**	**05/06**	**06/07**	**07/08**	**08/09**	**10/11**	**11/12**	**12/13**
Sales	19	38	63	70	51	97	172	267	442	642	966	1,056	1,131

Table 18: El Agro's sales (in millions of US-Dollars)
The sales correspond to the corporation as a whole (El Agro Group and subsidiaries)
Source: Data provided by El Agro

In the course of firm-level upgrading, annual sales have increased by a factor of 60 to more than one billion US-Dollars between the early 1990s and 2012–13 (Table 18). The following depicts the strategies underlying this development.

Knowledge-based network development

El Agro was one of the first to generalize agriculture production via land leasing and outsourcing field labor. It can be read as an example for rural entrepreneurs who readily risk the implementation of cutting-edge (information) technologies, form the core of a production network, and thus "push the economic cycle towards a positive phase" (Anlló et al. 2013c, 28, own translation; see Bisang and Campi 2013, 31).

First, this regards the company's role in promoting the development of means of production. It has contributed significantly to a generalization of the agribusiness development based on biotechnology, no-tillage, and precision farming. From the beginning, Santiago has been a driving force in Aapresid, the association of no-till farmers described in the previous chapter.

In 1995, El Agro started to develop in-house precision farming technology, including a software that uses GPS to measure soil characteristics and simulation models to tailor the use of agrochemicals more accurately to specific areas (El Agro 2013, 4). Santiago imagines that farming will be completely done by drones and robots in the future. European-like agriculture reminds him of gardening, he told the Financial Times. He instead likes to think of a plant as a modern factory, because of the "enormous technological disruption"[33] in agriculture.

In 2015, El Agro bought a 50 percent share of a joint venture (here named Agritech) with an Argentinian state-owned high-tech satellite and space technology company. Agritech works on combining remote sensing with communication and information technologies and agro-engineering to further improve precision farming.[34] Precision farming "has helped lower production costs by 30 percent and enhance competitiveness. We are creating a new necessity of our clients that increases the value added."[35]

In contrast to Agrigood, whose strategy includes the purchase of land (9.1.1), Santiago believes that capital can be invested more profitably in knowledge and technological expertise. He stresses that land ownership is not a prerequisite for getting rich in Argentina. Appropriating the name of the Brazilian landless workers movement (MST), he was cited in many newspapers as saying that he is a landless, too. "We do not have land and we do not have tractors, harvesting machines, nothing."[36] Santiago did not tell me, though, that his family are landowners who lease out around 10,000 ha to El Agro, as a production manager explained to me.[37] Together with the case of LAgricola, this corresponds to analyses, according to which corporations operating in Argentina on the basis of leasing have often enlarged their business based on initial landownership (Gras and Sosa Varrotti 2013).

Since 2005, El Agro has created trusts (in Argentina called *fideicomiso financiero*) for sowing campaigns, with which they attracted capitals from pension funds, among other things to invest in agriculture, El Agro being the managing core of such *pools de siembra*.

---

33 Interview with El Agro's former president, April 27, 2015, Buenos Aires.

34 Interview with a marketing and business manager of El Agro, April 27, 2015, Buenos Aires. Note that in 2017, the state-owned company bought back all shares, after the family owning El Agro had given up control over their company and sold a majority share to a multinational private equity investment company, as I will describe below.

35 Interview with El Agro's former president, April 27, 2015, Buenos Aires.

36 Interview with El Agro's former president, August 21, 2014, Buenos Aires.

37 Interview with a manager of El Agro responsible for primary production, April 28, anonymized town.

However, Santiago contends that a production in which landowners are incorporated as mere lessors has not been profitable since the late 2000s. Reasons include the elevation of *retenciones* in 2007 and increasing land prices. In response, El Agro has consolidated a business model described by Santiago as an asset-light "network of networks" based on "flexible governance structures," in which El Agro constitutes the managing nucleus. He differentiates this from "closed ecosystems" in which a farmer organizes everything on his or her own.[38]

In concrete terms, the company has reduced the area it leases-in at fixed prices and over which it controls grain and oilseed production at its own risk. At the same time, it has started "what we call associated sowing, in which we participate by 25, 30 percent, depending on the association."[39] It thus organizes the productive process by entering into associations with other formally independent actors. There are many variants of these associations. For example, they can be established with former *chacareros* who contribute land but do not have further capital to invest, while El Agro forms ties with *contratistas*, provides seeds, agrochemicals, and consulting services, someone else is assigned as the production manager, and so on. At the end of the season, everyone receives a percentage of the harvest agreed to beforehand. Chapter 10 provides an in-depth analysis of these relations.

The basic difference from former leasing contracts is that the landowners as 'associated partners' are not paid a fixed rent. As finance manager Graciela emphasizes, "we want to involve the people and share the risks [...]. Today, we are talking of a variable land rent, according to the yield."[40] In other words, a part of the production risk is transferred to landowners and other associates. Commercial manager Carla emphasizes that "this way, when you lease land and contribute the labor and the inputs and then when the harvest isn't good, you avoid things going wrong only for you."[41]

Santiago stresses that this business strategy is inspired by literatures that have also fed the GVC upgrading debate. In particular, he relies on Coase and Williamson's transaction cost theory as well as on Castell's knowledge society and network economy.[42] From these readings he has concluded that not all

38 Interview with El Agro's former president, August 21, 2014, Buenos Aires.

39 Interview with a manager of El Agro responsible for primary production, April 28, anonymized town.

40 Interview with a finance and controlling manager of El Agro, April 28, 2015, anonymized town.

41 Interview with a commercial manager of El Agro, June 15, 2016, anonymized town.

42 Santagio, anonymized speech, March 14, 2009, own translation.

transactions necessary for his business have to be a direct part of the company: "The farmer assembles products and services from a network of suppliers, much like an automotive company assembles a car [...] [El Agro] is and shall be the creator of such value systems." (Santiago, cited in El Agro 2013, 14)

Accompanying this strategy, the company has professionalized its management structure because its business model "is complex. So, we need people who are well prepared to lead it."[43] It already integrated a family-external management in the 1990s (El Agro 2013, 8). In 2011, it hired a CEO who formerly held a leading position at Syngenta. There is also a lower-ranked structure that works close to the 'network partners.'

> "Each area is run by an agricultural engineer who manages everything and who normally is from that area and knows it well, knows the landowner, knows the *contratistas*. [...] Our relationship with the landowners usually arises from this engineer. [...] They organize everything and then they report to the central production management."[44]

Chapter 10 discusses the different relations El Agro builds with these managers and 'network-partners' at the point of primary production in depth from a class analytical perspective.

Geographic and shareholder diversification

In addition to upgrading primary production in Argentina, El Agro diversified its investments geographically to lower risks further and to profit from other political economic contexts in countries that, for instance, have not levied high export taxes. "We have a vocation of regionalization. There is an issue of political risks, of capturing opportunities elsewhere [...]. Argentina has a very high tax pressure. Very high."[45]

In 2004, El Agro founded a firm in Uruguay, together with a local partner who initially held 45 percent of the shares. The firm produces and trades grains and oilseeds and sells agriculture services. Later, El Agro sold all its shares to the partner. In a similar vein, the company had produced soybeans in Paraguay since 2005, where it was not active anymore in 2018 either.

---

43 Interview with El Agro's former president, April 27, 2015, Buenos Aires.

44 Interview with a manager responsible for primary production of El Agro, April 28, anonymized town.

45 Interview with El Agro's former president, April 27, 2015, Buenos Aires.

In 2007, El Agro started a partnership with a private equity company based in Brazil which purchased 22 percent of the shares in El Agro. In the context of these investments, a holding was founded in Delaware, USA (El Agro LLC, see Figure 8 below), which in 2018 controlled all of El Agro's operations. Asked why the holding is based in Delaware, Carolina answers that "it was a part of their [the new investor's] conditions that we become a company that isn't headquartered in Argentina."[46] Accounting manager Dante adds that "this is due to tax issues."[47] However, none of my informants commented on the issue in depth.

The newly gained capital was used, among other things, to invest in operations in Brazil. El Agro bought the majority stake of an existing agribusiness and storage company. The latter increased its net earnings from 173 million US-Dollars to 515 million US-Dollars in the following five years (El Agro 2013, 15). In 2013, the business in Brazil was sold to the Japanese Mitsubishi, which had already acquired a 20 percent stake in 2011. Dante explains the deal saying that "Mitsubishi made a very interesting offer, and the truth is, it was a very big business to have entered and left in Brazil."[48] Graciela seconds that "it grew a lot, it was a very important business, and I think we found the right groom at the right moment of expansion [...], and we sold it at a moment of splendor."[49]

Following these investments and disinvestments, El Agro has concentrated mainly on its business in Argentina. However, the investments abroad have helped the company grow, Santiago says, and despite the geographical withdrawal, he is sure that it will go back to Brazil, or even to countries on the African continent, like Mozambique or Angola.

Becoming a one-stop shop

As indicated above, El Agro has reduced its primary production. In the 2009–10 season, it produced grains and oilseeds on over 250,000 ha in Argentina and neighboring countries. In the 2015–16 season, it had gone back down to 20,000 ha, 55,000 ha when including sharecropping (El Agro 2016). After former President Macri won the election in 2015 and reduced

46 Interview with El Agro's vice president, June 15, 2016, anonymized town.

47 Interview with an administration manager of El Agro, June 23, 2016, Buenos Aires.

48 Interview with an administration manager of El Agro, June 23, 2016, Buenos Aires.

49 Interview with a finance and controlling manager of El Agro, April 28, 2015, anonymized town.

export taxes on grains, production went up again to 80,000 ha, 100,000 ha when including sharecropping (El Agro 2018). This shows how the relatively asset light structure of the agriculture division, that does not fix much capital in land and machinery, facilitates the reorientation of investments on short terms and according to forseeable profits. El Agro involves other actors as associates when this is convenient to the company. When profit expectations suggest otherwise, it goes back to simply leasing-in their land. Business manager Mauricio points out that the strategy has never been to abandon agriculture but to gain the flexibility to reorient investments on relatively short terms and according to foreseeable profits. "We are talking about cycles and flows"[50] of the rewards to be gained from agriculture.

Yet in relative terms, primary production has lost quantitative importance for the company. The management believes that farming can provide high profits at times but, in general, it "has become a mature business with little growth potential" (El Agro 2013, 5) because new productive forces are quickly generalized among those farmers who have not been forced out of the market.

However, the years of lucrative soybean production have helped the company lay the basis for more profitable investments. "This [the reduction in agriculture] has not been a reduction of El Agro. The company has been strengthening itself and preparing for what follows."[51] This primarily means in-house chain integration. Today, El Agro operates as industrial, commercial, and finance capital in several subsidiaries that depend on the El Agro group (see Figure 8 below).[52]

A first business line that has been expanded is the provision of different agriculure-related services, including engineering and marketing consultancy, and the use of the above-mentioned GPS-software. Santiago explains that in contrast to primary production, "the profitability of services has not fallen. Services are still profitable." The subsidiary El Agro Consulting, for instance, has been selling farming consultancy to governments in

50 Interview with a marketing and business manager of El Agro, April 27, 2015, Buenos Aires.

51 Interview with a finance and controlling manager of El Agro, April 28, 2015, anonymized town.

52 The El Agro group was founded as an investment company after the Argentinian peso's peg to the US-Dollar was lifted in 2002. At the time, El Agro's debts were converted into debts in pesos and "as per market agreement the cost of the devaluation was divided between debtors and lenders, which meant a de facto partial debt write-down for the company. This was the moment when the professionalization of the network of knowledge paid off" (El Agro 2013, 9). El Agro hence benefitted form the 2001/02 crisis and used the moment to diversify its investments.

countries as far apart as Colombia and Kazakhstan since 2014. "I hope we can do it in Africa as well," Santiago says. But services sold within Argentina have more economic importance. Santiago describes El Agro as a radially integrated "ecosystem of services." He states that, in contrast to a time in agriculture when a farmer owned all means of production,

> "today, the producer needs an ecosystem around him that is more and more sophisticated and specialized. A seed supplier [...] an agrochemical supplier, a precision farming service, a financial service, logistics, risk management, cutting-edge technology and management practices, consulting, and so on. A knowledge-intensive ecosystem has grown around this producer [...]. [El Agro], today, is that ecosystem of services. We are a 'one-stop shop'."[53]

The notion of a "one-stop shop" has also been used by Gereffi and Fernandez-Stark in the context of an "upgrading trajectory" where companies become "able to offer a large spectrum of services ranging from low value added to high value services. These operations offer a 'one-stop shop' for clients and reduce overall transaction costs" (Gereffi and Fernandez-Stark 2016, 20).

According to Santiago, the focus on services has grown into an advantage over competitors. At the same time, competitors like LAgricola have become El Agro's clients. "They consume the services of [El Agro], so there is cooperation, not just competition."[54]

One crucial part of the 'one-stop shop' is an El Agro subsidiary founded in 2004, what is known as a Reciprocal Guarantee Company (SGR, in Spanish). It sells financial services to small and medium enterprises (SMEs). More precisely, it issues credit guarantees that grant SMEs access to higher credit volumes at more preferential rates, than what they would get by going directly to a bank or taking a loan from an input supplier.[55] These clients have to provide counter-guarantees, which may include surety bonds, mortgages, or promissory notes. For each completed transaction, they pay a commission to the SGR, which ranges from 1.5 to 2.5 percent of the warranty value. In addition to these gains for El Agro, investments in the risk fund of the SGR generate tax benefits for the investors who invest pre-tax. The main part of the risk-fund-capital comes from members of the El Agro-family, whose

53 Interview with El Agro's former president, August 21, 2014, Buenos Aires.

54 Interview with El Agro's former president, April 27, 2015, Buenos Aires.

55 In Argentina, SGRs are regulated by Law No. 24,467, which establishes that an SRG has to be constituted by participating partners, who obtain the financial service, and protective partners, who invest money in the risk fund (Art. 37). Only SMEs—i.e. those companies that do not exceed the limits established by Law No. 25,300—can be participating partners.

"money [...] is obviously not kept in a drawer. Of course, we invest it and it generates a profit [...], we buy bonds, shares, stocks, time deposits [...]. Those people always want the best option, the highest profitability, and at the same time it has to be safe, you know?"[56]

The SGR "came into play when there was no one else [laughs]"[57] and at the time of my study, it had become the largest privately-owned guarantor in Argentina. The most important purpose of the SGR is to link customers more closely to the company and to create loyalty. For Carolina, "it is a fantastic tool [...] and it has strengthened the chain a lot."[58] This is mainly because SGR-clients also buy other products and services at the 'one-stop shop,' which includes El Agro's commercial section. It has invested in infrastructures of capital circulation and installed 40 offices with adjacent storage plants in different areas over the Argentinian Pampas. From a catchment area with a roughly 100 km radius, "we receive grain, we process it, we dry it, we condition it, and we send it to the port via our logistics service [also via contractors]." El Agro has local commercial managers who "conduct the relations with the clients at each of our buying or selling points."[59] It stores and commercializes both its own grains and oilseeds and those produced by other farming companies.[60]

From 1999 on, El Agro has also traded farming inputs such as seeds, which are partly produced in-house, and agrochemicals like fertilizers and pesticides from its net of various local deposits. All managers I interviewed stressed that the company's activities as commercial capital are currently among the most profitable ones. This is one of the reasons why it has never fully withdrawn from agriculture: keeping a foot in this door helps establish close relationships to potential customers in the branch offices located everywhere. Especially the sowing associations with small producers "transform our partners into customers and our customers in partners, thus

56 Interview with an SGR manager of El Agro, April 28, 2015, anonymized town.

57 Interview with a marketing and business manager of El Agro, April 27, 2015, Buenos Aires.

58 Interview with El Agro's vice president, June 15, 2016, anonymized town.

59 Interview with a marketing and business manager of El Agro, April 27, 2015, Buenos Aires.

60 At the company level, the volume of grains and oilseeds traded grew from around 400,000 tons in 2001–02 to approximately 1.8 million tons in 2016–17 (El Agro 2008, 2017). Asked for its market position compared to the big traders, Dante explains that "the large exporters [like Cargill or Bunge] hold over 90 percent and the small storage facilities don't represent a percent. We are in between. We are neither large exporters nor small storage providers" (Interview with an administration manager of El Agro, June 23, 2016, Buenos Aires).

strengthening synergies between the different business units of the group" (El Agro 2018, 7 f.).

"We don't stop sowing, more than anything because it helps us to accompany producers. We are input sellers and grain traders. […] I don't think we should stop sowing, because it is something that prepares us to understand the logic of the producer, who is our end client, right?"[61]

"[It's] a tool to promote the commercialization of inputs […]. Selling agricultural products has a lot of potential […] it is about strategic positioning in the value chain."[62]

By concentrating on these services instead of primary production, El Agro releases its capital for other kinds of investments and circumvents the problem in agriculture production that the labor process pauses during the plants' growth. Now, with the services, Carla explains figuratively, El Agro is harvesting all year. The clients always need services and they "keep delivering grains throughout the year […] we are working all year long. As a company, we don't have much time to relax. This is due to El Agro's size."[63]

At the beginning, El Agro only resold inputs produced by large seed or agrochemical corporations. In 2013, however, after having sold the Brazil business, it bought an established company that develops and produces agrochemicals (here called ChemiAgro). "We wanted to integrate ourselves a little more into the value chain," Santiago explains, because processing industries bring even more profits than services.[64] "With services you can grow a lot in size, you need less capital, but at the same time the returns are lower."[65]

ChemiAgro produces herbicides, insecticides, fungicides, and growth regulators, among other things. Dante emphasizes that the new owners still have to work on the profitability of the company. But it was an investment in the future.[66] Even in years of non-profitable agriculture, someone will farm the fields and buy agrochemicals. In 2013, El Agro's then CEO commented:

---

61 Interview with El Agro's vice president, June 15, 2016, anonymized town.

62 Interview with a marketing and business manager of El Agro, April 27, 2015, Buenos Aires.

63 Interview with a commercial manager of El Agro, June 15, 2016, anonymized town.

64 Interview with El Agro's former president, April 27, 2015, Buenos Aires

65 Interview with El Agro's former president, August 21, 2014, Buenos Aires.

66 ChemiAgro has existed since 1978. Under El Agro's control, its sales rose from 62.2 million US-Dollars in 2013 to 120 million US-Dollars in 2017 (ChemiAgro 2013, 2017, own currency conversion). Its market share in Argentina rose from 2.3 percent in 2012 to 4.8 percent in 2015. Its main competitors are Bayer/Monsanto, Syngenta, Dow, Atanor, BASF, and DuPont (Interview with an administration manager of El Agro, June 23, 2016, Buenos Aires).

"There is a finite cake of profits to be made from the agribusiness value chain. So, we look at how this cake of profits is being divided up between the landowners, the farmers, the processors, and the inputs. Our analysis tells us that inputs are where the next money will be made, both volume-growth wise and margin-wise. [...] As a knowledge-driven network of professionals, we want to have this capacity in our network" (cited in El Agro 2013, 17).

In 2001, in corporation with other agribusiness companies, Santiago also co-founded a biotech company that develops new seeds, seed traits, and seed treatments, among other things, in order to make biotechnology "ever more fine-tuned to the application areas" (ibid., 7). But as a company, El Agro today only holds a 1 percent share.

On the other side of the value chain, El Agro has invested in the wheat processing industry, and it has its own brand for wheat products. It bought three mills in Argentina (one in 2001 and two in 2005) and another mill in Brazil. "They owed me money and I had to keep the mill," Santiago said, commenting on the takeover of the first mill. The other two mills were "a strategic thing. We learned about the business and decided to grow in it."[67] In the wheat value chain, Santiago concludes, "we are suppliers of inputs, technology, seeds, services, we process the wheat, and we sell pure flour as well as mixed versions [for instance for pizza dough]. [...] In this chain, we are very integrated."[68] In 2012, the company had furthermore invested 20 million US-Dollars in a pasta factory, which was sold again three years later, except for the more strategic part of the pasta business, the brand.[69]

Last but not least, in 2008, El Agro bought up a farming and trading company (here called NAC) which works like a smaller version of El Agro. Figure 8 shows the corporate structure in 2018. Until shortly before that, the Delaware holding was mainly controlled by members of the founding family. In 2016–17, however, a majority stake of El Agro LLC was sold to a private equity company headquartered in New York (El Agro 2018, 29).

Company data supports my informants in that investments in the production and commercialization of agrochemicals are more profitable and reliable for the company than in primary production. In absolute terms, the gross profits are higher in the case of agrochemicals than in the case of agriculture production (Table 19).

67 Interview with El Agro's former president, August 21, 2014, Buenos Aires.
68 Interview with El Agro's former president, April 27, 2015, Buenos Aires.
69 Interview with an administration manager of El Agro, June 23, 2016, Buenos Aires.

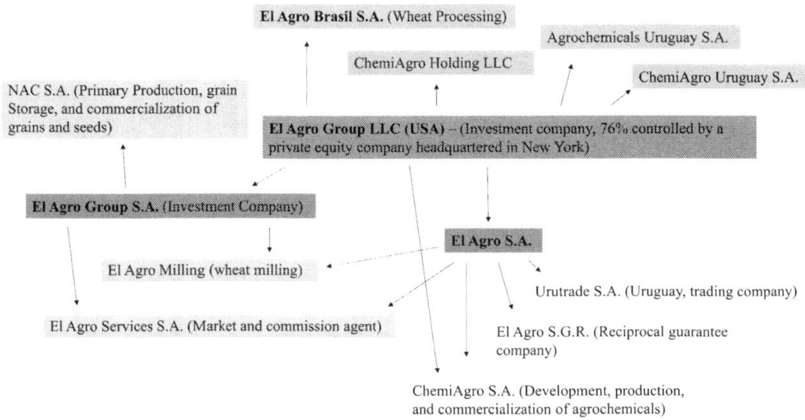

Figure 8: Corporate structure of El Agro and subsidiaries in 2018
The companies operate in Argentina unless the name indicates otherwise.
Source: own elaboration based on El Agro's 2008–2018 annual reports.

The same is true for the ratio of gross profits to direct production costs, according to the numbers published by El Agro (see Table 20). Today, ChemiAgro is an essential part of the corporation. In 2018, 21 percent of the total earnings and approximately 53 percent of the gross results came from the production and sale of agrochemicals.

My informants at El Agro often emphasized the company's net losses (see Table 19). There are several possible explanations, which do not contradict the extended capital accumulation under this company's roof (see also the limitations of the explanatory power of the data that I have mentioned in the case of Agrigood, Section 9.1.1). First, the presented data refers exclusively to El Agro S.A. and its subsidiaries in Argentina. The firms that are controlled by the holding in Delaware are not included. Dante explains that the balance sheets of the latter "are more private."[70] Thus, potential financial flows to the holding in Delaware are impossible to track for people outside the company. Berndt et al. (2019, 13) emphasize for other cases that such flows are "widespread, but difficult to quantify, practices to evade the state's fiscal grip." According to these authors, corporate actors regularly devalue income streams and overvalue expenses "in order to reduce their income and value added tax burdens" (ibid.). This also includes methods such as the un-

70 Interview with an administration manager of El Agro, June 23, 2016, Buenos Aires.

	2014		2016		2018	
	Millions of ARS	%	Millions of ARS	%	Millions of ARS	%
Total earnings	2,556.147	100	5,662.457	100	10,119.172	100
... thereof agriculture production	236.007	9.2	389.802	6.9	977.490	9.7
... thereof production and sale of inputs/agrochemicals	571.947	22.4	1,269.758	22.4	2,155.845	21.3
Costs of production	-2,260.006	100	-4,806.774	100	-9,042.320	100
...thereof agriculture production	-206.316	9.1	-327.371	6.8	-875.013	9.7
... thereof production and sale of inputs/agrochemicals	-436.055	19.29	-768.490	16.0	-1,580.510	17.5
Profits before interest payment and taxes	296.141	100	855.683	100	1,076.852	100
... thereof agriculture production	29.691	10.0	62.431	7.3	102.477	9.5
... thereof production and sale of inputs/agrochemicals	135.892	45.9	501.268	58.6	575.335	53.4
Finance costs (interests and exchange differences)	-239.272	_	-1,013.500	_	-3,623.601	_
Profits (Losses) before tax	56.869	_	-157.817	_	-2,552.514	_
Income tax benefit/expense	-28.221	_	50.538	_	625.999	_
Net profit/loss	28.648	_	-107.279	_	-1,926.515	_

Table 19: El Agro S.A.: earnings, costs, and profits (in millions of Argentine Pesos, ARS)
Source: own calculations based on El Agro's 2013–2018 annual reports

	2013	2014	2015	2016	2017	2018
Agriculture production	4.03	14.39	-0.005	19.07	12.35	11.7
Production and sale of inputs/agro-chemicals	66.6	31.16	52.01	65.22	19.23	36.40

Table 20: El Agro: ratio of gross profits to expenditures on production (in percent)
Source: own calculations based on El Agro's 2013–2018 annual reports

derreporting of harvest volumes and sales on black markets (ibid., 14), the gains of which do not appear in official financial reports. Another issue to note regarding the net losses is that they are partly due to high interest payments on debts. These debts finance investments in fixed capital which eventually increase both the capital base and the gross profits of the company.

In sum, El Agro's competitive strategies have been based, first, on technological and organizational upgrading at the point of primary production. The company grew with the agribusiness boom and when returns began to decline, it had already started to diversify its investments to become a 'one-stop shop.' Santiago says that El Agro is only just beginning to become an internationally known multinational company that serves as an example for others. "My dream is that ten years from now [...] I will be having a coffee in a bar in Angola or China and I will listen to producers in the area talk about [El Agro]."[71]

9.1.4 Summary

All three of the companies analyzed have managed to grow with agribusiness during the 1990s and 2000s. They have increased the profitability of their investments, each with firm-specific strategies.

First, this regards process upgrading in primary production.[72] All have grown to become large-scale grain and oilseed producers. To this end, Agrigood has significantly invested in land acquisition. El Agro and LAgricola have mainly produced on leased land, though building on previous land ownership. All have continuously invested in keeping up with the development of the productive forces and in some instances, they have played a pioneering role in them. Consider El Agro's investments in precision farming technology and its role in changing the organizational forms of doing agriculture. Company data (by LAgricola) suggests that the crop yields increased with these developments at a company level and that they outpace the national average.

Second, Agrigood, LAgricola, and El Agro have invested in higher profitable activities in upstream and downstream links of agro-industrial chains. The conditions for doing so were created by both expanded capital accumulation in agriculture, including through geographic expansion, and through

71 Santagio, anonymized speech, March 14, 2009, own translation.

72 For a critical discussion of capital-led process upgrading in agriculture see Section 8.1.

the opening of the companies to foreign investors. Agrigood has placed its main focus on the sugar-ethanol-energy complex in Brazil and on the rice processing industry in Argentina. LAgricola has focused on land transformation and real estate management services for European investors. In the case of El Agro, the company has concentrated on the production and sale of agrochemicals and on wheat processing in the recent past. All its investments are designed to strengthen and extend its identity as a 'one-stop shop.'

All three corporations might be interpreted as successful examples for process and functional upgrading at the firm level as defined by GVC scholars (see Chapter 3). My informants have also positively referred to the GVC metaphor as a tool for business development.

One can draw the conclusion from these examples that upgrading can actually work. However, the following sections and Chapter 10 point out several contradictions of firm-level upgrading and show that it is necessary to look beyond the latter to see patterns of winning and losing that go along with corporate developments. The GVC upgrading paradigm omits how companies can successfully upgrade, sometimes by making use of the GVC approach for the development of their strategies, while this may lead to a consolidation of social polarization. Chapter 10 further dives into what El Agro refers to as its 'network of networks' to analyze the class relations on which firm-level upgrading is built in this instance. But first, the following sections discuss limits and contradictions arising at other levels of the competitive strategies described. Although they can be read as examples of successful firm-level upgrading, I argue that the picture needs to be rounded out with the question, who benefits from firm-level moves into higher profit niches?

9.2 Up to where and for whom?

During my interviews, I asked my informants about disruptions, challenges, and limits to upgrading and whether they see potential disadvantages or risks built into their strategies. One point to keep in mind is that companies may not necessarily have an interest in communicating all possible drawbacks of their strategy. On the basis of interview statements and business reports, it is nevertheless feasible to identify contradictions in their trajectories. The following examines the ways in which my informants frame upgrading and its limits. I scrutinize their representations for underlying particular interests, and I shed critical light on the company developments portrayed. In this context, I also depict corporate ideologies that justify firm-level strategies where they clearly serve vested interests rather than broader populations—a fact that complicates the presumption of firms as partners in social upgrading.

9.2.1 Anyone can do it

On that note, there are different narratives surrounding the possibilities of value chain upgrading or its positive effects. A first one relates to converse statements quoted in this chapter's introduction, according to which there are no structural, socioeconomic hindrances to development at all. In this view, upgrading in agro-industrial chains is, in principle, possible for everyone. The conditions my interlocutors formulated are that, first, the right, i.e., non-business restrictive, political background is given for agribusiness to grow and that, second, entrepreneurs are keen to keep up with modern technologies. This is mirrored in Santiago's assertion according to which "we have to fight globalization with more globalization"[73] and socioeconomic development can be generated when large corporations pull small companies into GVCs. In this perspective, exploitation and capital power do not play a role; it is in the hands of those who have not yet benefited from globalization to change their situation through innovation. Furthermore, instead of problematizing the current dynamics of capitalist globalization, Santiago seeks to intensify the latter. Yet while he expects to be able to improve his own position in global capitalism, he claims that, in the end, the rising tide of economic growth lifts all boats. He explains that

> "the most progressive sectors or even Cristina's government [former President Kirchner] said that the big issue is who gets which part of the cake. But this is not the issue. The issue is whether or not there is cake, and how big it is. [...] If agricultural production grows, the number of trucks grows [...] everything moves: industry, services."[74]

The credo is, thus, more of the same form of growth and globalization that has shaped and reshaped geographies of uneven development.

73 Quote from an interview given by Santiago to students of the University of Buenos Aires (UBA) for the local journal of social sciences in 2016, own translation.
74 Ibid.

From another perspective, Santiago's remark quoted above that he is also landless likewise creates the impression that anyone can be successful in agribusiness. The underlying message is that this does not require property, only an open mind and competence in management. This narrative is an implicit de-legitimization of social struggles from below[75] and it abstracts from capital ownership or access to it as a precondition for leasing-in land and doing agribusiness. Tomas, who is a small-scale vegetable producer near Buenos Aires, brings the contradiction between corporations like El Agro and him and his peers to the point. In an interview he comments on Santiago's quote:

"Even if it would be true that he is a landless, the difference is that he is not poor. He has money that he can invest. [...] Here in this area, we don't own the land [on which we cultivate] and if the small producers cannot pay the rent, they don't even have a place to live. This is the double reality of the small producer. [...] I mean, they masquerade as humble people, but they are not. They're multinational corporations."[76]

Agrigood and LAgricola justify their land transformation and real estate businesses (see 9.1.1 and 9.1.2) as development projects. Both companies describe their activities in terms of a modernization of marginal, "underdeveloped" and "undermanaged or underutilized farmland (cultivated pastures and poorly managed agriculture)" (Agrigood 2018, 66). In Argentina, scholars, activists, and rural communities have criticized land appropriation by agribusiness and its justification as a shift from undermanagement to modernization. They have pointed to both the ongoing destruction of nature and sometimes violent displacements that accompany the geographical expansion of large-scale crop production. Especially in Argentina's northwest in provinces like Santiago del Estero, Chaco, and Salta, the land has long been cultivated extensively and, in indigenous communities, this has been done under collective use. However, the customary right that they claim cannot be enforced against companies who buy and monopolize the land (Leguizamón 2014).

The described land transformation strategies and the expansion into more peripheral areas has been analyzed as an expansion of the agribusi-

75 If the success (or lack thereof) is a reflection of personal skills in a modern knowledge society, and has nothing to do with land property, then the landless movement fights an enemy that does not exist.

76 Interview with a petty commodity producer and representative of APER, an association of regional peasants in the province of Buenos Aires, July 28, 2016, Parque Pereyra Iraola.

ness frontier (Barri and Wahren 2010; Cáceres and Gras 2017) and linked to land grabbing or real estate speculation (Sosa Varrotti 2015, 53), as well as to accumulation by dispossession and an increasing level of land conflicts (Cáceres 2015). Such strategies actively push forward a land concentration that is driven by international finance interests (Murmis and Murmis 2012). And it is worth underlining that such expansions of the "frontier regions" (Ouma 2016, 89) change property rights further to the benefit of big capital. Nevertheless, the interviewed company representatives either reinterpret the monopolization of land into a positive development, or, as in the following quote by Rogelio, deny such problems:

> "The issue of displacement of indigenous communities in Argentina is not a problem. This Wichi's thing that has appeared all over the media is in a small corner of Formosa and has been made an important political issue in the sense that it has gotten a lot of public awareness, but I would tell you that 95 percent of the area in Argentina does not have communities that have to be displaced in order to produce."[77]

In fact, Agrigood or LAgricola have never been directly associated with unlawful displacements or expropriations. However, new arable land that can be appropriated at a large scale without destroying nature and/or existing socio-cultural life clearly does not exist in Argentina, and the affected people so far have not been happy with the development that is taking place at these agribusiness frontiers. The denial of these conjunctures raises serious questions about the assumption that "public-private-civil society partnerships" (Gereffi and Luo 2014, 19) can achieve social upgrading for all, as the GVC approach suggests. What if capitalists do not even acknowledge that specific social problems exist?

These assessments of agribusiness as a developmental strategy that potentially benefits society render social relations of exploitation and power opaque and factor out inhered inequalities and environmental effects. From the depicted perspectives, the reasons for potential economic failure, exclusion, or uneven development are located outside the level of political economic relations and corporate action. Instead, if economic developments do not go well for some, this is implicitly attributed either to the individual who is not sufficiently open-minded to innovation, or to the business-hostile

77 Interview with the executive director of LAgricola, March 31, 2015, Buenos Aires. Wichi is the name of an indigenous community. Together with activists from other communities, Wichi-representatives camped out in the city center of Buenos Aires for several weeks while I was there in 2015. They demand the return of what they consider their territories.

state with its "attacks and closed policies."[78] The subtext is that a progressive society must be advanced by modern corporations, not by struggles from below, and that capitalist property relations are not part of the problem, rather the solution.

In this context, the ways in which my interlocutors address GVCs as a tool for corporate decision making or for sounding out investment opportunities contradict a fundamental concern especially of early chain research: the analysis of inequality as it is inscribed into the capitalist world system, though in ever changing ways. However, the intellectual shift of the GVC framework towards transaction cost economics (see Chapter 3) has enabled its integration into business worlds, both as a vehicle for corporate strategies and as an ideological tool. In the latter sense, it is used by my case companies to justify economic upgrading at the firm level as a path to development on which a rising tide of capitalist globalization can "lift all boats" (Webber 2010, 218).

Entry barriers (do not) matter

Another line of argument, namely that there actually are certain limits to upgrading set by stronger actors, seems to contradict these statements at first glance. Agrigood, for instance, mentions the competitive advantages of other firms as a potential threat to its own position: "Competitors may gain an advantage over us by [...] developing or using new products and production methods, introducing new products to the market sooner than we do, or securing exclusive rights to new technologies" (Agrigood 2018, 15).

However, the company does not consider the need to keep pace with such competitors to be a substantial problem. It rather poses this as an incentive to stay current: "Our success depends on the early identification of new developments and production methods and the continuous improvement of existing expertise to ensure that our product range keeps pace with technological change" (ibid.). Ultimately, leading competitive positions of other firms are regarded a challenge rather than an obstacle that makes it impossible for all economic actors to be on an equal footing.

My informants brought up entry barriers set by other actors in agriculture GVCs only upon explicit demand. In different interviews they then mentioned, for instance, that they would not put capital in the soy processing

78 Interview with the executive director of LAgricola, July 18, 2016, Buenos Aires.

industry because other corporations already form an oligopoly there. Miguel explains that the productivity is high in this industry. A profitable investment would require a massive amount of constant capital and a large scale of production.

> "In fact, Rosario […] is the largest soybean processing cluster in the world […] and competing against Cargill, Bunge, ADM, Dreyfus… just doesn't make sense. […] We could invest 200–300 million Dollars in a crushing plant but we would be less profitable than they are and we don't want that."[79]

However, none of my informants regards such entry barriers as a limit to their own upgrading strategies. When I asked Santiago, for instance, whether investments in soy processing are hampered by entry barriers placed by others, he answered: "No, they don't *put* entry barriers. The entry barrier is merely that they are very competitive." Only political entry barriers are regarded a problem, not the concentrated control over means of production. Santiago aims to make absolutely clear to me that competition and the corresponding search for innovation are a positive thing. And if an investment does not seem to work out, one should do something else. "This ecosystem is a very competitive ecosystem," he says. "It will always be that way. So, we have to be strong in what we do. And that's what gives us sustainability. […] I'm not worried about entry barriers."[80] Carolina adds in another interview that, "clearly, there are always niches."[81]

In sum, while these actors thus exemplify the impossibility to compete with global players in particular chain links, they do not regard this as a limit for themselves. Instead, they argue that, first, if it does not make sense to invest in a particular activity, one can simply invest somewhere else. Second, competitors who set high standards are not regarded as a problem, rather as an impetus to other actors to improve themselves. For the trajectories of my case companies, this is actually true; all of them managed to find higher profitable niches. For their businesses, entry barriers set by highly concentrated capitals in the soy chain are not a risk. However, they argue from the standpoints of relatively capitalized companies that are able to raise the financing necessary to fill such niches. As such, they are actors in the reproduction of capital-led uneven development.

79 Interview with an Agrigood manager, April 22, 2015, Buenos Aires.
80 Interview with El Agro's former president, August 21, 2014, Buenos Aires.
81 Interview with El Agro's vice president, June 15, 2016, anonymized town.

A facilitating state

Quite in line with neo-structural thinkers (see Leiva 2008; Webber 2010), Santiago asserts that the state needs to play an active role in developing local industries in global value chains. In his opinion, it must not do so by levying export taxes or by restricting companies' actions. Instead, it should create infrastructure and train people according to private actors' needs. Its main interest should be supporting industries with competitive advantages, such as agribusiness and related activities.

Several state-related problems which my interlocutors mention have also puzzled heterodox thinkers who, however, argue that the limits and failures of peripheral states need to be analyzed in the context of their political economy as well as of their insertion into global capitalism (Fernández and Ormaechea 2018). Other appeals to the state made by the interviewed managers more clearly reflect vested interests that my case companies have in specific policies that serve their strategies more than national or regional development in a broader sense.

The first set of problems includes issues such as economic instability and crisis susceptibility, inflation, meandering exchange rates, lack of investment, or deficits in infrastructure. Poor access to capital and low-risk credits was often mentioned as an obstacle that may prevent firms from upgrading. As Santiago puts it, "we have a problem with investment; access to credit is scarce and expensive." As an explanation, he adds that "the country has been sealed and the policies of closing have an impact on the economy."[82] The non-liberal fiscal policy of the former Kirchner administration, to which Santiago refers here, was mentioned as the reason for the poor access to capital in nearly all my interviews with company representatives. On the other hand, none of them assessed this situation in the context of the contradictions of world finance or the (international) political economy of the banking and credit system. Arrighi (2010), among many others, has analyzed the relation between finance power and the dynamics of uneven development. My interlocutors, in contrast, do not mention issues such as power relations between creditors and debtors and their particularities in peripheral economies, where there is a mutual interplay between lacking investments and relatively low effective demand for money capital on the one hand, and high interest rates on the other. My case companies therefore

82 Interview with El Agro's former president, August 21, 2014, Buenos Aires.

draw on a biased explanation for the uneven geographies of access to finance. Beyond that, in contrast to smaller local companies, their own access to international capital confers them an advantage, which reproduces the uneven access to capital within Argentina.

Another mentioned state shortcoming that effects economic competitiveness is the condition of infrastructure in Argentina and the related drawbacks. Agrigood, for instance, explains that

> "a substantial portion of agricultural production in the countries in which we operate is currently transported by truck, a means of transportation significantly more expensive than the rail transportation available to U.S. and other international producers. Our dependence on truck transportation may affect our position as a low-cost producer, such that our ability to compete in the world markets may be impaired" (Agrigood 2018, 23).

Basic transport infrastructure is indeed part of the territorialized uneven conditions for productivity and "the circulation of capital in built environments" which often require "state expenditures on projects that capital would find it difficult or impossible to undertake" (Harvey 2006, 101). This is especially the case in peripheral regions where investments in fixed capital like a railway is not promising in terms of the foreseen returns. In the words of Hadjimichalis (1984, 336), such conditions are "space-specific" parts of "the so-called 'total capital' available for each individual capitalist." Importantly, the availability of investments in spatial fixes like railway infrastructure that reduce the turnover time of capital are "particular to a location" (ibid.). They cannot be considered independently of accumulation dynamics and class struggles over state expenditures that actively co-determine the localized conditions in the geographical organization of capitalism. In Argentina, infrastructure is a much-discussed topic. From the perspective of my case companies, the state has not responded enough to business pressure to improve the conditions for doing business in this context. While they seek to expand infrastructure according to their needs, infrastructure in general lies in the interest of broader parts of the population.

Other remarks on state policies made by my interlocutors concern particular capital interests more exclusively. For example, this applies to already discussed issues like the *retenciones*, which all interviewed company representatives immediately listed when I asked about limits to upgrading. "Argentina is so competitive in producing soybeans," Rogelio says, "that even with bad international soybean prices we could produce well, if we didn't have the tax pressure that we're having."[83] Again, the logic is that with the export taxes, agribusiness cannot do well and thus, value chain development is not possible. As Santiago points out: "It's funny, but if Moyano [a labor leader in Argentina, secretary of the truck driver's union] is against lowering the *retenciones*, he's against the work of his own union members. In truth, everything moves [with the growth of agriculture production], industry, services, ..."[84] In fact, this argument is misleading, because agriculture production and therewith the quantity of commodities to be transported did not go down in Argentina with the export taxes. What did go down, though, was private profits, a part of which were redirected to the state. (For a discussion of the *retenciones* see Section 8.3.)

The current land law is regarded as a further limit to business development, especially by Agrigood and LAgricola, who engage in the real estate business and buy land with or for international capital. Remember that the current law restricts foreign land ownership in Argentina. Agrigood argues that "the adoption of laws and regulations that impose limitations on ownership of rural land by foreigners in the jurisdictions in which we operate may also limit the liquidity of our farmland holdings." In Rogelio's words, this "holds back growth in many locations."[85] Indeed, it does hold back company-level growth. Yet while Rogelio perceives this as a limit, the law can also be interpreted as an instrument to hold back the growth of land concentration in the hands of ever fewer investors.[86]

A last example of political measures that are named as potential restrictions consists of environmental legislation. Despite the fact that all my case companies present themselves as ecologically sustainable and responsible actors, Agrigood's assessment of this legislation is as follows:

83 Interview with the executive director of LAgricola, March 31, 2015, Buenos Aires.

84 Quote from an interview given by Santiago to students of the University of Buenos Aires (UBA) for the local journal of social sciences in 2016, own translation.

85 Interview with the executive director of LAgricola, March 31, 2015, Buenos Aires.

86 Note that there are also critical scholars who have put the current land law into question, though from a different perspective. For a critique see Gras (2013a, 67 ff.), who argues that this law has only partially addressed the land issue, as it is not accompanied by another legal instrument that addresses the role of land leasing for concentration processes. Above that, land titling policies in areas historically occupied by peasants in precarious tenure situations are not addressed either. In cases where the right of indigenous communities to the lands which they work has been recognized, this has depended to a great extent on these communities' strength in its struggles, not due to but despite the legal situation (ibid.).

"We are subject to extensive environmental regulation, and concerns regarding climate change may subject us to even stricter environmental regulations. [...] Such laws include compulsory maintenance of certain preserved areas within our properties, management of pesticides and associated hazardous waste and the acquisition of permits for water use and effluent disposal. [...] We could be exposed to criminal and administrative penalties in addition to the obligation to remedy the adverse effects of our operations on the environment and to indemnify third parties for damages. [...] [This could] adversely affect the availability of funds for capital expenditures and other purposes" (Agrigood 2018, 16).

In some GVC literatures, international standards including environmental regulation have been analyzed as a real potential barrier for small agriculture producers (Dolan and Humphrey 2000). Agrigood's concern, in contrast, seems instead to be motivated by the interest to lose as little as possible of its profits, among other things, at the cost of nature.

In closing of this section, state-related limits to upgrading as they are addressed by representatives of my case companies include problems that indeed affect regional development in a broader sense. However, as I have previously argued, an understanding of how the respective policies evolve requires a comprehensive understanding of nationally specific processes, (class) struggles and the building of hegemony in Argentina, as well as their intertwining with the historical dynamics of global capitalism and resulting geopolitical and geo-economic constraints (Fernández and Ormaechea 2018). Other complaints made against the state by my case companies appear to stem more directly from a concern that the state does not sufficiently serve their particular interests. It is furthermore noteworthy that issues like land concentration or competitive advantages of large corporations are not problematized as entry barriers by my case companies, while political measures that (could) reduce their profits are.

9.3 On ants and elephants

As I have sketched out in previous chapters, grain and oilseed production in Argentina is relatively atomized compared to other nodes in agro-industrial value chains, such as the soy processing industry. However, data provided by the INDEC and various studies have indicated a process of concentration and a discernible reduction of farming units with a simultaneous increase in total production over the past decades (see Chapter 6). The concentration and centralization of capital is crucial for determining who benefits from upgrading and, thus, the reproduction of uneven development on changing scales. However, while mainstream GVC research sees upgrading as a path to generating higher profits and thus to the induction of development (see Chapter 3), it has not paid adequate attention to the relationship between upgrading and capital concentration.

The following analyzes how in 'the jungle,' the 'elephants' do not generally help the 'ants,' to pick up Santiago's metaphor again. The upgrading trajectories of my case companies play a part in the relative reduction in the number of actors who control agricultural production in Argentina.

9.3.1 Upgrading and the concentration of capital

Process upgrading or the development of the productive forces in grain and oilseed production in Argentina has increased the productivity of labor and soils over the past decades. In the course of these changes, agribusiness has become more capital intensive and less labor intensive (Fernández 2012b, Neiman 2010b). This implies that the amount of capital that needs to be allocated in production has increased.

As a concrete example, the use of modern machinery speeds up the soy harvest and reduces the socially necessary labor time to produce a certain amount of this oilseed. Farming companies can hence produce the same amount of soy in shorter (labor-)times. However, unlike what the metaphor of increasing value added through process upgrading suggests, it is not the surplus value embodied in a particular unit of soybeans, say a ton, that increases. On the contrary, the surplus value embodied in this ton decreases as the socially necessary labor time to produce it shrinks and the constant capital that needs to be invested grows with the enhanced productivity.

But the total of the produced value increases when the scale of production is expanded. In fact, process upgrading in Argentina's agribusiness implies that production is only profitable above a certain scale, which is one of the reasons why especially farming units smaller than 500 ha have disappeared in this country's farming heartland (see Chapter 6). Large-scale farming companies like Agrigood, LAgricola, and El Agro have increased the value added under their control by extending the production volume and by diversifying their investments, not by adding more value per ton of soybeans. While other, smaller capitalist farmers could not compete, these companies remain competitive because of their capacity to control production on large scales. Importantly, these are not independent events, instead related processes.

Whether or not a firm can employ state-of-the-art means of production and produce on the scale necessary for being competitive depends on the capital it can raise. "Therefore the larger capital beats the smaller" (Marx 1990 [1867], 777). In a Marxist understanding, the development of the productive forces driven by capitalist competition inheres a tendency of capital to concentrate.[87] Capital concentration here refers to the increase of the amount of capital, including the means of production, controlled by individual capitalists. It is, in other words, extended accumulation. "The individual capitals grow, and with their growth the concentration of the means of production increases, in the proportion in which they form aliquot parts of the total social capital" (Marx 1990 [1867], 776).

As representatives of my case companies noted, their production has become relatively cheaper in the wake of process upgrading. At their scale, they can produce at production costs that are lower than those of a small farmer. The relatively higher profits these companies therefore make are further accelerated when process upgrading enhances soil productivity and therewith increases yields compared to other production areas.

However, the fact that the scale of grain and oilseed production in Argentina has increased does not necessarily imply that the farmed land and machinery are technically owned by one single firm. The next chapter discusses how process upgrading can inhere a differentiation of the social division of labor. The ownership structure within the total social capital can change and lead, for example, to the described outsourcing model. Companies like El Agro, however, still command the productive process.

Against the backdrop of these considerations, I reexamine Santiago's statement that as El Agro develops precision farming technologies, it "contributes to their [its clients'] competitiveness. We are creating a new need for them, leading to a relevant higher value added."[88] The fact that El Agro develops new means of production that are sold to its clients exemplifies how innovation and productivity improvement is not a matter of individual entrepreneurs in the first place; there is a "vast sector of industry specializing in innovation and dedicated to selling innovations to everyone else" (Harvey 2017, 120).

87 For a discussion of countertendencies see Krüger (2010, 135 ff.).

88 Interview with El Agro's former president, April 27, 2015, Buenos Aires.

But Santiago's position neglects several issues. First, the need that El Agro is creating for its clients requires the ability, i.e., the capital, to profitably invest in new constant capital on the client side. Second, a part of the value embodied, for instance, in a ton of soy produced by an Argentinian farmer who uses El Agro's precision farming services stems from the technology he or she buys from El Agro, which, thus, does not form part of his or her profit. Third, it also neglects the above-mentioned problem that the increase in the relative importance of constant capital requires a certain scale of production to be profitable. In this context, Carolina admits that the precision farming technology partly developed by El Agro has so far only been viable for producers that "are a little bigger."[89]

For these reasons, it can be stated in sum that the process upgrading devised and promoted by my case companies has made their businesses more profitable. However, this cannot easily be equated with a development that enhances the situation of agriculture producers in general. In capitalism, technology development does not happen as a conscious and democratic development that benefits the many. It does not serve to make production less time-consuming and easier for everyone or to satisfy social needs more quickly, but to increase (individual) accumulation. Many producers have not been able to stay competitive and have left the business at least as independent producers—not necessarily as *contratistas* or landowners. In this way, the role my case companies play in process upgrading is directly related to capital concentration and the difficulty that small producers face to stay in business.

Concentration or democratization?

In Section 9.1, I have shown that LAgricola and El Agro have long based the expansion of their companies on a land leasing model. Santiago has described this possibility as a democratization of agriculture. Following on his above cited self-description as landless, he explains that today, land cannot only be accessed by those who own it but also by other people. "It is a model that facilitates specialization, [...] creates social mobility, and democratizes access to land. [...] This is El Agro's model."[90]

89 Interview with El Agro's vice president, June 15, 2016, anonymized town.
90 Interview with El Agro's former president, August 21, 2014, Buenos Aires.

However, the kind of democratization he imagines is not to be confused with a democratic decision and control over what shall be produced on arable land and how. Santiago's picture does not address the question that control over land, be it through ownership or leasing contracts, depends on an actor's capital strength or position in highly uneven political economic relations. Second, when a small landowner does not have enough capital to invest in agricultural production in a profitable manner, due to the current state-of-the-art technology, the choices he or she can make are relatively limited. At any rate, independent production is not an available option in such a case.

Gras and Cáceres (2017) have therefore argued that capital concentration in Argentinian agribusiness is not necessarily linked to large land ownership. Network management as in the case of El Agro or other changing strategies of capital towards land should not be interpreted as a decrease in the concentration of control over and profits from agribusiness. Sosa Varotti (2015) similarly contends that in contemporary Argentina, control over the production process is more important for big agribusiness than is large landownership. As the following exemplifies, in this context, large companies have also been able to broaden their competitive strength through their bargaining power, which is based on their size.

The advantages of being a big player

Agrigood, LAgricola, and El Agro mention various advantages they have as large corporations compared to smaller producers which consolidate their competitive positions. First, this concerns the above-mentioned strategy of diversifying primary production geographically. In contrast to smaller producers that produce at one location only, they are able to lower or diversify the risk for the total business. Rogelio remarks that

> "[one year] it started raining a lot, which resulted in a huge agricultural loss. In our case, it was only one region [...] it did not hit us so much. But there were people who focus on one place only, producers who had only one field, and things became very complicated for them."[91]

And Eugenio, representative of the business association SRA adds: "The biggest companies have the ability to look further than the small producers,

91 Interview with the executive director of LAgricola, July 18, 2016, Buenos Aires.

so they go where it is most profitable. Uruguay and Brazil, for instance, did not have any kind of export withholdings."[92]

Second, large-scale producers are able to obtain an extra profit within the capital circuit compared to small producers, among other reasons because they can buy seeds, agrochemicals, and the like at relatively cheaper prices, below the average cost of production. Miguel explains that "obviously we are looking for the lowest costs [...] in long-term relationships [with input providers] where our scale allows us to have a competitive advantage and to benefit from the volume."[93] In general, Agrigood declares that "we have been able to obtain discounts for the acquisition of supplies and excess prices for our production in the farming sector" (Agrigood 2018, 72). When it comes to realizing the produced value, in Santiago's words, "you somehow have greater bargaining power, because of the volume of grains you originate."[94]

Third, Rogelio remarks that in contrast to small producers nearly all of LAgricola's production costs except for the fees paid to the *contratistas* are denominated in US-Dollars, which makes it less vulnerable to exchange rate fluctuations.[95] At the same time, large corporations have a greater ability to speculate, as their size allows them, for instance, to withhold harvests from the market and to "capitalize on fluctuations in the prices of commodities" (Agrigood 2018, 83). Furthermore, they can sell their products directly to the big dealers or even export on their own, thereby "avoiding the costs of an intermediary" (LAgricola 2018, 16). Rogelio summarizes all three points, saying that

> "our growth means that when we talk with Cargill, Dreyfus, Bunge as end-users or with Monsanto, Syngenta, BASF as input suppliers, we go with a big package. The truth is that we have a very good relationship with the big suppliers and with the big traders. That has allowed us to do good business, to have more favorable conditions than other companies. With the traders that finance us or that we can use for hedging or futures in Chicago [...] and with players like Syngenta, Monsanto, we have an excellent relationship [...] and well, to buy an input a little cheaper, to sell grains for a couple of Dollars more, or to get a financing at lower interest; when you take that to a large scale, the difference is even bigger."

92 Interview with a representative of the SRA, August 7, 2014, Rosario.
93 Interview with an Agrigood manager, April 22, 2015, Buenos Aires.
94 Interview with El Agro's former president, April 27, 2015, Buenos Aires.
95 Interview with the executive director of LAgricola, March 31, 2015, Buenos Aires.

As a fourth advantage, he goes on to explain that these relationships have helped the company to get a foot in other countries: "When we go to Colombia [...] we go hand in hand with Monsanto. They introduce us to people. Monsanto's CEO was eating in [then President of Colombia] Santos' house, so there is a very close relationship."[96] The access to international capitals, conditions of production, and markets "brings these actors into an unequal competition with those who are inserted in national capital circuits only" (Sosa Varrotti 2015, 52, own translation).

In sum, both the development of the means of production and the benefits for large corporations resulting from favorable relations to other corporations in upstream and downstream links of the chain have helped my case companies improve the profitability of their businesses. At the same time, however, the concentration of capital has contributed to both the exclusion of other actors from the production and appropriation of social wealth and to a deepening of unequal conditions of accumulation between agrarian capitals of different sizes.

9.3.2 Upgrading and the centralization of capital

I have argued before that, while it is possible for peripheral actors to climb a value chain, upgrading comes at the expense of other actors. This can mean, for instance, that it leads to an intensification of the exploitation of workers or that other firms' pieces of the cake shrink when firms like El Agro, Agrigood, and LAgricola enlarge theirs. Capital concentration has allowed my case companies to functionally upgrade to more profitable activities in agribusiness value chains, including different services and processing industries (9.1). Together with opening up to international investors, the reproduction of capital on an extended scale has built the base for investments in more capital-intensive chain nodes.

At the same time, they have also used a more direct form of prevailing over competitors: displacing other firms not through competitive advantages, instead by taking them over. In addition to developing the means of production, acquiring external companies becomes a further instrument for overcoming the limitations of corporate growth, and, thus, increasing this centralization of capital.

96 Interview with the executive director of LAgricola, March 31, 2015, Buenos Aires.

"It is concentration of capitals already formed, destruction of their individual independence, expropriation of capitalists by capitalists, transformation of many small into few large capitals. [...] Its field of action is therefore not limited by the absolute growth of social wealth, or in other words by the absolute limits of accumulation. Capital grows [...] in a single hand in one place, because it has been lost by many in another place. This is centralization proper, as distinct from accumulation and concentration" (Marx 1990 [1867], 777).

This tendency can be observed not only in famous cases like Bayer's acquisition of Monsanto. Takeovers are also made by smaller corporations, as my case companies have shown. Take Agrigood, whose history as a company started with the takeover of a 74,000-hectare farm. In the years to follow, the company bought at least 18 farming companies in Argentina, Brazil, and Uruguay (Agrigood 2018, 40 f.) Its rice business started with the acquisition of an established company in 2007.[97] The first sugar and ethanol mill Agrigood bought in Brazil in 2005 was also not built from scratch, instead taken over (see Section 9.1.1). As the company itself summarizes: "As a part of our business strategy, we have grown through acquisitions. We plan to continue growing by acquiring other farms and production facilities throughout South America" (Agrigood 2018, 11). El Agro's development inheres similar examples. The first wheat mill, for instance, was an acquisition, as Santiago says: "They owed me money and I had to take the mill." As for the other two mills that were integrated into the company later on, they were also "all bought up."[98] As I have shown in Section 9.1.3, El Agro also acquired the eighth largest agrochemical company in Argentina, and a company that works like a smaller version of itself, among other examples.

In these cases, functional upgrading at the firm level directly coincides with the centralization of capital and thus with a de-linking or "disarticulation" (Bair and Werner 2011a) of other actors from the value chain. It is the takeover of already existing wealth rather than the creation of new development opportunities outside the firm.

In sum, in contrast to the view of upgrading as benefiting a broad range of actors, firm-level upgrading may also entail the concentration and central-

97 In this context it should be briefly noted that Agrigood's presentation of its investments in the rice and sugar cane processing industries as automatic (since both need to be processed directly after the harvest) or as easy sledding is ideological; small producers, of course, could not easily do the same. From them, "we buy paddy rice for processing in our industry," Miguel explains (Interview with an Agrigood manager, July 20, 2016, Buenos Aires).

98 Interview with El Agro's former president, August 21, 2014, Buenos Aires.

ization of capital, and, therewith, the reproduction of uneven development. This entails the reproduction of barriers to entry for other actors and the narrowing down of the hands that control social production or, as for my case, the further development of agro-industrial chains in Argentina.

9.4 Geographical transfer of profits

It is generally agreed among critical scholars that several factors operate simultaneously on the geographical unevenness of capitalist development. Hadjimichalis (1984, 329) has proposed to analyze the "geographical transfer of value" (GTV) as one of them, using the labor theory of value in geographical terms. He understands GTV as

> "the tendency or process through which the value produced for exchange by workers at one locality: (a) is realized by the capitalists who have employed these workers, but profits have been reinvested elsewhere; and/or (b) is at least partially realized by the capitalists who have employed these workers and is added as excess profits to other capitalists in other localities" (Hadjimichalis 1984, 338).

Hadjimichalis refers to the first case "as direct and/or derived GTV" and to the second as "indirect and/or originating GTV" (ibid.). In both cases, his concern is that the exploitation of workers at one location may (partly) add to the profits "enjoyed by other capitalists in other areas" (ibid.). This can occur through violence and plunder but also through "abusive corporate tax behaviour" (Quentin and Campling 2018, 3 ff.), transfer-pricing, and multinational profit repatriation, among other mechanisms (Hadjimichalis 1984, 340).

Besides such deliberate actions, according to Hadjimichalis, indirect forms of GTV are necessarily rooted in the antagonistic social relations of capitalist production and circulation, and in the competition for the total surplus among capitalists across space. A company that controls production in regions with greater labor productivity can realize "aside from its own surplus value part of the nonrealized surplus value of other sectors and regions" (ibid., 341; see Quentin and Campling 2018).

There is a longstanding discussion among Marxists and other critics of the international political economy about how exactly value transfer works, whether it is a cause or effect of uneven development, and how much of a role it actually plays in the reproduction of geographical inequality. In highly simplified terms, representatives of dependency theories and world systems analysis have focused mainly on theories of unequal exchange between capitalist centers and peripheries and a profit drain or value transfer from the latter to the former (Amin 1975; Emmanuel 1972; Wallerstein 2000a). Harvey (2003, 137 ff.) has more recently argued that the plundering of social wealth—value transfer through "accumulation by dispossession"—has gained much significance in contemporary capitalism. Contributions that refer more closely to value theory have criticized approaches that are based primarily on exchange-theoretical conceptualizations of the global economy, arguing that they tend to treat the generation of surplus value as a question of income redistribution that ignores the social relations of production (Milios and Sotiropoulos 2009, ten Brink 2008).

Though in the awareness of these debates, it is not the intention of this study to take a position in relation to them. My primary concern here is to argue that my case-companies have played a role in the geographical transfer of profits, and that this further challenges the implicit link between upgrading and national/regional development as suggested by GVC scholars.

In this context, it is worth noting that the profits generated by my case companies in the course of firm-level upgrading do not remain completely on site. All three companies have—to different degrees—become corporations which employ capital invested from countries other than where it is being reproduced. Milios and Sotiropoulos (2009, 177) have argued that the position of capital in a corporation "may be occupied by more than one subject." In other words, the money invested in the labor force and means of production partly stems from shareholders, partly from a bank, i.e., finance or interest-bearing capital, and partly from the functioning capitalists who manage and control the productive processes. In class-analytical terms, the capital position may be composed of industrial capital and interest-bearing capital at the same time.[99]

As reflected in the operations of all of my case companies, this can also correspond to the sourcing of capital from different geographical places. In fact, the participation of international investors is one of the reasons why they have been able to invest in both newly built factories and acquisitions in different nodes in agribusiness value chains. This entails a "repatriation of a

99 In Marx's (1991, 504) words, "in the production process, the functioning capitalist represents capital against the wage-labourers as the property of others, and the money capitalist participates in the exploitation of labour as represented by the functioning capitalist."

part of the profits to the capital-exporting country" (Milios and Sotiropoulos 2009, 165).

In the case of El Agro, the holding is today headquartered in Delaware, and a 76 percent share is held by a private equity firm based in New York. Agrigood is a joint stock company that intends to "maintain our position as a leading agricultural company in South America by expanding and consolidating each of our business lines, creating value for our shareholders" (Agrigood 2018, 50). Its net profits are transferred to investors from Qatar, USA, and Europe, among others.[100] In the case of LAgricola, its most profitable business line is the provision of management services to a real estate fund headquartered in the US and owned by European investors. The profits made with the land transformation business are transferred to the investors, minus the management fees paid to LAgricola. Such management services are thus not directed towards economic development in situ.

Tax strategies have been described as another possible loophole for profit transfers. Quentin and Campling (2018) have pointed to the fact that multinational corporate groups (with various subsidiaries) are not taxed as such.

> "This is because, legally, corporate groups are not entities to which profits can arise. It is the profits of the individual companies making up the group that are taxed, rather than those of the group, and each group entity's gross revenues and deductible expenses potentially include intra-group payments. This means that multinational corporate groups can manipulate the distribution of functions and risks from entity to entity, to ensure that as much of the overall profits arise in low-tax jurisdictions as possible" (ibid., 35).

El Agro and Agrigood, for instance, have parent companies located in Delaware or Luxembourg, which are both known as tax shelters. I did not obtain access to information on the actual cash flows between the individual companies that form the groups. However, it has been shown how in other cases, such cash flows have consisted, for instance, in tax-deducible "management fees" (ibid.). In spite of the poor data situation in this instance, it is striking that any responses by my interlocutors to my question why their parent companies are located in Luxembourg or Delaware stated that it was because investors wanted this due to tax issues.[101] Miguel remarks that

---

100 This, in turn, reinforces capital concentration because "an investor from outside will not come and invest a thousand Dollars in a field, or two thousand or three thousand. He will always think of a little more. So, we needed more of the assets that were attractive to investors (Interview with an Agrigood manager, April 22, 2015, Buenos Aires).

101 Interview with an administration manager of El Agro, June 23, 2016, Buenos Aires.

> "this is an issue of being a public company and [...] if they [public companies] are based in a place they are subject to its law and taxes. All the legal analysis is not my strength obviously, but when a company goes public you have to adapt to a certain legal framework [...]. Every [individual company] pays its local taxes. Luxembourg is for our shareholders more than anything."[102]

This suggests that shareholders of my case companies seek to realize their 'shareholder value' (a term that diverts from the fact that it is actually a part of the profit that they appropriate) outside Argentina, where they are then also liable to be taxed. While this is indeed a problem that is difficult to grasp, the mainstream GVC upgrading literature has largely abstracted from the geographical transfer of profits. As my examples show, however, successful firm-level upgrading in situ can imply the outflow of a portion of the profits.

9.5 Firm upgrading, development in situ, and social betterment

In Chapter 8, I have argued that GVC research falls short when it presupposes companies to be carriers of socioeconomic progress without analyzing competitive strategies and corporate interests, which are not necessarily at the service of development beyond the firm level. The following section builds on this previous discussion and underlines two points based on interview statements and business reports of my case companies. The first is that capital strategies do not necessarily entail functional upgrading, and not necessarily in situ. The second is that the social responsibility that corporate actors set out to assume reaches its limits when it comes to demands posed by organized labor or social movements.

Capital strategies and upgrading in situ

The recent histories of my case companies have entailed successful upgrading at the firm level. According to the directors and managers I interviewed, it is both individual growth and Argentina's socioeconomic development that is of concern to them in this context. In practice, however, this does not imply that their competitive strategies are necessarily focused on economic activities on site. Instead, investments are predictably shifted to where

102 Interview with an Agrigood manager, April 22, 2015, Buenos Aires.

they promise the highest returns. Moreover, although functional upgrading forms a part of their strategies, this is not a straightforward process. As managers of all three enterprises emphasize, their investment foci are constantly meandering.

Rogelio explains that over the past years, the investors of Juaquimana (which is managed by LAgricola; see Section 9.1.2) have mainly opted to put money in land acquisitions in countries where this is easier and more promising than in Argentina.

> "Some investors are looking at Brazil, others want to see Paraguay, and there are investors who want to see Argentina. But today [in 2015], Argentina is not an open market. This is going to change, but today it is not an option. So, the projects we are seeing are where a foreigner can install himself [...] We are looking at investments in Paraguay and Colombia."[103]

I do not mention this example to suggest that the rural real estate business would have a more positive developmental effect when carried out in Argentina. What I aim to illustrate, instead, is that even if one accepted the premise that firm-level upgrading generally engenders broader gains, the problem remains that these concrete business decisions are not essentially shaped by an objective of local development. They are instead geared to profit expectations at given times and places. Argentina only plays a role in this picture insofar it is expected to reinstate a land law that will remove the tight corset from investors and further facilitate land concentration. In a similar vein, Miguel describes that "the contact with the investors is also a little bit what shapes your strategy or what gives you the vision, because they start asking you 'Che, why not Brazil?'"[104]

And while industrial processing is part of Agrigood's business strategy in Brazil (see 9.1.1), this is not necessarily a strategic priority. In Miguel's words: "What [investors] are looking for [...] is either secure returns in the long term, or high returns in the short term [...] but whether it is an investment in primary production, industrialization, or integration down to the consumer, there is no specific interest."[105] In Uruguay, for instance, the company exclusively engages in primary production. As regards "soybean, maize, and wheat production [in that country], the best option so far has been simply

103 Interview with the executive director of LAgricola, March 31, 2015, Buenos Aires.

104 Interview with an Agrigood manager, April 22, 2015, Buenos Aires.

105 Interview with an Agrigood manager, July 20, 2016, Buenos Aires

to produce the commodity, and not to industrialize it."[106] Contributing to a regionally uneven development, Uruguay thus only appears on the company map as a node where the peripheral activities of agro-industrial chains are carried out, because this is what is most lucrative at this point in time.

In Argentina, Agrigood is vertically integrated in the rice chain. But with respect to soybeans, Miguel remarks that "today, we are not obliged to [invest in processing]; the unprocessed soybeans are already efficient for us."[107]Again, this shows that functional upgrading is not a desirable goal per se. "Since we continued to get more cheap land with efficient soybeans, we continued to invest in soybean fields in Argentina as well as in sugarcane processing in Brazil. [...] It's not one or the other, it depends in each case where you maximize your results."[108]

As for El Agro, Santiago reiterates that there is no categorical interest in occupying particular chain nodes; it depends on where one can best grow individually with which activities.

> "[In Uruguay] our model works with more grain production and less services. [Question: What is the reason for this geographical difference?] Because there are tax issues, context issues [...] The model is precisely to adapt to the conditions of each country and do the business that suits each place. [Question: And how would you summarize the reasons for your strategy to make some of your investments in Uruguay instead of Argentina?] Well, no, we have a vocation for regionalization, due to political risks, but also to enable capturing opportunities elsewhere."[109]

In Argentina, compared to Agrigood and LAgricola, El Agro has withdrawn the most from agriculture at least before Macri's election, and invested in other, related, activities. Yet, Santiago does not regard this a landmark decision. He says he instead has a "radial integration" in mind which "sometimes is going to be with industry, sometimes with services, sometimes

106 Interview with an Agrigood manager, April 22, 2015, Buenos Aires.

107 Interview with an Agrigood manager, July 20, 2016, Buenos Aires.

108 Interview with an Agrigood manager, April 22, 2015, Buenos Aires. It is noteworthy that the company maintains this approach despite the fact that it is well aware of problems that are related to Argentina's dependency on agribusiness. In its 2018 annual report, it expresses the concern that "since the beginning of 2015, international commodity prices for Argentina's primary commodity exports have declined, which has had an adverse effect on Argentina's economic growth. A continued decline in the international prices for Argentina's main commodity exports could have a direct negative effect on our business, results of operation and financial condition, as well as on Argentina's economy" (Agrigood 2018, 24).

109 Interview with El Agro's former president, April 27, 2015, Buenos Aires.

with outsourcing [farming activities], sometimes with new products."[110] Accordingly, the company has recently invested and disinvested in several businesses, take, for instance the sale of the pasta company in Argentina and of its business in Brazil. As I have argued before, a positive general developmental effect of its recent focus on the production and commercialization of agrochemicals is doubtful, not only because it reinforces the centralization of capital but also because it inheres a strategic interest in maintaining Argentina's focus on the current agribusiness model with all its environmental, social, and health effects (see my discussion on process upgrading in agribusiness in Chapter 8).[111]

In conclusion, while mainstream GVC research treats functional upgrading as a generic path towards local development in so-called developing countries and presupposes companies as important driving forces in this process, the picture becomes more complicated when looking at economic strategies as they are actually defined and carried out by companies. My interlocutors' accounts indicate that their now multinational corporations have varied the destinations of investments rather than being attached to a particular location's development. Furthermore, based on profit interests, they point to a juxtaposition of vertical integration and non- or disintegration. While their accumulation strategies can and do inhere functional upgrading, many factors also lead to temporarily and spatially meandering courses of investment and disinvestment (see Werner 2016b) and, thus, reproduce what Smith (2001, 15960) has called the "'seesaw' geography of uneven development." These influencing factors have included changes in state regulations, lucrative takeover-offers from global players, or lower production costs in other countries.

As mentioned above, the argument I aim to make here is not that functional upgrading is in principle always a positive development as long as it is carried out in Argentina. What I seek to illustrate, instead, is that even if one accepted the premise that local firm-level upgrading generally engenders gains for the many, there remains a potential contradiction between actual corporate strategies and interests on the one hand and the objective

110 Ibid.

111 An issue that lies outside the scope of this book is that investment diversification within agribusiness value chains does not inhere economic diversification within Argentina. The term "reprimarization" (Giarracca and Teubal 2013, own translation) coined in Argentina rather criticizes an economic orientation primarily on agribusiness related activities and other primary sectors such as mining.

of local development on the other. GVC research thus falls short when it focuses on upgrading in situ and easily assumes that corporate actors invariably share this aim.

Social Upgrading and social conflict

I have previously argued that a presupposition of companies as co-providers of social upgrading neglects the antagonistic character of capital-labor relations. The following briefly discusses my case-companies' stances towards corporate social responsibility (CSR) on the one hand and their assessments of demands of labor and other social struggles on the other.

Company managers in my interviews often emphasized the importance of CSR with respect to both ecological and social standards. Agrigood, for example, notes that its practices are tailored to secure "neighboring community welfare," the "development, health and safety of our employees," and "enhanced working conditions" (Agrigood 2018, 73), among many other socially inclusive developments. "Our sustainable approach to farming requires that we take into account not only economic, but also social and environmental aspects specifically adapted to local circumstances" (ibid.), to be reached through the triad of efficiency, innovation, and sustainability. In its 2018 annual report, the company assures to its investors that it is "complying with local labor regulations," giving "special attention to education and poverty rates," and contributing to "hospitals, schools, and daycare centers" (ibid., 79). The document lists programs through which, for instance, schooling is funded for children from poor families, and powdered milk or processed rice are donated to various institutions. LAgricola and El Agro make similar statements on social responsibility.

A short note on such charitable measures: it should not be denied that they can actually help individual people enhance their educational, nutritional, or health situation. Yet at the same time, they can be a means of advertising, or also an investment in a better trained and healthier workforce. Most importantly, however, such donations are made with a surplus that was previously produced by workers and appropriated by the company. In other words, they do not touch exploitative social relations as a problem; instead, they are built upon them.

As another aspect of social enhancements for employees, my informants have underlined the importance of qualified labor for their business models. As for El Agro, being a company with a billion-dollar annual revenue, only about 800 people worked for it directly in 2016, most of them being managers, office and industrial-processing workers.[112] The outsourcing model explains this number.[113]

Santiago notes that the sharp minds that work for El Agro and which are needed for modern knowledge intensive agriculture are not only well paid but participate in the firm's reaps. He explains that this is because the productivity of well-trained people is higher. Furthermore, his company has to struggle for the best minds. In the informal conversations I had during a day spent at El Agro's headquarters, some employees reaffirmed that they were earning well. For Santiago, "the issue of salaries is a relative one. If we have better people, better quality, we are more productive."[114] Carolina adds that "it just seems to us that people have to do well. [...] Yes, we feel that people have to be well remunerated."[115]

However, as large parts of less qualified agribusiness labor are outsourced, this is not generalizable for rural workers (see Chapter 10).[116] Although the latter are in fact the direct producers of the grains and oilseeds that are cultivated in El Agro's network, they do not appear in Santiago's and Carolina's narratives. Miguel demonstrates how the focus on well-paid qualified labor in the public presentation of my case companies only shows a small cutout, as he answers to my question about the people working for Agrigood in Brazil, where the possibility to outsource rural labor does not exist. "There is a law that impedes contractor's services." Most of the workers on the sugarcane plantations are permanently employed and less qualified on average.

"Yes, remember that we are geographically very distributed from very poor inland areas in Argentina and Brazil to Sao Paulo and Buenos Aires, so there is a very wide difference within the human resources. We have people with minimal education in some places, I mean basic schooling or who never even finished school, and people with a Master's. We

112 Interview with an administration manager of El Agro, June 23, 2016, Buenos Aires. In comparison, Agrigood (2018, 120) reports to have nearly 7,800 employees, most of them in the sugarcane complex in Brazil.

113 See Chapter 10 for a discussion of how more people are included as wage-dependent workers in the production network controlled by El Agro, though their exploitation is veiled through various mechanisms.

114 Interview with El Agro's former president, August 21, 2014, Buenos Aires.

115 Interview with El Agro's vice president, June 15, 2016, anonymized town.

116 Dante has told me, for instance, that El Agro's network does not function without around 5,000 small producers and *contratistas*, who in turn employ rural wage workers (interview with an administration manager of El Agro, June 23, 2016, Buenos Aires).

have an education level that reflects a bit the countries where we are operating. The rural sector is a very poor sector in Argentina and Brazil [...] So in Brazil we also have field workers. [...] 4,000 or 5,000 [who work] at lower levels, from the tractor driver to someone who walks in the fields counting seeds."[117]

Apart from the question as to who works for my case companies and under what conditions, there is a further issue to consider. The presentation of corporate social responsibility is complemented by a portrayal of demands made by trade unions and social movements (for instance, for better salaries and labor conditions or for land reforms) as an economic risk. This is most clearly expressed in the business reports and financial statements, which are primarily addressed to potential investors.

El Agro (2018, 55), for instance, lists in its 2018 annual report the "risk of trade union action and/or higher labor costs." The company is especially concerned with demands that could affect the labor-intensive production in its agrochemical subsidiary. It calculates that more than half of the staff is unionized and

"in the past, the company has suffered from stoppages and interruptions as a result of strikes that where organized by the labor union, mainly caused by conflicts that arise outside of our company. [...] In the context of high inflation in Argentina, [...] [we] have experienced and could further experience a strong pressure to increase salaries and benefits granted to workers" (ibid., 55).

As for Agrigood, although the corporation writes that "historically, we had a positive relationship with trade unions" (ibid., 120), it informs potential investors of the risk that struggles for social enhancements could become a competitive disadvantage when compared globally:

"We may be subject to labor disputes from time to time that may adversely affect us. Our employees are represented by unions or equivalent bodies and are covered by collective bargaining or similar agreements which are subject to periodic renegotiation. We may not successfully conclude our labor negotiations on satisfactory terms, which may result in a significant increase in the cost of labor or may result in work stoppages or labor disturbances that disrupt our operations. Cost increases, work stoppages or disturbances that result in substantial amounts of raw product not being processed could have a material and adverse effect on our business, results of operation and financial condition" (ibid., 15 f.).

The report further bemoans deteriorating economic conditions, among other things, due to "the continued demand for salary increases" (ibid., 24).

117 Interview with an Agrigood manager, April 22, 2015, Buenos Aires.

Especially against the backdrop of economic crisis and growing levels of poverty and unemployment, it fears increasing protests and strikes, and pressure from unions, which could "increase our operating costs" (ibid.) when successful. The preoccupation is not only directed towards organized industrial workers' actions.

"Social movements, such as Movimento dos Trabalhadores Rurais SemTerra and Comissão Pastoral da Terra, are active in Brazil and advocate land reform and mandatory property redistribution by the Brazilian government. Land invasions and occupations of rural areas by a large number of individuals is common practice for these movements, and, in certain areas, including those in which we have invested or are likely to invest, police protection and effective eviction proceedings are not available to land owners. [...] [This could] have a material adverse effect on our results of operations [...]" (ibid., 35).

It is particularly telling in this context that Agrigood cannot exclude the possibility of being subjected to expropriation by the Brazilian government, which is, according to Article 184 of the Brazilian constitution, only possible if the land use is not in compliance with "social functions," defined as "(i) rational and adequate exploitation of land; (ii) adequate use of natural resources available and preservation of the environment; (iii) compliance with labor laws; and (iv) exploitation of land to promote welfare of owners and employees" (ibid.). The company notes that "disputing the Brazilian government's expropriation of land is usually time-consuming and the outcomes of such challenges are uncertain" (ibid.). The mere assumption of this possibility contradicts the above-cited assurance that all of its operations are in line with the ideas of CSR.

While opposing attempts to enhance the social situation of workers and landless people from below, Agrigood welcomes the fruits of class struggles from above: In February 2017, the Argentinian congress passed an amendment to the labor risk law, which makes it more difficult for workers to get benefits after suffering workplace accidents. The company is pleased to announce that now, "prior to filing a lawsuit resulting from work-related accidents, affected workers must go through jurisdictional medical commissions" (ibid., 26).

Besides the fact that upgrading at the firm level does not necessarily entail social improvements for a majority of workers, these quotes allude to antagonistic relations between the corporations analyzed in this chapter and (organized) labor and social movements that struggle against the adverse effects they experience as a result of particular corporate action. This reinforces my argument that GVC research needs to consider that inclusive social developments for which trade unions and other organizations or protesters fight is not per se in the interest of capital. This inherently conflictual relationship tends to be forgotten when imagining social upgrading as a project pushed forwards by "public-private-civil society partnerships, as well as regional partnerships involving countries and firms that lead international production networks" (Gereffi and Luo 2014, 19).

9.6 Interim conclusions

This chapter has built closely on the previous one, and it further substantiates observations made there. It has depicted economic strategies of three case companies and shown that it is quite possible for some enterprises of Argentinian origin to upgrade in agro-industrial value chains. Agrigood, LAgricola, and El Agro have been able to move into higher profit niches, be it by enhancing the production processes or by investing in chain nodes upstream and/or downstream of agriculture. Although they have pursued different agendas, all three corporations can thus be interpreted as successful examples for upgrading at the firm level as defined by GVC scholars. After all, it is not carved in stone who assumes higher profitable activities and who does not. Up to this point, my analysis does not contradict the upgrading paradigm. However, this study is not confined to telling success stories about company-developments. Instead, I have argued in this chapter that GVC research needs to put greater emphasis on the various contradictions that may arise not despite of but in the wake of upgrading.

In this vein, I have initially worked out in Section 9.2 how the managers I interviewed assess potential limits to upgrading. A first notable point is that this was not a matter of great concern to my interlocutors, except when it came to the limits they perceive in business-unfriendly state policies. One important line of argument was that there are no structural hindrances to development at all, as long as the wellbeing of agribusiness is assured. Against all odds, the latter is supposed to serve as a stepladder that enables value chain development in general. Even in cases where critics have directly associated economic strategies such as the rural real estate business with land concentration and (partly violent) displacements, my case companies instead portray their actions as the modernization of remote and underdeveloped areas.

Capital ownership or access to finance as a condition of upgrading trajectories has been implicitly veiled in all my interviews with company representatives. By the same token, not even entry barriers set by other actors' unassailable lead in particular chain nodes were mentioned as a problem. Instead, my informants depicted competitive advantages of others as a challenge that incites innovation, and they contended that there are always niches. This assessment, however, is made from the ideological standpoint of relatively capitalized companies that have so far been able to find such high profitable niches.

State policies were the only factor that the interviewed managers mentioned as being truly limiting. Here, on the one hand, problems like a lack of education or infrastructure were assessed from a biased perspective, wanting such state functions to work at their service. Other claims levied vis-à-vis the state, such as the removal of limitations in land acquisition, not only stem from particular interests, they would also directly be to the disadvantage of people, who, for instance, work the lands at agribusiness frontiers under precarious tenure situations.

In Sections 9.3, 9.4, and 9.5 I dealt with the contradictions inherent to the portrayed company developments, refuting the discourse according to which upgrading in Argentinian agribusiness is to the benefit of the many. Endorsing the conclusions drawn in Chapter 8, these sections have shown how concrete upgrading strategies are moved by capitals' vested interest to enhance accumulation and correspondingly tend to contradict broader socioeconomic interests.

In more detail, I have argued in Section 9.3 that the competitive strategies of my case companies have played a direct role in the concentration and centralization of capital in agro-industrial chains in Argentina, and therewith in the reproduction of uneven development on local and regional scales. While mainstream GVC research understands upgrading as a path to development, it has not paid adequate attention to the relation between upgrading and the concentration and centralization of capital. It therefore also tends to abstract from an increasingly unequal control over means of production and the resulting condensation of the produced social wealth in fewer hands. After all, when upgrading alters the geographies of capitalism, this may entail success for some as well as exclusion, disarticulation, or downgrading for others.

Section 9.4 has shown how firm-level upgrading in my cases is partly linked to the geographical transfer of profits away from Argentina, a circumstance that contradicts an orientation towards local development. The competitive strategies of all my case companies were partly made possibly by investments made from Europe, the US, Qatar, and other countries, where a part of the shareholder value is transferred after being produced in Argentina. Furthermore, they have all established a corporate structure with holdings that are located outside of Argentina, and therefore also outside of Argentina's tax jurisdiction.

In the last section of this chapter, I have evinced that capital strategies, functional upgrading in a particular location, and social development are not necessarily compatible endeavors. First, my case companies are expectedly spurred by the need to find profitable investment opportunities rather than by developing their country of origin. Their strategies are thus neither necessarily characterized by on-site investments nor by a straightforward interest in functional upgrading. Their economic activity is geared to profit expectations at a given time and place and consequently, this contributes to seesaw geographies of uneven development as opposed to pushing a country up the chain. Second, while my case companies have emphasized that they attach great importance to CSR measures, I have criticized the related practices. Even though such measures may in fact help individual people improve their health or nutrition, for example, they are built upon exploitative social relations that make welfare necessary in the first place instead of opposing exploitation. Furthermore, while my interlocutors have emphasized their efforts in creating high-level employment, they have abstracted from the work that is done on the fields (with the exception of one Agrigood manager, whom I asked about the company's employment of rural labor in Brazil). Finally, and most tellingly, El Agro's and Agrigood's reports have strongly turned against social actors who have struggled for social enhancements, including labor unions and the movement of landless workers in Brazil. On this basis I have reasserted my conclusion that GVC research needs to include the inherently conflictual relation between capital and these actors to avoid myopically assuming that social upgrading can easily be delivered by "public-private-civil society partnerships" (Gereffi and Luo 2014, 19). In conclusion, I can complement the general implications I have proposed for the debate on GVC development in Chapter 8.

First, adding to my previous argument that analyses of process upgrading need to consider how the latter may conflict with opportunities for a progressive development of the productive forces under democratic control, this chapter has shown that process upgrading at the firm level and a resulting differentiated control over productive forces can also enhance economic concentration and contribute to driving financially weak actors out the market.

Second, GVC research needs to put emphasis on the potential links between firm-level upgrading and the concentration and centralization of capital, and therewith on the potential (local) reproduction of uneven development going along with upgrading.

Third, while GVC research tends to abstract from the control over the means of production and capital in general, this chapter has shown that the capacity to upgrade cannot be understood independently of capital ownership or the access to capital, as in my cases, partly by attracting foreign investors. This inheres, on the other hand, that not everyone can upgrade, as not any small farmer could have developed in the same way as my case companies.

Fourth, local upgrading strategies can entail the transfer of a part of the gained profits to other places in the world. In general, the upgrading paradigm abstracts from the fact that upgrading capitals do not necessarily have a genuine interest in developing the countries in which they originate.

Fifth, capital interests should play a broader role in debates on entry barriers or competitive advantages. Not only leading monopolies but also upgrading companies that do have the capacity to position themselves within capitalist competition in a lucrative way may have an interest in maintaining an economic system that works to the detriment of many "ants," to carry Santiago's metaphor further.

Finally, this chapter has strengthened an argument made in Chapter 8, namely that GVC studies fall short when they presume firms as drivers of social development by deleting class conflicts from their theoretical agendas.

Profit-oriented corporate development should not be confused with social development. However, my case companies have partly used the GVC vocabulary exactly in this sense. While this of course does not directly lie in the hands of GVC scholars, the political and intellectual shift of the GVC framework (traced in Chapter 3) has at least made it possible to integrate it into business worlds, both as a vehicle for corporate strategies and as an ideological tool.

10. Upgrading, Class Differentiation, and Predominance by Consent—A Case Study

I introduced this book with the slogan *Together we add value*, a catchphrase of El Agro, which I portrayed as one of the leading agribusiness groups in Argentina in the last chapter. The company refers to itself as the managing nucleus of an innovative and knowledge-based network of partners who act collectively and mutually empower each other. This is also what its catchphrase conveys: *Partners* add value *together*—no one appropriates the fruits of someone else's labor. El Agro is a figurehead in Argentina, not only for having restructured its agriculture from a system based on family farming to a highly technologized, network-like industry, but also for making investments all along agro-industrial chains (see Chapter 9). Its emphasis on network partnership mirrors the idea of agribusiness-induced growth as it is outlined in the *Agribusiness Strategic Plan 2010–2020*, which sets out that the vitality of farming is based on "a complex network of agents connected to each other by a variety of contracts" (Ministry of Agriculture 2011, 43; see Chapter 7). Similarly, the INTA (cited in Tort 2010, 108) has posed that upgrading requires the "incorporation not only of technical-productive innovations but also of those that lead to the [...] organizational improvement of the set of actors in a value chain in order to 'build' competitiveness and benefits for all its members."

El Agro's path also resonates with what Gereffi and Fernandez-Stark (2016, 20) have contended to be an upgrading trajectory which occurs when large corporations "offer a 'one stop shop' for clients and reduce overall transaction costs" (see Chapter 9). Earlier, I have traced how upgrading in GVCs is regarded a development paradigm for enhancing the economic situation of firms and the social situation of workers (see Chapter 3).

Controversies persist among researchers who work on agrarian change in Argentina about how to evaluate companies like El Agro in connection with the network metaphor. First, and akin to mainstream GVC research, scholars have identified potential for development in agribusiness networks that are characterized by (a) a separation of land ownership and production, (b) the importance of services, (c) formalized contracting, and (d) competitiveness based on technological innovation (see Chapter 3; Bisang et al. 2008). The idea is that synergies among partners in such networks potentially allow everyone to be more efficient and thus attenuate existing social asymmetries.

Secondly, however, there are scholars who have analyzed agribusiness-networks from a critical stance. According to Hernández (2009, 39, own translation), the transition to a "globalized rurality" has impelled agrarian subjects to insert themselves into larger networks, requiring them to navigate the world of management techniques and financial mechanisms, whereas social asymmetries are reproducing (not diminishing) in this very context (see Hernández 2007, 349 f.). In contrast to affirmative approaches, she directs her interest to fragile parts within the scaffolding: While core activities are performed by innovative entrepreneurs, *contratistas* and small producers adopt a weak position in terms of power and decision making. In a similar vein, Gras and Sosa Varrotti (2013, 227) contend that networks controlled by mega-companies do not imply a neutral reduction of transaction costs but rather a transfer of risks to small producers. For Fernández (2016), on the other hand, it is generally questionable whether the description of firms like El Agro as networkers holds for analyzing social relations in agribusiness. For him, this rather poses an ideological mystification of what actually forms the core of agribusiness' success: capital concentration and resulting economies of scale that imply relatively higher profits.

This chapter draws from these critical assessments while taking a class analytical perspective. On the basis of a case study—an excerpt of the production network controlled by El Agro—it shows how a manifest change from an agriculture in the Pampean region, in which independently operating *chacareros*[1] played an important role in the 20th century, to modern agribusiness has entailed the (re)articulation of some former *chacareros* to

1 As a reminder: *Chacareros* have been described as traditional capitalized farmers who own the machinery needed for grain cultivation and cattle breeding, with a strong participation of family labor in direct production for both subsistence and the market. Until the mid-20th century, many of them leased-in land. Later, they gradually acquired land property through market purchases or colonization policies (Muzlera 2020). On the basis of INDEC data, Barsky and Gelman (2009, 461) have analyzed that in 1988, 91.3 percent of the production in the Argentinian Pampas was controlled by the respective landowners.

grain and oilseed production under new socioeconomic conditions. I argue that upgrading here works in and through a process of class differentiation, and I examine how changing relations of exploitation and domination benefit El Agro in particular. The concentrated control over the conditions of production is key in this context. In particular, I show how three interrelated strategies serve El Agro's growing control over capital—in connection to the expansion of capital property analyzed in the previous chapter: (a) the diversification of capital functions via investments in different links of agribusiness value chains; (b) the ties created to smaller capitals, intermediate classes and (outsourced) labor in a process of class differentiation; and (c) the capital-power to profit from these relations by appropriating surplus value at different points of the capital circuit. I seek to show that such dynamics of class differentiation are both results and conditions of firm-level upgrading: local agribusiness corporations like El Agro emerge in the context of—and they shape—the transformation of agriculture. However, this transformation does not only entail technological or organizational innovation and increasing areas of cultivation. Crucially, it also entails the reorganization of the social property and production relations. In this context, I argue that a class analytical gaze helps elucidating how corporations grow in part by establishing relations to other, smaller capitals, intermediate classes and wage workers in ways that expand control over the production and distribution of surplus value to the benefit of big capital.

My analysis builds directly on previous chapters. Critically examining corporate approaches to value chain development and cases of firm-level upgrading, this study has so far challenged the idea that upgrading is generally likely to lead to social equalization. I do not claim that (social) upgrading is impossible. Instead, for an empirically informed critique of this development strategy, the present chapter sets out to take a closer look at processes on the ground and to analyze the shaping of class relations and resulting unequal ramifications of upgrading. I aim to understand how, why, and for whom upgrading may entail advancement and for whom it instead entails either simple reproduction under the wings of big capital and/or different forms of exploitation. Pointing to contradictions that become apparent at the very level of "network-centric" (Lee and Gereffi 2015, 324) analyses, I argue that El Agro has climbed the value chain to adopt core-like activities, but this has not improved the conditions for achieving social equality in situ.

For reasons of feasibility, this analysis comprises an excerpt of activities directly related to primary production located in different sites within the

Pampean region. However, it includes effects on other parts of El Agro's business, such as the commercial section. My aim here is not to quantify inequality but to analyze the social relations behind it.

The chapter is structured as follows. First, I recall some key points with respect to the class dynamics of upgrading (10.1). Second, I focus on how El Agro's strategies work in and through a process of class differentiation. I examine how the ways in which means of production and labor power are combined and controlled among various actors—not necessarily under the roof of a single capital—have changed to El Agro's benefit in the context of an ongoing replacement of *chacareros* by agribusiness-led large-scale production. This entails cooperative and at the same exploitative relations to intermediate classes, which tend to be masked as a co-equal network-partnership (10.2). Section 10.3 then examines the ways in which El Agro does not neutrally coordinate but dominates and shapes these relations to its own benefit in the wake of upgrading. That notwithstanding, this goes along with a strong consensus building and the widespread rationalization of the analyzed social edifice as characterized by reciprocity. Finally, Section 10.4 turns to relatively poorly paid rural labor and working conditions in the fields. The outsourcing of seeding, fumigation, and harvesting is key in this context: Capital is, at the immediate level, detached from its direct relation of exploitation and domination to labor, as workers are instead employed by *contratistas*. This has adverse effects on the conditions for labor struggles that could achieve social improvements. In contrast to the vegetable oil industry, where a combative union has struggled for better wages, there have been no organized labor disputes at the point of grain and oilseed production.

In sum, the chapter examines how El Agro's strategies and the corresponding organization of the labor process rely essentially on a differentiation and perpetuation of exploitative relations—not *despite*, but in the wake of upgrading. At the same time, production is organized in a way that facilitates its harmonious appearance as a collective effort by partners: *Together we add value.*[2]

2 Like the previous chapter, this one tracks trends up to about 2018/2019.

10.1 The class dynamics of upgrading

Before I delve into the empirical analysis, the following recapitulates some conceptual key points which help in interpreting the class dynamics of upgrading in the analyzed case. In Chapter 3, I portrayed how the mainstream GVC approach entails the (implicit) assumption that upgrading leads to a general upward mobility, benefitting more than just firms. Various scholars have formulated sound criticism of the GVC framework and its understanding of governance and upgrading, among other things for a neglect of capital-labor relations or the treatment of labor as a mere input factor (Hammer and Riisgaard 2015, 84) rather than as part of a social relation. Selwyn, Campling, and others have recently pointed to the need for chain analysis to conceptualize both competitive capital accumulation and exploitation, and to take property relations and class dynamics as the social bases through which GVCs operate into account more generally (Campling et al. 2016; Campling and Selwyn 2018; Selwyn 2012). In this light, studies have questioned all too optimistic beliefs in companies or states as providers of social upgrading, which tend to neglect both capitalist imperatives of profit-maximization (Taylor et al. 2015, 12) and the problem that workers cannot "simply impose their demands on capital without the latter responding in kind" (Selwyn 2012, 7; see Anner 2015b, 154). To address these limitations, scholars have proposed to pay greater attention to the actual shaping of capital-labor relations (Bair and Werner 2015, 131; Smith et al. 2002, 42). This would require elucidating shifting patterns of exploitation that accompany firm-level upgrading, showing how conditions are potentially influenced by labor agency (Selwyn 2013; 2017; Taylor et al. 2015; Werner 2012), but also analyzing how the success of labor struggles can be constrained by historically and geographically specific political economic conditions. In this vein, it is necessary to consider where and why exploited classes may *not* successfully oppose their situations because the "organization of global capital structurally constrains and conditions labor agency in multiple ways" (Taylor et al. 2015, 11).

The present chapter ties into these discussions. It understands class as "constitutive of development processes and central to understanding inequality" (Campling et al. 2016, 1745). It is crucial to analyze class differentiation in order to scrutinize the reproduction of inequality in the wake of upgrading, without reducing value added to an unequal "money capture" between capitals, as Quentin and Campling (2018, 36) put it, or to returns on innovation and "barriers to entry" (Kaplinsky 2000, 122). Entry barriers are indeed a source of extra-profits to the detriment of other capitals, but uneven gains between actors in commodity chains are not merely based on power and uneven exchange, but crucially on exploitative social relations of production.

This assessment is based on the premise that the valorization of value is necessarily grounded in exploitation. As a reminder: value, here, is a characteristic attributed to commodities when they are exchanged and thus implicitly related to each other on the market as equals. Importantly, however, the valorization of value is not only characterized by market relations. To see "how capital itself is produced," one has to look into the "hidden abode of production," (Marx 1990 [1867], 279 f.) where the dominant social relations are class relations. In capitalism, production is dominantly aligned for continuous accumulation based on exploitation. The latter is understood as the appropriation of surplus value by those who essentially control the means of production—whereas surplus value is defined by the value workers produce during the period that exceeds the labor time necessary for the reproduction of their labor power's value under given historical conditions (Marx 1990 [1867], 274). This means that wage earners work longer hours than socially necessary (under given productive forces) to secure the reproduction of their labor power and their wellbeing. This produced surplus is the basis of capitalist profits, which are consequently always a result of the appropriation of alien labor.

Consequently, class is a *relational* concept: it defines the positioning of actors towards each other in the social relations of production and thus in the distribution of the produced value between capital and labor (Bernstein 2010; Campling et al. 2016; Carchedi 1998; 2001).[3] On this assumption, capitalist property relations are pivotal for the differentiated acquisition of the fruits of social labor.

At the same time, class relations appear in complex ways: both capital and labor are internally differentiated and, furthermore, there are intermediate classes (PKA 1974, 177 ff.). The fact that we find the basis of the "social edifice" in the "direct relationship of the owners of the conditions of production to the immediate producers" does not prevent this relation "from displaying endless variations and gradations in its appearance, as a result of innumerable different empirical circumstances, natural conditions, racial relations, his-

3 Here, the conceptualization of class differs from approaches that understand class in terms of a mere political category or in terms of distributional groups (see Wright 1979, 7 ff.).

torical influences acting from outside, etc., and these can only be understood by analyzing these empirically given conditions," (Marx 1991 [1894], 927 f.) which are constantly changing. Class is hence not only a relational but also a historically and geographically contingent concept: The production and circulation of capital is always a dynamic process and development in time and space includes ever changing social configurations. Clearly for Marx (1989 [1863], 517), "uniformity or similarity of reproduction—the repetition of production under the same conditions does not exist. Productivity itself changes and changes the conditions [of production]". In Harvey's (2017, 115) words, "capital is innately revolutionary [...] because it is value in motion under conditions of continuous growth and technological innovation." Systematic efforts to increase the extraction of surplus value comprise ongoing qualitative transformations of production systems (Altvater 1975, 149; Selwyn 2012, 23 ff.), which does not only entail technological innovation. Together with constant struggles over production, it also implies changing forms of the organization of production, including the ways in which capitals, intermediate classes, and labor are related to one another and hence labor power and means of production are combined in production networks. As a result, class relations can appear in convoluted ways and one of the tasks of their analysis "is to give precision to complexity and explore its ramifications" (Wright 2005, 12). Since capital is a social (not a natural) relation, these ramifications essentially depend on how firms organize the labor process and on whether or how such strategies are resisted under particular conditions.

As for changing social relations in agriculture, for example, Henry Bernstein (2006; 2010; 2016) has argued that, rather than assuming an ever-ongoing existence of farmers as a homogenous social group, research should analyze the class dynamics of agrarian change, which includes exiting the logic of juxtaposing agriculture and industry (see also Campling and Lerche 2016).[4] This will be further elaborated in the next section.

Briefly, my case study suggests examining shifting patterns of class differentiation in commodity chains and their ramifications. The diverse and at times complex relations of class places in production and circulation, which

4 Recent studies in different geographical settings have addressed class differentiation in this vein; see Claar (2018) on EU-trade policy and class dynamics in South African agriculture, Pattenden (2016) on rural labor relations in South India, Perez Niño (2016) on class dynamics in tobaco production in Mozambique, and Tsikata (2015) for a literature overview on agrarian economies in Sub-Saharan Africa.

in my case are often masked by the outward of El Agro's 'network' consisting of partners in sowing associations, need to be revealed through a closer analysis. Such a class analytical perspective can, in sum, enrich commodity chain research for examining the ways in which capital-labor relations, intra-capital competition, and the incorporation of intermediate classes in the circuit of capital shape the reproduction of inequality in the wake of upgrading strategies.

10.2 A case of upgrading in and through class differentiation

The decreasing viability of *chacareros*, a greatly romanticized figure, is a much-discussed issue in Argentina (Archetti and Stölen 1975; Balsa 2007; Barsky and Gelman 2001). Their presence was tightly connected to a series of state regulations, including price control mechanisms oriented at protecting small and medium agriculture producers (Giarracca and Teubal 2008). Before its dismantling, grain prices were controlled by the *Junta Nacional de Granos* (JNG), a public institution that centralized trade and controlled the ports. In 1991, the JNG was completely dissolved by the Menem administration in the context of a broader deregulation of the agrarian economy that also included the liberalization of foreign exchange and the promotion of the commodification of land, among other measures (see Chapter 6). "From that moment on, Argentina's agricultural sector became one of the least regulated globally" (Ainsuain and Echaguibel 2012, 84, own translation).

In the years to follow, the country's agrarian political economy has undergone major changes, as I have sketched in previous chapters. As for the examined case, this does not amount to a transformation from a "pre-capitalist" peasantry to capitalist farming—Pampean agriculture had been dominated by the latter throughout the past century, which had seen both big farmers and *chacareros*. "There is not only one path of capitalist development in agriculture," as Flammini (2001, 5, own translation) notes, and so there have been restructurings within the social fabric of capitalist agriculture in Argentina.

First, this concerns the tendency of capital concentration and the displacement of many formerly independent *chacareros* from the market, who could not hold their farms even under conditions of strong self-exploitation, as I discussed in previous chapters (see Barsky and Gelman 2009, 491). Over the past decades, especially production units smaller than 500 ha have tended to disappear (Barsky and Gelman 2009, 292; Murmis and Murmis

2012). Second, and of particular relevance to this chapter, upgrading strategies have entailed a reorganization of the production process: El Agro and similar enterprises have increased their efficiency also by the ways that they array production and relate to, coordinate, and control other social actors. This concerns the dependent inclusion of smaller capitals and intermediate classes in their production networks and the organization of field labor via *contratistas*, who own the means of production necessary for the respective tasks. Before I turn to the qualitative analysis of these relations, I must briefly specify some class-analytical concepts that are relevant for this study.

Class differentiation includes, first, capitals of different functions and related forms of appropriating surplus value. Industrial, in this case agrarian, capital makes profits that are based on the extraction of unpaid labor directly from the workers. Others participate thereof in form of an interest (finance capital), ground rent (landowners), or commercial profit (PKA 1974, 180 ff.).[5] As a part of its upgrading strategies, El Agro has assumed all of these capital functions (Section 10.1.1). The company's business model encompasses links with other (smaller) capitals and a myriad of actors in intermediate class positions. In this vein, class differentiation includes, second, capitals of varying competitive positions, and the relation between El Agro and some of its smaller clients is one between capitals of different scales.

Bernstein (2010, 110) has differentiated social positions that can neither be described as capital nor in terms of wage labor, and whose degrees of self-exploitation to the benefit of other capitals vary. Besides (a) emergent capitalist farmers who reproduce themselves as capital on larger scales (corresponding to Lenin's "rich peasants"), he has distinguished between (b) petty commodity producers who reproduce themselves as capitals on the same scale (corresponding to Lenin's "middle peasants") and (c) those who are struggling to reproduce themselves, becoming subject to a "simple reproduction squeeze" (corresponding to Lenin's "poor peasants") (ibid., 104).

5 In Marx's (1990 [1867], 709) words, "The capitalist who produces surplus-value, i.e. who extracts unpaid labour directly from the workers and fixes it in commodities, is admittedly the first appropriator of this surplus-value, but he is by no means its ultimate proprietor. He has to share it afterwards with capitalists who fulfil other functions in social production taken as a whole, with the owner of the land, and with yet other people. Surplus-value is therefore split up into various parts. Its fragments fall to various categories of person, and take on various mutually independent forms, such as profit, interest, gains made through trade, ground rent etc."

For the case study analyzed in this chapter, these theoretical determinations require amendments. First, there are farmers who are able to reproduce themselves as capital, though unlike El Agro they are not able to reduce their own work to capital functions. As far as they are still competitive, they are themselves expressions of capital concentration in Pampean agriculture. Nevertheless, in many instances, their description as emergent capitalists is misleading: while this is valid for some who have enlarged their production over the past years, others who had emerged to produce on fields larger than a few hundred hectares decades ago today face growing challenges producing independently at these scales.

Thus, to conceptually grasp class differentiation among agricultural actors whose role in the production and appropriation of surplus value is not necessarily based on a neat class divide between big capital and labor, I consider different variables. Consistent with Bernstein (2010), the first is the capacity—or incapacity—of actors to reproduce themselves as capital on an extended scale. This is related, secondly, to the employment of workers and the participation of own or family labor in the productive process and, thirdly, to the disposability of capital or means of production—in the present case especially the area on which a firm controls agricultural production and hence its relative position in the concentration and centralization of capital.

On this basis, I analyse as *medium-capitalized producers* those who own the means of production (and/or have the capital to buy the services and inputs) necessary to control production on average scales. They cannot reduce their own work to capital functions and thus they participate in the productive labor (mainly assuming coordinating tasks), yet they necessarily and systematically use wage labor. I then refer to those as *petty commodity producers* who own some means of production but use wage labor only on a limited scale. This can include *chacareros*, as well as farmers who produce grains on very small scales but mainly make a living, for example, by providing services.

In this vein, intermediate classes incorporated in the production network controlled by El Agro are not necessarily farmers (anymore). Instead, they are often (re)articulated to agribusiness production assuming a variety of particular tasks. This includes, for instance, (a) petty capitalist *contratistas*, labor contractors who partly work self-exploiting "in ways that represent indirect exploitation by capital or at least in ways that benefit capital" (ibid., 101), and (b) remunerated management service providers who work on a mainly (pseudo) self-employed basis for the company (see Craviotti and Gras 2006). In the words of El Agro's president Santiago, agriculture "has gone to a scheme where somehow the number of producers was reduced and many of those who were inside the ecosystem of production on their own came to participate as providers of particular services."[6] As Section 10.2.2. exemplifies, they contribute land or a part of the necessary means of production and labor power to such production associations. In the present case, El Agro then provides management, seeds, agrochemicals, and different services to these associations, and at the end of the season, everyone receives a share of the harvest agreed upon beforehand.

Lower down in the class hierarchy, among the workers who have nothing to sell but their labor power, there are socioeconomic and work process-related differentiations. Suffice it to say for this chapter that the latter concern, for instance, the inclusion in the reproduction of capital as qualified managerial labor or as field workers hired by *contratistas*, related working conditions, social and spatial scattering, and informality and super-exploitation.

Overall, I can say that in the analyzed case, process upgrading and capital concentration at the point of primary production have not led to a simultaneous concentration of the labor process under the roof of a single company.[7] Rather, I observe the simultaneity of cooperation among different social actors in a 'network' controlled by El Agro and a historically and geographically specific social edifice that benefits particular upgrading strategies. The possibility to climb the chain likewise is not generalizable for all class "places" within these social relations.

10.2.1 El Agro's capital functions

Chapter 3 portrayed how the GVC upgrading paradigm essentially sticks to the idea of company-led development. I have argued in previous chapters that it is therefore crucial to analyze capital-led upgrading strategies from a critical perspective. As for El Agro, readers can refer to Chapter 9 for a comprehensive description of its upgrading trajectory and of how this has encompassed the diversification of investments in several branches. For the present chapter, the crucial point to recall is how the corporate group has

---

6 Interview with El Agro's former president, August 21, 2014, Buenos Aires.

7 The fact that cooperation along GCCs does not necessarily take place under the auspices of a single firm has also been a key insight of the debate on global commodity chains as developed by Gereffi and Korzeniewicz (1994).

acted across class-analytical differentiations of capital functions, which has avowedly enhanced its accumulation capacity, allowing it to capture surplus value at different points of production and circulation in agro-industrial value chains.

First, as productive capital, it operates in agriculture, industrial processing, production of agrochemicals, technology development, and services. Despite investments in other chain nodes, El Agro has never fully retired from engaging in agriculture. One of the reasons to stay in this business even in times of low profit expectations is that the presence on the ground secures the company good contacts with clients for its other business lines. As commercial manager Carla puts it, it is the "most direct link with the one who is below producing the grain. If you are not producing the grain, you don't cross paths with him, you don't know what he needs, and you can't somehow energize your network."[8] Beyond agriculture, the provision of services (including engineering and marketing consultancy, the use of a GPS-software that allows to tailor agrochemicals accurately to specific areas, and logistics) has become an important business. The "one-stop shop" described in Chapter 9 has sprouted the company more stable profits than agriculture alone. However, as this model requires the ability, that is, the capital, to profitably invest in the related technologies and services on the client side, it also facilitates a further centralization of capital. The increase in the relative importance of constant capital requires a certain scale of production to be profitable. And a part of the surplus value embodied, for instance, in a ton of soy produced by a farmer who uses El Agro's services does not form part of his or her own but of El Agro's profit.

Secondly, as a one-stop shop provider, the company also operates as commercial capital. It trades seeds and agrochemicals, and it commercializes grains and oilseeds. The profits made through trade represent the appropriation of a part of the surplus value generated in (primary) production. As shown in Chapter 9, the commercial business is (a) more profitable for El Agro than primary production; (b), commercial profits are also more reliable than agrarian industrial profits because they can be reaped relatively independent of, for example, weather-related risks. Since primary producers buy seeds and agrochemicals independently of the outcome of the harvest, upgrading to become commercial capital means profiting from agriculture also when primary producers lose money, due to droughts or floods. At the same

8 Interview with a commercial manager of El Agro, June 15, 2016, anonymized town.

time, El Agro circumvents the problem of fixing capital in agriculture where the labor process pauses during the plants' growth. Today, manager Carla explains figuratively, the company is harvesting all year: clients always need a service, to buy inputs, or to sell grains.[9] El Agro has furthermore gained the capacity to largely determine the terms and conditions of commercialization especially in relation to small producers (Section 10.3). This power to govern the network is based on former accumulation and the resulting capacity to assume different capital functions. For instance, today, it can also provide its customers with the finance necessary for buying its inputs and therewith forge bonds with them at various points of the capital circuit.

This leads to the third function of El Agro as finance capital. It does not only hand over inputs to clients on credit but it also acts through a company-owned Reciprocal Guarantee Society (SGR, in Spanish). The SGR earns interest for providing clients with bank guarantees and the capital put in the SGR by El Agro's owner family is reinvested (see Chapter 9). Yet its main economic importance resides in its capacity to attract and maintain clients for the commercial section, since SGR users normally agree to buy inputs from and sell crops to the company. According to manager Ana, the SGR-clientele makes up a significant part of all deals: "I think more than 50 percent of the inputs we sell today, for you to get an idea, are funded through the SGR. This way we try to leverage each of [El Agro's] business lines […], it clearly helps you to get more customers."[10] This is also a competitive advantage vis-à-vis other companies. The SGR is El Agro's edge because "not all the grain traders and input sellers are able to offer an in-house financing tool."[11] Customer Agustina confirms that what she buys with money obtained via the SGR generally feeds back into El Agro's business: "I cannot have a firm that provides labor services and ask for money to buy a field. No. I can ask for a guarantee to renew a machine […] and these are machines that end up providing services to the network."[12]

Finally, although El Agro's grain and oilseed production is based on land leasing, the owning family has approximately 15,000 ha[13] that are leased out to the company. The family thus appropriates another part of the surplus in

9 Ibid.

10 Interview with a manager of El Agro's SGR, April 28, 2015, anonymized town.

11 Interview with a manager of El Agro's SGR, June 15, 2016, anonymized town.

12 Interview with a self-employed production manager, *contratista*, and medium-capitalized producer, July 07, 2016, anonymized town.

13 Interview with a commercial manager of El Agro, June 15, 2016, anonymized town.

form of agrarian rent. Historically, these land holdings were an important property basis on which the upgrading strategies were built (see Chapter 9)—a key difference from many of its 'partners.' The capacity to grow as a 'one-stop shop' with various capital functions is essentially based on previous property and accumulation, and on the resulting capacity to incorporate a qualified staff to manage the synergizing of these branches. The growing control over particular means of production and especially the SGR has enhanced El Agro's differentiated growth and ability to appropriate surplus at different points of the circuit of capital. On this basis, the socioeconomic gap with (smaller) capitalist producers and intermediate classes has increased.

10.2.2 El Agro's relations with smaller capitals and intermediate classes

The following tracks how El Agro's upgrading model encompasses links with smaller capitals and a myriad of actors who work in intermediate class positions: from clients with whom it cooperates and at the same time struggles over the produced surplus value from a dominant position to self-employed labor service providers. Here, the appropriation of surplus value is not based on an always neat class divide between capital and labor due to "various and complex combinations of employment and self-employment" (Campling et al. 2016, 1752, emphasis in the original). By shedding light on an excerpt of this social fabric, I aim to highlight that El Agro's property-based leading position is not designed to coordinate in a way that helps everyone to climb the value chain although some clients may benefit from these relations more than others. It is in a leading position because it is a "(temporary) winner of capitalist competition in a node (or more) of a GVC" (Quentin and Campling 2018, 41), while other actors in the network are treading water and/or working in sometimes disguised (wage) dependence of the company. El Agro's upgrading strategy is based on the existence of this contradictory unity of class "places" characterized by a differentiated control over means of production and labor power within the network. It profits from direct exploitation, from its value-capture based on different capital functions, and from "control relations (...) to appropriate a portion of the surplus value that 'small' firms relinquish" (Quentin & Campling 2018, 41). In these relations, the scope for small capitals and intermediate classes as well as their dependency and decision-making power vis-à-vis El Agro depend on their respective socioeconomic positions.

(Small) capitalist clients, petty commodity producers, and differentiated value capture

A first group of actors related to the company are smaller capitalist grain and oilseed producers who are linked to El Agro as clients of the SGR and the commercial section, and who often produce in association with the company. Barsky and Gelman (2009, 494) rightly point out that the current presence of these actors in the Pampean region is already a display of "a process of concentration of the use of the land, which is expressed not only in the highest social ranks" (ibid., 495). Estimations of how large a farming operation in the region must be, as a minimum, to be viable—under participation of own or family labor in direct production—are rare. At any rate, Fernández (2013b, 95) calculated in 2009 for the case of soy plantations that only around 11 percent were then smaller than 600 ha (down from over 40 percent in 2002), while production on nearly 2,000 ha or more had increased from less than 20 to more than 60 percent in the same period. Some of El Agro's clients do not own but lease-in land themselves.

Second, many landowners in Argentina's farming heartland see themselves unable to raise the capital or are unwilling to take the risk to produce independently of larger companies and therefore lease-out. Again, this does not mean that they are poor in absolute terms. Depending on where the land is located, a hectare in the Argentinian Pampas may be worth some hundred or up to several thousand US-Dollars. As Barsky and Gelman (2009, 503, own translation) put it, they may lack the capital for independent production but still live in favorable terms off their rents. As I demonstrated in Chapter 9, companies like El Agro avoid making deals with landowners at fixed prices and instead integrate them as 'partners' who receive a share of the harvest.

A third group of actors are the *contratistas*, whose particular role as brokers between capital and labor I discuss in more detail in Section 10.4. Suffice it to say here that many of these labor contractors are former *chacareros* who were unable to keep their farms (see Barsky and Gelman 2009, 496).[14] Today's *contratistas* in the province of Buenos Aires are often petty capitalists who own one or a few machines, hire workers, and/or work themselves in order to sell sowing, fumigation, or harvesting services. Some only have a single machine

14 In the province of Buenos Aires, nearly 70 percent of the contratistas used to be agriculture producers (Barsky and Gelman 2009, 496 f.). The strategy of outsourcing labor had already been adopted in the 1970s. Yet during the 1990s, it started to gain more importance in agribusiness.

they operate themselves as salaried labor service providers. By subcontracting labor to them, El Agro manages to control primary production without having equity relations with the *contratistas*. It can thus outsource the risk of fixing capital, for instance, in harvesters, and avoid being in direct relation with labor, while still appropriating a part of the surplus value (see 10.4).

On that general note, the actors linked to El Agro sometimes assume several of these roles. In socioeconomic or class-relational terms, they range from those whose position is rather close to the bourgeoisie, to those who work in the borderlines to remunerated labor. As I specify in Section 10.3, the respective capacities to control capital affects the dependency and decision-making power vis-à-vis El Agro.

Associations with (smaller) capitalist producers linked to El Agro imply business opportunities for the company mainly in terms of the quantity of goods and services they buy, that is, the extent to which in can participate in the produced surplus value.

One example is GrupoX, a company founded in the early 2000s by two partners. It is itself a merger of agrarian family businesses who together owned 3.000 ha of land and joined forces to be able to buy machinery. Throughout the years, GrupoX grew to produce grains and oilseeds on over 10,000 ha of mainly leased land, partly in association with El Agro. In 2016, however, it had to cut back its cultivation to 8,000 ha, because its structure was not able to cope with larger scales. The firm has 30 employees—a number that also was reduced from a peak of 50. Raúl explains: "I know that I have a limitation in the size and structure [...] and I am not [El Agro]."[15] However, he says that the relations with El Agro helped it expand in the first place. GrupoX is formally divided into five companies, such that they are small enough to access bank credits via the SGR. Vice versa, relations with GrupoX have allowed El Agro to expand its business as commercial capital: This client sells 65 percent of its grains to and buys 70 percent of its inputs from El Agro. In these deals, GrupoX has a greater leeway to set its own business terms, compared with petty commodity producers (see Section 10.3.).

On a smaller scale, Daniel and Fernando manage their own farms. Fernando contends that he has managed to increase his scale of production by 50 percent in the past two decades. Today, he owns around 4,000 ha of land on which he controls the production of grains and oilseeds, as well as

15 Interview with a representative of GrupoX, July 01, 2016, anonymized town.

some cattle breeding. His family owns machinery and employs six workers directly. Some of the production is in association with El Agro. According to Fernando, "today, you associate or you stagnate. And in this business, if you get stuck, you disappear."[16] In addition to primary production, Daniel runs a small sunflower oil press machine. Both are clients of El Agro's SGR and attractive customers of the one-stop shop. Osvaldo, for instance, sold to the company "80, 85 percent of the production and I bought 50 percent of my inputs."[17]

Agustina inherited a family firm together with her sister. In addition to their own work, the siblings employ 10 workers. Agustina recalls that an economic crisis at the beginning of the 2000s led her to begin synergizing different activities with El Agro and also to become a client of the SGR. She manages grain and oilseed production on around 5,000 ha of leased land—partly this is a management service on behalf of El Agro, and partly she produces in association with other local actors. Furthermore, she sells labor services to El Agro with her own fumigation machine and a seeder. Agustina explains that Santiago gives "the girl's machine a job" while she buys inputs from the company and sells both management services and her produce to it.[18]

As Section 10.3 discusses in greater depth, the smaller their property base, the more my interlocutors tend to act in favour of El Agro beyond these business relations. Alex is an example of a medium-capitalized producer. He manages a sowing pool that cultivated grains and oilseeds on 2,500 ha of leased land in 2016. All investors of the pool together own a sowing and a harvesting machine and a fumigator, and the firm employs four permanent workers. Only a part of this production is in association with El Agro. However, Alex says that he usually closes the majority of his deals in agrochemicals, services and so forth with the company, often even in cases when he could get better prices elsewhere in particular situations.[19]

Darío is a good example of how the centralization of capital has affected farmers. He used to produce independently on 1,500 ha of land owned by various family members, which is now mainly dedicated to grain and soy production in association with El Agro, as the family lacks capital and know-

16 Interview with two capitalist farmers, July 07, 2016, anonymized town.

17 Ibid.

18 Interview with a self-employed production manager, *contratista*, and medium-capitalized producer, July 07, 2016, anonymized town.

19 Interview with a medium-capitalized producer, July 14, 2016, anonymized town.

how for independent farming under today's conditions. In addition to his own (mainly coordinating) work and the field labor outsourced to *contratistas* (he does not own machinery), Darío hires two workers. When only considering the land ownership, he may appear a *medium-capitalized producer* but as most of the land is now controlled by El Agro via the sowing associations, he rather resembles a dependent rentier in the sense that his role in the sowing association is largely limited to contributing land. His own, independent farming activity is now limited to petty commodity production: cattle breeding and crop cultivation on a small piece of his land. At the size of this family business, Darío says, producing independently on a larger scale is too risky. Within the association, all the grains produced are sold to and all inputs are bought from El Agro. The SGR advances money for Darío's running costs.[20] After an interview we held at El Agro's headquarters, he invited me to spend the day with him on his farm in the province of Buenos Aires. He says he is one of the few figures left in the area who still live on site. His house is truly reminiscent of an old, beautiful, but somewhat dreary country residence that has seen better days.

Another of my interlocutors, Sergio, manages the belongings of his family, including 870 ha of land, which is constantly leased-out to El Agro *a porcentaje*, meaning that they receive a percentage of the harvest or of the profit (pursuant to their agreements) instead of a fixed rent. Despite this landownership, the family does not have enough money for independent production without risking too much, according to Sergio. As will be discussed in more detail in the next section, Sergio says that even though El Agro sometimes pays less of a lease for land in this association than other prospective lessees would do, he prefers to keep the good relation going with sometimes smaller but constant payments. Thus, in order to sustain the general advantage of being associated to El Agro, he puts up with commercial disadvantages from time to time. In addition to the rent income, he owns a farming machine and sells labor services to El Agro. Until the land lease is paid after the harvest, Sergio's family partly lives from money borrowed via El Agro's SGR.[21] This way, a part of what El Agro pays for rent comes back in form of an interest, paid to the SGR.

Further down in the hierarchy, Federico is an example for intermediate positions in the capital-labor relation that lean towards the latter. He ex-

20 Interview with a rentier and petty commodity producer, July 07, 2016, anonymized town.

21 Interview with a rentier and *contratista*, July 14, 2016, anonymized town.

plains that his family used to own some land, which they had to sell in the 1990s. Today, he co-manages the production of crops on 200 to 400 ha of leased land, in association with one of El Agro's area managers. Thanks to his academic education, his job here is agronomic consultancy. In addition, he sells fumigation services to El Agro with a machine he runs himself, since he does not have the capital to pay a worker. "I used to hire someone but I had to scale down" in 2014–15, a crisis season for Pampean agriculture.[22] Formally not employed (he sells fumigation services to El Agro, not his labor power directly), Federico is an empirical example of the fluid boundaries between petty capitalists and salaried service providers. Instead of being paid a fixed salary, he receives a previously determined share of the harvest. This means relatively good pay in times of good harvests, but also insecurity, for example, in the event of illness or in terms of possible weather conditions. For someone like Federico, a local crop shortfall obviously means a bigger slump than for a company with investments as diversified as those of El Agro. Yet despite the fact that most of the work he does is for this company, he explicitly perceives himself as an independent partner, not as a mere employee. As for such labor services, it is quite conceivable (though not quantifiable on the basis of the data I obtain) that they involve (self)exploitation and the appropriation of a part of the produced value by El Agro. At any rate, El Agro is able to accumulate capital based on these relations while Federico simply reproduces himself and his means of production.

In the end, all these actors form parts of El Agro's value capture strategies. However, although the narrative of network-partnership blurs existing differences, their particular socio-economic position determines their form of attractiveness as clients for El Agro, their dependency, and whether they are de facto exploited. The closer their socio-economic position to that of capital, the more they are mainly attractive for El Agro as commercial capital to capture a share of the produced surplus value in line with market conditions.

Dependent self-employment

Accompanying the one-stop-shop-strategy, El Agro has also professionalized its management. Beyond a top-management structure (that assumes capital functions), there is a lower-ranked one working close to the clients:

22 Interview with a petty commodity producer and self-employed contratista, July 01, 2016, anonymized town.

Area managers, who coordinate production or commercial branch offices, have become a centrepiece of El Agro's strategies (see Chapter 9). However, although they de facto work for the company, most of these managers are not formally employed or paid fixed salaries. Instead, they are independent 'entrepreneurs' or rather "own-account workers" (Hammer and Riisgaard 2015, 84). Note that, in this context, the term manager does not refer to those who are in top executive positions. It refers to management as qualified labor that assumes a necessary coordinating part in the productive process, "as with the conductor of an orchestra" (Marx 1991 [1894], 507). These area managers do not possess means of production and sell their labor power, although it is nevertheless their task to govern production and work as a representative of the company's interests (see ibid., 507 ff.). However, although they de facto work for El Agro, most of them are not paid fixed salaries.

Only some of my interlocutors who work as managers for El Agro have a formal employment contract. This is the case, for instance, of Ana and Carla, who work at the headquarters coordinating the SGR and the commercial business respectively. As for the area managers, they are not directly employed. They are *de jure* independent entrepreneurs and sell a service as formally self-employed 'partners,' although their enterprise consists in only working for El Agro. El Agro's former president Santiago told them to start their own business and associate themselves with the company. Graciela explains that this is because he wanted to have the flexibility to quickly change investment decisions. If the company decides to reduce primary production, it could not use a fixed staff. But it always maintains

"a certain structure of engineers, enough to be able to scale-up production quickly. About 10 years ago, it positioned itself with such a system of engineers as partners. They are not employees of the company. The engineer who manages the field is an independent person who works on a percentage. So, when it went well, both were doing well. When it didn't, both were doing badly."[23]

Instead of being paid a fixed salary, they hence receive forms of pay which tend to mystify their labor relation with El Agro, such as a piece wage for a specific management service, or a share of the produced harvest.[24] The labor

23 Interview with a finance and controlling manager of El Agro, April 28, 2015, anonymized town.

24 While the form of the wage in general does not lay open the separation of the working hours in paid and unpaid labor (PKA 1974, 239), Marx (1990 [1867], 629 ff.) has analyzed how piece wages tend to mystify the labor relation further because the commodity one sells in this case is not directly the labor force but a commodity in which the labor force is already embodied.

relation is concealed underneath the exchange of individual works among partners. For El Agro, this has the direct advantage that the necessary labor time is only paid insofar it is successfully embodied in a commodity, and not on a regular basis. Furthermore, these managers tend to be strongly committed to work, since their earnings do not come with a regular paycheck but depend on the business performance.

One example is Juan Manuel, who works as a sales manager in one of the company's commercial offices. He is responsible for attracting customers and he charges a commission for the crops he buys and the inputs he sells. In addition, he sells logistics services to El Agro with his own truck. He portrays his position as follows: "I officially belong to the network, not directly to the company. I am outside the company and inside the company at the same time."[25]

Similarly, Esteban, a production manager, charges the company a previously fixed part of the harvest for organizing both land for lease and the productive process. As he describes it, "I am part of the staff of [El Agro] but as I told you, I don't earn wages; I get a percentage of the production, which corresponds to a previously fixed fee."[26] Like most of my interlocutors quoted in this chapter, Esteban is financed by the SGR. Tellingly, he uses this financial service to advance the leases for the land on which El Agro controls production. Although he does not own capital, being an SGR-client thus allows him to appear as an associate who co-invests. This way he considers himself a business partner who contributes land to the production rather than a mere employee. El Agro, in turn, does not have to advance capital in the leases. Instead, the company even earns an interest via the SGR, thus increasing its share of the total profit.

Esteban also has a younger partner, Flavio, who helps him manage production. After an internship, El Agro recommended that he works with Esteban. But these two do not have a formal labor relation either. After a year of salaried employment, Esteban decided to reproduce the relation he has with El Agro downwards, assigning Flavio a percentage of the produce instead of a salary.

These relations show how the social boundaries between petty capitalists, remunerated service sellers, and qualified labor cannot only be fluid but

25 Interview with a local self-employed sales manager of El Agro, July 01, 2016, anonymized town.

26 Interview with a local self-employed production manager of El Agro, July 14, 2016, anonymized town.

therewith also make a de facto labor relation appear as a de jure partnership. I suggest that this and the related promise of ascendance also influence the strong identification with El Agro that both Juan Manuel and Esteban express and because of which they would sometimes even work for the company without asking for any remuneration at all. Esteban, for instance, considers some jobs that involve lengthy travel "like participating in an NGO *ad honorem*."[27] This voluntary work is further addressed in Section 10.3. The notion of belonging is further reinforced by the fact that the area managers I interviewed each have a very small—formally separated—business with which they cultivate grains in association with El Agro. Thus, even though they almost completely reproduce themselves as qualified workers, the additional existence as petty commodity producers influences their identities and additionally strengthens the sense of partnership to El Agro.

Another reason for this commitment lies in these local managers' personal biographies. As formerly independent farmers, both suffered severe crises during the 1990s and had to give up their farming operations. In this scenario, they met Santiago in the early 2000s, who offered them the described 'partnership' and helped them recapture the prospect of advancement after existential experiences of distress. Their relation to El Agro has allowed them to stay in agriculture—within "our network," as Esteban puts it. He remembers that "my family crashed 200 times and you get tired of being there, working, persisting in the activity with all the ups and downs, you get tired."[28] Santiago then told them: "Let's try something, let's go ahead. I see that you want to progress. I won't employ you. Let's make a partnership instead. Bring me crops and I'll pay you a commission. You can oversee your own things."[29] The gratitude that both express is combined with admiration. Juan Manuel highlights that "the fourth player that appeared 20 years ago is the brain," meaning that Santiago sees through market changes and knows, for example, "what is happening with the latest in biotech developments."[30] This high esteem for the then company president as an intellectual teacher and friend was present in nearly all of my interviews with actors related to

27 Interview with a local self-employed production manager of El Agro, July 14, 2016, anonymized town.
28 Ibid.
29 Interview with a local self-employed sales manager of El Agro, July 01, 2016, anonymized town.
30 Ibid.

El Agro. I discuss related ideological attributions to the network in Section 10.3.

In sum, by including these managers in the described way, El Agro avoids fixed salaries for qualified labor and diminishes the risk of having to pay them in case harvests are bad. Furthermore, the firm keeps the flexibility to spontaneously decide over the scale of production in function of commodity prices or political circumstances—without having a fixed staff. Concurrently, and importantly with regard to consensus-building, especially in times of good harvests, this relation has secured Esteban and Juan Manuel a good living, they say. Yet in contrast to El Agro, these managers have not accumulated capital but maintained their disguised employment within the production network over the past 20 years. This is based on a loss of control over critical means of production and the related economic need for a source of income.

As for the relations to intermediate classes in general, the next sections go on to examine how El Agro's upgrading is essentially based on this class differentiation. Its network coordination is not designed for equalization, rather it entails uneven gains, and power relations. Crucially, the concrete class position within this social edifice affects the extent to which the described actors exist in a dependent and exploitative relation to El Agro. Compared to capitalist clients, petty commodity producers qualify as 'network partners' only under stricter requirements. As individual clients, they are not as attractive in quantitative terms, but they are more dependent on El Agro—especially due to the SGR—and tend to act to the company's advantage, and to be so loyal to it that some voluntarily transfer a greater part of the surplus value than what is formally required. All in all, for El Agro, the economic advantages of the 'give and take' with its clients are unevenly greater.

10.3 A network partnership based on socioeconomic and power differences

In line with Quentin and Campling (2018, 41), I argue that governance power and the ability to hold a leading position within production networks is not separable from property relations and control over capital. And conversely, capital is coupled not only with domination over labor, it also considerably determines the scope for intermediate classes and for those who lose in the "struggle of inter-capitalist competition" (ibid.). Accordingly, a growing control over the conditions of production is a central aspect that allows corporations to "reproduce their dominance" (ibid.).

This does not preclude that other boats may also be lifted to a certain degree by a rising tide—or at least not drown. Actors like Fernando, for example, have expanded their scales of operation, even if they cannot concentrate capital the way El Agro can. And as mentioned before, the fact that El Agro has its nose ahead in the competitive struggle does not imply that all other actors are pushed out of the market. On the contrary, the functioning of the 'one-stop shop' requires the relative economic wellbeing of others as customers. However, El Agro's upgrading strategy is also built on the dependence of its 'partners' on the company—either because they need financial services controlled by El Agro or, like in the case of Esteban or Juan Manuel, they are de facto wage-dependent. El Agro widely determines the terms and conditions of the 'network partnership,' depending on the socioeconomic positions of the actors involved. The company is an example of firms that have gained the capital strength to exercise "control relations (including the threat and ability to exclude) to appropriate a portion of the surplus value that 'small' firms relinquish" (ibid.).

Inheriting control over intangible means of production

I first continue with the example of the self-employed managers. I have already noted that Esteban's and Juan Manuel's relation to El Agro is ambivalent in the sense that, at the individual level, El Agro saved them from ruin. Yet at the same time, they had to give up their existence as farmers due to a lack of competitiveness in the context of agribusiness development, and with it the control over their means of production, leading to a de facto wage dependency. In that sense, their socioeconomic position has been downgraded.

On this basis, and in addition to these managers' above-described dedicated work, the company benefits from its relation to them in yet another way. The business plan Santiago offered to them implies that both keep working in locations which they had already known well for decades before they met El Agro's former president. This knowledge and the ties to other people in the area, which they developed in over 20 years of their working lives, are intangible means of production—former labor embodied in these relations—now employed on behalf of El Agro. Juan Manuel and Esteban make available their information about particular production conditions as well as their personal contacts with landowners, *contratistas*, and small producers. The above-described connection to Sergio, for instance, whose family leases out land, was established by Esteban long before he started working for El Agro.

Oscar, another production manager, explains that this recourse to locally produced ties is crucial to win over customers for the 'one-stop shop.' "The relationship for instance between [El Agro and] a landowner or other actors is usually born from the knowledge of the person who is in charge in that area, who knows the area, who has long known the owners."[31] Commercial manager Carla adds that the area managers not only bring the contacts in the first place. The relations that are built by geographically and socially close locals are also more familiar and confidence-building than those that can be built by a big alien corporation. "I think that's what happens with our network model. You have to rely a lot on trust. You have to have control points but you also need the trust of producers, of contratistas, etc."[32]

In this way, El Agro benefits from the fact that Juan Manuel and Esteban lost the capacity to hold their own farms. While the connection to them is based on a strong mutual consensus, it nevertheless implies a centralization of productive relations that were previously woven and are now put at the service of the company.

Selective inclusion, control, and decision making-power

For El Agro "it is not useful to have partners who are crashing, whom you squeeze so much that the poor guy does not survive."[33] Especially the SGR is an important tool for bonding costumers, and "let's say to get more control in your chain"[34] by helping clients get a credit so that they then buy the company's inputs: "We always try to build this commercial synergy [...] to generate business, right?"[35] El Agro's capacity to profitably combine operations as productive, finance, and commercial capital is complemented by a resulting

31 Interview with a manager of El Agro responsible for primary production, April 28, anonymized town.

32 Interview with a commercial manager of El Agro, June 15, 2016, anonymized town.

33 Interview with a self-employed production manager, *contratista*, and medium-capitalized producer, July 07, 2016, anonymized town.

34 Interview with a manager of El Agro's SGR, April 28, 2015, anonymized town.

35 Interview with a manager of El Agro's SGR, June 15, 2016, anonymized town.

power to broadly determine the terms of conditions of doing business with clients.

In this context, it has to be considered again that the 'network partners' are not a homogeneous group. As a trend it can be observed that the bigger the business they control on their own, the more independent they are of El Agro's impositions. GrupoX, for example, has a simultaneously cooperative and competitive relationship with El Agro. Even though it has not been able to enlarge its capital base over the past years, it produces grains and oilseeds on several thousand hectares and is thus an important client that has greater leeway to set its own business terms, compared to petty commodity producers lower down in the hierarchy. Raúl says, for instance, that other input dealers sometimes have better prices. Then, he calls commercial manager Juan Manuel to see what he can do. The latter confirms that "our bigger customers never play a single deck. They give a little to Cargill, a little to [El Agro] […]." To win them over, "you have to be clear with the numbers, send them information, […] and offer them other commercial tools."[36]

Others qualify as "network partners" only under stricter requirements. The image of a win-win network which allows everyone to grow co-equally is thwarted when it comes to the question of who is actually "dis/articulated" (Bair and Werner 2011a; Bair et al. 2013) from/to the production network and under which terms and conditions. The decision over network inclusivity is a first example. For El Agro to accumulate capital, the customer relations need to be lucrative; they are built "because it benefits the business, not because you're good."[37] It is hence obvious that the company defines criteria according to which it selects customers, for instance of the SGR. Identifying potential clients is mainly the job of the area managers, whom Carla therefore calls "the eyes of the company." Potential clients will then be evaluated at the headquarters, financially and with respect to other characteristics, such as size of the enterprise, assessment of trustworthiness, and usefulness of the relation. Even though technically any small firm could become a client of the SGR, Carla stresses that El Agro is mainly interested in facilitating credits for those who buy inputs in considerable amounts or at least are not about to

36 Interview with a local self-employed sales manager of El Agro, July 01, 2016, anonymized town.

37 Interview with a local manager of El Agro's production, *contratista*, and petty commodity producer, July 07, 2016, anonymized town.

crash. This way, "the salesperson does not have to waste time with clients who are just *too* small [...] it's a way of seeing it as an optimization of resources."[38]

Ana contends, however, that the direct refusal of clients by the SGR is an exception—and so are cases in which El Agro has to initiate a legal process to take over a client's property with which he or she guaranteed a credit. This can also be explained by the pre-selection by local managers. "Generally, they won't send you a folder of a client whom they don't trust and whom you cannot support."[39] Juan Manuel seconds that he would turn down a requirement before forwarding it to the headquarters "if there is a story behind [...]. We talk honestly and there have been people to whom I said: 'Look, I can't give you this, look at the problems you've had.'"[40] After all, Carla argues, El Agro "isn't a concessionaire who wants to keep tractors or harvesters, and it isn't interested in taking over the clients' land or houses. In reality, this circuit of commercializing grains, selling inputs, and supporting clients financially, is more profitable than keeping a client's field."[41]

As a second example, El Agro has a certain dominance especially over its smaller customers with respect to making business decisions. For example, when Ana says she keeps an eye on "bad behavior," she is referring to the performance of an SGR client who is not generating sufficient profits for El Agro's commercial section. Even if "the idea is always to continue the business relationship and to continue to help them," she explains, "there are people who don't understand. They turn around, deliver their grains to someone else [...] or even don't pay you. Then in those cases you show a little bit of a firm hand."[42] Thus, in addition to the SGR's capacity to attract clients, it is also used to impose conditions on them. And despite the fact that all my interlocutors emphasize the freedom of decision making about with whom they want to do business, El Agro's employees dispel any doubts that they expect SGR clients to buy their inputs from this company instead of searching for potentially better prices somewhere else. Especially smaller clients have to prove that they are customers worth financing. This is expressed in Ana's testimony:

38 Interview with a commercial manager of El Agro, June 15, 2016, anonymized town.
39 Interview with a manager of El Agro's SGR, April 28, 2015, anonymized town.
40 Interview with a local self-employed sales manager of El Agro, July 01, 2016, anonymized town.
41 Interview with a commercial manager of El Agro, June 15, 2016, anonymized town.
42 Interview with a manager of El Agro's SGR, June 15, 2016, anonymized town.

"We give them lines of credit so that they can buy inputs, for example, and we ask them, as a commercial reciprocity, to deliver grains. [...] Suppose that we are evaluating a client who asks for working capital and inputs, and if it is the first time we have his dossier we always first try to have the customer bonded to us. Then we give him a very small limit of working capital, for inputs he buys from us, or we demand a little more in the delivery of grains. After the second year, if he has complied, we loosen the credit lines a little more [...] then a new sowing campaign arrives and the client has to qualify again to take a new credit. At that moment we consider the reciprocity [...] whether he bought the inputs and delivered grains. If not, that can obviously influence future decisions."[43]

In other words: No SGR client is directly forced to buy their inputs from and sell their grains and oilseeds to El Agro. But if they do not do so sufficiently, they might be filtered out as SGR clients. Hence, coercion lurks in the background. Here, a lack of control over sufficient capital or means of production to get a bank credit themselves on acceptable terms or to negotiate different terms directly engenders their dependency on El Agro's requirements. Commercial manager Carla states even more firmly that

"we need our clients to have a reciprocity with us. I ask them to buy our inputs. It does not work for me if the client takes the money and buys his inputs from the company next door. That is why everything is connected. We accompany the clients with their financial needs. But, give me something back. Make me a reciprocity. Give me your grains. Sign me a contract, commit to deliver x tons of soybeans, corn, or wheat [...] and buy the inputs. That's what we call reciprocity."[44]

Thus, although the service bought by the SGR is paid with a commission, El Agro's demands of its clients surpass the mere payment of the invoice. In this line, Carla also clarifies that she expects clients not to use the 'one-stop shop' selectively. This refers to cases in which prices for individual inputs such as particular agrochemicals are at times cheaper somewhere else. She insists:

"Don't judge me by a particular price. Measure me as a company for all the services I give you. I can assist you with credits, so measure me by other things than just by the price of a specific product. With this chicanery you already know with what kind of client you're dealing. To me, instead, a client who understands the situation and who keeps selling you his grains is super interesting."[45]

And since El Agro, which describes itself as the network-nucleus, is also the nodal point where the financial and other information about all clients con-

43 Ibid.

44 Interview with a commercial manager of El Agro, June 15, 2016, anonymized town.

45 Ibid.

verge, the management knows what can be reasonably demanded by a client. Asked whether El Agro therewith has the capacity to influence its clients' business strategies, Ana says "Yes! [Question: in what sense?] "Let's say we are always targeting at [selling] yet one more service."[46]

The next paragraph expands on how 'partners' meet these expectations often even without being directly obliged. Some transfer a greater part of the surplus value to El Agro than what is formally required.

"I have commercial loyalty"

A first aspect in this regard is that some interlocutors perform certain tasks for El Agro without asking for remuneration. One example that I have briefly mentioned above was given by Esteban, who considers some jobs he does for the company to be voluntary work. As an area manager, he says, he seeks to strengthen the network, to "empower everyone to do something more productive"—but at the same time he tries to prevent actors who are able to capitalize their business from competing in a way that conflicts with El Agro's interests. He explains that he himself would not enter into competition with the company. "I have my value judgments. I don't consider it right." For contrary cases, El Agro has an ethics committee "to evaluate conflicts." Esteban is a member of this committee and as such, he has had to settle disputes with people who, for instance, sold labor services to someone else while being employed by El Agro. His work as an arbiter, he says, "steals time and means lengthy travels. I paid for these travels, 1,200 km. Sometimes they [El Agro] paid for the hotel or so but most of the times I paid for it myself. If you accept that type [of work in a network]—it's like participating in an NGO *ad honorem*."[47] Agustina tells me that in her role as a local production manager, she often wins over new customers for the company. "Now, I don't turn around and ask them to pay me a commission for that. No. I mean, it's part of belonging to the network." After all, she says, she also gets important information from El Agro, so this is "give and take."[48]

46 Interview with a manager of El Agro's SGR, April 28, 2015, anonymized town.

47 Interview with a local self-employed production manager of El Agro, July 14, 2016, anonymized town.

48 Interview with a self-employed production manager, *contratista*, and medium-capitalized producer, July 07, 2016, anonymized town.

Second, all my respondents report that they close a majority—mostly around 70 percent—of their deals in grains and oilseeds, agrochemicals, etc. with El Agro, often also in cases when they could get better prices elsewhere. Thus, medium-capitalized and petty commodity producers at times transfer a greater part of the value produced to El Agro through trade than what the market demands. For some, this is because they want to maintain their overall good business relations with the company and therefore not displease it. Others, in addition, have moral concerns and feel (self) obliged to do so. As an example for the first case, Alex explains that

"there is a very good phrase, that says 'The tree does not cover the forest.' [...] Sometimes it does not suit you [to sell grains to El Agro] but we try to consider all advantages of being associated with them. If the conditions they offer are not very... if they are not really very much in disadvantage compared to others, we try to work always with them. If there is a really big difference in the cost of input or logistics or in the offer for grains, or whatever, we may put out our horns a little, but very little, we always try to give them priority."[49]

Similarly, Sergio stresses that for him, the most important advantage is to have a regular rent income. El Agro sometimes pays less of a lease for land than other prospective lessees would do. But to keep the relation going, he prefers smaller but constant payments over higher short-term earnings:

"There is a disadvantage in that sometimes there are people who want to lease your land and offer you more money. It happens. But really, for us to break the relationship we have with [El Agro] is not in our interest. Gaining another peso can be bread for today and hunger for tomorrow."[50]

Both Alex and Sergio thus say that in order to sustain the general advantage of being associated to El Agro, one has to put up with commercial disadvantages from time to time. The most emphasized advantages of being associated with the company in my interviews is the financing via the SGR. Furthermore, my interlocutors report that El Agro grants them access to information. For instance, they receive WhatsApp massages about *contratistas* with specific machinery operating in the region or advice about commercial tools. Others mention the importance of agronomic consultancy, or that they are learning to be better organized in administration.

However, for El Agro, the economic advantages of this 'give and take' are unevenly greater. As for the diffusion of information, most of my intervie-

---

49 Interview with a medium-capitalized producer, July 14, 2016, anonymized town.
50 Interview with a rentier and *contratista*, July 14, 2016, anonymized town.

wees consider this as a favor and do not attribute much importance to the fact that this is a part of the business strategy through which the company ensures that clients know about the technologies and services they can acquire and the grains that they can sell. It is a competitive advantage to be able to invest in staff that handles this kind of relationship maintenance. But most importantly, for the company there is no financial drawback to these relations; someone who buys more expensive agrochemicals or earns a lower land-rent, in contrast, does gain less money in particular instances—to the benefit of El Agro—, although they do it purposely to maintain a stable relationship with the company.

Nevertheless, for Agustina, giving El Agro priority is a "question of comradeship."[51] For others, it is rather a moral obligation. Federico sets out, for instance, that "I have commercial loyalty. Well, if the difference [in prices] is enormous, okay, perhaps. But for a small difference I would not [buy somewhere else], I would perhaps prefer to continue for a matter of commercial loyalty."[52] And Darío even reasons that he is

> "morally or ethically obliged to sell them my grains. I could not ask them for money [from the SGR] [...], then go sell my grains somewhere else, and tell them 'No, I sold it somewhere else because they offered me a good deal.' [...] Thus, my moral and ethical commitment is: if they finance me [the inputs for cultivating] 100ha, I sell [the harvest from] those 100ha to them [...] not to someone else. It doesn't seem right, you know, it doesn't seem right to me."

After all, he says, El Algro does him the favor of letting him know when wheat prices are good. Furthermore, "money has a cost [...] and even if people say that doing business is a war and it is often ugly, it seems necessary to me to have a minimum of good conduct."[53] Abstracting from the fact that he actually pays a fee for the financial service, which shows that the money does not have a cost for El Agro but instead earns it an interest, he thus derives from being financed via the SGR that he has a moral debt. In these cases, a formal obligation is not needed for my interlocutors to work to El Agro's advantage.

51 Interview with a self-employed production manager, *contratista*, and medium-capitalized producer, July 07, 2016, anonymized town.

52 Interview with a petty commodity producer and self-employed *contratista*, July 01, 2016, anonymized town.

53 Interview with a rentier and petty commodity producer, July 07, 2016, anonymized town.

On monsters and lice

El Agro thus gains from cooperating with medium-capitalized and petty capitalist producers through a variety of mechanisms. In contrast to the latter, it can, first, diversify the risks of agriculture production not only regionally but also across production associations: If production goes badly in one of these associations, for El Agro—in contrast to its partners—this is only a small part of the total business. Second, it can appropriate surplus at various points in the production and circulation of capital. The commercial business is more profitable and also more reliable; if small producers lose their harvest due to a flood, they have nevertheless bought inputs beforehand. Third, El Agro is able to reap extra profits, for instance, when clients pay above-market rates or when the company pays cheaper land rents. Extra profits are also made due to economies of scale: El Agro buys inputs at cheaper prices than small firms and when it contributes seeds or agrochemicals to production associations, the share of the gains received at the end of the harvest is calculated according to the size of this very production, without deducting El Agro's economies of scale. Fourth, the company has gained former chacareros—together with their intangible means of production—as dedicated self-employed managers. In sum, based on a diversification of its capital functions and a growing control over means of production and labor power in different branches, El Agro has become able to govern network relations with smaller capitals and intermediate classes at its own terms, conditions, and benefit. As Sosa Varrotti (2015, 54, own translation) puts it, by occupying the means that allow for being the nucleus of a network, "such mega-companies have the ability to influence or even subsume these other actors to their accumulation needs."

As a result of the uneven disposal over capital and a related uneven capacity to determine business conditions, the socioeconomic gap between the interviewed clients and El Agro has grown over the past years. While the company has strongly grown (see Chapter 9), other 'network partners' reproduce themselves as capitals at the same scales or have even lost their control over means of production. This does not mean, however, that my interlocutors call this situation into question. In interviews, they all address economic concentration in agribusiness and differences between themselves and El Agro. However, they do not problematize the status quo as in need of change, rather as something natural. Adverse ramifications of agribusiness development tend to be rationalized as individual problems that can potentially be remedied by the right behavior or even mitigated by being associated with El Agro.

As for the socioeconomic differences between himself and the company, Darío explains that

> "They are a monster and I am a louse, you see? [...] And well, they have more financial backing to withstand a collapse. For instance, [...] when it rains [...] I have had 50 percent of my field under water. I have endured such problems, but I did endure. [El Agro] is very big and it is not comparable."[54]

He recalls that it was once possible to live well and send one's children to university by producing on a 200ha farm, while today, he says, he works a lot and is still on the edge with his 1,200 ha. Alex describes the differences as follows: "First of all, the wallet. What happens is that we are very small and they are very big [...] there is no point of comparison. It's like comparing a [soccer] team from the D [league] with Boca [Juniors]."[55]

When it comes to the reasons for these differences, some interviewees point to El Agro's competitive position. Fernando, for instance, states that "as a big producer, you have more access to other types of commercialization than I do, economies of scale, everything."[56] Sergio adds that "a company of this size has access to input prices that are completely different from what we get." They also have the possibility, he goes on, "to hire suitable staff. Small producers cannot do that because of the salary costs."[57] Pointing to differentiated growth, Alex says that

> "in general, the biggest one is going to get the biggest advantage, I suppose, it's natural. It's the one who sets the conditions [...] you will adapt to these conditions, because it gives you a certain advantage. But as it imposes the conditions, it is going to bite a piece of the cake that's a little bit bigger, isn't it?"

Later in the interview he adds that "the nucleus of the network is [El Agro]. [...] All the little planets they have around them, they get something out of it. In the mass, the benefit goes to the *papá*, right?"[58] Again, the resulting uneven development is described as the ordinary run of things. Alex conveys that this is okay as long as he also benefits to some extent. In general, none of my

54 Interview with a rentier and petty commodity producer, July 07, 2016, anonymized town.
55 Interview with a medium-capitalized producer, July 14, 2016, anonymized town.
56 Interview with two capitalist farmers, July 07, 2016, anonymized town.
57 Interview with a rentier and *contratista*, July 14, 2016, anonymized town.
58 Interview with a medium-capitalized producer, July 14, 2016, anonymized town.

interviewees portray El Agro's core position as a problem. Taking the company's perspective from her position as a manager, Agustina instead sees it as a possible advantage for everyone:

> "At some point [...] the small producer felt like [El Agro] was looking at their business and taking them out of the system. In general terms, these small producers today end up leasing out to [El Agro], selling services to the network, and being more competitive than if they had kept sowing their small area alone."[59]

In this depiction, however, she omits that the concentration of capital and the private control of process upgrading created the situation in the first place in which petty commodity producers are often no longer able to produce independently.

Furthermore, many of my interviewees attribute growing economic differentiation to a matter of individual intelligence, instead of fundamental socioeconomic relations or a consequence of capitalist competition. Fernando, for instance, explains El Agro's development with the fact that "[Santiago] sees things before everyone else does. Many times, he explained things to us that he was going to do and we thought it was impossible [...]. And after a while we realized that everything became reality. So, it's like he has an ability to foresee the future." Daniel seconds that Santiago

> "keeps being a visionary for his time. And apart from that, he has a great capacity. He is a very intelligent man. He is super intelligent. [...] A lot of characteristics have come together in him that have distinguished him from others. [...] I think that was the big difference between him and us. [...] We don't have any of the characteristics that led [Santiago] to his success. [Question: Does this also refer to economic characteristics?] No, I am talking about intellectual capacity."[60]

In a similar vein, Darío states that Santiago "is a brilliant mind, I think. I've read a lot of things he wrote. He looks 100 years ahead."[61] Building on his family's property, Santiago's intelligence and innovative spirit have certainly contributed to El Agro's success. However, winning in capitalist competition cannot be explained primarily by intelligence; there are structural reasons as well as particular corporate strategies and state policies that cause capital to concentrate and centralize (Fernández 2013b). Nevertheless, many of

59 Interview with a self-employed production manager, *contratista*, and medium-capitalized producer, July 07, 2016, anonymized town.

60 Interview with two capitalist farmers, July 07, 2016, anonymized town.

61 Interview with a rentier and petty commodity producer, July 07, 2016, anonymized town.

my interlocutors take a meritocratic stance towards those who are downgraded or disarticulated from the system. Where El Agro's success is seen as an outcome of an exceptional brain, the disappearance of other producers is attributed to individual errors. For Agustina, "the producer who had the intelligence to stop being afraid and the courage to join the network is much better off today than the one who chose to renege against this associative model which exists anyways." In the same interview, Fernando makes a similar point saying that, "there are people who don't open up, who are directed inward and […] at a certain point they are not viable."[62]

In sum, my interlocutors portray themselves as being in a subordinate position vis-à-vis El Agro, but this does not lead them to criticize the political economy of agribusiness, from which they, too, benefit to a certain degree. Grosso modo, and in contrast to what the GVC upgrading paradigm suggests, they cannot follow El Agro's suit. At any rate, the latter's upgrading strategies are built on maintaining and deepening the described relations. Yet across different socioeconomic positions, they rationalize El Agro as a role model or a helping hand for those who are not too stubborn to open up to innovation and modernity[63]—leaving aside El Agro's role in the concentration and centralization of capital. Upgrading in Pampean agribusiness has in fact entailed a reproduction of capital on larger scales for some, while for others it has increased the dependency on the company, and at times, even resulted in their losing their farms.

However, these different actors are not just passive targets of the El Agro's network governance. As for my interlocutors, they have established themselves in the roles they play in this process. This may be partly explained by the fact that El Agro selected showcase clients as interview partners. At the same time, however, they do belong to some extent to the beneficiaries of competitive Pampean agriculture, as they have not been sorted out of the system that grants them material concessions; and those who do not merely work on a self-exploitative basis participate in the appropriation of surplus value. The fact that they learn from El Agro how to maneuver through the course of

62 Interview with two capitalist farmers, July 07, 2016, anonymized town.

63 Agribusiness associations such as Aapresid and CREA (analyzed in Chapter 8) have long promoted this discourse. Already in 2001, then Aapresid president Trucco, for instance, declared that "you cannot wait any longer or search for excuses. Whoever does not have an open mindset to face necessary changes will unfortunately find it very difficult to remain in business. We cannot distrust what is new; we have to understand it. We must understand the changes; they are realities, not preferences" (Víctor Trucco, cited in Müller 2001, own translation).

upgrading on their particular class positions is one of the reasons why, despite the uneven economic development and decision-making power, they have adopted mainstream ideas about upgrading in Pampean agribusiness, and network partnership is broadly perceived as a reciprocal relationship.

Network-reciprocity: a modern entrepreneurial ideology

In his *Great Transformation*, Polanyi (2001 [1944], 50 ff.) has prominently understood reciprocity as an institutional form to be found in symmetrical, egalitarian relationships without the pursuit of profit, reimbursement, or (re)payment principles. For him, reciprocity is imperiled in historical situations where the market economy becomes the dominant institutional form. El Agro reinterprets this notion by associating it with the expectation that customers of the SGR will contribute more in return for the financial service than 'just' the commission they pay. To recall Carla's words: "Make me a reciprocity in giving me your grains."[64] The reciprocity she demands is expressed in the requirement for 'partners' to be profitable customers. However, not only company representatives designate these relations as reciprocal. In fact, this was a core discourse in my interviews.

I analyze this narrative of network upgrading in reciprocity as an entrepreneurial ideology through which the relation between El Agro and its petty capitalist clients is construed as one of co-equal benefits. This corroborates the research on agrarian change in Argentina, according to which (a) the notion of network partnership suggests a socioeconomically homogeneous countryside that conceals exploitation (Villulla 2015), and (b) the related win-win discourse justifies the current economic relationship between agribusiness and *contratistas* and other small producers (Sosa Varrotti 2015). In this context, Gras and Hernández (2016b) have argued from a discourse-critical perspective that the idea of being part of a network is proactively spread by agribusiness actors as an identity marker.

My interviews indicate that the consolidation of the reciprocity metaphor as a dominant way of describing the social ties in place is strongly reinforced by the capacity of El Agro's leadership to generalize its ideas. In its publications, at conferences and trainings or meetings with customers, the company repeatedly emphasizes "the spirit of association in our business relations, involving the land owners, service providers, and others, where each of the

64 Interview with a commercial manager of El Agro, June 15, 2016, anonymized town.

parties adds value to the total business" (El Agro 2018, 6) in search of mutual benefits. To describe their relationship to the company, clients often adopt the language of El Agro's management, or they speak directly from Santiago's perspective. Agustina, for example, maintains: "[He] taught us that the best way to win in a business is that we all win."[65] Fernando and Daniel even quote Santiago straight: "If the client does well, I do well, too." And "if I want to do well, the whole chain has to do well."[66]

In fact, the mere instance that the company's profit strategies do not cause their bankruptcy is already regarded as an expression of mutual gains. The grain of truth in this win-win discourse is that the interviewed medium-capitalized and petty capitalist producers have to date been able to hold onto their businesses and, vice versa, El Agro would not do well with insolvent clients. But the way the former talk about the network goes beyond that. For Darío, for instance, this is not just a win-win-situation, but rather a "love-love relationship [that] allows you to sleep relatively peacefully."[67] When asked for advantages and disadvantages of being related to El Agro, Esteban says that "I would tell you that there is not one single [disadvantage], because the network is solidary."[68]

To reflect on this entrepreneurial ideology that conceals "the struggle and the contradiction" (Gramsci 2012 [1975]-e, 1326), I first come back to Polanyi, whose conception of reciprocity I quoted at the beginning to show how El Agro arrays vested interests in a language of mutual gains. As noted earlier, for Polanyi (2001 [1944], 136), marketization contradicts reciprocity, which is, however, recovered through pushes for social protection that contest the free market—the other site of the "double movement." His thinking backs up ideology critique in the sense that for Polanyi, the perpetuation of a market society could not work without collective ideologies that cover more than individual interests. He argues that economic interests cannot be the only social

65 Interview with a self-employed production manager, *contratista*, and medium-capitalized producer, July 07, 2016, anonymized town.
66 Interview with two capitalist farmers, July 07, 2016, anonymized town.
67 Interview with a rentier and petty commodity producer, July 07, 2016, anonymized town.
68 Interview with a local self-employed production manager of El Agro, July 14, 2016, anonymized town.

movens. Economic actors need to "win support from outside" (ibid., 159) by serving a "variety of interest other than its own" (ibid., 163).[69]

In this, there are linking points as well as differences to a Marxist and Gramscian understanding of the role of ideology. It was one of Polanyi's aims to show that the modern market society and its ideological concepts are not a natural phenomenon, rather a socially produced one, specific to a certain place and time. He shares this view with historical materialism. However, as Selwyn and Miyamura (2014, 641) have worked out vividly, these approaches differ in their understanding of the way that capitalism disrupts society and therewith also of how social relations are related to ideological patterns. For Polanyi (2001 [1944], 641 ff.), a core problem is the, though always incomplete, dis-embedding of the economy from social relations and the market's imperilment of social interests (ibid., 169). However, this juxtaposition of the economy and the social neglects that capital is itself a social relation. Polanyi's "conception of the market is detached from what Marxists call the social relations of production, and particularly from property relations, which underpin how surplus is produced, controlled and distributed" (Selwyn and Miyamura 2014, 652) within the capitalist mode of production. In this vein, Polanyi (2001 [1944], 159) deemphasizes class interests, arguing that ideology, among other forms of winning support from the outside, is important in terms of social change or perpetuation. From a Marxist perspective, on the other hand, ideology needs to be understood as dialectically related with the social relations of production, not merely because the capitalist structure implies ideological rationalizations and because the latter impact the former. The ideological is also a very part of—or terrain of—class struggles, on which the dominant propertied classes act under different conditions than exploited and dominated classes (see Chapter 2).

For the analyzed network, El Agro has gained the capacity to generalize its ideas. Concurrently, and in line with Gramsci's concept of (active or passive) consensus (Gramsci 2012 [1975]-b, 411), uneven property and power relations analyzed in this chapter can be compatible with a harmonious appearance and the consent of actors in different class places to the status quo. However, El Agro has not gained a hegemonic position in this network only

69 Stiglitz (preface to Polanyi 2001 [1944], viii) writes in his foreword to *The Great Transformation* that Polanyi sees an "interplay between ideologies and particular interests," in which the former serves as the "handmaiden" for the latter and "those interests used that ideology selectively."

by its economic and ideological-intellectual leadership. As for my interlocutors, they also actively decided to side with capital[70] due to the material concessions and gains they receive from modern agribusiness or sometimes the sheer economic need to do so under penalty of potential ruin. The ways that qualified labor relations are mystified and managers are motivated to run their own businesses as co-equal partners further contribute to the ideological legitimization of the status quo.

Briefly, the reciprocity narrative, analyzed here as an entrepreneurial ideology, portrays the social relationship between El Agro (as agro-industrial, commercial, and finance capital), smaller capitals, petty commodity producers, and remunerated service providers as one of co-equal partners. It therewith reinforces the veiling of the relations of exploitation and power differences on which the success of agribusiness in the Argentinian Pampas is based. Simply put, the created sense of belonging is stronger than the sense of inequality, and my interlocutors feel committed to El Agro in a way that often exceeds contractual obligations. The consent to the status quo of agribusiness across capital and intermediate classes also influences possible strategic alliances. As for the current situation, self-employed managers and petty capitalist producers in this network are more like El Agro's allies than people easily won over for alternatives to the current agribusiness model.

These considerations are also of more general relevance in the context of the debate on GVC upgrading and social progress. As I have previously sketched, the idea that upgrading can create benefits for all actors involved through public-private-civil society partnerships inheres a concept of civil society that is rather vague. From a Marxist perspective, civil society is fragmented by class and power relations. Depending on the state of class struggles and consensus building, this does not necessarily lead to struggles for social developments that benefit the many. As for the social relations analyzed so far, the promise of ascendance adds to a strong consent to the status quo. In a similar vein, a promise of social upgrading that abstracts from the actual social relations may entail the risk of becoming the rooster that announces a day that will never come (Gramsci 2012 [1975]-g), 1918).

70 This resonates with Marxist class analysis, according to which petty capitalists, due to advancement promises and/or material gains they have from the exploitation of workers, tend to have a predisposition—but are not determined—to identify with capital (PKA 1974). Bernstein (2006, 457) similarly poses that petty commodity production, "typically contains an aspiration to accumulation, even when this is likely to be realized by only a (small) minority of petty producers."

10.4 Upgrading in and through class differentiation (continued): the organization of wage labor in the fields

According to Quentin and Campling (2018, 44), the immediate promise of upgrading is to get more out of the "dirty work of exploiting productive labour," whereas some firms seek in the long-term to "leave behind altogether the risks attendant upon trying to make a profit at one of the core fault lines of capitalism, the one that subsists between productive workers and the owners of the means of production." As posited before, El Agro has partly shifted its source of profits away from extracting surplus value directly from workers by increasingly focusing on its commercial section. As I now discuss in more detail, it has also done so by outsourcing agriculture labor to *contratistas*, who are in charge of the direct production in the fields. The particular labor relations and conditions have much to do with big agribusiness corporations, even if there is no direct connection with the workers and the class-based exploitation of rural labor is rendered invisible in the description of modern agro-industries as sowing associations among partners.

This section focuses on the labor relations and conditions of those who—lower down in the class hierarchy, among the workers who have nothing to sell but their labor power—do the seeding and harvesting in the grain and oilseed fields of the Argentinian Pampas. Since El Agro outsources these tasks, it does not have a direct connection with the respective workers (mainly agricultural equipment operators). My analytical focus thus shifts from actors who are immediately associated with the company to consider more generally questions of outsourced rural labor in the context of economic upgrading. Here, I rely on the long-term ethnographic work conducted by Argentinian scholars. Villulla (2015) and Muzlera (2014) in particular have explored the working and living conditions of those who work harvests in detail. I also work with the limited available statistical data provided by state institutions. Primary production controlled by a leading company like El Agro—by its own account one of the first to implement the outsourcing model—likely correspondents to these general findings.

10.4.1 Scattered rural wage labor and contratistas

In my interviews, representatives of El Agro address high rates of informality in rural labor in Argentina as a problem. At the same time, they stress that the company attaches great importance to corporate social responsibility (CSR) and that it requires *contratistas* to employ workers on a formal basis (see Chapter 9 for a discussion of CSR). Ana, for instance, says that

> "there's an issue of document tracking, due to responsibility, as they say, corporate responsibility. Many times, the owner who is sowing has not registered his employee. And then it may happen that, if there is a problem, like a trial, this affects me collaterally. So, there are certain requirements; those who sow or those who harvest have to comply with documentation requirements."[71]

Suppose these conditions, which seem to arise from problem avoidance rather than from worrying about workers, are actually imposed on *contratistas*. Yet the possibility of non-compliance is outsourced to them along with the labor itself. Furthermore, this section demonstrates that the particularities of labor relations in the production of grains and oilseeds extend past the question of formalization. This will be discussed in the next sections.

In a book titled *Las cosechas son ajenas* (The harvests are alien) Villulla (2015, 2) discusses how the class-based exploitation of rural labor is rendered invisible in hegemonic discourses which, as in the case of El Agro, describe modern agro-industries as "the countryside," where "producers" work together as partners and everyone benefits from upgrading. Record crops and the related profits are frequently ascribed to innovative producers, machines, or GMO plants, leaving aside that the value is actually produced by those "who sowed and harvested the hundreds of millions of tons of grains in recent years: salaried workers" (Villulla 2012a, 68, own translation).

I will therefore discuss in the following sections the ramifications that modernized agribusiness in the Pampean region has on wage relations and working conditions. This includes (a) labor-extensive agribusiness and relative proletarianization (b) the actual organization of production that tends to obscure the capital-labor relation, (c) salaries and working conditions, and (d) the refusal of the responsible union (Argentine Union of Rural Workers and Stevedores, or UATRE in Spanish) to sustaining a combative stance in opposition to high rates of exploitation in agribusiness, compared to orga-

71 Interview with a manager of El Agro's SGR, April 28, 2015, anonymized town.

nized workers in the vegetable oil industry further downstream in the agro-industrial value chain.

Relative proletarianization

In Argentina, a sizeable body of scholarly research has pointed to the increasing labor productivity in agriculture and resulting job losses in the Pampean region, where industrial grain and oilseed production dominates the picture. Though exact data is rare and figures vary, there is a broad consensus that the demand for manual labor, be it by wage earners or *chacareros*, has been reduced considerably compared to pre-1970s levels (Acosta Reveles 2008; Basualdo 2011; Neiman 2010a; Neiman and Quaranta 2004; Villulla and Hadida 2012). Information on the reduction of the required labor time for grain cultivation since that decade range from 70 percent (Neiman and Quaranta 2004, 53) to over 90 percent in the case of maize (Villulla 2016b, no page).

With the expansion of agribusiness in the new millennium, the number of jobs has again increased. However, as Basualdo (2011) stresses, agribusiness growth has by far exceeded the increase in employment. Hence, a broad agreement that the need for manual labor in agriculture has decreased. However, Villulla and Hadida (2012, 127) have called for a class-analytical perspective on the issue, and to counter the impression labor does not play a role anymore in agribusiness. They assert that the expulsion of labor associated with the development of the means of production needs to be addressed in the broader context of both capital concentration and accumulation strategies that inhere a particular relation between capital and workers who, despite technology development, "deal with the inevitable materiality of capitalist production" (Villulla 2016b, no page, onw translation).

A first point to address is the process of relative proletarianization in Pampean agribusiness that has accompanied capital concentration. Again, in absolute terms, the demand for labor has been reduced with the increasing labor productivity, leading to a competition among workers. Relative to the remaining productive labor, however, a growing share is commanded by capital and done by wage workers. As Table 21 shows, the share of wage workers among the economically active population in Pampean agriculture grew by 11.9 percentage points from nearly 47 percent in 1991 to nearly 59 percent in 2010; the decreasing share consists of self-employed and family labor and of *patrones* (farm owners) (see Acosta Reveles 2008, 11).

Year	Activity	Total EAP	Wage workers	Patrón, self-employed, and family labor
1991	**Total**	100	64.68	35.33
	Agriculture, livestock, hunting, and forestry	100	**46.89**	53.09
2001	**Total**	100	70.31	29.69
	Agriculture, livestock, hunting, and forestry	100	**54.49**	45.51
2010	**Total**	100	71.33	28.67
	Agriculture, livestock, hunting, and forestry	100	**58.76**	41.24

Table 21: Share of wage workers in the economically active population (EAP) in the Pampean Region (1991–2010).
Source: own elaboration based on the National Population, Households, and Dwellings Census 1991, 2001, 2010 (INDEC)

More recent data are provided by the latest National Agricultural Census. However, it is limited to permanent workers in farming units. As Table 22 shows, the share of non-family wage workers among those who permanently work on farms grew by 15.11 percentage points from nearly 40 percent in 1988 to over 55 percent in 2018.

	Total	Farm Owner	Family Labor	External Wage Workers	Not Attributable
1988	100	40,52	19,5	39,98	0
2002	100	48,8	12,45	38,69	0,07
2018	100	34,97	9,51	55,07	0,45

Table 22: Share of actors who permanently work in farming units
Source: own elaboration based on INDEC data

The labor objectified in agriculture commodities is growingly done by workers who do not own means of production and who produce a surplus value that does not remain in their own hands. Upgrading strategies of companies like El Agro have driven this process, first, by contributing to the decreasing viability of small producers. Second, as the next section demonstrates, the growing relative importance of wage labor is directly linked to the outsourcing of labor to *contratistas*. Among the proletarians who earn their living by driving agriculture machines, this is furthermore accompanied by a shift from permanent employment to temporary work (Neiman 2012, Sánchez Enrique 2016).

Contratistas and (temporary) workers

Throughout the past years, the scholarly debate on GVCs has addressed the mediation of labor via contractors and its implications for working conditions (Barrientos 2013; Coe et al. 2010; Mieres 2018). It has shown that the organization of the labor process via labor intermediaries is not neutral in terms of control and domination, or in terms of constraints on possible class struggles from below.

Coe et al. (2010, 1055) have pointed to a growing "business of temporary staffing" in GPNs. They can be consulted for an overview of studies (a) on the role this has played in the flexibilization of labor, and the growing social insecurity and individualization among workers in particular, and (b) on how firms use temporary staffing to reduce labor costs and outsource risks. Looking mainly at industries in capitalist centers, where, in contrast to *contratistas* in Argentinian agribusiness, temporary labor is mainly brokered by large companies, they diagnose "rising penetration rates of agency work" (see Theodore and Peck 2002).

Hammer and Riisgaard (2015, 91) highlight that the management of labor through third party contractors has also become a central feature in factory regimes in the Global South. In this context, Phillips (2011) contends that subcontracted workers are often employed informally and under conditions of intensified exploitation. She calls this an "adverse incorporation" into global production and argues that labor-outsourcing companies are relieved "of responsibility for compliance with codes of conduct or labour laws" (ibid., 388). As for labor intermediation in agriculture, much of the research focuses on labor-intensive production, such as fresh fruits and vegetables, and on the recruitment of seasonal, often migrant workers who face poor working conditions and super-exploitation (Gertel and Sippel 2014; Uyan Semerci et al. 2015; Verité 2010). Barrientos (2013, 1063) has found in this context that within a 'tiered' labor force, contract workers in South African horticulture are made "the most flexible and lowest cost source of labour" through a "cascade systems of labour subcontracting."[72]

---

72 Since protection through national labor regulation is undermined by such "triangular employment relationship[s]," (ibid., 1067) she argues, global civil society campaigns are needed to put

Resonating with Coe's and Jordhus-Lier's (2011, 211) work on "constrained agency," scholars have also examined how labor brokerage influences workers' actions. Coe et al. (2010) assert that it changes patterns of labor control and that it conditions struggles. Temporarily hired workers are often precariously employed, which weakens their position in conflicts, and placed in multiple and often changing physical worksites, which hampers both organizing and sense of belonging. As a result, the authors argue, the temporary agency workforce tends to be politically disorganized and "highly fragmented, with very little sense of group solidarity" (see Hammer and Riisgaard 2015, 84 f.). For Bair and Werner (2015, 130), outsourcing is therefore a part of the "brutal assault on labour since the 1970s." In this vein, the strategy of organizing the labor process in Pampean agribusiness via *contratistas* tends to weaken or "disrupt labour's agency" (Campling et al. 2016, 1756), thereby undermining the preconditions for contesting capitalist control (see Quentin and Campling 2018, 41).

On that note, the following is a discussion of some of the particularities of the *contratismo* in Pampean grain and oilseed production.[73] In quantitative terms, data shows that between the harvest season of 2001–02 and that of 2016–17 the number of hectares worked by *contratistas* grew by over 50 percent to 22.3 million in the province of Buenos Aires, where El Agro is most active (Figure 9). The interim low in 2014–15 corresponds to a period of decline in the profitability of grain and oilseed production.

Villulla (2016a) finds that most *contratistas* participate in the productive labor themselves. Although they vary in size, most of them usually employ a maximum of four workers to operate a few large machines. Yet despite the participation of own and family labor, the trend of relative proletarianization can be observed here, too. Table 23 indicates that between the harvest season of 2001–02 and that of 2016–17, the number of wage workers employed by *contratistas* grew by 75 percent from nearly 9,100 to nearly 16,000. This corre-

---

pressure on commercial actors across GVCs. However, the role workers play in this vaguely conceptualized civil society remains undefined. Barrientos' diagnosis of the adverse effects of labor intermediation is insightful, yet the capital-labor relation and the role of class struggles remain obscure in this analysis (see Bair and Werner 2015, 131; Selwyn 2013).

73 To a certain degree, the partial recourse to *contratistas* has also permitted small producers (to the extent that they own enough land) to stay in business, since they could not raise the capital to buy ever more sophisticated and expensive agriculture machinery (Barsky and Gelman 2009, 496; Muzlera 2014, 58; Neiman 2012, 9).

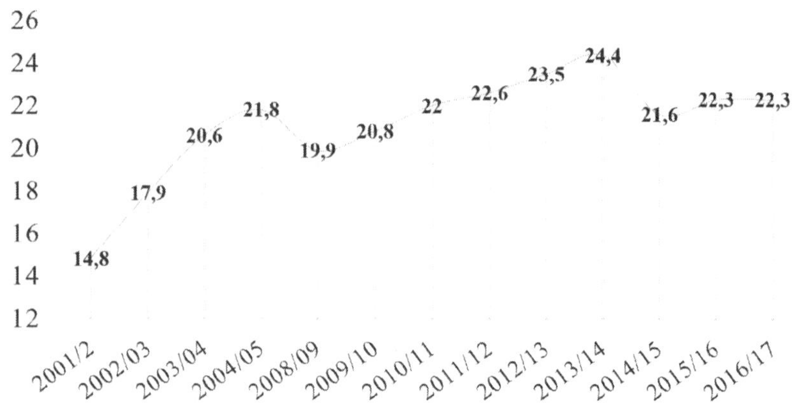

Figure 9: Area cultivated via *contratistas* in the Province of Buenos Aires (in millions of ha)
Data corresponds to the total of all work, including sowing, the application of agrochemicals, and harvesting.
Source: own elaboration based on the Provincial Agricultural Services Survey (2004–2017), Buenos Aires, Ministry of Economy

sponds to an increase in the share of productive labor done by wage workers from 58.6 percent to 65.7 percent.

Based on these developments, and in resonance with the above-quoted debate on labor intermediation in GVCs, local critical voices have analyzed the outsourcing of rural labor to *contratistas* as a strategy of flexibilization in the context of upgrading, which redefines the social relations of production and the terrain of labor struggles to the benefit of capital. It allows firms to reduce labor costs and related risks in an increasingly competitive and concentrated environment by reducing permanent employment (Aparicio and Benencia 1999; Neiman 2010a; Neiman and Quaranta 2004; Sánchez Enrique 2016).[74] Especially large firms like El Agro have pushed outsourcing, "moving labor in the region to a new stage" (Neiman and Quaranta 2004, 50).

Villulla (2015) concludes that this form of organizing production tends to conceal exploitation, for it defines capital and labor without them being in direct contact with one another (see Aparicio and Benencia 1999; Aparicio et al. 2004; Murmis 1995; Tort 1983). Instead, *contratistas* appear as the direct exploiters. Meanwhile, agribusiness companies apparently relate to them as

74 Neiman and Quaranta (2004, 47 f.) point out, however, that stable, well-paid, and secure conditions for workers in the countryside were rare already throughout the past century.

	Sowing Season											
	2001–02		2003–04		2005–06		2014–15		2015–16		2016–17	
Owners/ Asso-ciates	6,429	41.4 %	7,894	34.7 %	7,855	30.8 %	6,655	29.5 %	6.801	27.6 %	6,623	27.3 %
Family labor	–	–	–	–	–	–	2,310	10,2 %	1.557	6.3 %	1,704	7.0 %
Total wage workers	**9,088**	**58.6 %**	**14,872**	**65.3 %**	**17,626**	**69.2 %**	**13,590**	**60.3 %**	**16,299**	**66.1 %**	**15,917**	**65.7 %**
Perma-nent workers	5,708	36.8 %	9,307	40,8 %	12,123	47.6 %	7,928	35.1 %	8,411	34.1 %	8,386	34.6 %
Tempo-rary workers	3,380	21.8 %	5,565	24.5 %	5,503	21.6 %	5,662	25.1 %	7,888	32.0 %	7,531	31.1 %
Total	15,517	100 %	22,766	100 %	25,490	100 %	22,555	100 %	24,657	100 %	24,244	100 %

Table 23: Distribution of labor force in firms of *contratistas* in the Province of Buenos Aires
Source: own elaboration based on the Provincial Agricultural Services Survey, Ministry of Economy, extended after Bernhold and Palmisano (2017, 118)

'partners,' hence facilitating a network-driven narrative in which accumulation is not based on the exploitation of labor power at all.

Thus, companies like El Agro control the production process without having to employ workers directly and pay them in off seasons. At the same time, they avoid the risk of sinking fixed capital in means of production with long amortization rates, as *contratistas* are the ones who invest in the farming machinery and take on the respective debts and interests (Barsky and Gelman 2009, 496). Second, they shorten the turnover time of their own capital by not fixing it in expensive machinery, thus releasing it for other investments. Third, Villulla and Chen (2015) have shown that agribusiness capitals tend to appropriate larger parts of the produced surplus value than *contratistas*. This occurs through different mechanisms. In general, the former have more bargaining power when it comes to defining tariffs. According Villulla and Chen, the fees paid to *contratistas* for labor services have increased less than the latter's costs of machinery. Based on data from the Argentine Federation of Contractors of Agricultural Machinery (FACMA, in Spanish), they have calculated that between 2001–02 and 2013–14, the machinery prices increased by an average of 28 percent, while the fees paid to *contratistas* only increased by an average of 22 percent (ibid., 116). Companies also pressure them to work with state-of-the-art technology. El Agro (2013, 4), for instance, notes that to reach its goal of farming completely with precision agricultural methods, it targets "a successive upgrade of all machinery of the contractors with the respective equipment." *Contratistas* therefore work increasingly larger fields to be able to transfer the value of the machines to the produced commodities. In this context, Muzlera quotes a *contratista* bemoaning that

> "Clients are becoming more and more demanding. Some of them ask for illogical things. Before, you could talk with the landowner, but now 'estancias' [agricultural operations] have an administrator who obeys the orders of someone in Buenos Aires and you are in the middle. I used to thresh two 'estancias' in the south [of the Province of Buenos Aires] for more than 25 years, 4,000 or 5,000 hectares in total, it was a steady job. Now they demand new machines to give you the job and they hire four or five machine contractors to finish as soon as possible. You can never find the resources to pay back your machines this way" (Interview with a contratista, Muzlera 2014, 64).

Furthermore, large agribusiness firms are sometimes the ones who loan the *contratistas* the capital needed to purchase machinery, on which they earn interest. As Agrigood manager Miguel puts it, his company would earn lower profits if it owned machinery and hired workers directly. "This includes not only the cost of labor but also amortization, the financial cost of the fixed capital."[75]

In brief, it can be assumed that agribusiness companies like El Agro profit from productivity increases while risks and costs are outsourced to *contratistas*. This is critical with respect to labor because, as the next section shows, the economic pressure is passed on downwards to wage earners. After all, "the less well remunerated productive workers are, the greater the surplus available for appropriation" (Quentin and Campling 2018, 43).

Salaries and working conditions

Several studies have highlighted precarious working conditions of rural wage workers in different respects (Bardomás et al. 2010; Neiman 2010a; Neiman et al. 2006; Preda and Blanco 2010; Quaranta 2010; Villulla 2012b; 2015). The first is temporary employment and related economic insecurity. Table 24 indicates that within the group of wage earners hired by *contratistas*

75 Interview with an Agrigood manager, July 20, 2016, Buenos Aires.

in the province of Buenos Aires, permanent contracts have been gradually replaced by temporary employment, the share of the latter growing from 37.2 percent to 47.4 percent between the harvest season of 2001–02 and that of 2016–17.

	Sowing Season											
	2001–02		2003–04		2005–06		2014–15		2015–16		2016–17	
Total wage workers	**9,088**		**14,872**		**17,626**		**13,590**		**16,299**		**15,917**	
Permanent workers	5,708	62.8 %	9,307	62.5 %	12,123	68.8 %	7,928	58.3 %	8,411	51.4 %	8,386	52.6 %
Temporary workers	3,380	37.2 %	5,565	37.5 %	5,503	31.2 %	5,662	41.7 %	7,888	48.6 %	7,531	47.4 %

Table 24: Permanent and temporary workers in firms of *contratistas* in the Province of Buenos Aires
Source: own elaboration based on the Provincial Agricultural Services Survey, Ministry of Economy, extended after Bernhold and Palmisano (2017, 118)

According to Neiman and Quaranta (2004, 57), this is a general trend. While there has long been 'tiering' among permanent and seasonal workers in capitalist agriculture, the importance of non-permanent employment is on the rise, especially where technologized large-scale agribusiness dominates the picture and sophisticated machines allow for ever faster sowing and harvesting. Recent developments in local agrarian capitalism "have not resulted in the formation of a class of workers that is stable or permanent. Rather, a group of different types of non-permanent workers has grown" which cannot merely be explained by "productive cycles, rather by companies' strategies [...]" to lower labor costs (Neiman 2010a, 13, own translation; see Neiman 2012).

In line with these assessments, a survey held by the MTEySS in 2014 indicates that the replacement of permanent jobs with transitional ones accompanies modernized agribusiness. Accordingly, only 44 percent of the surveyed rural wage workers had permanent employment that year. It also reveals that permanent employment is rather related to those who have long worked in agriculture. 57 percent of those who started before 1990 declared that they have spent most of their working years in permanent jobs. Of those who started after 2014, only 27 percent have permanent contracts (MTEySS

2014, 12).[76] Accordingly, those who started at the higher levels of upgrading agribusiness face the least stable conditions. In sum, the available information allows me to assume the existence of seasonal underemployment (Neiman 2010b, 147) or what Marx has called a reserve army (see Bair and Werner 2015, 13), leading to a de facto competition among workers and a huge dependency on the jobs that exist.

Information on informal labor varies. It is broadly assumed that approximately 50 percent of agriculture labor is non-registered and without social security and health coverage in Argentina. In an article published by the MTEySS, Ohaco (2012, 82) estimated the rate of non-registered labor in crop and oilseed production to account for even more in 2010, namely for 66 percent. In contrast, Villulla (2010a, 165) considers that only 20–30 percent of these agriculture equipment operators are not registered with the National Registry of Agricultural Workers and Employers (RENATRE, in Spanish), which offers them the possibility of legal remedies. However, this does not necessarily imply that all *working hours* are registered. Neiman (2012), for his part, states that forms of partial registration have increased with the growing importance of *contratistas*. He argues that "the formalization of these outsourced jobs does not imply that the workers reach remunerations that place them above the conditions of poverty […] neither do they achieve stability in their jobs nor satisfactory access to social security" (ibid., 25). Hence, as aforementioned, even assuming that informality is relatively uncommon among workers in grain and oilseed production (and that El Agro takes care to avoid informality), this does not imply that salaries and working conditions have improved correspondingly with the growing productivity in agribusiness.

In general, salaries at the point of primary production belong to the lowest when compared nationally (Basualdo 2011, 26). However, among the rural proletariat, agriculture equipment operators are paid comparably well

76 I use this survey to emphasize a general tendency in Argentinian agriculture. However, it is only of limited information value for my study. First, workers were surveyed in several provinces (Buenos Aires, Corrientes, Entre Ríos, Mendoza, Misiones, Río Negro, San Juan, Santa Fe, Santiago del Estero, and Tucumán). Second, it includes different agricultural activities (grain and fruit production, livestock, and forestry). It is not possible to disaggregate grain and oilseed production. The survey suggests that the share of permanent employment is higher in the province of Buenos Aires than, for instance, in Santiago del Estero. However, this indication is not specified (ibid., 11).

monthly wages. But their salaries are still low compared to other industries (see Section 10.4.2) and when considering hourly wages.

Table 25 shows the wages for agriculture equipment operators as specified in the collective bargaining agreement (CBA) by the National Agricultural Work Commission (CNTA, in Spanish) which is composed of agribusiness representatives, the responsible labor union UATRE, and state representatives. Monthly and daily wages in current Argentine Pesos have grown considerably between 2007 and 2018. But these increases have been, to a large degree, inflation adjustments.

	2007, Dec 1	**2008, Sept 1**	**2010, Mar 1**	**2010, Nov 1**	**2012, Feb 1**	**2013, Nov 1**	**2014, Nov 1**	**2015, Oct 1**	**2016, Jul 1**	**2018, Jul 1**
Per month	1,744 (~560)	2,269 (~750)	2,745 (~711)	3,569 (~900)	4,462 (~1030)	7,171 (~1200)	9,690 (~1140)	11,636 (~1230)	12,403 (~826)	20,898 (~720)
Per day	76.9 (~24)	99.9 (~33)	120.9 (~31)	157.3 (~40)	196.6 (~45)	315.9 (~53)	426.9 (~50)	512.3 (~54)	546.4 (~36)	920.6 (~32)

Table 25: Wages of agricultural machine operators as agreed by the CNTA, in ARS and (USD)
Own currency conversion according to the exchange rate of the indicated dates.
Source: own elaboration based on UATRE data

To assess these wages, I converted them into US-Dollars, according to the exchange rates of the first day of each agreement. However, this is of limited informative value, since exchange rates are constantly changing. For example, the 11,636 Argentine Pesos agreed upon in October 2015 were worth approximately 1,230 US-Dollars at the time. By June 2016 they were worth only 770 US-Dollars.

	2008	**2010**	**2012**	**2014**	**2016**	**2018**	**2019**
Basic total family basket (poverty line, in ARS)	1,962.83	2,953.96	4,479.95	7,906.31	13,250.99	24,652.8	30,175.03
Ratio of CNTA wage to TBB	0.84	0.87	1.2	1.23	1.26	1.04	0.91

Table 26: Poverty line in the Pampean Region in relation to CNTA wages
Source: own elaboration based on Villulla et al. (2019, 56)

Table 26 provides a different comparison, namely the poverty line for an average family in the Pampean region. Accordingly, those seed and harvest workers who were employed all year long had an income that allowed a couple with two children to live above the poverty line in the displayed years between 2012 and 2018. Between 2008 and 2011, their wages for an eight-hour day were on average below the region's basic family basket, referred to as the poverty line in the following. In 2011, the new Agricultural Labour Law was enacted, which regulates the eight-hour day (allowing up to 30 overtime hours per week and 200 per year), among other things. Even though actual practice has not changed in many instances, this law implied a change in the correlation of forces between agricultural "patrones" and the government, which, in turn, expressed "a general, albeit limited, change in the correlation of forces between capital and labour" to the benefit of the latter (Villulla et al. 2019, 57, own translation). After Macri took power, real wages dropped again significantly, and have been back below the poverty line since 2019.

Another question is what these workers really earn throughout the year, given the importance of temporary labor. According to the aforementioned survey held by the MTEySS, many rural workers have to manage to live off seasonal salaries all year long, since "other branches of the local economy do not show dynamism or the capacity to create jobs" (MTEySS 2014, 10, own translation). Based on interview material, Villulla (2015) and Muzlera (2014) assume that this is to some extent remedied in the case of agricultural machine operators. During the working seasons, some gain more than the collective agreement stipulates. According to Muzlera, they often receive a bonus on top of the salary at the end of the season. His interviewees earned an average of 33,000 Argentine Pesos in the 2008–09 season, 54,000 in that of 2010–11, and—after adverse weather conditions—40,500 in 2011–12 (ibid., 67). Similarly, Villulla (2015, 111) calculated 35,000 Argentine Pesos for harvester operators and 20,000 for tractor drivers in 2009. In years of a good harvest, this corresponds to the collective agreement when converted into months although, according to Villulla's account, this is not the case of tractor drivers, whose earnings (converted to monthly 1,667 Argentine Pesos) were below the agreement in 2009.

Even though these wages are higher compared to other rural workers, Villulla (2018) opposes the discourse by agribusiness actors that their workers earn "very well," such that "class struggle loses its meaning" (Manager of a leading agribusiness company in Argentina, cited in ibid., 71 f.).

First, it is questionable to describe salaries that are above the family-poverty line in most—but not in all—years as "very well." Second, the author points to rising exploitation rates. Salaries have not increased correspondingly with the growing labor productivity in agribusiness, particularly in the new millennium (Villulla 2015, 84 ff.; Aparicio 2005), such that the share of the produced value appropriated by capital has increased. In this context, we may note that the wages agreed upon by the CNTA grew less than the price of the basic total family basket (Table 26)—just in the years after the *retenciones* were eliminated or reduced by the Macri administration, which raised the incomes of grain and oilseed producers. Third, especially when considering hourly wages, which are explicitly not defined in the collective agreement, the high rates of exploitation become apparent. Villulla (2015) has found in an ethnographic study that workers often spend three or more months on the road and work up to 16 hours per day, without respite, day after day. They sleep in trailers in the fields where they are available around the clock, thus actually spending 24 hours at work. Some even report that they work up to 48 hours straight at harvest time (Villulla 2018, 74 ff.).[77] Clearly, the reduced need for human labor has hence not led to a shortening of the workdays of individual laborers. Instead of distributing the remaining work among several workers with several monthly salaries, agribusiness companies have thus substantially reduced labor costs. "No machine or seed dictated that the work that could be done by two workers in two eight-hour shifts is done by only one who works twice as much" (Villulla and Hadida 2012, 127, own translation, see Neiman 2010b). In brief, the relatively livable salaries come along with high exploitation rates and long workdays to acquire the basic family basket.[78]

As regards the working conditions, one historical improvement is that the development of the productive forces and the high level of mechaniza-

77 As described in Chapter 6, the legal background is that agricultural workers were excluded from the Law of Employment under the neoliberal military dictatorship in 1976. In 1980, the Agricultural Labor Law (22,248) was enacted, which explicitly did not contain a legal restriction of daily working hours. Today, this is still mirrored in the non-fixing of hourly wages in the collective agreement. In 2011, a new Agricultural Labor Law (26,727) was enacted, which regulates the eight-hour day (allowing up to 30 overtime hours per week and 200 per year). However, this has not always changed the actual practice (see Sánchez Enrique 2016).

78 See Villulla (2018) for several testimonies. One worker said to him, for instance that "you have to do it [work long hours] either way, because with the salary you have from the government [as agreed upon by the CNTA] you cannot live" (ibid., 79).

tion in grain and oilseed production have made most of the labor process less physically demanding than other agriculture activities (Neiman and Quaranta 2004, 54).[79] For instance, from the standpoint of immediate material conditions, qualified labor in a harvesting cabin or driving a tractor is more comfortable than manual labor in horticulture. On the other hand, it is also more individualizing and isolating, aside from the fact that workers are constantly exposed to agrochemicals. Furthermore, while the work in the field as such is monotonous, the rural proletarians are required to be flexible in terms of territorial mobility. As mentioned above, they sometimes spend months away from home during working seasons, seasonally migrating up to 2,000 km in trailers. As a consequence, not only is the reproductive labor at home mostly left to women (Muzlera 2014, 69). Scholars have analyzed associated family problems and emotional effects of the continuous absence for both families and workers (Villulla 2015; Muzlera 2014). As discussed below, these labor relations and conditions also have an impact on the conditions for labor struggles.

10.4.2 (Absent) Class struggle from below

Commodity chain analysis in the world systems tradition has assumed labor relations to be worse in peripheral contexts than in capitalist centers. Hopkins and Wallerstein (1982, 126) characterize one feature of periphery formation as "low-wage labor-in-relation-to-capital," where workers earn "little more than is needed [...] to maintain or reproduce" themselves. In this way, the critique of the functional and geographical division of labor in the capitalist world system is concurrently a critique of the miserable conditions under which a majority of people works, above all, at the periphery. However, scholars have identified a shortcoming in this approach, namely that it leaves the definition of labor exploitation somewhat unclear. It is based on "external factors and exchange, thus ignoring local social relations and class struggle" (Hadjimichalis 1984).

---

79 A description of working conditions that considers various tasks of the entire production process is beyond the scope of this chapter. Readers can refer to Villulla (2015). As for the fact that most of this work is qualified labor by trained machine operators, Neimand and Quaranta (2004, 54) analyze that as a historical process of disqualification and reassessment, since people who used to know how to run an entire farm today only perform one particular task.

In fact, Hopkins and Wallerstein do not actually neglect class struggle. Hopkins (1982, 84) argued early on that "there is some urgency to our getting to work on the theoretical connections (the processes) linking class as a category of production to class as a category, respectively, of social formations and of political actors or agencies." He further maintains that the conditions for political class formation and struggles from below are "continually transformed in the course of capitalist development" (ibid.). However, and this is what Hadjimichalis' critique aims at, the primary or principal contradiction moving WSA is that between center and periphery or, in class-analytical terms, between core capital and peripheral labor. Class struggle from below is then mainly conceived as a political struggle against exchange-based exploitation, underrating the social relations of production as inherently contradictory and exploitative relations between capital and labor. The assertion that working conditions are, at large, worse at the periphery is therefore right and one-sided at the same time. It is subject to "a mainly technological explanation of the sources of increased productivity and, hence, of wage increases" (Hadjimichalis 1984). In other words, the world systems tradition tends to explain enhanced conditions for labor as an outcome of core-like activities located there.

This section maintains that the state of capitalist development and competition at a particular place and time determines the conditions for labor to achieve concessions in many ways. However, class struggle is not merely a struggle over distribution but also over production. Within particular conditions of peripheral development, workers at the periphery can struggle for social improvements and thus play a developmental role (Selwyn 2012), whereas labor in the center can also lose ground when dwindling in organizational strength to confront strategies from above. It is therefore necessary to "contribute to a dispassionate and realistic analysis of the social conditions" of labor in capitalism and the challenges that "diverse forms of fragmentation present" (Bernstein 2006, 457) for those who want to achieve "labour-led development" (Selwyn 2017, 101 ff.).

As noted before, in the Pampean region, the labor union responsible for grain and oilseed production (UATRE) has been far from sustaining a combative stance in opposition to high rates of exploitation. To be precise, this does not mean that there are no social struggles confronting agribusiness in Argentina. On the contrary, there have been plenty of conflicts, for instance, around the expansion of the agribusiness frontier and related dispossessions and displacements of local peasants (Cáceres 2015, Gürcan 2016).

Other examples are the *Madres de Izuzaingó* or the collective *Paren de Fumigar* who have campaigned against the aerial application of agrochemicals and their environmental and health effects. Furthermore, there are cooperatives of vegetable producers who protest against the privileging of big agribusiness in the Argentinian political economy[80] as well as the successful resistance against a projected new Monsanto/Bayer seed plant in Córdoba (Agosto 2014, Berndt et al. 2019). Argentinian members of the international movement La Vía Campesina struggle for an agriculture where the direct producers define what is produced and how.[81] However, at a congress held by CLOC–Vía Campesina in Buenos Aires in 2015, participants complained that their political work has no connection to a unionized working class in Pampean agribusiness.

As for the wage workers in grain and oilseed production, Villulla (2015) has identified individual forms of protest against particular working conditions or dismissals. This includes legal action, spontaneously leaving the workplace in the middle of a harvest, or destroying machine parts. There are also cases where workers have joined forces locally to achieve the formalization of their employment relationships (Villulla 2016b).[82] Individual action can lead to better deals individually. However, the capitalist relations of production leave individual workers in a weaker position vis-à-vis capital, although this can be changed by repealing isolation (see PKA 1974, 40).

However, since the beginning of the neoliberalization of rural labor relations, including the violent persecution of union leaders, under the military dictatorship that seized power in 1976, the agribusiness scenario in Argentina's farming heartland has been characterized by an absence of collective class struggle from below. This adds not only to the socio-political invisibilization of workers (Villulla 2012a, 69) but, above all, to a consolidation of overall comparably low wages.

There is no single reason for this absence of collective labor disputes; there instead is an array of economic, practical, and political-cultural constraints to both organizing and the development of class solidarity. A

80 Interview with a petty commodity producer and representative of APER, an association of regional peasants in the province of Buenos Aires, July 28, 2016, Parque Pereyra Iraola.

81 Ernesto says that the land should "be cultivated according to the needs of the people and not according to the profit interests of finance capital and transnational corporations" (Interview with a member of the CLOC–La Vía Campesina, April 13, 2015, Buenos Aires).

82 See Villulla (2015, 23 ff.) for a history of the rural labor movement in the Pampean region, including successful unionizing in the 1970s.

conjunction of (a) the locally specific social relations of production, (historical) domination and disciplining of labor, (b) the organization of the work process in the wake of upgrading, (c) the type of activity, (d) technological changes, (e) actual unionism, and (f) questions of culture and identity together constrain the possibilities to translate a need for change into actual political class formation (see Neiman 2010a, 9 f.; Villulla 2012a). Currently, this has brought forth "workers with less bargaining power who [...] are willing to work under conditions that would not be acceptable for other workers" (Neiman 2010a, 4, own translation).

In detail, a first aspect is the above-mentioned (seasonal) underemployment that leads to a de facto competition among workers and which further weakens their position to struggle for benefits that they themselves could gain from upgrading. This is reinforced by the practice of extending working days instead of increasing the number of workers.

A second issue is the nature of the labor process as regards both technological development and geographically dispersed working units. Grain and oilseed workers today work on modern machines, which has not only increased the labor productivity but also reinforced the notion that "the worker does not employ the means of production, but the means of production employ the worker [...]," degrading him or her "to the level of an appendage of a machine" (Marx 1990 [1867], 798 f.). Villulla (2012a, 86) has analyzed the related monotonous work on a seeder or harvester, where a worker works alone and cannot spontaneously stop or talk to a colleague, as a disciplining effect (see Harvey 2017, 110). The individualization of labor at the immediate workplace is supplemented by the above-described geographical fragmentation: There is no automatic encounter of larger groups of workers, and hence no workplace-related space to foster a culture of solidarity.

Third, this is crucially reinforced by the outsourcing of labor, through which agribusiness capital is detached from a direct relation to labor and therewith from potential conflicts. Subcontracting thereby has "deleterious impacts on labor's terms and conditions and the exercise of effective agency" (Taylor et al. 2015, 11). This concerns the way in which these particular relations of production tend to conceal their exploitative character: In contrast to other industries, agribusiness workers in Pampean agribusiness are not only spatially scattered but also socially dispersed in terms of *whom* they work for. The fact that they are not directly related to firms like El Agro, but work for *contratistas*, blurs class differences both objectively and subjectively, as *contratistas* and workers are often acquaintances from the village and share the physical work on the field. The social difference between them is often much smaller than with El Agro or similar firms (Villulla 2016a, 74).

These relations also play a role in consensus building. Muzlera (2014, 67) has maintained that the above-mentioned bonuses are often paid to workers in form of a percentage of the profit, which does not only serve as an incentive to work more efficiently but also forces a sense of common "interests between the employees and the owner of the equipment." He contends that this does not only work as a material concession but that workers also often feel they owe their employers (ibid.). In the same vein, Villulla (2010a, 154) has observed a commonly greater solidarity between workers and *contratistas* than among workers, who often do not know each other. Here, in addition to material conditions, extra-economic, cultural aspects play a role, too. This regards legitimizing or naturalizing discourses promoted by public and media institutions or agribusiness associations, which may influence how social actors build a collective sense, as well as a common cultural life in the countryside—with children attending the same schools and workers and employers going to the same church, commercial center, or celebration (Villulla 2010a, 159; 2012a, 84 f.).

Fourth, workers are in many aspects not a homogeneous group, not only with respect to potentially differing political ideas, but crucially to different socioeconomic situations. This includes the fact that some wage workers are the sons of *contratistas* who hope to take over the family enterprise at some point (Villulla 2010a, 157).

This brings me to the fifth issue: The responsible labor union UATRE has not made efforts during my research period to bridge socioeconomic, cultural, and work process-related fragmentations within the rural working class—which are even bigger between machine operators and other rural workers, and vis-à-vis migrant workers—as part of a collective commitment to achieve better salaries and working conditions. An analysis of the UATRE and its history would lead too far away from the scope of this study. Suffice it to recall that after the initial flexibilization of labor and the fierce repression against unionists during the last military dictatorship, organized agriculture workers have not reappeared as protagonists in social struggles in the Pampean region. For example, UATRE did not oppose the deepening of flexibilization during the 1990s. On the contrary, it openly supported the Menem administration (Villulla 2010b, 19 ff.) under the leadership of Gerónimo Venegas, who was the union's general secretary from 1991 until his death in 2017.[83] After his passing, the conservative daily *La Nación* raved that Venegas was the closest trade unionist to former President Maurico Macri and the only union leader to openly campaign for Macri's presidency in 2015 (Balinotti 2017). In a nutshell, "the leadership of [UATRE] is more concerned with guaranteeing order than transforming it" (Villulla 2015, 78, own translation).

UATRE is therefore viewed by critical scholars as a pro-neoliberal and business-oriented institution. It has served its clientele with social assistance[84] and campaigns for formalization, yet it has not been a space for the collective development of demands and struggles (Gomez 2008, 28; Jordán 2014; Neiman et al. 2006, 82; Villulla 2015).

	2004	2006	2008	2009	2013	2015	2016
Total collective bargaining agreements	348	930	1,231	1,331	1,699	1,957	1,731
Agriculture	21	31	26	23	80	77	62
Mining	13	24	50	48	–	–	–
Manufacturing industry	134	313	389	469	596	660	660
Share of collective bargaining agreements	100	100	100	100	100	100	100
Agriculture	6.0	3.3	2.1	1.7	4.70	3.93	3.58
Mining	3.7	2.6	4.1	3.6	–	–	–
Manufacturing industry	38.5	33.7	31.6	35.2	35.10	33.73	38.13

Table 27: Collective bargaining agreements negotiated in agriculture, mining, and manufacturing industries
Since 2013, agriculture and mining have been counted together.
Source: own elaboration based on MTEySS data

One expression of this is that considerably fewer collective agreements on salaries and working conditions were negotiated in agriculture than, for instance, in the manufacturing industry (Table 27). In 2016, the latter accounted for over 38 percent of the collective agreements, agriculture and mining together for only for 3.6 percent. The quantity of agreements does

83 Villulla (2020b) offers both a literature overview and an in-depth analysis of the internal conflicts within the union that finally led to a strong internal cohesion and to a pro-Menem positioning.

84 Since qualified workers in grain and oilseed production generally do not belong to those agriculture workers who live in misery, they are not the addressees of the union's social services. Thus, these UATRE-policies instead contribute to a political fragmentation and further obstruct their sense of belonging to a rural working class (Villulla 2015, 74 ff.).

not yet say much about their content. As the next section demonstrates, however, in the analyzed years, workers in grain and oilseed production have really performed worse in terms of salaries and working conditions than their colleagues downstream in the chain, in the vegetable oil industry.

In summary, the adverse conditions for labor to organize for social progress are in part a direct result of the particular upgrading strategies in agribusiness. Above all, this concerns the mediation of the capital-labor relation via contractors. Following my discussion in the previous section, this calls further into question the GVC approach, according to which CSR and private-public-civil society partnerships work for social improvement in the context of economic upgrading (Gereffi and Lee 2016). I have argued before that this agenda is ideological in that it neglects capitalist competition, exploitation, and domination and hence unfoundedly presupposes that state and corporate actors are interested in achieving development benefits for all (Selwyn 2012). This section has further argued that, although workers may have an objective interest in organizing as a class, they do not automatically struggle for social upgrading either—be it for subjective reasons or due to objective constraints. As this chapter demonstrates economic upgrading itself can be designed to create such adverse conditions.[85]

Excursus to the vegetable oil industry: "when they didn't understand us, we went on strike"

For comparison, a brief excursus to a node downstream in the agro-industrial value chain in Argentina is useful: the vegetable oil industry. Here, wages have developed considerably better in recent years than in agriculture.

85 Of course, these constraints are not solely attributable to individual corporate upgrading strategies. As I have argued earlier, the concrete agro-industrial value chain development has been pursued within a political context tailored to back agribusiness interests, starting with the military dictatorship (1976–1983), later under the Menem administration during the 1990s, and also the Kirchner administrations, which never fully scratched agribusiness-friendly policies (Berndt and Bernhold 2018).

86 F.T.C.I.O.D y A.R.A. is short (in Spanish) for the Argentine Workers' Federation of the Industrial Oilseed and Cotton Complex. It organizes 21 unions that operate in different regions in Argentina. The CBA is negotiated by the F.T.C.I.O.D y A.R.A., the Argentine Oilseed Industry Chamber (CIARA), the Argentine Chamber of Biofuels (CARBIO), and the Chamber of the Vegetable Oil Industry of Córdoba (CIAVEC), and then ratified by the national government. According to the MTEySS, in 2014, a total of 23,950 people worked in the vegetable oil processing industry. This comprises both mills that produce edible and industrial oils. As I have already mentioned in

	2007, May 1	2008, Aug 1	2010, Dec 27	2012, Jan 24	2014, Apr 1	2015, Apr 1	2016 Oct 1	2018 Dec 1	2019, Jan 1
Per month	1,315 – 1,667	2,000 – 2,490	4,700 – 6,019	6,000 – 7,583	10,500 – 13,628	13,420 – 17,417	19,000 – 24,659	35,628 – 46,239	43,822 – 56,874
Monthly average private sector	2,075	2,682	4,074	6,973	11,634	15,277	20,295	31,112	–

Table 28: Basic wages in the vegetable oil industry as per CBA (in ARS)
The two values for monthly wages correspond to wage categories defined by different qualifications.
Source: own elaboration based on F.T.C.I.O.D y A.R.A. and MTEySS data[86]

In 2008, the monthly wages agreed to in the respective collective bargaining agreements were still roughly the same for agricultural equipment operators and workers in the vegetable oil industry. In 2018, however, the latter's agreed monthly wages were on average twice as high as those of their counterparts in the countryside (see Tables 25 and 28). In the listed years (after 2016), even the lowest wage category figured at the top of wage competition in Argentina, exceeding the average in the private sector (Table 28).[87] In addition to these basic wages, workers in this industry have received extra payments. The 2018 agreement, for instance, included a one-off payment of 33,734 Argentine Pesos.

A narrative put forward by the union in press releases and interviews is that a worker's wage is to be measured by what people need to live. "We think that the salary must suit the needs, not a particular work you do," union secretary Victor says. Correspondingly, he reports that, as a result of his colleagues' struggles, the work covered by the collective agreement extends from computer and machine operators to those who load and unload ships and trucks, and even includes cleaning staff.[88]

Chapter 8, there is another oil workers' union in San Lorenzo that negotiates agreements for this location only and which organizes approximately 5,000 workers.

87 According to union lawyer Pepe, a majority of the workers in this industry belongs to the higher wage category (interview with two lawyers of the F.T.C.I.O.D y A.R.A., August 3, 2016, Buenos Aires).

88 Interview with the secretary general of the F.T.C.I.O.D y A.R.A., August 9, 2016, Buenos Aires.

The wage differences compared to rural workers are not merely due to the respective industry's position within the value chain.[89] Instead, the fact that workers in the oilseed processing industry are highly organized and the F.T.C.I.O.D y A.R.A. has been among the most combative unions in Argentina plays an important role here. As mentioned above, wages were roughly the same before 2008 and Silvio explains that vegetable oil workers "used to have the worst wages in the country, historically very bad. They did not have agreements like the steel workers in the 70s or the workers in the petrochemical industry." In the same interview, Pepe seconds that "the salaries were very low and if they [the business associations] could, they would reduce them again and return to those terms."[90]

According to the F.T.C.I.O.D y A.R.A., the change that took place over the past decade is "due to the change of our union policy." The workers' federation had long existed (since 1947) but during the 1990s, Victor contends, there was not much room for union action. Furthermore, similar to the rural workers, large parts of the labor in this industry were outsourced, so that it was hard to organize people. "We were very divided, very atomized, and we were really, ehm, within a totally adverse power relationship." Even when the soy crushing industry became more important in the Argentinian political economy in the new millennium, Victor goes on to explain, the situation of workers did not change, because after the 2001 crisis in Argentina, "there was also no collective bargaining." From 2004 on, the union began to organize more industrial action "with one or two-day strikes once or twice a year."[91]

The first agreement for a 20 percent salary increase was negotiated with the company Dreyfus. Here, Silvio says, "we learned from the company's financial reports that the labor cost was only something like 0.2 percent."[92] In 2009, the first collective bargaining of the federation took place at the national level. Since then, the collective agreement has covered all companies nationwide (except for those in San Lorenzo), regardless of their size.[93]

89 As I have briefly shown in Chapter 6, the vegetable oil industry is monopolized by a couple of multinational corporations.

90 Interview with two lawyers of the F.T.C.I.O.D y A.R.A., August 3, 2016, Buenos Aires; see Chapter 8 for an analysis of business associations that work along agribusiness GVC's and their discourses on union struggles.

91 Interview with the secretary general of the F.T.C.I.O.D y A.R.A., August 9, 2016, Buenos Aires.

92 Interview with two lawyers of the F.T.C.I.O.D y A.R.A., August 3, 2016, Buenos Aires.

93 In Chapter 8, I outlined how CIARA and CARBIO, who represent multinational groups such as Dreyfus, Cargill, and Bunge, justify their rejection of this trade union policy with the protection of smaller companies. According to them, unions are to blame for capital concentration, because

The most well-known conflict took place in 2015. That year, "we were on strike for 25 days in a row," Victor stresses.[94] Business associations had entered the negotiations with a 24 percent wage increase offer, well below the 42 percent demanded by the union (Vivas 2015). After 19 days of striking and paralyzing Argentina's agro-export hub, the Rosario port, CIARA, CARBIO, and F.T.C.I.O.D y A.R.A agreed to a 36 percent salary increase. However, the Kirchner-administration still in office at the time did not ratify the agreement. It had set a nation-wide upper limit of 27.8 percent. The union, however, continued to strike and after a total of 25 days of work stoppage, it had pushed through 36 percent.[95]

Silvio emphasizes that the F.T.C.I.O.D y A.R.A systematically managed to break all salary caps during the past years through "direct disputes with both the capital side and government representatives."[96] Time and again, Victor adds, both the business associations and the government entered the negotiations with proposals below inflation adjustments. "What happens is that they're gonna have to move us before that works for them." The conflicts have not only revolved around wages. According to Victor, struggles have also led to a change in overtime regulations, for example. In contrast to the agriculture machine operators, the earnings of the oil workers are based on three rotating eight-hour shifts (with a nighttime surcharge). The unionist says that the shared struggle also changed the solidarity among and the self-consciousness of their coworkers.

"When we weren't united within the factory, the company didn't ask you whether you wanted to stay. They just decided: 'This weekend, you work.' [...] When the workers started

---

they burden small companies with high labor costs. The union, on the other hand, argues that, based on their analyses of balance sheets published by companies, labor costs are proportionately low throughout the industry and that returns are the same in relation to the investments. Thus, they say, when small companies crash, this is due to capitalist competition and not to workers' struggles. And "if there is a particular company that has problems, we can discuss these problems, but we do not condition the collective bargaining on the problem of one company or plant" (ibid.).

94 According to the secretary general, the struggles had long abandoned a purely economic logic: the companies organized in CIARA and CARBIO lost more money during the strike than if they had "offered us something coherent from the beginning." Interview with the secretary general of the F.T.C.I.O.D y A.R.A., August 9, 2016, Buenos Aires.

95 The increase of the basic wage from 10,500/13,628 Argentine Pesos (2014) to 13,420/17,417Argentine Pesos (2015) in fact corresponds to the governments upper limit (see Table 28). However, this was complemented by additional payments of 880 or 993 Argentine Pesos, leading to real wage increases by 36.2 percent to 14,300/18,410 Argentine Pesos in 2015.

96 Interview with two lawyers of the F.T.C.I.O.D y A.R.A., August 3, 2016, Buenos Aires.

to defend themselves [...] there was really also a cultural change. You cannot mistreat a worker [...]. This cultural change started after a couple of years."[97]

Another difference from rural workers is that labor in the vegetable oil industry is largely based on permanent contracts. Even when production drops, Victor says, "as the labor cost is still low, and before they risk a conflict with the workers, the companies' prefer to hold them in any activity." Further changes reported by the union representative include successful campaigns against labor outsourcing, which had especially gained importance during the 1990s. Since 2008, non-outsourcing was contractually defined. Asked how this was achieved, Victor answers that the union first tried to negotiate for years, "and well, when they didn't understand us, we went on strike. And then, afterwards, it was an ant's job, sitting down each and every day with the company."[98] According to Silvio, non-outsourcing "implied an absolute change in the conditions of both work and union activities."[99]

With this short account of labor struggles in the vegetable oil industry, I do not mean to assert that everything is well in this link of the agro-industrial value chain, nor that labor struggles can easily lead to social betterment within the capitalist world system, regardless of the actual historical and geographical conditions. Even if the *Aceiteros*, as these unionists call themselves, have achieved improvements for themselves, this does not alter the oligopolistic power in this chain link and its impact on other nodes. And although the gained salaries lie above the Argentinian average, they are not rich wages.[100]

Furthermore, the conditions of labor struggles for a greater share of the value are incomparably better in the vegetable oil industry than in primary production. Workers are not as socially and geographically dispersed, and it is easier to organize and build solidarity among coworkers who face companies like Bunge or Dreyfus and their respective profits instead of rural

97 Interview with the secretary general of the F.T.C.I.O.D y A.R.A., August 9, 2016, Buenos Aires.

98 Ibid.

99 Interview with two lawyers of the F.T.C.I.O.D y A.R.A., August 3, 2016, Buenos Aires.

100 Furthermore, F.T.C.I.O.D y A.R.A. reported numerous layoffs in 2018, for example, in plants run by Bunge and Cargill. In a call for a national strike in September 2018, the federation noted that "the agro-export companies are among the few that benefit from the current economic situation, and their profits continue to grow with each devaluation of the Dollar." At the same time, however, "being the great winners of the economic model [...] they still plan to lower the 'labor costs,' they have dismissed dozens of people, and they challenge our rights" (F.T.C.I.O.D y A.R.A 2018, own translation).

contratistas. And *in* labor struggles, they also have a geographical advantage, namely that when these workers paralyze plants or a port at one location, they already address an important part of the companies operating in this chain link, and a delicate part of the country's export economy.

However, better salaries are not given to the *Aceiteros* automatically. They have struggled for this. I thus argue in sum that social improvement in the wake of upgrading is a question of "the strength of productivity gains and how the benefits from increasing productivity are distributed between capital and labour," (Harvey 2017, 108) depending on both the *conditions for* and the *practice of* labor action—in other words, the dialectics of economic development and class struggles.

This view differs from the GVC social upgrading agenda in that it addresses class contradictions and takes into account that neither state, nor capital, nor other civil society actors can automatically be regarded as allies for social development. As the examples of UATRE and F.T.C.I.O.D y A.R.A. show, unions, too, can position themselves differently in this struggle.

10.5 Interim conclusions

This chapter has argued that an analysis of the class dynamics of upgrading can help shed light on the question as to whom upgrading benefits and for whom it may instead entail a perpetuation of exploitation or dependent simple reproduction. This includes elucidating the historically and geographically specific control over means of production and labor power and, in this context, the shifting relations between capital(s), intermediate classes, and workers, as well as the related patterns of exploitation and power. Upgrading, I suggest, may serve capital without improving the conditions for achieving social equalization in situ. It can even have a detrimental impact on the conditions for social struggles.

To expand on this, I focused on relations of production and exchange that have been built in a network led by El Agro, a company that has successfully climbed the agro-industrial value chain in the past several years (Chapter 9). My analysis has shown how network upgrading in this case has worked in and through class differentiation (not merely through technological innovation), built on a reorganization of the labor and valorization process, i.e., new forms of organizing the control over means and production and labor power, to create a social edifice that serves El Agro in an uneven manner.

The complexity of these relations is not easy to see through, which may reinforce the appearance that the social product derives from a collective and mutually benefitting performance. Yet unlike what El Agro's initially quoted slogan *Together we add value* suggests, its unevenly high profits are based on the concentration—and diversification of functions—of capital, as well as on a related differentiated power to appropriate parts of the surplus value generated in medium capitalized and petty capitalist production.

In Section 10.2, I first analyzed how the diversification of capital functions has increased El Agro's ability to appropriate surplus value at different points of the circuit of capital. By complementing agriculture production with industrial processing, trading, and the provision of services, the company has also made its profits less dependent on natural cycles and the risks associated with crop cultivation. At the same time, the continuation of primary production helps to maintain the everyday relationships with producers on the ground and thus to bond clients to its 'one stop shop'. This also allows to keep open the possibility of a quick expansion according to foreseeable profits, and once primary production seems lucrative, El Agro has access to several landowners ready to lease-out their lands. The company thus (potentially) controls much land without having to fix too much capital in this means of production.

My case study further showed how the capacity to concentrate and centralize capital is closely connected to class differentiation. In detail, in Sections 10.2 and 10.3, I examined the company's links to actors, who are connected to it as clients, *contratistas*, or production associates, as well as to dependently self-employed managers. In a sense, this corresponds to a "network-centric" (Lee and Gereffi 2015, 324) analysis. In doing so, however, I pointed to class-based contradictions immanent in these relationships, thus contributing to an empirical ideology critique of network upgrading as a development strategy. As for the relation to other (smaller) capitals and intermediate classes, the scope for El Agro's clients, their dependency and their decision-making power vis-à-vis the company depend on their particular position in the social edifice. In general, the closer their class position to that of El Agro, the more they are independent clients that cooperate and at the same time compete over the produced surplus value. The less capital the clients control, the more they are subject to direct capital power (being one of the most important players in the region, El Agro can set prices and determine the terms and conditions of the 'partnerships'). This tends to be complemented by more indirect control mechanisms (some producers express a moral debt or a 'network pressure' to work to El Agro's advantage). Furthermore, especially in relation to petty commodity producers, El Agro uses sowing associations to gain control over their land while at the same time binding them as clients. In some cases, the relation also involves direct benefitting from self-exploitation. Ultimately, El Agro's grip on these actors can be attributed to their lack of control over capital. El Agro, in turn, bases its network-governance on control over capital—especially the company-owned SGR is important in this context.

I also analysed the role of qualified management workers without formal employment. El Agro's relation to them implies a centralization of their intangible means of production that are now put at the service of big capital. In different areas, they are deployed to organize land for lease, procure costumers and maintain the company's good image. Although they are de facto qualified workers, El Agro avoids fixed salaries, and their pay depends on the overall business results. For this and other reasons (linked to their biographies and personal ties to company-president Santiago), they are committed enough to El Agro to even do some of their work without any remuneration at all. The fact that they constitute a hybrid of qualified workers and petty capitalist producers further reinforces the sense of a partnership with El Agro that blurs real existing class differences.

I have previously sketched how the mainstream GVC literature suggests that "the scope and speed of upgrading and the gains from it largely depend on a firm's position and the types of governance," (ibid.) which range from low to high levels of power asymmetry in (arm's length) market, modular, relational, captive, or hierarchical relations respectively (Sturgeon 2009, 117, see Chapter 3). I have criticized the underlying understanding of governance for how it abstracts from property relations and class interests in GVC development. As a consequence, it discounts how uneven development among capitals and intermediate classes is likely to be reproduced *through* firm-level upgrading.

Indeed, some of the linkages between El Agro and its clients can be described as arm's length market relations (e.g., where smaller capitalist firms buy services from El Agro), others as captive (e.g., where El Agro provides remunerated service providers with detailed instructions). However, these descriptions do not provide an explanation of (a) for the ways in which the social relations of production and exploitation have changed and reproduced in Argentinian agriculture over the past decades and (b) the class and power differences that exist between the portrayed actors. Here, my analysis sits well with a proposal made by Campling and Selwyn (2018, 427) who argue that lead firm control should be "situated in a theorization of the dynamics of competitive capital accumulation" instead of portraying ideal-types of governance.

I have shown that my case company dominates the shaping of these network relations. It is able, for instance, to determine the inclusivity and terms and conditions for clients to its own advantage. My argument here is that its power to govern is based on property relations. Its competitive position and extended control over productive, commercial, and finance capital, which, in combination, allows for the binding of clients, has a bearing on the ability to control transactions and on its uneven capacities to appropriate surplus value. Vice versa, other actors do not control the means of production necessary to make business decisions independently of companies like El Agro. Again, the mechanisms through which El Agro profits from dependent 'partners' include benefitting from self-exploitation and the outsourcing of particular investment risks while enjoying related productivity gains. Some clients voluntarily emit a greater part of the surplus value than formally required although El Agro's expectations linger in the background.

The company has, in other words, become an example for lead firms that concentrate on "core competencies," and it establishes powerful relations to 'partners' in which they "outsource risks, costs of production and supply, and preside, at a distance, over heightened labour-exploitation. They have also contributed to their ability to capture value from other actors within the chain" (Selwyn 2016b, 13; see Nolan et al. 2002, 107 f.).

However, class differentiation, here, does not mean that El Agro is the only profiteer. Although the company is the biggest beneficiary of this social edifice, other actors in the network also capture or in some cases even increase 'their' share of the pie. Some capitalist farmers are themselves an expression of concentration in agribusiness, albeit to an unequal extent. In general, medium-capitalized and even petty commodity producers belong to those who have so far managed—to varying degrees—to profit from the unpaid work of rural laborers. Furthermore, the system provides remunerated service providers like manager Esteban with material concessions or shares of the profit—especially in times of good harvests. This also plays a role in the formation of a consensus towards the status quo under El Agro's economic, intellectual, and political-cultural leadership, as I have considered in reference to Gramsci's hegemony theory. In this context, and entangled with (a) the social stratification that tends to be mystified as a co-equal partnership and (b) particular material interests and concessions, I have highlighted the ideological significance of capital-led reciprocity discourses that both justify and perpetuate El Agro's uneven benefits. Due to all these factors, the sense of cohesion between capital and intermediate classes tends to be stronger in the analyzed case than a sense of inequality.

Lower down in the class hierarchy, I have analyzed labor relations and working conditions of the wage dependent agriculture machine operators who are hired via *contratistas* (Section 10.4). Capital concentration in Pampean agribusiness has gone along with a process of relative proletarianization. Relatedly, in one of the most dynamic branches of the Argentinian economy, hourly wages of those who do the seeding, fumigation, and harvesting in the fields are relatively poor. These required labors are increasingly done by qualified, non-permanently employed wage earners whose salaries are lower than those of colleagues in the vegetable oil industry, and for which they have to accept adverse conditions, including long working shifts and months of absence from home.

These relations are not a leftover of pre-upgrading times, but an essential part of the accumulation strategies pushed by companies like El Agro. They are part of the very basis upon which the El Agro's upgrading strategies are built. Since the company does not employ rural workers directly, it benefits from low salaries without being in direct contact with labor and thus also with possible conflicts.

I have argued that upgrading can possibly lead to a broader enhancement of working and living conditions, which, however, is not generalizable. Capital interests first and foremost lie in accumulation, not in social development. Material concessions are made when profits are abounding and capital has an interest in making these concessions, or when they are fought for. In this context, I have demonstrated that firm-level upgrading can even weaken the position of the direct producers. In particular, the way of organizing labor has created adverse conditions for potential struggles that could result in more benefits that workers could gain from upgrading. This concerns both material and political-ideological conditions. First, many workers lack a secured employment. Second, rural labor is fragmented and scattered both geographically and socially, in terms of who people work for. The social, personal, and ideological-cultural closeness to petty capitalist *contratistas*, who often share the physical labor, is often greater than class solidarity. Together with the political orientation of the responsible union (UATRE), these aspects constrain collective organizing. In contrast, at the point of oilseed processing—where labor is highly organized—concessions to workers stipulated in CBAs have been among the most far-reaching in the past years at the national level.

With respect to the debate on social upgrading in GVCs and the assumption that it is to be achieved through private-public-civil society partnerships, I have drawn the following conclusions:

First, this chapter has shown that class relations are a crucial factor when it comes to evaluating possible ways to sical betterment for more than just firms. It has thus addressed a class-analytical blind spot in the mainstream GVC literature, which tends to result in an arbitrary or illusive presumption of state and corporate actors as supporters of social upgrading. Second, depending on the state of class struggles and hegemony formation, petty capitalist producers within the civil society are also not (necessarily or automatically) attracted to changing the status quo. Third, as for workers, even though they may have an objective interest in organizing for labor struggles, this cannot be presupposed either—be it for subjective reasons or objective constraints. As this chapter has shown, economic upgrading itself can be designed to create such adverse conditions. Without considering these problems, the social upgrading agenda entails the risk of becoming a rooster who crows a day that will never come (Gramsci 2012 [1975]-g), 1918). At any rate, in Argentina, unionists in the oilseed processing industry have shown that labor struggles can bring about improvements.

In closing, I would like to point out that the considerations made in this chapter rest upon a particular case study, which I do not aim to overgeneralize. This includes the danger to overestimate El Agro's position or to neglect its subordination vis-à-vis global players such as Monsanto/Bayer, Cargill, or Bunge. Furthermore, the geographically particular web of social relations analyzed here cannot necessarily be transferred to other historical and geographical contexts; class differentiation is not the same everywhere and many determinants mediate between structural tendencies and local dynamics (see Bernstein 2010, 109). However, my study can be a model for exploring other constellations, with other local and historical peculiarities to be considered. Furthermore, it allows to support the general conclusions that there is a need for GVC research to analyze property relations or the "class dynamics of development" (Campling et al. 2016), both at the network level and across broader geographies, and to examine how upgrading works in and through class differentiation.

11. Conclusions

At the heart of this book lay the aim to analyze the mainstream GVC approach and its focus on upgrading as a development strategy. This was based in particular on in-depth empirical research into upgrading strategies in Argentinian agro-industrial value chains and their ramifications. By situating my work within critical chain studies and taking inspiration from Marxist, social-relational theories of capitalism, I devised an immanent, ideology-critical and at the same time empirical methodology, which I used to trace contradictions mainly within two (implicit) assumptions of GVC research: (a) that upgrading can engender general socioeconomic development within capitalism, provided the right institutional or business environment, and (b) that state and corporate actors are the key developmental figures in this process. The rationale of my empirical research design was twofold. First, as elsewhere, government and agribusiness circles in Argentina have pushed the concept of agro-industrial value chain development, maintaining that it is foundational to an overall sustainable progress. Second, agro-industries in this South American country have indeed seen organizational, technological, and functional developments that can well be described as upgrading—a fact that makes it all the more pertinent to ask: *cui bono*?

On these grounds, the theoretical part of my study discussed how transformations made to the chain approach, which has its origins in the critique of global political economy in the world-systems tradition, turned the GVC framework into a policy device that is generally affirmative of capitalism and usable for business analysis. These changes have allowed corporate actors to use it both on practical and ideological terrains. However, instead of rejecting the chain analytic, I situated my own work in critical chain studies and reviewed concepts necessary for analyzing the reproduction of uneven development in global chains (Chapters 3 and 4).

Foundational to the empirical part of my ideology critique (Chapters 7–10) was my following the above-named assumptions of the GVC agenda into the empirical world of grain and oilseed value chains in Argentina. Through a variety of methods, including interviews, document analysis, participant observation, and quantitative data analysis, to respond to my research questions, I examined

(a) the realpolitik of upgrading on the ground. This included practices and strategic approaches to GVC development of the government under former President Cristina Fernández de Kirchner. The main focus, however, was on multiple agribusiness associations and three case companies. I analyzed their ideas, successes, and the limitations they face with respect to GVC development, as well as the contradictions that arise in using upgrading as a general development strategy.

(b) the ways in which these strategies come along with particular class- and power dynamics and resulting unequal socioeconomic outcomes.

I showed how upgrading, put into practice by corporate actors, can well be successful when measured by the mainstream GVC framework's definition. However, at the same time, this success entails the reproduction of uneven development and a consolidation of exploitative social relations on the ground, although in ever changing forms. Moreover, I argued that there are limits to upgrading that cannot be adequately grasped with the analytics offered by mainstream GVC research and which require the thinking tools of a critical political economy.

In the remainder of this concluding chapter, I retrace in more detail the main arguments made to respond to my problem statement. Subsequently, I reflect on the implications of my results for future GVC research. This involves thinking about desiderata, which require an engagement with debates on questions of uneven development, which I could not thoroughly address.

I commenced this study with a detailed account of my understanding of what constitutes the methodology of an empirical ideology critique. From a historical materialist perspective, I argued that grasping ideology with respect to the GVC approach involves scrutinizing (a) its role in veiling or omitting obstacles to emancipatory social practices and (b) its structural—and not accidental—detachment from the historically and geographically specific, but nonetheless structured capitalist socioeconomic forms and actions under which uneven development reproduces itself. On this basis, I set out that an immanent ideology critique aims at unveiling both particular interests that are portrayed as general interests and the omission of disturbing counter-facts that contradict the notion that upgrading can lead to general socioeconomic development. It is immanent—not internal—critique in the sense that it examines how the GVC approach comes into conflict with both its own objectives and with an actual social practice that entails exploitation and uneven development. Making sense of this social practice requires theoretical tools that, I have suggested, draw from a social-relational critique of political economy. At the same time, immanent critique preserves the elements which the examined theory itself offers for the analysis of uneven development.

Gazing through this kaleidoscope, I then analyzed the conceptual evolution of the GVC approach. Whether it is called global commodity- or value chain analysis, it remains an invaluable tool for mapping geo-economic power differences and their ramifications for socioeconomic prospects in peripheral chain nodes. Based on empirical studies, it has repeatedly revealed the effects of power structures on uneven development across global and local space and therewith helped remedy the limits of analyzing national economies. However, I pointed to several shortcomings of today's mainstream GVC approach, which—besides its tautological explanation of power or chain governance—focuses on management and inter-firm coordination in chains, while at the same time seeking to explain uneven development and to remedy it through upgrading. I have argued that there is a contradiction inherent to this paradigm, in that upgrading by definition has a competitive component and thus cannot logically be possible for all. The move into higher profit niches implies that firms increase exploitation and/or win over a greater piece of the pie at the expense of other firms elsewhere. Furthermore, mainstream chain analysis structurally omits social root causes of inequality and thus comes into conflict with its own aspiration to remedy this very problem. Its presumption of states and firms as key developmental agents ignores class dynamics and capitalist competition, and therewith neglects counter-facts that may contradict the agenda of economic and social upgrading. In a word, the GVC approach moves structural dynamics of global capitalism, systemic exploitation, and class agency off the scholarly radar. It thus excludes analytical tools that can explain inequality and the ways of contesting it. On these grounds, I posed that the idea of upgrading as a general development strategy becomes ideological in the sense of the

Gramscian rooster who, in affirming prevailing social-property relations, crows for a day that will never come.

My empirical discussions in Chapters 7–10 demonstrated that these contradictions also reveal a chasm between the upgrading paradigm and actual social practice in agro-industrial value chains in Argentina. The GVC approach has facilitated both the transformation of chain analysis into a policy template and its incorporation into business worlds, which are not necessarily inclined to general development.

Before I commenced with my analysis of practical approaches to agro-industrial value chain development, Chapter 6 contextualized them within the political economy of grain and oilseed value chains in Argentina. Over the past decades, the production, processing, and trade of especially soybeans have increased in importance in this country. Although the policies of two Kirchner governments have differed from previous and later market-radical approaches, especially through redistributive elements, they continuously facilitated a development of export-oriented agribusiness in Argentina that has benefitted big players in different chain nodes in particular. At the same time, small-scale production has become less and less viable and the concerns, for instance, of rural workers and indigenous groups who are protesting against the violent encroachment of the agribusiness frontier on lands they have traditionally cultivated, have largely gone ignored.

As I problematized in the subsequent chapter, this status quo was more corroborated than contested by a 2011 governmental strategy plan, which set out the goal of combining Argentina's world leadership in agro-industrial value chains with a socially and ecologically sustainable development in situ. On the basis of this document as well as of interviews with state representatives, I showed that the proposed government policies did not ultimately include strategies to limit capital power or to address the relational question of winning and losing in the context of current agro-industrial development. While state actors mentioned socioeconomic challenges, their problem-solving approaches remained conditioned by a technocratic belief in the feasibility of socioeconomic change via top-down innovation and educational advancement. At the same time, corporate interests, social conflicts, and other potential obstructions of a sustainable catch-up-industrialization were widely omitted. Thus, the strategies advocated by the Kirchner government were clad in the language of inclusive value chain development, while at the same time tailored to a continuation and deepening of an agro-industrial model that has reinforced capital concentration. This, I have argued, contradicts the assumption of states as developmental actors generally prone to ensuring harmonious growth.

After this consideration of state-led initiatives, the main focus of my empirical analysis was on business actors. To elaborate on my research questions further, I began with an examination of the strategies for, and the limits to, value chain development as they are formulated by agribusiness associations organized in the chain-wide federations ACSOJA and ArgenTrigo. I described these associations as corporate-practical expressions of the GVC framework. They use the value chain metaphor for their defining business strategies, and also for ideologically embedding their agency in an agribusiness development discourse that claims general upward mobility. Furthermore, the agro-industrial chain is a terrain of their own political class-formation. In contrast to labor unions, ACSOJA and ArgenTrigo have organized their business associations alongside grain and soybean value chains. Here, alliances among capital fractions are manufactured and interests are harmonized in order to advocate their positions on the ideological terrain and to lobby for their concerns together within the extended state; moreover, these largely end up being the concerns of the dominant actors within these chains.

I showed that the policies they claim and the ways in which they approach upgrading are strongly characterized by specific rather than universal interests, which puts into question the assumption of the GVC upgrading paradigm, that business actors can generally be won over as interested partners for a project of broader socioeconomic development. To recall three examples: first, ACSOJA's and ArgenTrigo's proposals for further process upgrading in grain and oilseed production are tailored to a consolidation of industrial large-scale agribusiness, ignoring both potential destructive social and environmental effects and alternative proposals for a technology development oriented at sustainable agriculture. A second example concerns social upgrading. Here, beyond taking charge of economic growth, the analyzed corporate actors do not see themselves as responsible for social questions, a fact that challenges the idea of corporate responsibility and public-private-civil society partnerships for social upgrading upheld by GVC scholars. Third, while many of the business associations depict geo-economic and geopolitical constraints as a limit to upgrading, and thus implicitly problematize the roles they play in the capitalist world system, it is not their goal to generally change center-periphery relations, rather to benefit from their particular positions or to create a core-like position for themselves.

The next chapter built directly on this analysis by zooming in more closely on the competitive strategies of three case companies: Agrigood, El Agro, and LAgricola. These examples illustrate the possibility of fairly successful and, in a sense, intriguing trajectories of firm-level upgrading through agro-industrial value chain development in Argentina. Capitalist development is always a dynamic process and center-periphery relations are never carved in stone. In this sense, all three companies have been able to move into higher profit niches, be it by enhancing production processes or by investing in chain nodes upstream and downstream of agriculture. El Agro's economic performance in particular was also accompanied by the intellectual work of former company president Santiago, who has advertised for an understanding of agribusiness as a modern, knowledge-based network industry, a fact that has earned him consulting assignments internationally. Despite these successes, though, these three examples also illustrate some of the contradictions that come with firm-level upgrading. This concerns both the direct contribution of upgrading strategies to a reproduction of uneven development and its ideological justification.

On that note, my analysis first demonstrated that the portrayed upgrading strategies have played a direct role in the concentration and centralization of capital in agro-industrial chains in Argentina. They have thus contributed to an increasingly unequal control over means of production and the produced social wealth. In other words, their activities have played a part in shaping the uneven geographies of capitalism, in which upgrading for some and the disarticulation or downgrading for others are two sides of the same coin. With respect to land concentration, Agrigood in particular has lobbied for a new land law that would allow further large-scale acquisitions in Argentina and which would thus be to the direct detriment of local actors who are using that land today. Adding to this, I showed that firm-level upgrading can be linked to the geographical transfer of profits away from Argentina, as well as to investment strategies abroad, which are obviously not oriented towards local development needs. Third, the analysis of my case companies again demonstrated that accumulation interests are not easily compatible with the concerns of social development. For example, while all my case companies emphasized the importance of CSR measures, in annual reports, they have taken hostile attitudes towards social movements and labor struggles for social betterment that could restrict their profits. On this basis, I reasserted my conclusion that the mainstream GVC understanding of social upgrading achieved by public-private-civil society partnerships is myopic, as it neglects the inherently exploitative and conflictual relation between capital and labor, and it also ignores marginalized actors in the process. Finally, I pointed to the ideological justification of these corporate strategies along different lines of argumentation, including 'anyone can do it' stories and the vindication of company activities as a modernization of remote and underdeveloped areas. I concluded from this chapter that successful firm-level upgrading cannot be easily understood as a part of a general development strategy, as it can instead directly contribute to the reproduction of uneven development and its ideological justification.

El Agro also played a major part in my last empirical chapter. Here, I further examined the contradictions inherent to firm-level upgrading, but at the same time, I shifted the focus to discussing the third set of my research questions on the basis of a case study. I analyzed the ways in which El Agro's strategies of network-upgrading are based on and shape class and power relations. Inspired by Marxist social-relational approaches, this chapter argued that an analysis of the class dynamics of upgrading can help shed light on the question of who benefits from upgrading and for whom it may instead entail a perpetuation of exploitation or dependent simple reproduction. I devised the concept of 'upgrading in and through class differentiation,' the analysis of which included elucidating the historically and geographically specific control over means of production and labor power and, in this context, the shifting relations between capital(s), intermediate classes, and workers. Ultimately, upgrading is not merely based on innovation—but crucially also on the restructuring of the social relations of production. El Agro is linked to a myriad of smaller capitalist actors and intermediate classes, who are linked to the company as clients, labor contractors (*contratistas*), production associates, or dependently self-employed qualified workers. Unlike what its slogan 'Together we add value' suggests, my analysis of these relations highlighted that El Agro's ability to lead this production network to its own advantage is based on social property relations. In contrast to other actors in the network, the company has been able to concentrate capital and to diversify its capital functions. On the basis of its capacity to offer financial services, for instance, it binds clients to its commercial section and defines the terms and conditions of commercial transactions. Another example is that the company benefits from voluntary work done by self-employed managers, who now exist in a de facto labor relationship with El Agro, as they have lost their own farms and with them, the means necessary for independent production. Yet despite these uneven relations, I found a strong consensus towards El Agro's economic, intellectual, and political-cultural leadership, and a wide-spread ideological perception of the network as reciprocal.

Lower down in the class hierarchy, I analyzed labor relations and working conditions of the wage-dependent agriculture machine operators who are hired via *contratistas*. I showed that, first, capital concentration in Pampean agribusiness has gone along with a process of relative proletarianization. Second, in one of the most dynamic branches of the Argentinian economy, salaries and working conditions of those who do the seeding, fumigation, and harvesting in the fields are relatively poor. These conditions are not a leftover of pre-upgrading times, but part of the very basis upon which agribusiness upgrading strategies are built. Thus, not only does economic upgrading not generally lead to better salaries and working conditions. Corresponding corporate strategies, which are primarily profit strategies, are also likely to undermine the conditions for achieving social betterment. For Pampean agricultural production, I showed that the way in which the capital-labor relation is intermediated by *contratistas* inheres adverse conditions for struggles for benefits that workers could gain from upgrading. In contrast, downstream in the agro-industrial value chain, at the point of oilseed processing—where labor is highly organized and combative—concessions to workers have been among the most far-reaching in Argentina in the years I studied.

In sum, my final empirical chapter has shown that class relations are a crucial factor when it comes to evaluating 'who gets what' from upgrading. The latter builds on exploitative relations, which constantly shift in form but do not disappear under capitalist conditions. Upgrading in and through class differentiation, again, contradicts the assumption that a general upward mobility is possible under capitalist relations of production.

Following on from this recapitulation of how I answered my research questions throughout the individual chapters, the next few paragraphs summarize my conceptual contributions and the core arguments which I have advanced in reference to GVC research. Here, I point to some general implications for future commodity or value chain research that I have deduced from both my empirical and theoretical discussions.

With my conceptualization and use of what I called 'empirical ideology critique,' I made both a methodological contribution and a contribution to debates on GVC development. Methodologically, I suggested how an ideology-critical approach can be underpinned using qualitative social research by following basic assumptions of the theory under scrutiny into the empirical world, in my case grain and oilseed value chains in Argentina. I was thus able to demonstrate that key assumptions of the GVC approach contain theoretical contradictions and shortcomings that are also strongly challenged when subjected to empirical analysis. Therewith, my study also contributed to critical scholarship on export-led agribusiness in Argentina, whose results are often dismissed by agribusiness actors in reference to the potentials of value chain development.

Some overall conclusions can be drawn from my research results, which I argue must be considered for GVC analysis, if it is not to play the role of the Gramscian rooster. As a premise, it must be noted that the detailed results of my empirical study cannot necessarily be transferred to other historical and geographical contexts. Thus, when I consider general implications for GVC research, they are not derived from an 'overgeneralization' of my cases, rather from conceptual conclusions. For example, the particular class dynamics which I analyzed in the case of El Agro's network-upgrading are historically and geographically specific. At the same time, my analysis allows for the conclusion to be drawn that class relations in general need to be a part of the value chain research basis.

On that note, my study provided solid grounds to support an argument made by scholars from different angles, including Bair et al. (2013), Campling and Quentin (2018), Fernández and Trevignani (2015), and Selwyn (2016a): instead of narrowly focusing on inter-firm relations, assuming firms to be developmental agents, and declaring what they need to change to engender inclusive progress, GVC scholars need to remember the structural conditions of the global political economy and how they play out on the ground, produced and reproduced in everyday practice by social agents. In this line, my study advocates for a social-relational value chain approach that sets out to analyze how relations of exploitation and domination unfold in GVCs. Based thereon, a number of considerations resulting from my study are listed below.

First, I argued that historical materialist thinking implicitly assigns a high significance to the notion of class interest. My research underscored that a GVC theory which abstracts from actual capital (dis)interests and strategies is likely to result in illusive assumptions about development. Capitalist firms that are able to upgrade do not generally have a genuine interest in broader socioeconomic development. This argument is related to various issues.

1. The value chain metaphor is frequently used by business actors (be it for strategic planning, on the ideological terrain, or for political class-formation) who are not inclined to advancing general development. I demonstrated how corporate strategies designed with reference to value chain development may instead obstruct forms of upgrading that serve the many. As a consequence, GVC research needs to consider how the upgrading paradigm may in practice be turned into a tool for designing strategies that end up reproducing exploitative social relations and uneven development.
2. In this context, I pointed out the need to analyze contradictions that arise from, and not despite, upgrading. One example is the relation between upgrading and the concentration and centralization of capital. Another is firm-level upgrading that involves a geographical transfer of profits.
3. I have furthermore illustrated the need to scrutinize process upgrading as a development of productive forces that can turn into destructive forces. In Argentinian agriculture, for example, the relationship of forces has allowed for a GMO-based process upgrading that serves agrarian capital but opposes the concerns of locals, workers, peasant organizations and eco-movements. Some of these actors have argued that enhancing the production processes in a for-need system would mean food sovereignty and more lifetime, not an increasing loss of livelihood.
4. Finally, my research underscored Selwyn's (2013) critique of the social upgrading agenda, arguing that the idea of public-private-civil society partnerships neglects antagonistic class relations and systemic exploitation. I illustrated how business actors may refuse to see themselves as having any responsibility when it comes to social questions, and they may even openly oppose struggles for better working and other social conditions.

These examples feed into a second characteristic of a social-relational GVC approach, which I espouse, namely a dialectical understanding of capitalist structure and agency, and thus also of value chain development. Such an understanding acknowledges that capitalism is a dynamic system in which monopolization is a general tendency, but it is not carved in stone and upgrading can actually work. Besides my illustration of successful trajectories of upgrading in grain and oilseed value chains in Argentina, I also do not dispute the possibility of a national or regional development that, depending on class struggles, includes concessions made to workers and broader social improvements within national or regional scales. However, I argued that upgrading is a dialectical process, in the sense that successful upgrading at the same time entails the perpetuation of inequality, exploitation, or also exclusion. It is a differentiation within a continuous context of global social relations of production and distribution. As El Agro moves into core-like positions within the grain value chain, for example, it reproduces uneven development and consolidates exploitation. When and where different social actors are affected by this is the result of many variables mediating between structural tendencies of global capitalism and local agency, which I do not claim to entirely grasp with this book.

However, building on Marxist chain studies, I have advanced the concept of upgrading in and through class differentiation to argue that social property relations and exploitation are key to these dynamics. On the basis of a local example, I showed that upgrading is both based on and shapes the particular web of class relations, and that the power to govern a network of production is related to spatio-temporal patterns of private control over capital and means of production. I argued that an analysis of the production, appropriation and distribution of value requires an understanding of the social property relations.

While I consider this study a potential model for exploring other class constellations, with other local and historical peculiarities to be considered, it also opened up many questions. First, this concerns the question of how an understanding of the (local) class dynamics of capitalist development can be fruitfully combined with an analysis of the political economy on a global level—both theoretically and empirically. Taking the dialectic of production and exchange into account, such a research design would entail analyzing, among other things, the geographies of, and the relations between, (a) control over capital and over the development of means of production, differentiated among core and peripheral capitals (b) complex and meandering class dynamics and struggles over the production and appropriation of value, and (c) the capacity to control the transfer of profits across space. For my future empirical research, I would like to elaborate on these questions while following agro-industrial value chains from Argentina to meat industries in Europe.

Second, my empirical discussion supported the argument that GVC research must engage with theories of capitalist states and geopolitics. In this context, I am interested in further studying the making of geopolitical environments in a way that takes underlying conflicting capital interests into account.

Third, my study has followed critical chain scholars who argue that labor is developmental. Social betterment understood as a question of class struggles deserves greater attention in value chain analysis. I showed that in Argentinian grain and oilseed value chains, agribusiness actors have advanced their political class-formation, while the conditions for workers to struggle vary strongly between different chain nodes, due to different capital-labor relations as well as labor process-related and political-cultural reasons. However, this research needs to be expanded to include labor relations in different chain nodes and their relation to each other. Although there are growing literatures on these issues, there is a need for further in-depth analysis into the conditions for labor struggles, taking both capital power and particular conditions resulting from uneven capitalist evelopment into account. Yet, labor struggles can also not be simply presumed as given. With respect to actual social relations of exploitation and domination, which do not necessarily translate into struggles against these relations, I referred to Gramsci's hegemony theory and the related question of the manufacturing of consent on class-structured economic, political, cultural, and ideological terrains of struggle.

As can be seen, this study has provided me with a lot of food for thought for future research. With regard to the present, I hope to have offered a helpful contribution both to critical scholarly research on agro-industries in Argentina and to a critical theory of global chains, that seeks to understand the mechanisms of exploitation and uneven development and calls them into question.

Abbreviations

AACREA	Argentine Association of Regional Consortiums of Agricultural Experimentation
AAPRESID	Argentinian No-Till Farmers Association
ABA	Argentinian Banking Association
ACSOJA	Argentinian Soy Chain Association
ArgenTrigo	Argentinian Wheat Chain Associations
ARS	Argentinine Peso
BDCC	Buyer Driven Commodity Chain
CAFMA	Chamber of Agricultural Machinery Manufacturers
CARBIO	Argentinian Chamber of Biodiesel
CASAFE	Argentinian Chamber of Agricultural Health and Fertilizers
CIARA-CEC	Chamber of the Argentinian Oil Industry–Center for Cereal Exporters
CLOC	Latin American Coordination of Rural Organizations
CNA	National Agricultural Census
CNTA	National Agricultural Work Commission
CONABIA	National Advisory Commission on Agricultural Biotechnology
CSR	Corporate Social Responsibility
EAP	Economically Active Population
EBITDA	Earnings Before Interest, Tax, Depreciation, and Amortization
ECLAC	UN Economic Commission for Latin America and the Caribbean
EOI	Export Oriented Industrialization
FAA	Argentine Agrarian Federation
FADA	Agricultural Foundation for the Development of Argentina
FADEEAC	Argentine Federation of Freight Transport
FAIM	Argentine Milling Industry Federation
F.T.C.I.O.D y A.R.A.	Argentine Workers' Federation of the Industrial Oilseed and Cotton Complex
GCC	Global Commodity Chain
GIZ	German Society for International Cooperation
GMO	Genetically Modifies Organism

GPN	Global Production Network
GVC	Global Value Chain
IAPI	Argentine Trade Promotion Institute
IDB	Inter-American Development Bank
ILO	International Labor Organization
IMF	International Monetary Fund
INDEC	Argentinian National Statistics Institute
INTA	National Agricultural Technology Institute
ISAAA	International Service for the Acquisition of Agri-biotech Applications
ISI	Import Substitution Industrialization
JNG	National Grain Board
MAGyP	Ministry of Agriculture, Livestock, and Fishing (Renamed to Ministry of Agroindustry in December 2015. In 2018, it became a secretariat of the Ministry of Production and Labor)
MML	Movement of Agricultural Women in Struggle
MTEySS	Ministry of Labor, Employment, and Social Security (In 2018, it became a secretariat of the Ministry of Production and Labor)
NIC	Newly Industrialized Countries
OECD	Organization for Economic Co-operation and Development
PEA	Argentina Agribusiness Leader. Federal and Participative Agri-Food and Agribusiness Strategic Plan 2010–2020
PDCC	Producer Driven Commodity Chain
R&D	Research and Development
RENATRE	National Registry of Agricultural Workers and Employers
ROE	Register of Export Operations
RR	RoundupReady
SGR	Reciprocal Guarantee Society
SMEs	Small and Medium Enterprises
SRA	Argentine Rural Society
UATRE	Argentinian Union of Rural Workers and Stevedores
UIFRA	Union of Pasta Manufacturers of the Republic of Argentina
UNCTAD	United Nations Conference on Trade and Development
UNIDO	United Nations Industrial Development Organization
USAID	United States Agency for International Development
USD	US-Dollar
WAP	Wireless Application Protocol
WSA	World-systems Analysis
WTO	World Trade Organization

List of Interview Partners and Anonymized Company Documents

1	Agustina	Interview with a self-employed production manager, *contratista*, and medium-capitalized producer, July 07, 2016, anonymized town.
2	Alejandro	Interview with a representative of CIARA-CEC, August 29, 2014, Buenos Aires.
3	Alfredo	Interview with a representative of ACSOJA, August 7, 2014, Rosario.
4	Alex	Interview with a medium-capitalized producer, July 14, 2016, anonymized town.
5	Ana I	Interview with a manager of El Agro's SGR, April 28, 2015, anonymized town.
6	Ana II	Interview with a manager of El Agro's SGR, June 15, 2016, anonymized town.
7	Benicio	Interview with three representatives of the INTA, May 05, 2015, Buenos Aires.
8	Bruno	Interview with three representatives of the INTA, May 05, 2015, Buenos Aires.
9	Carla	Interview with a commercial manager of El Agro, June 15, 2016, anonymized town.
10	Carlos	Interview with an economist at the grain stock exchange in Buenos Aires, May 26, 2016, Buenos Aires.
11	Carolina	Interview with El Agro's vice president, June 15, 2016, anonymized town.
12	Celina	Interview with a member of the CLOC–La Vía Campesina, April 13, 2015, Buenos Aires.
13	Cristian	Interview with a representative of CARBIO, June 6, 2016, Buenos Aires.
14	Dalina	Interview with a representative of FAIM, May 26, 2016, Buenos Aires.
15	Daniel	Interview with two capitalist farmers, July 07, 2016, anonymized town.

16	Dante	Interview with an administration manager of El Agro, June 23, 2016, Buenos Aires.
17	Darío	Interview with a rentier and petty commodity producer, July 07, 2016, anonymized town.
18	Diego	Interview with two representatives of ArgenTrigo, May 12, 2016, Buenos Aires.
19	Eugenio	Interview with a representative of the SRA, August 7, 2014, Rosario.
20	Ernesto	Interview with a member of the CLOC–La Vía Campesina, April 13, 2015, Buenos Aires.
21	Esteban	Interview with a local self-employed production manager of El Agro, July 14, 2016, anonymized town.
22	Emma	Interview with three representatives of the INTA, May 05, 2015, Buenos Aires.
23	Fabio	Interview with a representative of CAFMA, May 13, 2016, Buenos Aires.
24	Federico	Interview with a petty commodity producer and self-employed *contratista*, July 01, 2016, anonymized town.
25	Flavio	Interview with a local self-employed production manager of El Agro, July 14, 2016, anonymized town.
26	Fernando	Interview with two capitalist farmers, July 07, 2016, anonymized town.
27	Graciela	Interview with a finance and controlling manager of El Agro, April 28, 2015, anonymized town.
28	Hernando	Interview with a representative of the grain stock exchange in Rosario, August 12, 2014, Rosario.
29	José	Interview with a representative of the MAGyP, Sub-secretariat for value added, April 21, 2015, Buenos Aires.
30	Juan Manuel	Interview with a local self-employed sales manager of El Agro, July 01, 2016, anonymized town.
31	Julieta	Interview with two representatives of CIARA-CEC, June 2, 2016, Buenos Aires.
32	Juri	Interview with a representative of the truck drivers' union, August 17, 2016, Rosario.
33	Lea	Interview with a representative of the Argentine Ministry of Agroindustry, Secretariat of Family Agriculture, June 17, 2016, Buenos Aires.
34	Lisa	Interview with two representatives of ArgenTrigo, May 12, 2016, Buenos Aires.
35	Lucas	Interview with a representative of UIFRA, April 27 2016, Buenos Aires.

36	Luis	Interview with a representative of ABA, August 26, 2014, Buenos Aires.
37	Manilo	Interview with two representatives of FADEEAC, June 6, 2016, Buenos Aires.
38	Marcos	Interview with two representatives of CIARA-CEC, June 2, 2016, Buenos Aires.
39	Mauricio	Interview with a marketing and business manager of El Agro, April 27, 2015, Buenos Aires.
40	Miguel I	Interview with an Agrigood manager, April 22, 2015, Buenos Aires.
41	Miguel II	Interview with an Agrigood manager, July 20, 2016, Buenos Aires.
42	Oscar	Interview with a manager of El Agro responsible for primary production, April 28, anonymized town.
43	Pepe	Interview with two lawyers of the F.T.C.I.O.D y A.R.A, August 3, 2016, Buenos Aires
44	Raúl	Interview with a representative of GrupoX, July 01, 2016, anonymized town.
45	Renerio	Interview with a representative of AACREA, August 27, 2014, Buenos Aires.
46	Roberto	Interview with two representatives of FADEEAC, June 6, 2016, Buenos Aires.
47	Rogelio I	Interview with the executive director of LAgricola, March 31, 2015, Buenos Aires.
48	Rogelio II	Interview with the executive director of LAgricola, July 18, 2016, Buenos Aires.
49	Santiago I	Interview with El Agro's former president, August 21, 2014, Buenos Aires.
50	Santiago II	Interview with El Agro's former president, April 27, 2015, Buenos Aires.
51	Sergio	Interview with a rentier and *contratista*, July 14, 2016, anonymized town.
52	Silvio	Interview with two lawyers of the F.T.C.I.O.D y A.R.A, August 3, 2016, Buenos Aires.
53	Tomas	Interview with a petty commodity producer and representative of APER, an association of regional peasants in the province of Buenos Aires, July 28, 2016, Parque Pereyra Iraola.
54	Vanessa	Interview with a representative of the INTA, April 22, 2015, Buenos Aires.
55	Victor	Interview with the secretary general of the F.T.C.I.O.D y A.R.A, August 9, 2016, Buenos Aires.

Agrigood	In the case of **Agrigood**, I accessed annual reports of the years 2013, 2015, and 2018.
El Agro	In the case of **El Agro**, I accessed annual reports of the years 2008–2018. Where the reference is "El Agro 2013," this refers to a publication written by an external academic. However, it was written in cooperation with El Agro and is advertised by the company.
LAgricola	In the case of **LAgricola**, I accessed annual reports of the years 2010–2018.

Statistical Datebases

UN Comtrade	https://comtrade.un.org/ (last accessed June 01, 2022)
CIARA	http://ciaracec.com.ar/ciara/Estadisticas (last accessed June 01, 2022)
FAOSTAT	http://www.fao.org/faostat/en/ (last accessed June 01, 2022)
INDEC	https://www.indec.gob.ar/ (last accessed June 01, 2022)
ISAAA GM Approval Database	http://www.isaaa.org/gmapprovaldatabase/ (last accessed June 01, 2022)
Ministry of Production and Labor	https://www.agroindustria.gob.ar/sitio/areas/ss_mercados_agropecuarios/exportaciones/ (last accessed June 01, 2022)
Provincial Agricultural Services Survey	http://www.estadistica.ec.gba.gov.ar/dpe/index.php/economia/agricultura-ganaderia-y-pesca/servicios-agropecuarios/47-encuesta-provincial-de-servicios-agropecuarios (last accessed June 01, 2022)

List of Tables

List of Figures

Literature

Acosta Reveles, Irma-Lorena (2008). Capitalismo Agrario y Sojización en la Pampa Argentina. Las Razones el Desalojo Laboral. *Revista Lavboratorio. Estudios sobre Cambio Estructural y Desigualdad Social*, 10 (22), 8–12.

Acosta Reveles, Irma-Lorena (2012). The Limits and Contradictions of Agricultural Technology in Latin America: Lessons from Mexico and Argentina. *Perspectives on Global Development and Technology*, 1, 386–400.

Adorno, Theodor W. (1973). *Negative Dialectics*. London: Routledge.

Adorno, Theodor W. (1977 [1969]). Introduction. In Theodor W. Adorno, Hans Albert, Ralf Dahrendorf, Jürgen Habermas, Harald Pilot and Karl R. Popper (eds.). *The Positivist Dispute in German Sociology*, 1–67. London: Heinemann.

Adorno, Theodor W. (1997 [1972]). Beitrag zur Ideologienlehre. In Rolf Tiedemann (ed.). Theodor W. Adorno. Gesammelte Schriften, volume 8, 457–77. Frankfurt: Suhrkamp.

Agosto, Patricia (ed.). (2014). *Malvinas. Un Pueblo en Lucha Contra Monsanto*. Buenos Aires: Ediciones América Libre.

Ainsuain, Oscar, and Mariana Echaguibel (2012). *A 100 Años del Grito de Alcorta. Soja, Agronegocios y Explotación*. Buenos Aires: CICCUS.

Alonso, Lucas Leonel, Alicia Estela Ronco and Damián José Mariano (2014). Niveles de Glifosato y Atrazina de Lluvia de la Región Pampeana. Paper presented at V. Congreso SETAC, October 22–25, in Neuquén, Argentina.

Altieri, Miguel A. (ed.). (2018 [1995]). *Agroecology. The Science of Sustainable Agriculture*. Boca Raton: CRC Press.

Altvater, Elmar (1975). Wertgesetz und Monopolmacht. In Wolfgang Fritz Haug (ed.). *Zur Theorie des Monopols. Staat und Monopole (I)*, Argument-Sonderband 6, 129–98. Berlin: Argument

Amin, Samir (1975). *Die ungleiche Entwicklung. Essay über die Gesellschaftsformationen des peripheren Kapitalismus*. Hamburg: Hoffmann und Campe.

Andreucci, Diego, Melissa Garcia-Lamarca, Jonah Wedekind and Erik Swyngedouw (2017). "Value Grabbing": A Political Ecology of Rent. *Capitalism Nature Socialism*, 28 (3), 28–47.

Anlló, Guillermo, Roberto Bisang and Mercedes Campi (eds.). (2013a). *Claves para Repensar el Agro Argentino*. Buenos Aires: Eudeba.

Anlló, Guillermo, Roberto Bisang and Mercedes Campi (2013b). El modelo de Organización de la Producción Agrícola: De la Integración Vertical a la Agricultura en Red. In Guillermo Anlló, Roberto Bisang and Mercedes Campi (eds.). *Claves Para Repensar El Agro Argentino*, 152–202. Buenos Aires: Eudeba.

Anlló, Guillermo, Roberto Bisang and Mercedes Campi (2013c). ¿Schumpeter de Visita en las Pampas Argentinas? In Guillermo Anlló, Roberto Bisang and Mercedes Campi (eds.). *Claves Para Repensar El Agro Argentino*, 11–30. Buenos Aires: Eudeba.

Anlló, Guillermo, Roberto Bisang and Guillermo Salvatierra (2010). *Cambios Estructurales en las Actividades Agropecuarias. De lo Primario a las Cadenas Globales de Valor*. Buenos Aires: CEPAL.

Anner, Mark (2015a). Labor Control Regimes and Worker Resistance in Global Supply Chains. *Labor History*, 56 (3), 292–307.

Anner, Mark (2015b). Social Downgrading and Worker Resistance in Apparel Global Value Chains. In Kirsty Newsome, Phil Taylor, Jennifer Bair and Al Rainnie (eds.). *Putting Labour in its Place. Labour Process Analysis and Global Value Chains*, 152–70. London: Palgrave.

Anner, Mark (2019). Squeezing Workers' Rights in Global Supply Chains: Purchasing Practices in the Bangladesh Garment Export Sector in Comparative Perspective. *Review of International Political Economy*, 27 (2), 320–47.

Anner, Mark (2021). Preisdruck in globalen Wertschöpfungsketten und seine Auswirkungen auf Gewalt und Belästigung am Arbeitsplatz. *WSI Mitteilungen*, 1, 28–36.

Aparicio, Susana Teresa (2005). Trabajo y Trabajadores en el Sector Agropecuario de la Argentina. In Norma Giarracca and Miguel Teubal (eds.). *El Campo en la Encrucijada*, 193–221. Buenos Aires: Alianza.

Aparicio, Susana Teresa, and Roberto Rodolfo Benencia (1999). Empleo Rural en la Argentina. In Susana Teresa Aparicio and Roberto Rodolfo Benecia (eds.). *Empleo Rural en Tiempos de Flexibilidad*, 29–81. Buenos Aires: La Colmena.

Aparicio, Susana Teresa, Paula Berenguer and Victor Rau (2004). Modalidades de Intermediación en los Mercados de Trabajo Rurales en Argentina. *Cuadernos de Desarrollo Rural*, 53, 59–79.

Appelbaum, Richard P., David Smith and Brad Christerson (1994). Commodity Chains and Industrial Restructuring in the Pacific Rim: Garment Trade and Manufacturing. In Gary Gereffi and Miguel Korzeniewicz (eds.). *Commodity Chains and Global Capitalism*, 187–204. Westport: Praeger.

Arancibia, Florencia (2013). Challenging the Bioeconomy: The Dynamics of Collective Action in Argentina. *Technology in Science*, 35 (2), 79–92.

Archetti, Eduardo, and Kristi Stölen (1975). *Explotación Familiar y Acumulación de Capital en el Campo Argentino*. Buenos Aires: Siglo Veintiuno Editores.

Arrighi, Giovanni (1990). The Developmentalist Illusion. In William G. Martin (ed.). *Semiperipheral States in the World-Economy*, 11–42. Westport: Greenwood Press.

Arrighi, Giovanni (2010). *The Long Twentieth Century. Money, Power and the Origins of our Times*. London: Verso.

Arrighi, Giovanni, and Jessica Drangel (1986). The Stratification of the World-Economy: An Exploration of the Semiperipheral Zone. *Review* (Fernand Braudel Center), 10, 9–74.

Ávila-Vázquez, Medardo, and Flavia Silvina Difilippo (2016). Agricultura Tóxica y Salud en Pueblos Fumigados de Argentina. Crítica y Resistencias. *Revista de conflictos sociales latinoamericanos*, 2, 23–45.

Azcuy Ameghino, Eduardo (2000). Las reformas económicas neoliberales y el sector agropecuario pampeano (1991–1999). *Ciclos*, 10 (20), 191–219.

Azcuy Ameghino, Eduardo, and Diego A. Fernández (2019). *El Censo Nacional Agropecuario 2018. Visión General y Aproximación a la Región Pampeana*. Documento de Trabajo. Centro Interdisciplinario de Estudios Agrarios. Facultad de Ciencias Económicas, Universidad de Buenos Aires.

Azpiazu, Daniel, Pablo Manzanelli and Martín Schorr (2011). *Concentración y Extranjerización. La Argentina en la Posconvertibilidad*. Buenos Aires: Capital Intelectual.

Azpiazu, Daniel, and Martín Schorr (2010). *Hecho en Argentina. Industria y Economía, 1976–2007*. Buenos Aires: Siglo Veintiuno Editores.

Bair, Jennifer (2005). Global Capitalism and Commodity Chains: Looking Back, Going Forward. *Competition & Change*, 9 (2), 153–80.

Bair, Jennifer (2008). Analysing Global Economic Organization: Embedded Networks and Global Chains Compared. *Economy and Society*, 73 (3), 339–64.

Bair, Jennifer (2009). Global Commodity Chains: Genealogy and Review. In Jennifer Bair (ed.). *Frontiers of Commodity Chain Research*, 1–34. Stanford: Stanford University Press.

Bair, Jennifer (2010). On Difference and Capital: Gender and the Globalization of Production. *Signs: Journal of Women in Culture and Society*, 36 (1), 203–26.

Bair, Jennifer (2014). Editor's Introduction: Commodity Chains in and of the World-System. *Journal of World-System's Research*, 20 (1), 1–10.

Bair, Jennifer, and Enrique Dussel Peters (2006). Global Commodity Chains and Endogenous Growth: Export Dynamism and Development in Mexico and Honduras. *World Development*, 34 (2), 203–21.

Bair, Jennifer, and Marion Werner (2011a). Commodity Chains and the Uneven Geographies of Global Capitalism: A Disarticulations Perspective. Guest Editorial. *Environment and Planning A*, 43, 988–97.

Bair, Jennifer, and Marion Werner (2011b). The Place of Disarticulations: Global Commodity Production in La Laguna, Mexico. *Environment and Planning A*, 43, 998–1015.

Bair, Jennifer, and Marion Werner (2015). Global Production and Uneven Development: When Bringing Labour in isn't Enough. In Kirsty Newsome, Phil Taylor, Jennifer Bair and Al Rainnie (eds.). *Putting Labour in its Place. Labour Process Analysis and Global Value Chains*, 119–34. London: Palgrave.

Bair, Jennifer, and Marion Werner (2017). New Geographies of Uneven Development in Global Formation: Thinking with Chase-Dunn. *Journal of World-System's Research*, 23 (2), 604–19.

Bair, Jennifer, Marion Werner, Christian Berndt and Marc Boeckler (2013). Dis/articulating Producers, Markets, and Regions: New Directions in Critical Studies of Commodity Chains. *Environment and Planning A*, 45 (11), 2544–52.

Balinotti, Nicolás (2017). Gerónimo Venegas: Un Sindicalista Histórico que se Alineó con Macri. *La Nación*, June 27, 2017.

Balsa, Javier (2007). *El Desvanecimiento del Mundo Chacarero. Transformaciones Sociales en la Agricultura Bonaerense: 1937–1988*. Bernal: Universidad de Quilmes.

Bamber, Penny, and Karina Fernandez-Stark (2013). Global Value Chains, Economic Upgrading, and Gender: The Horticulture Industry. In Cornelia Staritz and José Gulherme Reis (eds.). *Global Value Chains, Economic Upgrading and Gender: Case Studies of the Horticulture, Tourism, and Call Center Industries*, 11–42. Washington, D.C.: World Bank.

Bamber, Penny, and Karina Fernandez-Stark (2014). Inclusive Value Chain Interventions in the High-Value Agrifood Sector in Latin America. In René A. Hernandez, Jorge Mario Martínez-Piva and Nanno Mulder (eds.). *Global Value Chains and World Trade. Prospects and Challenges for Latin America*, 137–62. Santiago de Chile: ECLAC, GIZ.

Bamber, Penny, Karina Fernandez-Stark, Gary Gereffi and Andrew Guinn (2014). *Connecting Local Producers in Developing Countries to Regional and Global Value Chains: Update*. OECD Trade Policy Papers. Paris: OECD Publishing.

Ban, Cornel (2013). Brazil's Liberal Neo-Developmentalism: New Paradigm or Edited Orthodoxy? *Review of International Political Economy*, 20 (2), 298–331.

Bardomás, Silvia, Mariela Blanco and Guillermo Neiman (2010). Las Ocupaciones y Tareas de los Trabajadores en las Empresas del Sector Agropecuario. In Guillermo Neiman (ed.). *Estudio Sobre la Demanda de Trabajo en el Agro Argentino*, 301–11. Buenos Aires: CICCUS.

Barri, Fernando (2009). El Modelo Sojero de Desarrollo en la Argentina. Consecuencias Sociales y Ambientales en la Era de los Agronegocios. Paper presented at XXVII Congreso de la Asociación Latinoamericana de Sociología, August 31–September 4, in Buenos Aires, Argentina.

Barri, Fernando, and Juan Wahren (2010). El Modelo Sojero de Desarrollo en la Argentina: Tensiones y Conflictos en la Era del Neocolonialismo de los Agronegocios y el Cientificismo-Tecnológico. *Realidad Económica*, 255, 43–65.

Barrientos, Stephanie (2007). *Global Production Systems and Decent Work*. Working Paper No. 77. Geneva: ILO.

Barrientos, Stephanie (2013). "Labour Chains": Analysing the Role of Labour Contractors in Global Production Networks. *The Journal of Development Studies*, 49 (8), 1058–71.

Barrientos, Stephanie (2019). *Gender and Work in Global Value Chains. Capturing the Gains?* Cambridge: Cambridge University Press.

Barrientos, Stephanie, Catherine Dolan and Anne Tallontire (2003). A Gendered Value Chain Approach to Codes of Conduct in African Horticulture. *World Development*, 31 (9), 1511–26.

Barrientos, Stephanie, Gary Gereffi and Dev Nathan (2012). *Economic and Social Upgrading in Global Value Chains: Emerging Trends and Pressures. Capturing the Gains Summit Briefing*. Manchester: University of Manchester.

Barrientos, Stephanie, Gary Gereffi and Arianna Rossi (2011a). Economic and Social Upgrading in Global Production Networks: A New Paradigm for a Changing World. *International Labour Review*, 150 (3–4), 319–40.

Barrientos, Stephanie, Frederick Mayer, John Pickles and Anne Posthuma (2011b). Decent Work in Global Production Networks: Framing the Policy Debate. *International Labour Review*, 150 (3–4), 300–17.

Barrientos, Stephanie, and Sally Smith (2007). Do Workers Benefit from Ethical Trade? Assessing Codes of Labour Practice in Global Production Systems. *Third World Quarterly*, 28 (4), 713–29.

Barsky, Osvaldo, and Jorge Gelman (2001). *Historia del Agro Argentino. Desde la Conquista hasta Fines del Siglo XX*. Buenos Aires: Grijalbo-Mondadori.

Barsky, Osvaldo, and Jorge Gelman (2009). *Historia del Agro Argentino. Desde la Conquista hasta Comienzos del Siglo XXI*. Buenos Aires: Sudamericana.

Basualdo, Eduardo (2006). La Reestructuración de la Economía Argentina durante las últimas Décadas de la Sustitución de Importaciones a la Valorización Financiera. In Eduardo Basualdo and Enrique Arcero (eds.). *Neoliberalismo y Sectores Dominantes. Tendencias Globales y Experiencias Nacionales*, 123–77. Buenos Aires: CLACSO.

Basualdo, Eduardo (2011). *Rentabilidad, Empleo y Condiciones de Trabajo en el Sector Agropecuario*. Documento de Trabajo No 8. Buenos Aires: CTA.

Basualdo, Eduardo (2013). El Auge de la Producción Agropecuaria Pampeana durante el Predominio Sojero: Evolución y Características Estructurales. In Federico Basualdo, Mariano A. Barrera and Eduardo Basualdo (eds.). *Las Producciones Primarias en la Argentina Reciente. Minería, Petróleo y Agro Pampeano*, 199–256. Buenos Aires: Atuel.

Berger, Mauricio, and Francisco Ortega (2009). Poblaciones Expuestas a Agrotóxicos: Autoorganización Ciudadana en la Defensa de la Vida y la Salud. *Physis*, 20 (1), 119–43.

Berndt, Christian (2013). Assembling Market B/orders: Violence, Dispossession, and Economic Development in Ciudad Juárez, Mexico. *Environment and Planning A*, 45 (11), 2646–62.

Berndt, Christian (2015). Behavioural Economics, Experimentalism and the Marketization of Development. *Economy and Society*, 44 (4), 567–91.

Berndt, Christian (2018). Uneven Development, Commodity Chains and the Agrarian Question. *Progress in Human Geography*, Virtual issue, 1–14.

Berndt, Christian, and Christin Bernhold (2018). Lateinamerikanischer Neostrukturalismus: Sojaboom und wirtschaftliche Konzentration in Argentinien. *Zeitschrift für Wirtschaftsgeographie*, 62 (1), 30–45.

Berndt, Christian, Marion Werner and Victor Ramiro Fernandez (2019). Postneoliberalism as Institutional Recalibration: Reading Polanyi through Argentina's Soy Boom. *Environment and Planning A*, Online first, 1–21.

Bernhardt, Thomas, and William Milberg (2011). Does Economic Upgrading Generate Social Upgrading? Insights from the Horticulture, Apparel, Mobile Phones and Tourism Sector. Capturing the Gains Working Paper 7. 05.06.2022 https://ssrn.com/abstract=1987694.

Bernhold, Christin (2022). Social Partners for Social Upgrading? On Corporate Strategies in Argentinian Agro-Industrial Value Chains. *Mitteilungen der Österreichischen Geographischen Gesellschaft*, 23, 235–64.

Bernhold, Christin and Tomás Palmisano (2017). Relaciones Sociales, Concentración de Capital y Construcción de Consenso en el Agronegocio. Un Caso de Estudio. *Revista Interdisciplinaria de Estudios Agrarios*, 46, 105–40.

Bernhold, Christin, and Tomás Palmisano (2022): Capital concentration in and through class differentiation: A case study from Pampean agribusiness. *Journal of Agrarian Change*, 22 (2), 341–61.

Bernhold, Christin, and Christian Stache (2021): Die Anatomie der deuschen Fleischindustrie. *Z. Zeitschrift Marxistische Erneuerung*, 125, 174–86.

Bernstein, Henry (2006). Is There an Agrarian Question in the 21st Century? *Canadian Journal of Development Studies*, 27 (4), 449–60.

Bernstein, Henry (2010). *Class dynamics of agrarian change. Agrarian change and peasant studies*. Halifax and Winnipeg: Fernwood Publishing.

Bernstein, Henry (2016). Agrarian Political Economy and Modern World Capitalism: The Contributions of Food Regime Analysis. *The Journal of Peasant Studies*, 43 (3), 611–47.

Bernstein, Henry, and Terence J. Byres (2001). From Peasant Studies to Agrarian Change. *Journal of Agrarian Change*, 1 (1), 1–56.

Bernstein, Henry, and Liam Campling (2006a). Commodity Studies and Commodity Fetishism I: Trading Down. *Journal of Agrarian Change*, 6 (2), 239–64.

Bernstein, Henry, and Liam Campling (2006b). Commodity Studies and Commodity Fetishism II: "Profits with Principles"? *Journal of Agrarian Change*, 6 (3), 414–47.

Berterretche, Juan Luis (2015). Vuelve a Crecer el Enclave Sojero Sudamericano y la Violencia También Crece. *Tareas*, 149, 85–103.

Bhaskar, Roy (2008). *A Realist Theory of Science*. London: Verso.

Bhaskar, Roy, and Alex Callinicos (2003). Marxism and Critical Realism. *Journal of Critical Realism*, 1 (2), 89–114.

Bisang, Roberto (2003). Diffusion Process in Networks: The Case of Transgenic Soybean in Argentina. Paper presented at The First Globelics Conference. Innovation Systems and Development Strategies for the Third Millenium, November 3–6, in Río de Janeiro, Brazil.

Bisang, Roberto (2007). El Desarrollo Agropecuario en las últimas Décadas: ¿Volver a Creer? In Bernardo Kosacoff (ed.). *Crisis, Recuperación y Nuevos Dilemas. La Economía Argentina 2002–2007*, 191–266. Buenos Aires: CEPAL.

Bisang, Roberto, Guillermo Anlló and Mercedes Campi (2008). Una Revolución (No Tan) Silenciosa. Claves Para Repensar el Agro en Argentina. *Desarollo Económico*, 48, 1–41.

Bisang, Roberto, and Mercedes Campi (2013). El Desarrollo Agrario Argentino en las últimas Décadas: Fases en el Establecimiento de un Nuevo Paradigma Productivo. In Guillermo Anlló, Roberto Bisang and Mercedes Campi (eds.). *Claves Para Repensar El Agro Argentino*, 31–93. Buenos Aires: Eudeba.

Bisang, Roberto, Nelson Illescas, Carolina Pontelli, Diego Taraborelli and Augustin Tejeda Rodriguez (2013). Argentina y las Cadenas Globales de Valor Agroalimentarias. In Guillermo Anlló, Roberto Bisang and Mercedes Campi (eds.). *Claves Para Repensar El Agro Argentino*, 285–330. Buenos Aires: Eudeba.

Boris, Dieter (2002). Die argentinische Tragödie. *Zeitschrift Sozialismus*, Supplement 12, 1–32.

Boris, Dieter, and Anne Tittor (2006). *Der Fall Argentinien. Krise, soziale Bewegungen und Alternativen*. Hamburg: VSA.

Bravo, Ana Lucia, Hugo F. Mereles Centurión, Diego Domínguez, Pablo Sabatino, Carla Mariela Poth, Javier Rodríguez and Leonel Javier (eds.). (2010). *Los Señores de la Soja: La Agricultura Transgénica en América Latina*. Buenos Aires: CICCUS.

Brewer, Benjamin D. (2011). Global Commodity Chains and World Income Inequalities: The Missing Link of Inequality and the "Upgrading" Paradox. *Journal of World-System's Research*, 17 (2), 308–27.

Brown, Sandy (2013). One Hundred Years of Labor Control: Violence, Militancy, and the Fairtrade Banana Commodity Chain in Colombia. *Environment and Planning A*, 45 (11), 2572–91.

Cáceres, Daniel M. (2015). Accumulation by Dispossession and Socio-Environmental Conflicts Caused by the Expansion of Agribusiness in Argentina. *Journal of Agrarian Change*, 15 (1), 116–47.

Cáceres, Daniel M. (2018). Biotecnología y Poder. ¿Usan los Cultivos Transgénicos Menos Agroquímicos? *Revista Interdisciplinaria de Estudios Agrarios*, 48, 29–56.

Cáceres, Daniel M., and Carla Gras (2017). El Acaparamiento de Tierras como Proceso Dinámico. Las Estrategias de los Actores en Contextos de Estancamiento Económico. *Población and Sociedad*, 24 (2), 163–94.

Campi, Mercedes (2013). Tecnología y Desarrollo Agrario. In Guillermo Anlló, Roberto Bisang and Mercedes Campi (eds.). *Claves Para Repensar El Agro Argentino*, 95–149. Buenos Aires: Eudeba.

Campling, Liam, and Jens Lerche (2016). Introduction to the Special Issue The Political Economy of Agrarian Change: Essays in Appreciation of Henry Bernstein. *Journal of Agrarian Change*, 16 (3), 365–9.

Campling, Liam, Satoshi Miyamura, Jonathan Pattenden and Benjamin Selwyn (2016). Class Dynamics of Development: A Methodological Note. *Third World Quarterly*, 37 (10), 1745–67.

Campling, Liam, and Benjamin Selwyn (2018). Value Chains and the World Economy: Genealogies and Reformulations. In Andreas Nölke and Christian May (eds.). *Handbook of the International Political Economy of the Corporation*, 416–34. Cheltenham: Elgaronline.

Carballo González, Carlos, Felipe Boucau and Carlos Moreira (2012). Plan Estrategico Agroalimentario y Agroindustrial 2010–2020. Desafios Crecientes para un Desarrollo Rural Sustentable. Paper presented at XVI Jornadas Nacionales de Extension Rural y VIII Del Mercosur, Asociacion Argentina de Extension Rural, November 7–9, in Concordia, Argentina.

Carchedi, Guglielmo (1998). Classes and Class Analysis. In Erik Olin Wright (ed.). *The Debate on Classes*, 105–25. London: Verso.

Carchedi, Guglielmo (2001). *For Another Europe. A Class Analysis of European Economic Integration*. London: Verso.

Carrizo, Cecilia, and Mauricio Berger (2012). Citizens' Rights and Environmental Genocide. *Environmental Justice*, 5 (2), 105–10.

CASAFE (2016). *Mercado de Productos Fitosanitarios, Año 2016*. Buenos Aires: CASAFE.

Cattaneo, Oliver, Gary Gereffi and Cornelia Staritz (2010). Global Value Chains in a Postcrisis World: Resilience, Consolidation, and Shifting End Markets. In Olivier Cattaneo, Gary Gereffi and Cornelia Staritz (eds.). *Global Value Chains in a Postcrisis World: A Development Perspective*, 3–20. Washington, D.C.: The World Bank.

Challies, Edward R. T., and Warwick E. Murray (2011). The Interaction of Global Value Chains and Rural Livelihoods: The Case of Smallholder Raspberry Growers in Chile. *Journal of Agrarian Change*, 11 (1), 29–59.

Charmaz, Kathy (2006). *Constructing Grounded Theory. A Practical Guide Through Qualitative Analysis*. London: Sage Publications.

Chase-Dunn, Christopher (1998). *Global Formation. Structures of the World-Economy*. Boston: Rowman and Littlefield Publishers.

Claar, Simone (2018). *International Trade Policy and Class Dynamics in South Africa. The Economic Partnership Agreement*. London: Palgrave.

Clarín (2008). "No Somos Golpistas ni Oposición," Dijo Miguens de la Sociedad Rural. Dura Réplica a Cristina en los Discursos. *Clarín*, April 03, 2008.

Clelland, Donald (2014). The Core of The Apple: Degrees of Monopoly and Dark Value in Global Commodity Chains. *Journal of World-System's Research*, 20 (1), 82–111.

Coe, Neil M. (2011). Geographies of Production II: A Global Production Network A-Z. *Progress in Human Geography*, 36 (3), 389–402.

Coe, Neil M., Peter Dicken and Martin Hess (2008). Global Production Networks: Realizing the Potential. *Journal of Economic Geography*, 8 (3), 271–95.

Coe, Neil M., and Martin Hess (2013). Global Production Networks, Labour and Development. *Geoforum*, 44, 4–9.

Coe, Neil M., Katharine Jones and Kevin Ward (2010). The Business of Temporary Staffing: A Developing Research Agenda. *Geography Compass*, 4 (8), 1055–68.

Coe, Neil M., and David Jordhus-Lier (2011). Constrained Agency? Re-evaluating the Geographies of Labour. *Progress in Human Geography*, 35 (2), 211–33.

Cohan, Luciano, and Ramiro Costa (2011). *Panorama General de las Nuevas Formas de Organización del Agro: Las Principales Cadenas Agroalimentarias. Documentos de proyecto*. Santiago de Chile: United Nations, ECLAC.

Constantino, Agostina (2016). El Capital Extranjero y el Acaparamiento de Tierras: Conflictos Sociales y Acumulación por Desposesión en Argentina. *Revista de Estudios Sociales*, 55, 137–49.

Conte, Analía S., Mariana Etchepareborda, Mariela Marino and Fernando Vazquez Róvere (2009). Oleaginización de la Agricultura Argentina. 05.06.2022 http://ffyl1.uncu.edu.ar/IMG/pdf/oleaginizac_en_la_agric_argentina-Conte_2_.pdf.

Craviotti, Carla (2016). Which Territorial Embeddedness? Territorial Relationships of Recently Internationalized Firms of the Soybean Chain. *The Journal of Peasant Studies*, 43, 331–47.

Craviotti, Carla, and Carla Gras (2006). De Desafiliaciones y Desligamientos: Trayectorias de Productores Familiares Expulsados de la Agricultura Pampeana. *Desarrollo Económico*, 46 (181), 117–34.

Da Silva, Carlos A., and Doyle Baker (2009). Introduction. In Carlos A. da Silva, Doyle Baker, Andrew W. Shepherd, Chaikb Jenane and Sergio Miranda-da-Cruz (eds.). *Agro-Industries for Development*, 1–9. Oxfordshire: FAO and UNIDO.

Da Silva, Carlos A., Doyle Baker, Andrew W. Shepherd, Chaikb Jenane and Sergio Miranda-da-Cruz (eds.). (2009). *Agro-Industries for Development*. Oxfordshire: FAO and UNIDO.

Daly, Jack, Danny Hamrick, Penny Bamber and Karina Fernandez-Stark (2018). *Jamaica in the Arabica Coffee Global Value Chain*. Durham: Duke Global Value Chains Center.

Dannenberg, Peter, and Elmar Kulke (2014). Editorial: Dynamics in Agriculture Value Chains. *Die Erde*, 145 (3), 121–6.

Daviron, Benoit, and Peter Gibbon (2002). Global Commodity Chains and African Export Agriculture. *Journal of Agrarian Change*, 2 (2), 137–61.

Debbané, Anne-Marie (2013). Dis/articulations and the Hydrosocial Cycle: Postapartheid Geographies of Agrarian Change in the Ceres Valley, South Africa. *Environment and Planning A*, 45 (11), 2553–71.

Dedrick, Jason, Kenneth L. Kraemer and Greg Linden (2009). Who Profits from Innovation in Global Value Chains? A Study of the iPod and Notebook PCs. *Industrial and Corporate Change*, 19 (1), 81–116.

Delvenne, Pierre, Federico Vasen and Ana María Vara (2013). The "Soy-ization" of Argentina: The Dynamics of the "Globalized" Privatization Regime in a Peripheral Context. *Technology in Society*, 35, 153–62.

Dicken, Peter (2003). *Global Shift: Transforming the World Economy*. New York: Guilford Press.

Dicken, Peter, Philip F. Kelly, Kris Olds and Henry Wai-Chung Yeung (2001). Chains and Networks, Territories and Scales: Towards a Relational Framework for Analysing the Global Economy. *Global Networks*, 1 (2), 89–112.

Dolan, Catherine, and John Humphrey (2000). Governance and Trade in Fresh Vegetables: The Impact of UK Supermarkets on the African Horticultural Industry. *Journal of Development Studies*, 37 (2), 147–76.

Dolan, Catherine, and John Humphrey (2004). Changing Governance Patterns in the Trade in Fresh Vegetables between Africa and the United Kingdom. *Environment and Planning A*, 36, 491–509.

Dolan, Catherine, and Meenu Tewari (2001). From What We Wear to What We Eat. Upgrading in Global Value Chains. *IDS Bulletin*, 32 (3), 94–104.

Domínguez, Diego, and Pablo Sabatino (2006). Con la Soja al Cuello: Crónica de un País Hambriento Productor de Divisas. In Héctor Alimonda (ed.). *Los Tormentos de la Materia. Aportes Para una Ecología Política Latinoamericana*, 249–74. Buenos Aires: CLACSO.

Domínguez, Diego, and Pablo Sabatino (2010). La Muerte que Viene en el Viento. La Problemática de la Contaminación por Efecto de la Agricultura Transgénica en Argentina y Paraguay. In Ana Lucia Bravo, Hugo F. Mereles Centurión, Diego Domínguez, Pablo Sabatino, Carla Mariela Poth, Javier Rodríguez and Leonel Javier (eds.). *Los Señores de la Soja: La Agricultura Transgénica en América Latina*, 31–121. Buenos Aires: CICCUS.

Dünhaupt, Petra, and Hansjörg Herr (2021). Ökonomisches Upgrading in globalen Wertschöpfungsketten. Wie viel Raum bleibt Entwicklungsländern für Industriepolitik? *WSI Mitteilungen*, 74 (1), 53–60.

Dussel Peters, Enrique (2008). GCCs and Development: A Conceptual and Empirical Review. *Competition & Change*, 12 (1), 11–27.

Ebenau, Matthias, and Santiago Gatica (2013). Las Teorías Dependentistas en Escena: Análisis Crítico de la Inserción Argentina en el Sistema Económico Internacional. Paper presented at XI Congreso Nacional de Ciencia Política, Sociedad Argentina de Análisis Político, Universidad Nacional de Entre Ríos, July 17–20, in Paraná, Argentina.

Elms, Deborah K., and Patrick Low (eds.). (2013). *Global Value Chains in a Changing World*. Geneva: WTO Publications.

Emmanuel, Arghiri (1972). *Unequal Exchange: A Study of the Imperialism of Trade*. New York: Monthly Review Press.

Engels, Friedrich (2001 [1890]). Engels to Joseph Bloch in Königsberg. In Karl Marx and Friedrich Engels. *Collected Works (MECW)*, volume 49, 33–7. New York: International Publishers.

FADA (2017). *El Campo Argentino en Numeros*. Buenos Aires: FADA.

Farole, Thomas, and Deborah Winkler (2014). *Making Foreign Direct Investment Work for Sub-Saharan Africa: Local Spillovers and Competitiveness in Global Value Chains. Directions in Development*. Washington D.C.: The World Bank.

Féliz, Mariano (2013). El Neodesarrollismo y la Trampa de la Renta Extraordinaria. El Caso de Argentina, 2002–2012. *Revista Contrapunto*, 2 (5), 113–29.

Féliz, Mariano (2014). Neodevelopmentalism, Accumulation by Dispossession and International Rent. Argentina, 2003–2013. Paper presented at Workshop "100th Anniversary of 'The Accumulation of Capital'", March 7–9, in Berlin, Germany.

Fernández, Diego A. (2011). Reflexiones Sobre el Crecimiento Agricola Pampeano a la Luz del Concepto de la Renta Diferencial de Segundo Tipo. *Documentos del CIEA*, 6, 5–29.

Fernández, Diego A. (2012a). La Organización de la Gran Empresa Mediante Nuevos Instrumentos Financieros en la Primera Década del Siglo XXI. In Eduardo Azcuy Ameghino, Pedro Castillo, Diego A. Fernández, Lucía Ortega, José Pierri, Fernando Romero Wimer and Juan Manuel Villulla (eds.). *Estudios Agrarios y Agroindustriales*, 93–135. Buenos Aires: Ediciones Imago Mundi.

Fernández, Diego A. (2012b). Vinculaciones entre los Procesos de Cambio Tecnológico y Concentración Económica en la Agricultura Pampeana en la Década del 90. *Documentos del CIEA*, 8, 99–114.

Fernández, Diego A. (2013a). Sojización del Sector Agropecuario y Concentración de la Producción: Una Historia a Partir de los Números a Nivel de Empresa. In Gabriela Martínez Dougnac (ed.). *De Especie Exótica a Monocultivo. Estudios Sobre la Expansión de la Soja en Argentina*, 211–41. Buenos Aires: Imago Mundi.

Fernández, Diego A. (2013b). Tendencias y Evidencias Sobre el Avance del Proceso de Concentración Económica en las Región Pampeana Tras 2002. *Documentos del CIEA*, 9, 77–99.

Fernández, Diego A. (2014). Nota Sobre el Componente Especulativo en la Formación del Precio de los Granos. *Cuadernos del CIMBAGE*, 14, 1–26.

Fernández, Diego A. (2016). Las Grandes Empresas Productoras de Granos: conforman 're-des productivas'? Paper presented at Pre-congreso ALASRU, La Sociología Rural en la Encrucijada: Vigencia de la Cuestión Agraria, Actores Sociales y Modelos de Desarrollo en la Región, October 18–21, in Santiago del Estero, Argentina.

Fernández, Diego A. (2017). Un Análisis Sobre Distintas Estrategias de Persistencia de las Unidades de Producción Chacareras en la Región Pampeana Argentina. *Agrociencia Uruguay*, 21 (2), 105–15.

Fernández, Víctor Ramiro (2015). Global Value Chains in Global Political Networks: Tool for Development or Neoliberal Device? *Review of Radical Political Economics*, 42 (2), 209–30.

Fernández, Víctor Ramiro, and Emilia Ormaechea (2018). The State in the Capitalist Periphery: From the Structuralist Vacuum to the Neo-Structuralist Deviations and Beyond. In Víctor Ramiro Fernández and Gabriel Brondino (eds.). *Development in Latin America. Critical Discussions from the Periphery*, 123–55. London: Palgrave.

Fernández, Víctor Ramiro, and Cristhian Rubén Seiler (2016). Procesos de Acumulación, Industria y Pyme. El Caso Argentino y los Límites del Neodesarrollismo. *Sociedad y Economía*, 30, 225–53.

Fernández, Víctor Ramiro, and Manuel Facundo Trevignani (2015). Cadenas de Valor Globales y Desarrollo: Perspectivas Criticas desde el Sur Global. *Revista de Ciências Sociais*, 58 (2), 499–536.

Fernandez-Stark, Karina, Penny Bamber and Gary Gereffi (2011). The Fruit and Vegetable Global Value Chain: Economic Upgrading and Workforce Development. In Gary Gereffi, Karina Fernandez-Stark and Phil Psilos (eds.). *Skills for Upgrading: Workforce Development and Global Value Chains in Developing Countries*, 13–74. Durham: Duke Center on Globalization, Governance & Competitiveness, RTI International.

Fernandez-Stark, Karina, Penny Bamber and Gary Gereffi (2012). *Inclusion of Small- and Medium-sized Producers in High-value Agro-food Value Chains*. Durham: Duke Center on Globalization, Governance & Competitiveness.

Fernandez-Stark, Karina, Penny Bamber and Gary Gereffi (2014). Global Value Chains in Latin America: A Development Perspective for Upgrading. In René A. Hernandez, Jorge Mario Martínez-Piva and Nanno Mulder (eds.). *Global Value Chains and World Trade. Prospects and Challenges for Latin America*, 79–106. Santiago de Chile: ECLAC, GIZ.

Fessehaie, Judith, and Mike Morris (2018). *Global Value Chains and Sustainable Development Goals: What Role for Trade and Industrial Policies? Programme on Inclusive Economic Transformation*. Geneva: ICTSD.

Figueroa, Adolfo (1993). Agricultural Development in Latin America. In Osvaldo Sunkel (ed.). *Development from Within: Toward a Neostructuralist Approach for Latin America*, 287–314. Colorado: Lynne Rienner Publishers.

Finnegan, Liam Klein (2017). *Glyphosate: The Fragile Power Behind Argentina's Soy Complex*. Ås: Department of Plant Sciences, Norwegian University of Life Science.

Fischer, Karin, Christian Reiner and Cornelia Staritz (eds.). (2021). *Globale Warenketten und ungleiche Entwicklung. Arbeit, Kapital, Konsum, Natur*. Wien: Mandelbaum.

Flammini, María Alejandra (2001). Algunas Reflexiones Sobre los Cambios Económico-Sociales del Agro Pampeano en el Siglo XX. *Mundo Agrario*, 1 (2), 1–8.
Flecker, Jörg (2021). Die Qualität der Arbeit in dynamischen Ketten und Netzen. Wie ist soziale Aufwertung möglich? In Karin Fischer , Christian Reiner and Cornelia Staritz (eds.). *Globale Warenketten und Ungleiche Entwicklung. Arbeit, Kapital, Konsum, Natur*, 149–66. Wien: Mandelbaum.
Flick, Uwe (2006). *Qualitative Sozialforschung. Eine Einführung*. Reinbek: Rowohlt.
Fold, Niels (2002). Lead Firms and Competition in 'Bi-polar' Commodity Chains: Grinders and Branders in the Global Cocoa–chocolate Industry. *Journal of Agrarian Change*, 2 (2), 228–47.
Fold, Niels, and Bill Pritchard (2005). *Cross-continental Food Chains*. London: Routledge.
Foster, John Bellamy, Brett Clark and Richard York (2010). *The Ecological Rift. Capitalism's War On The Earth*. New York: Monthly Review Press.
Frank, André Gunder (1969a). *Kapitalismus und Unterentwicklung in Lateinamerika*. Frankfurt am Main: EVA.
Frank, André Gunder (1969b). *Latin America: Underdevelopment or Revolution: Essays on the Development of Underdevelopment and the Immediate Enemy*. New York: Monthly Review Press.
Frank, André Gunder (1973). *Lumpenburgesia: Lumpendesarrollo. Dependencia Clase y Politica en Latinoamerica*. Buenos Aires: Ediciones Periferia.
Gaggero, Alejandro, Martín Schorr and Andrés Wainer (2014). *Restriccion Eterna. El Poder Economico Durante el Kirchnerismo*. Buenos Aires: Futuro Anterior Ediciones.
GEPCyD (2011). La Violencia Rural en la Argentina de los Agronegocios: Crónicas Invisibles del Despojo. *Revista NERA*, 14 (19), 8–23.
GER, Grupo de Estudios Rurales (2004). Desalojos y Arrinconamientos de Campesinos y Comunidades Indígenas en la Argentina. *Realidad Económica*, 203, 111–20.
Gereffi, Gary (1983). *The Pharmaceutical Industry and Dependency in the Third World*. Princeton: Princeton University Press.
Gereffi, Gary (1994a). Capitalism, Development and Global Commodity Chains. In Leslie Sklair (ed.). *Capitalism and Development*, 211–31. London: Routledge.
Gereffi, Gary (1994b). The Organization of Buyer-Driven Global Commodity Chains: How U.S. Retailers Shape Overseas Production Networks. In Gary Gereffi and Miguel Korzeniewicz (eds.). *Commodity Chains and Global Capitalism*, 95–122. Westport: Praeger.
Gereffi, Gary (1996). Global Commodity Chains: New Forms of Coordination and Control Among Nations and Firms in International Industries. *Competition & Change*, 4, 427–39.
Gereffi, Gary (1999). International Trade and Industrial Upgrading in the Apparel Commodity Chain. *Journal of International Economics*, 48 (1), 37–70.
Gereffi, Gary (2001a). Beyond the Producer-driven/Buyer-driven Dichotomy. The Evolution of Global Value Chains in the Internet Era. *IDS Bulletin*, 32 (3), 30–40.
Gereffi, Gary (2001b). Shifting Governance Structures in Global Commodity Chains, With Special Reference to the Internet. *American Behavioral Scientist*, 44 (10), 1617–37.

Gereffi, Gary (2012). Latin America's Prospects for Upgrading in Global Value Chains. Paper presented at El Colegio de Mexico, March 14–15, in Mexico City, Mexico.

Gereffi, Gary (2014). Global Value Chains in a Post-Washington Consensus World. *Review of International Political Economy*, 21 (1), 9–37.

Gereffi, Gary, and Jennifer Bair (2010). *Strengthening Nicaragua's Position in the Textile-Apparel Value Chain: Upgrading in the Context of the CAFTA-DR Region. USAID, CARANA and the National Free Zones Commission (CNZF/Government of Nicaragua)*. Durham: Duke Center on Globalization, Governance & Competitiveness.

Gereffi, Gary, Penny Bamber, Stacey Frederick and Karina Fernandez-Stark (2013). *Costa Rica in Global Value Chains: An Upgrading Analysis*. Durham: Duke Center on Globalization, Governance & Competitiveness.

Gereffi, Gary, and Karina Fernandez-Stark (2016). *Global Value Chain Analysis: A Primer*. Durham: Duke Center on Globalization, Governance & Competitiveness.

Gereffi, Gary, Karina Fernandez-Stark and Penny Bamber (2015). *Global Value Chains in Latin America: Opportunities and Challenges for Upgrading*. Durham: Duke Center on Globalization, Governance & Competitiveness.

Gereffi, Gary, Karina Fernandez-Stark and Phil Psilos (2011). *Skills for upgrading: Workforce Development and Global Value Chains in Developing Countries*. Durham: Duke Center on Globalization, Governance & Competitiveness.

Gereffi, Gary, and Gary Hamilton (2009). Global Commodity Chains, Market Makers, and the Rise of Demand-Responsive Economies. In Jennifer Bair (ed.). *Frontiers of Commodity Chain Research*, 136–61. Stanford: Stanford University Press.

Gereffi, Gary, John Humphery, Raphael Kaplinsky and Timothy J. Sturgeon (2001a). Introduction: Globalisation, Value Chains and Development. *IDS Bulletin*, 32 (2), 1–8.

Gereffi, Gary, John Humphrey, Raphael Kaplinsky and Timothy J. Sturgeon (eds.). (2001b). Globalisation, Value Chains and Development. *IDS Bulletin*, 32 (3).

Gereffi, Gary, John Humphrey and Timothy J. Sturgeon (2005). The Governance of Global Value Chains. Review of International Political Economy, 12 (1), 78–104.

Gereffi, Gary, and Raphael Kaplinsky (eds.). (2001). *The Value of Value Chains: Spreading the Gains from Globalisation*. Sussex: Institute of Development Studies (IDS).

Gereffi, Gary, and Miguel Korzeniewicz (1990). Commodity Chains and Footwear Exports in the Semiperiphery. In William G. Martin (ed.). *Semiperipheral States in the World-Economy*, 45–68. New York: Greenwood Press.

Gereffi, Gary, and Miguel Korzeniewicz (eds.). (1994). *Commodity Chains and Global Capitalism*. Westport: Praeger.

Gereffi, Gary, Miguel Korzeniewicz and Roberto Korzeniewicz (1994). Introduction: Global Commodity Chains. In Garyy Gereffi and Miguel Korzeniewicz (eds.). *Commodity Chains and Global Capitalism*, 1–14. Westport: Praeger.

Gereffi, Gary, and Joonkoo Lee (2012). Why the World Suddenly Cares About Global Supply Chains. *Journal of Supply Chain Management*, 48 (3), 24–32.

Gereffi, Gary, and Joonkoo Lee (2016). Economic and Social Upgrading in Global Value Chains and Industrial Clusters: Why Governance Matters. *Journal of Business Ethics*, 133, 25–38.

Gereffi, Gary, and Xubei Luo (2014). *Risks and Opportunities of Participation in Global Value Chains*. Policy Research Working Paper. Washington, D.C.: The World Bank.

Gertel, Jörg, and Sarah Ruth Sippel (2014). Seasonality and Temporality in Intensive Agriculture. In Jörg Gertel and Sarah Ruth Sippel (eds.). *Seasonal Workers in Mediterranean Agriculture. The Social Costs of Eating Fresh*, 3–22. London: Routledge.

Giancola, Silvana Inés, Maria Laura Salvador, Melina Covacevich and Gabriela Iturrioz (2009). *Analisis de la Cadena de Soja en la Argentina. Estudios Socioeconomicos de los Sistemas Agroalimentarios y Agroinsustriales*. Buenos Aires: INTA.

Giarracca, Norma (2002). El Movimiento de Mujeres Agropecuarias en Lucha: Protesta Agraria y Género Durante el último Lustro en Argentina. In Norma Giarraca (ed.). *Una Nueva Ruralidad en América Latina*, 129–51. Buenos Aires: CLACSO.

Giarracca, Norma, and Tomás Palmisano (2013). Tres Lógicas de Producción de Alimentos: ¿Hay Alternativas al Agronegocio? In Norma Giarraca and Miguel Teubal (eds.). *Actividades Extractivas en Expansión: ¿Reprimarización de la Economía Argentina?*, 159–72. Buenos Aires: Antropofagia.

Giarracca, Norma, and Miguel Teubal (2006). Democracia y Neoliberalismo en el Campo Argentino. Una Convivencia Difícil. In Hubert C. de Grammont (ed.). *La Construcción de la Democracia en el Campo Latinoamericano*, 69–94. Buenos Aires: CLACSO.

Giarracca, Norma, and Miguel Teubal (2008). Del Desarrollo Agroindustrial a la Expansión del 'Agronegocio': El Caso Argentino. In Bernardo Mançano Fernandes (ed.). *Campesinato e Agronegócio na América Latina: A Questão Agraria Atual*. São Paulo: Expressão Popular.

Giarracca, Norma, and Miguel Teubal (eds.). (2011). *Del Paro Agrario a las Elecciones de 2009. Tramas, Reflexiones y Debates*. Buenos Aires: Antropofagia.

Giarracca, Norma, and Miguel Teubal (eds.). (2013). *Actividades Extractivas en Expansión ¿Reprimarización de la Economía Argentina?* Buenos Aires: Antropofagia.

Gibbon, Peter (2001a). Agro-Commodity Chains. An Introduction. *IDS Bulletin*, 32 (3), 60–8.

Gibbon, Peter (2001b). Upgrading Primary Production: A Global Commodity Chain Approach. *World Development*, 29 (2), 345–63.

Gibbon, Peter (2008). Governance, Entry Barriers, Upgrading: A Re-Interpretation of Some GVC Concepts from the Experience of African Clothing Exports. *Competition & Change*, 12 (1), 29–48.

Gibbon, Peter, and Stefano Ponte (2005). *Trading Down: Africa, Value Chains, and the Global Economy*. Philadelphia: Temple University Press.

Girbal-Blacha, Noemí María (2013). El Poder de la Tierra en la Argentina. De la Cultura Agrícola al Agronegocio. *Estudios Rurales – Centro de Estudios de la Argentina Rural/UNQ*, 3 (4), 103–15.

Glassman, Jim (2011). The Geo-political Economy of Global Production Networks. *Geography Compass*, 5 (4), 154–64.

Gómez Lende, Sebastián, and Guillermo Velázquez (2018). Soybean Agribusiness in Argentina (1990–2015): Socio-Economic, Territorial, Environmental, and Political Implications. In Gokhan Egilmez (ed.). *Agricultural Value Chain*, 117–36. London: IntechOpen.

Gomez, Marcelo (2008). La Soja de la Discordia. Los Sentidos y Estrategias en la Movilización de la Pequeño Burguesía. Lavboratorio. *Estudios sobre Cambio Estructural y Desigualdad Social*, 10 (22), 22–35.

Gorenstein, Silvia, and Ricardo Daniel Ortiz (2017). La Tierra en Disputa. Agricultura, Acumulación y Territorio en la Argentina Reciente. *Revista Latinoamericana de Estudios Rurales*, 1 (2), 1–26.

Gramsci, Antonio (2012 [1975]-a). Gefängnishefte, volume 2. Hamburg: Argument.

Gramsci, Antonio (2012 [1975]-b). Gefängnishefte, volume 3. Hamburg: Argument.

Gramsci, Antonio (2012 [1975]-c). Gefängnishefte, volume 4. Hamburg: Argument.

Gramsci, Antonio (2012 [1975]-d). Gefängnishefte, volume 5. Hamburg: Argument.

Gramsci, Antonio (2012 [1975]-e). Gefängnishefte, volume 6. Hamburg: Argument.

Gramsci, Antonio (2012 [1975]-f). Gefängnishefte, volume 7. Hamburg: Argument.

Gramsci, Antonio (2012 [1975]-g). Gefängnishefte, volume 8. Hamburg: Argument.

Gramsci, Antonio (2012 [1975]-h). Gefängnishefte, volume 9. Hamburg: Argument.

Gras, Carla (2012). Los Empresarios de la Soja: Cambios y Continuidades en la Fisonomía y Composición Interna de las Empresas Agropecuarias. *Mundo Agrario*, 12 (24), 1–32.

Gras, Carla (2013a). *Agronegocios en el Cono Sur. Actores Sociales, Desigualdades y Entrelazamientos Transregionales*. Working Paper Series. Berlin: desiguALdades Research Network.

Gras, Carla (2013b). Expansión Agrícola y Agricultura Empresarial. *Revista de Ciencias Sociales*, 26 (32), 73–92.

Gras, Carla, and Daniel M. Cáceres (2017). El Acaparamiento de Tierras como Proceso Dinámico. Las Estrategias de los Actores en Contextos de Estancamiento Económico. *Población & Sociedad*, 24 (2), 163–94.

Gras, Carla, and Valeria Hernández (2013a). *El Agro como Negocio. Producción, Sociedad y Territorios en la Globalización*. Buenos Aires: Editorial Biblos.

Gras, Carla, and Valeria Hernández (2013b). El Modelo Agribusiness y sus Traducciones Territoriales. In Carla Gras and Valeria Hernández (eds.). *El Agro como Negocio. Producción, Sociedad y Territorios en la Globalización*, 49–66. Buenos Aires: Editorial Biblos.

Gras, Carla, and Valeria Hernández (2013c). Los Pilares del Modelo Agribusiness y sus Estilos Empresariales. In Carla Gras and Valeria Hernández (eds.). *El Agro como Negocio. Producción, Sociedad y Territorios en la Globalización*, 17–46. Buenos Aires: Editorial Biblos.

Gras, Carla, and Valeria Hernández (2016a). Hegemony, Technological Innovation and Corporate Identities: 50 Years of Agricultural Revolutions in Argentina. *Journal of Agrarian Change*, 16 (4), 675–83.

Gras, Carla, and Valeria Hernández (2016b). *Radiografía del Nuevo Campo Argentino. Del Terrateniente al Empresario Transnacional*. Buenos Aires: Siglo Veintiuno Editores.

Gras, Carla. and Andrea Patricia Sosa Varrotti (2013). El Modelo de Negocios de las Principales Megaempresas Agropecuarias. In Carla Gras and Valeria Hernández (eds.). *El Agro como Negocio. Producción, Sociedad y Territorios en la Globalización*, 215–36. Buenos Aires: Editorial Biblos.

Grosso, Susana, María Eva Bellini, Laura Qüesta, Martine Guibert, Silvia Lauxmann and Fabiana Rotondi (2010). Impactos de los "Pools de Siembra" en la Estructura Social Agraria: Una Aproximación a las Transformaciones en los Espacios Centrales de la Provincia de Santa Fe (Argentina). *Revista de estudios regionales y mercado de trabajo*, 6, 115–38.

Grugel, Jean, and Maria Pia Riggirozzi (2007). The Return of the State in Argentina. *International Affairs*, 83 (1), 87–107.

Gürcan, Efe Can (2016). Theorizing Food Sovereignty From a Class Analytical Lens: The Case of Agrarian Mobilization in Argentina. Paper presented at American Sociological Association (ASA) Annual Meeting, August 20–23, in Seattle, USA.

Hadjimichalis, Costis (1984). The Geographical Transfer of Value: Notes on the Spatiality of Capitalism. *Environment and Planning D*, 2, 329–45.

Hall, Stuart (1983). The Problem of Ideology: Marxism Without Guarantees. In Betty Matthews (ed.). Marx: 100 Years On, 57–84. London: Lawrence & Wishart.

Hammer, Nikolaus, and Lone Riisgaard (2015). Labour and Segmentation in Value Chains. In Kirsty Newsome, Phil Taylor, Jennifer Bair and Al Rainnie (eds.). *Putting Labour in its Place. Labour Process Analysis and Global Value Chains*, 83–97. London: Palgrave.

Harris, Nigel (1987). *The End of the Third World: Newly Industrialising Countries and the Decline of an Ideology*. Harmondsworth: Penguin.

Harvey, David (2003). *The New Imperialism*. Oxford, New York: Oxford University Press.

Harvey, David (2005). *Spaces of Neoliberalization. Towards a Theory of Uneven Geographical Development*. Stuttgart: Franz-Steiner.

Harvey, David (2006). *Spaces of Global Capitalism*. London: Verso.

Harvey, David (2007). In What Ways Is New "Imperialism" Really New? *Historical Materialism*, 15, 57–70.

Harvey, David (2010a). *The Enigma of Capital and the Crises of Capitalism*. Oxford: Oxford University Press.

Harvey, David (2010b). *The Crisis of Capitalism*. London: Royal Society for the encouragement of Arts, Manufactures and Commerce (RSA).

Harvey, David (2017). *Marx, Capital and the Madness of Economic Reason*. London: Profile Books.

Hawel, Marcus (2008). The Ideology-Critical Method of Immanent Critique. *Goethe Institut*. 05.06.2022 https://web.archive.org/web/20140513024459/http://www.goethe.de/ges/phi/eth/en3352666.htm.

Helfferich, Cornelia (2009). *Die Qualität qualitativer Daten. Manual für die Durchführung qualitativer Interviews*. Wiesbaden: VS Verlag für Sozialwissenschaften.

Henderson, Jeffrey, Peter Dicken, Martin Hess, Neil Coe and Henry Wai-Chung Yeung (2002). Global Production Networks and the Analysis of Economic Development. *Review of International Political Economy*, 9 (3), 436–64.

Hermida, Gonzalo (2018). *Evolución de la Producción de Granos en Argentina*. Buenos Aires: Bolsa de Cereales.

Hernández, René A., Jorge Mario Martinez-Piva and Nanno Mulder (eds.). (2014). *Global Value Chains and World trade. Prospects and Challenges for Latin America*. Santiago de Chile: ECLAC, GIZ.

Hernández, Valeria (2007). El Fenómeno Económico y Cultural del Boom de la Soja y el Empresario. *Desarollo Económico*, 47 (187), 331–65.

Hernández, Valeria (2009). La Ruralidad Globalizada y el Paradigma de los Agronegocios en las Pampas Gringas. In Carla Gras and Valeria Hernández (eds.). *La Argentina Rural: De la Agricultura Familiar a los Agronegocios*, 39–64. Buenos Aires: Biblos.

Herrigel, Johanna (2018). *Shifting Global Market Frontiers. Performing Global Fresh Vegetable Commodity Chains in Tanzania*. PhD Thesis. Zürich: Department of Geography, University of Zürich.

Höffler, Heike, and Booker W. Owuor Ochieng (2009). *High Commodity Prices – Who Gets the Money? A Case Study on the Impact of High Food and Factor Prices on Kenyan Farmers*. Berlin: Heinrich Böll Stiftung.

Hopkins, Terence (1982). Notes On Class Analysis and the World-System. In Terence Hopkins and Immanuel Wallerstein (eds.). *World-Systems Analysis. Theory and Methodology*, 83–9. Beverly Hills: Sage Publications.

Hopkins, Terence, and Immanuel Wallerstein (1977). Patterns of Development of the Modern World-System. *Review* (Fernand Braudel Center), 1 (2), 111–45.

Hopkins, Terence, and Immanuel Wallerstein (1982). Structural Transformations of the World-Economy. In Terence Hopkins and Immanuel Wallerstein (eds.). *World-Systems Analysis. Theory and Methodology*, 121–42. Beverly Hills: Sage Publications.

Hopkins, Terence, and Immanuel Wallerstein (1986). Commodity Chains in the World Economy Prior to 1800. *Review* (Fernand Braudel Center), 10 (1), 157–70.

Hopkins, Terence, and Immanuel Wallerstein (1994). Commodity Chains: Construct and Research. In Gary Gereffi and Miguel Korzeniewicz (eds.). *Commodity Chains and Global Capitalism*, 17–20. Westport: Praeger.

Horkheimer, Max (1972 [1937]). Traditional and Critical Theory. In Max Horkheimer (ed.). *Critical Theory: Selected Essays*, 188–243. New York: Seabury.

Horkheimer, Max, and Theodor W. Adorno (2004 [1944]). *Dialektik der Aufklärung. Philosophische Fragmente*. Frankfurt am Main: Fischer Taschenbuch.

Humphrey, John (2004). *Upgrading in Global Value Chains*. Working Paper No. 28. Geneva: ILO.

Humphrey, John (2006a). *Global Value Chains in the Agrifood Sector*. Wien: UNIDO.

Humphrey, John (2006b). Policy Implications of Trends in Agribusiness Value Chains. *The European Journal of Development Research*, 18 (4), 572–92.

Humphrey, John, Neil McCulloch and Masako Ota (2004). The Impact of European Market Changes on Employment in The Kenyan Horticulture Sector. *Journal of International Development*, 16 (1), 63–80.

Humphrey, John, and Hubert Schmitz (2000). *Governance and Upgrading: Linking Industrial Cluster and Global Value Chain Research*. IDS Working Paper 120. Brighton: Institute of Development Studies (IDS).

Humphrey, John, and Hubert Schmitz (2001). Governance in Global Value Chains. *IDS Bulletin*, 32 (3), 19–29.

Iglesias, Daniel Humberto (2002). *Cadenas de Valor como Estrategia: Las Cadenas de Valor en el Sector Agroalimentario*. Buenos Aires: INTA.

INTA (2004). *El INTA Que Queremos. Plan Estrategico Institucional 2005–2015*. Buenos Aires: INTA.

ISAAA (2019). *Global Status of Commercialized Biotech/GM Crops in 2019: Biotech Crops Drive Socio-Economic Development and Sustainable Environment in the New Frontier*. ISAAA Brief No. 55. Ithaca, New York: ISAAA.

Isaksen, Robert K. (2018). Without Foundation or Neutral Standpoint: Using Immanent Critique to Guide a Literature Review. *Journal of Critical Realism*, 17 (2), 97–117.

Jaeggi, Rahel (2009). Was ist Ideologiekritik? In Rahel Jaeggi und Tilo Wesche (eds.). *Was ist Kritik?*, 266–95. Frankfurt am Main: Suhrkamp.

Jordán, Angélica (2014). Formas de Organización Sindical y Prácticas Gremiales en el Complejo Agroindustrial Frutícola de la Provincia de Entre Ríos (Argentina). *Trabajo y Sociedad*, 4, 205–26.

Kaplinsky, Raphael (2000). Globalisation and Unequalisation: What Can Be Learned from Value Chain Analysis? *The Journal of Development Studies*, 37 (2), 117–46.

Kaplinsky, Raphael (2006). How can Agricultural Commodity Producers Appropriate a Greater Share of Value Chain Incomes? In Alexander Sarris and David Hallam (eds.). *Agricultural Commodity Markets and Trade. New Approaches to Analyzing Market Structure and Instability*, 356–79. Cheltenham: FAO and Edward Elgar.

Kaplinsky, Raphael, and Masuma Farooki (2010). Global Value Chains, the Crisis, and the Shift of Markets from North to South. In Olivier Cattaneo, Gary Gereffi and Cornelia Staritz (eds.). *Global Value Chains in a Postcrisis World: A Development Perspective*, 125–53. Washington, D.C.: The World Bank.

Kaplinsky, Raphael, and Mike Morris (2001). *A Handbook for Value Chain Research*. 05.06.2022 https://www.researchgate.net/publication/42791981.

Kaplinsky, Raphael, Anne Terheggen and Julia Tijaja (2011). China as a Final Market: The Gabon Timber and Thai Cassava Value Chains. *World Development*, 37 (7), 1177–90.

Kay, Cristóbal (2016). La Transformación Neoliberal del Mundo Rural: Procesos de Concentración de la Tierra y del Capital y la Intensificación de la Precariedad del Trabajo. *Revista Latinoamericana de Estudios Rurales*, 1 (1), 1–26.

Knorringa, Peter, and Lee Pegler (2006). Globalisation, Firm Upgrading and Impacts on Labour. *Tijdschrift voor Exonomische en Sociale Geografie*, 97 (5), 470–79.

Komlosy, Andrea (2021). Zyklen der Globalisierung: Textile Güterketten im historischen Wandel. In Karin Fischer, Christian Reiner and Cornelia Staritz (eds.). *Globale Warenketten und Ungleiche Entwicklung. Arbeit, Kapital, Konsum, Natur*, 99–117. Wien: Mandelbaum.

Korf, Benedikt (2018). Die Ironie der Entwicklungstheorie. *Geographische Zeitschrift*, 106 (2918/3), 150–74.

Korzeniewicz, Roberto P., and William Martin (1994). The Global Distribution of Commodity Chains. In Gary Gereffi and Miguel Korzeniewicz (eds.). *Commodity Chains and Global Capitalism*, 67–91. Westport: Praeger.

Krüger, Stephan (2010). *Allgemeine Theorie der Kapitalakkumulation. Konjunkturzyklus und langfristige Entwicklungstendenzen*. Hamburg: VSA.

Kuckartz, Udo (2012). *Qualitative Inhaltsanalyse. Methoden, Praxis, Computerunterstützung*. Weinheim: Beltz.

Kuijpers, Rob, and Johan Swinnen (2016). Value Chains and Technology Transfer to Agriculture in Developing and Emerging Economies. *American Journal of Agricultural Economics*, 84 (5), 1403–18.

Lapegna, Pablo (2016). Genetically Modified Soybeans, Agrochemical Exposure, and Everyday Forms of Peasant Collaboration in Argentina. *The Journal of Peasant Studies*, 43 (2), 517–36.

Lapegna, Pablo (2017). The Political Economy of the Agroexport Boom under the Kirchners: Hegemony and Passive Revolution in Argentina. *Journal of Agrarian Change*, 17, 313–29.

Lattuada, Mario (2002). El Peronismo y los Sectores Sociales Agrarios. La Resignificación del Discurso como Articulador de los Cambios en las Relaciones de Dominación y la Permanencia de las Relaciones de Producción. *Mundo Agrario*, 3 (5), 1–19.

Lattuada, Mario, and Guillermo Neiman (2005). *El Campo Argentino. Crecimiento con Exclusion*. Buenos Aires: Capital Intelectual.

Lavarello, Pablo (2012). La Recuperación de la Producción Industrial de Maquinaria Agrícola. Estrategias Empresariales y Grado de Integración Nacional en la Producción. *Voces en el Fénix*, 3 (12), 50–5.

Lee, Joonkoo, and Gary Gereffi (2015). Global Value Chains, Rising Power Firms and Economic and Social Upgrading. *Critical Perspectives on International Business*, 11 (3/4), 219–339.

Lee, Joonkoo, Gary Gereffi and Stephanie Barrientos (2011). Global value chains, Upgrading and Poverty Reduction. *Capturing the Gains. Briefing Note*, 3, 1–6. 05.06.2022 https://ssrn.com/abstract=1990232.

Lee, Naeyoung, and Jeffrey Cason (1994). Automobile Commodity Chains in the NICs: A Comparison of South Korea, Mexico, and Brazil. In Gary Gereffi and Miguel Korzeniewicz (eds.). *Commodity Chains and Global Capitalism*, 223–43. Westport: Praeger.

Leguizamón, Amalia (2014). Modifying Argentina: GM Soy and Socio-environmental Change. *Geoforum*, 53, 149–60.

Leiva, Fernando I. (2008). *Latin American Neostructuralism. The Contradictions of Post-Neoliberal Development*. Minneapolis: University of Minnesota Press.

Lence, Sergio H. (2010). The Agricultural Sector in Argentina: Major Trends and Recent Developments. In Julian M. Alston, Bruce A. Babcock and Philip G. Pardey (eds.). *The Shifting Patterns of Agricultural Production and Productivity Worldwide*, 209–448. Ames: The Midwest Agribusiness Trade Research and Information Center Iowa State University.

Liu, Weidong, and Peter Dicken (2006). Transnational Corporations and "Obligated Embeddedness": Foreign Direct Investment in China's Automobile Industry. *Environment and Planning A*, 38 (7), 1229–47.

Llach, Juan José, Marcela Harriague and Ernesto O'Connor (2004). *La Generación de Empleo en las Cadenas Agroindustriales*. Buenos Aires: Fundacion Producir Conservando.

Lódola, Agustín, and Rafael Brigo (2013). Contratistas de Servicio Agropecuarios, Difusión Tecnológica y Redes Agroalimentarias: Una Larga y Productiva Relación. In Guillermo Anlló, Roberto Bisang and Mercedes Campi (eds.). *Claves Para Repensar El Agro Argentino*, 203–50. Buenos Aires: Eudeba.

Lódola, Agustín, Rafael Brigo and Fernando Morra (2010). *Evolución de las Cadenas Agroalimentarias*. Buenos Aires: Mimeo.

López, Andrés, Daniel Ramos and Cecilia Simkievich (2008). *The Impact of China's Global Expansion on Latin America. A Study of the Impact of China's Global Expansion on Argentina. Soybean Value Chain analysis: Final Report*. Buenos Aires: Centro de Investigaciones para la Transformación.

Losch, Bruno (2002). Global Restructuring and Liberalization: Côte d'Ivoire and the End of the International Cocoa Market? *Journal of Agrarian Change*, 2 (2), 206–27.

Lütten, John (2015). Struktur, Handlung, Herrschaft. Zur Diskussion über Herrschaftsverhältnisse in der Kritik der politischen Ökonomie. *Z. Zeitschrift Marxistische Erneuerung*, 104, 119–29.

Luxemburg, Rosa (1913). *Die Akkumulation des Kapitals. Ein Beitrag zur ökonomischen Erklärung des Imperialismus*. Berlin: Buchhandlung Vorwärts Paul Singer.

Mahutga, Matthew C. (2014). Global Production Networks and International Inequality: Making a Case for a Meso-Level Turn in Macro-Comparative Sociology. *Journal of World-System's Research*, 20 (1), 11–37.

Malm, Andreas (2016). *Fossil Capital. The Rise of Steam Power and the Roots of Global Warming*. London: Verso.

Martínez Dougnac, Gabriela (2013). De los Márgenes al Boom. Apuntes para una Historia de la Sojización In Gabriela Martínez Dougnac (ed.). *De Especie Exótica a Monocultivo. Estudios sobre la Expansión de la Soja en Argentina*, 1–38. Buenos Aires: Imago Mundi.

Martínez Dougnac, Gabriela (2016). Monocultivo Sojero, Concentración Económica, Acaparamiento y Despojo de Tierras: Formas Actuales de la Expansión del Capital en la Agricultura Argentina. Rosario: Legem.

Marx, Karl (1975 [1844]). Contribution to the Critique of Hegel's Philosophy of Law. Introduction. In Karl Marx and Friedrich Engels. *Collected Works (MECW)*, volume 3, 175–87. New York: International Publishers.

Marx, Karl (1986 [1857–61]). Grundrisse: Foundations of the Critique of Political Economy. Economic Manuscripts of 1857–58. In Karl Marx and Friedrich Engels. *Collected Works (MECW)*, volume 28. New York: International Publishers.

Marx, Karl (1989 [1863]). Theories of Surplus Value. In Karl Marx and Friedrich Engels. *Collected Works (MECW)*, volume 32. New York: International Publishers.

Marx, Karl (1989 [1875]). Critique of the Gotha Programme. In Karl Marx and Friedrich Engels. *Collected Works (MECW)*, volume 24, 75–99. New York: International Publishers.

Marx, Karl (1990 [1867]). *Capital. A Critique of Political Economy. Volume I*. London: Penguin.

Marx, Karl (1991 [1894]). *Capital. A Critique of Political Economy. Volume III*. London: Penguin.

Marx, Karl, and Friedrich Engels (1976 [1846]). The German Ideology. Critique of Modern German Philosophy According to Its Representatives Feuerbach, B. Bauer and Stirner, and of German Socialism According to Its Various Prophets. In Karl Marx and Friedrich Engels. *Collected Works (MECW)*, volume 5, 19–539. New York: International Publishers.

Massey, Doreen (1995). *Spatial Divisions of Labour: Social Structures and the Geography of Production*. London: Routledge.

Mather, Charles (2008). Upgrading in South Africa's Squid Value Chain. In Christian Stringer and Richard Le Heron (eds.). *Agri-Food Commodity Chains and Globalising Networks*, 9–22. Burlington: Ashgate.

Mattisek, Annika, Paul Reuber and Carmela Pfaffenbach (2013). *Methoden der empirischen Humangeographie*. Braunschweig: Westermann.

McMichael, Philip (2005). Global Development and the Corporate Food Regime. In Frederick H. Buttel and Philip McMichael (eds.). *New Directions in the Sociology of Global Development (Research in Rural Sociology and Development)*, 269–303. Bingley: Emerald Group Publishing Limited.

McMichael, Philip (2016). Commentary: Food regime for thought. *The Journal of Peasant Studies*, 43 (3), 648–70.

Mieres, Fabiola (2018). Migration, Recruitment and Forced Labour in a Globalising World. In Anna Triandafyllidou (ed.). *Handbook of Migration and Globalisation*, 155–69. Cheltenham: Edward Elgar.

Milberg, William, and Deborah Winkler (2011). Economic and Social Upgrading in Global Production Networks: Problems of Theory and Measurement. *International Labour Review*, 150 (3–4), 341–65.

Milios, John, and Dimitris P. Sotiropoulos (2009). *Rethinking Imperialism. A Study of Capitalist Rule*. Hampshire: Palgrave.

Ministry of Agriculture, Livestock, and Fisheries (MAGyP) (2011). *Argentina Agribusiness Leader. Federal and Participative Agri-Food and Agribusiness Strategic Plan 2010–2020*. Buenos Aires.

Ministry of Economy, MECON (2011). Complejo Oleaginoso. Buenos Aires.

Ministry of Treasury, Secretaría de Política Económica (2016). Informes de Cadenas de Valor. Maquinaria Agricola. Buenos Aires.

Ministry of Treasury, Secretaría de Política Económica (2017). Informes de Cadenas de Valor. Oleaginosa. Buenos Aires.

Ministry of Treasury, Secretaría de Política Económica (2018). Informes de Cadenas de Valor. Trigo. Buenos Aires.

Ministry of Treasury, Secretaría de Política Económica (2019). Informes de Cadenas de Valor. Cereales: Maíz. Buenos Aires.

Morgan, Kevin (2018). Strategic Coupling: East Asian Industrial Transformation in the New Global Economy. *Regional Studies*, 52 (3), 458–9.

MTEySS (2014). *Encuesta sobre Empleo, Protección Social y Condiciones de Trabajo de los Asalariados Agrario. Acceso a Políticas de Protección y Seguridad Social de los Asalariados Agrarios.*

Principales Resultados. Buenos Aires: MTEySS, Subsecretaría de Programación Técnica y Estudios Laborales.

Müller, Héctor (2001). La Innovación es el Camino. *La Nación*, August 18, 2001.

Murmis, Miguel (1995). *Pobreza Rural: Datos Recientes y Diversidad de Situaciones Ocupacionales*. Buenos Aires: PROINDER, SAPyA.

Murmis, Miguel, and Maria R. Murmis (2012). Land Concentration and Foreign Land Ownership in Argentina in the Context of Global Land Grabbing. *Canadian Journal of Development Studies*, 33 (4), 490–508.

Murphy, James T. (2012). Global Production Networks, Relational Proximity, and the Sociospatial Dynamics of Market Internationalization in Bolivia's Wood Products Sector. *Annales of the Association of Amercian Geographers*, 102 (1), 208–33.

Muzlera, José (2014). Capitalization Strategies and Labor in Agricultural Machinery Contractors in Argentina. In Alessandra Bonanno and Josefa Salete Barbosa Cavalcanti (eds.). *Labor Relations in Globalized Food. Research in Rural Sociology and Development*, volume 20, 57–74. Bingley: Emerald Group Publishing.

Muzlera, José (2020). Chacarero pampeano (Region Pampeana, Argentina, siglo XX). In José Muzlera and Alejandra Salomón (eds.). *Diccionario del agro iberoamericano*, 2nd edition, 281–92. Buenos Aires: TeseoPress.

Neilson, Jeffrey (2014). Value Chains, Neoliberalism and Development Practice: The Indonesian Experience. *Review of International Political Economy*, 21 (1), 38–69.

Neilson, Jeffrey, Bill Pritchard and Henry Wai-Chung Yeung (2014). Global Value Chains and Global Production Networks in the Changing International Political Economy: An Introduction. *Review of International Political Economy*, 21 (1), 1–8.

Neiman, Guillermo (2010a). Los Estudios sobre el Trabajo Agrario en la última Década: Una Revisión para el Caso Argentino. *Mundo Agrario*, 10 (20), 1–19.

Neiman, Guillermo (2010b). Los Nuevos Escenarios Productivos y Consecuencias sobre los Mercados de Trabajo en el Contexto de la Restructuración de la Agricultura Argentina. *Revista Atlántida*, 2, 139–52.

Neiman, Guillermo (2012). Caso de Argentina. In Fernando Soto Baquero and Emilio Klein (eds.). *Politicas de Mercado de Trabajo y Pobreza Rural en América Latina*, 3–36. Roma: FAO, CEPAL, ILO.

Neiman, Guillermo, Silvia Bardomás, Matias Berger, Mariela Blanco, Dora Jiménez and German Quaranta (2006). *Los Asalariados del Campo en la Argentina. Diagnóstico y Políticas*. Buenos Aires: CICCUS.

Neiman, Guillermo, and German Quaranta (2004). Restructuring and Functional Flexibilization of Agricultural Labor on Argentina. *Latin American Perspectives*, 31 (4), 45–61.

Newman, Susan (2012). Global Commodity Chains and Global Value Chains. In Alfredo Saad-Filho, Ben Fine and Marco Boffo (eds.). *The Elgar Companion to Marxist Economics*, 155–61. Northampton: Edward Elgar.

Nibert, David (ed.). (2017). *Animal Oppression and Capitalism*. Santa Barbara: Praeger.

Nocelli Pac, Santiago (2017). *Evolución de Siembra Directa en Argentina. Campaña 2016–2017.* Rosario: Aapresid.

Nohlen, Dieter, and Franz Nuscheler (1993). Was heißt Entwicklung? In Dieter Nohlen and Franz Nuscheler (eds.). *Handbuch der dritten Welt*, 55–75. Bonn: JHW Dietz.

Nolan, Peter, Dylan Sutherland and Jin Zhang (2002). The Challenge of the Global Business Revolution. *Contributions to Political Economy*, 21, 91–110.

OECD (2014). *Global Value Chains: Challenges, Opportunities, and Implications for Policy. Report prepared for submission to the G20 Trade Ministers Meeting*. Sydney: OECD, WTO, World Bank Group.

Ohaco, Moira (2012). Precariedad y No Registro en los Trabajadores Asalariados Rurales de la Argentina. In Ministerio de Trabajo, Empleo y Seguridad Social (ed.). *Investigaciones sobre protección social y relaciones laborales Argentina 2012*, 73–94. Buenos Aires: MTEySS.

Otero, Gerardo (2012). The Neoliberal Food Regime in Latin America: State, Agribusiness Transnational Corporations and Biotechnology. *Canadian Journal of Development Studies*, 33 (3), 282–94.

Ouma, Stefan (2010). Global Standards, Local Realities: Private Agrifood Governance and the Restructuring of the Kenyan Horticulture Industry. *Economic Geography*, 86 (2), 197–222.

Ouma, Stefan (2016). From Financialization to Operations of Capital: Historicizing and Disentangling the Finance–Farmland-Nexus. *Geoforum*, 72, 82–93.

Ouma, Stefan (2017). The Difference that "capitalism" Makes: On the Merits and Limits of Critical Political Economy in African Studies. *Review of African Political Economy*, 44 (153), 499–509.

Özveren, Eyüp (1994). The Shipbuilding Commodity Chain, 1590–1790. In Gary Gereffi and Miguel Korzeniewicz (eds.). *Commodity Chains and Global Capitalism*, 20–33. Westport: Praeger Publishers.

Paganelli, Alejandra, Victoria Gnazzo, Silvia L. López and Andrés E. Carrasco (2010). Glyphosate-Based Herbicides Produce Teratogenic Effects on Vertebrates by Impairing Retinoic Acid Signaling. *Chemical Research in Toxicology*, 23, 1586–95.

Palmisano, Tomás (2014). *Los Señores de la Tierra. Transformaciones Económicas, Productivas y Discursivas en el Mundo del Agronegocio Bonaerense*. PhD Thesis. Buenos Aires: Facultad de Ciencias Sociales, Universidad de Buenos Aires.

Palpacuer, Florence (2008). Bringing the Social Context Back In: Governance and Wealth Distribution in Global Commodity Chains. *Economy and Society*, 37 (3), 393–419.

Parnreiter, Christof (2007). *Historische Geographien, Verräumlichte Geschichte. Mexico City und das Mexikanische Städtenetz von der Industrialisierung bis zur Globalisierung*. Stuttgart: Franz Steiner.

Parnreiter, Christof (2011). Städte, Warenketten und die ungleiche Geographie der Weltwirtschaft. In Bernd Belina, Norbert Gestring, Wolfgang Müller and Detlev Sträter (eds.). *Urbane Differenzen. Disparitäten innerhalb und zwischen Städten*, 186–206. Münster: Westfälisches Dampfboot.

Parnreiter, Christof (2013). 20 Jahre NAFTA. Mexikos gescheitertes upgrading in globalen Güterketten. *Zeitschrift für Wirtschaftsgeographie*, 57 (4), 216–36.

Parnreiter, Christof (2019). Global Cities and the Geographical Transfer of Value. *Urban Studies*, 56 (1), 81–96.

Parnreiter, Christof, and Christin Bernhold (2020). Global Commodity Chains. In Audrey Kobayashi (ed.): *International Encyclopedia of Human Geography*, 2nd edition, 169–76. Amsterdam: Elsevier.

Pattenden, Jonathan (2016). Working at the Margins of Global Production Networks: Local Labour Control Regimes and Rural-based Labourers in South India. *Third World Quarterly*, 37 (10), 1809–33.

Peck, Jamie (2012). Economic Geography: Island Life. *Dialogues in Human Geography*, 2 (2), 113–33.

Peck, Jamie, and Nik Theodore (2007). Variegated Capitalism. *Progress in Human Geography*, 31 (6), 731–72.

Pelizzon, Sheila (1994). The Grain Flour Commodity Chain, 1590–1790. In Gary Gereffi and Miguel Konzeniewicz (eds.). *Commodity Chains and Global Capitalism*, 34–47. Westport: Praeger Publishers.

Pengue, Walter (2004). Transgenic Crops in Argentina and its Hidden Costs. In Enrique Ortega and Sergio Ulgiati (eds.). *Proceedings of IV Biennial International Workshop "Advances in Energy Studies"*, 91–101. Campinas: Unicamp.

Pengue, Walter (2005). Transgenic Crops in Argentina: The Ecological and Social Debt. *Bulletin of Science, Technology and Society*, 25 (4), 314–22.

Peretti, Miguel (1999). Competitividad de la empresa agropecuaria argentina en la década de los 90. *Revista Argentina de Economía Agraria*, 2 (1), 27–41.

Pérez Niño, Helena (2016). Class Dynamics in Contract Farming: The Case of Tobacco Production in Mozambique. *Third World Quarterly*, 37 (10), 1787–808.

Pérez, Ramón Padilla (ed.). (2017). *Política Industrial Rural y Fortalecimiento de Cadenas de Valor*. Santiago de Chile: CEPAL.

Pertierra Cánepa, Francisco María (2014). *Fideicomiso y Negocios*. Buenos Aires: Alfaomega.

Phillips, Nicola (2011). Informality, Global Production Networks and the Dynamics of "adverse incorporation". *Global Networks*, 11 (3), 380–97.

Pietrobelli, Carlo, and Roberta Rabellotti (ed.). (2006). *Upgrading to Compete. Global Value Chains, Clusters, and SMEs in Latin America*. Washington, D.C.: Inter-American Development Bank, David Rockefeller Center for Latin American Studies, Harvard University.

Pietrobelli, Carlo, and Cornelia Staritz (2013). *Challenges for Global Value Chain Interventions in Latin America. Competitiveness and Innovation Division*. Washington, D.C.: Inter-American Development Bank.

Piva, Adrián (2015). *Economía y Política en la Argentina Kirchnerista*. Buenos Aires: Batalla de Ideas.

PKA, Projekt Klassenanalyse (1974). *Materialien zur Klassenstruktur der BRD*. Hamburg: VSA.

Polanyi, Karl (2001 [1944]). *The Great Transformation. The Political and Economic Origins of Our Time*. Boston: Beacon Press.

Ponte, Stefano (2002). Brewing a Bitter Cup? Deregulation, Quality and the Re-organization of Coffee Marketing in East Africa. *Journal of Agrarian Change*, 2 (2), 248–72.

Ponte, Stefano (2009). Governing through Quality: Conventions and Supply Relations in the Value Chain for South African Wine. *Sociologia Ruralis*, 39 (3), 236–57.

Ponte, Stefano, and Joachim Ewert (2009). Which Way is "Up" in Upgrading? Trajectories of Change in the Value Chain for South African Wine. *World Development*, 37 (10), 1637–50.

Ponte, Stefano, and Peter Gibbon (2005). Quality Standards, Conventions and the Governance of Global Value Chains. *Economy and Society*, 34 (1), 1–31.

Ponte, Stefano, and Timothy J. Sturgeon, Timothy (2014). Explaining Governance in Global Value Chains: A Modular Theory-building Effort. *Review of International Political Economy*, 21 (1), 195–223.

Poth, Carla (2010). El Modelo Biotecnológico en América Latina. Un Análisis sobre las Posturas de los Gobiernos de Lula y Kirchner en Torno a los Organismos Genéticamente Modificados y su Relación con los Movimientos Sociales. In Ana Lucia Bravo, Hugo F. Mereles Centurión, Diego Domínguez, Pablo Sabatino, Carla Mariela Poth, Javier Rodríguez and Leonel Javier (eds.). *Los Señores de la Soja: La Agricultura Transgénica en América Latina*, 261–308. Buenos Aires: CICCUS.

Poulantzas, Nicos (2000 [1978]). *State, Power, Socialism*. London: Verso.

Preda, Graciela, and Mariela Blanco (2010). La Demanda de Mano de Obra en Trigo y Soja, Provincia de Cordoba. In Guillermo Neiman (ed.). *Estudio Sobre la Demanda de Trabajo en el Agro Argentino*, 65–79. Buenos Aires: CICCUS.

Pretty, Jules, James Morrison and Rachel Hine (2003). Reducing Food Poverty by Increasing Agricultural Sustainability in the Development Countries. *Agriculture, Ecosystems and Environment*, 95 (1), 217–34.

Prowse, Martin, and Jason Moyer-Lee (2014). A Comparative Value Chain Analysis of Smallholder Burley Tobacco Production in Malawi – 2003/04 and 2009/10. *Journal of Agrarian Change*, 14 (3), 323–46.

Psilos, Phil, and Gary Gereffi (2011). Workforce Development in the Global Economy: Linking Skills and Capabilities to Upgrading. In Gary Gereffi, Karina Fernandez-Stark and Phil Psilos (eds.). *Skills for Upgrading: Workforce Development and Global Value Chains in Developing Countries*, 1–12. Durham: Duke Center on Globalization, Governance and Competitiveness, RTI International.

Purcell, Thomas, Estefania Martinez-Esguerra and Nora Fernandez (2018). The Value of Rents: Global Commodity Chains and Small Cocoa Producers in Ecuador. *Antipode*, 50 (3), 641–61.

Quaranta, German (2010). Estructura Ocupacional, Caracteristicas de la Demanda y Perfil de la Oferta Laboral en el Agro Argentino a Principios de la Década Acutual. In Guillermo Neiman (ed.). *Estudio Sobre la Demanda de Trabajo en el Agro Argentino*, 13–49. Buenos Aires: CICCUS.

Quark, Amy (2014). Private Governance, Hegemonic Struggles, and Institutional Outcomes in the Transnational Cotton Commodity Chain. *Journal of World-System's Research*, 20 (1), 38–63.

Quentin, David, and Liam Campling (2018). Global Inequality Chains: Integrating Mechanisms of Value Distribution into Analyses of Global Production. *Global Networks*, 18 (1), 33–56.

Raikes, Philip, and Peter Gibbon (2000). "Globalisation" and African export crop agriculture. *The Journal of Peasant Studies*, 27 (2), 50–93.

Raikes, Philip, Michael Friis Jensen and Stefano Ponte (2000). Global Commodity Chain Analysis and the French Filière Approach: Comparison and Critique. *Economy and Society*, 29 (3), 390–417.

Rapoza, Kenneth (2018). It Might Be Time To Get Out Of Argentina. *Forbes*. 05.06.2022 https://www.forbes.com/sites/kenrapoza/2018/05/03/it-might-be-time-to-get-out-of-argentina/#.

Raynolds, Laura T. (1994). Institutionalizing Flexibility: A Comparative Analysis of Fordist and Post-Fordist Models of Third World Agro-Export Production. In Gary Gereffi and Miguel Konzeniewicz (eds.). *Commodity Chains and Global Capitalism*, 143–61. Westport: Praeger.

Rebossio, Alejandro (2013). Argentina Deja De Exportar Trigo Para Que No Suba El Pan. *El País*, 15 July 2013.

Reitz, Tilman (2004). Ideologiekritik. In Wolfgang Fritz Haug (ed.). *Historisch-Kritisches Wörterbuch des Marxismus*, 690–717. Hamburg: Argument.

Rivera Quiñones, Miguel A. (2014). Macroeconomic Governance in Post-Neoliberal Argentina and the Relentless Power of TNCs: The Case of the Soy Complex. In Cara Levey, Daniel Ozarow and Chris Wylde (eds.). *Argentina Since the 2001 Crisis. Recovering the Past, Reclaiming the Future*, 67–86. New York: Palgrve Mcmillan.

Rodríguez, Adriana Mabel, and Elisabeth J. Jacobo (2010). Glyphosate Effects on Floristic Composition and Species Diversity in the Flooding Pampa Grassland (Argentina). *Agriculture, Ecosystems and Environment*, 138 (3–4), 222–31.

Rodríguez, Javier (2006). Los Complejos Agroalimentarios y el Empleo: Una Controversia Teórica y Empírica. *Realidad Económica*, 2018, 107–35.

Rolf, Steven (2015). Locating the State: Uneven and Combined Development, the States System and the Political. In Radhika Desai (ed.). *Theoretical Engagements in Geopolitical Economy*, 113–53. Bingley: Emerald Group Publishing Limited.

Romero, Fernando Gabriel (2016). *El Imperialismo y el Agro Argentino. Historia Reciente del Capital Extranjero en el Complejo Agroindustrial Pampeano*. Buenos Aires: CICCUS.

Ronco, Alicia Estela, Damian José Gabriel Marino, Mariana Abelando, Pablo Almada and Carina Diana Apartin (2016). Water Quality of the Main Tributaries of the Paraná Basin: Glyphosate and AMPA in Surface Water and Bottom Sediments. *Environmental Monitoring and Assessment*, 188 (458), 1–13.

Sábato, Jorge F. (1988). *La Clase Dominante en la Argentina Moderna. Formación y Características*. Buenos Aires: CISEA.

Salido, Joaquín, and Tom Bellhouse (2016). *Economic and Social Upgrading: Definitions, Connections and Exploring Means of Measurement*. United Nations: ECLAC.

Sánchez Enrique, Daniela Verónica (2016). Trabajo Rural Temporario y Fragmentación Normativa en Argentina. Revista Pilquen. *Sección Ciencias Sociales*, 19 (2), 25–37.

Sarandón, Santiago Javier, and Claudia Cecilia Flores (2014). La Insustentabilidad del Modelo Agrícola Actual. In Santiago Javier Sarandón and Claudia Cecilia Flores (eds.). *Agroecología: Bases Teóricas para el Diseño y Manejo de Agroecosistemas Sustentables*, 13–41. La Plata: Universidad Nacional de La Plata.

Schmalz, Stefan (2009). Spielarten der Weltsystemanalyse: Der Ansatz von Giovanni Arrighi. Paper presented at Kapitalismustheorien, ÖGPW and DVPW, Sektion Politik und Ökonomie, April 24–25, in Wien, Austria.

Schmitz, Hubert (2004). *Local Enterprises in the Global Economy: Issues of Governance and Upgrading*. Cheltenham: Edward Elgar.

Schmitz, Hubert (2006). Learning and Earning in Global Garment and Footwear Chains. *European Journal of Development Research*, 18 (4), 546–71.

Schnepf, Randall D., Erik Dohlman and Christine Bolling (2001). *Agriculture in Brazil and Argentina: Developments and Prospects for Major Field Crops. Agriculture and Trade Report*. Washington, D.C.: Market and Trade Economics Division, Economic Research Service, USDA.

Schoenberger, Erica (1991). The Corporate Interview as a Research Method in Economic Geography. *Professional Geographer*, 43 (2), 180–9.

Schorr, Martín (ed.). (2013). *Argentina en la Posconvertibilidad: ¿Desarrollo o Crecimiento Industrial? Estudios de Economia Politica*. Buenos Aires: Editorial Miño y Dávila.

Schorr, Martín (2016). La Política Económica del Macrismo. El Carácter Social. *Revista Anfibia*. 05.06.2022 http://www.revistaanfibia.com/ensayo/el-caracter-social/.

Schorr, Martín, Pablo Manzanelli and Eduardo Basualdo (2012). *Elite Empresaria y Régimen Economico en la Argentina. Las Grandes Firmas en la Posconvertibilidad*. Documento de Trabajo. Buenos Aires: FLACSO.

Schrank, Andrew (2004). Ready-to-wear Development? Foreign Investment, Technology Transfer, and Learning-by-watching in the Apparel Trade. *Social Forces*, 83 (1), 123–56.

Schumpeter, Joseph Aloïs (2003 [1943]). *Capitalism, Socialism and Democracy*. New York: Taylor & Francis.

Selwyn, Benjamin (2012). *Workers, State and Development in Brazil. Powers of Labour, Chains of Value*. Manchester: Manchester University Press.

Selwyn, Benjamin (2013). Social Upgrading and Labour in Global Production Networks: A Critque and an Alternative Conception. *Competition and Change*, 17 (1), 75–90.

Selwyn, Benjamin (2014a). Commodity Chains, Creative Destruction and Global Inequality: A Class Analysis. *Journal of Economic Geography*, 15 (2), 253–274.

Selwyn, Benjamin (2014b). *The Global Development Crisis*. Cambridge: Polity Press.

Selwyn, Benjamin (2016a). Global Value Chains and Human Development: A Class-relational Framework. *Third World Quarterly*, 37 (10), 1768–86.

Selwyn, Benjamin (2016b). *Global Value Chains or Global Poverty Chains? A new research agenda*. CGPE Working Paper Series. Brighton: University of Sussex.

Selwyn, Benjamin (2017). *The Struggle for Development*. Cambridge: Polity Press.

Selwyn, Benjamin, and Dara Leyden (2021a). Oligopoly-Driven Development: The World Bank's 'Trading for Development in the Age of Global Value Chains' in Perspective. *Competition & Change*, Online First, 1–23.

Selwyn, Benjamin, and Dara Leyden (2021b). World Development under Monopoly Capitalism. *Monthly Review* 73 (6), 15–28.

Selwyn, Benjamin, and Satoshi Miyamura (2014). Class Struggle or Embedded Markets? Marx, Polanyi and the Meanings and Possibilities of Social Transformation. *New Political Economy*, 19 (5), 639–61.

Shaikh, Anwar (2006). *Globalization and the Myth of Free Trade. History, theory, and empirical evidence*. London: Routledge.

Silici, Laura (2014). *Agroecology. What it Is and What it has to Offer*. IIED Issue Paper. London: IIED.

Smith, Adrian, Al Rainnie, Mick Dunford, Jane Hardy, Ray Hudson and David Sadler (2002). Networks of Value, Commodities and Regions: Reworking Divisions of Labour in Macro-regional Economies. *Progress in Human Geography*, 26 (1), 41–63.

Smith, David A., and Matthew C. Mahutga (2009). Trading Up the Commodity Chain? The Impact of Extractive and Labor-Intensive Manufacturing Trade on World-System Inequalities. In Jennifer Bair (ed.). *Frontiers of Commodity Chain Research*, 63–82. Stanford: Stanford University Press.

Smith, John (2016). *Imperialism in the Twenty-First Century. Globalization, Super-Exploitation, and Capitalism's Final Crisis*. New York: Monthly Review Press.

Smith, Neil (2001). Geography of Uneven Development. In Neil J. Smelser and Paul B. Baltes (eds.). *International Encyclopedia of the Social and Behavioral Sciences*, 15958–62. Amsterdam: Elsevier.

Soendergaard, Niels (2018). Modern Monoculture and Periphery Processes: a World Systems Analysis of the Brazilian soy expansion from 2000–2012. *Revista de Economia e Sociologia Rural*, 56 (1), 69–89.

Sommer, Michael, and Dieter Wolf (2008). *Imaginäre Bedeutungen und Historische Schranken der Erkenntnis. Eine Kritik an Cornelius Castoriadis*. Hamburg: Argument.

Sosa Varrotti, Andrea Patricia (2015). Las Megaempresas en las Redes de Producción del Agronegocio Argentino. Un Análisis Estructural. *Teoria e Cultura*, 10 (2), 45–59.

Sowers, Elizbeth, Paul S. Ciccantell and David Smith (2014). Comparing Critical Capitalist Commodity Chains in the Early Twenty-first Century: Opportunities For and Constraints on Labor and Political Movements. *Journal of World-System's Research*, 20 (1), 112–39.

Stache, Christian (2017). *Kapitalismus und Naturzerstörung. Zur kritischen Theorie des gesellschaftlichen Naturverhältnisses*. Opladen: Budrich UniPress.

Stache, Christian, and Christin Bernhold (2021). The bourgeois meat hegemony. A contribution to explaining the persistence of animal super-exploitation in capitalism. *Österreichische Zeitschrift für Soziologie*, 46, 167–86.

Stahl, Titus (2013). *Immanente Kritik. Elemente einer Theorie sozialer Praktiken*. Frankfurt: Campus.

Stamm, Andreas (2008). Agribusiness and Poverty Reduction: What can be Learned from the Value Chain Approach? In Christian Stringer and Richard Le Heron (eds.). *Agri-Food Commodity Chains and Globalising Networks*, 23–34. Burlington: Ashgate.

Starosta, Guido (2010). Global Commodity Chains and the Marxian Law of Value. *Antipode*, 42 (2), 433–65.

Steen, Cynthia, Rich Magnani and Lara Goldmark (2005). *Competitive Strategies for Agriculture-related MSEs: From Seeds to Supermarket Shelves*. microREPORT 37. Washington, D.C.: USAID.

Sturgeon, Timothy J. (2001). How Do We Define Value Chains and Production Networks? *IDS Bulletin*, 32 (3), 9–18.

Sturgeon, Timothy J. (2009). From Commodity Chains to Value Chains. In Jennifer Bair (ed.). *Frontiers of Commodity Chain Research*, 110–35. Stanford: Stanford University Press.

Sunkel, Osvaldo (1993). Introduction: In Search of Development Lost. In Osvaldo Sunkel (ed.). *Development from Within: Toward a Neostructuralist Approach for Latin America*, 1–4. Colorado: Lynne Rienner Publishers.

Sunkel, Osvaldo, and Joseph Ramos (1993). Toward a Neostructuralist Synthesis. In Osvaldo Sunkel (ed.). *Toward a Neostructuralist Approach for Latin America*, 5–19. Colorado: Lynne Rienner Publishers.

Suwandi, Intan (2019). *Value Chains: The New Economic Imperialism*. New York: Monthly Review Press.

Svampa, Maristella, and Enrique Viale (2014). *Maldesarrollo. La Argentina del Extractivismo y el Despojo*. Buenos Aires: Katz.

Taglioni, Daria, and Deborah Winkler (2016). *Making Global Value Chains Work for Development. Trade and Development Series*. Washington, D.C.: World Bank.

Talbot, John M. (2009). The Comparative Advantages of Tropical Commodity Chain Analysis. In Jennifer Bair (ed.). *Frontiers of Commodity Chain Research*, 93–103. Stanford: Stanford University Press.

Taylor, Marcus (2007). Rethinking the Global Production of Uneven Development. *Globalizations*, 4 (4), 529–42.

Taylor, Marcus (2010). Book Review: Frontiers of Commodity Chain Research, edited by Jennifer Bair. *Journal of Agrarian Change*, 10 (4), 611–5.

Taylor, Phil, Kirsty Newsome, Jennifer Bair and Al Rainnie (2015). Putting Labour in its Place: Labour Process Analysis and Global Value Chains. In Kirsty Newsome, Phil Taylor, Jennifer Bair and Al Rainnie (eds.). *Putting Labour in its Place. Labour Process Analysis and Global Value Chains*, 1–26. London: Palgrave.

ten Brink, Tobias (2008). *Geopolitik. Geschichte und Gegenwart kapitalistischer Staatenkonkurrenz*. Münster: Westfälisches Dampfboot.

Teubal, Miguel (2006). Expansión del Modelo Sojero en la Argentina. De la Producción de Alimentos a los Commodities. *Realidad Económica*, 220, 71–96.

Teubal, Miguel (2008). Soja y Agronegocios en la Argentina: La Crisis del Modelo. *Lavboratorio. Estudios sobre Cambio Estructural y Desigualdad Social*, 10 (22), 5–7.

Teubal, Miguel, and Tomás Palmisano (2010). El Conflicto Agrario: Características y Proyecciones. In Norma Giarracca and Miguel Teubal (eds.). *Del Paro Agrario a las Elecciones de 2009. Tramas, Reflexiones y Debates*, 193–252. Buenos Aires: Antropofagia.

Theodore, Nik, and Jamie Peck (2002). Staffing Industry: Growth Imperatives and Limits to Contingency. *Economic Geography*, 78 (4), 463–93.

Tort, María Isabel (1983). *Los Contratistas de Maquinaria Agrícola, una Modalidad de Organización Económica del Trabajo Agrícola en la Pampa Húmeda*. Buenos Aires: CEIL.

Tort, María Isabel (2010). Las Tecnologías de Gestión en los Productores Bonaerenses de Soja. In Juan Manuel Villulla and Diego A. Fernández (eds.). *Sobre la Tierra. Problemas del Desarrollo Agropecuario Pampeano*, 107–14. Buenos Aires: Facultad de Ciencias Económicas de la Universidad de Buenos Aires.

Trienkens, Jacques (2011). Agricultural Value Chains in Developing Countries. A Framework for Analysis. *International Food and Agribusiness Management Review*, 14 (2), 51–82.

Tsikata, Dzodzi (2015). *The Social Relations of Agrarian Change*. London: IIED, IDS, ODI.

Turzi, Mariano (2017). *The Political Economy of Agricultural Booms. Managing Soybean Production in Argentina, Brazil, and Paraguay*. Basingstoke: Palgrave.

UNCTAD (2011). *Price Formation in Financialized Commodity Markets: The Role of Information*. Wien: UNCTAD.

UNIDO (2002). *Industrial Development Report 2002/2003: Competing through innovation and learning*. Wien: UNIDO.

USDA (2019). *Oilseeds: World Markets and Trade*. Washington, D.C.: USDA.

USDA (2022). *Oilseeds: World Markets and Trade*. Washington, D.C.: USDA.

Uyan Semerci, Pinar, Emre Erdoğan and Sinem Kavak (2015). *Seasonal Agricultural Work in Turkey*. Istanbul: Support to Life. International Humanitarian Aid.

Verité (2010). *Immigrant Workers in US Agriculture: The Role of Labor Brokers in Vulnerability to Forced Labor*. Amherst: Verité.

Vicente, Lucia (2014). Resistencias Populares a las Leyes de Semilla en América Latina. In Patricia Agosto (ed.). *Malvinas. Un Pueblo en Lucha Contra Monsanto*, 179–202. Buenos Aires: América Libre.

Villulla, Juan Manuel (2009). Apuntes Críticos para el Debate sobre el Conflicto Agrario de 2008. Paper presented at VI Jornadas Interdisciplinarias de Estudios Agrarios y Agroindustriales, CIEA, CONICET: Facultad de Ciencias Económicas, Universidad de Buenos Aires, November 11–13, in Buenos Aires, Argentina.

Villulla, Juan Manuel (2010a). El Proletariado Agrícola de la Pampa Sojera y las Condiciones Históricas de su Estrellato Invisible. In Juan Manuel Villulla and Diego A. Fernández (eds.). *Sobre la Tierra. Problemas del Desarrollo Agropecuario Pampeano*, 137–67. Buenos Aires: Universidad de Buenos Aires.

Villulla, Juan Manuel (2010b). La Contención del Conflicto Obrero contra el "Neoliberalismo" en los ´90. El Caso de la UATRE y los Trabajadores Agrícolas Pampeanos. *Theomai*, 22, 18–35.

Villulla, Juan Manuel (2012a). Dominación, Explotación y Disciplinamiento: Conceptos Fundamentales para el Estudio del Proletariado Agrícola Pampeano, 1970–2010. In Eduardo Azcuy Ameghino, Pedro Castillo, Diego A. Fernández, Lucía Ortega, José Pierri, Fernando Romero Wimer and Juan Manuel Villulla (eds.). *Estudios Agrarios y Agroindustriales*, 67–92. Buenos Aires: Imago Mundi.

Villulla, Juan Manuel (2012b). Las Formas del Salario en la Agricultura Pampeana: Su Rol en el Disciplinamiento, el Aumento de la Productividad y el Abaratamiento de la Fuerza de Trabajo. *Mundo Agrario*, 13 (25), 1–23.

Villulla, Juan Manuel (2015). *Las Cosechas Son Ajenas. Historia de los Trabajadores Rurales Detras del Agronegocio*. Buenos Aires: Editorial Cienflores.

Villulla, Juan Manuel (2016a). Intermediación Laboral en la Agricultura Pampeana Argentina: Trabajadores Asalariados y Contratistas. *EUTOPÍA*, 9, 63–79.

Villulla, Juan Manuel (2016b). Mi Amigo Invisible. *Crisis*. 05.06.2022 https://revistacrisis.com.ar/notas/mi-amigo-invisible.

Villulla, Juan Manuel (2018). Pergamino, Iowa y los Salarios en la Agricultura Pampeana: Viejos Mitos y Nuevas Realidades. *Realidad Económica*, 47 (316), 69–97.

Villulla, Juan Manuel, and Yi Erh Chen (2015). Costos y Tarifas de los Contratistas de Cosecha en la Agricultura Pampeana, 1991–2014. *Revista Interdisciplinaria de Estudios Agrarios*, 42 (1), 99–141.

Villulla, Juan Manuel, Diego Fernández, and Bruno Capdevielle (2019). *Los números rojos de la Argentina verde. El campo entre el conflicto por las retenciones y la gestión de Cambiemos*. Buenos Aires: Facultad de Ciencias Económicas de la Universidad de Buenos Aires.

Villulla, Juan Manuel, and Florencia Hadida (2012). Salto Tecnológico, Tiempos de Trabajo y Puestos Laborales en la Agricultura Pampeana, 1970–2010. *Documentos del CIEA*, 8, 115–28.

Vivas, Úrsula (2015). Continúa la Histórica Huelga Aceitera. *La Izquierda Diario*, May 22, 2015.

Volkind, Pablo (2009). Los Trabajadores Agrícolas Pampeanos: Procedencia, Tareas y Condiciones Laborales, 1890–1914. *Documentos del CIEA*, 4, 35–61.

Wallerstein, Immanuel (1974a). Dependence in an Interdependent World: The Limited Possibilities of Transformation within the Capitalist World Economy. *African Studies Review*, 17 (1), 1–26.

Wallerstein, Immanuel (1974b). *The Modern World System. Capitalist Agriculture and the Origins of the European World-Economy in the Sixteenth Century*. New York: Academic Press.

Wallerstein, Immanuel (1974c). The Rise and Future Demise of the World Capitalist System: Concepts for Comparative Analysis. *Comparative Studies in Society and History*, 16 (4), 387–415.

Wallerstein, Immanuel (1975). Class-Formation in the Capitalist World-Economy. *Politics and Society*, 5 (3), 367–75.

Wallerstein, Immanuel (1988). The Bourgeois(ie) as Concept and Reality. *New Left Review*, 167, 91–106.

Wallerstein, Immanuel (1994). Development. Lodestar or Illusion? In Leslie Sklair (ed.). *Capitalism and Development*, 3–20. London: Routledge.

Wallerstein, Immanuel (2000a). *The Essential Wallerstein*. New York: The New Press.

Wallerstein, Immanuel (2000b). Introduction to Special Issue on Commodity Chains in the World Economy, 1590–1790. *Review* (Fernand Braudel Center), 23 (1), 1–13.

Wallerstein, Immanuel (2004). *World-Systems Analysis. An Introduction*. Durham: Duke University Press.

Wallerstein, Immanuel (2009a). Crisis of the Capitalist System: Where Do We Go from Here? *Monthly Review Online*. 05.06.2022 https://mronline.org/2009/11/12/crisis-of-the-capitalist-system-where-do-we-go-from-here/.

Wallerstein, Immanuel (2009b). Protection Networks and Commodity Chains in the Capitalist World-Economy. In Jennifer Bair (ed.). *Frontiers of Commodity Chain Research*, 83–9. Stanford: Stanford University Press.

Wallerstein, Immanuel (2012a). *Das moderne Weltsystem II – Der Merkantilismus. Europa zwischen 1600 und 1750*. Wien: Promedia.

Wallerstein, Immanuel (2012b). *Das moderne Weltsystem IV – Der Siegeszug des Liberalismus (1789–1914)*. Wien: Promedia.

Webber, Jeffery (2010). Neostructuralism, Neoliberalism, and Latin America's Resurgent Left. *Historical Materialism*, 18 (2010), 208–29.

Werner, Marion (2012). Beyond Upgrading: Gendered Labor and the Restructuring of Firms in the Dominican Republic. *Economic Geography*, 88 (4), 403–22.

Werner, Marion (2016a). *Global Displacements. The Making of Uneven Development in the Caribbean*. New Jersey: Wiley-Blackwell.

Werner, Marion (2016b). Global Production Networks and Uneven Development: Exploring Geographies of Devaluation, Disinvestment, and Exclusion. *Geography Compass*, 10 (11), 457–69.

Werner, Marion (2018). Geographies of Production I: Global Production and Uneven Development. *Progress in Human Geography*, Online First, 1–11.

Werner, Marion, Jennifer Bair and Victor Ramiro Fernandez (2014). Linking Up to Development? Global Value Chains and the Making of a Post-Washington Consensus. *Development and Change*, 45 (6), 1219–47.

Williamson, Oliver Eaton (1989). *Transaction Cost Economics*. Amsterdam: North Holland.

Wilson, Bradley (2013). Breaking the Chains: Coffee, Crisis, and Farmworker Struggle in Nicaragua. *Environment and Planning A*, 45 (11), 2592–609.

Wolf, Dieter (2013). Wie der Waren- und Geldfetisch den Zusammenhang von gesellschaftlichem Sein und Bewusstsein bestimmt. 05.06.2022 http://www.dieterwolf.net/pdf/Warenfetisch_Geldfetisch_Sein_Bewusstsein.pdf.

World Bank (2016). *Argentina. Country Environmental Analysis. Series of technical reports of the World Bank in Argentina, Paraguay and Uruguay*. Washington, D.C.: World Bank Group.

World Bank (2020). *World Development Report 2020. Trading for Development in the Age of Global Value Chains*. Washington, D.C.: World Bank.

Wright, Erik Olin (1979). *Class Structure and Income Determination*. New York: Academic Press.

Wright, Erik Olin (2005). Foundations of a Neo-Marxist Class Analysis. In Erik Olin Wright (ed.). *Approaches to Class Analysis*, 4–30. Cambridge: Cambridge University Press.

Wright, Melissa (2006). Disposable Women and Other Myth of Global Capitalism. London: Routledge.

Yeung, Henry Wai-Chung (2015). Regional Development in the Global Economy: A Dynamic Perspective of Strategic Coupling in Global Production Networks. *Regional Science Policy and Practice*, 7 (1), 1–23.

Yeung, Henry Wai-Chung, and Neil Coe (2015). Toward a Dynamic Theory of Global Production Networks. *Economic Geography*, 91 (1), 29–58.

Index